ABBREVIATED RAIL TIMES

FOR GREAT BRITAIN

for Principal Stations on Main Lines and Rural Routes

Winter Edition

10 December 2017 to 19 May 2018

Cut here or use a photocopier to make a bookmark to save memorising details.

KEY:

DAYS OF RUNNING

⚒	Mondays to Saturdays
Ⓐ	Mondays to Fridays
Ⓑ	Daily except Saturdays
Ⓒ	Saturdays and Sundays
①②	Mondays, Tuesdays
③④	Wednesdays, Thursdays
⑤⑥	Fridays, Saturdays
⑦	Sundays
①–④	Mondays to Thursdays

SERVICES

[12]	Through service (first and standard class seats)
[2]	Through service (standard class seats only)
🛏	Sleeping car
🍴	Restaurant car
🍸	Snacks and drinks available
2	Standard class only
🚌	Bus or coach service
⛴	Shipping service

OTHER SYMBOLS

[R]	Reservation compulsory
✈	Airport
|	Train does not stop
▬	Separates two trains in the same column between which no connection is possible
→	Continued in later column
←	Continued from earlier column
v.v.	Vice Versa

Cover picture: No. 222015 departs Derby with empty coaching stock on 12th December 2015. Other views of this area can be seen in Middleton Press' latest album, Derby to Chesterfield. (John Whitehouse)

Compiled by:
European Rail Timetable Ltd
Director and Editor-in-Chief: John Potter, 28 Monson Way, Oundle, Northamptonshire, PE8
Tel: 01832 270198 (Monday to Friday 0900-1700) *www.europeanrailtimetable.eu*

D1513338

Published by:
MP Middleton Press
Easebourne Lane
Midhurst, West Sussex, GU29 9AZ
Tel: 01730 813169
sales@middletonpress.co.uk *www.middletonpress.co.uk*

ISBN 978 1 910356 13 5
Data and monochrome diagrams
Copyright © 2017 European Rail Timetable Ltd
Print Managed by Jellyfish Print Solutions Ltd, Hampshire, SO32 2NW

Every care has been taken to rende ... 'antly being made by the administrations concerned and neither the publishers nor the ... or inaccuracies.

80003450771

Heritage Railways

CONTENTS

FOREWORD

The production of the *Comprehensive Rail Times* in two volumes became necessary, due to the printer's requirements, in May 2016. The factors have now altered and we can revert to a single volume, but the paper has to be thinner to allow this.

We regret that the *Abbreviated Rail Times* will be discontinued after this issue. If you wish to continue with the same style, it can be found in the Great Britain section of the *European Rail Timetable*, whose details can be found on page 1.

Please promote our new *Rail Times* widely, so that the orders remain sufficient to enable us to keep it in production. Few nations now retain one. We are proud of our heritage and determined to keep the Rail Times available as long as possible.

We always recommend confirmation of train times by visiting *www.nationalrail.co.uk* or telephoning 03457 484950.

Vic Bradshaw-Mitchell

NEWSLINES

Three Saturday Chiltern Railways services (**Table 128**) from London to Birmingham continue through to Kidderminster at 1710, 1810 and 1940 and also three Sunday services at 1810, 1940 and 2040. The 1055 on Saturdays from Birmingham to London starts back from Kidderminster at 1011 and two services on Sundays start back from Kidderminster at 0940 and 1113.

Great Western Railway is starting its winter timings from January 1st instead of December 11th and this will affect our **Tables 120A, 130, 131, 132, 132a, 133, 134, 136, 138** and **140** which all start from this date.

Table 130 sees an additional Saturday train from Paddington to Moreton in Marsh at 1222 and an early train on Sundays at 0839 from Worcester Shrub Hill to Paddington, replacing the 1023 departure.

Staying with GWR, the Slough to Windsor & Eton Central service (**Table 131A**) has been re-cast on Mondays to Fridays and the Reading to London Gatwick service is doubled on Sundays with two trains per hour.

TransPennine Express has added additional trains on Sundays from Manchester Airport to Glasgow Central (**Table 154**) at 1100 and 1858. On Saturdays, the 0723 from Lancaster to Manchester Airport starts back from Glasgow at 0421.

Tables 156, 190 and **191** are affected by the closure of the route between Preston to Blackpool North for electrification and other improvement work until March 25th. A replacement bus service is operating.

East Midlands Trains has added two extra trains each way on the Nottingham – Derby – Matlock corridor on Sundays (**Table 172**).

In **Table 175**, Northern (Arriva Rail North) has enhanced its Leeds – Harrogate – York service on Sundays with additional hourly services between Leeds and Knaresborough. On weekdays additional half hourly services are planned to start from March 26th between Leeds and Harrogate, which would give Harrogate a train every 15 minutes during most of the day.

Northern has also put in place enhanced Sunday services from Ilkley to Bradford and Bradford to Skipton with seven additional services each way bringing the total on both services to fourteen (**Table 176**).

Staying with Northern, the service from Lincoln to Sheffield (**Table 179**) also benefits from additional Sunday services up from four each way to thirteen.

...continued on page 5.

INDEX OF PLACES by table number

🚃 Connection by train from the nearest station shown in this timetable.
⛴ Connection by boat from the nearest station shown in this timetable.

🚌 Connection by bus from the nearest station shown in this timetable.
180 / 186 Consult both indicated tables to find the best connecting services.

(continued...) Virgin Trains East Coast (**Table 180**) has put in place a major timetable revision on its services from London Kings Cross on Saturdays with twenty four additional trains bringing the total number of services to 151, only six fewer than on Mondays to Fridays.

Grand Central Trains (**Tables 182** and **183**) now has one train each way with an additional stop at Peterborough on most days of the week.

TransPennine Express has introduced additional Sunday services from Manchester Airport to Cleethorpes (**Table 193**) at 0751 and 0955 and the 1155 service to Doncaster has been extended to Cleethorpes. Also in **Table 193**, the seasonal Summer Sunday services from Sheffield to Manchester and v.v., through the Hope Valley, will now run year round.

Northern has increased its Sunday offering between Middlesbrough and Newcastle (**Table 210**) with three extra trains each way.

Northern has also changed its Sunday offering on the Middlesbrough to Whitby route (**Table 211**), with the four train service completely re-cast and all trains now going to and from Darlington or Newcastle.

Northern has doubled the Bishop Auckland to Saltburn service (**Table 212**) on Mondays to Saturdays. On Sundays, one additional train is provided.

Lastly for Northern, the Sunday service from Newcastle to Carlisle (**Table 213**) has been completely re-cast with an additional two trains each way.

Turning finally to Scotland, Abellio ScotRail has increased its offering on Mondays to Fridays on the Carlisle – Dumfries – Glasgow route (**Table 214**) by adding a service from Dumfries to Glasgow at 0513 (returning at 2013) together with services from Dumfries to Carlisle at 0713, 1102, 1304, 1602 and 1841 (returning at 0955, 1220, 1430 1727 and 2017).

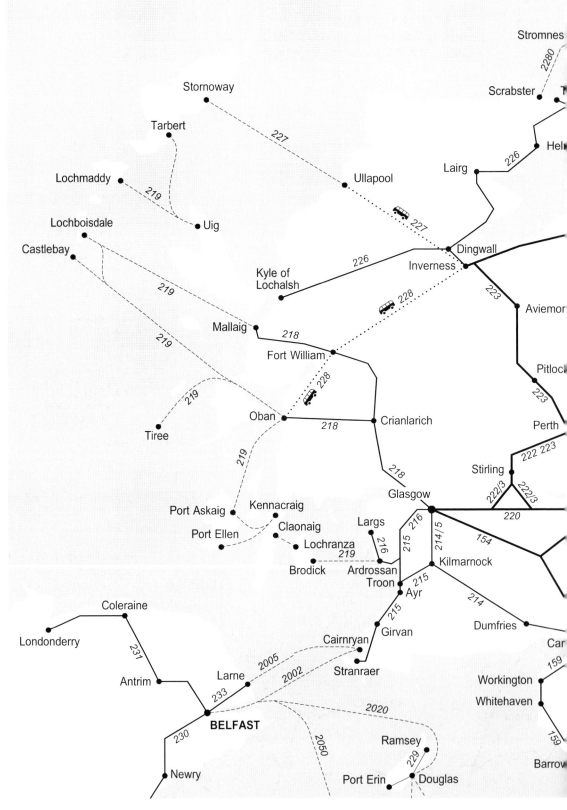

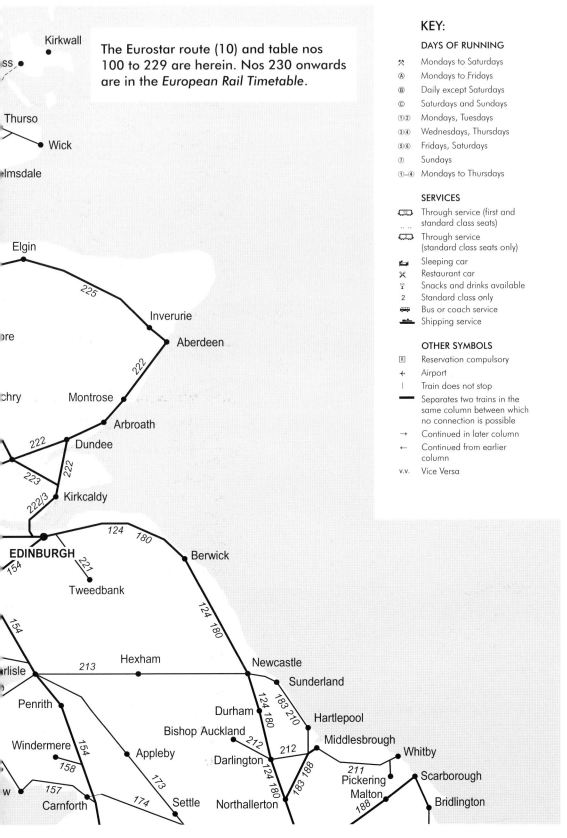

KEY:

Kirkwall

ss

The Eurostar route (10) and table nos 100 to 229 are herein. Nos 230 onwards are in the *European Rail Timetable*.

Thurso

Wick

Imsdale

Elgin

225

Inverurie

re

Aberdeen

222

chry   Montrose

Arbroath

222   Dundee

223   222

222/3   Kirkcaldy

124   180

EDINBURGH

154   221

Tweedbank

Berwick

124   180

154

Hexham   Newcastle

rlisle   213   Sunderland

Penrith   124 180   183 210

Durham   Hartlepool

Bishop Auckland

212   Middlesbrough

Windermere   154   212

Appleby   Darlington   Whitby

158   Northallerton   124 180   183 188   211   Scarborough

173   Pickering

157   Malton

w   174   Settle   Northallerton   188   Bridlington

Carnforth

7

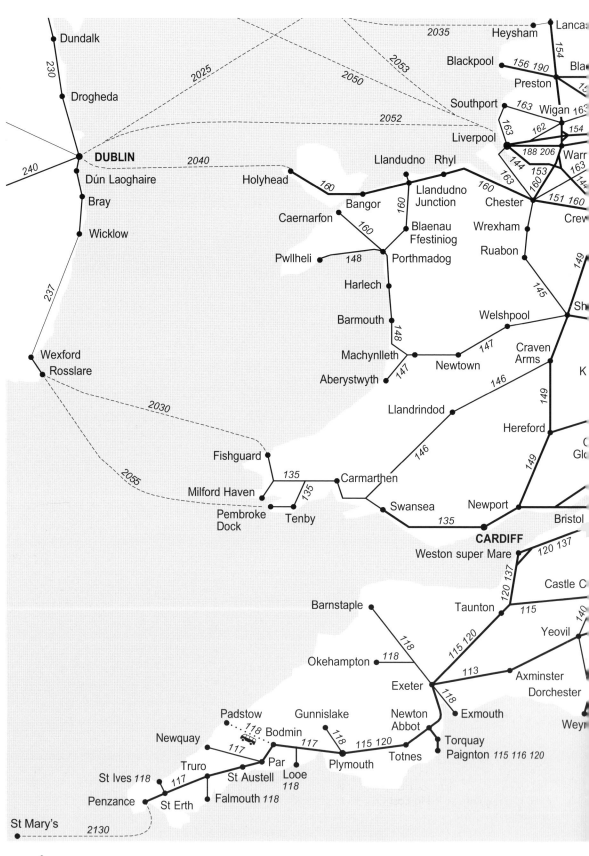

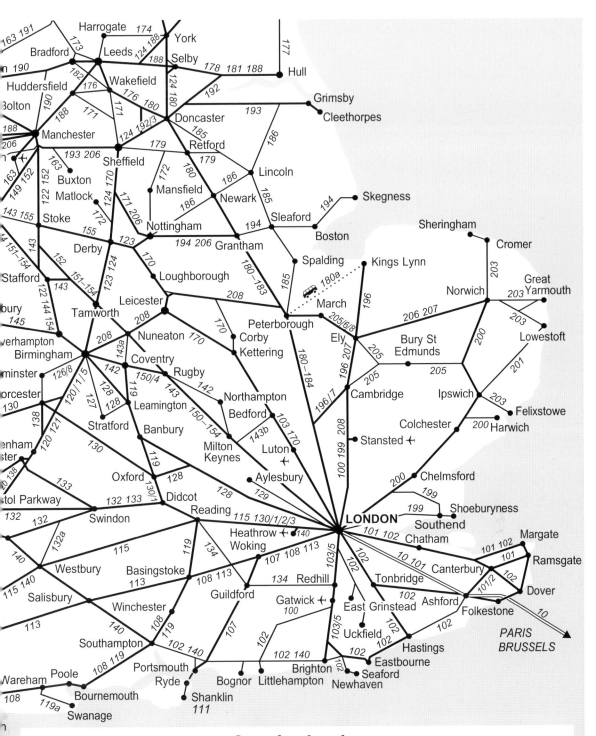

Crossing London

London termini are linked by buses and underground trains, but some journeys involve a change. Those travelling between the Midlands and most of Sussex are likely to be advised to travel by Underground, via Victoria. However, those using King's Cross can cross the road to St. Pancras, where there is a regular service to East Croydon. Mid-Surrey and many Sussex stations are served from there. See table no. 103.

LONDON - LILLE - PARIS and BRUSSELS *by Eurostar*

Minimum check-in time is 30 minutes, but passengers are advised to allow longer due to immigration procedures. Not available for London - Ebbsfleet - Ashford or v.v. Special fares payable that include three classes of service: business premier, standard premier and standard. All times shown are local times (France and Belgium are one hour ahead of Great Britain). All Eurostar services are [R], non-smoking and convey ✕ in Business Premier and Standard Premier, 🍸 in Standard.

Service December 10 - May 26. No service December 25.

Services from Paris depart ±12 minutes earlier January 7 - February 3 and 6-9 minutes earlier February 4 - May 26.

km	km	*train number*	9080	9108	9002	9110	9110	9110	9110	9110	9004	9006	9008	9008	9112	9010	9010	9116	9116	9116	9014	9014	9018	9128	9020
		notes	①–⑤	①⑤	⑥	①–⑤	①–⑤	①–⑤	②③④	⑥	①–⑤		⑥	①–⑤		⑦				⑥⑦			⑧		⑥
		notes	O	KK		EE j	FF	GG	E¶		j	T	g	j	J	y	R	LL	MM	k	E	D			
0	0	**London** St Pancras ....d.	0540	0613	0618	0647	0647	0650	0650	0657	0701	0728	0752	0755	0804	0819	0831	0854	0854	0858	0922	0924	1024	1058	1101
35	35	Ebbsfleet International ....d.	0558	0630	|	0704	0707	0707	0707	|	|	|	0812	0812	|	0838	|	0912	0912	0915	|	0941	1042	1115	|
90	90	Ashford International ....d.	0624	0652	0655	0725	0728	0728	0728	0728	|	|	|	|	|	|	|	|	|	|	0955	|	|	|	|
166	166	Calais Fréthun ....a.	|	|	|	0859	0859	0859	0859	|	|	|	|	|	|	|	|	|	1056	1059	|	|	|	|	|
267	267	Lille Europe ....a.	|	0849	|	0930	0930	0930	0930	0926	|	|	|	|	1026	|	|	1123	1127	1130	|	|	|	1326	|
	373	**Brussels** Midi / Zuid ....a.	|	0922	|	1007	1007	1007	1007	1005	|	|	|	|	1105	|	|	1202	1205	1208	|	|	|	1405	|
492		**Paris** Nord ....a.	0917	...	0947	...	...	...	...	...	1017	1047	1117	1117	...	1147	1147	...	...	...	1247	1248	1347	...	1417

train number	9022	9060	9024	9132	9028	9030	9136	9032	9032	9140	9036	9038	9040	9042	9150	9044	9152	9046	9152	9048	9050	9054	9158	9054	9056
notes							⑦§					⑤⑦		⑧				①–⑤							⑦
notes	S	B			M	L	E	c	AA			k		N	NN	X	PP	b	G	C	P	Q	q	DD	x
London St Pancras ....d.	1131	1201	1224	1258	1331	1401	1404	1422	1431	1504	1531	1601	1631	1701	1704	1731	1755	1801	1804	1831	1901	1925	1934	2001	2031
Ebbsfleet International ....d.	|	|	1242	1315	|	|	|	|	|	|	|	|	|	|	|	|	|	|	|	|	|	|	|	|	|
Ashford International ....d.	|	|	|	|	|	|	|	1455e	|	|	|	|	|	|	|	|	1828e	|	|	|	|	|	|	|	|
Calais Fréthun ....a.	|	|	|	1459	|	|	|	|	|	|	|	|	|	|	|	|	|	|	|	|	|	|	2129	|	|
Lille Europe ....a.	|	|	|	1530	|	|	1626	|	|	1726	|	|	|	|	1926	|	2026	|	2026	|	|	|	2200	|	|
Brussels Midi / Zuid ....a.	|	|	|	1608	|	|	1705	|	|	1805	|	|	|	|	2005	|	2105	|	2105	|	|	|	2238	|	|
Paris Nord ....a.	1447	1517	1547	...	1647	1717	...	1747	1747	...	1847	1917	1947	2020	...	2047	...	2117	...	2147	2217	2317	...	2317	2347

train number	9109	9005	9007	9113	9009	9011	9117	9013	9015	9019	9125	9021	9023	9131	9027	9133	9031	9035	9037	9141	9141	9039	9039	9145	9043
notes	①	①	①–⑥	①–⑥	①–⑤	⑥⑦								⑦		①–⑥		⑥⑦	⑤	⑦	①–⑥			⑦	
notes	p	BB	h	n	j	k		CC		V	K	U		d	F	j		t	d	k	j	W	Y	E§	
Paris Nord ....d.	...	0643	0713	...	0743	0813	...	0843	0913	1013	...	1043	1113	...	1213	...	1313	1413	1443	...	...	1513	1513	...	1613
Brussels Midi / Zuid ....d.	0656	|	|	0756	|	|	0852	|	|	|	1056	|	|	1156	|	1252	|	|	|	1452	1456	|	|	1556	|
Lille Europe ....d.	0735	|	|	0835	|	|	0930	|	|	|	1135	|	|	1235	|	1330	|	|	|	1530	1535	|	|	1635	|
Calais Fréthun ....d.	|	|	|	|	|	|	1001	|	|	|	|	|	|	|	|	1401	|	|	|	1601	|	|	|	|	|
Ashford International ....a.	|	|	|	|	|	|	|	|	|	|	|	|	1207r	|	|	|	|	|	|	|	|	|	1607	|	|
Ebbsfleet International ....a.	|	|	|	|	|	|	|	|	1018	|	|	|	|	|	|	1345	1418	|	|	1545	1545	1618	|	|	1718
London St Pancras ....a.	0759	0802	0832	0857	0900	0930	0957	1000	1039	1130	1157	1200	1239	1258	1330	1405	1439	1530	1602	1605	1605	1639	1640	1657	1739

train number	9045	9045	9149	9149	9149	9047	9153	9153	9153	9153	9051	9159	9159	9053	9055	9163	9163	9059	9061	9063					
notes	⑦	⑦	⑦	①–⑥			①–⑤	⑦	⑧		⑧	⑦					①–⑥		⑦	⑧					
notes	HH	JJ	D f	D ⁝	E		D ⁝	D d	E	AA	q	E	H	A	q	D q	E	q	w	q					
Paris Nord ....d.	1643	1643	...	...	...	1713	...	...	...	...	1813	...	...	1843	1913	...	...	2013	2043	2113	...	...	...	...	...
Brussels Midi / Zuid ....d.	|	|	1656	1656	1656	|	1756	1756	1756	1756	|	1853	1856	|	|	1952	1952	|	|	|	...	...	...	...	...
Lille Europe ....d.	|	|	1734	1735	1735	|	1835	1835	1835	1835	|	1930	1935	|	|	2030	2030	|	|	|	...	...	...	...	...
Calais Fréthun ....d.	|	|	|	|	|	|	|	|	|	|	|	2001	|	|	|	2101	2101	|	|	|	...	...	...	...	...
Ashford International ....a.	1737	|	|	1734	1734	|	|	1835e	|	|	|	|	|	|	2007r	|	|	|	|	|	...	...	...	...	...
Ebbsfleet International ....a.	|	|	1745	|	|	|	1845	|	1845	|	1918	1945	|	|	|	2045	2045	2118	|	2218	...	...	...	...	...
London St Pancras ....a.	1812	1800	1803	1806	1806	1832	1903	1910	1903	1910	1939	2003	1957	2004	2039	2103	2103	2139	2200	2239	...	...	...	...	...

A – ⑤⑦ Dec. 10 - Mar. 31 (also Dec. 26, Jan. 1). ②③④⑤⑦ Apr. 1 - May 26 (not Apr. 1, May 6).

B – Dec. 23, 30. ①⑤ Apr. 6 - May 4 (also May 11).

C – ⑤⑦ Dec. 10 - Jan. 6 (not Dec. 24, Jan. 2). ⑦ Jan. 7 - Feb. 3 (also Jan. 22 - 26, Jan. 29 - Feb. 2). ⑧ Feb. 4 - Apr. 29. ⑤⑦ Apr. 30 - May 26 (also May 7).

D – Dec. 10 - Mar. 31.

E – Apr. 1 - May 26.

F – ⑤⑥⑦ Dec. 10 - Mar. 31 (also Dec. 21, 26, Jan. 1, 2). ①⑤⑥⑦ Apr. 1 - May 26.

G – ①–⑤ Dec. 10 - Jan. 6. ⑤ Jan. 7 - Feb. 3. ①–⑤ Apr. 1 - May 26 (not Apr. 2, May 7).

H – ⑤⑦ Dec. 10 - Jan. 6 (also Dec. 26, Jan. 1). ⑦ Jan. 7 - Feb. 3. ⑤⑦ Feb. 4 - Mar. 31. ⑦ Apr. 1 - May 26 (also Apr. 2).

J – ⑤ Dec. 10 - Jan 6, Feb. 4 - Mar. 31.

K – ①–⑤ Dec. 10 - Jan. 6 (not Jan. 1). ⑤ Jan. 7 - Feb. 3. ①–⑤ Feb. 4 - Mar. 31 (also Apr. 2).

L – Dec. 22, 29. ⑤ Feb. 4 - May 26.

M – Daily Dec. 10 - Jan. 6. ④⑤ Jan. 7 - Feb. 3. Daily Feb. 4 - May 26.

N – ⑧ Apr. 1 - May 26 (not Apr. 2).

O – ①–⑤ (not Dec. 26, Jan. 1, Apr. 2, 30, May 1, 7, 8, 10, 11, 21).

P – Daily Dec. 10 - Jan. 6 (not Dec. 24, 31). ⑧ Jan. 7 - Feb. 3 (not Jan. 22 - 26, Jan. 29 - Feb. 2). ⑥⑦ Feb. 4 - Mar. 31. Daily Apr. 1 - May 26.

Q – ①–⑤ Jan. 22 - Feb. 2. ①–④ Feb. 4 - Apr. 27.

R – ①⑤⑥ Dec. 9 - March 31 (not Jan. 1).

S – ⑤⑥⑦ Dec. 9 - Mar. 31 (also Dec. 21, 26, Jan. 1, 2). Daily Apr. 1 - May 26 (not May 15, 16, 17, 22, 23, 24).

T – ⑥ Apr. 1 - May 5. ①–⑥ May 12 - 26.

U – Dec. 22, 29. ⑤ Apr. 1 - May 26.

V – Daily Dec. 10 - Jan. 6. ①⑤ Jan. 7 - Feb. 3. Daily Feb. 4 - May 26.

W – Daily Dec. 10 - Jan. 6. ⑧ Jan. 7 - Feb. 3. Daily Feb. 4 - Mar. 31.

X – Daily Dec. 10 - Mar. 31 (not Dec. 24, 31). ⑥ Apr. 1 - May 26 (also Apr. 1, 2).

Y – Daily Apr. 1 - May 26.

AA – Dec. 26.

BB – ① Dec. 10 - Apr. 23 (also May 14; not Jan. 1, Apr. 2).

CC – ①–⑤ Dec. 10 - May 26 (also Dec. 23, 30; not Dec. 26, Jan. 1, Apr. 2, May 7).

DD – Daily Dec. 10 - Feb. 3 (not Dec. 24, 26, 31, Jan. 1). ⑤⑥⑦ Feb. 4 - Apr. 29. ①–⑥ Apr. 30 - May 26.

EE – Dec. 10 - Jan. 6.

FF – Jan. 7 - Feb. 3.

GG – Feb. 4 - Mar. 31.

HH – ⑦ Dec. 10 - Mar. 31 (also Dec. 26, Jan. 1).

JJ – ⑦ Apr. 1 - May 26 (also Apr. 2, May 7; not Apr. 1, May 6).

KK – Apr. 1 - May 26 (not Apr. 2, May 7, 11, 21).

LL – ①–⑤ Dec. 10 - Mar. 31 (not Dec. 26, Jan. 1). ②③④ Apr. 1 - May 26.

MM – ①⑤ Apr. 1 - May 26.

NN – Daily Dec. 10 - Mar. 31. ⑥⑦ Apr. 1 - May 26 (also Apr. 2).

PP – ⑦ Dec. 10 - Mar. 31 (also Jan. 1, Apr. 1, 2, May 7; not Dec. 24, 31).

b – Not Dec. 26, Apr. 2, May 7.

c – Not Dec. 26.

d – Also Jan. 1.

e – Not Feb. 25.

f – Also Dec. 26, Jan. 1.

g – Also May 7.

h – Not Dec. 24, 26, 31, Jan. 1, Apr. 2, May 1, 7, 8, 10, 11.

j – Not Dec. 26, Jan. 1, Apr. 2, May 7.

k – Also Dec. 26, Jan. 1, Apr. 2, May 7.

m – Also Dec. 26, Jan. 1, Apr. 2, May 7; not Apr. 1, May 6.

n – Not Dec. 26, Jan. 1, Apr. 2, May 1, 7, 10, 11.

p – Not Jan. 1, Apr. 2, May 7, 21.

q – Not Dec. 24, 31.

r – Not Dec. 26, Feb. 25.

t – Also Jan. 1, Apr. 2.

w – Also Dec. 26, Apr. 2, May 7; not Dec. 24, 31, Apr. 1, May 6.

x – Also Dec. 26, Jan. 1, May 7.

y – Also Dec. 26, Jan. 1, Apr. 2.

z – Also Dec. 26, Jan. 1, Apr. 2, May 7; not Apr. 1, May 6.

¶ – Not May 1, 10.

§ – Also Apr. 2, May 7.

⁝ – Not Dec. 26, Jan. 1.

This page is from the European Rail Timetable Winter 2017-2018 edition. For more details see page 85.

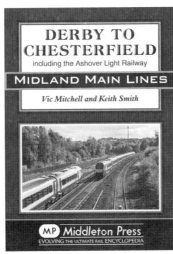

GREAT BRITAIN

Operators: Passenger services are provided by a number of private passenger train companies operating the **National Rail** (www.nationalrail.co.uk) network on lines owned by the British national railway infrastructure company **Network Rail**. The following Network Rail codes are used in the table headings to indicate the operators of trains in each table:

AW	Arriva Trains Wales	GR	Virgin Trains East Coast	ME	Merseyrail	SW	South Western Railway
CC	c2c	GW	Great Western Railway	NT	Arriva Rail North	TL	Thameslink Railway
CH	Chiltern Railways	HT	Hull Trains	NY	North Yorkshire Moors Railway	TP	TransPennine Express
CS	Caledonian Sleeper	IL	Island Line	SE	Southeastern	VT	Virgin Trains West Coast
EM	East Midlands Trains	LE	Greater Anglia	SN	Southern	XC	Arriva Cross Country
GC	Grand Central Railway	LM	London Midland	SR	Abellio ScotRail		

Timings: Except where indicated otherwise, timings are valid **December 10, 2017 - May 19, 2018**.
As service patterns at weekends (especially on ⑦) usually differ greatly from those applying on Mondays to Fridays, the timings in most tables are grouped by days of operation: Ⓐ = Mondays to Fridays; ⚒ = Mondays to Saturdays; ⑥ = Saturdays; ⑦ = Sundays. Track engineering work, affecting journey times, frequently takes place at weekends, so it is advisable to confirm your journey details locally if planning to travel in the period between the late evening of ⑥ and the late afternoon of ⑦. Confirm timings, too, if you intend travelling on public holidays (see page 4) as there may be alterations to services at these times. Suburban and commuter services are the most likely to be affected; the majority of long-distance and cross-country trains marked Ⓐ and ⚒ run as normal on these dates. No trains (except limited Gatwick and Heathrow Express services) run on **December 25**, with only a limited service on certain routes on **December 26**. In Scotland, only trains between Edinburgh / Glasgow and England run on **January 1**.

Services: Unless indicated otherwise (by '2' in the train column or '2nd class' in the table heading), trains convey both **first** (1st) and **standard** (2nd) classes of seated accommodation. Light refreshments (snacks, hot and cold drinks) are available from a **buffet car** or a **mobile trolley service** on board those trains marked 🍷 and 🍴: the latter also convey a **restaurant car** or serve meals to passengers at their seats (this service is in some cases available to first-class ticket holders only). Note that catering facilities may not be available for the whole of a train's journey. **Sleeping-cars** (🛏) have one berth per compartment in first class and two in standard class.

Reservations: Seats on most long-distance trains and berths in sleeping-cars can be reserved in advance when purchasing travel tickets at rail stations or directly from train operating companies (quote the departure time of the train and your destination). Seat reservation is normally free of charge.

100 LONDON AIRPORT LINKS

Gatwick ✈

GATWICK EXPRESS: Daily non-stop rail service from / to **London Victoria**. Journey time: 30 minutes (35 minutes on ⑦).

From **London** Victoria: 0002, 0030, 0500 and every 15 minutes until 2045, 2100⑥, 2115Ⓑ, 2130⑥, 2145Ⓑ, 2200, 2215, 2230, 2300, 2330, 2345.
From **Gatwick Airport**: 0020, 0035, 0050, 0135, 0545, 0600 and every 15 minutes until 2045, then 2-3 trains per hour until 2330⑥, 2335Ⓐ, 2350⑦.

Other rail services via Gatwick Airport: London Victoria - Eastbourne Table **102**; Bedford - Brighton Table **103**; London Victoria - Brighton Table **105**; Reading - Gatwick Airport Table **134**.

Heathrow ✈

HEATHROW EXPRESS: Daily non-stop rail service **London** Paddington - **Heathrow** Terminal 5 and v.v. Journey times: **Heathrow** Central ♣, 15 minutes, **Heathrow** Terminal 5, 21 minutes.
From **London** Paddington: 0510⚒/0625⑦ and every 15 minutes until 2155, then every 30 minutes (15 minutes on ⑤⑦) until 2325.
From **Heathrow** Terminal 5 (5 mins. later from Heathrow Central): 0507⚒/0618⑦ and every 15 minutes until 2212, then every 30 minutes (15 mins. on ⑤⑦) until 2342⚒ / 2348⑦.

HEATHROW CONNECT: Daily rail service **London** Paddington - **Heathrow** Central ♣ and v.v. Journey time 32 minutes.
From **London** Paddington: on ⚒ at 0442, 0513, 0533 and every 30 minutes until 2103 (additional later trains on ⑤⑥); on ⑦ at 0612, 0712, 0812, 0907 and hourly until 2312.
From **Heathrow** Central ♣: on ⚒ at 0529, 0557 and every 30 minutes until 2127 (additional later trains on ⑤⑥); on ⑦ at 0713 and hourly until 2313.

♣ – Heathrow Central serves Terminals 1, 2 and 3. A free rail transfer service operates every 15 minutes Heathrow Central - Heathrow **Terminals 4 and 5 and v.v.**

PICCADILLY LINE: London Underground service between **Kings Cross St Pancras** and all Heathrow terminals via Central London. Journey time: 50 - 58 minutes.
Frequent trains (every 4 - 10 minutes) 0530⚒/0730⑦ - 2300⚒/2330⑦.

RAILAIR LINK 🚌 **Reading** railway station - **Heathrow Airport** (Service **X25**).
From **Reading**: Services call at Heathrow Terminal 5 (±40 minutes), Heathrow Terminal 1 (±50 minutes) and Heathrow Terminal 3 (±56 minutes):
On Ⓐ at 0400, 0500, 0530, 0555, 0608, 0620, 0640, 0700, 0720, 0740, 0800, 0820, 0840, 0905 and every 20 minutes until 1805, 1835, 1905, 1935, 2005, 2035, 2105, 2205, 2305.
On Ⓒ at 0400, 0500, 0545, 0615, 0645 and every 30 minutes until 1915, 1945, 2025, 2055, 2205, 2305.
From **Heathrow Airport** Bus Station: Services call at Heathrow Terminal 5 (±10 minutes) and Reading Railway Station (±50 minutes).
On Ⓐ at 0005, 0500, 0600, 0630, 0657, 0720 and every 20 minutes until 1000, 1015, and every 20 minutes until 1755, 1815, 1835, 1855, 1915, 1940, 2010, 2040, 2110, 2140, 2215, 2305.
On Ⓒ at 0005, 0500, 0600, 0700, 0730 and every 30 minutes until 1900, 1920, 1950, 2020, 2050, 2130, 2200, 2305.

RAILAIR LINK 🚌 **Woking** rail station - **Heathrow Airport** (Service **701**).
From **Woking**: Services call at Heathrow Terminal 5 (±25 - 45 minutes) and Heathrow Central Bus Station (±40 - 60 minutes).
0300, 0400, 0500, 0600, 0640, 0740, 0845, 0945, 1050, 1135 and hourly until 1735, 1845, 1945, 2045, 2130, 2220.
From **Heathrow** Central Bus Station: Services call at Heathrow Terminal 5 (±15 minutes) and Woking (±45 - 65 minutes).
0545, 0645, 0745, 0845, 0950, 1040, 1140, 1230 and hourly until 1630, 1735, 1835, 1940, 2040, 2130, 2215, 2315.

Luton ✈

Thameslink Railway services Brighton - Gatwick Airport - London St Pancras - Luton Airport Parkway ◧ - Luton ◧ - Bedford: Table **103**.
East Midlands Trains services London St Pancras - Luton Airport Parkway ◧ - Luton ◧ - Leicester - Nottingham / Derby / Sheffield: Table **170**.
◧ – A frequent shuttle 🚌 service operates between each of the railway stations and the airport terminal.

🚌 service **Milton Keynes** - **Luton Airport** and v.v. (Stagecoach route **99**. Journey 55 minutes) for connections from / to **Birmingham**, **Liverpool** and **Manchester** (Table **150**).
From **Milton Keynes** railway station: on Ⓐ at 0645, 0745, 0900 and hourly until 1600, 1710, 1740, 1810, 1910, 2010, 2110, 2210; on ⑥ at 0635, 0755, 0900 and hourly until 1600, 1710, 1810, 1910, 2010, 2110; on ⑦ at 0900 and hourly until 2100.
From **Luton Airport**: on Ⓐ at 0545, 0655, 0755, 0915 and hourly until 1715, 1820, 1920, 2020, 2120; on ⑥ at 0535, 0700, 0800, 0915 and hourly until1715, 1820, 1920, 2020; on ⑦ at 0815 and hourly until 2015.

Stansted ✈

STANSTED EXPRESS: Daily rail service from / to **London** Liverpool St. Journey time ± 45 minutes.
From **London** Liverpool Street: on ⚒ at 0440, 0510 and every 15 minutes until 2255, 2325; on ⑦ at 0410, 0440, 0510, 0540, 0610 and every 15 minutes until 2255, 2325.
From **Stansted Airport**: on ⚒ at 0030, 0600 and every 15 minutes until 2345, 2359; on ⑦ at 0030, 0530, 0600, 0630, 0700 and every 15 minutes until 2345, 2359.

Most trains call at **Tottenham Hale** for London Underground (Victoria Line) connections to / from Kings Cross, St Pancras, Euston, and Victoria stations.
For *Cross Country* services to / from Cambridge, Peterborough, Leicester and Birmingham see Table **208**.

City ✈

DOCKLANDS LIGHT RAILWAY from / to **Bank** (interchange with London Underground: Central, Circle, District, Northern, and Waterloo & City Lines).
Trains run every 7 - 10 minutes 0530 - 0030 on ⚒, 0700 - 2330 on ⑦. Journey time: ± 22 minutes.

Inter - Airport 🚌 links

Operator: National Express ✆ 08717 81 81 81. www.nationalexpress.com

Gatwick North Terminal - **Heathrow** Central. Journey time: 65 - 85 minutes
0015, 0035, 0240, 0340, 0535, 0540, 0600, 0615, 0635, 0700, 0720Ⓐ, 0735Ⓒ, 0800Ⓐ, 0815Ⓒ, 0820Ⓐ, 0835, 0905, 0935, 0940, 1015, 1025, 1035, 1100, 1120, 1135, 1140, 1215, 1235, 1245, 1300, 1315, 1335, 1340, 1415, 1435, 1455, 1515, 1530, 1535, 1540, 1545, 1615, 1635, 1645, 1705Ⓐ, 1715Ⓒ, 1720, 1735, 1740, 1815, 1835, 1900, 1920, 1935, 1950, 1955, 2015, 2030, 2035, 2130, 2205, 2225, 2230, 2240, 2305, 2315, 2340, 2355.

Heathrow Central - **Gatwick** North Terminal.
0055, 0155, 0245, 0300, 0320, 0335, 0400, 0430, 0440, 0510, 0535, 0540, 0605, 0630, 0640, 0700, 0715, 0730Ⓐ, 0740, 0805, 0825, 0840, 0925, 0945Ⓒ, 0955, 1000Ⓐ, 1005, 1025, 1040, 1055, 1110, 1125, 1155, 1205, 1215, 1225, 1240, 1255, 1325, 1340, 1355, 1405, 1415, 1425, 1440, 1455, 1525, 1555, 1605, 1610, 1630, 1640, 1655, 1710, 1735, 1755Ⓒ, 1805, 1825, 1910Ⓒ, 1920Ⓒ, 1925Ⓐ, 1935Ⓐ, 1945Ⓒ, 1955Ⓒ, 2005, 2040, 2055, 2110, 2200, 2255, 2355.

Gatwick North Terminal - **Stansted**. Journey time: 3 hours
0340, 0535, 0720Ⓐ, 0735Ⓒ, 0935, 1135, 1335, 1535, 1735, 1935, 2205.

Stansted - **Gatwick** North Terminal.
0140, 0405, 0605, 0815, 1015, 1215, 1415, 1615Ⓒ, 1625Ⓐ, 1815Ⓒ, 1825Ⓐ, 2115.

Heathrow Central - **Luton**. Journey time: 1–1½ hours
0005, 0550Ⓐ, 0605Ⓒ, 0730, 0750Ⓐ, 0805Ⓒ, 1005, 1205, 1405, 1605, 1805, 2005, 2205.

From **Luton** to **Heathrow** Central.
0355, 0555, 0740Ⓐ, 0755Ⓒ, 0955, 1155, 1355, 1555, 1755, 1955, 2155.

Heathrow Central - **Stansted**. Journey time: 1½ hours
0505, 0705, 0905, 1105, 1305, 1505, 1705, 1905, 2105, 2335.

Stansted - **Heathrow** Central.
0140, 0405, 0605, 0815, 1015, 1215, 1415, 1615Ⓒ, 1625Ⓐ, 1815Ⓒ, 1825Ⓐ, 2115.

Stansted - **Luton**. Journey time: 1½ hours
0100, 0615Ⓐ, 0645Ⓒ, 0920, 1200, 1400, 1630, 1900, 2200.

Luton - **Stansted**.
0300, 0630, 0910, 1130, 1355, 1620, 1855Ⓒ, 1905Ⓐ, 2055.

Special fares are payable for high-speed services. For slower services see Table **102**.

Via Faversham

km		Ⓐ	Ⓐ	ⒶF	Ⓐ	ⒶF		ⒶF	Ⓐ	Ⓐ	Ⓐ	Ⓐ	Ⓐ	Ⓐ	Ⓐ		Ⓐ	Ⓐ	ⒶA	Ⓐ	Ⓐ	Ⓐ	⑥	⑥F	⑥	⑥F	⑥
0	**London** St Pancras d.		0655	0722	0755	0825		1525	1555	1625	1658	1725	1755	1825	1855		2125	2155	2225	2255	2325	2355		0725	0755	0825	0852
9	Stratford Int'l d.		0702	0729	0805	0832	and at	1532	1602	1632	1705	1732	1802	1832	1902	and at	2132	2202	2232	2302	2332	0002		0732	0802	0832	0859
35	Ebbsfleet Int'l d.		0713	0740	0816	0843	the same	1543	1613	1643	1716	1743	1813	1844	1913	the same	2143	2213	2243	2313	2343	0013		0743	0813	0843	0913
52	Rochester d.		0731	0758	0834	0901	minutes	1601	1631	1701	1734	1758	1830	1902	1931	minutes	2201	2231	2301	2331	0001	0031		0801	0831	0901	0931
54	Chatham d.		0735	0801	0837	0904	past each	1604	1634	1704	1738	1802	1834	1906	1934	past each	2204	2234	2304	2334	0004	0034		0804	0834	0904	0934
70	Sittingbourne d.		0752	0818	0854	0921	hour until	1621	1651	1721	1755	1820	1852	1924	1953	hour until	2221	2251	2321	2351	0021	0051		0821	0851	0921	0951
83	Faversham a.		0801	0826	0903	0929	♣	1629	1700	1730	1803	1828	1900	1932	2006	♣	2229	2300	2329	0002	0030	0100		0829	0900	0929	1000
100	Herne Bay a.		...	0842	...	0944		1646	...	...	...	1843	1915	1948	...		2246	...	2346	...	...	...		0844	...	0944	...
118	**Margate** a.		...	0859	...	0959		1702	...	...	..	1857	1931	2004	...		2302	...	0002	...	...	...		0859	...	0959	...

	⑥F	⑥	⑥F		⑥F	⑥	⑥	⑥	⑥	⑥	⑥	⑥	⑦	⑦F	⑦F	⑦F	⑦F	⑦F	⑦		⑦K	⑦	⑦	⑦	⑦	⑦	⑦
London St Pancras d.	0927	0955	1022		2025	2055	2125	2155	2225	2255	2325	2355		0825	0927	1027	1125	1225	1252		2025	2055	2125	2155	2225	2255	2325
Stratford Int'l d.	0934	1002	1032	and at	2032	2102	2132	2202	2232	2302	2332	0002		0832	0934	1034	1132	1232	1259	and at	2032	2102	2132	2202	2232	2302	2332
Ebbsfleet Int'l d.	0945	1013	1043	the same	2043	2113	2143	2213	2243	2313	2343	0013		0843	0945	1045	1143	1243	1313	the same	2043	2113	2143	2213	2243	2313	2343
Rochester d.	1002	1031	1101	minutes	2101	2131	2201	2231	2301	2331	0001	0031		0901	1002	1102	1201	1301	1331	minutes	2101	2131	2201	2231	2301	2334	0001
Chatham d.	1005	1034	1104	past each	2104	2134	2204	2234	2304	2334	0004	0034		0904	1005	1105	1204	1304	1334	past each	2104	2134	2204	2234	2304	2337	0004
Sittingbourne d.	1022	1051	1121	hour until	2121	2151	2221	2251	2321	2351	0021	0051		0921	1022	1122	1221	1321	1351	hour until	2121	2151	2221	2251	2321	2355	0021
Faversham a.	1030	1100	1129	♣	2129	2200	2229	2300	2329	0001	0030	0100		0929	1030	1130	1229	1329	1404	♣	2129	2204	2229	2304	2329	0004	0030
Herne Bay a.	1044	...	1144		2144	...	2244	...	2344	*0040*	...	...		0944	1044	1144	1244	1344	...		2144	...	2244	...	2344	...	...
Margate a.	1059	...	1159		2159	...	2259	...	2359	*0057*	...	...		0959	1059	1159	1259	1359	...		2159	...	2259	...	2359	...	...

	Ⓐ	Ⓐ	Ⓐ	Ⓐ	Ⓐ	Ⓐ	Ⓐ	Ⓐ	Ⓐ	Ⓐ	Ⓐ	ⒶG	Ⓐ	ⒶG		ⒶG	Ⓐ	Ⓐ	ⒶG	Ⓐ	Ⓐ	Ⓐ	Ⓐ	ⒶG	⑥	⑥	⑥	⑥
Margate d.		...	*0443*	*0517*	0605	0634	0703	...	...	0826	...	0926	...	1030		1730	...	1826	1838	1930	...	2030	...	2130		...	...	0630
Herne Bay d.		...	*0459*	*0533*	0619	0648	0717	...	...	0843	...	0943	...	1044	and at	1744	...	1843	1854	1944	...	2044	...	2144		...	...	0644
Faversham d.		0458	0528	0558	0634	0702	0731	0759	0828	0859	0926	0959	1026	1059	the same	1759	1829	1859	1928t	1959	2028	2059	2126	2159		0528	0628	0659
Sittingbourne d.		0507	0537	0607	0642	0710	0739	0807	0837	0907	0937	1007	1037	1107	minutes	1807	1837	1907	1937	2007	2037	2107	2137	2207		0537	0637	0707
Chatham d.		0524	0554	0624	0659	0727	0758	0824	0854	0924	0954	1024	1054	1124	past each	1824	1854	1924	1954	2024	2054	2124	2154	2224		0554	0654	0724
Rochester d.		0528	0558	0628	0703	0730	0802	0828	0858	0928	0958	1028	1058	1128	hour until	1828	1858	1928	1958	2028	2058	2128	2158	2228		0558	0658	0728
Ebbsfleet Int'l a.		0546	0616	0646	0717	0747	0817	0847	0916	0946	1016	1046	1116	1146	♣	1849	1916	1946	2016	2046	2116	2146	2216	2246		0616	0716	0746
Stratford Int'l a.		0558	0628	0658	0729	0800	0830	0859	0928	0959	1030	1059	1129	1159		1902	1928	1959	2028	2102	2128	2159	2228	2258		0628	0728	0758
London St Pancras a.		0606	0636	0707	0737	0807	0838	0907	0936	1006	1037	1106	1140	1206		1910	1936	2006	2036	2109	2136	2207	2236	2306		0636	0736	0806

	⑥	⑥H	⑥	⑥G		⑥	⑥G	⑥	⑥G	⑥	⑥G	⑥	⑥G	⑦	⑦	⑦		⑦	⑦H	⑦G	⑦	⑦G		⑦	⑦G	⑦	⑦G
Margate d.	...	0730	...	0830		...	1830	...	1930	...	2030	...	2130		...	...	...	0830	0930	1030	...	1130		...	2030	...	2130
Herne Bay d.	...	0744	...	0844	and at	...	1844	...	1944	...	2044	...	2144		...	...	...	0844	0944	1044	...	1144	and at	...	2044	...	2144
Faversham d.	0728	0759	0828	0859	the same	1826	1859	1926	1959	2026	2059	2126	2159		0659	0759	...	0859	0959	1059	1129	1159	the same	2029	2059	2129	2159
Sittingbourne d.	0737	0807	0837	0907	minutes	1837	1907	1937	2007	2037	2107	2137	2207		0707	0807	...	0907	1007	1107	1137	1207	minutes	2037	2107	2137	2207
Chatham d.	0754	0824	0854	0924	past each	1854	1924	1954	2024	2054	2124	2154	2224		0724	0824	...	0924	1024	1124	1154	1224	past each	2054	2124	2154	2224
Rochester d.	0758	0828	0858	0928	hour until	1858	1928	1958	2028	2058	2128	2158	2228		0728	0828	...	0928	1028	1128	1158	1228	hour until	2058	2128	2158	2228
Ebbsfleet Int'l a.	0816	0846	0916	0946	♣	1916	1946	2016	2046	2116	2146	2216	2246		0746	0846	...	0946	1046	1146	1216	1246	♣	2116	2146	2216	2246
Stratford Int'l a.	0829	0858	0929	0958		1928	1958	2028	2102	2128	2158	2228	2258		0758	0858	...	0958	1058	1159	1228	1258		2128	2159	2228	2258
London St Pancras a.	0836	0906	0936	1006		1936	2006	2036	2109	2136	2206	2236	2306		0806	0906	...	1006	1106	1207	1236	1306		2136	2207	2236	2306

Via Ashford and Dover

km		Ⓐ	②–⑤	Ⓐ	Ⓐ	ⒶD	Ⓐ	Ⓐ	ⒶD	Ⓐ		Ⓐ	ⒶD	Ⓐ	Ⓐ	Ⓐ	Ⓐ	Ⓐ	Ⓐ	Ⓐ	Ⓐ	Ⓐ	Ⓐ	Ⓐ	ⒶD	Ⓐ
0	**London** St Pancras d.		0012	0640	0704	0725	0737	0812	0837	0909		1612	1637	1650	1707	1720	1737	1750	1807	1820	1837	1850	1907	1920	1937	2012
9	Stratford International d.		0019	0647	0711	0732	0744	0819	0844	0916	and at	1619	1644	1657	1714	1727	1744	1757	1814	1827	1845	1857	1914	1927	1944	2019
35	Ebbsfleet International d.		0030	0659	0722	|	0755	0830	0855	0927	the same	1630	1655	|	1726	|	1756	|	1826	|	1856	|	1926	|	1955	2030
90	Ashford International d.		0050	0722	0742	0801	0817	0852	0915	0952	minutes	1652	1718	1726	1747	1756	1817	1826	1847	1856	1917	1926	1947	1956	2015	2052
112	**Folkestone** Central d.		...	|	|	0819	0837	|	0930	|	past each	|	1733	|	1803	|	1835	|	1903	|	1934	|	2003	|	2030	|
124	**Dover** Priory a.		...	|	|	0830	0847	|	0941	|	hour until	|	1744	|	1815	|	1845	|	1915	|	1944	|	2015	|	2041	|
112	Canterbury West d.		...	0740	0758	|	|	0909	|	1009	♠	1709	|	1742	...	1812	|	1842	...	1912	...	1942	...	2012	|	2109
140	Ramsgate a.		...	0803	0818	0910	0924	0927	1018	1027		1731	1823	1801	...	1831	1925	1901	...	1931	...	2001	...	2031	2118	2131
149	**Margate** a.		...	...	0831	0926	...	0939	1030	1039		1742	1837	1815	...	1845	...	1915	...	1945	...	2015	...	2045	2130	2142

	Ⓐ	Ⓐ	Ⓐ	ⒶB	Ⓐ	②–⑤	①	Ⓐ	⑥	⑥	⑥D	⑥	⑥D	⑥		⑥D	⑥	⑥	⑥	⑥	⑥	⑥	⑥	⑥	⑦	⑦
London St Pancras d.	2037	2112	2137	2212	2237	2312	2312	2337		0012	...	...	0637	0708		1937	2012	2037	2112	2137	2212	2237	2312	2337		0012
Stratford International d.	2044	2119	2144	2219	2244	2319	2319	2344		0019	...	...	0644	0715	and at	1944	2019	2044	2119	2144	2219	2244	2319	2344		0019
Ebbsfleet International d.	2055	2130	2155	2230	2255	2330	2330	2355		0030	...	...	0655	0726	the same	1955	2030	2055	2130	2155	2230	2255	2330	2355		0030
Ashford International d.	2115	2152	2215	2252	2315	2352	2352	0015		0050	0615	0632	0715	0752	minutes	2015	2052	2115	2152	2215	2252	2315	2352	0015		0050
Folkestone Central d.	2130	|	2230	|	2330	|	|	0030		...	0630	|	0730	|	past each	2030	|	2130	|	2230	|	2330	|	0030		...
Dover Priory a.	2141	|	2241	|	2341	|	|	0041		...	0641	|	0741	|	hour until	2041	|	2141	|	2241	|	2341	|	0041		...
Canterbury West d.	|	2209	|	2309	|	0009	*0034*p	|		...	|	0651	|	0809	♠	|	2109	|	2209	|	2309	|	0009	|		...
Ramsgate a.	2219	2227	2322	2330	0019	0030	0043	0121		...	0718	0713	0818	0827		2119	2127	2219	2227	2321	2327	0021	0027	0121		...
Margate a.	...	2239	...	2340	...	0039r	0058	...		...	0730	0725	0830	0839		2130	2139	...	2239	...	2339	...	0039	...		...

	⑦D	⑦D	⑦		⑦D	⑦	⑦	⑦	⑦	⑦	⑦	⑦	⑦
London St Pancras d.	...	0837	0909		1937	2012	2037	2112	2137	2212	2237	2312	2337
Stratford International d.	...	0844	0916	and at	1944	2019	2044	2119	2144	2219	2244	2319	2344
Ebbsfleet International d.	...	0855	0927	the same	1955	2030	2055	2130	2155	2230	2255	2330	2355
Ashford International d.	0815	0915	0952	minutes	2015	2052	2115	2152	2215	2252	2315	2352	0015
Folkestone Central d.	0830	0930	|	past each	2030	|	2130	|	2230	|	2330	|	...
Dover Priory a.	0841	0941	|	hour until	2041	|	2141	|	2241	|	2341	|	...
Canterbury West d.	|	|	1009	♠	|	2109	|	2209	|	2309	|	0009	...
Ramsgate a.	0918	1018	1027		2118	2127	2218	2227	2318	2327	0018	0027	...
Margate a.	0930	1030	1039		2130	2139	...	2239	...	2339	...	0039	...

	Ⓐ	Ⓐ	Ⓐ	Ⓐ	Ⓐ	Ⓐ	Ⓐ	Ⓐ	Ⓐ
Margate d.		...	...	...	0546	...	0615	...	0646
Ramsgate d.		...	0455	...	0558	...	0628	0614	0658
Canterbury West d.		...	0518	...	0618	...	0648	|	0718
Dover Priory d.		...	|	0545	|	0618	|	0648	|
Folkestone Cent. d.		...	|	0556	|	0629	|	0659	|
Ashford Int'l d.		0513	0543	0613	0636	0646	0706	0716	0736
Ebbsfleet Int'l a.		0532	0602	0632	0655	0705	|	0735	|
Stratford Int'l a.		0544	0614	0644	0707	0717	0734	0747	0804
London St Pancras a.		0551	0621	0651	0714	0725	0742	0754	0813

	Ⓐ	Ⓐ	Ⓐ	Ⓐ	Ⓐ	Ⓐ	Ⓐ	ⒶE	Ⓐ		ⒶE	Ⓐ	Ⓐ	Ⓐ	Ⓐ	Ⓐ	Ⓐ	Ⓐ	Ⓐ	Ⓐ	Ⓐ	Ⓐ	⑥	⑥	⑥	⑥
Margate d.	...	0716	0656	0749	...	0851	...	0859	0953		1702	1753	...	1853	...	1953	...	2053	2100	2153	...	2253		...	...	0553
Ramsgate d.	...	0728	0712	0801	...	0903	0932	0912	1005	and at	1713	1805	...	1905	...	2005	...	2105	2112	2205	2212	2305		0505	...	0605
Canterbury West d.	...	0748	|	0825	...	0923	0952	|	1025	the same	|	1825	...	1925	...	2025	...	2125	|	2225	|	2325		0525	...	0625
Dover Priory d.	0716	|	0748	|	0849	|	|	0949	|	minutes	1749	|	1849	|	1949	|	2049	|	2149	|	2249	|		|	0549	|
Folkestone Central d.	0727	|	0759	|	0900	|	|	1000	|	past each	1800	|	1900	|	2000	|	2100	|	2200	|	2300	|		|	0600	|
Ashford International d.	0744	0806	0816	0843	0916	0943	1010	1016	1043	hour until	1816	1843	1916	1943	2016	2043	2116	2143	2216	2243	2316	2341		0543	0616	0643
Ebbsfleet International a.	|	|	0835	0902	0935	1002	|	1035	1102	♠	1835	1902	1935	2002	2035	2102	2135	2202	2235	2302	2335	...		0602	0635	0702
Stratford International a.	0812	0834	0847	0914	0947	1014	1038	1047	1114		1847	1914	1947	2014	2047	2114	2147	2214	2247	2314	2347	...		0614	0647	0714
London St Pancras a.	0820	0842	0854	0921	0954	1021	1046	1055	1121		1854	1921	1954	2021	2054	2121	2154	2221	2254	2321	2354	...		0621	0654	0721

	⑥	⑥	⑥	⑥	⑥	⑥	⑥E		⑥	⑥E	⑥	⑦	⑦	⑦	⑦		⑦	⑦	⑦	⑦	⑦E		⑦E	⑦	⑦E
Margate d.	...	0653	0657	0753	...	0853	0859		2153	2159	2253		...	...	0753	...	...	0853	...	0953	0959		2059	2153	2159
Ramsgate d.	0612	0705	0712	0805	0812	0905	0912	and at	2205	2212	2305		...	0712	0805	...	0812	0905	0912	1005	1012	and at	2112	2205	2212
Canterbury West d.	|	0725	|	0825	|	0925	|	the same	2225	|	2325		...	|	0825	...	|	0925	|	1025	|	the same	|	2225	|
Dover Priory d.	0649	|	0749	|	0849	|	0949	minutes	|	2249	|		...	0749	|	...	0849	|	0949	|	1049	minutes	2149	|	2249
Folkestone Central d.	0700	|	0800	|	0900	|	1000	past each	|	2300	|		...	0800	|	...	0900	|	1000	|	1100	past each	2200	|	2300
Ashford International d.	0716	0743	0816	0843	0916	0943	1016	hour until	2243	2316	2341		0743	0816	0843	...	0916	0943	1016	1043	1116	hour until	2216	2243	2315
Ebbsfleet International a.	0735	0802	0835	0902	0935	1002	1035	♠	2302	2335	...		0802	0835	0902	...	0935	1002	1035	1102	1135	♠	2235	2302	...
Stratford International a.	0747	0814	0847	0914	0947	1014	1047		2314	2347	...		0814	0847	0914	...	0947	1014	1047	1114	1147		2247	2314	...
London St Pancras a.	0754	0821	0855	0921	0954	1021	1055		2321	2354	...		0821	0854	0921	...	0954	1021	1054	1121	1154		2254	2321	...

A – ② departure from London St Pancras is operated by 🚌 after Faversham (Faversham d. 2336, Herne Bay d. 0012, Margate a. 0043).
B – ② departure from London St Pancras is operated by 🚌 after Ramsgate (Ramsgate d. 2335, Margate a. 2354).
D – To London St Pancras (see upper table).
E – From London St Pancras (see upper table).
F – To London St Pancras (see lower table).
G – From London St Pancras (see lower table).
H – From Ashford International (see lower table).
K – To Ashford International (see lower table).
p – Connection by 🚌 from Ashford; continues to Ramsgate (arr. 0112) and Margate (arr. 0131).
r – Not ②.
t – Arrives 1910.
♠ – Timings may vary by up to ± 4 minutes.
♣ – Timings may vary by up to ± 3 minutes.

Typical off-peak journey time in hours and minutes
READ DOWN ↓ READ UP ↑

Journey times may be extended during peak hours on Ⓐ (0600 - 0900 and 1600 - 1900) and also at weekends.
The longest journey time by any train is noted in the table heading.

LONDON VICTORIA - RAMSGATE

Longest journey: 2 hours 10 minutes SE

km	↓	Station	↑
0	0h00	d.**London** Victoria.....a.	1h57
18	0h17	d.Bromley South.......d.	1h40
53	0h47	d.Rochester..............d.	1h12
55	0h50	d.Chatham.................d.	1h10
72	1h09	d.Sittingbourne..........d.	0h50
84	1h21	d.Faversham..............d.	0h42
101	1h36	d.Herne Bay..............d.	0h26
119	1h49	d.Margate..................d.	0h10
128	1h59	a.**Ramsgate**.............d.	0h00

From London Victoria: on Ⓐ at 0007②–⑥ **f**, 0522, 0552, 0622 **g**, 0652 **g**, 0736, 0837 and hourly until 1437, 1537, 1607, 1637 **g**, 1636 **c**, 1657, 1727, 1730 **c m**, 1752 **c m**, 1757 **m**, 1812 **c**, 1827, 1844 **c**, 1857, 1937, 2037, 2137, 2207 **f g**, 2237 **f**, 2307 **f**; on ⑥ at 0007, 0707 **g**, 0737 and hourly until 2237, 2307; on ⑦ at 0007, 0745 and hourly until 2045, 2104 **h**, 2145, 2204 **h**, 2245, 2304 **h**, 2345 **h**.

From Ramsgate: on Ⓐ at 0432, 0506, 0539, 0608, 0629 **m c**, 0632, 0651 **m c**, 0703, 0708 **m c**, 0719 **b**, 0754 and hourly until 1354, 1450, 1545, 1648, 1705, 1748, 1848, 1954, 2050, 2154, 2310 **h**; on ⑥ at 0430, 0554 and hourly until 2154, 2310 **h**; on ⑦ at 0705, and hourly until 2105, 2120 **g**, 2235.

b – To London Blackfriars, not Victoria.
c – From/to London Cannon Street, not Victoria.
f – On Tuesday nights/Wednesday mornings does not call at Herne Bay or Margate.
h – To Faversham.
g – Change at Faversham.
m – To/from Margate.

LONDON VICTORIA - DOVER

Longest journey: 2 hours 10 minutes SE

km	↓	Station	↑
0	0h00	d.**London** Victoria.....a.	2h02
18	0h17	d.Bromley South.......d.	1h43
53	0h47	d.Rochester..............d.	1h17
55	0h50	d.Chatham.................d.	1h15
72	1h09	d.Sittingbourne..........d.	0h58
84	1h21	d.Faversham..............d.	0h47
99	1h37	d.Canterbury East.....d.	0h27
124	1h58	a.**Dover** Priory..........d.	0h00

From London Victoria: on Ⓐ at 0522 **g**, 0552 **g**, 0622, 0652, 0734, 0807, 0834 and at the same minutes past each hour until 1407, 1437 **g**, 1507, 1537 **g**, 1607, 1636 **c g**, 1637, 1657 **g**, 1708 **c**, 1727, 1730 **c g**, 1757, 1827, 1857, 1927 **b**, 1937 **g**, 2007, 2034 **e**, 2107, 2134 **e**, 2207; on ⑥ at 0522, 0634, 0707, 0734 and at the same minutes past each hour until 1934, 2007, 2034 **e**, 2107, 2134 **e**, 2207; on ⑦ at 0745, 0804 **e**, 0845, 0904 **e** and at the same minutes past each hour until 2004 **e**, 2045, 2104 **h**, 2145.

From Dover Priory: on Ⓐ at 0430, 0500 **g**, 0545 **b**, 0605 **g**, 0628 **g**, 0702, 0735, 0820, 0852, 0920, 0952 and at the same minutes past each hour until 1520, 1551, 1620, 1651 **g**, 1720, 1751, 1820, 1851, 1920, 2005, 2105, 2205, 2305 **h**; on ⑥ at 0520, 0620, 0652 and at the same minutes past each hour until 1920, 2005, 2105, 2205, 2305 **h**; on ⑦ at 0705, 0805, 0903 **e**, 0905 and at the same minutes past each hour until 2005, 2103 **e**, 2105, 2203 **e**, 2235 **g**.

b – From/to London Blackfriars, not Victoria. **c** – From London Cannon Street, not Victoria. **e** – To/from Canterbury East. **g** – Change at Faversham. **h** – To Faversham.

LONDON CHARING CROSS - CANTERBURY WEST

Longest journey: 1 hour 55 minutes SE

km	↓	Station	↑
0	0h00	d.**London** C Cross...a.	1h46
1	0h03	d.**London** Waterloo ‡ a.	1h42
3	0h08	d.**London** Bridge......a.	1h36
36	0h32	d.Sevenoaks.............d.	1h13
48	0h40	d.Tonbridge..............d.	1h04
90	1h20	a.Ashford Int'l...........d.	0h27
113	1h38	a.**Canterbury** West...d.	0h00

From London Charing Cross: on Ⓐ at 0530 **d**, 0635 **c**, 0709, 0737, 0816, 0922, 0940 **d**, 1010, 1040 **d** and at the same minutes past each hour until 1609, 1638, 1709, 1738, 1800 **d**, 1807 **c g**, 1840, 1910, 1940 **d**, 2010, 2110, 2210 **e**, 2310 **e**, 2340 **e h**; on ⑥ at 0602, 0710, 0740 **d**, 0810 and at the same minutes past each hour until 1910, 2010, 2110, 2210, 2310, 2340 **d**; on ⑦ at 0810, 0840 **d** and at the same minutes past each hour until 1710 then hourly until 2210.

From Canterbury West: on Ⓐ at 0518 **d**, 0600, 0634 **c g**, 0703, 0718 **d**, 0736, 0806 **d**, 0836 **d**, 0906 **d**, 0937, 1006 **d**, 1042 and at the same minutes past each hour until 1506 **d**, 1542, 1606 **d**, 1641, 1706 **d**, 1740, 1806 **d**, 1836, 1939, 2039, 2139; on ⑥ at 0539, 0637, 0737, 0806 **d**, 0840, 0906 **d**, 0938, 1006 **d**, 1042 at the same minutes past each hour until 1942, 2006 **d**, 2039, 2139, 2239 **k**; on ⑦ at 0740, 0840, 0906 **d**, 0943 and at the same minutes past each hour until 1843, 1906 **d**, 1940, 2040, 2140.

c – To/from London Cannon Street.
d – Change trains at Ashford.
e – On ① change trains at Ashford for 🚌 connection to Canterbury.
g – Does not call at London Bridge.
h – On ②–⑤ change trains at Ashford.
k – To Tonbridge.
‡ – London Waterloo East.

LONDON CHARING CROSS - DOVER

Longest journey: 2 hours 06 minutes SE

km	↓	Station	↑
0	0h00	d.**London** C Cross...a.	1h58
1	0h03	d.**London** Waterloo ‡ a.	1h53
3	0h08	d.**London** Bridge......a.	1h42
36	0h32	d.Sevenoaks.............d.	1h18
48	0h40	d.Tonbridge..............d.	1h06
90	1h20	d.Ashford Int'l...........d.	0h29
113	1h40	d.Folkstone Central...d.	0h12
124	1h52	a.**Dover** Priory..........d.	0h00

From London Charing Cross: on Ⓐ at 0530, 0636 **c d**, 0709, 0738, 0836 **b**, 0940 and hourly until 1240, 1310 **d**, 1340, 1410, 1440, 1510, 1540, 1609, 1638, 1650 **f**, 1724 **b c**, 1738 **d**, 1745 **c f**, 1800, 1832 **b c**, 1910, 1940, 2040, 2140, 2240, 2340; on ⑥ at 0740 and hourly until 2340; on ⑦ at 0840 and hourly until 2240.

From Dover Priory: on Ⓐ at 0429 **b c**, 0529, 0559 **b c**, 0628, 0711 **b c f**, 0725, 0758, 0825, 0858, 0925, 0958 and hourly until 1458, 1556, 1625, 1658, 1725, 1758, 1825, 1858, 1958, 2058, 2158 **e**; on ⑥ at 0458 and hourly until 2058, 2158 **e**; on ⑦ at 0759 and hourly until 2059.

b – Does not call at London Bridge.
c – From/to London Cannon Street.
d – Change trains at Ashford.
e – Terminates at Tonbridge.
f – To/from Folkestone Central.
‡ – London Waterloo East.

LONDON VICTORIA - ASHFORD INTERNATIONAL

Longest journey: 1 hours 40 minutes SE

km	↓	Station	↑
0	0h00	d.**London** Victoria.....a.	1h29
18	0h17	d.Bromley South.......d.	1h14
28	0h28	d.Swanley.................d.	1h03
56	0h52	d.West Malling..........d.	0h42
64	1h03	d.Maidstone East......d.	0h30
68	1h09	d.Bearsted................d.	0h25
95	1h31	a.**Ashford** Int'l..........d.	0h00

From London Victoria: on Ⓐ at 0022 ②–⑤, 0555, 0637, 0707, 0752, 0822, 0852 and every 30 minutes until 1622, 1652, 1712, 1742, 1747 **b**, 1818, 1842, 1904 **b**, 1922, 1952, 2022, 2052, 2122, 2152, 2222, 2252, 2322; on ⑥ at 0022, 0622, 0722, 0752 and every 30 minutes until 2322; on ⑦ at 0022, 0736 and hourly until 2336.

From Ashford International: on Ⓐ at 0514, 0532 **b**, 0547, 0601, 0617, 0624 **b**, 0640, 0656, 0711, 0748, 0830, 0910, 0930, 1010, 1038 and at the same minutes past each hour until 1538, 1602, 1638, 1702, 1738, 1802, 1838, 1900, 1938, 2002, 2038, 2102, 2132, 2232; on ⑥ at 0532, 0610, 0638 and at the same minutes past each hour until 2038, 2110, 2132, 2232; on ⑦ at 0646 and hourly until 2146.

b – From/to Blackfriars, not Victoria.

LONDON CHARING CROSS - HASTINGS

Longest journey: 1 hour 53 minutes SE

km	↓	Station	↑
0	0h00	d.**London** C Cross...a.	1h43
1	0h03	d.**London** Waterloo ‡ a.	1h39
3	0h08	d.**London** Bridge......a.	1h35
36	0h34	d.Sevenoaks.............d.	1h09
48	0h43	d.Tonbridge..............d.	1h00
55	0h55	d.Tunbridge Wells.....d.	0h49
89	1h33	d.Battle....................d.	0h16
100	1h45	a.**Hastings**...............d.	0h00

From London Charing Cross: on Ⓐ at 0628, 0715, 0743 **c**, 0818, 0840 **c**, 0914 **c**, 0945 and every 30 minutes until 1545, 1621 **c** *, 1642, 1702 **c d**, 1714 *, 1737 **c d** *, 1756 *, 1828 **c d** *, 1845, 1905 **c d**, 1915, 1945, 2015, 2045, 2145, 2245, 2345; on ⑥ at 0715, 0745, 0815, 0845 and every 30 minutes until 2015, 2045, 2145, 2245, 2345; on ⑦ at 0825, 0855, and every 30 minutes until 1925, 1955, 2025, 2125, 2225, 2325.

From Hastings: on Ⓐ at 0517, 0537 **c d**, 0548 **c d**, 0604 *, 0620 *, 0628 *, 0643 **c d** *, 0703 *, 0725 **c d** *, 0744, 0804 **c d** *, 0814, 0847, 0929, 0947, 1031, 1050 and at the same minutes past each hour until 1450, 1531 **d**, 1545 **c d**, 1619, 1645, 1719, 1750, 1819, 1846, 1950, 2050, 2150; on ⑥ at 0548, 0620, 0650, 0720, 0750, 0820, 0850, 0931, 0950 and at the same minutes past each hour until 1650, 1720, 1750, 1820, 1850, 1950, 2050, 2150; on ⑦ at 0650, 0720, 0750, 0831, 0850 and at the same minutes past each hour until 1831, 1850, 1950, 2050, 2150.

c – From/to London Cannon Street.
d – Does not call at London Bridge.
* – Does not call at Sevenoaks and Tonbridge. Frequent trains call at these stations.
‡ – London Waterloo East.

LONDON VICTORIA - EASTBOURNE

Longest journey: 1 hour 44 minutes SN

km	↓	Station	↑
0	0h00	d.**London** Victoria.....a.	1h26
17	0h16	d.East Croydon.........d.	1h09
43	0h33	d.Gatwick Airport......d.	0h53
61	0h50	d.Haywards Heath....d.	0h34
81	1h06	d.Lewes....................d.	0h19
106	1h27	a.**Eastbourne**...........d.	0h00

From London Victoria: on Ⓐ at 0005 ②–⑤, 0532, 0647, 0747, 0817, 0847, 0917 and every 30 minutes until 1647, 1723 **b**, 1727, 1757, 1823 **b**, 1846, 1917, 1947, 2017, 2047, 2117, 2147, 2247; on ⑥ at 0005, 0747 and every 30 minutes until 2147, 2247; on ⑦ at 0005, 0847 and hourly until 2247.

From Eastbourne: on Ⓐ at 0508, 0543 **b**, 0621 **b**, 0654 **g**, 0712 **g b**, 0731 **g**, 0757, 0818, 0853, 0931, 0955, 1035, 1055 and at the same minutes past each hour until 1435, 1453, 1535, 1553, 1635, 1653, 1733, 1755, 1831, 1859, 1931, 1955, 2031, 2131, 2216; on ⑥ at 0503, 0628, 0655, 0735, 0755 and at the same minutes past each hour until 1935, 1955, 2035, 2135, 2218; on ⑦ at 0658, 0755, 0900 and hourly until 2100.

b – From/to London Bridge, not Victoria. **g** – Does not call at Gatwick Airport.

ASHFORD - HASTINGS - EASTBOURNE - BRIGHTON

Longest journey: 2 hours 07 minutes SN

km	↓	Station	↑
0	0h00	d.**Ashford** Int'l ‡.......a.	1h46
25	0h23	d.Rye ‡......................d.	1h24
42	0h42	d.**Hastings**...............d.	1h04
50	0h52	d.Bexhill.....................d.	0h52
67	1h07	a.**Eastbourne**...........d.	0h37
67	1h15	d.**Eastbourne**...........a.	0h32
93	1h35	d.Lewes.....................d.	0h12
106	1h48	a.**Brighton**...............d.	0h00

From Ashford International: on Ⓐ at 0614, 0715, 0833, 0853 **h**, 0933 and hourly until 1933, 1959 **h**, 2033, 2133, 2234 **h**; on ⑥ at 0615, 0733 and hourly until 2133, 2234 **h**; on ⑦ at 0811, 0916 and hourly until 2116, 2234 **h**.

From Brighton: on Ⓐ at 0450 **k**, 0512 **e**, 0546 **h**, 0554 **k**, 0615, 0732 and hourly until 1532, 1632, 1709 **h**, 1730, 1832, 1932, 2030; on ⑥ at 0510 **e**, 0520 **h**, 0553 **k**, 0632 and hourly until 2032; on ⑦ at 0709 **e**, 0722 **h**, 0748 **k**, 0812 and hourly until 2012.

e – Change at Eastbourne. **h** – Ashford - Hastings and v.v. **k** – Eastbourne - Ashford.
‡ – Additional services operate on Ⓐ: Ashford - Rye at 0635, 0741, 1800, 1902; Rye - Ashford at 0706, 0814, 1831, 1933.
☛ Additional local services are available Brighton/Lewes - Eastbourne - Hastings v.v.

Typical off-peak journey time in hours and minutes

READ DOWN ↓   **READ UP** ↑

Journey times may be extended during peak hours on Ⓐ (0600 - 0900 and 1600 - 1900) and also at weekends.
The longest journey time by any train is noted in the table heading.

LONDON BRIDGE - UCKFIELD   Longest journey : 1 hour 19 minutes   SN

km					
0	0h00	↓	d.**London** Bridge ......a.	↑	1h15
16	0h16		d.East Croydon ....d.		0h59
32	0h29	↓	d.Oxted ....d.		0h44
57	0h55		d.Eridge △ ....d.		0h17
70	1h01	↓	d.Crowborough ....d.		0h12
74	1h15		a.**Uckfield** ....d.	↑	0h00

From London Bridge : on Ⓐ at 0526 e, 0602, 0638, 0703, 0755, 0902, 1008 and hourly until 1508, 1538, 1608, 1638, 1708, 1806, 1817 x, 1908, 2004, 2104, 2204, 2304; on ⑥ at 0608 and hourly until 2208, 2304.
From Uckfield : on Ⓐ at 0516, 0540, 0630, 0705, 0731, 0801, 0833, 0934 and hourly until 1534, 1633, 1732, 1832, 1900, 1933, 2004, 2034, 2134, 2234; on ⑥ at 0634 and hourly until 2234.
On ⑦ services run Oxted - Uckfield and v.v. only. Connections available from / to London Victoria (see East Grinstead Table).
From Oxted at 0937 ⑦ and hourly until 2237 ⑦. From Uckfield at 1034 ⑦ and hourly until 2134 ⑦, 2234 e.

e – East Croydon - Uckfield and v.v.   **x** – Change at Oxted.   △ – Spa Valley Railway (🚂 Eridge - Tunbridge Wells West : 8 km). ✆ 01892 537715. www.spavalleyrailway.co.uk

LONDON VICTORIA - EAST GRINSTEAD   Longest journey : 60 minutes   SN

km					
0	0h00	↓	d.**London** Victoria.....a.	↑	0h56
17	0h17		d.East Croydon ....d.		0h37
33	0h37	↓	d.Oxted ....d.		0h16
42	0h43	↓	d.Lingfield ....d.		0h12
48	0h54		a.**East Grinstead** ▽ .d.	↑	0h00

From London Victoria : on Ⓐ at 0526, 0547, 0624, 0654, 0710, 0718 b, 0732, 0750 b, 0824 b, 0853 and every 30 minutes until 1653, 1713 b, 1723, 1744 b, 1753, 1823, 1847 b, 1853 and every 30 minutes until 2323; on ⑥ at 0523, 0623, 0653 and every 30 minutes until 2253, 2324; on ⑦ at 0747, 0853, 0923, 0953 and every 30 minutes until 1953, 2053, 2153, 2236.
From East Grinstead : on Ⓐ at 0545 b, 0555, 0613 b, 0632, 0640 b, 0702, 0716 b, 0733, 0749 b, 0807, 0817 b, 0837 and every 30 minutes until 1807, 1817 b, 1837, 1847 c, 1907, 1917 c, 1937, 1947 c, 2007, 2037, 2107, 2137, 2207, 2237, 2254; on ⑥ at 0637 and every 30 minutes until 2237, 2257; on ⑦ at 0820, 0912, and every 30 minutes until 2012, 2112, 2212, 2309.

b – From / to London Bridge (not Victoria).   ▽ – Bluebell Railway (🚂 East Grinstead - Sheffield Park : 18 km). ✆ 01825 720800. www.bluebell-railway.com
c – East Grinstead - East Croydon.

LONDON VICTORIA - LITTLEHAMPTON   Longest journey : 1 hour 47 minutes   SN

km					
0	0h00	↓	d.**London** Victoria.....a.	↑	1h42
17	0h16		d.East Croydon ....a.		1h25
43	0h33	↓	d.Gatwick Airport ....a.		1h09
61	0h50		d.Haywards Heath ......a.		0h54
82	1h06	↓	d.Hove ....a.	↑	0h35
96	1h21		d.Worthing ....d.		0h21
114	1h41		a.**Littlehampton** ....d.	↑	0h00

From London Victoria : on Ⓐ at 0747, 0817, 0847 and every 30 minutes until 1617, 1657 b g, 1718, 1741 b g, 1746, 1810 b g, 1817 g, 1846, 1917, 1947, 2017, 2047, 2147; on ⑥ at 0747, 0817, 0847 and every 30 minutes until 2017, 2047, 2147; on ⑦ at 0817 and hourly until 2117.
From Littlehampton : on Ⓐ at 0552 b, 0629 b g, 0640 g, 0700 g, 0729, 0814, 0851, 0914, 0947, 1014, 1051 and at the same minutes past each hour until 1514, 1549, 1614, 1651, 1714, 1751, 1814, 1914, 2014, 2114; on ⑥ at 0545, 0614, 0651 and at the same minutes past each hour until 1814, 1914, 2014, 2114; on ⑦ at 0715 and hourly until 2015.

b – From / to London Bridge (not Victoria).   **g** – Does not call at Gatwick Airport.

LONDON VICTORIA - BOGNOR REGIS   Longest journey : 1 hour 57 minutes   SN

km					
0	0h00	↓	d.**London** Victoria.......d.	↑	1h50
17	0h16		d.East Croydon ....d.		1h30
43	0h37	↓	d.Gatwick Airport ....d.		1h08
61	1h03		d.Horsham ....d.		0h50
94	1h30	↓	d.Arundel................d.		0h16
110	1h40		d.Barnham ....d.		0h07
116	1h46		a.**Bognor Regis** ....d.	↑	0h00

From London Victoria : on Ⓐ at 0602, 0803, 0832, 0902, 0932, 1006 and every 30 minutes until 1636, 1702 g, 1734 g, 1803 g, 1834 g, 1902, 1932, 2002, 2032, 2102, 2117 k, 2217 k; on ⑥ at 0736, 0806, 0836 and every 30 minutes until 1836, 1902, 1932, 2002, 2032, 2117 k, 2217 k; on ⑦ at 0702 and hourly until 2202.
From Bognor Regis : on Ⓐ at 0605, 0640 g, 0717 g, 0755, 0826, 0856, 0930, 0956 and at the same minutes past each hour until 1456, 1527, 1556, 1630, 1656, 1730, 1756, 1833 k, 1936 k, 2033 k; on ⑥ at 0630, 0656 and at the same minutes past each hour until 1756, 1833 k, 1930, 1940 k, 2040 k; on ⑦ at 0652, 0759 and hourly until 2159.

g – Does not call at Gatwick Airport.   **k** – Does not call at Arundel and Horsham.

SEAFORD - BRIGHTON   Longest journey : 42 minutes   SN

km					
0	0h00	↓	d.**Seaford** ....a.	↑	0h36
4	0h05		d.Newhaven Harbour...d.		0h30
5	0h07	↓	d.Newhaven Town ......d.		0h28
15	0h19		d.Lewes ....d.		0h18
22	0h26	↓	d.Falmer ....d.		0h09
28	0h35		a.**Brighton** ....d.	↑	0h00

From Seaford : on Ⓐ at 0509, 0544, 0627, 0717, 0733, 0759, 0855, 0925, 0954 and at the same minutes past each hour until 1654, 1720, 1757, 1824, 1841, 1859, 1917, 1937, 1957, 2028, 2057, 2128, 2157, 2220, 2257, 2325; on ⑥ at 0505, 0628, 0657, 0725, 0757 and at the same minutes past each hour until 1957, 2028, 2057, 2128, 2157, 2220, 2257, 2325; on ⑦ at 0757, 0828, 0857, 0928, 0957 and every 30 minutes until 2127, 2154, 2227, 2253.
From Brighton : on Ⓐ at 0545, 0639, 0652, 0717, 0740, 0810, 0845, 0910 and every 30 minutes until 1710, 1745, 1802, 1822, 1838, 1908, 1940, 2010, 2040, 2104, 2140, 2204, 2234, 2336; on ⑥ at 0552, 0610, 0640 and every 30 minutes until 2040, 2104, 2140, 2204, 2236, 2336; on ⑦ at 0715, 0749, 0817, 0849, 0917, 0947 and every 30 minutes until 2147, 2209, 2239.

BRIGHTON - PORTSMOUTH HARBOUR   Longest journey : 1 hour.49 minutes   SN

km	✕	⑦			✕	⑦
0	0h00	0h00	↓	d.**Brighton** ....d.	↑	1h19	1h36
2	0h04	0h10		d.Hove ....d.		1h15	1h31
16	0h22	0h31	↓	d.Worthing ....d.		0h57	1h10
35	0h39	0h54		d.Barnham ....d.		0h39	0h48
45	0h47	1h02	↓	d.Chichester...........d.		0h31	0h39
59	1h02	1h23		d.Havant ....d.		0h17	0h19
71	1h14	1h37	↓	a.**Portsmouth** S ▽ ..d.		0h04	0h04
72	1h18	1h41		a.**Portsmouth** Hbr ..d.	↑	0h00	0h00

From Brighton : on Ⓐ at 0553, 0635, 0715, 0737 t, 0803, 0904, 1003 and hourly until 1503, 1603 p, 1705, 1800 t, 1900 p t, 2003 t, 2103 t, 2133 t, 2203 t; on ⑥ at 0601, 0703 and hourly until 1903 t, 1956 t, 2103 t, 2133 t, 2203 t; on ⑦ at 0715 r, 0719, 0820 r, 0830 and hourly until 2030, 2125, 2144.
From Portsmouth Harbour : on Ⓐ at 0528 t, 0604, 0701, 0720, 0829 and hourly until 1629, 1640, 1729, 1827, 1932 p, 2032 p, 2115 p t, 2215 t, 2240 t; on ⑥ at 0629, 0648, 0729 and hourly until 1929, 2028, 2111 t, 2215 t, 2244 t; on ⑦ at 0714 and hourly until 1914, 2011, 2114, 2144.

p – To / from Portsmouth & Southsea only.   **t** – Runs in ⑦ (slower) timings.
r – Runs in ✕ (faster) timings.   ▽ – Portsmouth and Southsea.

BRIGHTON - SOUTHAMPTON CENTRAL   Longest journey : 2 hours 1 minute   SN

km	✕	⑦			✕	⑦
0	0h00	0h00	↓	d.**Brighton** ....d.	↑	1h45	1h50
2	0h04	0h04		d.Hove ....d.		1h41	1h46
16	0h18	0h25	↓	d.Worthing ....d.		1h23	1h25
35	0h39	0h48		d.Barnham ....d.		1h00	1h03
45	0h46	0h56	↓	d.Chichester...........d.		0h52	0h54
59	1h04	1h08		d.Havant ....d.		0h38	0h42
75	1h19	1h25	↓	d.Fareham ....d.		0h23	0h24
98	1h52	1h56		a.**Southampton** C ..d.	↑	0h00	0h00

From Brighton : on Ⓐ at 0512 t, 0530 t, 0627, 0705, 0730, 0833, 0859, 0933 and hourly until 1633, 1702, 1733, 1828, 1930 t, 2030 t; on ⑥ at 0515, 0527 t, 0634, 0733, 0833, 0900, 0933 and hourly until 1633, 1700, 1733, 1833, 1929 t, 2030 t; on ⑦ at 0800, 0900, 1000, 1100, 1110 r, 1200, 1300, 1400, 1500, 1546 r, 1600, 1700, 1746 r, 1800, 1900, 2000, 2100.
From Southampton Central : on Ⓐ at 0610, 0733, 0832 and hourly until 1332, 1426, 1434, 1532 and hourly until 2032 t, 2113 t; on ⑥ at 0632 and hourly until 1332, 1426, 1434, 1532 and hourly until 1732, 1832 t, 1932 t, 2032 t, 2113 t; on ⑦ at 0730, 0827, 0831 r, 0930, 1030, 1130, 1230, 1304 r, 1330, 1430, 1506 r, 1530, 1630, 1730, 1830, 1927 r, 1930, 2029, 2130.

r – Runs in ✕ (faster) timings.   **t** – Runs in ⑦ (slower) timings.

LONDON WATERLOO - READING   Longest journey : 1 hour 35 minutes   SW

km					
0	0h00	↓	d.**London** Waterloo ..a.	↑	1h22
16	0h16		d.Richmond.............d.		1h03
18	0h20	↓	d.Twickenham..........d.		0h58
30	0h33		d.Staines ....d.		0h36
46	0h53	↓	d.Ascot ....d.		0h28
70	1h20		a.**Reading** ....d.	↑	0h00

From London Waterloo : on Ⓐ at 0505, 0550, 0620, 0650, 0720, 0750, 0807, 0820, 0837, 0850 and every 30 minutes until 1550, 1605, 1620, 1635, 1650, 1720, 1735, 1750, 1805, 1820, 1835, 1850, 1905, 1920, 1935, 1950 and every 30 minutes until 2350; on ⑥ at 0505, 0550 and every 30 minutes until 2350; on ⑦ at 0709, 0809 and every 30 minutes until 2339.
From Reading : on Ⓐ at 0542, 0612, 0623, 0642, 0654, 0712, 0723, 0742, 0812, 0842, 0912, 0925, 0942, 0956, 1012 and every 30 minutes until 1712, 1723, 1742, 1753, 1812, 1842, 1852, 1912 and every 30 minutes until 2242, 2312; on ⑥ at 0542 and every 30 minutes until 2242, 2312; on ⑦ at 0754, 0824, 0854 and every 30 minutes until 2154, 2224, 2254.

LONDON WATERLOO - WINDSOR   Longest journey : 1 hour 09 minutes   SW

km					
0	0h00	↓	d.**London** Waterloo ..a.	↑	0h56
16	0h20		d.Richmond.............d.		0h34
18	0h24	↓	d.Twickenham..........d.		0h30
30	0h39		d.Staines ....d.		0h15
41	0h53	↓	a.**Windsor** ▷ ....d.	↑	0h00

From London Waterloo : on Ⓐ at 0558 and every 30 minutes until 2328; on ⑥ at 0558 and every 30 minutes until 2328; on ⑦ at 0644, 0744, 0825, 0844 and at the same minutes past each hour until 1944, 2025, 2044, 2144, 2244.
From Windsor and Eton Riverside : on Ⓐ at 0553, 0623 and every 30 minutes until 2223, 2253; on ⑥ at 0553, 0623 and every 30 minutes until 2223, 2253; on ⑦ at 0701, 0801, 0901, 0934, 1001, 1034 and at the same minutes past each hour until 2101, 2201, 2301.

▷ – Windsor and Eton Riverside.

BEDFORD - LUTON ✈ - LONDON - GATWICK ✈ - BRIGHTON

Additional trains are available London Bridge - Brighton and v.v.

Other services: Bedford - Luton Airport - London St Pancras see Table **170**; London Victoria - Gatwick Airport - Brighton see Table **105**; London Victoria - Gatwick Airport *Gatwick Express* see Table **100**.

km			Ⓐ	Ⓐ	Ⓐ	Ⓐ	Ⓐ	Ⓐ	Ⓐ	Ⓐ	Ⓐ	Ⓐ	Ⓐ	Ⓐ	Ⓐ	Ⓐ	Ⓐ	Ⓐ	Ⓐ	Ⓐ	Ⓐ	Ⓐ	Ⓐ	Ⓐ		Ⓐ	Ⓐ	Ⓐ
0	**Bedford** d.	Ⓐ	0040	0140	0220	0240	0320	0340	0416	0446	0518	0544	0600	0618	0654	0658	0730	0734	0748	0804	0824	0840	0854	0910	and at	1440	1454	1510
31	Luton d.		0104	0204	0244	0304	0344	0404	0440	0510	0542	0604	0624	0638	0714	0722	0750	0758	0812	0828	0848	0904	0918	0934	the same	1504	1518	1534
33	Luton Airport ✈ d.		0107	0207	0247	0307	0347	0407	0443	0513	0544	|	0627	0641	|	0725	|	0800	0815	0831	0851	0907	0921	0937	minutes	1507	1521	1537
48	St Albans City d.		0119	0219	0259	0319	0359	0419	0455	0525	0556	0616	0638	0652	0726	0738	0802	0812	0828	0843	0903	0918	0933	0948	past	1518	1533	1548
80	**London** St Pancras d.		0154	0254	0324	0354	0424	0454	0523	0553	0620	0636	0658	0716	0746	0758	0822	0834	0850	0906	0924	0942	0954	1012	each	1542	1554	1612
85	**London** Blackfriars d.		0205	0305	0335	0405	0435	0505	0535	0603	0630	0646	0708	0728	0756	0808	0832	0844	0900	0916	0936	0952	1006	1022	hour	1552	1606	1622
101	East Croydon d.		0236	0336	0406	0437	0506	0532	0602	0632	0702	0716	0736	0758	0826	0838	0858	0912	0931	0949	1004	1019	1034	1049	until	1619	1634	1651
127	Gatwick Airport ✈ d.		0259	0359	0425	0504	0527	0548	0618	0648	0717	0732	0754	0814	0842	0852	0914	0928	0958	1005	1033	1035	1101	1105		1635	1701	1707
145	Haywards Heath d.		...	...	...	0519	0542	0602	0634	0704	0731	0748	0808	0830	0858	...	0928	0945	...	1019	...	1049	...	1119	♥	1649	...	1721
166	**Brighton** a.		...	...	...	0537	0602	0622	0654	0726	0750	0808	0823	0850	0918	...	0948	1006	...	1039	...	1109	...	1139		1709	...	1743

	Ⓐ	Ⓐ	Ⓐ	Ⓐ	Ⓐ	Ⓐ	Ⓐ	Ⓐ	Ⓐ	Ⓐ	Ⓐ	Ⓐ	Ⓐ	Ⓐ	Ⓐ	Ⓐ	Ⓐ	Ⓐ	Ⓐ	Ⓐ	Ⓐ	Ⓐ	Ⓐ	Ⓐ		⑥	⑥	⑥	⑥
Bedford d.	1524	1550	1608	1626	1640	1708	1720	1734	1800	1810	1824	1840	1854	1908	1940	2010	2040	2110	2140	2152	2222	2240	2310	2340	⑥	0040	0140	0220	0240
Luton d.	1548	1610	1632	1650	1704	1732	1744	1758	1819	1834	1848	1904	1918	1932	2004	2034	2104	2134	2204	2216	2246	2306	2334	0004		0104	0204	0244	0304
Luton Airport ✈ d.	1551	1613	1635	1652	1707	1735	1747	1801	1822	1837	1851	1907	1921	1935	2007	2037	2107	2137	2207	2219	2249	2309	2337	0007		0107	0207	0247	0307
St Albans City d.	1603	1624	1647	1704	1718	1748	1758	1812	1834	1848	1903	1918	1933	1946	2018	2048	2118	2148	2218	2230	2300	2321	2349	0019		0119	0219	0259	0319
London St Pancras d.	1624	1646	1710	1729	1742	1810	1820	1836	1855	1912	1925	1942	1955	2012	2042	2112	2142	2212	2242	2254	2324	2354	0024	0054		0154	0254	0324	0354
London Blackfriars d.	1636	1658	1720	1740	1752	1820	1830	1846	1906	1922	1936	1952	2006	2022	2052	2122	2152	2222	2252	2308	2336	0005	0035	0105		0205	0305	0335	0405
East Croydon d.	1704	1726	1748	1809	1825	1850	1901	1918	1939	1951	2010	2021	2039	2051	2121	2151	2221	2251	2321	2339	0006	0032	0106	0136		0236	0336	0406	0436
Gatwick Airport ✈ d.	1728	1742	1814	1824	1850	1906	1926	1935	2000	2007	2025	2037	2054	2107	2137	2207	2237	2307	2337	2357	0026	0058f	0140j	0155r		0255	0355	0425	0455
Haywards Heath d.	...	1758	1832	1840	...	1920	...	1949	...	2021	...	2051	2110	2121	2153	2221	2253	2321	2355	0011	0043	...	...	0215t		...	...	...	...
Brighton a.	...	1819	1852	1903	...	1942	...	2010	...	2041	...	2111	2124	2141	2213	2243	2315	2343	0015	0031	0103	...	...	0230t		...	...	...	...

	⑥	⑥	⑥	⑥	⑥	⑥	⑥	⑥	⑥	⑥		⑥	⑥	⑥	⑥	⑥	⑥	⑥	⑥		⑥	⑥	⑥	⑥	⑥	⑥	⑥	⑥
Bedford d.	0320	0340	0412	0450	0520	0540	0554	0610	0624	0640	and at	1754	1810	1824	1840	1854	1910	1940	2010	...	2040	2110	2140	2152	2222	2240	2310	2340
Luton d.	0344	0404	0436	0514	0544	0604	0618	0634	0648	0704	the same	1818	1834	1848	1904	1918	1934	2004	2034	...	2104	2134	2204	2216	2246	2306	2334	0004
Luton Airport ✈ d.	0347	0407	0439	0517	0547	0607	0621	0637	0651	0707	minutes	1821	1837	1851	1907	1921	1937	2007	2037	...	2107	2137	2207	2219	2249	2309	2337	0007
St Albans City d.	0359	0419	0451	0528	0558	0618	0633	0648	0703	0718	past	1833	1848	1903	1918	1933	1948	2018	2048	...	2118	2148	2218	2230	2300	2321	2349	0019
London St Pancras d.	0424	0456	0526	0554	0624	0642	0654	0712	0725	0742	each	1854	1912	1924	1942	1954	2012	2042	2112	...	2142	2212	2242	2254	2324	2354	0024	0054
London Blackfriars d.	0435	0505	0535	0606	0636	0652	0706	0722	0736	0752	hour	1906	1922	1936	1952	2006	2022	2052	2122	...	2152	2222	2252	2308	2336	0005	0035	0105
East Croydon d.	0506	0532	0602	0634	0704	0719	0734	0749	0804	0819	until	1934	1951	2004	2021	2034	2051	2121	2151	...	2221	2251	2321	2339	0004	0032	0106	0136
Gatwick Airport ✈ d.	0526	0548	0618	0650	0720	0735	0802	0805	0833	0835		2001	2007	2033	2037	2102	2107	2137	2207	...	2237	2307	2337	2357	0024	0054	0126	0155
Haywards Heath d.	0543	0603	0633	0703	0733	0751	...	0819	...	0849	♥	...	2021	...	2051	2118	2121	2153	2221	...	2253	2321	2353	0011	0041	0109	...	...
Brighton a.	0606	0624	0654	0724	0755	0811	...	0839	...	0909		...	2041	...	2111	2132	2141	2213	2241	...	2313	2341	0013	0031	0101	0129	...	...

		⑦	⑦	⑦	⑦	⑦	⑦	⑦	⑦	⑦		⑦	⑦	⑦	⑦	⑦	⑦	⑦	⑦	⑦	⑦	⑦	⑦	⑦	⑦	⑦	⑦	⑦
Bedford d.	⑦	...	0558	0628	0658	0728	0750	0806	0820	0836		1636	1650	1706	1720	1736	1806	1836	1906	1936	2006	2028	2058	2128	2158	2228	2300	2340
Luton d.		...	0622	0652	0722	0752	0814	0830	0844	0900	and at	1700	1714	1730	1744	1800	1830	1900	1930	2000	2030	2052	2122	2152	2222	2252	2324	0004
Luton Airport ✈ d.		...	0625	0655	0725	0755	0817	0833	0847	0903	the same	1703	1717	1733	1747	1803	1833	1903	1933	2003	2033	2055	2125	2155	2225	2255	2327	0007
St Albans City d.		...	0637	0707	0737	0807	0829	0845	0859	0915	minutes	1715	1729	1745	1759	1815	1845	1915	1945	2015	2045	2107	2137	2207	2237	2307	2339	0019
London St Pancras d.		...	0712	0742	0812	0842	0856	0912	0926	0942	past	1742	1756	1812	1826	1842	1912	1942	2012	2042	2112	2142	2212	2242	2310	2340	0014	0054
London Blackfriars d.		0652	0722	0752	0822	0852	0906	0922	0936	0952	each	1752	1806	1822	1836	1852	1922	1952	2022	2052	2122	2152	2222	2252	2322	2352	0025	0105
East Croydon d.		0723	0753	0821	0856	0926	0939	0956	1009	1026	hour	1826	1839	1856	1909	1926	1956	2026	2056	2126	2156	2226	2256	2326	2357	0029	0059	0136
Gatwick Airport ✈ d.		0744	0818	0842	0912	0942	0954	1012	1024	1042	until	1842	1854	1912	1924	1942	2012	2042	2112	2142	2212	2242	2312	2342	0020	0048	0130	0200
Haywards Heath d.		0758	0834	0856	0926	0956	...	1028	...	1056		1856	...	1928	...	1956	2028	2056	2128	2156	2228	2256	2328	2356	0036	...	...	0215
Brighton a.		0818	0854	0916	0948	1016	...	1048	...	1116		1916	...	1948	...	2016	2048	2116	2148	2216	2248	2316	2348	0016	0056	...	...	0230

		②–⑤	Ⓐ	Ⓐ	Ⓐ	Ⓐ	Ⓐ	Ⓐ	Ⓐ	Ⓐ	Ⓐ	Ⓐ	Ⓐ	Ⓐ	Ⓐ	Ⓐ	Ⓐ	Ⓐ	Ⓐ	Ⓐ	Ⓐ	Ⓐ	Ⓐ	Ⓐ	Ⓐ	Ⓐ	Ⓐ	
Brighton d.	Ⓐ	0010	...	...	...	...	...	0415	...	0510	0530	0544	0606	0619	0657	0722	0748	0800	0818	0833	0905	0935	1005	1035	...	1105	...	and at
Haywards Heath d.		0025	...	...	...	...	...	0429	...	0531	0551	0603	0629	0642	0720	0746	0809	0822	0839	0856	0926	0956	1026	1056	...	1126	...	the same
Gatwick Airport ✈ d.		0039	0118	0218	0318	0351	0420	0452	0525	0548	0608	0617	0643	0700	0738	0801	0823	0839	0853	0910	0940	1010	1040	1110	1108	1140	1138	minutes
East Croydon d.		0100	0140	0240	0340	0410	0442	0517	0547	0603	0623	0639	0658	0723	0754	0824	0839	0854	0910	0925	0955	1025	1055	1125	1138	1155	1208	past
London Blackfriars d.	★	0129	0209	0309	0409	0439	0510	0546	0612	0630	0652	0708	0726	0754	0822	0850	0910	0922	0938	0954	1024	1054	1124	1154	1208	1224	1238	each
London St Pancras d.		0140	0220	0320	0420	0450	0520	0556	0622	0640	0702	0718	0736	0804	0832	0900	0920	0932	0948	1004	1034	1104	1134	1204	1218	1234	1248	hour
St Albans City d.		0214	0254	0354	0454	0514	0554	0618	0644	0703	0723	0743	0757	0825	0852	0920	0940	0952	1009	1025	1055	1125	1155	1225	1239	1255	1309	until
Luton Airport ✈ d.		0226	0306	0406	0506	0526	0606	0630	0656	0714	0734	0754	0808	0837	0903	0929	0952	1003	1021	1037	1107	1137	1206	1237	1251	1307	1321	
Luton d.		0229	0309	0409	0509	0529	0609	0633	0659	0717	0737	0757	0811	0840	0906	0932	0955	1006	1024	1040	1110	1140	1210	1240	1254	1310	1324	♣
Bedford a.		0255	0337	0435	0535	0557	0637	0701	0724	0743	0803	0823	0837	0905	0926	0957	1020	1025	1053	1105	1135	1205	1235	1305	1319	1335	1349	

	Ⓐ	Ⓐ	Ⓐ	Ⓐ	Ⓐ	Ⓐ	Ⓐ	Ⓐ	Ⓐ	Ⓐ	Ⓐ	Ⓐ	Ⓐ	Ⓐ	Ⓐ	Ⓐ	Ⓐ	Ⓐ	Ⓐ	Ⓐ	Ⓐ	Ⓐ	Ⓐ	Ⓐ	Ⓐ	Ⓐ	Ⓐ	Ⓐ	Ⓐ
Brighton d.	...	1505	...	1535	...	1602	...	1635	...	1701	...	1735	...	1805	1835	...	1905	...	1933	...	2003	...	2033	2105	2131	2202	2230	2305	2337
Haywards Heath d.	...	1526	...	1556	...	1623	...	1656	...	1722	...	1756	...	1826	1856	...	1926	...	1954	...	2026	...	2054	2126	2152	2223	2251	2326	2358
Gatwick Airport ✈ d.	1508	1540	1538	1610	1608	1640	1638	1710	1710	1740	1745	1810	1815	1840	1910	1917	1940	1947	2010	2018	2040	2047	2110	2140	2209	2238	2307	2340	0015
East Croydon d.	1538	1555	1608	1625	1638	1656	1703	1725	1739	1755	1804	1825	1834	1855	1925	1934	1955	2008	2025	2038	2055	2108	2125	2155	2225	2255	2325	2356	0038
London Blackfriars d.	1608	1622	1638	1652	1708	1722	1736	1752	1810	1822	1836	1852	1906	1924	1954	2008	2024	2038	2054	2108	2124	2138	2154	2222	2252	2322	2352	0024	0104
London St Pancras d.	1618	1632	1648	1702	1718	1732	1746	1802	1820	1832	1846	1902	1916	1934	2004	2018	2034	2048	2104	2118	2134	2148	2204	2232	2302	2332	0002	0034	0114
St Albans City d.	1639	1650	1709	1720	1736	1750	1806	1820	1842	1850	1906	1920	1936	1955	2025	2039	2055	2109	2125	2139	2155	2209	2225	2257	2327	2357	0027	0108	0148
Luton Airport ✈ d.	1651	|	1721	|	1748	|	1818	|	1854	|	1919	|	1948	2007	2037	2051	2107	2121	2137	2151	2207	2221	2237	2309	2339	0009	0039	0120	0200
Luton d.	1654	1702	1724	1732	1751	1802	1821	1832	1857	1902	1922	1932	1951	2010	2040	2054	2110	2124	2140	2154	2210	2224	2240	2312	2342	0012	0042	0123	0203
Bedford a.	1719	1723	1749	1753	1813	1823	1846	1853	1926	1923	1948	1953	2013	2035	2105	2119	2135	2150	2205	2219	2235	2249	2305	2340	0008	0038	0108	0149	0229

		⑥	⑥	⑥	⑥	⑥	⑥	⑥	⑥	⑥	⑥	⑥	⑥	⑥	⑥	⑥	⑥	⑥	⑥	⑥		⑥	⑥	⑥	⑥	⑥	⑥	⑥
Brighton d.	⑥	0010	...	...	...	...	...	...	0533	0605	0602	0635	0632	0705	0737	0734	0805	...	0835	...	and at	2005	...	2033	...	2105	2133	2205
Haywards Heath d.		0025	...	...	...	...	...	...	0554	0626	0620	0656	0647	0726	0756	0751	0826	...	0856	...	the same	2026	...	2054	...	2126	2154	2226
Gatwick Airport ✈ d.		0039	0121	0221	0321	0421	0455	0525	0610	0640	0638	0710	0708	0740	0810	0808	0840	0838	0910	0908	minutes	2040	2038	2110	2108	2140	2210	2240
East Croydon d.		0100	0140	0240	0340	0440	0517	0547	0625	0655	0708	0725	0738	0755	0825	0838	0855	0908	0925	0938	past	2055	2108	2125	2138	2155	2225	2255
London Blackfriars d.	☆	0129	0209	0309	0409	0509	0542	0614	0654	0724	0738	0754	0808	0824	0854	0908	0924	0938	0954	1008	each	2124	2138	2154	2208	2224	2252	2322
London St Pancras d.		0140	0220	0320	0420	0520	0552	0624	0704	0734	0748	0804	0818	0834	0904	0918	0934	0948	1004	1018	hour	2134	2148	2204	2218	2234	2302	2332
St Albans City d.		0214	0254	0354	0454	0554	0625	0645	0725	0755	0809	0825	0839	0855	0925	0939	0955	1009	1025	1039	until	2155	2209	2225	2239	2259	2327	2357
Luton Airport ✈ d.		0226	0306	0406	0506	0606	0637	0657	0737	0807	0821	0837	0851	0907	0937	0951	1007	1021	1037	1051		2207	2221	2237	2251	2311	2339	0009
Luton d.		0229	0309	0409	0509	0609	0640	0700	0740	0810	0824	0840	0854	0910	0940	0954	1010	1024	1040	1054	♥	2210	2224	2240	2254	2314	2342	0012
Bedford a.		0255	0335	0436	0537	0635	0708	0725	0805	0835	0849	0905	0919	0935	1005	1019	1035	1049	1105	1119		2235	2249	2305	2319	2340	0008	0038

	⑥	⑥	⑥		⑦	⑦	⑦	⑦	⑦	⑦	⑦	⑦	⑦	⑦		⑦	⑦	⑦	⑦	⑦	⑦	⑦	⑦	⑦	⑦	⑦	⑦	⑦
Brighton d.	2233	2305	2337	⑦	0010	0606	0636	0703	0736	0804	0844	...	0914	...	and at	...	1844	...	1914	1944	2014	2044	2114	2144	2214	2244	2312	2342
Haywards Heath d.	2254	2326	2358		0026	0624	0654	0724	0754	0824	0903	...	0933	...	the same	...	1903	...	1933	2003	2033	2103	2133	2203	2233	2303	2331	0002
Gatwick Airport ✈ d.	2310	2340	0015		0039	0638	0708	0738	0808	0838	0917	0929	0947	0959	minutes	1859	1917	1929	1947	2017	2047	2117	2147	2217	2247	2317	2345	0015
East Croydon d.	2325	2356	0038	♡	0100	0657	0727	0757	0827	0856	0933	0947	1003	1017	past	1917	1933	1947	2003	2033	2103	2133	2203	2233	2303	2333	0002	0038
London Blackfriars d.	2352	0024	0104		0129	0724	0754	0824	0854	0924	1008	1022	1038	1052	each	1952	2008	2022	2038	2108	2138	2208	2238	2308	2338	0008	0032	0104
London St Pancras d.	0002	0034	0114		0140	0734	0804	0834	0904	0934	1018	1032	1048	1102	hour	2002	2018	2032	2048	2118	2148	2218	2248	2318	2348	0018	0044	0114
St Albans City d.	0027	0108	0148		0214	0808	0838	0908	0938	1008	1043	1057	1113	1127	until	2027	2043	2057	2113	2143	2213	2243	2322	2352	0022	0052	0118	0148
Luton Airport ✈ d.	0039	0120	0200		0226	0820	0850	0920	0950	1020	1055	1109	1125	1139		2039	2055	2109	2125	2155	2225	2255	2334	0004	0034	0104	0130	0200
Luton d.	0042	0123	0203		0229	0823	0853	0923	0953	1023	1058	1112	1128	1142	♥	2042	2058	2112	2128	2158	2228	2258	2337	0007	0037	0107	0133	0203
Bedford a.	0108	0149	0229		0255	0849	0919	0949	1019	1049	1125	1138	1154	1208		2108	2124	2138	2154	2226	2254	2324	0003	0033	0103	0133	0159	0229

f – Arrives 0053 on ⑥ mornings.
j – Arrives 0127 on ⑥ mornings.
r – Arrives 0155 on ⑥ mornings.
t – ②–⑤ mornings only.

★ – Additional services on Ⓐ from Gatwick to Bedford at 0916 and 1008.
☆ – Additional service on ⑥ from Gatwick to Bedford at 0738.
♡ – Additional services on ⑦ from Blackfriars to Bedford at 0008; Brighton to Blackfriars at 0536; from Gatwick to Bedford at 0859.

♥ – Timings may vary by up to 2 minutes.

For explanation of standard symbols see page 1

LONDON - GATWICK ✈ - BRIGHTON

km			②–⑤	Ⓐ	Ⓐ	Ⓐ	Ⓐ	Ⓐ	Ⓐ	Ⓐ	Ⓐ	Ⓐ	Ⓐ	Ⓐ	Ⓐ	Ⓐ	Ⓐ	Ⓐ	Ⓐ		Ⓐ	Ⓐ	Ⓐ	Ⓐ	Ⓐ	Ⓐ	Ⓐ
0	**London** Victoria.....d.	Ⓐ	0005	0452	0606	0615	0617	0630	0715	0736	0800	0807	0821	0830	0838	0900	0920	0930	0950	and at the same	1550	1600	1620	1630	1647	1706	1730
17	East Croydon.........d.		0027	0519	0623	|	0635	|	|	0752	|	0823	0841	|	0854	|	0936	|	1006	minutes past	1606	|	1636	|	1703	1723	|
43	Gatwick Airport ✈..d.		0045	0548	|	0646	0706	0704	0750	0808	0833	|	0857	0902	0910	0932	0952	1002	|	each hour until	|	1632	1652	1702	1719	|	1807
82	**Brighton** ....a.		0118	0626	0705	0716	0741	0736	0820	0838	0857	0912	0938	0927	0942	0954	1017	1024	1047	✣	1646	1654	1720	1732	1756	1812	1839

	Ⓐ	Ⓐ	Ⓐ	Ⓐ	Ⓐ	Ⓐ	Ⓐ	Ⓐ	Ⓐ	Ⓐ	Ⓐ	Ⓐ	Ⓐ	Ⓐ	Ⓐ	Ⓐ	Ⓐ	Ⓐ	Ⓐ	⑤	①–④	⑤	①–④	⑤	Ⓐ		⑥	⑥	⑥
London Victoria .....d.	1742	1800	1815	1830	1844	1900	1920	1930	1950	2000	2020	2030	2050	2100	2120	2130	2150	2200	2220	2230	2230	2250	2250	2307	2332	⑥	0005	0100	0400
East Croydon..........d.	|	|	|	1847	|	|	1936	|	2007	|	2036	|	2106	|	2136	|	2206	|	2238	|	|	2306	2306	2323	2350		0027	0124	0424
Gatwick Airport ✈...d.	1815	1837	1847	|	1917	1932	1952	2002	2023	2032	2051	2102	2122	2132	2152	2202	2222	2232	2254	2302	2305	2322	2324	|	0015		0045	0151	0449
Brighton ....a.	1848	1912	1921	1939	1953	2002	2019	2027	2049	2057	2119	2127	2148	2158	2216	2230	2248	2300	2321	2327	2331	2346	2349	0003	0053		0118	0226	0517

	⑥	⑥	⑥	⑥	⑥	⑥	⑥	⑥	⑥	⑥	⑥	⑥		⑥	⑥	⑥	⑥	⑥	⑥	⑥	⑥	⑥	⑥	⑥	⑥	⑥	⑥
London Victoria .....d.	0502	0532	0600	0630	0700	0720	0730	0750	0800	0820	0830	0850	and at the same	2000	2020	2030	2050	2100	2120	2130	2150	2200	2220	2230	2250	2307	2332
East Croydon..........d.	0524	0548	|	|	|	0736	|	0806	|	0836	|	0906	minutes past	|	2036	|	2106	|	2136	|	2206	|	2236	|	2306	2324	2349
Gatwick Airport ✈...d.	0553	0622	0632	0702	0732	0751	0802	|	0832	0852	0902	|	each hour until	2032	2052	2102	2122	2132	2152	2202	2222	2232	2252	2302	2322	|	0013
Brighton ....a.	0630	0706	0702	0727	0757	0816	0824	0846	0854	0916	0924	0946	✣	2054	2118	2124	2146	2157	2221	2227	2247	2259	2318	2327	2346	0003	0050

		⑦	⑦	⑦	⑦	⑦	⑦	⑦	⑦	⑦	⑦	⑦	⑦	⑦	⑦		⑦	⑦	⑦	⑦	⑦	⑦	⑦	⑦	⑦	⑦	
London Victoria .....d.	⑦	0005	0100	0400	0502	0547	0632	0726	0832	0907	0927	0932	1006	1027	1032	and at the same	1906	1927	1932	2006	2027	2032	2106	2127	2227	2332	...
East Croydon..........d.		0028	0126	0426	0525	0610	0655	0748	0853	0923	0942	0949	1022	1042	1049	minutes past	1923	1942	1949	2023	2042	2049	2123	2142	2242	2353	...
Gatwick Airport ✈...d.		0046	0154	0453	0550	0633	0723	0813	0913	0939	1006	|	1038	1106	|	each hour until	1939	2006	|	2039	2106	|	2139	2207	2306	0015	...
Brighton ....a.		0117	0225	0522	0620	0709	0759	0851	0951	1003	1043	1024	1103	1143	1124	✣	2003	2043	2024	2103	2143	2124	2203	2243	2345	0052	...

		Ⓐ	Ⓐ	Ⓐ	Ⓐ	Ⓐ	Ⓐ	Ⓐ	Ⓐ	Ⓐ	Ⓐ	Ⓐ	Ⓐ	Ⓐ	Ⓐ	Ⓐ		Ⓐ	Ⓐ	Ⓐ	Ⓐ	Ⓐ		Ⓐ	Ⓐ	Ⓐ	Ⓐ
Brighton ....d.	Ⓐ	0523	0614	0630	0640	0646	0712	0729	0744	0815	0830	0846	0918	0928	0948	0958	and at the same	1418	1429	1448	1458	1518	...	1526	1548	1618	1648
Gatwick Airport ✈...a.		0554	0651	0703	0716	|	0747	0800	0819	0846	0905	0913	0942	0952	1013	|	minutes past	1442	1452	1512	|	1542	...	1552	1612	1643	1712
East Croydon..........a.		0611	0716	|	|	0738	|	|	|	|	|	0928	|	1008	|	1038	each hour until	|	1507	|	1537	|	...	1607	|	|	|
London Victoria .....a.		0629	0735	0741	0754	0758	0823	0839	0855	0923	0939	0949	1016	1026	1045	1056	✣	1515	1524	1546	1554	1615	...	1626	1647	1717	1747

	Ⓐ	Ⓐ	Ⓐ	Ⓐ	Ⓐ	Ⓐ	Ⓐ	Ⓐ	Ⓐ	Ⓐ	Ⓐ	Ⓐ	Ⓐ	Ⓐ	Ⓐ	Ⓐ	Ⓐ	Ⓐ	Ⓐ	⑤	Ⓐ	Ⓐ	⑤			⑥	⑥	⑥	⑥
Brighton ....d.	1720	1728	1750	1758	1818	1828	1848	1859	1915	1928	1948	1958	2020	2028	2048	2058	2120	2128	2149	2158	2226	2255	2310	...	⑥	0350	0523	0550	0556
Gatwick Airport ✈...a.	1745	1752	1814	1822	1843	1852	1912	1939	1942	1952	2013	2022	2042	2052	2113	2122	2142	2152	2213	2222	2248	2319	2353	...		0502	0552	0625	0632
East Croydon..........a.	|	1807	|	1837	|	1909	|	2002	|	2008	|	2038	|	2107	|	2137	|	2207	|	2237	|	|	0020	...		0528	0607	0640	0648
London Victoria .....a.	1822	1824	1852	1856	1926	1928	1951	2020	2015	2026	2044	2056	2117	2125	2145	2156	2214	2224	2243	2256	2321	2354	0042	...		0556	0624	0657	0710

	⑥	⑥	⑥	⑥	⑥	⑥	⑥	⑥	⑥		⑥	⑥	⑥	⑥	⑥	⑥	⑥	⑥	⑥	⑥	⑥	⑥	⑥	⑥	⑥	⑥	⑥
Brighton ....d.	0609	0618	0628	0648	0658	0718	0728	0748	0758	and at the same	1818	1828	1848	1858	1918	1928	1948	1958	2018	2028	2048	2058	2118	2128	2148	2158	2218
Gatwick Airport ✈...a.	0655	0642	0652	0712	|	0742	0752	0812	|	minutes past	1842	1852	1912	1922	1942	1952	2013	2023	2042	2053	2114	2123	2142	2152	2213	2224	2242
East Croydon..........a.	0711	|	0707	|	0737	|	0807	|	0837	each hour until	|	1907	|	1937	|	2007	|	2038	|	2108	|	2138	|	2207	|	2239	|
London Victoria .....a.	0727	0715	0724	0746	0754	0815	0824	0845	0854	✣	1915	1924	1945	1954	2015	2024	2045	2055	2115	2125	2145	2155	2215	2224	2245	2256	2315

	⑥	⑥		⑦	⑦	⑦	⑦		⑦	⑦	⑦	⑦	⑦	⑦	⑦	⑦		⑦	⑦	⑦	⑦	⑦	⑦		⑦	⑦	⑦
Brighton ....d.	2255	2308	⑦	0350	0613	0706	0747	...	0825	0838	0910	0859	0935	1010	0959	1035	and at the same	1910	1859	1935	2010	1959	2035	...	2104	2204	2305
Gatwick Airport ✈...a.	2319	2353		0501	0647	0742	0829	...	|	0900	|	0940	0956	|	1040	1056	minutes past	|	1940	1957	|	2040	2057	...	2140	2240	2346
East Croydon..........a.	|	0019		0527	0705	0804	0857	...	0903	0915	0945	1001	1013	1045	1101	1113	each hour until	1945	2001	2014	2045	2101	2114	...	2201	2301	0018
London Victoria .....a.	2355	0041		0555	0727	0825	0914	...	0924	0932	1003	1018	1030	1103	1118	1130	✣	2003	2018	2031	2105	2118	2130	...	2218	2319	...

✣ – Timings may vary by ± 3 minutes.

☛ For other services London - Gatwick Airport - Brighton and v.v. see Tables **100** and **103**.

 🍷 on most trains

LONDON - GUILDFORD - PORTSMOUTH

km			①	Ⓐ	Ⓐ	Ⓐ	Ⓐ	Ⓐ	Ⓐ	Ⓐ	Ⓐ	Ⓐ	Ⓐ		Ⓐ	Ⓐ	Ⓐ	Ⓐ	Ⓐ	Ⓐ	Ⓐ	Ⓐ	Ⓐ	Ⓐ	Ⓐ
0	**London** Waterloo....... **113** d.	Ⓐ	0050	...	0500	0520	0615	0645	0730	0800	0830	0900	0930	and at	1600	1630	1700	1730	1800	1815	1830	1900	1930	2000	2030
39	Woking...................... **113** d.		0118	...	0553	0611	0643	0713	0756	0825	0855	0925	0955	the same	1625	1656	1725	1756	|	|	1858	1925	1955	2025	2055
49	Guildford ....d.		0126**s**	0509	0604	0630**a**	0655	0725	0805	0839	0907	0934	1004	minutes	1634	1705	1737	1808	1834	1851	1908	1937	2004	2034	2104
69	Haslemere..........................d.		|	0524	0628	0655	0720	0753	0825	0856	0925	0949	1021	past each	1651	1724	1754	1826	1852	1906	1926	1953	2023	2055	2122
88	Petersfield..........................d.		|	0545	0645	0711	0736	0811	0836	0907	0936	1000	1032	hour until	1702	1735	1805	1837	1903	1923	1937	2004	2034	2106	2133
107	Havant ....a.		0200**s**	0600	0659	0727	0751	0826	0849	0919	0949	1014	1049		1714	1749	1819	1850	1915	1940	1951	2016	2048	2118	2145
118	**Portsmouth** & Southsea ... a.		0214**s**	0616	0716	0746	0807	0843	0902	0932	1003	1028	1102	♥	1728	1802	1832	1903	1929	1959	2004	2029	2101	2132	2158
120	**Portsmouth** Harbour ....a.		0219	0620	0720	0751	0812	0848	0907	0937	1008	1033	1107		1738	1809	1839	1910	1936	...	2010	2034	2106	2137	2202

	Ⓐ	Ⓐ	Ⓐ	Ⓐ	Ⓐ	Ⓐ	Ⓐ		⑥	⑥	⑥	⑥	⑥	⑥		⑥	⑥	⑥	⑥	⑥		⑥	⑥	⑥	⑥
London Waterloo .... **113** d.	2100	2130	2200	2230	2245	2315	2345	⑥	...	0520	0645	0730	0800	0830		1900	1930	2000	2030	2100	...	2130	2200	2230	2245
Woking .... **113** d.	2125	2155	2225	2256	2313	2343	0013		...	0613	0713	0755	0825	0855	and at	1925	1955	2025	2055	2125	...	2155	2225	2255	2313
Guildford.............................d.	2134	2204	2234	2305	2325	2352	0025		0515	0625	0725	0804	0834	0904	the same	1934	2004	2034	2104	2134	...	2204	2234	2304	2325
Haslemere ....d.	2155	2225	2255	2325	2350	0012	0050		0530	0645	0745	0821	0849	0921	minutes	1949	2021	2049	2121	2155	...	2225	2255	2325	2350
Petersfield ....d.	2206	2236	2306	2336	0006	0023	0106		0546	0701	0801	0832	0900	0932	past each	2000	2032	2100	2132	2206	...	2236	2306	2336	0006
Havant.................................a.	2218	2248	2318	2348	0020	0036	0121		0601	0719	0816	0849	0915	0949	hour until	2015	2049	2115	2144	2218	...	2248	2318	2348	0020
Portsmouth & Southsea ....a.	2232	2303	2331	0002	0038	0050	0138		0618	0735	0832	0902	0928	1002		2028	2102	2128	2158	2232	...	2302	2331	0002	0037
Portsmouth Harbour..........a.	2237	2308	2336	0007	...	0055	...		0622	0740	0837	0907	0933	1007		2033	2107	2133	2203	2236	...	2308	2336	0007	...

	⑥	⑥		⑦	⑦	⑦	⑦		⑦	⑦	⑦		⑦	⑦	⑦	⑦		⑦	⑦	⑦	⑦	⑦	⑦	⑦	⑦
London Waterloo .... **113** d.	2315	2345	⑦	...	0800	0830	0900	...	0930	1000	1030	and at	1800	1830	1900	1930	...	2000	2030	2100	2130	2200	2230	2300	2330
Woking .... **113** d.	2343	0013		0732	0835	0904	0935	...	1004	1032	1102	the same	1832	1902	1932	2002	...	2032	2102	2132	2202	2232	2302	2332	0003
Guildford.............................d.	2352	0025		0741	0845	0914	0945	...	1014	1042	1112	minutes	1842	1912	1942	2012	...	2042	2112	2142	2212	2242	2312	2342	0012
Haslemere ....d.	0012	0050		0807	0912	0929	1012	...	1029	1107	1127	past each	1907	1927	2007	2027	...	2107	2127	2207	2227	2307	2327	0007	0027
Petersfield ....d.	0023	0106		0823	0928	0940	1028	...	1040	1123	1138	hour until	1923	1938	2023	2038	...	2123	2138	2223	2238	2323	2338	0023	0038
Havant.................................a.	0036	0121		0838	0943	0952	1043	...	1052	1138	1150		1938	1950	2038	2050	...	2138	2150	2238	2250	2338	2350	0038	0050
Portsmouth & Southsea ....a.	0049	0137		0853	0958	1006	1058	...	1105	1153	1204	♥	1953	2004	2053	2104	...	2153	2204	2253	2304	2353	0004	0053	0104
Portsmouth Harbour..........a.	0054	...		0857	1003	1011	1103	...	1111	1158	1211		1958	2011	2058	2109	...	2158	2208	2258	2309	2358	0009	0058	0109

		Ⓐ	Ⓐ	Ⓐ	Ⓐ	Ⓐ	Ⓐ	Ⓐ	Ⓐ	Ⓐ	Ⓐ	Ⓐ	Ⓐ	Ⓐ	Ⓐ	Ⓐ		Ⓐ	Ⓐ	Ⓐ	Ⓐ	Ⓐ	Ⓐ	Ⓐ	Ⓐ
Portsmouth Harbour..........d.	Ⓐ	0425	0519	...	0550	0615	...	0642	...	0713	0745	0815	0845	0915	0945	1015	and at	1445	1515	...	1545	1615	...	1645	1715
Portsmouth & Southsea ....d.		0430	0524	...	0555	0620	...	0647	...	0718	0750	0820	0850	0920	0950	1020	the same	1450	1520	...	1550	1620	...	1650	1720
Havant.................................d.		0446	0540	...	0611	0634	0650	0700	0711	0732	0804	0834	0904	0934	1004	1034	minutes	1504	1534	1554	1604	1634	1656	1704	1734
Petersfield ....d.		0503	0557	0612	0629	0648	0707	0714	0725	0746	0818	0848	0918	0948	1018	1048	past each	1518	1548	1610	1618	1648	1710	1718	1748
Haslemere ....d.		0526	0616	0630	0647	0702	0726	0734	0740	0800	0832	0902	0932	1002	1032	1102	hour until	1532	1602	1624	1637	1702	1732	1737	1802
Guildford ....d.		0549	0631	0653	0707	0717	0745	0752	0803	0815	0853**c**	0917	0947	1017	1047	1117		1547	1617	1647	1700	1717	1747	1800	1817
Woking .... **113** a.		0600	0640	0703	0715	0725	0755	|	0811	0826	|	0927	0959	1025	1057	1125	♥	1557	1625	1657	1711	1725	1758	1811	|
London Waterloo .... **113** a.		0629	0713	0736	0745	0754	0824	0831	0841	0856	0931	0955	1029	1054	1124	1151		1624	1651	1727	1743	1754	1827	1843	1859

	Ⓐ	Ⓐ	Ⓐ	Ⓐ	Ⓐ	Ⓐ	Ⓐ	Ⓐ	Ⓐ	Ⓐ			⑥		⑥	⑥	⑥	⑥	⑥		⑥	⑥	⑥	⑥	⑥
Portsmouth Harbour..........d.	1745	1815	1845	1915	1945	2015	2045	2119	2219	2319	⑥	...	0443	...	0519	0619	0645	0715	0745	and at	1615	1645	...	1719	1745
Portsmouth & Southsea ....d.	1750	1820	1850	1920	1950	2020	2050	2124	2224	2324		...	0448	...	0524	0624	0650	0720	0750	the same	1620	1650	1710	1724	1750
Havant.................................d.	1804	1834	1904	1934	2004	2034	2104	2140	2240	2340		...	0504	...	0540	0640	0704	0734	0804	minutes	1634	1704	1726	1740	1804
Petersfield ....d.	1818	1848	1918	1948	2018	2048	2118	2157	2257	2357		...	0520	...	0557	0657	0718	0748	0818	past each	1648	1718	1743	1757	1818
Haslemere ....d.	1832	1902	1932	2002	2032	2102	2132	2215	2315	0015		...	0539	...	0615	0715	0732	0802	0832	hour until	1702	1732	1802	1815	1832
Guildford ....d.	1855	1921	1947	2017	2047	2117	2147	2239	2339	0037		...	0602	...	0634	0734	0747	0817	0847		1717	1747	1817	1834	1847
Woking .... **113** a.	1903	1929	1957	2025	2058	2125	2157	2249	2349	...		...	0611	...	0644	0744	0757	0826	0857	♣	1725	1757	1825	1844	1857
London Waterloo .... **113** a.	1929	1959	2024	2050	2129	2151	2227	2319	0033	...		...	0640	...	0713	0813	0823	0851	0923		1751	1823	1851	1913	1923

	⑥	⑥	⑥	⑥	⑥	⑥	⑥	⑥	⑥			⑦	⑦	⑦	⑦	⑦	⑦	⑦	⑦	⑦		⑦	⑦	⑦	⑦
Portsmouth Harbour..........d.	1815	1845	1915	1945	2015	2045	2119	2219	2319	⑦	...	0648	0732	0748	0832	0848	0932	0948	1032	1048		2132	2148	2232	2248
Portsmouth & Southsea ....d.	1820	1850	1920	1950	2020	2050	2124	2224	2324		...	0653	0737	0753	0837	0853	0937	0953	1037	1053	and at	2137	2153	2237	2253
Havant.................................d.	1834	1904	1934	2004	2034	2104	2140	2240	2340		...	0707	0750	0807	0850	0907	0950	1007	1050	1107	the same	2150	2207	2250	2307
Petersfield ....d.	1848	1918	1948	2018	2048	2118	2157	2257	2357		...	0724	0804	0824	0904	0924	1004	1024	1104	1124	minutes	2204	2224	2304	2324
Haslemere ....d.	1902	1932	2002	2032	2102	2132	2215	2315	0015		...	0742	0817	0842	0917	0942	1017	1042	1117	1142	past each	2217	2242	2317	2342
Guildford ....d.	1917	1947	2017	2047	2117	2149	2239	2339	0037		...	0805	0835	0905	0935	1005	1035	1106	1135	1205	hour until	2235	2305	2335	0005
Woking .... **113** a.	1925	1957	2025	2059	2125	2157	2249	2349	...		...	0813	0842	0915	0942	1015	1042	1113	1142	1213		2242	2313	2342	0013
London Waterloo .... **113** a.	1951	2023	2050	2127	2152	2227	2318	0032	...		...	0850	0916	0948	1014	1046	1114	1149	1214	1244		2314	2344	0014	...

a – Arrives 0624.
c – Arrives 0847.

♣ – London Waterloo arrivals may vary by ± 6 minutes.
♥ – Timings may vary by ± 3 minutes.

① – Mondays ② – Tuesdays ③ – Wednesdays ④ – Thursdays ⑤ – Fridays ⑥ – Saturdays ⑦ – Sundays Ⓐ – Not Saturdays 17

108 LONDON - SOUTHAMPTON - BOURNEMOUTH - WEYMOUTH

🍷 on most trains. SW

km			②–⑤	Ⓐ	Ⓐ	Ⓐ	Ⓐ	Ⓐ	Ⓐ	Ⓐ	Ⓐ	Ⓐ	Ⓐ		Ⓐ	Ⓐ	Ⓐ	Ⓐ	Ⓐ	Ⓐ	Ⓐ	Ⓐ	Ⓐ	Ⓐ	Ⓐ
0	**London** Waterloo .... 113 d.	Ⓐ	0005	...	...	...	0530	0630	0703	0735	0805	0835	0905		1635	1705	1735	1805	1835	1905	1935	2005	2035	2105	2135
39	Woking .... 113 d.		0037	...	...	...	0601	0657	0730	0800	|	0900	|	and	1700u	|	|	|	|	|	2000	|	2100	2132	2200
77	Basingstoke .... 119 d.		0056	...	...	0540	0621	0718	0750	0820	0849	|	0949	at	|	|	|	|	|	1949	|	2049	|	2152	|
107	Winchester .... 119 d.		0113	...	...	0559	0638	0734	0806	0837	0905	0933	1005	the	1733	1800	1830	1900	1930	2005	2033	2105	2133	2208	2233
120	**Southampton** Airport.. 119 d.		0126	...	...	0613	0653	0749	0815	0852	0914	0942	1014	same	1742	1809	1839	1909	1939	2014	2042	2115	2142	2222	2242
128	**Southampton** Central. 119 d.		0137	...	...	0625	0701	0759	0827	0901	0924	0951	1024	minutes	1753r	1821r	1851r	1919	1951r	2024	2051	2125	2151	2231	2251
149	Brockenhurst .... 119 d.		0153s	...	0615	0644	0718	0820	0846	0918	0938	1005	1038	past	1808	|	|	1936	|	2038	2108	2144	2205	2250	2305
174	**Bournemouth** .... 119 d.		0215	0611	0644	0711	0746	0848	0913	0945	1004r	1024r	1104r	each	1824	1850	1921	2007r	2021	2104r	2127r	2212	2224r	2317	2329r
183	Poole .... d.		...	0624	0657	0724	0758	0900	0926	0958	1014	1037	1114	hour	1837	1903	1934	2019	2034	2115	2139	2223	2237	2329	2342
193	Wareham .... 119a d.		...	0638	0711	0738	0812	0912	0940	1010	1028	1050	1128	until	1849	1917	1946	2033	2046	2127	2151	...	2249	...	2354
219	Dorchester South ....d.		...	0658	0731	0758	0833	0933	1000	1026	1054	1106	1149	♠	1908	1937	2003	2054	2102	2147	2212	...	2309	...	0014
230	**Weymouth** .... a.		...	0709	0742	0809	0844	0944	1011	1035	1106	1115	1202		1919	1950	2015	2107	2115	2200	2223	...	2320	...	0025

	Ⓐ	Ⓐ	Ⓐ		⑥	⑥	⑥	⑥	⑥	⑥	⑥	⑥	⑥	⑥	⑥		⑥	⑥	⑥	⑥	⑥	⑥	⑥	⑥	⑥
London Waterloo .... 113 d.	2205	2235	2305	⑥	0005	...	...	...	0530	...	0630	...	0735	0805	0835		1835	1905	1935	2005	2035	2105	2135	2205	2235
Woking .... 113 d.	2232	2300	2332		0037	...	...	...	0601	...	0657	...	0800	|	0900	and	1900	|	2000	|	2100	2132	2200	2232	2300
Basingstoke .... 119 d.	2252	|	2353		0056	...	...	...	0621	...	0718	...	0821	0849	|	at	|	1949	|	2049	|	2152	|	2252	|
Winchester .... 119 d.	2308	2333	0012		0113	...	...	...	0641	...	0734	...	0838	0905	0933	the	1933	2005	2033	2105	2133	2208	2233	2308	2333
Southampton Airport ... 119 d.	2322	2342	0028		0126	...	...	...	0656	...	0748	...	0851	0914	0942	same	1942	2014	2042	2114	2142	2222	2242	2322	2342
Southampton Central .. 119 d.	2330	2351	0038		0137	...	...	0621	0705	0721	0800r	0819	0900	0924	0951	minutes	1951	2024	2051	2124	2151	2230	2251	2330	2351
Brockenhurst .... 119 d.	2349	0005	0054s		0153s	...	0615	0640	0722	0740	0817	0840	0917	0938	1005	past	2005	2038	2105	2143	2205	2249	2305	2349	0005
Bournemouth .... 119 d.	0016	0022	0118		0215	0611	0644	0711r	0749	0811r	0844	0911r	0944	1004r	1024r	each	2024r	2104r	2124r	2210	2224r	2317	2326r	0016	0022
Poole ....d.	0028	0035	0130		...	0624	0657	0724	0802	0824	0857	0924	0957	1014	1037	hour	2037	2114	2137	2223	2237	2329	2339	0030	0035
Wareham .... 119a d.	...	...	...		...	0638	0711	0738	0814	0838	0909	0938	1009	1028	1049	until	2049	2128	2149	...	2249	...	2350	...	...
Dorchester South ....d.	...	...	...		...	0658	0731	0758	0834	0858	0929	0958	1027	1049	1105	♠	2105	2149	2209	...	2309	...	0011	...	...
Weymouth ....a.	...	...	...		...	0709	0742	0809	0845	0909	0940	1009	1035	1100	1113		2113	2200	2220	...	2320	...	0022	...	...

	⑥		⑦	⑦	⑦	⑦	⑦	⑦	⑦	⑦	⑦		⑦	⑦	⑦	⑦	⑦		⑦	⑦	⑦	⑦	⑦	⑦
London Waterloo .... 113 d.	2305	⑦	0005	...	...	...	0754	0835	0854	0935	0954		1435	1454	1535	1605	1635		2005	2035	2105	2135	2205	2305
Woking .... 113 d.	2332		0037	...	...	...	0828	0909	0928	1009	1028	and	1507	1528	1607	1637	1707	and	2037	2107	2137	2207	2237	2337
Basingstoke .... 119 d.	2352		0056	...	0748	...	0848	0929	0948	1029	1048	at	1528	1548	1628	1657	1728	at	2057	2128	2157	2228	2257	2357
Winchester .... 119 d.	0011		0113	...	0808	...	0908	0946	1008	1046	1108	the	1544	1608	1644	1714	1744	the	2114	2144	2214	2244	2314	0014
Southampton Airport ... 119 d.	0025		0126	...	0827	...	0927	0955	1027	1055	1127	same	1553	1627	1653	1727	1753	same	2127	2153	2227	2253	2327	0028
Southampton Central .. 119 d.	0035		0137	...	0835	0903	0935	1003	1035	1103	1135	minutes	1603	1635	1703	1736	1803	minutes	2136	2203	2236	2303	2336	0042
Brockenhurst .... 119 d.	0051s		0153s	...	0857	0917	0957	1018	1057	1118	1157	past	1617	1657	1717	1757	1817	past	2157	2217	2257	2317	2355	0058s
Bournemouth .... 119 d.	0115		0215	0839	0927r	0939r	1024	1039r	1124	1139r	1224	each	1639r	1724	1739r	1825	1839r	each	2225	2239r	2325	2339r	0022	0122
Poole ....d.	0127		...	0851	0936	0951	1033	1051	1133	1151	1233	hour	1651	1733	1751	1834	1851	hour	2234	2251	2334	2351	0034	0134
Wareham .... 119a d.	...		...	0903	...	1003	...	1103	...	1203	...	until	1703	...	1803	...	1903	until	...	2303	...	0003	...	...
Dorchester South ....d.	...		...	0924	...	1024	...	1124	...	1224	...		1724	...	1824	...	1924		...	2325	...	0025	...	...
Weymouth ....a.	...		...	0935	...	1035	...	1135	...	1235	...		1735	...	1835	...	1935		...	2336	...	0036	...	...

		Ⓐ	Ⓐ	Ⓐ	Ⓐ	Ⓐ	Ⓐ	Ⓐ	Ⓐ	Ⓐ	Ⓐ	Ⓐ	Ⓐ	Ⓐ		Ⓐ	Ⓐ	Ⓐ	Ⓐ	Ⓐ	Ⓐ	Ⓐ	Ⓐ	Ⓐ	Ⓐ
Weymouth ....d.	Ⓐ	...	...	...	...	0555	...	0625	0655	...	0725	0755	0820	0903		1703	1720	1803	1820	1903	1920	2010	2110	2210	2310
Dorchester South ....d.		...	...	...	...	0607	...	0637	0707	...	0737	0807	0833	0913	and	1713	1733	1813	1833	1913	1937	2022	2122	2222	2322
Wareham .... 119a d.		...	...	...	...	0627	...	0657	0727	...	0757	0827	0853	0928	at	1728	1753	1828	1853	1928	1957	2042	2142	2242	2342
Poole ....d.		0500	0545	0611	...	0641	...	0711	0741	0755	0811	0841	0907	0940	the	1740	1807	1840	1907	1940	2009	2054	2154	2254	2354
Bournemouth .... 119 d.		0515	0557	0625	0634	0656	0704	0726	0759r	0810	0825	0859r	0918	0955	same	1759r	1822r	1859r	1922r	1959r	2022r	2112r	2212r	2312r	0003
Brockenhurst .... 119 d.		0538	0614	|	0703	|	0733	|	0815	0841	0852	0915	0941	1011	minutes	1815	1845	1915	1945	2015	2045	2140	2240	2340	...
Southampton Central .. 119 d.		0555	0630	0700r	0730j	0730r	0800j	0800r	0830	0900	*0916*	0930	1000r	1030r	past	1830	1900	1930	2000	2030	2100	2200	2300	2359	...
Southampton Airport ... 119 d.		0603	0638	0708	0738	0738	0808	0808	0838	0908	*0923*	0938	1008	1038	each	1838	1908	1938	2008	2038	2108	2208	2308	0010	...
Winchester .... 119 d.		0618	0648	0718	0748	0748	0818	0818	0848	0918	*0932*	0948	1018	1048	hour	1848	1918	1948	2018	2048	2118	2218	2324	...	...
Basingstoke .... 119 a.		0634	|	|	|	|	0834	0834	|	0935	*0946*	|	1034	|	until	|	1934	|	2034	|	2134	2234	2343	...	...
Woking .... 113 a.		0653	|	|	|	|	0853	0853	0922	0954	...	1020	|	1119	♠	1925	|	2019	|	2119	|	2254	0018	...	...
London Waterloo .... 113 a.		0725	0747	0816	0850	0850	0925	0925	0953	1023	...	1049	1120	1149		1952	2020	2048	2125	2149	2222	2323	0104	...	...

		⑥	⑥	⑥	⑥	⑥	⑥	⑥	⑥	⑥	⑥	⑥	⑥		⑥	⑥	⑥	⑥	⑥	⑥	⑥	⑥	⑥	⑥	⑥
Weymouth ....d.	⑥	...	...	...	0542	0620	0655	0720	0803	0820	0903	0920	1003		1703	1720	1803	1820	1903	1920	2010	...	2110	2210	2310
Dorchester South ....d.		...	...	...	0552	0633	0707	0733	0813	0833	0913	0933	1013	and	1713	1733	1813	1833	1913	1933	2022	...	2122	2222	2322
Wareham .... 119a d.		...	...	...	0610	0653	0727	0753	0828	0853	0928	0953	1028	at	1728	1753	1828	1853	1928	1953	2042	...	2142	2242	2342
Poole ....d.		...	...	0528	0624	0707	0741	0807	0840	0907	0940	1007	1040	the	1740	1807	1840	1907	1940	2007	2054	...	2154	2254	2354
Bournemouth .... 119 d.		...	...	0542	0642r	0722r	0759r	0822r	0859r	0922r	0959r	1022r	1059r	same	1759r	1822r	1859r	1922r	1959r	2022r	2112r	...	2212r	2312r	0003
Brockenhurst .... 119 d.		...	...	0610	0710	0745	0815	0845	0915	0945	1015	1045	1115	minutes	1815	1845	1915	1945	2015	2045	2140	...	2240	2340	...
Southampton Central .. 119 d.		0512	0600	0630	0730	0800	0830	0900	0930	1000	1030	1100	1130	past	1830	1900	1930	2000	2030	2100	2200	2230	2300	2359	...
Southampton Airport ... 119 d.		0520	0608	0638	0738	0808	0838	0908	0938	1008	1038	1108	1138	each	1838	1908	1938	2008	2038	2108	2208	2238	2308	0010	...
Winchester .... 119 d.		0534	0623	0652	0748	0818	0848	0918	0948	1018	1048	1118	1148	hour	1848	1918	1948	2018	2048	2118	2218	2255	2324	...	...
Basingstoke .... 119 a.		0550	0639	0708	|	0834	|	0934	|	1034	|	1134	|	until	|	1934	|	2034	|	2134	2234	2311	2343	...	...
Woking .... 113 a.		0628	0658	0727	0821	|	0919	|	1019	|	1119	|	1219	♠	1919	|	2019	|	2120	|	2253	2332	0018	...	...
London Waterloo .... 113 a.		0705	0729	0753	0849	0920	0949	1020	1049	1120	1149	1221	1251		1949	2020	2049	2124	2149	2222	2322	0003	0104	...	...

		⑦	⑦	⑦	⑦	⑦	⑦	⑦	⑦		⑦	⑦	⑦	⑦	⑦		⑦	⑦	⑦	⑦	⑦	⑦	⑦	⑦
Weymouth ....d.	⑦	...	...	...	0748	...	0848	...	0948		...	1248	...	1348	...		1748	...	1848	...	1958	2058	2158	2258
Dorchester South ....d.		...	...	...	0800	...	0900	...	1000	and	...	1300	...	1400	...	and	1800	...	1900	...	2010	2110	2210	2310
Wareham .... 119a d.		...	...	...	0820	...	0920	...	1020	at	...	1320	...	1420	...	at	1820	...	1920	...	2030	2130	2230	2330
Poole ....d.		...	0650	0750	0832	0855	0932	0955	1032	the	1255	1332	1355	1432	1455	the	1832	1855	1932	1955	2050j	2150j	2250j	2350j
Bournemouth .... 119 d.		...	0706r	0806r	0850r	0906	0950r	1006	1050r	same	1306	1350r	1406	1450r	1506	same	1850r	1906	1950r	2006	2106	2206	2308r	0003
Brockenhurst .... 119 d.		...	0734	0834	0909	0934	1009	1034	1109	minutes	1334	1409	1434	1509	1534	minutes	1909	1934	2009	2034	2134	2234	2336	...
Southampton Central .. 119 d.		0655	0755	0855	0925	0955	1025	1055	1125	past	1355	1425	1455	1525	1555	past	1925	1955	2025	2055	2155	2255	2354	...
Southampton Airport ... 119 d.		0703	0803	0903	0933	1003	1033	1103	1133	each	1403	1433	1503	1533	1603	each	1933	2003	2033	2103	2203	2303	...	...
Winchester .... 119 d.		0723	0823	0923	0942	1023	1042	1123	1142	hour	1423	1442	1523	1542	1617	hour	1942	2017	2042	2117	2218	2323	...	...
Basingstoke .... 119 a.		0742	0842	0942	0958	1042	1058	1142	1158	until	1442	1458	1542	1558	1633	until	1958	2033	2058	2133	2235	2342	...	...
Woking .... 113 a.		0802	0902	1002	1019	1102	1118	1202	1218		1502	1518	1602	1618	1653		2018	2053	2118	2153	2254	0002	...	...
London Waterloo .... 113 a.		0846	0941	1039	1050	1139	1150	1237	1249		1537	1549	1637	1649	1724		2049	2124	2149	2224	2325	0033	...	...

Brockenhurst - Lymington Pier (for ⛴ to Isle of Wight).
Journey 11 minutes. Trains call at Lymington Town 6 minutes later:
Ⓐ: 0559 and every 30 minutes until 0929, 1012 and every 30 minutes until 1812, 1848 and every 30 minutes until 2218.
⑥: 0612, 0642 and every 30 minutes until 2112, 2148, 2218.
⑦: 0859, 0929 and every 30 minutes until 2059, 2129, 2159.

Lymington Pier - Brockenhurst.
Journey 11 minutes. Trains call at Lymington Town 2 minutes later:
Ⓐ: 0614 and every 30 minutes until 0944, 1027 and every 30 minutes until 1827, 1903 and every 30 minutes until 2203, 2236.
⑥: 0627, 0657 and every 30 minutes until 2127, 2203, 2236.
⑦: 0914, 0944 and every 30 minutes until 2114, 2144, 2214.

j – Arrives 8 – 9 minutes earlier.
r – Arrives 4 – 5 minutes earlier.
s – Calls to set down only.
u – Calls to pick up only.
♠ – Timings may vary by ± 4 minutes.
☛ For ⛴ services Weymouth / Poole – Jersey / Guernsey / St Malo and v.v., see Table **2100**.

111 PORTSMOUTH - RYDE - SHANKLIN

2nd class IL

Through fares including ferry travel are available. Allow 10 minutes for connections between trains and ferries. Operator: Wightlink ✆ 0333 999 7333. www.wightlink.co.uk

⛴

Portsmouth Harbour - Ryde Pierhead:
0515Ⓐ, 0615⚒, 0715 and hourly until 1815, 1920, 2020, 2120, 2245.

Ryde Pierhead - Portsmouth Harbour — Journey time: ± 20 minutes
0547Ⓐ, 0647⚒, 0747 and hourly until 2147, 2310.

Service from December 18, 2017. Additional services operate on Ⓐ and on public holidays.

Ryde Pierhead - Shanklin: *14 km*
⚒: 0549, 0607, 0649, 0707, 0749, 0807, 0849, 0907, 0949, 1007, 1049*, 1107, 1149*, 1207*, 1249*, 1307*, 1349, 1407, 1449*, 1507*, 1549*, 1607*, 1649, 1707, 1749, 1807, 1849, 1907, 1949, 2007, 2049, 2149.
⑦: 0649, 0749, 0849, 0949, 1049*, 1149*, 1249*, 1307*, 1349, 1407, 1449*, 1507*, 1549*, 1607*, 1649, 1707, 1749, 1807, 1849, 1949, 2049, 2149.

Shanklin - Ryde Pierhead — Journey time: ± 24 minutes
⚒: 0618, 0638, 0718, 0738, 0818, 0838, 0918, 0938, 1018, 1038*, 1118, 1138*, 1218*, 1238*, 1318*, 1338, 1418, 1438*, 1518*, 1538*, 1618*, 1638, 1718, 1738, 1818, 1838, 1918, 1938, 2018, 2118, 2238.
⑦: 0718, 0818, 0918, 1018, 1118, 1218*, 1318*, 1338, 1418, 1438*, 1518*, 1538*, 1618*, 1638, 1718, 1738, 1818, 1918, 2018, 2118, 2238.

* – Also calls at Smallbrook Junction (connection with **Isle of Wight Steam Railway**, see note △) 9 minutes from Ryde / 15 minutes from Shanklin, when Steam Railway is operating.

△ – **Isle of Wight Steam Railway** (🚂 Smallbrook Junction - Wootton: *9 km*). ✆ 01983 882204. www.iwsteamrailway.co.uk

SW 🍸 on most services London - Axminster and v.v.

LONDON - SALISBURY - EXETER 113

km			Ⓐ	Ⓐ	Ⓐ	Ⓐ	Ⓐ	Ⓐ	Ⓐ	Ⓐ B	Ⓐ	Ⓐ	Ⓐ B	Ⓐ	Ⓐ	Ⓐ	Ⓐ	Ⓐ	Ⓐ	Ⓐ	Ⓐ W	Ⓐ	Ⓐ	Ⓐ	Ⓐ W	Ⓐ B
0	**London** W'loo.... **108** d.	Ⓐ	...	...	...	...	*0630*	0710	0820	0920	1020	1120	1220	1250	1320	1350	1420	1520	1550	1620	1650	1720	1750	1820	1850	1920
39	Woking .... **108** d.		...	...	...	...	*0657*	0736	0846	0946	1046	1146	1246	1316	1346	1416	1446	1546	1616	1646	1716**u**	1746**u**	|	1846	1918	1946
77	Basingstoke .... **108** d.		...	...	...	...	0722	0757	0907	1007	1107	1207	1307	1338	1407	1438	1507	1607	1638	1707	1738	1807	1838	1907	1939	2007
107	Andover .... d.		...	...	...	...	0744	0819	0924	1024	1124	1224	1324	1400	1424	1500	1524	1624	1700	1729	1800	1829	1900	1929	2001	2029
134	**Salisbury** .... a.		...	...	...	...	0803	0839	0943	1042	1142	1242	1343	1419	1442	1520	1542	1642	1720	1748	1820	1850	1920	1948	2021	2049
134	**Salisbury** .... d.		...	...	0608	0740	0808	0847	0947	1047	1147	1247	1347	1424	1447	1523	1547	1647	1723	1753	1823	1854	1924	1953	2025	2053
169	Gillingham .... d.		...	0551	0642	0811	0837	0917	1017	1117	1217	1317	1417	|	1517	1552**f**	1617	1717	1753**f**	1819	1851	1919	1955**f**	2022	2052	2119
190	Sherborne .... d.		...	0606	0657	0826	...	0932	1032	1132	1232	1332	1432	◧	1532	1607	1632	1732	1808	1834	1906	1934	2010	2037	2107	2134
197	**Yeovil** Junction .... a.		...	0611	0703	0832	...	0938	1038	1138	1238	1338	1438	|	1538	1613	1638	1738	1813	1840	1912	1939	2016	2043	2113	2140
197	**Yeovil** Junction .... d.		...	0615	0707	0839	...	0939	1039	1139	1239	1339	1439	|	1539	1620	1639	1739	...	1843	1917	1941	2021	2044	2117	2141
200	**Yeovil** Pen Mill **140** a.		...	|	|	|	...	|	|	|	|	|	|	1539	|	1627	|	|	...	|	1925	|	2026	|	2123	|
211	Crewkerne .... d.		...	0624	0716	0849	...	0949	1049	1149	1249	1349	1449	...	1549	▬	1649	1749	...	1853	...	1950	...	2054	...	2151
233	Axminster .... d.		0552	0656**c**	0737	0903	...	1003	1103	1203	1303	1403	1503	...	1603	Ⓐ	1703	1803	...	1907	...	2004	...	2108	...	2205
249	Honiton .... d.		0607	0712	0753**f**	0916	...	1016	1116	1216	1316	1416	1516	...	1616	1707	1716	1818	...	1919	...	2017	...	2120	...	2219
277	**Exeter** St Davids ..△ a.		0635	0742	0821	0944	...	1042	1143	1243	1343	1443	1544	...	1643	1733	1742	1843	...	1946	...	2043	...	2147	...	2247

	Ⓐ	Ⓐ	Ⓐ	①–④	⑤		⑥	⑥	⑥	⑥	⑥	⑥	⑥ B	⑥		⑥		⑥ B	⑥	⑥	⑥	⑥	⑥	⑥	⑥ B	⑥
London Waterloo **108** d.	2020	2120	2220	2340	2340	⑥	...	...	...	...	0710	0820	0920	1020	...	1120	...	1220	1320	1420	1520	1620	1720	1820	1920	2020
Woking .... **108** d.	2046	2149	2249	0008	0008		...	...	...	...	0736	0846	0946	1046	...	1146	...	1246	1346	1446	1546	1646	1746	1846	1946	2046
Basingstoke .... **108** d.	2107	2214	2311	0028	0028		...	...	...	...	0759	0907	1007	1107	...	1207	...	1307	1407	1507	1607	1707	1807	1907	2007	2107
Andover .... d.	2129	2236	2333	0050	0050		...	...	...	...	0821	0924	1024	1124	...	1224	...	1324	1424	1524	1624	1724	1824	1924	2024	2129
Salisbury .... a.	2148	2255	2353	0110	0110**s**		...	...	...	...	0842	0942	1042	1142	...	1242	...	1342	1442	1542	1642	1742	1843	1943	2042	2148
Salisbury .... d.	2206	2303	...	...	|		...	...	0615	0745	0847	0947	1047	1147	...	1247	...	1347	1447	1547	1647	1747	1847	1947	2047	2153
Gillingham .... d.	2235	2327**s**	...	...	0136**s**		...	...	0642	0811	0917	1017	1117	1217	...	1317	...	1417	1517	1617	1717	1817	1919	2017	2117	2220
Sherborne .... d.	2250	2342**s**	...	...	0151**s**		...	...	0657	0826	0932	1032	1132	1232	...	1332	...	1432	1532	1632	1732	1832	1934	2032	2132	2235
Yeovil Junction .... a.	2255	2348	...	...	0157		...	...	0703	0832	0938	1038	1138	1238	...	1338	...	1438	1538	1638	1738	1838	1939	2038	2138	2241
Yeovil Junction .... d.	2257	...	...	...	...		...	0615	0707	0839	0939	1039	1139	1239	...	1339	...	1439	1539	1639	1739	1839	1941	2039	2139	2242
Yeovil Pen Mill. **140** a.	|	...	...	...	...		...	|	|	|	|	|	|	|	...	|	...	|	|	|	|	|	|	|	|	|
Crewkerne .... d.	2306	...	...	...	...		...	0624	0716	0849	0949	1049	1149	1249	...	1349	...	1449	1549	1649	1749	1849	1950	2049	2149	2252
Axminster .... d.	2320	...	...	...	...		0552	0656**c**	0738	0903	1003	1103	1203	1303	...	1403	...	1503	1603	1703	1803	1903	2005	2103	2203	2305
Honiton .... d.	2332	...	...	...	...		0607	0712	0754**f**	0916	1016	1116	1216	1316	...	1416	...	1516	1616	1716	1817	1916	2017	2117	2217	...
Exeter St Davids ... △ a.	0001	...	...	...	...		0635	0742	0822	0944	1042	1142	1242	1342	...	1442	...	1542	1642	1742	1842	1942	2045	2142	2245	...

	⑥	⑥	⑥		⑦	⑦	⑦	⑦	⑦	⑦	⑦ B	⑦	⑦	⑦	⑦	⑦	⑦	⑦ B	⑦	⑦	⑦	⑦	⑦	⑦ e	⑦	⑦
London Waterloo **108** d.	2120	2220	2340	⑦	...	...	0815	0915	1015	1115	1215	1315	1415	1515	1615	1715	1745	1815	1845	1915	1945	2015	2045	2115	2215	2335
Woking .... **108** d.	2149	2249	0008		...	...	0847	0947	1046	1146	1246	1346	1446	1546	1646	1746	|	1846	|	1946	|	2046	|	2146	2246	0008
Basingstoke .... **108** d.	2214	2311	0028		...	0805	0908	1008	1107	1207	1307	1407	1507	1607	1707	1807	|	1907	|	2007	|	2107	|	2207	2307	0040
Andover .... d.	2236	2333	0050		...	0827	0930	1025	1129	1224	1329	1424	1529	1624	1729	1824	1849	1929	1949	2024	2049	2129	|	2226	2329	0102
Salisbury .... a.	2255	2353	0110		...	0846	0946	1045	1145	1245	1345	1445	1545	1645	1745	1845	1905	1945	2005	2045	2105	2145	2205	2245	2348	0122
Salisbury .... d.	2303	...	...		0706	0851	0951	1051	1151	1251	1351	1451	1551	1651	1751	1851	...	1951	...	2051	...	2151	...	2251	...	...
Gillingham .... d.	2327**s**	...	...		0731	0921	1021	1121	1221	1321	1421	1521	1621	1721	1821	1921	...	2021	...	2121	...	2221	...	2322	...	...
Sherborne .... d.	2342**s**	...	...		0746	0936	1036	1136	1236	1336	1436	1536	1636	1736	1836	1936	...	2036	...	2136	...	2236	...	2337	...	...
Yeovil Junction .... a.	2349	...	...		0751	0941	1041	1141	1241	1341	1441	1541	1641	1741	1841	1941	...	2041	...	2141	...	2242	...	2343	...	...
Yeovil Junction .... d.	...	...	...		0753	0943	1043	1143	1243	1343	1443	1543	1643	1743	1843	1943	...	2043	...	2143	...	...	...	2344	...	...
Yeovil Pen Mill. **140** a.	...	...	...		|	|	|	|	|	|	|	|	|	|	|	|	...	|	...	|	...	...	...	|	...	...
Crewkerne .... d.	...	...	...		0802	0952	1052	1152	1252	1352	1452	1552	1652	1752	1852	1952	...	2052	...	2152	...	...	...	2354	...	...
Axminster .... d.	...	...	...		0816	1006	1106	1206	1306	1406	1506	1606	1706	1806	1906	2006	...	2106	...	2206	...	...	...	0008	...	...
Honiton .... d.	...	...	...		0831	1018	1118	1218	1318	1418	1518	1618	1718	1818	1918	2018	...	2118	...	2220	...	...	...	0020	...	...
Exeter St Davids ... △ a.	...	...	...		0859	1045	1145	1245	1345	1445	1545	1645	1745	1845	1945	2045	...	2146	...	2248	...	...	...	0046	...	...

		Ⓐ	Ⓐ	Ⓐ	Ⓐ	Ⓐ	Ⓐ	Ⓐ	Ⓐ	Ⓐ	Ⓐ B	Ⓐ	Ⓐ	Ⓐ	Ⓐ B	Ⓐ	Ⓐ	Ⓐ	Ⓐ B	Ⓐ	Ⓐ	Ⓐ	Ⓐ	Ⓐ	Ⓐ	Ⓐ
Exeter St Davids ... ▽ d.	Ⓐ	...	...	...	...	0510	...	0641	0725	...	0823	0925	1025	1125	1225	1325	1425	...	1525	...	...	1624	1725	1746	1825	...
Honiton .... d.		...	...	...	...	0541	0619	0712	0752	...	0855	0955	1055	1155	1255	1355	1455	...	1555	...	...	1656**f**	1755	1819	1859	...
Axminster .... d.		...	...	...	...	0552	0630	0723	0803	...	0906	1006	1106	1206	1306	1406	1506	...	1606	...	...	1707	1806	1829	1910	...
Crewkerne .... d.		...	...	...	...	0605	0643	0736	0816	...	0919	1019	1119	1219	1319	1419	1519	...	1619	...	...	1720	1819	...	1923	...
Yeovil Pen Mill. **140** d.		...	...	...	0541	|	|	|	|	...	|	|	|	|	|	|	|	1544	|	1631	1653	|	|	...	|	1927
Yeovil Junction .... a.		...	...	...	0546	0614	0652	0745	0825	...	0927	1027	1127	1227	1327	1427	1527	1549	1627	1636	|	1728	1827	...	1931	|
Yeovil Junction .... d.		...	...	0514	0550	0620	0653	0750	0829	...	0929	1029	1129	1229	1329	1429	1529	1553	1629	...	1646**b**	1730	1829	...	1933	1917**b**
Sherborne .... d.		...	...	0520	0556	0626	0700	0756	0835	...	0935	1035	1135	1235	1335	1435	1535	1559	1635	...	◧	1736	1835	...	1939	◧
Gillingham .... d.		...	...	0536	0612	0642	0715	0812	0851	0918	0951	1051	1151	1251	1351	1451	1551	1617	1651	...	|	1752	1851	...	1955	|
Salisbury .... a.		...	...	0601	0639	0707	0740	0837	0916	0942	1016	1116	1216	1316	1416	1516	1616	1643	1716	...	1817	1822	1923	...	2022	2042
Salisbury .... d.		0515	0543	0606	0645	0715	0745	0847	0921	0947	1021	1121	1221	1321	1421	1521	1621	1647	1721	...	1827	1827	1926	...	2026	...
Andover .... d.		0535	0603	0626	0705	0735	0805	0906	0938	1006	1038	1138	1238	1338	1438	1538	1638	1706	1738	...	1844	1844	1945	...	2045	...
Basingstoke .... **108** a.		0558	0626	0649	0728	0758	0828	0928	0955	1028	1055	1155	1255	1355	1455	1555	1655	1729	1755	...	1901	1901	2008	...	2108	...
Woking .... **108** a.		0618	0646	|	|	0818	0848	0949	1015	1049	1115	1215	1315	1415	1515	1615	1715	1749	1815	...	1921	1921	2029	...	2129	...
London Waterloo **108** a.		0649	0716	0739	0814	0846	0917	1019	1049	1119	1149	1249	1349	1449	1549	1649	1749	1816	1849	...	1950	1950	2100	...	2204	...

	Ⓐ	Ⓐ	Ⓐ	Ⓐ	Ⓐ		⑥	⑥	⑥	⑥	⑥	⑥	⑥	⑥	⑥ B	⑥	⑥	⑥	⑥ B	⑥	⑥	⑥ B	⑥	⑥	⑥	⑥
Exeter St Davids ... ▽ d.	1925	...	2025	2125	2257	⑥	...	...	...	...	0510	...	0641	0725	0824	0925	1025	1125	1225	1325	1425	1525	1625	1725	1825	1924
Honiton .... d.	1955	...	2057	2159	2332**f**		...	...	...	...	0541	0619	0713	0755	0855	0955	1055	1155	1255	1355	1455	1555	1655	1757	1855	1955
Axminster .... d.	2006	...	2108	2210	2343		...	...	...	...	0552	0630	0724	0806	0906	1006	1106	1206	1306	1406	1506	1606	1706	1808	1906	2006
Crewkerne .... d.	2019	...	2121	2223	2356		...	...	...	...	0605	0643	0737	0819	0919	1019	1119	1219	1319	1419	1519	1619	1719	1821	1919	2019
Yeovil Pen Mill. **140** d.	|	2030	|	|	|		...	...	...	...	|	|	|	|	|	|	|	|	|	|	|	|	|	|	|	|
Yeovil Junction .... a.	2028	2035	2129	2231	0004		...	...	...	...	0614	0652	0745	0827	0927	1027	1127	1227	1327	1427	1527	1627	1727	1829	1927	2027
Yeovil Junction .... d.	2029	...	2131	2233	0006		...	...	...	...	0620	0653	0750	0829	0929	1029	1129	1229	1329	1429	1529	1629	1729	1831	1929	2029
Sherborne .... d.	2036	...	2137	2239	|		...	...	...	...	0626	0700	0756	0835	0935	1035	1135	1235	1335	1435	1535	1635	1735	1837	1935	2035
Gillingham .... d.	2051	...	2153	2255	|		...	...	...	...	0642	0715	0812	0851	0951	1051	1151	1251	1351	1451	1551	1651	1751	1853	1951	2051
Salisbury .... a.	2122	...	2218	2329	0043		...	...	...	...	0707	0740	0837	0916	1016	1116	1216	1316	1416	1516	1616	1716	1816	1918	2016	2116
Salisbury .... d.	2126	...	2226	...	...		0515	0547	0621	0647	0721	0747	0847	0921	1021	1121	1221	1321	1421	1521	1621	1721	1821	1926	2026	2126
Andover .... d.	2145	...	2245	...	...		0535	0606	0638	0706	0738	0806	0906	0938	1038	1138	1238	1338	1438	1538	1638	1738	1838	1945	2045	2145
Basingstoke .... **108** a.	2207	...	2307	...	...		0558	0628	0655	0728	0755	0828	0928	0955	1055	1155	1255	1355	1455	1555	1655	1755	1855	2008	2108	2207
Woking .... **108** a.	2228	...	*2331*	...	...		0618	0649	0715	0749	0817	0849	0949	1015	1115	1215	1315	1415	1515	1615	1715	1815	1915	2029	2129	2228
London Waterloo **108** a.	2258	...	*0008*	...	...		0649	0719	0749	0819	0849	0919	1019	1049	1149	1249	1349	1449	1549	1649	1749	1849	1949	2104	2204	2257

	⑥	⑥	⑥		⑦	⑦	⑦	⑦	⑦	⑦	⑦	⑦	⑦	⑦	⑦	⑦	⑦ B	⑦	⑦	⑦ F	⑦	⑦	⑦	⑦	⑦	⑦
Exeter St Davids ... ▽ d.	2025	2125	2257	⑦	...	...	...	...	...	0925	1025	1125	1225	1325	1425	...	1525	...	1625	...	1725	1825	1925	2025	2125	2315
Honiton .... d.	2056	2157	2332**f**		...	...	...	...	0858	0957	1057	1157	1257	1357	1457	...	1557	...	1657	...	1757	1857	1957	2057	2159	2340**s**
Axminster .... d.	2107	2208	2343		...	...	...	...	0909	1009	1109	1209	1309	1409	1509	...	1609	...	1709	...	1809	1909	2009	2109	2210	2351**s**
Crewkerne .... d.	2120	2221	2356		...	...	...	...	0922	1022	1122	1222	1322	1422	1522	...	1622	...	1722	...	1822	1922	2022	2122	2223	0012**s**
Yeovil Pen Mill. **140** d.	|	|	|		...	...	...	...	|	|	|	|	|	|	|	...	|	...	|	...	|	|	|	|	|	|
Yeovil Junction .... a.	2129	2229	0004		...	...	...	...	0930	1030	1130	1230	1330	1430	1530	...	1630	...	1730	...	1830	1930	2030	2131	2232	0021**s**
Yeovil Junction .... d.	2130	2231	0006		...	...	0732	...	0932	1032	1132	1232	1332	1432	1532	...	1632	...	1732	...	1832	1932	2032	2132	2233	|
Sherborne .... d.	2137	2237	|		...	...	0738	...	0938	1038	1138	1238	1338	1438	1538	...	1638	...	1738	...	1838	1938	2038	2138	2240	|
Gillingham .... d.	2152	2253	|		...	...	0754	0854	0954	1054	1154	1254	1354	1454	1554	1621	1654	1721	1754	...	1854	1954	2054	2154	2256	|
Salisbury .... a.	2223	2329	0041		...	...	0820	0920	1020	1120	1220	1320	1420	1520	1620	1647	1720	1747	1820	...	1920	2020	2120	2220	2321	0057
Salisbury .... d.	2227	...	...		0645	0727	0827	0927	1027	1129	1227	1327	1427	1527	1627	1652	1727	1752	1827	1852	1927	2027	2127	2227	...	...
Andover .... d.	2247	...	...		0702	0746	0846	0946	1044	1146	1244	1346	1444	1546	1644	1709	1746	1809	1844	1909	1946	2044	2146	2246	...	...
Basingstoke .... **108** a.	2309	...	...		0719	0808	0908	1002	1106	1204	1306	1402	1506	1602	1706	1726	1802	1826	1906	1926	2002	2106	2203	2308	...	...
Woking .... **108** a.	*2332*	...	...		0739	0828	0928	1028	1128	1228	1328	1428	1528	1628	1728	1748	1828	1848	1928	1948	2028	2128	2228	*0002*	...	...
London Waterloo **108** a.	*0003*	...	...		0820	0912	1011	1104	1204	1304	1359	1459	1559	1659	1759	1819	1859	1919	1959	2019	2059	2159	2259	*0033*	...	...

☛ Full service **London** Waterloo - **Salisbury** and v.v.:

From **London** Waterloo on ⚒ at 0710, 0750, 0820, 0850 and every 30 minutes until 1920, 1950, 2020, 2120, 2220, 2340; on ⑦ at 0815 and hourly until 2215, 2335 (also 1745, 1845, 1945, 2045. Please see timings above for calling points between London and Salisbury).

From **Salisbury** on Ⓐ at 0515, 0543, 0606, 0645, 0715, 0745, 0815, 0847, 0921, 0947 and at the same minutes past each hour until 1747, 1827, 1847, 1926, 2026, 2126; on ⑥ at 0515, 0547, 0621, 0647, 0720, 0747, 0821, 0847, 0921, 0947 and at the same minutes past each hour until 1847, 1926, 2026, 2126; on ⑦ at 0645, 0727, 0827, 0927, 1027, 1129, 1227 and hourly until 2127 (also 1652, 1752, 1852).

B – Conveys 🚃12 London Waterloo - Bristol and v.v. (Table **140**).
F – From Frome (Table **140**).
W – To Westbury (Table **140**).

b – Calls at Yeovil Junction before Yeovil Pen Mill.
c – Arrives 0643.
e – Does not call at Exeter Central.

f – Arrives 5–7 minutes earlier.
s – Calls to set down only.
u – Calls to pick up only.

◧ – Via Westbury (Table **140**).
△ – Trains to Exeter St Davids also call at **Exeter Central** 5–6 minutes earlier
▽ – Trains from Exeter St Davids also call at **Exeter Central** 4–5 minutes later.

① – Mondays ② – Tuesdays ③ – Wednesdays ④ – Thursdays ⑤ – Fridays ⑥ – Saturdays ⑦ – Sundays Ⓑ – Not Saturdays 19

LONDON - EXETER - PAIGNTON and PLYMOUTH

GW

km		Ⓐ 2 B★	Ⓐ 2★	Ⓐ 2	Ⓐ	Ⓐ	Ⓐ 🍷	Ⓐ 2 D★	Ⓐ 🍷		Ⓐ 2D	Ⓐ 🍷	Ⓐ 🍷★	Ⓐ 🍷	Ⓐ 🍴		Ⓐ 🍴	Ⓐ 🍴	Ⓐ D2	Ⓐ 2★	Ⓐ 🍷	Ⓐ 🍷
0	**London** Paddington 132 d.	...	...	...	0633	0703	0730	...	0903	...	...	1003	1035	1103	1203	...	1234	1303	...	...	1403	1503
58	**Reading** 132 d.	...	...	...	0701	0730	0757	...	0931	...	...	1032	1102	1133	1233	...	1301	1331**u**	...	...	1430**u**	1533**u**
85	Newbury d.	...	...	...	|	0748	|	...	|	...	...	|	1122	|	|	...	1317	|	...	...	|	|
154	Westbury 139 d.	...	...	...	|	0827	|	...	|	...	...	|	|	1224	|	...	1356	|	...	...	|	1623
186	Castle Cary 139 d.	...	...	...	|	|	|	...	1027	...	...	|	1209	|	|	...	1414	|	...	...	|	1641
	Bristol Temple M. 132 120a 120 d.	...	0524	0643	|	|	0912	0855	|	...	0955	|	|	|	|	...	|	|	1358	...	|	|
230	Taunton 120a 120 d.	...	0620	0739	0818	0904	0945	1001	1050	...	1100	|	1231	1300	|	...	1435	1448	1459	...	1550	1703
253	Tiverton Parkway 120 d.	...	0635	0755	|	0917	|	|	1103	...	1116	|	|	1313	|	...	...	1501	1515	...	1603	1716
279	**Exeter** St Davids 120 a.	...	0652	0812	0841	0931	1009	1031	1117	...	1132	1203	1255	1327	1405	...	...	1515	1533	...	1617	1732
279	**Exeter** St Davids 116 120 d.	0628	0655	0814	0844	0932	1011	1032	1118	...	1135	1208	1257	1329	1409	...	...	1516	...	1550	1619	1737
311	Newton Abbot 116 120 d.	0654	0728	0835	0905	0953	1032	1101	1139	...	1157	1229	1324	1350	1430	...	...	1539	...	1621	1640	1758
321	Torquay 116 120 d.	|	|	|	|	1005	|	1113	|	...	|	|	1335	|	|	...	...	|	...	|	|	|
324	**Paignton** 116 120 a.	|	|	|	|	1011	|	1120	|	...	|	|	1343	|	|	...	...	|	...	|	|	|
325	Totnes 120 d.	0707	0742	0849	|	...	1044	...	1152	...	1209	|	...	1403	|	...	...	1551	...	1633	1653	1810
363	**Plymouth** 120 a.	0737	0811	0919	0941	...	1111	...	1219	...	1240	1303	...	1430	1505	...	...	1618	...	1705	1720	1837
	Newquay **117** a.	...	|	|	|	...	|	...	...	...	|	|	...	...	|	...	...	...	...	...	|	|
	Penzance **117** a.	...	1016	1120	1137	...	1313	...	...	...	1439	1511	...	...	1709	...	...	...	...	...	1932	2040

	Ⓐ 🍷	Ⓐ 🍷	Ⓐ 🍷	Ⓐ 🍷★	Ⓐ 🍴	Ⓐ 🍷	①–④ 🍷	⑤ 🍷	①–④ 🍴		⑤ 🍴	Ⓐ 🍷	Ⓐ 🍷	Ⓐ 2	Ⓐ 2	Ⓐ 🍷	Ⓐ A	⑥ 2★	⑥ 2★		⑥ 2	⑥ 🍷
London Paddington 132 d.	1603	1633	1703	1733	1803	1807	1833	1833	1903	...	1903	2003	2103	...	...	2145	2345‡	...	...	...	...	0730
Reading 132 d.	1633	1702	1730**u**	1800	1830	1839	1901	1901	1933	...	1933**u**	2031	2132	...	...	2213	0046**u**	...	...	...	...	0758
Newbury d.	|	1720	1747	1816	1847	1904	1917	1917	1949	...	1949	2047	2148	...	...	|	|	...	...	...	...	|
Westbury 139 d.	|	1805	|	1902	|	1958	2005	2005	|	...	|	2127	2227	...	...	|	|	...	...	...	...	|
Castle Cary 139 d.	|	1823	|	1920	|	...	2023	2023	|	...	|	2145	2245	...	...	|	|	...	...	...	...	|
Bristol Temple M. 132 120a 120 d.	|	|	|	|	|	...	|	|	|	...	|	|	|	2154	2306	2336	|	0524	0645	...	...	0915
Taunton 120a 120 d.	1752	1846	1855	1943	1951	...	2045	2045	2053	...	2053	2207	2308	2312	0013**s**	0036**s**	0238	0620	0736	...	...	0949
Tiverton Parkway 120 d.	1805	1859	1908	1956	|	...	2058	2058	2106	...	2106	2220	2321	2328	0030**s**	0049**s**	|	0635	0751	...	...	|
Exeter St Davids 120 a.	1819	1913	1922	2010	2014	...	2112	2112	2120	...	2120	2234	2335	2346	0052	0104	0307	0652	0808	...	...	1012
Exeter St Davids 116 120 d.	1824	...	1925	2019	2016	...	...	2114	2122	...	2123	2236	2337	...	...	...	0411	0655	0810	...	0928	1016
Newton Abbot 116 120 d.	1845	...	1946	2058	2037	...	...	2135	2143	...	2144	2257	2358	...	...	...	0432	0728	0838	...	0949	1037
Torquay 116 120 d.	|	...	|	2112	|	...	...	|	|	...	|	|	|	...	...	...	|	|	|	...	|	|
Paignton 116 120 a.	|	...	|	2119	|	...	...	|	|	...	|	|	|	...	...	...	|	|	|	...	|	|
Totnes 120 d.	1858	...	1959	...	2050	...	...	|	2155	...	2157	2309	0010	...	...	...	|	0742	0850	...	1001	1050
Plymouth 120 a.	1928	...	2026	...	2117	...	...	2211	2222	...	2224	2336	0037	...	...	...	0511	0811	0921	...	1032	1116
Newquay **117** a.	|	...	|	...	|	...	...	...	|	...	|	...	...	...	...	...	|	|	|	...	|	|
Penzance **117** a.	2129	...	2226	...	2310	...	...	...	*0041*	...	0045	...	...	...	...	...	0755**j**	1017	1122	...	1236	1316

	⑥ 🍷	⑥ 🍷	⑥ 🍷	⑥ 2★	⑥ 🍷	⑥ 🍷	⑥ 🍷	⑥ 🍷		⑥ 🍷	⑥ 🍷	⑥ 2★	⑥ 🍷	⑥ 🍷	⑥ 🍷	⑥ 🍷	⑥ 🍷	⑥ 🍷★	⑥ 2	⑥ 🍷	⑦ 2★	⑦ 2★
London Paddington 132 d.	0803	0903	1003	...	1103	1203	1233	1303	...	1403	1503	...	1603	1703	1630	1803	1903	2003	...	2030	...	...
Reading 132 d.	0832	0931	1031	...	1131	1232	1300	1331	...	1431	1531	...	1631	1731	1658	1831	1931	2030	...	2058	...	...
Newbury d.	0850	|	|	...	|	|	1316	|	...	|	|	...	|	|	|	|	1947	2046	...	|	...	...
Westbury 139 d.	0929	|	|	...	1221	|	1355	|	...	|	1620	...	|	1821	|	|	2026	2126	...	|	...	...
Castle Cary 139 d.	0947	|	|	...	1239	|	1413	|	...	|	1638	...	|	1839	|	|	2044	2144	...	|	...	...
Bristol Temple M. 132 120a 120 d.	|	|	|	*1144*	|	|	|	|	...	|	|	*1645*	|	|	1818	|	|	|	2201	2216	0726	0828
Taunton 120a 120 d.	1011	1046	|	*1216*	1301	|	1434	1446	...	1548	1701	*1718*	1746	1902	1908	1946	2107	2207	2307	2316	0820	0932
Tiverton Parkway 120 d.	1024	1059	|	*1228*	1314	|	...	1459	...	1601	1714	*1731*	1759	1915	1921	|	2120	2220	2322	2329	0835	0947
Exeter St Davids 120 a.	1039	1113	1206	*1241*	1328	1405	...	1513	...	1615	1728	*1744*	1813	1929	1935	2009	2134	2234	2341	2345	0852	1004
Exeter St Davids 116 120 d.	...	1117	1210	1253	1330	1408	...	1516	...	1618	1730	1753	1816	1934	1940	2013	2137	2238	...	...	0853	1004
Newton Abbot 116 120 d.	...	1139	1231	1322	1351	1429	...	1537	...	1639	1751	1822	1837	1955	2001	2034	2158	2306	...	...	0919	1031
Torquay 116 120 d.	...	|	|	|	|	|	...	|	...	|	|	|	|	|	2015	|	|	|	...	...	|	|
Paignton 116 120 a.	...	|	|	|	|	|	...	|	...	|	|	|	|	|	2024	|	|	|	...	...	|	|
Totnes 120 d.	...	1152	|	1335	1404	|	...	1550	...	1652	1805	1835	1850	2008	...	2047	2211	2318	...	...	0930	1043
Plymouth 120 a.	...	1222	1306	1405	1431	1504	...	1616	...	1721	1831	1905	1920	2034	...	2113	2238	2345	...	...	1001	1110
Newquay **117** a.	...	...	|	|	...	|	...	|	...	|	|	|	...	|	...	|	...	...	...	...	|	|
Penzance **117** a.	...	...	1510	1606	...	1706	...	1818	...	1922	2035	2108	...	2242	...	2322	...	...	...	...	1214	1314

	⑦ 🍷★	⑦ 🍷	⑦ 2	⑦ 🍷	⑦ 🍷	⑦ 🍷★	⑦ 🍷		⑦ 🍷	⑦ 🍷	⑦ 2★	⑦ 🍷	⑦ 🍷		⑦ 🍷	⑦ 🍷	⑦ 2	⑦ 🍷	⑦ 🍷★	⑦ 🍷	⑦ 🍷	⑦ 🍷	⑦ A
London Paddington 132 d.	0757	0857	...	0957	1057	1133	1157	...	1257	1303	...	1357	1457	...	1557	1657	...	1757	1857	1903	1957	2057	2350‡
Reading 132 d.	0836	0932	...	1032	1132	1210	1232	...	1332	1338	...	1432	1532	...	1632	1732	...	1832	1932	1938	2032	2132	0038**u**
Newbury d.	|	0947	...	|	|	|	1248	...	|	|	...	1448	|	...	1648	|	...	1848	|	|	2048	|	|
Westbury 139 d.	|	1021	...	|	|	1303	|	...	1419	|	...	|	|	...	1722	|	...	1927	|	|	2127	|	|
Castle Cary 139 d.	|	|	...	1133	|	1322	|	...	|	|	...	1536	|	...	1741	|	...	|	2028	|	2144	|	|
Bristol Temple M. 132 120a 120 d.	1000	|	...	|	|	|	|	...	|	1455	...	|	|	...	|	|	1830	|	|	2055	|	|	|
Taunton 120a 120 d.	1032	1057	...	1154	1246	1343	1353	...	1455	1529	...	1557	1651	...	1804	1849	1933	2001	2050	2148	2206	2246**s**	|
Tiverton Parkway 120 d.	1046	1111	...	|	|	1357	1406	...	|	|	...	|	1704	...	1818	1902	1948	2016	2104	2202	2219	2300**s**	|
Exeter St Davids 120 a.	1100	1125	...	1219	1313	1412	1420	...	1518	1553	...	1623	1718	...	1835	1917	2005	2029	2119	2218	2235	2319	0305
Exeter St Davids 116 120 d.	1104	1125	1215	1221	1314	1413	1423	...	1521	1555	1605	1625	1721	...	1836	1919	...	2030	2120	...	2236	...	0435
Newton Abbot 116 120 d.	1132	1146	1237	1242	1336	1440	1445	...	1542	1616	1637	1644	1740	...	1858	1938	...	2053	2147	...	2257	...	0456
Torquay 116 120 d.	|	|	|	|	|	1451	|	...	|	|	|	|	|	...	|	|	...	|	|	...	|	...	|
Paignton 116 120 a.	|	|	|	|	|	1501	|	...	|	|	|	|	|	...	|	|	...	|	|	...	|	...	|
Totnes 120 d.	1144	1200	1249	1256	|	...	1457	...	1554	|	1651	1700	1754	...	|	1952	...	2106	2201	...	2310	...	|
Plymouth 120 a.	1214	1229	1319	1326	1412	...	1525	...	1622	1653	1721	1729	1820	...	1934	2019	...	2133	2229	...	2339	...	0535
Newquay **117** a.	|	|	|	...	|	...	|	...	|	...	|	|	|	...	|	|	...	|	...	...	...	...	|
Penzance **117** a.	1416	*1447*	1524	...	1609	...	1729	...	1823	...	1935	*1935*	2028	...	*2138*	2221	...	2333	...	...	...	...	0859

A – THE NIGHT RIVIERA – Conveys 🛏 1, 2. cl and (2).
See also note ‡.
B – To Par (Table **117**).
D – To/from Cardiff (Table **120a**).

a – Via Trowbridge (Table **140**).
j – Arrives 0750 on ⑥ mornings.
s – Stops to set down only.

t – Arrives 2339 on ⑤.
u – Stops to pick up only.

NOTES CONTINUE ON NEXT PAGE →

EXETER - PAIGNTON

2nd class GW

km		Ⓐ	Ⓐ	Ⓐ	Ⓐ	Ⓐ	Ⓐ	Ⓐ	Ⓐ	Ⓐ	Ⓐ	Ⓐ		Ⓐ	Ⓐ	Ⓐ	Ⓐ	Ⓐ	Ⓐ	Ⓐ	Ⓐ	Ⓐ
0	**Exeter** St Davids 115 120 d.	0534	0611	0718	0750	0900	0958	1032	1058	1158	1249	1303	...	1358	1501	1558	1628	1655	1728	1751	1836	1933
20	Dawlish 115 120 d.	0555	0631	0738	0810	0924	1019	1048	1118	1227	|	1324	...	1427	1521	1619	1648	1715	1753	1812	1902	1959
24	Teignmouth 115 120 d.	0600	0636	0743	0815	0929	1024	1053	1123	1232	|	1329	...	1432	1526	1624	1653	1720	1758	1817	1907	2004
32	Newton Abbot 115 120 d.	0609	0645	0752	0824	0937	1032	1101	1132	1240	1311	1338	...	1440	1535	1632	1702	1729	1807	1826	1916	2013
42	Torquay 115 120 d.	0620	0656	0803	0836	0948	1044	1113	1143	1252	1322	1349	...	1452	1546	1644	1713	1740	1818	1837	1927	2024
45	**Paignton** 🚂 115 120 a.	0626	0706	0810	0844	0955	1051	1120	1150	1300	1329	1356	...	1459	1553	1651	1720	1748	1825	1844	1934	2030

	Ⓐ	Ⓐ	Ⓐ	⑥	⑥	⑥	⑥	⑥	⑥	⑥	⑥	⑥	⑥	⑥	⑥	⑥	⑥	⑥	⑥	⑥	⑥	⑥
Exeter St Davids 115 120 d.	2019	2129	2246	0518	0538	0611	0754	0837	0859	0958	1022	1045	1059	1159	1258	1358	1430	1459	1601	1655	1734	1827
Dawlish 115 120 d.	2043	2149	2307	0538	0558	0631	0814	0850	0926	1018	1037	|	1120	1226	1319	1424	1445	1519	1621	1715	1754	1847
Teignmouth 115 120 d.	2050	2154	2312	0543	0603	0636	0819	0855	0931	1023	1042	|	1125	1231	1324	1429	1450	1524	1626	1720	1759	1852
Newton Abbot 115 120 d.	2058	2203	2320	0551	0611	0645	0828	0906	0939	1033	1050	1106	1141**b**	1239	1332	1437	1459	1540**b**	1642**b**	1729	1808	1901
Torquay 115 120 d.	2112	2214	2330	0602	0622	0656	0839	0916	0950	1044	1100	1117	1152	1251	1344	1449	1510	1551	1653	1740	1820	1912
Paignton 🚂 115 120 a.	2119	2221	2337	0611	0631	0706	0848	0925	0958	1051	1108	1126	1201	1259	1352	1456	1518	1600	1701	1750	1830	1921

	⑥	⑥	⑥	⑥	⑦	⑦	⑦	⑦	⑦	⑦	⑦	⑦	⑦	⑦	⑦	⑦	⑦	⑦	⑦	⑦	⑦	⑦
Exeter St Davids 115 120 d.	1900	1917	2018	2150	0845	0954	1053	1159	1302	1326	1359	1413	1502	1531	1600	1657	1713	1757	1857	1957	2102	2202
Dawlish 115 120 d.	1913	1938	2038	2210	0912	1014	1113	1219	1317	1339	1419	1427	1517	1543	1615	1712	1725	1817	1917	2017	2117	2222
Teignmouth 115 120 d.	1918	1943	2043	2215	0917	1019	1118	1224	1322	1344	1424	1433	1522	1548	1620	1717	1730	1822	1922	2022	2122	2227
Newton Abbot 115 120 d.	1925	1952	2052	2223	0926	1037**b**	1127	1233	1330	1352	1435	1440	1530	1556	1629	1726	1738	1831	1931	2031	2131	2236
Torquay 115 120 d.	1935	2003	2103	2234	0937	1049	1138	1244	1341	1404	1446	1451	1542	1607	1640	1737	1749	1842	1942	2042	2142	2247
Paignton 🚂 115 120 a.	1943	2013	2110	2242	0944	1054	1145	1252	1348	1411	1453	1501	1550	1615	1647	1744	1756	1849	1949	2049	2149	2255

a – Arrives 2321.
b – Arrives 9 minutes earlier.
🚂 – Dartmouth Steam Railway (Paignton - Kingswear). See page 101 for contact details.

PLYMOUTH and PAIGNTON - EXETER - LONDON

GW

km			Ⓐ 🍷a	Ⓐ 🍷	Ⓐ 🍷	Ⓐ 2	Ⓐ 🍷	Ⓐ ☆	Ⓐ 🍷	Ⓐ ✕	Ⓐ 🍷	Ⓐ 🍷☆	Ⓐ 2☆	Ⓐ 2D	Ⓐ 🍷	Ⓐ 🍷	Ⓐ 🍷	Ⓐ 🍷☆	Ⓐ ✕	Ⓐ2 D☆	Ⓐ ✕	Ⓐ 2	Ⓐ 🍷
	Penzance **117** d.	Ⓐ	...	...	...	...	...	...	...	0505	0541	...	0600	...	0645	0741	0900	...	1000	...	*1051*	1141	1204
	Newquay **117** d.		...	...	...	...	...	...	...	|	|	...	|	...	|	|	|	...	|	...	|	|	|
0	**Plymouth** 120 d.		...	...	0451	...	0553	0529	...	0653	0745	...	0809	...	0851	0949	1100	...	1201	...	1255	1343	1356
38	Totnes 120 d.		...	...	|	...	|	0556	...	|	0815	...	0839	...	0921	1019	|	...	1228	...	1322	1412	|
	Paignton 116 120 d.		...	...	0527	...	|	|	...	|	|	0748	|	...	|	|	|	1132	|	1253	|	|	|
	Torquay 116 120 d.		...	...	|	...	|	|	...	|	|	0755	|	...	|	|	|	1138	|	1259	|	|	|
52	Newton Abbot 116 120 d.		...	...	|	...	0629	0609	...	0731	0828	0808	0852	...	0934	1032	|	1150	1241	1312	1335	1424	1432
84	**Exeter** St Davids 116 120 a.		...	...	0546	...	0650	0634	...	0750	0849	0840	0916	...	0953	1052	1152	1215	1300	1336	1354	...	1453
84	**Exeter** St Davids 120 d.		...	...	0552	0600	0652	0636	0628	0752	0851	0842	...	0933	0955	1054	1155	1217	1302	1338	1359	...	1455
110	Tiverton Parkway 120 d.		...	...	0607	0617	|	0651	0643	|	0906	|	...	0950	1010	1109	|	1232	1317	1355	1414	...	1510
133	Taunton 120a 120 d.		...	...	0622	0634	0717	0705	0657	0816	0920	0907	...	1011	1028	1123	|	1246	1331	1411	1428	...	1524
205	**Bristol** Temple M. 120a 120 132 a.		0515	...	|	0741	|	|	0758	|	|	0957	...	1111	|	|	|	|	|	1514	|	...	|
	Castle Cary d.		|	...	0644	...	|	0727	|	|	0941	|	...	...	|	|	|	1307	|	...	|	...	|
	Westbury d.		0600	0616	0703	...	|	0752	|	|	1001	|	...	...	1105	|	|	1327	|	...	1504	...	|
	Newbury a.		0650	0706	0745	...	|	0830	|	|	|	|	...	...	|	|	|	1404	|	...	|	...	|
337	**Reading** 132 a.		0718	0737	0807	...	0833	0854	0915	0933	1052	1110	...	...	1151	1242	1331	1423	1451	...	1550	...	1653
395	**London** Paddington 132 a.		0747	0809	0837	...	0900	0923	0943	1002	1121	1137	...	...	1221	1314	1400	1454	1521	...	1621	...	1721

	Ⓐ 🍷	Ⓐ 🍷☆	Ⓐ 🍷	Ⓐ 2	Ⓐ 🍷	Ⓐ 🍷	Ⓐ 2☆	Ⓐ ✕	Ⓐ 2☆	①–④ 2	⑤ 2	Ⓐ 🍷	Ⓐ 🍷	Ⓐ 🍷	Ⓐ 🍷	Ⓐ 2☆	Ⓐ 2☆	Ⓐ A		⑥ 2	⑥ 🍷	⑥ 🍷	⑥ 🍷
Penzance **117** d.	...	...	*1257*	1257	1400	*1449*	...	1600	...	1644	1644	...	1742	...	...	...	*1916*	2145‡	⑥	...	...	...	...
Newquay **117** d.	...	...	|	|	|	|	...	|	...	|	|	...	|	...	...	...	|	|		...	...	...	...
Plymouth 120 d.	...	...	1500	1508	1600	1657	1735	1803	...	1844	1844	...	1944	...	...	...	2125	2354		...	0540	0657	...
Totnes 120 d.	...	...	1527	1537	1627	1728	1806	1831	...	1913	1913	...	2012	...	...	...	2154	0022		...	0607	|	...
Paignton 116 120 d.	...	1454	|	|	|	|	|	|	1852	|	|	...	|	2014	...	*2035*	|	|		...	|	|	...
Torquay 116 120 d.	...	1500	|	|	|	|	|	|	1857	|	|	...	|	2020	...	*2040*	|	|		...	|	|	...
Newton Abbot 116 120 d.	...	1512	1540	1549	1640	1741	1819	1844	1909	1926	1926	...	2025	2031	...	*2053*	2206	0036		...	0620	0733	...
Exeter St Davids 116 120 a.	...	1537	1559	...	1659	1800	1848	1903	1939	1948	1948	...	2044	2050	...	*2128*	2240	0057		...	0639	0752	...
Exeter St Davids 120 d.	...	1539	1601	...	1702	1802	...	1905	1939	...	1948	1955	2046	2052	...	2149	...	0106		0600	0643	0756	0729
Tiverton Parkway 120 d.	...	|	1616	...	1717	1817	...	1920	|	...	2005	2010	2101	2105	...	2206	...	|		0617	0659	0811	0744
Taunton 120a 120 d.	1533	1604	1630	...	1731	1831	...	1934	2010	...	2021	2026	2115	2119	2132	2223	...	0142		0634	0713	0825	0759
Bristol Temple M. 120a 120 132 a.	|	|	|	...	|	|	...	|	2054	...	...	|	2147	2152	2235	2313	...	|		0742	|	|	0856
Castle Cary d.	1555	1625	|	...	|	1852	...	|	...	...	...	2047	|	...	|	...	...	|		...	0734	|	|
Westbury d.	1615	1645	|	...	|	1912	...	|	...	...	...	2107	|	...	|	...	...	|		...	0756	|	|
Newbury a.	1651	|	|	...	|	1948	...	|	...	...	...	2143	|	...	|	...	...	|		...	0834	|	|
Reading 132 a.	1715	1737	1745	...	1852	2008	...	2052	...	...	...	2202	2307	...	2353	...	...	0400s		...	0851	0942	1011
London Paddington 132 a.	1752	1807	1816	...	1920	2037	...	2122	...	...	...	2237	2342t	...	0033	...	...	0507z		...	0921	1010	1039

	⑥ 🍷	⑥ 2☆	⑥ 🍷	⑥ 🍷☆	⑥ 🍷		⑥ 🍷	⑥ 🍷	⑥ 🍷	⑥ 🍷	⑥ 🍷	⑥ 🍷	⑥ 🍷	⑥ 🍷	⑥ 🍷	⑥ 2☆	⑥ 🍷	⑥ 2☆	⑥ 🍷	⑥ 2☆		⑦ 2	⑦ 🍷
Penzance **117** d.	*0540*	...	0650	...	0759	...	0900	...	1000	1058	*1141*	...	*1255*	1400	*1452*	...	1552	1644	1740	1906	⑦	...	...
Newquay **117** d.	|	...	|	...	|	...	|	...	|	|	|	...	|	|	|	...	|	|	|	|		...	...
Plymouth 120 d.	0750	0808	0851	...	1001	...	1100	...	1159	1254	1355	...	1500	1600	1656	1740	1754	1844	1941	2115		...	...
Totnes 120 d.	0817	0838	0919	...	1031	...	|	...	1229	1322	|	...	1527	1627	1727	1809	1821	1913	2009	2144		...	...
Paignton 116 120 d.	|	|	|	0918	|	...	|	...	|	|	|	...	|	|	|	|	|	|	|	|		...	...
Torquay 116 120 d.	|	|	|	0925	|	...	|	...	|	|	|	...	|	|	|	|	|	|	|	|		...	...
Newton Abbot 116 120 d.	0830	0851	0932	0939	1044	...	|	...	1242	1335	1431	...	1540	1640	1740	1821	1834	1926	2022	2157		...	...
Exeter St Davids 116 120 a.	0849	0916	0951	1011	1103	...	1152	...	1301	1354	1450	...	1603	1659	1759	1850	1853	1955	2041	2223		...	...
Exeter St Davids 120 d.	0852	...	0954	1015	1107	...	1156	1201	1305	1357	1453	...	1603	1703	1802	...	1856	...	2045	...		0801	0838
Tiverton Parkway 120 d.	0907	...	1010	1030	1122	...	|	1217	1320	|	1509	...	1619	1718	1817	...	1912	...	2100	...		0818	0853
Taunton 120a 120 d.	0921	...	1024	1045	1136	...	|	1231	1334	1422	1523	1530	1633	1733	1831	...	1926	...	2114	...		0834	0906
Bristol Temple M. 120a 120 132 a.	|	...	|	1126	|	...	|	|	|	|	|	|	|	|	|	...	|	...	2146	...		0937	|
Castle Cary d.	0942	...	|	|	|	...	|	1252	|	1443	|	1553	|	|	1853	...	1947	...	|	...		...	0928
Westbury d.	1002	...	1103	|	|	...	|	1313	|	1503	|	1613	|	|	1914	...	2007	...	|	...		...	0951
Newbury a.	|	...	|	|	|	...	|	1351	|	|	|	1651	|	|	1947	...	|	...	|	...		...	1027
Reading 132 a.	1052	...	1149	1246	1251	...	1331	1411	1449	1549	1641	1710	1751	1849	2005	...	2059	...	2304	...		...	1046
London Paddington 132 a.	1121	...	1221	1314	1321	...	1400	1438	1521	1621	1710	1744	1821	1922	2037	...	2131	...	2343	...		...	1123

	⑦ 2	⑦ 🍷☆	⑦ 🍷	⑦ 🍷	⑦ 🍷	⑦ 🍷	⑦ 🍷	⑦ 2☆	⑦ 🍷	⑦ 🍷	⑦ 🍷	⑦ 🍷☆	⑦ 2	⑦ 🍷	⑦ 2☆	⑦ 🍷	⑦ 🍷	⑦ 🍷	⑦ 🍷	⑦ 🍷	⑦ 🍷	⑦ 2☆	⑦ A
Penzance **117** d.	...	...	0807	...	0947	1100	...	1205	1256	...	...	...	1339	...	1437	1500	...	1613	...	1731	...	1900	2115‡
Newquay **117** d.	...	...	|	...	|	|	...	|	|	...	...	...	|	...	|	|	...	|	...	|	...	|	|
Plymouth 120 d.	...	0840	1009	1100	1145	1300	1347	1408	1455	1510	1542	...	1551	1610	1638	1700	1749	1815	1845	1930	2004	2115	2320
Totnes 120 d.	...	0907	1038	1127	1214	1328	1415	1437	1525	|	1609	...	1620	1637	1707	1728	1816	|	1912	1957	|	2144	2348
Paignton 116 120 d.	...	|	|	|	|	|	|	|	|	|	|	1545	|	|	|	|	|	|	|	|	|	|	|
Torquay 116 120 d.	...	|	|	|	|	|	|	|	|	|	|	1550	|	|	|	|	|	|	|	|	|	|	|
Newton Abbot 116 120 d.	...	0921	1052	1140	1228	1341	1428	1449	1538	1547	1623	1605	1633	1655v	1720	1740	1830	|	1925	2010	2040	2157	0001
Exeter St Davids 116 120 a.	...	0946	1111	1159	1247	1400	1447	1514	1557	1606	1644	1632	1653	1714	1745	1800	1849	1907	1944	2029	2200	2222	0023
Exeter St Davids 120 d.	0934	0949	1114	1201	1249	1403	1450	...	1600	1608	1645	1634	...	1717	1749	1801	1851	1913	1947	2031	2102	...	0059
Tiverton Parkway 120 d.	0951	|	1129	1216	|	1417	|	...	1616	1623	1701	|	...	1732	|	1819	|	|	2002	2047	2117	...	|
Taunton 120a 120 d.	1008	1012	1142	1230	1315	1432	1513	...	1631	1637	1714	1658	...	1746	1819	1834	1914	1940	2015	2100	2129	...	|
Bristol Temple M. 120a 120 132 a.	1110	|	|	|	|	|	|	...	|	1720	|	1758	...	1822	1919	|	|	|	|	|	2200	...	|
Castle Cary d.	...	|	1203	|	|	|	1535	...	|	|	1736	|	...	|	...	|	|	|	2037	2126	|	...	|
Westbury d.	...	1049	1223	|	1359	|	1553	...	|	|	1756	|	...	|	...	|	1951	|	2056	2145	|	...	|
Newbury a.	...	1123	1300	|	1432	|	1632	...	|	|	1833	|	...	|	...	|	2024	|	|	2220	|	...	|
Reading 132 a.	...	1138	1320	1347	1450	1550	1650	...	1749	1844	1852	1914	...	1944	...	1950	2045	2101	2145	2240	2326	...	0403s
London Paddington 132 a.	...	1222	1401	1428	1528	1628	1728	...	1828	1921	1930	1958	...	2021	...	2028	2128	2143	2228	2328	0005	...	0503

← **NOTES** (continued from previous page)

v – Arrives 1649.
z – Arrives 0503 on Ⓐ.

★ – Also calls at Dawlish (10–15 minutes after Exeter) and Teignmouth (15–18 minutes after Exeter).
☆ – Also calls at Teignmouth (7–10 minutes after Newton Abbot) and Dawlish (12–15 minutes after Newton Abbot).
‡ – Passengers may occupy cabins at London Paddington from 2230 and at Penzance from 2045⑦/2115Ⓐ.

PAIGNTON - EXETER

GW 2nd class — 116

		Ⓐ	Ⓐ	Ⓐ	Ⓐ	Ⓐ	Ⓐ	Ⓐ	Ⓐ	Ⓐ	Ⓐ	Ⓐ	Ⓐ	Ⓐ	Ⓐ	Ⓐ	Ⓐ	Ⓐ	Ⓐ	Ⓐ	Ⓐ	Ⓐ	Ⓐ	Ⓐ	Ⓐ
Paignton 🚂 115 120 d.	Ⓐ	0603	0634	0710	0748	0820	0912	0934	1021	1033	1120	1213	1308	1421	1513	1612	1629	1657	1726	1752	1834	1852	1937	2035	2135
Torquay 115 120 d.		0608	0639	0715	0755	0825	0917	0939	1026	1038	1125	1218	1313	1426	1518	1617	1634	1702	1731	1757	1839	1857	1942	2040	2141
Newton Abbot 115 120 d.		0621	0652	0734b	0808	0838	0939b	0950	1039	1051	1137	1231	1325	1439	1531	1631	1647	1715	1744	1810	1852	1919	1954	2053	2153
Teignmouth 115 120 d.		0628	0659	0741	0815	0845	0945	|	1046	1058	1145	1238	1333	1446	1538	1638	1655	1722	1751	1817	1859	1916	2002	2100	*2213*
Dawlish 115 120 d.		0633	0704	0746	0822	0850	0950	|	1051	1103	1150	1243	1338	1451	1543	1643	1700	1727	1756	1822	1904	1921	2007	2105	*2218*
Exeter St Davids 115 120 a.		0703	0733	0810	0840	0912	1014	*1020*	1113	1128	1211	1313	1408	1513	1612	1711	1717	1751	1819	1844	1932	1939	2029	2128	*2240*

	Ⓐ	Ⓐ		⑥	⑥	⑥	⑥	⑥	⑥	⑥	⑥	⑥	⑥	⑥	⑥	⑥	⑥	⑥	⑥	⑥	⑥	⑥	⑥	⑥	⑥
Paignton 🚂 115 120 d.	2245	2355	⑥	0613	0634	0702	0806	0904	0918	0930	1016	1100	1121	1213	1242	1313	1355	1408	1513	1544	1613	1711	1752	1852	1924
Torquay 115 120 d.	2250	2359		0618	0639	0708	0811	0909	0925	0935	1021	1105	1126	1218	1247	1318	1401	1413	1518	1549	1618	1716	1757	1857	1929
Newton Abbot 115 120 d.	2303	0013		0630	0652	0719	0834c	0922	0939	0948	1033	1118	1139	1231	1307	1338b	1412	1438f	1531	1608b	1631	1729	1810	1910	1942
Teignmouth 115 120 d.	2310	0020		0638	0659	0726	0841	0929	0947	0955	1040	1125	1147	1238	1315	1346	1419	1445	1538	1615	1638	1736	1817	1917	1949
Dawlish 115 120 d.	2315	0025		0643	0704	0731	0846	0934	0954	1000	1045	1130	1152	1243	1320	1351	1424	1450	1543	1620	1643	1741	1822	1922	1954
Exeter St Davids 115 120 a.	2337	0048		0705	0733	0742	0909	1003	1011	1017	1114	1147	1214	1313	1336	1413	1435	1513	1612	1634	1713	1810	1844	1945	2025

	⑥	⑥	⑥	⑥	⑥	⑥		⑦	⑦	⑦	⑦	⑦	⑦	⑦	⑦	⑦	⑦	⑦	⑦	⑦	⑦	⑦	⑦	⑦	⑦
Paignton 🚂 115 120 d.	1951	2020	2044	2120	2245	2330	⑦	0949	1059	1149	1256	1352	1418	1457	1545	1555	1619	1654	1749	1820	1855	1955	2053	2153	2300
Torquay 115 120 d.	1956	2025	2050	2125	2250	2335		0954	1104	1154	1301	1357	1423	1501	1550	1600	1624	1659	1754	1826	1900	2000	2058	2158	2305
Newton Abbot 115 120 d.	2007	2037	2102	2138	2301	2347		1007	1116	1208	1314	1409	1437	1516	1616	1612	1637	1712	1807	1837	1913	2014	2111	2210	2318
Teignmouth 115 120 d.	2015	2045	|	2145	...	2354		1014	1122	1216	1321	1416	1444	1523	1614	1619	1644	1719	1814	|	1920	2022	2118	2217	2325
Dawlish 115 120 d.	2020	2050	|	2150	...	2359		1019	1127	1221	1326	1421	1449	1528	1619	1624	1649	1724	1819	|	1925	2027	2123	2222	2330
Exeter St Davids 115 120 a.	2037	2112	2122	2212	...	0022		1040	1140	1242	1342	1441	1511	1541	1632	1640	1711	1740	1839	1856	1938	2049	2139	2242	2351

b – Arrives 7–11 minutes earlier.
c – Arrives 0822.
f – Arrives 1424.
🚂 – Dartmouth Steam Railway (Paignton - Kingswear). ✆ 01803 555 872. www.dartmouthrailriver.co.uk

① – Mondays ② – Tuesdays ③ – Wednesdays ④ – Thursdays ⑤ – Fridays ⑥ – Saturdays ⑦ – Sundays Ⓐ – Not Saturdays 21

117 PLYMOUTH - NEWQUAY and PENZANCE — GW, XC

km		Ⓐ	②–⑤	①	②–⑤	①	Ⓐ	Ⓐ	Ⓐ	Ⓐ	Ⓐ	Ⓐ	Ⓐ 2	Ⓐ	Ⓐ	Ⓐ 2	Ⓐ	Ⓐ	Ⓐ	Ⓐ	Ⓐ	Ⓐ	Ⓐ
			A			A	🍷	2 K	2	2	2	🍷	K	2	🍷	B	🍷	2	2	🍷	2	2	2
	London Paddington **115** d.		2345p	...	...	2350p	...	...	...	...	...	0633	...	...	0730	*0903*	1003	...	...	1203	...	...	*1303*
	Bristol Temple Meads **115 120** d.		|	...	...	|	...	...	0524	...	0643	|	...	...	0912	0955	*1045*	...	*1144*	*1245*	...	*1345*	*1445*
0	**Plymouth** d.		0549	0600	0628	0628	0702	0753	0814	...	0921	0945	1034	...	1119	1243	1313	...	1355	1511	...	1557	1701
7	Saltash d.		|	|	|	|	0715	0802	0824	...	0931	|	1043	...	|	1252	|	...	1404	|	...	1612	1714
29	Liskeard d.		0615	0623	0651	0709	0736	0821	0843	...	0950	1010	1102	...	1144	1311	1338	...	1423	1536	...	1633	1736
43	Bodmin Parkway 🚂 d.		0629	0635	0703	0723	0749	0833	0855	...	1002	1023	1114	...	1157	1323	1351	...	1435	1549	...	1645	...
49	Lostwithiel d.		0635	0641	0708	0729	0755	0840	0900	...	1007	|	1119	...	|	1329	|	...	1440	|	...	1650	...
56	Par ♡ d.		0643	0648	0715	0738	0803	0848	0908	0917	1015	|	1126	1140	1208	1336	1402	1407	1447	1600	1610	1658	...
89	**Newquay** ♡ a.		|	|	|	|	|	...	|	1009	|	|	|	1231	|	|	|	1459	|	|	1702	|	...
63	St Austell d.		0652	0655	0721	0746	0811	...	0916	...	1022	1039	1134	...	1215	1343	1409	...	1454	1608	...	1706	...
86	Truro d.		0710	0711	0738	0806	0829	...	0934	...	1040	1057	1155	...	1233	1400	1427	...	1511	1625	...	1723	...
101	Redruth d.		0723	0723	0749	0820	0841	...	0947	...	1053	1109	1208	...	1246	1413	1439	...	1524	1638	...	1736	...
107	Camborne d.		0731	0730	0755	0827	0848	...	0953	...	1059	1116	1214	...	1253	1419	1447	...	1530	1645	...	1742	...
119	St Erth d.		0745	0743	0807	0845	0902	...	1008	...	1110	1127	1225	...	1303	1430	1501	...	1541	1659	...	1754	...
128	**Penzance** a.		0755	0752	0816	0859	0912	...	1016	...	1120	1137	1234	...	1313	1439	1511	...	1550	1709	...	1804	...

	Ⓐ	Ⓐ	Ⓐ	Ⓐ	Ⓐ		Ⓐ	Ⓐ	Ⓐ	Ⓐ	Ⓐ	Ⓐ	⑤	①–④
	🍷	2	2	🍷	C		🍷	2	D	🍷	C	🍷	🍷	2
London Paddington **115** d.	1403	...	...	1503	...	...	1603	...	...	1703	...	1803	1903	*1903*
Bristol Temple Meads **115 120** d.	*1513*e	...	*1544*	|	1645	...	|	...	1744	|	1844	|	*1945*	*1945*
Plymouth d.	1725	...	1755	1840	1901	...	1932	...	1949	2028	2050	2121	2229	2242
Saltash d.	1736	...	1804	|	|	...	1942	...	|	2039	|	|	2240	2251
Liskeard d.	1756	...	1823	1905	1924	...	1959	...	2012	2059	2113	2146	2300	2310
Bodmin Parkway 🚂 d.	1809	...	1835	1919	1936	...	2012	...	2024	2112	2125	2200	2314	2324
Lostwithiel d.	1815	...	1840	|	|	...	|	...	|	|	2131	|	2320	2329
Par ♡ d.	1823	1829	1847	1930	1946	...	2023	2028	2034	2123	2137	2211	2329	2336
Newquay ♡ a.	|	1921	|	|	|	...	|	2120	|	|	|	|	|	|
St Austell d.	1831	...	1855	1942	1952	...	2030	...	2041	2130	2144	2219	2336	2344
Truro d.	1848	...	1911	2000	2018	...	2048	...	2102	2148	2203	2236	2358	2359
Redruth d.	1901	...	1924	2012	2029	...	2100	...	2118	2200	2214	2249	0013	0014
Camborne d.	1908	...	1930	2020	2035	...	2108	...	2125	|	2220	|	0021	0020
St Erth d.	1922	...	1942	2030	2046	...	2119	...	2135	2215	2232	|	0035	0031
Penzance a.	1932	...	1951	2040	2054	...	2129	...	2143	2226	2241	2310	0045	0041

	⑥	⑥	⑥	⑥	⑥	⑥	⑥	⑥	⑥
		2	A	2		2	2	2	2
London Paddington **115** d.	⑥	...	2345p	...	...	...	...	...	...
Bristol Temple Meads **115 120** d.		...	|	...	...	0524	...	0645	...
Plymouth d.		...	0540	...	0628	0818	...	0923	0950
Saltash d.		...	|	...	|	0828	...	0932	1000
Liskeard d.		...	0606	...	0651	0847	...	0951	1021
Bodmin Parkway 🚂 d.		...	0620	...	0703	0859	...	1003	1033
Lostwithiel d.		...	0627	...	0708	0904	...	|	1039
Par ♡ d.		0610	0635	0652	0714	0911	0917	1015	1046
Newquay ♡ a.		|	|	0744	|	|	1009	|	|
St Austell d.		0617	0644	...	0721	0919	...	1022	1053
Truro d.		0635	0705	...	0737	0936	...	1040	1110
Redruth d.		0648	0718	...	0748	0949	...	1053	1124
Camborne d.		0654	0726	...	0755	0955	...	1059	1130
St Erth d.		0704	0740	...	0807	1007	...	1110	1142
Penzance a.		0715	0750	...	0815	1017	...	1122	1152

	⑥	⑥	⑥	⑥	⑥	⑥	⑥		⑥	⑥	⑥	⑥	⑥	⑥	⑥	⑥	⑥	⑥	⑥	⑥	⑥	⑥	⑥
	2 K	🍷	2	2	🍷	2	2 K		🍷	2	2	🍷	🍷	2	2	🍷	C	2 K	2	D	🍷	C	🍷
London Paddington **115** d.	...	0730	...	*0903*	1003	...	...	...	1203	...	...	1303	1403	...	...	1503	...	...	...	*1603*	1703	...	1803
Bristol Temple Meads **115 120** d.	*0812*e	0915	...	*1044*	*1044*	...	*1144*	...	*1244*	...	*1345*	|	*1512*e	...	*1544*	|	1645	...	...	1744	|	1844	|
Plymouth d.	1033	1120	...	1245	1310	...	1409	...	1510	...	1555	1621	1726	...	1752	1839	1855	1910	...	1948	2040	2058	2121
Saltash d.	1044	|	...	1254	|	...	1418	...	|	...	1604	|	|	...	1806	|	|	1919	...	|	2050	|	|
Liskeard d.	1103	1145	...	1313	1335	...	1437	...	1535	...	1624	1646	1751	...	1826	1904	1921	1938	...	2011	2110	2125	2146
Bodmin Parkway 🚂 d.	1115	1158	...	1325	1348	...	1449	...	1548	...	1636	1659	1804	...	1838	1917	1933	1950	...	2023	2124	2137	2200
Lostwithiel d.	1120	|	...	1330	|	...	1454	...	|	...	1641	|	|	...	1843	|	|	1955	...	2028	|	|	|
Par ♡ d.	1128	1209	1212	1337	1400	1405	1501	...	1559	1610	1648	|	1815	1820	1850	1928	1944	2003	2015	2035	2136	2147	2211
Newquay ♡ a.	|	|	1304	|	|	1457	|	...	|	1702	|	|	|	1912	|	|	|	|	2107	|	|	|	|
St Austell d.	1137	1216	...	1345	1407	...	1508	...	1606	...	1656	1714	1822	...	1858	1935	1953	2010	...	2041	2144	2201	2219
Truro d.	1155	1235	...	1402	1425	...	1526	...	1625	...	1713	1733	1841	...	1915	1954	2011	2028	...	2102	2203	2218	2238
Redruth d.	1208	1247	...	1415	1437	...	1539	...	1637	...	1726	1745	1853	...	1928	2006	2024	2041	...	2113	2215	2229	2250
Camborne d.	1214	1255	...	1421	1445	...	1545	...	1645	...	1732	1753	1901	...	1934	2014	2031	2047	...	2119	|	2235	2258
St Erth d.	1225	1306	...	1433	1500	...	1555	...	1656	...	1744	1808	1912	...	1946	2025	2043	2058	...	2131	2232	2245	2312
Penzance a.	1236	1316	...	1442	1510	...	1606	...	1706	...	1754	1818	1922	...	1956	2035	2052	2108	...	2140	2242	2254	2322

		⑦	⑦	⑦	⑦	⑦	⑦	⑦	⑦	⑦ 2		⑦	⑦	⑦	⑦	⑦	⑦	⑦	⑦	⑦	⑦	⑦	⑦
		2 h	2 g	2	2	2	🍷	2	F	K		🍷	2	🍷	2	🍷	2 K	🍷	E	2	🍷	C	🍷
London Paddington **115** d.	⑦	...	...	...	...	...	0757	...	*0857*	*0957*	...	1057	...	1157	...	1257	*1303*	1457	...	*1557*	1657	...	1757
Bristol Temple Meads **115 120** d.		...	...	...	0726	0828	1000	...	1057	|	...	*1154*	...	*1254*	...	*1344*	*1455*	*1614*e	1644	|	*1744*	1844	|
Plymouth d.		0906	0910	...	1005	1110	1217	...	1255	1331	...	1415	1450	1525	...	1625	1733	1825	1853	1940	2025	2050	2135
Saltash d.		0916	0920	...	1015	1122	|	...	|	1339	...	|	1459	|	...	|	1743	|	|	1949	|	|	|
Liskeard d.		|	0938	...	1036	1141	1243	...	1318	1358	...	1439	1518	1555	...	1650	1804	1852	1916	2008	2049	2113	2200
Bodmin Parkway 🚂 d.		0950	0950	...	1048	1153	1256	...	1330	1410	...	1453	1530	1609	...	1703	1816	1906	1928	2020	2102	2125	2213
Lostwithiel d.		0956	0956	...	1052	1158	|	...	|	|	...	|	1536	|	...	|	1821	|	|	2025	|	|	|
Par ♡ d.		1003	1003	1018	1101	1206	1308	1315	1340	1421	...	|	1544	1621	1630	1714	1829	1917	1938	2033	2113	2135	2226
Newquay ♡ a.		|	|	1110	|	|	|	1407	|	|	...	|	|	|	1728	|	|	|	|	|	|	|	|
St Austell d.		1010	1010	...	1109	1215	1316	...	1351	1429	...	1509	1551	1629	...	1722	1836	1925	1945	2040	2120	2143	2234
Truro d.		1030	1028	...	1132	1234	1336	...	1409	1444	...	1527	1610	1647	...	1740	1854	1941	2001	2057	2137	2200	2249
Redruth d.		1043	1041	...	1145	1247	1347	...	1420	1458	...	1538	1623	1659	...	1753	1907	1954	2012	2111	2151	2211	2304
Camborne d.		1049	1047	...	1151	1253	1355	...	1427	1504	...	1546	1629	1707	...	1801	1913	2004	2021	2117	2157	2220	2311
St Erth d.		1105	1101	...	1205	1304	1406	...	1437	1515	...	1557	1640	1719	...	1812	1923	2016	2031	2128	2209	2230	2322
Penzance a.		1114	1110	...	1214	1314	1416	...	1447	1524	...	1609	1650	1729	...	1823	1935	2028	2039	2138	2221	2242	2333

A – THE NIGHT RIVIERA – Conveys 🛏 1, 2. cl and (2).
See also note ‡ on page 101.
B – From Cardiff Central (Tables **115** and **120a**).
C – From Glasgow Central (Table **120**).
D – From Aberdeen (Tables **222** / **120**).
E – From Edinburgh (Table **120**).
F – From Birmingham New Street (Table **120**).

H – From York (Table **120**).
J – From Dundee (Tables **222** / **120**).
K – From Exeter St Davids (Table **115**).
M – From Manchester Piccadilly (Table **120**).

e – Change at Exeter St Davids.
g – Until Mar. 25.
h – From Apr. 1.

j – Arrives 0906.
p – Previous night.

♡ – Par - Newquay: *'The Atlantic Coast Line'*.

🚂 – Bodmin & Wenford Railway (Bodmin Parkway - Bodmin General - Boscarne Junction *10 km*). ✆ 01208 73555. www.bodminrailway.co.uk

118 BRANCH LINES and BUS CONNECTIONS IN DEVON and CORNWALL — 2nd class GW

EXETER - EXMOUTH *'The Avocet Line'* *18 km*

From Exeter St Davids: on ⚒ at 0544, 0606Ⓐ, 0629, 0708, 0736Ⓐ, 0744⑥, 0815, 0845, 0915, 0948 and at the same minutes past each hour until 1615, 1646, 1715, 1745⑥, 1753Ⓐ, 1814⑥, 1821Ⓐ, 1847⑥, 1850Ⓐ, 1931⑥, 1933Ⓐ, 2031⑥, 2034Ⓐ, 2131Ⓐ, 2140⑥, 2231Ⓐ, 2240⑥, 2309⑥, 2326Ⓐ; on ⑦ at 0830, 0940, 1013, 1044, 1122**a**, 1145, 1226**a**, 1247, 1322**a**, 1348, 1446, 1518, 1546, 1622**a**, 1646, 1716, 1746, 1846, 1951, 2052, 2148, 2248, 2325.

From Exmouth: on ⚒ at 0001①, 0004②–⑥, 0614, 0643Ⓐ, 0712Ⓐ, 0718⑥, 0751, 0821, 0852, 0921, 0953 and at the same minutes past each hour until 1653, 1723, 1753⑥, 1801Ⓐ, 1823⑥, 1832Ⓐ, 1854⑥, 1859Ⓐ, 1939, 2007⑥, 2015Ⓐ, 2111Ⓐ, 2116⑥, 2207Ⓐ, 2219⑥, 2307Ⓐ, 2317⑥, 2345⑥; on ⑦ at 0910, 1019, 1054**b**, 1124, 1154**b**, 1228, 1255, 1324, 1358, 1427, 1523, 1555**b**, 1623, 1655, 1723, 1755, 1823, 1923, 2028, 2128, 2228, 2330.

Journey: 37 – 40 minutes. Trains call at Exeter Central 3 – 4 minutes from Exeter St Davids.

a – Starts from Exeter Central. **b** – Terminates at Exeter Central.

EXETER - BARNSTAPLE *'The Tarka Line'* *63 km*

From Exeter St Davids: on ⚒ at 0548Ⓐ, 0554⑥, 0648Ⓐ, 0654⑥, 0831, 0927, 1027, 1127, 1227, 1327, 1427, 1527, 1657, 1757, 1852⑥, 1900Ⓐ, 2100, 2253⑤; on ⑦ at 0843, 0954, 1205, 1408, 1604, 1807, 2001.

From Barnstaple: on ⚒ at 0005⑥, 0658Ⓐ, 0705⑥, 0843, 0943, 1043, 1143, 1243, 1343, 1443, 1543, 1708⑥, 1713Ⓐ, 1811⑥, 1814Ⓐ, 1916, 2024, 2216Ⓐ, 2230⑥; on ⑦ at 1000, 1129, 1323, 1529, 1721, 1926, 2130.

Journey: 65 minutes. Trains call at ***Crediton*** *(11 minutes from Exeter / 54 minutes from Barnstaple) and* ***Eggesford*** *(40 minutes from Exeter / 25 minutes from Barnstaple).*

PLYMOUTH - GUNNISLAKE *'The Tamar Valley Line'* *24 km*

From Plymouth: on Ⓐ at 0506, 0641, 0840, 1054, 1254, 1454, 1637, 1823, 2131;
on ⑥ at 0640, 0854, 1054, 1254, 1454, 1638, 1823, 2131;
on ⑦ at 0920, 1117, 1306, 1511, 1741.

From Gunnislake: on Ⓐ at 0551, 0731, 0929, 1145, 1345, 1545, 1729, 1913, 2221;
on ⑥ at 0731, 0945, 1145, 1345, 1545, 1729, 1913, 2221;
on ⑦ at 1010, 1207, 1358, 1605, 1835.

Journey: 45 – 60 minutes

LISKEARD - LOOE *'The Looe Valley Line'* *14 km*

From Liskeard:
on Ⓐ at 0605, 0714, 0850, 1012, 1115, 1216, 1320, 1424, 1541, 1641, 1806, 1920;
on ⑥ at 0610, 0713, 0820, 0956, 1108, 1216, 1339, 1442, 1551, 1655, 1758, 1925;
on ⑦ from April 1 at 1012, 1126, 1247, 1402, 1523, 1635, 1750, 2015.

From Looe:
on Ⓐ at 0637, 0746, 0929, 1044, 1147, 1249, 1352, 1458, 1613, 1715, 1842, 1952;
on ⑥ at 0638, 0746, 0855, 1028, 1143, 1248, 1411, 1517, 1623, 1727, 1830, 2000;
on ⑦ from April 1 at 1044, 1158, 1319, 1434, 1555, 1712, 1825, 2050.

Journey: 28 – 33 minutes.

EXETER - OKEHAMPTON *Service runs only summer ⑦.* 40 km

From Exeter St. Davids:
From Okehampton:
Journey: 40 – 42 minutes. Trains call at ***Crediton*** *(approx. 10 minutes from Exeter).*

GW, XC — PENZANCE and NEWQUAY - PLYMOUTH — 117

		Ⓐ	Ⓐ	Ⓐ	Ⓐ	Ⓐ	Ⓐ	Ⓐ	Ⓐ	Ⓐ		Ⓐ	Ⓐ	Ⓐ	Ⓐ	Ⓐ	Ⓐ	Ⓐ	Ⓐ	Ⓐ	Ⓐ	Ⓐ
		🍷	2	🍷	2**B**	**D**	🍷	🍷	**D**	🍷		**E**	2	🍷	2	2**K**	2	🍷	2**K**	🍷	2	2
Penzance d.	Ⓐ	0505	0519	0541	0600	0628	0645	0741	0828	0900	...	0935	...	1000	1051	1141	...	1204	1257	1400	...	1449
St Erth d.		|	|	|	0609	0636	0655	0751	0836	0910	...	0943	...	1010	1100	1150	...	1214	1306	1410	...	1458
Camborne d.		|	0538	0558	0621	0646	0706	0805	0846	0921	...	0956	...	1021	1112	1202	...	|	1318	1421	...	1511
Redruth d.		0526	|	0605	0627	0652	0713	0812	0852	0928	...	1003	...	1028	1118	1208	...	1228	1324	1428	...	1517
Truro d.		0538	0553	0618	0639	0704	0726	0825	0904	0941	...	1015	...	1041	1130	1219	...	1241	1335	1441	...	1528
St Austell d.		0556	...	0635	0656	0720	0743	0843	0920	0958	...	1031	...	1058	1147	1236	...	1259	1352	1458	...	1545
Newquay ♡ d.		|	...	|	|	|	|	|	|	|	...	|	1013	|	|	|	1303	|	|	|	1501	|
Par ♡ d.		|	...	0643	0702	0727	0751	0850	0927	1005	...	1038	1102	1106	1153	1243	1352	|	1359	1506	1547	1552
Lostwithiel d.		|	...	0651	0709	|	0758	|	|	|	...	1045	...	|	1200	1249	...	|	1405	|	...	1558
Bodmin Parkway 🚂 d.		0612	...	0657	0715	0737	0805	0902	0937	1017	...	1051	...	1117	1206	1255	...	1315	1411	1517	...	1604
Liskeard d.		0625	...	0711	0728	0753	0818	0915	0950	1030	...	1104	...	1130	1219	1308	...	1328	1424	1530	...	1617
Saltash d.		|	...	0731	0746	|	0838	0935	|	|	...	|	...	|	1237	1328	...	|	1444	|	...	1637
Plymouth a.		0649	...	0741	0803	0820	0848	0945	1018	1054	...	1127	...	1155	1246	1337	...	1352	1453	1555	...	1651
Bristol Temple Meads **115 120** a.		*0926*	...	|	...	1025	*1124*	|	1224	*1324*	...	1355	...	*1426*	*1523*	...	...	*1623*	*1724*	*1823*	...	*1923*
London Paddington **115** a.		1002	...	1121	...	...	1221	1314	...	1400	...	...	...	1521	*1621*	...	...	1721	*1816*	1920	...	*2037*

	Ⓐ	Ⓐ	①–④	⑤	Ⓐ	Ⓐ	Ⓐ	Ⓐ		①–④	⑤	Ⓐ	Ⓐ	Ⓐ		⑥	⑥	⑥	⑥	⑥	⑥	⑥
	🍷	2	2**B**	2**C**	2	🍷	2	2		2	🍷	2	**A**			2	2	**D**	🍷	2	2	🍷
Penzance d.	1600	...	1644	1644	...	1742	...	1916	...	2018	2018	...	2145	2210	⑥	0520	0540	0630	0650	...	0739	0759
St Erth d.	1610	...	1653	1653	...	1752	...	1925	...	2027	2027	...	2155	2218		|	0549	0638	0700	...	0748	0809
Camborne d.	1621	...	1706	1706	...	1807	...	1938	...	2042	2042	...	2208	2231		0538	0602	0651	0712	...	0802	0824
Redruth d.	1628	...	1712	1712	...	1814	...	1944	...	2050	2050	...	2216	2238		0544	0608	0657	0719	...	0808	0831
Truro d.	1641	...	1725	1725	...	1826	...	1956	...	2103	2103	...	2229	2249		0556	0619	0709	0732	...	0820	0844
St Austell d.	1659	...	1742	1742	...	1844	...	2013	...	2120	2120	...	2247	2305		...	0636	0725	0749	...	0837	0902
Newquay ♡ d.	|	...	|	|	1722	|	1924	|	...	|	|	2126	|	|		...	|	|	|	0747	|	|
Par ♡ d.	1706	...	1748	1748	1811	1851	2013	2019	...	2127	2127	2216	2256	2312		...	0643	0732	0756	0838	0844	0909
Lostwithiel d.	1714	...	1755	1755	...	|	...	2026	...	2134	2134	...	|	2319		...	0650	0739	0804	...	0851	|
Bodmin Parkway 🚂 d.	1720	...	1801	1801	...	1903	...	2032	...	2140	2140	...	2308	2325		...	0656	0746	0810	...	0857	0920
Liskeard d.	1733	1749	1814	1814	...	1916	...	2045	...	2153	2153	...	2324	2337		...	0710	0758	0823	...	0910	0933
Saltash d.	|	1806	1832	1832	...	|	...	2104	...	2211	2211	...	|	|		...	0728	|	|	...	0931	|
Plymouth a.	1758	1818	1842	1842	...	1940	...	2119	...	2221	2224	...	2347	0001		...	0745	0821	0847	...	0942	0957
Bristol Temple Meads **115 120** a.	*2025*	*2025*	|	|	...	2147	...	...	...	...	...	...	|	...		...	|	1025	*1124*	...	...	|
London Paddington **115** a.	2122	...	*2237*e	*2237*e	...	2342**k**	...	...	...	...	...	...	0503**t**	...		...	*1121*	...	1221	...	...	1321

	⑥	⑥	⑥	⑥	⑥	⑥	⑥	⑥	⑥	⑥	⑥	⑥	⑥		⑥	⑥	⑥	⑥	⑥	⑥	⑥	⑥
	D	🍷	**E**	2	🍷	2	🍷	2	2	🍷	🍷	2	2		🍷	2**B**	2	🍷	2	2**B**	2	
Penzance d.	0828	0900	0943	...	1000	1036	1058	1141	...	1255	1400	...	1452	...	1552	1644	...	1740	...	1906	...	2129
St Erth d.	0836	0910	0951	...	1010	1046	1108	1150	...	1304	1410	...	1501	...	1602	1653	...	1750	...	1915	...	2138
Camborne d.	0846	0922	1001	...	1022	1100	1120	1203	...	1317	1422	...	1514	...	1614	1706	...	1805	...	1928	...	2149
Redruth d.	0852	0929	1007	...	1029	1106	1127	1209	...	1323	1429	...	1520	...	1621	1712	...	1812	...	1935	...	2156
Truro d.	0904	0942	1019	...	1042	1117	1140	1222	...	1336	1442	...	1531	...	1634	1725	...	1825	...	1946	...	2209
St Austell d.	0920	1000	1035	...	1059	1134	1157	1239	...	1353	1459	...	1548	...	1652	1742	...	1842	...	2003	...	2226
Newquay ♡ d.	|	|	|	1013	|	|	|	|	1306	|	|	1500	|	...	|	|	1720	|	1915	|	2120	|
Par ♡ d.	0927	1007	1041	1102	1107	1141	|	1245	1355	1400	1506	1550	1555	...	1659	1748	1810	1849	2005	2010	2212	2233
Lostwithiel d.	|	|	1048	...	|	1148	|	1252	...	1407	|	...	1601	...	1706	1755	...	|	...	2016	2219	|
Bodmin Parkway 🚂 d.	0937	1018	1055	...	1118	1154	1213	1258	...	1413	1518	...	1607	...	1713	1801	...	1901	...	2022	2225	2244
Liskeard d.	0950	1031	1107	...	1131	1207	1226	1311	...	1426	1531	...	1620	...	1726	1814	...	1914	...	2035	2238	2258
Saltash d.	|	|	|	...	|	1226	|	1330	...	1443	|	...	1640	...	|	1832	...	|	...	2055	2258	|
Plymouth a.	1017	1055	1130	...	1155	1236	1250	1341	...	1455	1554	...	1650	...	1749	1841	...	1937	...	2109	2313	2322
Bristol Temple Meads **115 120** a.	1225	*1325*	1355	...	*1425*	...	*1525*	*1625*	...	*1725*	*1825*	...	*1924*	...	*2022*	...	...	2146	...	...	...	...
London Paddington **115** a.	...	1400	...	...	1521	...	1621	*1710*	...	*1821*	1922	...	*2037*	...	2131	...	...	2343	...	...	...	...

		⑦	⑦	⑦	⑦	⑦	⑦	⑦	⑦		⑦	⑦	⑦	⑦	⑦		⑦	⑦	⑦	⑦	⑦	⑦
		🍷	**F**	🍷	2	🍷	2**B**	**E**	🍷		2**B**	2	2	🍷	**G**		🍷	2	🍷	2**B**	2	**A**
Penzance d.	⑦	0807	0930	0947	...	1100	1205	1230	1256	...	1339	1437	...	1500	1530	...	1613	...	1731	1900	2005	2115
St Erth d.		0816	0938	0956	...	1110	1214	1238	1306	...	1349	1447	...	1510	1538	...	1624	...	1740	1909	2014	2125
Camborne d.		0833	0948	1009	...	1124	1226	1251	1320	...	1402	1500	...	1523	1549	...	1637	...	1753	1921	2027	2139
Redruth d.		0839	0954	1015	...	1130	1232	1258	1326	...	1408	1506	...	1530	1555	...	1644	...	1800	1927	2033	2146
Truro d.		0853	1011**f**	1028	...	1143	1244	1309	1339	...	1419	1517	...	1542	1607	...	1657	...	1812	1939	2045	2201
St Austell d.		0909	1027	1045	...	1200	1300	1326	1357	...	1436	1534	...	1600	1623	...	1714	...	1831	1956	2102	2219
Newquay ♡ d.		|	|	|	1112	|	|	|	|	...	|	|	1510	|	|	...	|	1738	|	|	|	|
Par ♡ d.		0917	1034	1053	1201	1207	1306	1332	1403	...	1443	1540	1559	1607	1630	...	1720	1827	1838	2003	2109	|
Lostwithiel d.		|	|	|	...	|	1313	1339	|	...	1449	1547	...	|	|	...	|	...	|	2009	2115	|
Bodmin Parkway 🚂 d.		0929	1044	1106	...	1219	1319	1346	1416	...	1455	1553	...	1618	1640	...	1732	...	1849	2015	2122	2235
Liskeard d.		0942	1057	1119	...	1233	1333	1358	1429	...	1508	1609	...	1631	1652	...	1746	...	1902	2028	2136	2250
Saltash d.		0958	|	|	...	|	1354	|	|	...	1526	1626	...	|	|	...	1802	...	|	2047	2154	|
Plymouth a.		1006	1120	1143	...	1257	1403	1423	1453	...	1534	1636	...	1656	1715	...	1811	...	1926	2100	2204	2314
Bristol Temple Meads **115 120** a.		|	1323	*1354*	...	*1526*	*1625*	1647	*1721*	...	*1822*	1919	...	|	1922	...	*2025*	...	*2200*	...	...	|
London Paddington **115** a.		1401	...	1528	...	1628	...	...	1828	...	*1930*	...	...	2028	*2128*	...	2143	...	2328	...	...	0503

A – THE NIGHT RIVIERA – Conveys 🛏 1, 2. cl and (2). See also note ‡ on page 101.
B – To Exeter St Davids (Table **115**).
C – To Taunton (Table **115**).
D – To Glasgow Central (Table **120**).
E – To Manchester Piccadilly (Table **120**).
F – To Edinburgh (Table **120**).
G – To Leeds (Table **120**).
H – To Dundee (Tables **120** / **222**).
K – To Newton Abbot (Table **115**).
e – Change at Exeter St Davids.
f – Arrives 1004.
k – Arrives 2339 on ⑤.
t – Arrives 0507 on ⑥ mornings.
♡ – Par - Newquay: *'The Atlantic Coast Line'*.
🚂 – Bodmin & Wenford Railway (Bodmin Parkway - Bodmin General - Boscarne Junction *10 km*). ✆ 01208 73555. www.bodminrailway.co.uk

GW 2nd class — BRANCH LINES and BUS CONNECTIONS IN DEVON and CORNWALL — 118

Rail tickets are generally not valid on 🚌 services shown in this table.

BODMIN PARKWAY - PADSTOW — *Plymouth City Bus 🚌 service 11A*

From Bodmin Parkway station:
on ⚒ at 0612, 0652**n**, 0707**p**, 0747**n**, 0807**p**, 0907**p**, 1007 and hourly until 1607⑥, 1612Ⓐ, 1722, 1812;
on ⑦ at 0756, 0956, 1156, 1356, 1556, 1751.

From Padstow Bus Terminus:
on ⚒ at 0625, 0730, 0830**p**, 0930 and hourly until 1430, 1520**n**, 1530**p**, 1630, 1730, 1830, 1920;
on ⑦ at 0905, 1105, 1305, 1505, 1705, 1905.

Journey: 68 minutes. Buses also make calls in Bodmin town centre and at Bodmin General station, and call at ***Wadebridge*** *(35 minutes after Bodmin / 25 minutes after Padstow).*

TRURO - FALMOUTH DOCKS — *'The Maritime Line'* — *20 km*

From Truro:
on ⚒ at 0604, 0631, 0714, 0747, 0820, 0851 and at the same minutes past each hour until 1620, 1651, 1727, 1759, 1831, 1902, 2004, 2105, 2208Ⓐ, 2212⑥;
on ⑦ at 0912, 1036, 1136, 1237, 1344, 1440, 1547, 1705, 1815, 1946, 2103, 2204.

From Falmouth Docks:
on ⚒ at 0631, 0715, 0747, 0820, 0850 and at the same minutes past each hour until 1620, 1650, 1727, 1759, 1831, 1902, 1929Ⓐ, 1934⑥, 2031, 2132, 2239⑥, 2311Ⓐ;
on ⑦ at 0940, 1103, 1203, 1304, 1411, 1509, 1617, 1735, 1842, 2013, 2130, 2233.

Trains call at ***Falmouth Town*** *22 minutes after Truro and 3 minutes after Falmouth Docks.*

Journey: 25 minutes.

c – Until Mar. 25.
k – From April 1.
n – Schooldays - check locally for details.
p – School holidays (check locally for details) and ⑥.

ST AUSTELL - EDEN PROJECT — *First Kernow 🚌 service 101*

From St Austell bus station:
on Ⓐ at 0847, 0928, 1040, 1147, 1242, 1412, 1454, 1550, 1645, 1735;
on ⑥ at 0847, 0928, 1040, 1140, 1235, 1417, 1504, 1553, 1640, 1737;
on ⑦ at 0847, 0937, 1030, 1130, 1225, 1330, 1441, 1535, 1625, 1737.

From Eden Project:
on Ⓐ at 0907, 1105, 1208, 1330, 1432, 1515, 1615, 1715, 1800;
on ⑥ at 0907, 1102, 1205, 1315, 1437, 1525, 1615, 1705, 1800;
on ⑦ at 0907, 0957, 1055, 1150, 1247, 1400, 1505, 1555, 1654, 1800.

Journey: 20 minutes.

ST ERTH - ST IVES — *'The St Ives Bay Line'* — *7 km*

From St Erth: on Ⓐ at 0706, 0759, 0852, 0938 and every 30 minutes until 1648, 1717, 1748 and every 30 minutes until 2048, 2123, 2158;
on ⑥ at 0650, 0800, 0859, 0935, 1013, 1048, 1118, 1148 and every 30 minutes until 1648, 1717, 1759, 1859, 1950, 2030, 2103, 2147;
on ⑦ at 1030**k**, 1113**k**, 1142**k**, 1156**c**, 1213**k**, 1230**c**, 1245**k**, 1316, 1346, 1416, 1448, 1518, 1548, 1618, 1648, 1725, 1755, 1830, 1930.

From St Ives: on Ⓐ at 0725, 0815, 0922, 0953, 1033 and every 30 minutes until 1703, 1731, 1803, 1833, 1905, 1932, 2003, 2033, 2103, 2137, 2231;
on ⑥ at 0712, 0815, 0920, 0950, 1027, 1103, 1133, 1203, 1233 and every 30 minutes until 1703, 1732, 1817, 1925, 2007, 2047, 2120, 2205;
on ⑦ at 1047**k**, 1127**k**, 1157**k**, 1213**c**, 1229**k**, 1245**c**, 1300**k**, 1331, 1401, 1430, 1503, 1533, 1603, 1633, 1703, 1740, 1810, 1850, 1950.

Journey: 15 minutes.

119 BIRMINGHAM - READING - SOUTHAMPTON - BOURNEMOUTH

Most services convey 🍷 XC

km			⚒	⚒	⑥	Ⓐ	⑥	Ⓐ	⚒	⑥	Ⓐ	⚒	Ⓐ	⑥	⚒	Ⓐ	⑥	Ⓐ	⑥	⚒	⚒		⚒	⚒
									A											E				
	Manchester Piccadilly **122** .. d.	⚒	...	...	0511	0511	...	...	...	...	...	0727	...	...	0827	...	...	0927	0927	...	1027	...	...	1127
	Newcastle **124** ... d.		...	...	|	|	...	...	...	...	...	|	0625	0623	|	0725	0735	|	|	0835	|	...	0935	|
	York **124** ... d.		...	...	|	|	...	...	...	...	...	|	0727	0727	|	0826	0835	|	|	0935	|	...	1035	|
	Leeds **124** ... d.		...	...	|	|	...	...	...	0616	0616	|	|	|	|	|	|	|	|	|	|	...	|	|
	Sheffield **124** ... d.		...	...	|	|	...	0601	...	0718	0718	|	0821	0820	|	0924	0924	|	|	1024	|	...	1124	|
	Derby **124** ... d.		...	...	|	|	0648	0648	0706	0751	0750	|	0853	0853	|	0953	0953	|	|	1053	|	...	1153	|
0	**Birmingham** New St. **142 150** d.		0604	0633	0704	0704	0733	0733	0804	0833	0833	0904	0933	0933	1004	1033	1033	1104	1104	1133	1204	...	1233	1304
13	Birmingham Intl ✈ ... **142 150** d.		0614	|	0714	0714	|	|	0814	|	|	0914	|	|	1014	|	|	1114	1114	|	1214	...	|	1314
30	Coventry ... **142 150** d.		0625	|	0725	0725	|	|	0825	|	|	0925	|	|	1025	|	|	1125	1125	|	1225	...	|	1325
45	Leamington Spa ... **128** d.		0637	0700	0738	0738	0801	0800	0838	0900	0900	0938	1000	1000	1038	1100	1100	1138	1138	1200	1238	...	1300	1338
77	Banbury ... **128** d.		0654	0719	0755	0755	0819	0817	0855	0919	0920	0955	1019	1019	1055	1119	1119	1155	1155	1219	1255	...	1319	1355
114	Oxford ... a.		0714	0741	0814	0814	0839	0839	0914	0940	0941	1015	1040	1041	1114	1141	1141	1214	1214	1241	1314	...	1341	1414
114	Oxford ... **131** d.		0716	0743	0816	0816	0843	0843	0916	0943	0943	1016	1043	1043	1116	1143	1143	1216	1216	1243	1316	...	1343	1415
158	**Reading** ... **131** a.		0741	0809	0841	0840	0909	0908	0941	1008	1010	1041	1109	1110	1140	1208	1206	1242	1241	1309	1340	...	1409	1441
158	**Reading** ... d.		0746**a**	0820	0846	0846	...	...	0946**b**	1020	1020	1046**a**	...	...	1146	1220	1220	1250	1246	...	1346	...	1418	1446**b**
183	Basingstoke ... **108** a.		0808	0841	0908	0908	...	...	1008	1039	1039	1108	...	...	1208	1239	1240	1308	1308	...	1408	...	1440	1508
213	Winchester ... **108** a.		0824	0856	0924	0925	...	...	1024	1054	1054	1124	...	...	1224	1254	1255	1323	1324	...	1424	...	1455	1524
226	**Southampton** Airport ✈. **108** a.		0833	0908	0932	0933	...	...	1032	1108	1107	1133	...	...	1232	1308	1308	1332	1332	...	1434	...	1509	1532
234	**Southampton** Central ... **108** a.		0844	0917	0940	0943	...	...	1043	1117	1117	1143	...	...	1241	1317	1317	1341	1341	...	1441	...	1517	1541
255	Brockenhurst ... **108** a.		0859	...	0957	0958	...	...	1058	...	...	1158	...	...	1257	...	...	1356	1357	...	1457	...	...	1557
280	**Bournemouth** ... **108** a.		0914	...	1011	1013	...	...	1113	...	...	1213	...	...	1312	...	...	1411	1412	...	1512	...	...	1612

	⚒	⚒	⑥	Ⓐ	⚒	Ⓐ	⑥	⚒	⚒	⚒		⚒	⚒	⚒	⚒	⑥	Ⓐ	⚒	⑥	Ⓐ		Ⓐ	⑥	Ⓐ
									G															
Manchester Piccadilly **122** ... d.	...	1227	...	...	1327	...	...	1427	...	1527	...	...	1627	...	1727	...	...	1827	...	...	...	1927	1927	*2007*
Newcastle **124** ... d.	1035	|	1135	1135	|	1234	1235	|	1335	|	...	1435	|	1505	|	1635	1635	|	1732	1732	...	|	|	|
York **124** ... d.	1135	|	1235	1235	|	1335	1335	|	1435	|	...	1535	|	1605	|	1735	1735	|	1835	1835	...	|	|	|
Leeds **124** ... d.	|	|	|	|	|	|	|	|	|	|	...	|	|	1640	|	|	|	|	|	|	...	|	|	|
Sheffield **124** ... d.	1224	|	1324	1324	|	1424	1424	|	1524	|	...	1624	|	1724	|	1824	1824	|	1924	1924	...	|	|	|
Derby **124** ... d.	1253	|	1353	1353	|	1453	1453	|	1553	|	...	1653	|	1753	|	1853	1853	|	1954	1954	...	|	|	|
Birmingham New St. **142 150** d.	1333	1404	1433	1433	1504	1533	1533	1604	1633	1704	...	1733	1804	1833	1904	1933	1933	2004	2033	2033	...	2104	2104	2204
Birmingham Intl ✈ ... **142 150** d.	|	1414	|	|	1514	|	|	1614	|	1714	...	|	1814	|	1914	|	|	2014	|	|	...	2114	2114	2214
Coventry ... **142 150** d.	|	1425	|	|	1525	|	|	1625	|	1725	...	|	1825	|	1925	|	|	2025	|	|	...	2125	2125	2225
Leamington Spa ... **128** d.	1400	1438	1500	1500	1538	1601	1602	1638	1700	1738	...	1801	1838	1900	1938	2003	2002	2038	2100	2100	...	2138	2138	2238
Banbury ... **128** d.	1419	1455	1522	1519	1555	1619	1620	1655	1719	1755	...	1819	1855	1919	1955	2020	2022	2055	2120	2119	...	2155	2155	2255
Oxford ... a.	1440	1514	1541	1540	1614	1640	1640	1714	1740	1814	...	1841	1914	1941	2014	2040	2040	2115	2141	2140	...	2214	2214	2314
Oxford ... **131** d.	1443	1516	1543	1543	1616	1643	1643	1716	1743	1816	...	1843	1915	1943	2016	2043	2042	2116	2143	2143	...	2216	2218	2316
Reading ... **131** a.	1508	1541	1609	1611	1641	1708	1710	1740	1810	1843	...	1910	1941	2009	2041	2108	2107	2142	2214	2216	...	2242	2245	2349
Reading ... d.	...	1546**a**	1620	1620	1646	...	...	1750	...	1850	...	...	1946**c**	...	2046**c**	...	...	2150	2222	2222	...	2248	2250	...
Basingstoke ... **108** a.	...	1608	1640	1640	1708	...	...	1808	...	1908	...	...	2009	...	2109	...	...	2209	2239	2239	...	2305	2307	...
Winchester ... **108** a.	...	1624	1655	1658	1724	...	...	1824	...	1924	...	...	2024	...	2124	...	...	2226	2256	2256	...	2324	2324	...
Southampton Airport ✈.. **108** a.	...	1632	1708	1708	1732	...	...	1833	...	1932	...	...	2033	...	2133	...	...	2234	2312	2312	...	2336	2332	...
Southampton Central ... **108** a.	...	1641	1717	1716	1741	...	...	1843	...	1941	...	...	2041	...	2140	...	...	2242	2320	2320	...	2343	2341	...
Brockenhurst ... **108** a.	...	1657	...	...	1757	...	...	1858	...	1957	...	...	2058	...	2156	...	...	2258	...	...	...	...	...	...
Bournemouth ... **108** a.	...	1712	...	...	1815	...	...	1912	...	2012	...	...	2115	...	2215	...	...	2319	...	...	...	...	...	...

		⑦	⑦	⑦	⑦	⑦	⑦	⑦	⑦	⑦	⑦	⑦	⑦	⑦	⑦	⑦	⑦	⑦	⑦	⑦	⑦	⑦	⑦	⑦
																			E				G	
Manchester Piccadilly **122** ... d.	⑦	...	...	0827	0927	1027	...	1127	...	1226	...	1327	...	1427	...	1527	...	1627	...	1727	...	1827	...	1927
Newcastle **124** ... d.		...	...	|	|	|	...	|	...	|	...	|	...	|	1335	|	1436	|	1524	|	1635	|	1735	|
York **124** ... d.		...	...	|	|	|	...	|	...	|	...	|	...	|	1435	|	1535	|	1625	|	1735	|	1835	|
Leeds **124** ... d.		...	...	|	|	|	...	|	...	|	...	|	...	|	|	|	|	|	|	|	|	|	|	|
Sheffield **124** ... d.		...	...	|	|	|	...	|	...	|	...	|	1422	|	1524	|	1624	|	1724	|	1824	|	1924	|
Derby **124** ... d.		...	...	|	|	|	...	|	...	|	1355	|	1453	|	1553	|	1654	|	1754	|	1854	|	1956	|
Birmingham New St. **142 150** d.		...	0904	1004	1104	1204	1233	1304	1333	1404	1433	1504	1533	1604	1633	1704	1733	1804	1833	1904	1933	2004	2033	2104
Birmingham Intl ✈ ... **142 150** d.		...	0914	1014	1114	1214	1245	1314	|	1414	1445	1514	|	1614	1645	1714	|	1814	1845	1914	1945	2014	|	2114
Coventry ... **142 150** d.		...	0925	1025	1125	1225	1255	1325	|	1425	1455	1525	|	1625	1655	1725	|	1825	1855	1925	1955	2025	|	2124
Leamington Spa ... **128** d.		...	0938	1038	1138	1238	1308	1338	1359	1438	1509	1538	1559	1638	1709	1738	1759	1838	1909	1938	2009	2038	2100	2136
Banbury ... **128** d.		...	0955	1055	1155	1255	1325	1355	1416	1455	1527	1555	1616	1655	1726	1755	1817	1855	1926	1955	2026	2055	2119	2153
Oxford ... a.		...	1014	1114	1214	1314	1343	1414	1435	1514	1545	1614	1635	1714	1744	1814	1835	1914	1944	2014	2044	2114	2138	2211
Oxford ... **131** d.		...	1016	1116	1216	1316	1345	1416	1436	1516	1547	1616	1636	1716	1745	1816	1838	1916	1946	2016	2045	2116	2140	2212
Reading ... **131** a.		...	1042	1140	1240	1341	1410	1440	1502	1540	1611	1640	1701	1739	1810	1840	1905	1939	2008	2040	2113	2140	2206	2238
Reading ... d.		0952	1052	1152	1252	1352	...	1452	...	1552	...	1652	...	1752	...	1852	...	1952	...	2052	...	2152	...	...
Basingstoke ... **108** a.		1011	1109	1208	1308	1408	...	1508	...	1608	...	1708	...	1808	...	1909	...	2009	...	2108	...	2209	...	...
Winchester ... **108** a.		1026	1124	1224	1324	1424	...	1524	...	1624	...	1724	...	1824	...	1924	...	2024	...	2124	...	2223	...	...
Southampton Airport ✈.. **108** a.		1035	1133	1233	1333	1433	...	1533	...	1633	...	1733	...	1833	...	1933	...	2033	...	2133	...	2233	...	...
Southampton Central ... **108** a.		1042	1142	1242	1342	1443	...	1542	...	1642	...	1740	...	1842	...	1940	...	2041	...	2142	...	2242	...	...
Brockenhurst ... **108** a.		1106	1206	1306	1406	1506	...	1603	...	1706	...	1806	...	1903	...	2006	...	2106	...	2206	...	...	...	...
Bournemouth ... **108** a.		1126	1226	1326	1426	1526	...	1626	...	1726	...	1826	...	1926	....	2026	...	2126	...	2226	...	...	...	...

A – From Nottingham (Table **121**).
E – From Edinburgh Waverley (Table **124**).
G – To Guildford (Table **134**).

a – Departs 6 minutes later on Ⓐ.
b – Departs 6 minutes later on ⑥.
c – Departs 4 minutes later on Ⓐ.

119a WAREHAM - SWANAGE

SWR ⊠

Service shown is for 2017 - the 2018 service is due to begin late May / early June

km		a	a		a	a
0	**Wareham** ... **108** d.	1115	1315	...	1515	1715
9	Norden ... a.	1136	1336	...	1536	1736
10	Corfe Castle ... a.	1138	1338	...	1538	1738
18	**Swanage** ... a.	1200	1357	...	1600	1757

	a	a	a		a
Swanage ... d.	1023	1223	1423	...	1623
Corfe Castle ... d.	1040	1240	1440	...	1640
Norden ... d.	1046	1246	1443	...	1646
Wareham ... **108** a.	1110	1310	1510	...	1710

a – ②③④⑥⑦ June 13 - Sept. 3. Heritage diesel train.

⊠ – Operated by Swanage Railway. National rail tickets **not** valid. Passengers are strongly advised to reserve seats online. Additional steam trains run Norden - Corfe Castle - Swanage and v.v. www.swanagerailway.co.uk ✆ 01929 425800.

XC Most services convey 🍷 — BOURNEMOUTH - SOUTHAMPTON - READING - BIRMINGHAM — 119

		⑥	Ⓐ	ⒶG	⑥G	Ⓐ	⑥	Ⓐ	⑥	Ⓐ	⑥	Ⓐ	⑥	Ⓐ	⑥	⑥	Ⓐ	⚒	⚒	⚒	⚒	⚒	Ⓐ	⑥	⚒	Ⓐ
Bournemouth 108 d.		...	...	...	...	...	...	...	0625	0630	0637	...	...	0730	0747	...	...	0845	...	0945	...	1045	...	...	1145	...
Brockenhurst 108 d.		...	...	...	...	...	...	...	0639	0645	0655	...	...	0750	0802	...	...	0900	...	1000	...	1100	...	...	1200	...
Southampton Central 108 d.	⚒	0509	0515	...	...	0615	0620	...	0653	0715	0720	...	0747	0815	0820	...	...	0916	0946	1017	...	1117a	1146	1147	1217a	...
Southampton Airport ✈ 108 d.		0516	0522	...	...	0622	0627	...	0701	0722	0727	...	0754	0822	0827	...	...	0923	0954	1024	...	1124a	1153	1154	1224a	...
Winchester 108 d.		0525	0531	...	...	0631	0636	...	0709	0731	0736	0812	0803	0831	0836	...	...	0932	1003	1033	...	1133a	1202	1203	1233a	...
Basingstoke 108 d.		0541	0547	...	...	0647	0652	...	0725	0747	0752	0828	0819	0847	0852	...	...	0949a	1019	1049a	...	1149a	1218	1219	1249a	...
Reading a.		0600	0605	...	...	0704	0708	...	0742	0804	0808	0844	0835	0904	0908	...	...	1008	1037	1107	...	1208b	1237	1235	1308b	...
Reading 131 d.		0615	0615	0645	0645	0715	0715	0746	0747	0815	0815	0850	0845	0915	0914	0945	0945	1015	1045	1115	1145	1215	1245	1245	1315	1345
Oxford 131 a.		0637	0637	0706	0710	0736	0738	0810	0810	0837	0838	0913	0910	0937	0938	1010	1013	1038	1110	1138	1210	1238	1311	1310	1338	1411
Oxford d.		0639	0638	0708	0712	0739	0740	0812	0812	0839	0840	0915	0912	0939	0940	1012	1015	1039	1112	1139	1212	1239	1313	1312	1339	1413
Banbury 128 d.		0657	0657	0726	0729	0757	0757	0830	0829	0857	0857	0934	0929	0957	0957	1029	1032	1057	1129	1157	1229d	1257	1331	1329	1357	1431
Leamington Spa 128 d.		0714	0714	0743	0747	0814	0814	0847	0847	0914	0914	0951	0947	1014	1015	1047	1050	1114	1147	1214	1247d	1314	1348	1347	1414	1450
Coventry 142 150 d.		0727	0727	|	|	0827	0827	|	|	0927	0927	|	|	1027	1027	|	|	1127	|	1227	|	1327	|	|	1427	|
Birmingham Intl ✈ 142 150 d.		0738	0738	|	|	0838	0838	|	|	0938	0938	|	|	1038	1038	|	|	1138	|	1238	|	1338	|	|	1438	|
Birmingham New St. 142 150 a.		0748	0748	0812	0818	0848	0848	0918	0918	0948	0948	1018	1018	1048	1048	1118	1118	1148	1218	1248	1318	1348	1418	1418	1448	1518
Derby 124 a.		|	|	0905	0905	|	|	1005	1006	|	|	1105	1105	|	|	1205	1205	|	1305	|	1405	|	1505	1505	|	1605
Sheffield 124 a.		|	|	0944	0944	|	|	1044	1044	|	|	1144	1144	|	|	1244	1244	|	1344	|	1444	|	1544	1544	|	1644
Leeds 124 a.		|	|	|	|	|	|	|	|	|	|	|	|	|	|	|	|	|	|	|	|	|	|	|	|	|
York 124 a.		|	|	1039	1040	|	|	1139	1139	|	|	1240	1239	|	|	1339	1340	|	1440	|	1540	|	1639	1639	|	1740
Newcastle 124 a.		|	|	1145	1145	|	|	1245	1246	|	|	1345	1345	|	|	1446	1445	|	1544	|	1646	|	1745	1745	|	1847
Manchester Piccadilly 122 a.		0926	0939	...	...	1026	1026	...	...	1126	1126	...	...	1226	1226	...	...	1326	...	1426	...	1526	...	...	1626	...

	⑥	⚒	ⒶE	⑥	⚒	⚒	⚒	Ⓐ	⑥	⚒	Ⓐ	⑥	⚒	⑥	Ⓐ	Ⓐ		⑥	⑥	Ⓐ	Ⓐ	⑥	Ⓐ	⑥	Ⓐ	⑥
Bournemouth 108 d.	...	1245	...	...	1345	...	1445	...	...	1545	...	...	1645	...	...	1745	...	1747	...	...	1845	1847	...	...	1945	1947
Brockenhurst 108 d.	...	1300	...	...	1400	...	1500	...	...	1600	...	...	1700	...	...	1800	...	1802	...	...	1900	1902	...	...	2000	2002
Southampton Central 108 d.	...	1316	1346	1347	1417a	...	1516	1546	1547	1617a	...	...	1717a	1747	1746	1815	...	1820	...	...	1916	1920	...	...	2017	2019
Southampton Airport ✈ 108 d.	...	1323	1354	1354	1424a	...	1523	1553	1554	1624a	...	...	1724a	1754	1753	1822	...	1827	...	...	1923	1927	...	...	2024	2026
Winchester 108 d.	...	1332	1403	1403	1433a	...	1532	1602	1603	1633a	...	...	1733a	1803	1802	1831	...	1836	...	...	1932	1936	...	...	2033	2036
Basingstoke 108 d.	...	1349a	1419	1419	1449a	...	1548a	1618	1618	1649a	...	...	1749a	1818	1818	1847	...	1852	...	...	1949	1952	...	...	2049	2052
Reading a.	...	1408b	1436	1435	1507	...	1607b	1634	1635	1708	...	...	1807b	1835	1835	1904	...	1908	...	...	2005	2009	...	...	2106	2108
Reading 131 d.	1345	1415	1445	1445	1515	1545	1615	1645	1645	1715	1745	1745	1815	1845	1845	1915	...	1915	1945	1945	2015	2015	2045	2045	2111	2115
Oxford 131 a.	1410	1438	1509	1510	1538	1611	1638	1708	1710	1738	1808	1810	1838	1910	1911	1938	...	1938	2010	2009	2036	2038	2112	2110	2134	2138
Oxford d.	1412	1439	1513	1512	1539	1612	1639	1713	1712	1739	1810	1812	1839	1912	1913	1939	...	1940	2012	2013	2039	2040	2114	2112	2136	2139
Banbury 128 d.	1429	1457	1532	1529	1557	1629	1657	1733	1729	1757	1827	1829	1857	1929	1930	1957	...	1957	2030	2032	2057	2057	2133	2129	2154	2157
Leamington Spa 128 d.	1447	1514	1550	1547	1614	1647	1714	1751	1747	1814	1845	1847	1914	1947	1948	2014	...	2015	2048	2050	2114	2115	2153	2149	2212	2214
Coventry 142 150 d.	|	1527	|	|	1627	|	1727	|	|	1827	|	|	1927	|	|	2027	...	2027	|	|	2127	2127	|	2201	2225	2226
Birmingham Intl ✈ 142 150 d.	|	1538	|	|	1638	|	1738	|	|	1838	|	|	1938	|	|	2038	...	2038	|	|	2138	2138	|	2211	2235	2237
Birmingham New St. 142 150 a.	1518	1548	1618	1618	1648	1718	1748	1818	1818	1848	1918	1918	1948	2018	2018	2048	...	2048	2116	2123	2148	2148	2218	2221	2245	2247
Derby 124 a.	1606	|	1705	1705	|	1805	|	1905	1905	|	2005	2005	|	2124	2109	|	...	|	...	...	|	|	...	...	...	...
Sheffield 124 a.	1644	|	1742	1745	|	1844	|	1940	1947	|	2040	2049	|	2159	2152	|	...	|	...	...	|	|	...	...	...	...
Leeds 124 a.	|	|	1834	1828	|	|	|	|	|	|	|	|	|	|	|	|	...	|	...	...	|	|	...	...	...	...
York 124 a.	1740	|	1901	1901	|	1940	|	2038	2042	|	2141	2144	|	2246	2251	|	...	|	...	...	|	|	...	...	...	...
Newcastle 124 a.	1841	|	2001	2002	|	2042	|	2144	2147	|	2247	2247	|	...	...	|	...	|	...	...	|	|	...	...	...	...
Manchester Piccadilly 122 a.	...	1726	...	...	1826	...	1924	...	...	2026	...	...	2126	...	...	2227	...	2233	...	...	2326	2329	...	...	...	...

	⑥	Ⓐ		⑦	⑦	⑦	⑦	⑦G	⑦	⑦	⑦	⑦	⑦	⑦E	⑦	⑦	⑦	⑦	⑦	⑦	⑦	⑦	⑦	⑦	⑦	⑦
Bournemouth 108 d.	...	...	⑦	...	...	0940	1040	...	1140	...	1240	...	1340	...	1440	...	1540	...	1640	...	1740	...	1840	...	1940	...
Brockenhurst 108 d.	...	...		...	...	0957	1057	...	1157	...	1257	...	1357	...	1457	...	1557	...	1657	...	1757	...	1857	...	1957	...
Southampton Central 108 d.	...	...		...	0915	1015	1115	...	1215	...	1315	...	1415	...	1515	...	1615	...	1715	...	1815	...	1915	...	2015	...
Southampton Airport ✈ 108 d.	...	...		...	0922	1022	1122	...	1222	...	1322	...	1422	...	1522	...	1622	...	1722	...	1822	...	1922	...	2022	...
Winchester 108 d.	...	...		...	0931	1031	1131	...	1231	...	1331	...	1431	...	1531	...	1631	...	1731	...	1831	...	1931	...	2031	...
Basingstoke 108 d.	...	...		...	0947	1047	1147	...	1247	...	1347	...	1447	...	1547	...	1647	...	1747	...	1847	...	1947	...	2047	...
Reading a.	...	...		...	1004	1103	1203	...	1304	...	1403	...	1505	...	1603	...	1703	...	1803	...	1903	...	2003	...	2103	...
Reading 131 d.	2145	2145		0912	1011	1111	1211	1254	1311	1341	1411	1441	1511	1541	1611	1641	1711	1741	1811	1841	1911	1941	2011	2041	2111	2141
Oxford 131 a.	2210	2225		0935	1035	1135	1235	1315	1335	1404	1435	1504	1535	1604	1635	1704	1735	1804	1835	1903	1935	2003	2035	2104	2134	2202
Oxford d.	2212	2230		0937	1037	1137	1237	1317	1337	1406	1437	1506	1537	1606	1637	1706	1737	1806	1837	1906	1937	2006	2037	2106	2137	2206
Banbury 128 d.	2229	2248		0955	1055	1155	1255	1335	1355	1424	1455	1524	1555	1624	1655	1724	1755	1824	1855	1924	1955	2024	2055	2124	2155	2224
Leamington Spa 128 d.	2247	2305		1012	1112	1212	1312	1352	1412	1441	1512	1541	1612	1641	1712	1741	1812	1841	1912	1941	2012	2041	2112	2141	2212	2241
Coventry 142 150 d.	|	2317		1029	1129	1228	1327	|	1427	1454	1527	1554	1627	1654	1727	1754	1827	1854	1927	1954	2027	2054	2127	2153	2224	2254
Birmingham Intl ✈ 142 150 d.	|	2327		1040	1141	1240	1338	|	1438	1504	1538	1604	1638	1704	1738	1804	1838	1904	1938	2004	2038	2104	2138	2203	2234	2304
Birmingham New St. 142 150 a.	2317	2356		1050	1151	1250	1348	1419	1448	1514	1548	1614	1648	1714	1748	1814	1848	1914	1948	2014	2048	2115	2148	2214	2243	2314
Derby 124 a.	...	...		|	|	|	|	1501	|	1601	|	1702	|	1802	|	1903	|	2001	|	...	|	...	|	...	...	...
Sheffield 124 a.	...	...		|	|	|	|	1547	|	1648	|	1749	|	1845	|	1940	|	2041	|	...	|	...	|	...	...	...
Leeds 124 a.	...	...		|	|	|	|	|	|	|	|	1850	|	|	|	|	|	|	|	...	|	...	|	...	...	...
York 124 a.	...	...		|	|	|	|	1638	|	1740	|	1921	|	1940	|	2039	|	2143	|	...	|	...	|	...	...	...
Newcastle 124 a.	...	...		|	|	|	|	1744	|	1841	|	2019	|	2042	|	2145	|	2312	|	...	|	...	|	...	...	...
Manchester Piccadilly 122 a.	...	...		1240	1329	1429	1524	...	1629	...	1730	...	1829	...	1928	...	2028	...	2129	...	2226	...	2324	...	...	...

E – To Edinburgh Waverley (Table **124**).
G – From Guildford (Table **134**).

a – Departs 3–5 minutes later on ⑥.
b – Arrives 3 minutes earlier on Ⓐ.

d – Departs 3 minutes later on Ⓐ.

GW 2nd class — BRISTOL - TAUNTON — 120a

Service from Jan. 1 (for service until Dec. 31 please contact National Rail Enquiries ✆ +44 (0) 3457 48 49 50).

km			ⒶB	ⒶB	ⒶA	Ⓐ	Ⓐ	ⒶB	ⒶB	Ⓐ	Ⓐ	Ⓐ	ⒶB	Ⓐ	Ⓐ	Ⓐ	Ⓐ	ⒶF	Ⓐ	ⒶF	Ⓐ	Ⓐ	ⒶB	ⒶB	ⒶC		⑥B	⑥
	Cardiff Central 136 d.	Ⓐ	...	...	...	...	...	0800	0900	1000	1100	1200	1300	1400	1500	1600	1700	...	1800	...	1900	2000	...	...	...	⑥	...	...
0	**Bristol** T M 120 132 d.		0524	0643	0718	0748	0826	0855	0955	1054	1153	1253	1358	1453	1553	1654	1755	1820	1856	1917	1955	2055	2154	2306	2336		0524	0618
31	Weston-s-Mare 132 d.		0547	0706f	0749	0825	0901	0929f	1024	1122	1221	1323	1426	1528f	1627	1728	1830	1900	1930	2002	2029	2135j	2229	2342	0006s		0547	0646
43	Highbridge ‡ d.		0557	0717	0800	0836	0911	0940	1035	1133	1232	1334	1437	1538	1638	1739	1841	1911	1940	2013	2039	2145	2240	2354	0017s		0557	0657
53	Bridgwater d.		0605	0725	0808	0844	0919	0948	1043	1141	1240	1342	1445	1546	1646	1747	1849	1919	1948	2020	2047	2153	2248	0002	0024s		0605	0705
72	**Taunton** 120 132 a.		0618	0738	0823	0857	0932	1001	1059	1155	1253	1355	1458	1601	1659	1801	1903	1930	2002	2031	2101	2210	2300	0014	0035		0618	0718

	⑥B	⑥A	⑥	⑥	⑥	⑥	⑥	⑥	⑥	⑥	⑥	⑥	⑥	⑥	⑥F	⑥B	⑥C		⑦B	⑦B	⑦	⑦A	⑦	⑦	⑦	⑦B	⑦	⑦
Cardiff Central 136 d.	...	...	0800	0900	1000	1100	1200	1300	1400	1500	1600	1700	1800	1900	...	...	...	⑦	...	...	...	...	...	...	...	...	...	...
Bristol T M 120 132 d.	0645	0718	0858	0955	1055	1153	1253	1353	1453	1555	1654	1754	1853	1953	2054	2201	2216		0726	0828	1022	1110	1305	1555	1655	1830	1905	2025
Weston-s-Mare 132 d.	0708	0751	0932	1023	1124	1222	1323	1424	1528	1624	1725f	1822	1924	2023	2130	2234	2246s		0749	0858	1054	1142	1332	1629	1726	1901	1940	2059
Highbridge ‡ d.	|	0802	0943	1034	1135	1233	1334	1435	1538	1635	1736	1833	1935	2034	2140	2245	2257s		|	0909	1105	1153	1343	1639	1739	1911	1950	2109
Bridgwater d.	|	0810	0951	1042	1143	1241	1342	1443	1546	1643	1744	1841	1943	2042	2148	2253	2304s		0805	0917	1113	1201	1351	1647	1744	1919	1958	2117
Taunton 120 132 a.	0734	0823	1005	1057	1156	1255	1357	1457	1600	1657	1758	1856	1957	2057	2159	2306	2315		0818	0930	1126	1214	1404	1701	1759	1931	2011	2130

		Ⓐ	Ⓐ	ⒶB	ⒶD	ⒶF	Ⓐ	Ⓐ	Ⓐ	Ⓐ	ⒶB		Ⓐ	Ⓐ	Ⓐ	ⒶB	Ⓐ	Ⓐ	Ⓐ	Ⓐ	Ⓐ	ⒶA	ⒶF	Ⓐ		⑥	⑥B	⑥F
Taunton 120 132 d.	Ⓐ	0512	0602	0634	0657	0712	0735	0836	0916	*0935*	1011	...	1104	1204	1308	1411	1457	1607	1706	1808	1917	2035	2132	2245	⑥	0539	0634	0654
Bridgwater d.		0524	0614	0646	0707	0724	0747	0848	0932	*0947*	1023	...	1116	1218	1320	1423	1509	1619	1718	1820	1929	2047	2143	2257		0551	0646	0705
Highbridge ‡ d.		0532	0621	0654	0715	0732	0755	0856	0940	*0954*	1031	...	1124	1226	1328	1431	1516	1627	1726	1828	1936	2055	2151	2305		0559	0654	0713
Weston-s-Mare 132 d.		0546f	0636f	0708	0726	0743	0807	0911	0952	1010	1043	...	1138f	1241f	1341	1445	1543b	1639	1738	1840	1951f	2107	2202	2317		0611	0708	0726
Bristol T M 120 132 a.		0620	0708	0741	0758	0819	0842	0943	1021	1042	1111	...	1204	1309	1412	1514	1612	1713	1812	1913	2020	2139	2232	2351		0644	0742	0756
Cardiff Central 136 a.		0715	0821	...	...	...	...	...	1122	...	1213	...	1315	1413	1523	1614	1722	1811	1916	2014	...	...	...	...		...	...	...

	⑥	⑥C	⑥	⑥	⑥	⑥	⑥	⑥		⑥	⑥	⑥	⑥	⑥	⑥	⑥		⑦B	⑦B	⑦	⑦	⑦	⑦E	⑦	⑦B	⑦F	⑦	⑦
Taunton 120 132 d.	0735	0759	0912	1011	1104	1207	1307	1407	...	1507	1607	1706	1808	1907	2017	2135	⑦	0834	1008	1136	1334	1519	1658	1719	1819	1856	2024	2136
Bridgwater d.	0747	0809	0924	1023	1116	1219	1319	1419	...	1519	1619	1718	1820	1919	2029	2147		0846	1020	1148	1346	1531	1709	1730	1831	1906	2036	2148
Highbridge ‡ d.	0755	0817	0932	1031	1124	1227	1327	1427	...	1527	1627	1726	1828	1927	2037	2155		0854	1027	1155	1353	1538	1717	1737	1838	1914	2044	2155
Weston-s-Mare 132 d.	0807	0829	0944	1043	1140f	1239	1341	1439	...	1539	1639	1740	1840	1940	2050	2206		0907	1039	1210f	1406	1550	1729	1750	1849	1925	2059f	2207
Bristol T M 120 132 a.	0839	0856	1012	1111	1209	1309	1411	1509	...	1609	1711	1810	1909	2010	2124	2241		0937	1110	1244	1439	1620	1758	1819	1919	1950	2133	2240
Cardiff Central 136 a.	...	...	1117	1217	1318	1417	1517	1615	...	1717	1815	1917	2013	...	2232	...		...	...	...	...	...	...	...	...	...	...	...

A – To/from Gloucester (Table **138**).
B – To/from Penzance, Paignton, Plymouth or Exeter St Davids (see Table **115**).
C – [12] 🍷 London Paddington - Exeter St Davids and v.v. (Table **115**).
D – [12] 🍷 Plymouth - London Paddington (Table **115**).

E – [12] 🍷 Paignton - London Paddington (Table **115**).
F – To/from London Paddington (Table **132**).

b – Arrives 1527.
f – Arrives 4–6 minutes earlier.

j – Arrives 2127.
s – Calls to set down only.

‡ – Highbridge and Burnham.

Block 1 — ⒶⒶⒶⒶⒶⒶⒶⒶ★d ⒶⒶⒶⒶⒶⒶA ⒶⒶⒶⒶ★ ⒶB Ⓐ

Glasgow Central 124 ...d.	0601 0748 0900
Edinburgh Waverley 124 ...d.	0606 0707 0810 0908 1010 1106
Newcastle 124 ...d.	0645 0740 0841 0942 1042 1144 1241
York 124 ...d.	0743 0845 0944 1045 1145 1245 1345
Leeds 124 ...d.	0600 0705 0811 0911 1011 1111 1211 1311 1411
Sheffield 124 ...d.	0652 0753 0854 0954 1054 1155 1255 1355 1455
Derby 124 ...d.	0610 0727 0828 0928 1030 1130 1228 1328 1428 1528
Manchester P'dilly 122 ...d.	0600 0707 0807 0907 1007 1107 1207 1307 1407 1507
0 Birmingham New St 121 d.	0642 0712 0742 0812 0842 0917 0942 1017 1042 1117 1142 1217 1242 1317 1342 1417 1442 1517 1542 1612 1642
73 Cheltenham Spa 121 138 a.	0721 0751 0824 0850 0924 0958 1024 1059 1124 1157 1224 1259 1324 1358 1424 1524 1558 1624 1649 1724
135 Bristol Parkway 138 a.	0754 0826 0854 0925 0954 1030 1054 1131 1154 1229 1254 1331 1354 1428 1454 1529 1554 1630 1654 1725 1754
145 Bristol Temple Meads 138 a.	0805 0839 0910 0939 1008 1043 1110 1141 1205 1242 1309 1342 1408 1443 1510 1541 1611 1643 1710 1740 1807
145 Bristol Temple M 120a 115 d.	0634 0810 0844 0944 1045 1115 1144 1245 1345 1445 1513 1544 1645 1713 1744
217 Taunton 120a 115 a.	0707 0842 0914 1015 1117 1158 1214 1316 1416 1515 1544 1614 1716 1744 1815
240 Tiverton Parkway 115 a.	0719 0854 0926 1028 1129 1210 1226 1328 1428 1528 1556 1626 1728 1756 1827
266 Exeter St Davids 115 a.	0732 0907 0940 1042 1144 1224 1240 1343 1443 1543 1612 1640 1742 1811 1841
298 Newton Abbot 115 a.	0754 0927 0959 1104 1205 1248 1259 1403 1503 1603 1704 1811 1905
308 Torquay 115 a.	0939 1300 1847
311 Paignton 115 a.	0947 1308 1855
312 Totnes 115 a.	0807 1014 1117 1219 1311 1416 1516 1615 1716 1823 1917
350 Plymouth 115 a.	0833 1042 1144 1247 1338 1443 1543 1645 1742 1849 1943
Newquay 117 ...a.	
Penzance 117 ...a.	2054 2143

Block 2 — Ⓐ Ⓐb ⒶD ⒶⒶⒶⒶ Ⓐc Ⓐ   ⑥   ⑥⑥⑥⑥⑥⑥⑥⑥★d ⑥⑥⑥⑥⑥⑥

Glasgow Central 124 ...d.	1100 1300 1500 • 0601
Edinburgh Waverley 124 ...d.	1208 1307 1408 1508 1606 1707 • 0606 0707
Newcastle 124 ...d.	1343 1442 1541 1641 1741 1843 • 0645 0741 0843
York 124 ...d.	1445 1545 1645 1745 1845 1945 • 0620 0745 0845 0945
Leeds 124 ...d.	1511 1611 1711 1811 1911 2011 • 0600 0711 0811 0911 1011
Sheffield 124 ...d.	1555 1655 1758 1858 1958 2058 • 0650 0756 0854 0954 1055
Derby 124 ...d.	1628 1729 1829 1930 2029 2129 • 0610 0726 0828 0931 1029 1130
Manchester P'dilly 122 ...d.	1607 1705 1805 1907 • 0600 0707 0807 0907 1007
Birmingham New St 121 d.	1712 1742 1812 1842 1912 1942 2012 2042 2112 2212 • 0642 0712 0742 0812 0842 0912 0942 1012 1042 1112 1142 1212
Cheltenham Spa 121 138 a.	1751 1824 1850 1924 1950 2024 2125 2151 2250 • 0724 0750 0824 0851 0924 0951 1024 1051 1124 1153 1224 1251
Bristol Parkway 138 a.	1828 1854 1932 1954 2030 2054 2125 2201 2233 2320 • 0753 0824 0853 0924 0953 1029 1054 1125 1153 1229 1253 1324
Bristol Temple Meads 138 a.	1841 1906 1942 2009 2042 2105 2136 2214 2243 2339 • 0805 0824 0906 0939 1004 1042 1109 1139 1204 1242 1309 1338
Bristol Temple M 120a 115 d.	1844 1945 2049 2113 2144 • 0608 0812 0845 0944 1044 1112 1144 1244 1345
Taunton 120a 115 a.	1915 2016 2119 2143 2215 • 0715 0842 0915 1016 1115 1159 1215 1316 1415
Tiverton Parkway 115 a.	1927 2029 2131 2155 2227 • 0727 0854 0927 1029 1127 1211 1227 1329 1427
Exeter St Davids 115 a.	1942 2043 2145 2209 2241 • 0740 0907 0940 1043 1141 1225 1241 1343 1441
Newton Abbot 115 a.	2002 2103 2205 2228 2301 • 0759 0928 1000 1109 1201 1250 1300 1403 1502
Torquay 115 a.	• 0939 1302
Paignton 115 a.	• 0947 1310
Totnes 115 a.	2014 2116 2217 2240 2318 • 0812 1012 1122 1213 1312 1417 1514
Plymouth 115 a.	2040 2146 2245 2307 2344 • 0838 1039 1151 1240 1339 1445 1541
Newquay 117 ...a.	
Penzance 117 ...a.	2241

Block 3 — ⑥A ⑥⑥⑥ ⑥★ ⑥ ⑥B ⑥⑥ ⑥D ⑥⑥ ⑥c   ⑦   ⑦⑦⑦

Glasgow Central 124 ...d.	0748 0900 1100 1300 1500
Edinburgh Waverley 124 ...d.	0806 0908 1005 1108 1206 1309 1405 1508 1605
Newcastle 124 ...d.	0942 1044 1142 1244 1344 1444 1544 1644 1744
York 124 ...d.	1045 1145 1245 1345 1445 1545 1645 1745 1845
Leeds 124 ...d.	1111 1211 1311 1411 1511 1611 1711 1811 1911
Sheffield 124 ...d.	1155 1255 1355 1455 1555 1655 1755 1858 1955
Derby 124 ...d.	1230 1328 1430 1528 1628 1728 1829 1929 2028
Manchester P'dilly 122 ...d.	1107 1207 1307 1407 1507 1607 1706 1805 1907
Birmingham New St 121 d.	1242 1312 1342 1412 1442 1512 1542 1612 1642 1712 1742 1812 1842 1912 1942 2012 2042 2112 • 0930
Cheltenham Spa 121 138 a.	1325 1350 1424 1451 1524 1550 1624 1650 1724 1750 1824 1850 1924 1950 2024 2051 2124 2150 • 1008
Bristol Parkway 138 a.	1354 1426 1454 1524 1554 1629 1653 1725 1753 1853 1925 1954 2029 2053 2122 2158 2231 • 1037
Bristol Temple Meads 138 a.	1405 1441 1509 1538 1607 1643 1707 1739 1804 1843 1905 1939 2005 2042 2104 2133 2212 2241 • 1048
Bristol Temple M 120a 115 d.	1444 1512 1544 1645 1710 1744 1844 1944 2044 2111 2145 • 0844 0948 1057
Taunton 120a 115 a.	1516 1542 1614 1717 1740 1815 1915 2015 2115 2141 2215 • 0915 1019 1129
Tiverton Parkway 115 a.	1528 1554 1626 1730 1752 1827 1927 2027 2127 2153 2229 • 0927 1031 1141
Exeter St Davids 115 a.	1543 1609 1640 1744 1805 1841 1944 2040 2143 2207 2244 • 0939 1044 1154
Newton Abbot 115 a.	1603 1700 1810 1830 1904 2005 2100 2204 2226 2311 • 0959 1103 1214
Torquay 115 a.	1841
Paignton 115 a.	1849
Totnes 115 a.	1616 1712 1823 1916 2017 2112 2220 2238 2327 • 1012 1116 1226
Plymouth 115 a.	1643 1739 1851 1942 2043 2138 2250 2305 2356 • 1037 1142 1252
Newquay 117 ...a.	2056e
Penzance 117 ...a.	2140 2254 • 1447

Block 4 — ⑦⑦⑦⑦⑦⑦★⑦⑦⑦⑦⑦⑦⑦⑦⑦★a ⑦B ⑦⑦ ⑦c ⑦

Glasgow Central 124 ...d.	1055 1202 1348 1455 1708
Edinburgh Waverley 124 ...d.	0908 1008 1104 1208 1308 1408 1508 1608 1708
Newcastle 124 ...d.	0935 1039 1140 1240 1340 1441 1540 1640 1740 1840 1941
York 124 ...d.	0933 1033 1141 1241 1341 1441 1541 1641 1741 1841 1941 2011
Leeds 124 ...d.	0810 0900 1000 1100 1211 1311 1411 1511 1611 1711 1811 1911 2011
Sheffield 124 ...d.	0854 0957 1057 1157 1257 1357 1455 1555 1655 1755 1855 1955 2054
Derby 124 ...d.	0928 1033 1129 1229 1332 1429 1526 1627 1727 1826 1927 2027 2126
Manchester P'dilly 122 ...d.	1307 1407 1507 1607 1707 1807 1907 2007
Birmingham New St 121 d.	1030 1130 1212 1312 1342 1412 1442 1512 1542 1612 1642 1712 1742 1812 1842 1912 1942 2012 2042 2112 2142 2212
Cheltenham Spa 121 138 a.	1109 1209 1251 1351 1423 1450 1524 1550 1624 1650 1724 1751 1824 1851 1924 1951 2024 2051 2124 2151 2223 2252
Bristol Parkway 138 a.	1139 1239 1320 1420 1453 1523 1559 1620 1654 1720 1803 1820 1854 1921 2003 2020 2056 2120 2159 2233 2252 2322
Bristol Temple Meads 138 a.	1151 1250 1331 1431 1508 1534 1611 1631 1708 1731 1814 1835 1908 1932 2014 2031 2106 2130 2210 2244 2302 2333
Bristol Temple M 120a 115 d.	1154 1254 1344 1444 1544 1614 1644 1744 1844 1944 2019 2044 2144
Taunton 120a 115 a.	1225 1325 1414 1514 1614 1644 1714 1817 1916 2017 2058 2114 2214
Tiverton Parkway 115 a.	1235 1336 1426 1526 1626 1656 1726 1829 1928 2029 2111 2126 2227
Exeter St Davids 115 a.	1252 1352 1439 1539 1640 1709 1739 1845 1945 2043 2127 2139 2245
Newton Abbot 115 a.	1312 1412 1459 1600 1701 1730 1800 1905 2007 2101 2153 2200 2305
Torquay 115 a.	1748
Paignton 115 a.	1756
Totnes 115 a.	1325 1425 1511 1612 1714 1812 1917 2019 2113 2218 2318
Plymouth 115 a.	1352 1452 1537 1638 1742 1838 1943 2045 2141 2237 2246 2346
Newquay 117 ...a.	
Penzance 117 ...a.	2039 2242

A – From Dundee (Table 222).
B – From Aberdeen (Table 222).
D – To Cardiff Central (Table 121).

a – Also calls at Weston-super-Mare (a. 2036).
b – Also calls at Gloucester (a. 1901).
c – Also calls at Gloucester (a. 2202 on Ⓐ and ⑦, 2200 on ⑥).
d – Also calls at Weston-super-Mare (a. 1132 on Ⓐ, 1129 on ⑥).
e – Arrives 2052 from Jan. 6.
★ – Also calls at Dawlish (10–15 minutes after Exeter) and Teignmouth (15–18 minutes after Exeter).

Ⓐ	Ⓐ E	Ⓐ	Ⓐ	Ⓐ D	Ⓐ	Ⓐ ☆e	Ⓐ	Ⓐ	Ⓐ	Ⓐ	Ⓐ B	Ⓐ ☆		Ⓐ	Ⓐ	Ⓐ A	Ⓐ	Ⓐ	Ⓐ	Ⓐ	Ⓐ ☆a
Penzance 117 d.	...	...	...	...	...	...	...	...	0628	...	...	...	...	0828	...	...	0935	...	...	...	...
Newquay 117 d.	...	...	...	...	...	...	...	...	|	...	...	...	...	|	...	...	|	...	...	...	...
Plymouth 115 d.	...	...	0520	...	0625	...	0725	...	0825	...	0925	...	...	1025	...	1125	1150	1225	...	1325	...
Totnes 115 d.	...	...	0545	...	0650	...	0750	...	0850	...	0950	...	...	1050	...	1150	1215	1251	...	1351	...
Paignton 115 d.	...	...	|	...	|	0702	|	...	|	...	|	1007	...	|	...	|	|	|	...	|	1404
Torquay 115 d.	...	...	|	...	|	0708	|	...	|	...	|	1013	...	|	...	|	|	|	...	|	1410
Newton Abbot 115 d.	...	...	0602	...	0703	0719	0803	...	0903	...	1003	1024	...	1103	...	1203	1228	1304	...	1404	1421
Exeter St Davids 115 d.	...	...	0624	...	0724	0745	0824	...	0924	...	1024	1050	...	1124	...	1224	1250	1324	...	1424	1448
Tiverton Parkway 115 d.	...	...	0637	...	0737	0758	0837	...	0938	...	1037	1103	...	1137	...	1238	1306	1338	...	1438	1502
Taunton 120a 115 d.	...	...	0651	...	0751	0812	0851	...	0951	...	1051	1117	...	1151	...	1251	1322	1351	...	1451	1515
Bristol Temple Meads 120a 115 a.	0620	...	0726	...	0827	0855	0926	...	1025	...	1124	1152	...	1224	...	1324	1355	1426	...	1523	1556
Bristol Temple Meads 138 d.	0627	0700	0730	0800	0830	0900	0930	1000	1030	1100	1130	1200	...	1230	1300	1330	1400	1430	1500	1530	1600
Bristol Parkway 138 d.	0639	0710	0740	0810	0840	0910	0940	1010	1040	1110	1140	1210	...	1240	1310	1340	1410	1440	1510	1540	1610
Cheltenham Spa 121 138 d.	0710	0741	0811	0841	0912	0942	1011	1041	1111	1142	1211	1241	...	1311	1341	1411	1441	1511	1542	1611	1641
Birmingham New Street 121 a.	0756	0826	0856	0926	0958	1023	1056	1126	1158	1226	1256	1326	...	1356	1423	1456	1523	1556	1623	1656	1723
Manchester P'dilly 122 a.	|	0959	|	1059	|	1159	|	1259	|	1359	|	1459	...	|	1559	|	1659	|	1800	|	1859
Derby 124 a.	0841	...	0939	...	1038	...	1138	...	1241	...	1339	...	...	1440	...	1540	...	1641	...	1739	...
Sheffield 124 a.	0917	...	1017	...	1118	...	1217	...	1317	...	1418	...	...	1517	...	1618	...	1718	...	1818	...
Leeds 124 a.	1000	...	1100	...	1201	...	1300	...	1400	...	1500	...	...	1600	...	1700	...	1802	...	1903	...
York 124 a.	1030	...	1130	...	1230	...	1330	...	1430	...	1530	...	...	1630	...	1730	...	1831	...	1930	...
Newcastle 124 a.	1129	...	1228	...	1329	...	1430	...	1529	...	1629	...	...	1729	...	1833	...	1933	...	2034	...
Edinburgh Waverley 124 a.	1305	...	1409	...	1508	...	1606	...	1705	...	1807	...	...	1905	...	2008	...	2108	...	2213	...
Glasgow Central 124 a.	1415	...	...	...	1615	...	...	...	1811	...	...	...	...	2015	...	...	...	2224	...	...	...

Ⓐ / ⑥	Ⓐ	Ⓐ	Ⓐ	Ⓐ	Ⓐ	Ⓐ	Ⓐ	Ⓐ b	Ⓐ	Ⓐ	⑥ c	⑥	⑥	⑥ D	⑥		⑥ ☆	⑥	⑥	⑥	⑥
Penzance 117 d.	...	...	...	...	...	...	...	...	...	...	...	...	...	...	...	...	...	...	...	0630	...
Newquay 117 d.	...	...	...	...	...	...	...	...	...	...	...	...	...	...	...	...	...	...	...	|	...
Plymouth 115 d.	1425	...	1525	...	1625	...	1725	...	1825	...	...	...	0525	...	0625	...	...	0725	...	0825	...
Totnes 115 d.	1450	...	1551	...	1651	...	1750	...	1850	...	...	...	0550	...	0650	...	...	0750	...	0850	...
Paignton 115 d.	|	...	|	...	|	...	|	...	|	2014	...	...	|	...	|	...	0702	|	...	|	...
Torquay 115 d.	|	...	|	...	|	...	|	...	|	2020	...	...	|	...	|	...	0708	|	...	|	...
Newton Abbot 115 d.	1503	...	1604	...	1704	...	1803	...	1903	2031	...	...	0603	...	0703	...	0719	0803	...	0903	...
Exeter St Davids 115 d.	1524	...	1624	1654	1725	...	1825	...	1924	2052	...	...	0623	...	0723	...	0745	0823	...	0923	...
Tiverton Parkway 115 d.	1537	...	1638	1708	1739	...	1838	...	1937	2105	...	...	0637	...	0737	...	0758	0837	...	0937	...
Taunton 120a 115 d.	1551	...	1651	1722	1751	...	1851	...	1951	2119	...	...	0650	...	0750	...	0811	0850	...	0950	...
Bristol Temple Meads 120a 115 a.	1623	...	1724	1754	1823	...	1923	...	2025	2152	...	...	0722	...	0824	...	0849	0925	...	1025	...
Bristol Temple Meads 138 d.	1630	1700	1730	1800	1830	1900	1930	2000	2030	2200	0615	0700	0730	0800	0830	...	0900	0930	1000	1030	1100
Bristol Parkway 138 d.	1640	1710	1740	1810	1840	1910	1940	2010	2040	2210	0625	0710	0740	0810	0840	...	0910	0940	1010	1040	1110
Cheltenham Spa 121 138 d.	1711	1742	1811	1841	1911	1941	2011	2056	2117	2242	0711	0741	0811	0841	0911	...	0941	1011	1041	1111	1141
Birmingham New Street 121 a.	1756	1823	1856	1923	1956	2022	2051	2137	2202	2343	0756	0825	0856	0926	0956	...	1025	1056	1126	1156	1226
Manchester P'dilly 122 a.	|	1959	|	2058	|	2200	|	...	...	...	|	0959	|	1059	|	...	1159	|	1259	|	1359
Derby 124 a.	1839	...	1940	...	2040	...	2141	...	...	...	0841	...	0939	...	1038	...	...	1138	...	1238	...
Sheffield 124 a.	1918	...	2018	...	2118	...	2224	...	...	...	0917	...	1017	...	1117	...	...	1217	...	1317	...
Leeds 124 a.	2005	...	2101	...	2203	...	2315	...	...	...	1000	...	1100	...	1200	...	...	1300	...	1400	...
York 124 a.	2030	...	...	...	...	...	...	...	...	...	1030	...	1130	...	1230	...	...	1330	...	1430	...
Newcastle 124 a.	2128	...	...	...	...	...	...	...	...	...	1129	...	1228	...	1329	...	...	1429	...	1529	...
Edinburgh Waverley 124 a.	2302	...	...	...	...	...	...	...	...	...	1301	...	1405	...	1503	...	...	1602	...	1703	...
Glasgow Central 124 a.	...	...	...	...	...	...	...	...	...	...	1415	...	...	...	1615	...	...	...	...	1811	...

⑥ / ⑦	⑥ B	⑥ ☆	⑥	⑥	⑥ A	⑥	⑥		⑥	⑥	⑥ ☆a	⑥	⑥	⑥	⑥	⑥	⑥	⑥	⑥	⑥	⑦ c
Penzance 117 d.	...	...	0828	...	...	0943	...	...	...	...	...	...	...	...	...	...	...	...	...	...	...
Newquay 117 d.	...	...	|	...	...	|	...	...	...	...	...	...	...	...	...	...	...	...	...	...	...
Plymouth 115 d.	0925	...	1025	...	1125	1148	1225	...	...	1325	...	1425	...	1525	...	1625	...	1725	...	1825	...
Totnes 115 d.	0950	...	1050	...	1150	1213	1251	...	...	1350	...	1450	...	1551	...	1650	...	1751	...	1850	...
Paignton 115 d.	|	1006	|	...	|	|	|	...	...	|	1355	|	...	|	...	|	...	|	...	|	...
Torquay 115 d.	|	1012	|	...	|	|	|	...	...	|	1401	|	...	|	...	|	...	|	...	|	...
Newton Abbot 115 d.	1003	1023	1103	...	1203	1225	1303	...	...	1403	1412	1503	...	1604	...	1703	...	1804	...	1903	...
Exeter St Davids 115 d.	1023	1049	1123	...	1223	1248	1323	...	...	1424	1437	1523	...	1624	1653	1723	...	1824	...	1923	...
Tiverton Parkway 115 d.	1037	1102	1136	...	1236	1302	1337	...	...	1437	1450	1537	...	1638	1707	1737	...	1838	...	1937	...
Taunton 120a 115 d.	1050	1117	1150	...	1250	1315	1350	...	...	1451	1503	1550	...	1651	1721	1750	...	1851	...	1950	...
Bristol Temple Meads 120a 115 a.	1124	1154	1225	...	1325	1355	1425	...	...	1525	1549	1625	...	1725	1755	1825	...	1924	...	2022	...
Bristol Temple Meads 138 d.	1130	1200	1230	1300	1330	1400	1430	...	1500	1530	1600	1630	1700	1730	1800	1830	1900	1930	2000	2030	0915
Bristol Parkway 138 d.	1140	1210	1240	1310	1340	1410	1440	...	1510	1540	1610	1640	1710	1740	1810	1840	1910	1940	2010	2040	0925
Cheltenham Spa 121 138 d.	1211	1241	1311	1341	1411	1441	1511	...	1541	1611	1641	1712	1741	1813	1841	1911	1941	2013	2041	2111	1012
Birmingham New Street 121 a.	1256	1326	1356	1426	1456	1526	1556	...	1626	1656	1726	1756	1826	1856	1926	1956	2026	2051	2138	2152	1049
Manchester P'dilly 122 a.	|	1459	|	1559	|	1659	|	...	1759	|	1859	|	1959	|	2059	|	2202	|	...	...	|
Derby 124 a.	1338	...	1438	...	1540	...	1640	...	...	1738	...	1840	...	1939	...	2040	...	2143	...	...	1137
Sheffield 124 a.	1418	...	1517	...	1618	...	1717	...	...	1817	...	1917	...	2021	...	2119	...	2223	...	...	1218
Leeds 124 a.	1500	...	1600	...	1700	...	1801	...	...	1901	...	2004	...	2104	...	2201	...	2325	...	...	1259
York 124 a.	1530	...	1630	...	1729	...	1830	...	...	1930	...	2030	...	2159	...	...	...	...	...	...	1327
Newcastle 124 a.	1629	...	1729	...	1830	...	1932	...	...	2035	...	2128	...	...	...	...	...	...	...	...	1427
Edinburgh Waverley 124 a.	1803	...	1905	...	2005	...	2107	...	...	2209	...	2257	...	...	...	...	...	...	...	...	1602
Glasgow Central 124 a.	...	...	2015	...	...	...	2220	...	...	...	...	...	...	...	...	...	...	...	...	...	...

⑦	⑦	⑦ B	⑦	⑦ ☆a	⑦	⑦		⑦	⑦	⑦	⑦	⑦	⑦ d		⑦	⑦	⑦	⑦	⑦	⑦	⑦	⑦
Penzance 117 d.	...	...	...	...	0930	...	...	...	...	...	...	...	1230	...	...	...	...	...	1530	...	...	...
Newquay 117 d.	...	...	...	...	|	...	...	...	...	...	...	...	|	...	...	...	...	...	|	...	...	...
Plymouth 115 d.	...	0925	1025	...	1125	1200	...	1225	1252	1325	...	1425	1435	...	1524	...	1625	...	1725	...	1825	...
Totnes 115 d.	...	0950	1050	...	1150	|	...	1250	|	1351	...	1451	1501	...	1550	...	1650	...	1750	...	1852	...
Paignton 115 d.	...	|	|	1050	|	|	...	|	|	|	...	|	|	...	|	...	|	...	|	1820	|	...
Torquay 115 d.	...	|	|	1056	|	|	...	|	|	|	...	|	|	...	|	...	|	...	|	1826	|	...
Newton Abbot 115 d.	...	1003	1103	1108	1203	1236	...	1303	1327	1404	...	1504	1513	...	1603	...	1703	...	1803	1837	1905	...
Exeter St Davids 115 d.	...	1023	1123	1133	1223	1256	...	1323	1347	1424	...	1524	1532	...	1624	...	1726	...	1823	1858	1925	...
Tiverton Parkway 115 d.	...	1037	1137	1147	1237	1310	...	1337	|	1438	...	1537	1546	...	1637	...	1739	...	1837	1911	1938	...
Taunton 120a 115 d.	...	1050	1152	1200	1250	1323	...	1350	|	1451	...	1551	1559	...	1651	...	1753	...	1850	1924	1952	...
Bristol Temple Meads 120a 115 a.	...	1124	1224	1244	1323	1354	...	1421	1440	1526	...	1625	1647	...	1726	...	1827	...	1922	1957	2025	...
Bristol Temple Meads 138 d.	1030	1130	1230	1300	1330	1400	...	1430	1500	1530	1600	1630	1700	...	1730	1800	1830	1900	1930	2000	2030	2210
Bristol Parkway 138 d.	1040	1140	1240	1310	1340	1410	...	1440	1510	1540	1610	1640	1710	...	1740	1810	1840	1910	1940	2009	2040	2220
Cheltenham Spa 121 138 d.	1111	1211	1311	1341	1411	1441	...	1511	1540	1611	1641	1712	1741	...	1811	1841	1911	1941	2011	2040	2111	2249
Birmingham New Street 121 a.	1148	1249	1348	1427	1448	1527	...	1548	1627	1649	1726	1749	1827	...	1848	1926	1948	2027	2049	2118	2148	2340
Manchester P'dilly 122 a.	|	|	|	1559	|	1659	...	|	1759	|	1859	|	1959	...	|	2100	|	2200	|	...	|	...
Derby 124 a.	1238	1337	1439	...	1537	...	...	1638	...	1740	...	1839	...	...	1940	...	2039	...	2141	...	2240	...
Sheffield 124 a.	1318	1417	1517	...	1618	...	...	1717	...	1819	...	1920	...	...	2018	...	2116	...	2218	...	2318	...
Leeds 124 a.	1401	1459	1602	...	1659	...	...	1802	...	1903	...	2004	...	...	2107	...	2202	...	2259	...	0008	...
York 124 a.	1427	1527	1627	...	1727	...	...	1827	...	1930	...	2030	...	...	2131	...	...	...	...	...	...	...
Newcastle 124 a.	1526	1625	1725	...	1825	...	...	1925	...	2031	...	2131	...	...	...	...	...	...	...	...	...	...
Edinburgh Waverley 124 a.	1655	1758	1856	...	1957	...	...	2100	...	2210	...	2303	...	...	...	...	...	...	...	...	...	...
Glasgow Central 124 a.	1813	...	2019	...	...	...	...	2212	...	...	...	...	...	...	...	...	...	...	...	...	...	...

A – To Dundee (Table **222**).
B – To Aberdeen (Table **222**).
D – From Cardiff Central (Table **121**).
E – From Bath Spa (d. 0609).

a – Also calls at Weston-super-Mare (d. 1538 on Ⓐ, 1529 on ⑥, 1221 on ⑦).
b – Also calls at Gloucester (d. 2046).
c – Also calls at Gloucester (d. 0700 on ⑥, 1000 on ⑦).
d – Also calls at Weston-super-Mare (d. 1629).

e – Also calls at Weston-super-Mare (d. 0835).
k – Also calls at Weston-super-Mare (d. 1033).

☆ – Also calls at Teignmouth (7 – 10 minutes after Newton Abbot) and Dawlish (12 – 15 minutes after Newton Abbot).

121 BIRMINGHAM - CARDIFF

AW, XC

km			Ⓐ 2	Ⓐ	Ⓐ	Ⓐ 2	Ⓐ 🍷	Ⓐ 2	Ⓐ		Ⓐ 🍷	Ⓐ 2	Ⓐ 🍷	Ⓐ 2	Ⓐ 🍷	Ⓐ 🍷	Ⓐ 2	Ⓐ 🍷	Ⓐ 2 B	Ⓐ 🍷	Ⓐ 🍷	Ⓐ 2
	Nottingham **123** d.	Ⓐ	...	...	...	...	0600	...	0704	...	0812	...	0910	...	1010	1110	...	1210	...	1310	1410	...
	Derby **123** d.		...	...	...	...	0636	...	0736	...	0837	...	0936	...	1037	1137	...	1237	...	1337	1436	...
0	**Birmingham** New Street **120** d.		...	0500	0537	...	0730	...	0830	...	0930	...	1030	...	1130	1230	...	1330	...	1430	1530	...
73	Cheltenham **120 138** d.		0537	0602	0643	0746	0811	0846	0910	...	1010	1045	1110	1146	1210	1310	1345	1410	...	1510	1610	1645
83	**Gloucester** **138** d.		0550	0614	0701**d**	0758	0825**c**	0858	0925**c**	...	1025**c**	1058	1125**c**	1158	1225**c**	1325**c**	1358	1425	1448	1525**c**	1625**c**	1658
115	Lydney 🚂 d.		0609	0633	0720	0817	|	0917	|	...	1044	1117	|	1218	|	1344	1417	|	1507	|	1644	1717
127	Chepstow d.		0619	0642	0729	0827	0851	0927	0951	...	|	1127	1151	1227	1251	|	1427	1451	1517	1551	1653	1727
138	Caldicot d.		0626	0651	0738	0835	|	0935	|	...	|	1135	|	1236	|	|	1435	|	1525	|	|	1735
155	Newport **132 136 149** a.		0641	0705	0752	0850	0912	0951	1011	...	1111	1150	1210	1251	1309	1410	1450	1510	1540	1612	1711	1750
174	**Cardiff** Central **132 136 149** a.		0700	0721	0808	0907	0927	1011	1028	...	1128	1213	1226	1312	1325	1426	1515	1530	1558	1630	1730	1810

	Ⓐ 🍷	Ⓐ 2	Ⓐ	Ⓐ 2	Ⓐ	Ⓐ 🍷 A	Ⓐ 2	Ⓐ	Ⓐ	Ⓐ	⑤ 2	①–④ 2		⑥ 2	⑥	⑥	⑥ 2	⑥ 🍷		⑥ 2	⑥	⑥ 🍷
Nottingham **123** d.	1510	...	1610	...	1710	...	...	1810	1910	*2040*	...	...	⑥	...	...	...	...	0558	...	...	0658	0809
Derby **123** d.	1537	...	1637	...	1737	...	...	1837	1937	2129	...	...		...	...	...	...	0636	...	...	0736	0837
Birmingham New Street **120** d.	1630	...	1730	...	1830	1842	...	1930	2030	2212	...	...		...	0500	0542	...	0730	...	...	0830	0930
Cheltenham **120 138** d.	1714	1745	1817	1845	1913	1925	1945	2011	2110	2251	2300	2300		...	0603	0642	0745	0810	...	0845	0910	1010
Gloucester **138** d.	1725	1758	1831	1900	1925	|	1958	2025**c**	2121	...	2313	2313		0550	0614	0657**c**	0758	0822	...	0858	0922	1022
Lydney 🚂 d.	1744	1817	|	1920	|	|	2017	|	2140	...	2333	2333		0609	0633	0716	0817	|	...	0917	|	1041
Chepstow d.	|	1827	|	1929	|	|	2027	|	2149	...	2342	2342		0619	0642	0726	0827	0848	...	0927	0948	|
Caldicot d.	|	1835	|	1937	|	|	2035	|	2158	...	2351	2351		0627	0651	0734	0835	|	...	0935	|	|
Newport **132 136 149** a.	1811	1849	1914	1953	2011	2047	2050	2110	2212	...	0006	0006		0642	0705	0748	0850	0906	...	0950	1005	1106
Cardiff Central **132 136 149** a.	1828	1909	1933	2012	2028	2103	2110	2128	2235**a**	...	0026	0034		0703	0721	0804	0910	0923	...	1009	1021	1124

	⑥ 2	⑥ 🍷	⑥ 2	⑥ 🍷	⑥ 🍷		⑥ 2	⑥ 🍷	⑥ B	⑥ 🍷		⑥ 🍷	⑥ 2	⑥ 🍷	⑥ 2	⑥	⑥ 2	⑥	⑥ 🍷 A	⑥ 2	⑥	⑥
Nottingham **123** d.	...	0910	...	1010	1110	...	...	1210	...	1310	...	1410	...	1510	...	1610	...	1710	...	...	1810	1910
Derby **123** d.	...	0936	...	1037	1137	...	...	1237	...	1337	...	1437	...	1537	...	1637	...	1737	...	...	1837	1937
Birmingham New Street **120** d.	...	1030	...	1130	1230	...	...	1330	...	1430	...	1530	...	1630	...	1730	...	1830	1842	...	1930	2030
Cheltenham **120 138** d.	1045	1110	1146	1210	1310	...	1345	1410	...	1510	...	1610	1645	1710	1745	1816	1845	1910	1925	1945	2010	2110
Gloucester **138** d.	1058	1122	1158	1222	1322	...	1358	1422	1442	1522	...	1622	1658	1722	1758	1827	1858	1922	|	1958	2022	2121
Lydney 🚂 d.	1117	|	1217	|	1341	...	1417	|	1501	|	...	1641	1717	1741	1817	|	1917	|	|	2017	|	2140
Chepstow d.	1127	1148	1227	1248	|	...	1427	1449	1511	1548	...	1651	1727	|	1827	|	1927	|	|	2027	|	2150
Caldicot d.	1135	|	1235	|	|	...	1435	|	1519	|	...	|	1735	|	1835	|	1934	|	|	2035	|	2158
Newport **132 136 149** a.	1150	1205	1250	1305	1406	...	1450	1509	1535	1606	...	1708	1750	1806	1850	1910	1950	2003	2044	2050	2109	2217
Cardiff Central **132 136 149** a.	1206	1223	1307	1321	1422	...	1509	1526	1553	1625	...	1724	1810	1824	1912	1930	2011	2020	2100	2107	2126	2242

	⑥ 🍷	⑥ 2		⑦ 2	⑦ 🍷	⑦ 🍷	⑦ 2	⑦ 🍷	⑦ 🍷	⑦ 2	⑦ 🍷		⑦ 🍷	⑦ 2	⑦	⑦	⑦ 2	⑦	⑦	⑦ 2	⑦	⑦ 2
Nottingham **123** d.	...	...	⑦	...	...	0954	...	1111	1210	...	1310	...	1410	...	1510	1610	...	1710	1810	...	*1910*	...
Derby **123** d.	2028	...		...	...	1018	...	1136	1236	...	1338	...	1434	...	1534	1634	...	1735	1835	...	2027	...
Birmingham New Street **120** d.	2112	...		...	1012	1112	...	1230	1330	...	1430	...	1530	...	1630	1730	...	1830	1930	...	2112	...
Cheltenham **120 138** d.	2151	...		...	1052	1152	1221	1310	1410	1419	1510	...	1610	1619	1711	1810	1835	1912	2010	2019	2152	...
Gloucester **138** d.	2200	2309		1048	1105	1205	1233	1323	1424**c**	1434	1523	...	1623	1637**c**	1723	1823	1848	1928	2022	2033	2202	2233
Lydney 🚂 d.	...	2328		1107	|	|	1252	|	|	1453	|	...	|	1656	|	|	1907	|	|	2052	...	2252
Chepstow d.	...	2338		1117	|	|	1302	|	|	1503	|	...	|	1707	|	|	1917	|	|	2102	...	2302
Caldicot d.	...	2346		1125	|	|	1310	|	|	1511	|	...	|	1713	|	|	1925	|	|	2110	...	2310
Newport **132 136 149** a.	...	0011		1139	1147	1244	1325	1406	1501	1526	1606	...	1704	1729	1806	1906	1947	2006	2106	2125	...	2330
Cardiff Central **132 136 149** a.	...	0038		1206	1209	1307	1350	1427	1528	1551	1629	...	1726	1752	1829	1927	2014	2030	2127	2148	...	2351

		Ⓐ C	Ⓐ 2	Ⓐ	Ⓐ 2	Ⓐ 🍷 A	Ⓐ		Ⓐ	Ⓐ 2	Ⓐ 🍷	Ⓐ 2	Ⓐ		Ⓐ 🍷	Ⓐ 2	Ⓐ 🍷	Ⓐ 2	Ⓐ 🍷	Ⓐ 🍷	Ⓐ 2	Ⓐ 🍷
Cardiff Central **132 136 149** d.	Ⓐ	...	0612	0640	0705	0700	0745	...	0845	0912	0945	1009	1045	...	1145	1212	1245	1312	1345	1445	1512	1545
Newport **132 136 149** d.		...	0628	0655	0723	0714	0802	...	0900	0928	1000	1027	1100	...	1200	1228	1301	1328	1400	1500	1528	1600
Caldicot d.		...	0641	0708	0738	|	|	...	|	0940	|	1040	|	...	|	1242	|	1343	|	|	1541	|
Chepstow d.		...	0650	0716	0749	|	|	...	0918	0949	1018	1049	|	...	1218	1251	1318	1352	|	1518	1550	1618
Lydney 🚂 d.		...	0659	0725	0758	|	0825	...	|	0958	|	1058	1125	...	|	1300	|	1401	1425	|	1559	|
Gloucester **138** d.		0710	0722	0746	0821	|	0849**c**	...	0950**c**	1021	1050**c**	1121	1150**c**	...	1248**c**	1322	1350**c**	1422	1450**c**	1550**c**	1622	1650**c**
Cheltenham **120 138** d.		0721	0734	0757	0834	0841	0900	...	1001	1031	1101	1132	1201	...	1258	1333	1401	...	1501	1601	1631	1701
Birmingham New Street **120** a.		0816	*0826*	0845	...	0926	0945	...	1045	...	1145	...	1245	...	1345	...	1445	...	1545	1645	...	1745
Derby **123** a.		...	...	0934	...	...	1034	...	1134	...	1234	...	1334	...	1434	...	1534	...	1634	1734	...	1834
Nottingham **123** a.		...	...	1003	...	...	1103	...	1203	...	1303	...	1403	...	1503	...	1603	...	1703	1803	...	1903

	Ⓐ 2	Ⓐ 🍷		Ⓐ 2	Ⓐ 🍷	Ⓐ 2	Ⓐ 🍷	Ⓐ	Ⓐ	Ⓐ 2	Ⓐ	Ⓐ 2		⑥	⑥ C	⑥ 2	⑥	⑥ 2	⑥ 🍷 A	⑥	⑥	⑥ 2
Cardiff Central **132 136 149** d.	1610	1645	...	1712	1745	1808	1845	1950	2105	2112	2150	2320	⑥	...	...	0610	0640	0707	0700	0745	0845	0910
Newport **132 136 149** d.	1627	1700	...	1728	1800	1824	1900	2005	2121	2127	2205	2338		...	...	0626	0655	0723	0715	0800	0900	0925
Caldicot d.	1640	|	...	1741	|	1837	|	2018	|	2141	|	0001		...	...	0639	0708	0736	|	|	|	0937
Chepstow d.	1649	|	...	1750	1818	1846	1917	2026	|	2150	|	0010		...	...	0648	0716	0745	|	|	0918	0947
Lydney 🚂 d.	1658	1725	...	1759	|	1855	|	2035	|	2159	|	0019		...	...	0657	0725	0754	|	0825	|	0955
Gloucester **138** d.	1723**c**	1750**c**	...	1821	1846	1921**c**	1945	2059**c**	2204	2223	2247	0039		0700	0707	0721	0746	0822	|	0850**c**	0950**c**	1021
Cheltenham **120 138** d.	1732	1801	...	1830	1857	1931	1957	2111	2215	2234	2258	...		0711	0718	0734	0757	0835	0841	0901	1001	1032
Birmingham New Street **120** a.	...	1845	...	...	1945	...	2040	2151	2305	...	2359	...		0756	0808	...	0845	...	0926	0945	1045	...
Derby **123** a.	...	1934	...	...	2034	...	2132	*2251*	...	...	...	...		0841	...	...	0934	...	...	1034	1134	...
Nottingham **123** a.	...	2004	...	...	2103	...	2208	*2327*	...	...	...	...		...	...	...	1003	...	...	1103	1203	...

	⑥ 🍷	⑥ 2	⑥		⑥ 🍷	⑥ 2	⑥ 🍷	⑥ 2 🍷	⑥ 🍷	⑥ 🍷	⑥ 2	⑥ 🍷	⑥ 2	⑥ 🍷	⑥ 2	⑥ 🍷	⑥ 2	⑥ 🍷	⑥	⑥	⑥ 2	⑥ 2
Cardiff Central **132 136 149** d.	0945	1010	1045	...	1145	1209	1245	1312	1345	1445	1508	1545	1608	1645	1709	1745	1808	1845	2000	2050	2111	2318
Newport **132 136 149** d.	1000	1027	1100	...	1200	1227	1300	1327	1400	1500	1527	1600	1624	1700	1725	1800	1827	1900	2015	2105	2127	2337
Caldicot d.	|	1040	|	...	|	1240	|	1341	|	|	1538	|	1637	|	1738	|	1840	|	2028	|	2140	2359
Chepstow d.	1018	1049	|	...	1218	1249	1318	1350	|	1518	1547	1618	1646	|	1747	1818	1849	1918	2036	|	2149	0008
Lydney 🚂 d.	|	1058	1125	...	|	1258	|	1359	1425	|	1556	|	1655	1725	1756	|	1858	|	2045	|	2158	0017
Gloucester **138** d.	1050**c**	1122	1150**c**	...	1248**c**	1322	1350**c**	1420	1450**c**	1550**c**	1621	1650**c**	1723**c**	1750**c**	1824**c**	1846	1921	1946	2107	2149	2219	0040
Cheltenham **120 138** d.	1101	1132	1201	...	1259	1332	1401	...	1501	1601	1632	1701	1733	1801	1833	1857	1931	1957	2118	2200	...	...
Birmingham New Street **120** a.	1145	...	1245	...	1345	...	1445	...	1545	1645	...	1745	...	1845	...	1945	...	2042	2207	2242	...	...
Derby **123** a.	1235	...	1334	...	1434	...	1535	...	1634	1734	...	1835	...	1932	...	2034	...	2133	2253	...	...	...
Nottingham **123** a.	1303	...	1403	...	1503	...	1603	...	1703	1803	...	1903	...	2004	...	2103	...	2208	2327	...	...	...

		⑦ 2	⑦	⑦	⑦ 2	⑦	⑦		⑦ 2	⑦ 🍷	⑦ 🍷	⑦ 2	⑦ 🍷		⑦ 🍷	⑦ 2	⑦ 🍷	⑦ D	⑦	⑦ 2	⑦	⑦ 2
Cardiff Central **132 136 149** d.	⑦	1030	1045	1145	1225	1245	1345	...	1425	1445	1545	1625	1645	...	1745	1824	1845	1945	...	2024	2045	2226
Newport **132 136 149** d.		1048	1106	1205	1247	1305	1405	...	1445	1505	1605	1645	1703	...	1804	1846	1903	2003	...	2046	2105	2246
Caldicot d.		1102	|	|	1300	|	|	...	1458	|	|	1658	|	...	|	1859	|	|	...	2059	|	2259
Chepstow d.		1111	|	|	1309	|	|	...	1507	|	|	1707	|	...	|	1908	|	|	...	2108	|	2308
Lydney 🚂 d.		1120	|	|	1318	|	|	...	1516	|	|	1716	|	...	|	1917	|	|	...	2117	|	2317
Gloucester **138** d.		1142	1150	1248	1340	1348	1448	...	1540	1548	1648	1740	1748	...	1848	1942**c**	1950	2049	...	2142	2148	2342
Cheltenham **120 138** d.		1155	1201	1258	1352	1358	1458	...	1550	1558	1658	1750	1758	...	1858	1955	2000	2100	2111	...	2159	...
Birmingham New Street **120** a.		...	1243	1341	...	1441	1541	...	...	1641	1741	...	1841	...	1941	...	2043	2144	2148	...	2242	...
Derby **123** a.		...	1333	1434	...	1533	1634	...	...	1733	1833	...	1933	...	2034	...	2133	...	2240	...	...	...
Nottingham **123** a.		...	1400	1500	...	1600	1700	...	...	1800	1900	...	2000	...	2100	...	2200	...	...	...	...	...

A – (12) Manchester Piccadilly - Bristol Temple Meads - Cardiff Central and v.v. (Tables **120** / **122**).
B – (2) 🍷 Gloucester - Fishguard Harbour (Table **135**).
C – (12) Gloucester - Stansted Airport (Table **208**).
D – (12) Cardiff - Leicester (Table **208**).

a – Arrives 2230 on ⑤.
c – Arrives 4–6 minutes earlier.
d – Arrives 8 minutes earlier.

🚂 – DEAN FOREST RAILWAY (Lydney Junction - Parkend. *7 km*). ✆ 01594 845840. www.deanforestrailway.co.uk. Lydney Junction station is 10 minutes walk from the National Rail station.

km			Ⓐ	Ⓐ	Ⓐ	Ⓐ	Ⓐ	Ⓐ	Ⓐ	Ⓐ	Ⓐ	Ⓐ	Ⓐ	Ⓐ	Ⓐ	Ⓐ	Ⓐ	Ⓐ	Ⓐ	Ⓐ	Ⓐ	Ⓐ	Ⓐ	Ⓐ
										A												H		
	Bournemouth **119** d.	Ⓐ	...	...	...	...	...	...	...	...	0630	...	0730	...	0845	...	0945	...	1045	...	1145	...	1245	...
	Southampton Central **119** d.		...	...	...	...	0515	...	0615	...	0715	...	0815	...	0916	...	1017	...	1117	...	1217	...	1316	...
	Reading **119** d.		...	...	...	...	0615	...	0715	...	0815	...	0915	...	1015	...	1115	...	1215	...	1315	...	1415	...
	Paignton **120** d.		...	...	...	...	|	...	|	...	|	0702	|	...	|	...	|	1007	|	...	|	...	|	...
	Exeter St Davids **120** d.		...	..	...	...	|	...	|	...	|	0745	|	...	|	...	|	1050	|	...	|	1250	|	...
	Bristol T Meads **120** d.		...	...	...	...	|	0700	|	0800	|	0900	|	1000	|	1100	|	1200	|	1300	|	1400	|	1500
0	**Birmingham** New Street **150** d.		0557	0622	0657	0731	0757	0831	0857	0931	0957	1031	1057	1131	1157	1231	1257	1331	1357	1431	1457	1531	1557	1631
20	Wolverhampton **150** d.		0616	0641	0715	0750	0815	0849	0915	0949	1015	1049	1115	1149	1215	1249	1315	1349	1415	1449	1515	1549	1615	1649
46	Stafford d.		0632	0655	0731	0802	0833	0902	0928	1002	1028	1102	1128	1202	1228	1302	1328	1402	1428	1502	1528	1603	1628	1702
72	Stoke on Trent **152** d.		0651	0714	|	0820	0854	0920	0944	1020	1044	1120	1144	1220	1244	1320	1344	1420	1444	1520	1544	1620	1644	1720
104	Macclesfield **152** d.		0712	0731	|	0837	0911	|	1002	|	1102	|	1202	|	1302	|	1402	|	1502	|	1602	|	1702	|
123	Stockport **152** d.		0726	0750	0824	0850	0927	0950	1014	1050	1114	1150	1214	1250	1314	1350	1414	1450	1514	1550	1614	1650	1714	1751
132	**Manchester** Piccadilly **152** a.		0734	0800	0834	0859	0939	0959	1026	1059	1126	1159	1226	1259	1326	1359	1426	1459	1526	1559	1626	1659	1726	1800

	Ⓐ	Ⓐ	Ⓐ	Ⓐ	Ⓐ		Ⓐ	Ⓐ	Ⓐ	Ⓐ	Ⓐ	Ⓐ		⑥	⑥	⑥	⑥	⑥	⑥	⑥	⑥	⑥	⑥	⑥
																					A			
Bournemouth **119** d.	1345	...	1445	...	1545	...	...	1645	...	1745	1845	...	⑥	...	...	...	...	...	...	...	...	0637	...	0747
Southampton Central **119** d.	1417	...	1516	...	1617	...	...	1717	...	1815	1916	...		...	...	...	...	0509	...	0620	...	0720	...	0820
Reading **119** d.	1515	...	1615	...	1715	...	...	1815	...	1915	2015	...		...	...	...	...	0615	...	0715	...	0815	...	0914
Paignton **120** d.	|	1404	|	...	|	...	...	|	...	|	|	...		...	...	...	...	|	...	|	...	|	0702	|
Exeter St Davids **120** d.	|	1448	|	...	|	...	1654	|	...	|	|	...		...	...	...	...	|	...	|	...	|	0745	|
Bristol T Meads **120** d.	|	1600	|	1700	|	...	1800	|	1900	|	|	...		...	...	...	...	|	0700	|	0800	|	0900	|
Birmingham New Street **150** d.	1657	1731	1757	1831	1857	...	1931	1957	2031	2057	2157	2230		0557	0631	0657	0731	0757	0831	0857	0931	0957	1031	1057
Wolverhampton **150** d.	1715	1749	1815	1849	1915	...	1949	2015	2049	2115	2215	2248		0615	0649	0715	0749	0815	0849	0915	0949	1015	1049	1115
Stafford d.	1728	1802	1828	1902	1928	...	2002	2028	2102	2129	2228	2301		0628	0702	0731	0802	0828	0902	0928	1002	1028	1102	1128
Stoke on Trent **152** d.	1744	1820	1844	1920	1944	...	2020	2044	2119	2146	2244	2320		0645	0720	|	0820	0844	0920	0944	1020	1044	1120	1144
Macclesfield **152** d.	1802	|	1902	|	2002	...	|	2102	|	2203	2302	|		0706	0737	|	0837	0902	|	1002	|	1102	|	1202
Stockport **152** d.	1815	1850	1914	1951	2014	...	2049	2114	2150	2216	2316	|		0719	0750	0816	0850	0914	0950	1014	1050	1114	1150	1214
Manchester Piccadilly **152** a.	1825	1859	1924	1959	2026	...	2058	2126	2200	2227	2326	0011		0728	0759	0829	0859	0926	0959	1026	1059	1126	1159	1226

	⑥	⑥	⑥		⑥	⑥	⑥	⑥	⑥	⑥	⑥	⑥	⑥	⑥	⑥	⑥	⑥	⑥	⑥	⑥	⑥		⑥	⑥
										H														
Bournemouth **119** d.	...	0847	...	...	0947	...	1047	...	1147	...	1247	...	1347	...	1447	...	1547	...	1647	...	1747	...	1847	...
Southampton Central **119** d.	...	0918	...	...	1017	...	1120	...	1220	...	1318	...	1420	...	1518	...	1620	...	1720	...	1820	...	1920	...
Reading **119** d.	...	1015	...	...	1115	...	1215	...	1315	...	1415	...	1515	...	1615	...	1715	...	1815	...	1915	...	2015	...
Paignton **120** d.	...	|	...	...	|	1006	|	...	|	...	|	...	|	1355	|	...	|	...	|	...	|	...	|	...
Exeter St Davids **120** d.	...	|	...	...	|	1049	|	...	|	1248	|	...	|	1437	|	...	|	1653	|	...	|	...	|	*1923*
Bristol T Meads **120** d.	1000	|	1100	...	|	1200	|	1300	|	1400	|	1500	|	1600	|	1700	|	1800	|	1900	|	...	|	*2030*
Birmingham New Street **150** d.	1131	1157	1231	...	1257	1331	1357	1431	1457	1531	1557	1631	1657	1731	1757	1831	1857	1931	1957	2031	2057	...	2157	2231
Wolverhampton **150** d.	1149	1215	1249	...	1315	1349	1415	1449	1515	1549	1615	1649	1715	1749	1815	1849	1915	1949	2015	2049	2117	...	2215	2249
Stafford d.	1202	1228	1302	...	1328	1402	1428	1502	1528	1602	1628	1702	1728	1802	1828	1902	1928	2002	2028	2102	2130	...	2228	2302
Stoke on Trent **152** d.	1220	1244	1320	...	1344	1420	1444	1520	1544	1620	1644	1720	1744	1820	1844	1920	1944	2020	2044	2120	2147	...	2244	2320
Macclesfield **152** d.	|	1302	|	...	1402	|	1502	|	1602	|	1702	|	1802	|	1902	|	2002	2037	2102	2138	2205	...	2302	2339
Stockport **152** d.	1250	1314	1350	...	1414	1450	1514	1550	1614	1650	1714	1750	1814	1850	1914	1950	2014	2050	2114	2153	2221	...	2314	2354
Manchester Piccadilly **152** a.	1259	1326	1359	...	1426	1459	1526	1559	1626	1659	1726	1759	1826	1859	1924	1959	2025	2059	2124	2202	2233	...	2329	0010

		⑦	⑦	⑦	⑦	⑦	⑦	⑦	⑦	⑦	⑦		⑦	⑦	⑦	⑦	⑦	⑦	⑦	⑦	⑦	⑦	⑦	⑦
											F			F				H						
Bournemouth **119** d.	⑦	...	...	...	...	0940	...	1040	...	1140	...	...	1240	...	1340	...	1440	...	1540	...	1640	...	1740	1840
Southampton Central **119** d.		...	...	...	0915	1015	...	1115	...	1215	...	...	1315	...	1415	...	1515	...	1615	...	1715	...	1815	1915
Reading **119** d.		...	...	0912	1011	1111	...	1211	...	1311	...	...	1411	...	1511	...	1611	...	1711	...	1811	...	1911	2011
Paignton **120** d.		...	...	|	|	|	...	|	1050	|	...	...	|	...	|	...	|	...	|	...	|	...	|	|
Exeter St Davids **120** d.		...	...	|	|	|	...	|	1133	|	1256	...	|	1347	|	...	|	1532	|	...	|	...	|	|
Bristol T Meads **120** d.		...	...	|	|	|	...	|	1300	|	1400	...	|	1500	|	1600	|	1700	|	1800	|	1900	|	|
Birmingham New Street **150** d.		0901	1001	1101	1157	1257	1331	1357	1431	1457	1531	...	1557	1631	1657	1731	1757	1831	1857	1931	1957	2031	2057	2157
Wolverhampton **150** d.		0919	1019	1119	1216	1316	1349	1415	1449	1515	1549	...	1615	1649	1715	1749	1815	1849	1915	1949	2015	2053	2117	2215
Stafford d.		0933	1033	1132	1229	1329	1402	1428	1502	1528	1602	...	1628	1702	1729	1802	1828	1902	1928	2002	2028	2106	2130	2228
Stoke on Trent **152** d.		0952	1052	1152	1246	1345	1420	1445	1521	1545	1619	...	1645	1721	1746	1821	1847	1921	1947	2021	2045	2122	2146	2245
Macclesfield **152** d.		1010	1109	1210	1305	1405	|	1502	|	1605	|	...	1705	|	1805	|	1905	|	2005	|	2103	|	2204	2302
Stockport **152** d.		1026	1123	1230	1317	1417	1451	1515	1550	1617	1650	...	1717	1750	1817	1850	1918	1950	2017	2050	2115	2151	2216	2315
Manchester Piccadilly **152** a.		1037	1133	1240	1329	1429	1500	1524	1559	1629	1659	...	1730	1759	1829	1859	1928	1959	2028	2100	2129	2200	2226	2324

		Ⓐ	Ⓐ	Ⓐ	Ⓐ	Ⓐ	Ⓐ	Ⓐ	Ⓐ	Ⓐ	Ⓐ	Ⓐ	Ⓐ	Ⓐ	Ⓐ	Ⓐ	Ⓐ	Ⓐ	Ⓐ	Ⓐ	Ⓐ	Ⓐ	Ⓐ	Ⓐ
Manchester Piccadilly **152** d.	Ⓐ	0511	0600	0627	0707	0727	0807	0827	0907	0927	1007	1027	1107	1127	1207	1227	1307	1327	1407	1427	1507	1527	1607	1627
Stockport **152** d.		|	0608	0635	0716	0736	0816	0836	0916	0935	1016	1036	1116	1136	1216	1236	1316	1336	1416	1436	1516	1536	1616	1636
Macclesfield **152** d.		|	|	0648	|	0749	|	0849	|	0949	|	1049	|	1149	|	1249	|	1349	|	1449	|	1549	|	1649
Stoke on Trent **152** d.		0607	|	0706	0744	0807	0844	0907	0944	1007	1045	1107	1144	1207	1244	1307	1344	1407	1444	1507	1544	1607	1644	1707
Stafford d.		0625	0700	0724	0801	0825	0902	0925	1000	1025	1102	1125	1201	1225	1301	1326	1401	1425	1501	1525	1603	1625	1702	1725
Wolverhampton **150** d.		0641	0716	0745	0816	0841	0916	0942	1017	1041	1116	1141	1216	1241	1317	1341	1417	1441	1517	1541	1617	1641	1717	1741
Birmingham New Street **150** a.		0657	0733	0807	0833	0858	0933	0958	1033	1058	1133	1158	1233	1258	1333	1358	1433	1458	1533	1558	1633	1658	1733	1758
Bristol T Meads **120** a.		|	0910	...	1008	|	1110	|	1205	|	1309	|	1408	|	1510	|	1611	|	1710	|	1807	|	1906	|
Exeter St Davids **120** a.		|	...	...	...	|	1224	|	...	|	...	|	...	|	1612	|	...	|	1811	|	...	|	...	|
Paignton **120** a.		|	...	...	...	|	1308	|	...	|	...	|	...	|	...	|	...	|	1855	|	...	|	...	|
Reading **119** a.		0840	...	...	...	1041	...	1140	...	1242	...	1340	...	1440	...	1541	...	1640	...	1740	...	1843	...	1940
Southampton Central **119** a.		0943	...	...	...	1143	...	1241	...	1341	...	1441	...	1541	...	1641	...	1741	...	1843	...	1940	...	2041
Bournemouth **119** a.		1013	...	...	...	1213	...	1311	...	1411	...	1511	...	1611	...	1711	...	1815	...	1912	...	2011	...	2115

	Ⓐ	Ⓐ	Ⓐ	Ⓐ	Ⓐ	Ⓐ	Ⓐ	Ⓐ	Ⓐ	Ⓐ			⑥	⑥	⑥		⑥	⑥	⑥	⑥	⑥	⑥	⑥	⑥
	A		F																					
Manchester Piccadilly **152** d.	1705	1727	1805	1827	1907	1927	2007	2027	2127	2207	...	⑥	0511	0600	0707	...	0727	0807	0827	0907	0927	1007	1027	1107
Stockport **152** d.	1714	1735	1813	1836	1916	1936	2017	2036	2136	2216	...		|	0608	0716	...	0736	0816	0836	0916	0937	1016	1036	1116
Macclesfield **152** d.	1728	|	1826	|	|	1949	|	2049	2149	2229	...		|	0621	|	...	0749	|	0849	|	0950	|	1049	|
Stoke on Trent **152** d.	1745	|	1844	1907	1944	2007	2045	2107	2208	2247	...		0608	0640	0744	...	0807	0844	0907	0944	1008	1044	1107	1144
Stafford d.	1802	1825	1901	1925	2001	2025	2102	2125	2226	2304	...		0626	0700	0801	...	0825	0901	0925	1001	1025	1101	1125	1201
Wolverhampton **150** d.	1816	1841	1917	1941	2017	2044	2116	2141	2242	2318	...		0641	0716	0817	...	0841	0917	0941	1017	1041	1117	1141	1217
Birmingham New Street **150** a.	1833	1858	1933	1958	2033	2100	2133	2200	2259	2336	...		0657	0733	0833	...	0858	0933	0958	1033	1058	1133	1159	1233
Bristol T Meads **120** a.	2009	|	2105	|	2214	|	|	...	...	...	...		|	0906	1004	...	|	1109	|	1204	|	1309	|	1405
Exeter St Davids **120** a.	...	|	2209	|	...	|	|	...	...	...	...		|	...	...	...	|	1225	|	...	|	...	|	...
Paignton **120** a.	...	|	...	|	...	|	|	...	...	...	...		|	...	...	...	|	1310	|	...	|	...	|	...
Reading **119** a.	...	2041	...	2142	...	2242	*2349*	...	...	...	...		0841	...	...	...	1041	...	1138	...	1241	...	1340	...
Southampton Central **119** a.	...	2140	...	2242	...	2343	...	...	...	...	...		0940	...	...	...	1141	...	1241	...	1341	...	1441	...
Bournemouth **119** a.	...	2215	...	2319	...	...	...	...	...	...	...		1011	...	...	...	1212	...	1312	...	1412	...	1512	...

A – To / from Cardiff (Table **121**).
C – To / from Newquay (Tables **117** and **120**).
F – To / from Plymouth (Table **120**).
H – From Penzance (Tables **117** and **120**).

122 MANCHESTER - BIRMINGHAM

Most services convey 🍷 XC

	⑥		⑥	⑥	⑥	⑥	⑥		⑥	⑥	⑥	⑥	⑥	⑥ A	⑥	⑥ F	⑥	⑥	⑥	⑥	⑥	⑥	⑥
Manchester Piccadilly 152 d.	1127	...	1207	1227	1307	1327	1407	...	1427	1507	1527	1607	1627	1706	1727	1805	1827	1907	1927	2007	2027	2107	2127
Stockport 152 d.	1136	...	1216	1236	1316	1336	1416	...	1436	1516	1536	1616	1636	1715	1736	1813	1836	1916	1936	2016	2035	2116	2135
Macclesfield 152 d.	1149	...	|	1249	|	1349	|	...	1449	|	1549	|	1649	1727	|	1826	|	|	1949	|	2049	|	2149
Stoke on Trent 152 d.	1207	...	1244	1307	1344	1407	1444	...	1507	1544	1607	1644	1707	1745	1807	1844	1907	1944	2007	2045	2107	2144	2207
Stafford d.	1225	...	1301	1325	1401	1425	1501	...	1526	1601	1625	1701	1725	1801	1825	1901	1925	2001	2025	2102	2125	2202	2230
Wolverhampton 150 d.	1241	...	1317	1341	1417	1441	1517	...	1541	1617	1641	1717	1741	1817	1841	1917	1941	2017	2041	2115	2142	2217	2245
Birmingham New Street 150 a.	1258	...	1333	1358	1433	1458	1533	...	1558	1633	1658	1733	1758	1833	1858	1933	1959	2033	2058	2131	2159	2233	2301
Bristol T Meads **120** a.	|	...	1509	|	1607	|	1707	...	|	1804	|	1905	|	2005	|	2104	|	2212	|	...	...	...	...
Exeter St Davids **120** a.	|	...	1609	|	...	|	1805	...	|	...	|	...	|	...	|	2207	|	...	|	...	...	...	...
Paignton **120** a.	|	...	...	|	...	|	1849	...	|	...	|	...	|	...	|	...	|	...	|	...	...	...	...
Reading **119** a.	1441	...	...	1540	...	1641	...	...	1739	...	1842	...	1941	...	2041	...	2142	...	2245	...	...	...	...
Southampton Central **119** a.	1541	...	...	1641	...	1741	...	...	1841	...	1941	...	2041	...	2140	...	2242	...	2341	...	...	...	...
Bournemouth **119** a.	1612	...	...	1712	...	1812	...	...	1912	...	2012	...	2112	...	2215	...	2319	...	...	...	...	...	...

		⑦	⑦	⑦	⑦	⑦	⑦	⑦	⑦	⑦	⑦	⑦	⑦	⑦	⑦ F	⑦	⑦	⑦	⑦	⑦	⑦	⑦	⑦
Manchester Piccadilly 152 d.	⑦	0827	0927	1027	1127	1226	1307	1327	1407	1427	1507	1527	1607	1627	1707	1727	1807	1827	1907	1927	2007	2107	2207
Stockport 152 d.		0836	0936	1036	1136	1235	1316	1336	1416	1436	1516	1536	1616	1636	1716	1736	1816	1836	1916	1936	2016	2116	2216
Macclesfield 152 d.		|	0949	1049	1149	1249	|	1349	|	1449	|	1549	|	1649	|	1749	|	1849	|	1949	2029	2129	2229
Stoke on Trent 152 d.		|	1007	1107	1207	1307	1344	1407	1444	1507	1544	1607	1644	1707	1744	1807	1844	1907	1944	2007	2047	2147	2247
Stafford d.		0926	1025	1127	1225	1325	1401	1425	1501	1525	1601	1625	1701	1725	1801	1825	1901	1925	2001	2025	2104	2204	2304
Wolverhampton 150 d.		0941	1041	1142	1241	1341	1415	1441	1515	1541	1615	1641	1715	1741	1815	1841	1915	1941	2015	2041	2117	2222	2319
Birmingham New Street 150 a.		0957	1057	1158	1257	1357	1431	1457	1531	1557	1631	1657	1731	1757	1831	1857	1931	1957	2031	2057	2133	2240	2336
Bristol T Meads **120** a.		|	|	|	|	|	1611	|	1708	|	1814	|	1908	|	2014	|	2106	|	2210	|	2302	...	...
Exeter St Davids **120** a.		|	|	|	|	|	1709	|	...	|	...	|	...	|	2127	|	...	|	...	|	...	...	...
Paignton **120** a.		|	|	|	|	|	1756	|	...	|	...	|	...	|	...	|	...	|	...	|	...	...	...
Reading **119** a.		1140	1240	1341	1440	1540	...	1640	...	1739	...	1840	...	1939	...	2040	...	2140	...	2238	...	...	...
Southampton Central **119** a.		1242	1342	1443	1542	1642	...	1740	...	1842	...	1940	...	2041	...	2142	...	2242	...	...	...	...	...
Bournemouth **119** a.		1326	1426	1526	1626	1726	...	1826	...	1926	...	2026	...	2126	...	2226	...	...	...	...	...	...	...

A – To Cardiff Central (Table **121**).

F – To Plymouth (Table **120**).

123 BIRMINGHAM - NOTTINGHAM

XC

km			Ⓐ	Ⓐ	Ⓐ	Ⓐ	Ⓐ	Ⓐ	Ⓐ	Ⓐ		Ⓐ	Ⓐ	Ⓐ	Ⓐ	Ⓐ			⑥	⑥	⑥	⑥	⑥
	Cardiff Central **121** d.	Ⓐ	...	...	...	...	...	0640	...	0745	and at	...	1745	1845	*1950*	...	...	⑥	...	...	...	...	...
0	**Birmingham** New Street **124** d.		0619	0649	0719	0749	0819	0849	0919	0949	the same	1919	1949	2049	2203	2309	...		0619	0649	0719	0749	0819
28	Tamworth **124** d.		0639	0707	0739	0807	0836	0909	0936	1007	minutes	1936	2009	2109	2227	2328	...		0639	0707	0739	0807	0836
48	Burton-on-Trent **124** d.		0651	0720	0750	0819	0848	0921	0948	1019	past each	1948	2021	2121	2239	2340	...		0651	0719	0750	0819	0848
67	**Derby** **124** a.		0704	0735	0805	0836	0900	0934	1000	1034	hour until	2000	2034	2132	2251	2353	...		0703	0735	0805	0835	0900
67	**Derby** d.		0708	0743	0810	0840	0908	0940	1008	1040		2008	2040	2138	2259	2357	...		0709	0740	0809	0840	0908
93	**Nottingham** a.		0738	0809	0834	0906	0928	1003	1028	1103		2028	2103	2208	2327	0016	...		0738	0806	0834	0906	0928

	⑥	⑥	⑥	⑥		⑥	⑥	⑥	⑥	⑥	⑥		⑦	⑦	⑦	⑦	⑦	⑦	⑦	⑦	⑦	⑦	⑦
Cardiff Central **121** d.	0640	...	0745	...	and at	1645	...	1745	1845	2000	...	⑦	...	1045	1145	1245	1345	1445	1545	1645	1745	1845	*1945*
Birmingham New Street **124** d.	0849	0919	0949	1019	the same	1849	1919	1949	2049	2210	2249		1149	1249	1349	1449	1549	1649	1749	1849	1949	2049	2203
Tamworth **124** d.	0909	0936	1007	1036	minutes	1909	1936	2009	2109	2227	2308		1207	1307	1407	1509	1607	1707	1807	1909	2007	2106	2219
Burton-on-Trent **124** d.	0921	0948	1019	1048	past each	1921	1948	2021	2121	2239	2320		1219	1319	1419	1521	1619	1719	1819	1921	2019	2119	|
Derby **124** a.	0934	1000	1034	1100	hour until	1932	2000	2034	2133	2253	2333		1234	1333	1434	1533	1634	1733	1833	1933	2034	2133	2240
Derby d.	0940	1008	1040	1108	▽	1940	2008	2040	2140	2259	...		1240	1340	1440	1540	1640	1740	1840	1940	2040	2140	...
Nottingham a.	1003	1028	1103	1128		2004	2028	2103	2208	2327	...		1300	1400	1500	1600	1700	1800	1900	2000	2100	2200	...

		Ⓐ	Ⓐ A	Ⓐ	Ⓐ	Ⓐ	Ⓐ	Ⓐ		Ⓐ	Ⓐ	Ⓐ	Ⓐ	Ⓐ	Ⓐ		⑥	⑥ A	⑥	⑥	⑥	⑥	⑥
Nottingham d.	Ⓐ	0600	0637	0704	0737	0812	0841	0910	and at	1841	1910	1940	2040	2139	...	⑥	0558	0637	0658	0737	0809	0841	0910
Derby a.		0632	0659	0731	0802	0833	0907	0931	the same	1906	1931	2006	2104	2208	...		0630	0659	0729	0802	0829	0909	0931
Derby **124** d.		0636	0706	0736	0806	0837	0910	0936	minutes	1910	1937	2010	2110	2212	2245		0636	0706	0736	0806	0837	0912	0936
Burton-on-Trent **124** d.		0648	0717	0750	0818	0849	0921	0950	past each	1921	1949	2021	2124	2223	2256		0648	0717	0750	0818	0849	0924	0949
Tamworth **124** d.		0701	0730	0803	0830	0902	0933	1002	hour until	1933	2003	2033	2134	2235	2307		0701	0730	0802	0830	0902	0935	1002
Birmingham New Street **124** a.		0725	0753	0825	0855	0924	0955	1024	▲	1955	2025	2055	2157	2301	2326		0724	0752	0824	0855	0924	0956	1024
Cardiff Central **121** a.		0927	...	1028	...	1128	...	1230		...	2235a	...	...	...	...		0923	...	1021	...	1124	...	1224

		⑥	⑥	⑥	⑥	⑥	⑥		⑦	⑦	⑦		⑦	⑦	⑦		⑦	⑦	⑦	⑦	⑦	⑦	⑦
Nottingham d.	and at	1841	1910	1941	2037	2139	...	⑦	0954	1111	1210	...	1310	1410	1510	...	1610	1710	1810	1910	2010	2110	...
Derby a.	the same	1906	1932	2007	2102	2208	...		1012	1131	1230	...	1330	1429	1530	...	1630	1729	1830	1930	2030	2130	...
Derby **124** d.	minutes	1910	1937	2011	2110	2212	2226		1018	1136	1236	...	1338	1434	1534	...	1634	1735	1835	1935	2035	2137	2226
Burton-on-Trent **124** d.	past each	1921	1949	2022	2124	2222	2237		1029	1147	1247	...	1349	1447	1547	...	1647	1747	1847	1947	2047	2148	2237
Tamworth **124** d.	hour until	1933	2002	2034	2135	2235	2247		1042	1200	1300	...	1400	1500	1600	...	1700	1800	1900	1959	2059	2200	2247
Birmingham New Street **124** a.	△	1955	2024	2055	2156	2302	2306		1102	1221	1320	...	1422	1520	1621	...	1719	1819	1921	2021	2118	2223	2305
Cardiff Central **121** a.		...	2242	...	...	...	...		1307	1427	1528	...	1629	1726	1829	...	1927	2030	2127	...	...	...	...

A – To Bournemouth (Table **119**).

a – On ⑤ arrives 2230.

▲ – Cardiff arrivals may vary ± 4 minutes.

△ – Cardiff arrivals may vary ± 6 minutes.

▽ – Nottingham arrivals may be up to 3 minutes later after 1700.

BIRMINGHAM - SHEFFIELD - LEEDS - YORK - NEWCASTLE - EDINBURGH - GLASGOW

km	Ⓐ	Ⓐ	Ⓐ	Ⓐ	Ⓐ	Ⓐ	Ⓐ	Ⓐ	Ⓐ	Ⓐ	Ⓐ	Ⓐ	Ⓐ	Ⓐ	Ⓐ	Ⓐ	Ⓐ	Ⓐ	Ⓐ	Ⓐ	Ⓐ	Ⓐ	Ⓐ
								H	G				A			B		C		B		D	
	Plymouth **120** d.		...	...	...	...	...	...	...	...	0520	...	0625	...	0725	...	0825	...	0925	...	1025	...	1125	...
	Bristol Temple Meads **120** d.		...	...	...	...	...	...	0627	...	0730	...	0830	...	0930	...	1030	...	1130	...	1230	...	1330	...
	Southampton Central **119** d.		...	...	...	...	...	...	|	...	|	...	|	...	|	...	|	0946	|	...	|	1146	|	...
	Reading **119** d.		...	...	...	...	...	...	|	0645	|	0746	|	0850	|	0945	|	1045	|	1145	|	1245	|	1345
0	**Birmingham** New Street **123** d.		...	...	0600	0630	0703	0730	0803	0830	0903	0930	1003	1030	1103	1130	1203	1230	1303	1330	1403	1430	1503	1530
28	Tamworth **123** d.		...	...	|	|	0719	|	0819	|	|	|	1019	|	|	|	1219	|	|	|	1419	|	|	|
48	Burton on Trent **123** d.		...	...	|	|	0731	|	0829	|	0927	|	|	|	1126	|	|	|	1328	|	|	|	1526	|
67	**Derby** **123 170** d.		...	0556	0635	0713	0744	0813**c**	0844	0916**a**	0944**b**	1016**a**	1044**b**	1116**a**	1144**b**	1216**a**	1244	1316**a**	1344**b**	1416**a**	1444**c**	1516**a**	1544**c**	1616**a**
105	Chesterfield **170** d.		...	0617	0654	0732	0803	0832	0903	|	1003	|	1103	|	1203	|	1303	|	1403	|	1503	|	1603	|
125	**Sheffield** **170** d.		...	0633	0709	0754**d**	0822**b**	0847	0921**c**	0947	1021**c**	1047	1121	1147	1221**c**	1247	1321**c**	1347	1421	1447	1521**c**	1547	1621	1647
154	Doncaster **180** d.		...	0703**c**	|	0825	|	0919	|	1019	|	1119	|	1219	|	1320	|	1420**b**	|	1519	|	1619	|	1720
171	Wakefield Westgate **180** d.		...	|	0737	|	0848	|	0947	|	1047	|	1147	|	1247	|	1347	|	1447	|	1547	|	1647	|
187	**Leeds** **190 180** d.		...	|	0757**b**	|	0908**d**	|	1008**d**	|	1108**d**	|	1208**d**	|	1308**d**	|	1408**d**	|	1508**d**	|	1608**d**	|	1708**d**	|
199	**York** **190 180** a.		...	0723	0823	0847	0930	0940	1030	1039	1130	1139	1230	1240	1330	1340	1430	1440	1530	1539	1630	1639	1730	1740
	York **180** d.		0625	0732	0829	0850	0932	0949	1032	1048	1132	1149	1232	1248	1332	1346	1432	1448	1532	1548	1632	1648	1732	1748
270	Darlington **180** d.		0655**c**	0800	0857	0917	0958	1016	1100	1115	1159	1216	1300	1315	1401	1416	1500	1515	1600	1615	1700	1715	1800	1816
305	Durham **180** d.		0713	0818	0913	0934	1017	1033	1117	1132	1216	1233	1317	1332	1417	1433	1517	1532	1617	1632	1717	1732	1817	1833
328	**Newcastle** **180** a.		0730	0836	0928	0947	1029	1046	1129	1145	1228	1245	1329	1345	1430	1445	1529	1544	1629	1645	1729	1745	1833	1847
	Newcastle **180** d.		0735	...	0935	...	1035	...	1137	...	1238	...	1338	...	1435	...	1537	...	1635	...	1737	...	1840	...
384	Alnmouth **180** a.		|	...	0959	...	|	...	|	...	|	...	1402	...	|	...	1601	...	1702	...	1801	...	|	...
436	Berwick upon Tweed **180** a.		0820	...	1021	...	|	...	1223	...	|	...	1423	...	|	...	1623	...	|	...	1823	...	1922	...
528	**Edinburgh** Waverley **180 220** a.		0902	...	1106	...	1204	...	1305	..	1409	...	1508	...	1606	...	1705	...	1807	...	1905	...	2008	...
599	Motherwell **220** a.		0959	...	1154	...	...	...	1354	...	...	...	1554	...	...	...	1754	...	...	...	1953	...	...	...
620	**Glasgow** Central **220** a.		1025	...	1215	...	...	...	1415	...	...	...	1615	...	...	...	1811	...	...	...	2015	...	...	...

	Ⓐ	Ⓐ	Ⓐ	Ⓐ	Ⓐ	Ⓐ	Ⓐ	Ⓐ	Ⓐ	Ⓐ	Ⓐ	⑥	⑥	⑥	⑥	⑥	⑥	⑥	⑥	⑥	⑥	⑥	⑥	⑥
																				G		E		
Plymouth **120** d.	1225	...	1325	...	1425	...	1525	...	1625	...	1725		...	...	...	...	...	...	...	...	0525	...	0625	...
Bristol Temple Meads **120** d.	1430	...	1530	...	1630	...	1730	...	1830	...	1930		...	...	...	...	...	...	0615	...	0730	...	0830	...
Southampton Central **119** d.	|	1346	|	...	|	1546	|	...	|	1746	|		...	...	...	...	...	...	|	...	|	0653	|	0747
Reading **119** d.	|	1445	|	1545	|	1645	|	1745	|	1845	|		...	...	...	...	...	...	|	0645	|	0747	|	0845
Birmingham New Street **123** d.	1603	1630	1703	1730	1803	1830	1903	1930	2003	2030	2103		...	...	0558	0630	0703	0730	0803	0830	0903	0930	1003	1030
Tamworth **123** d.	1620	|	|	|	1819	|	|	|	2019	|	2119		...	...	0614	0646	0719	0746	0819	|	|	|	1019	|
Burton on Trent **123** d.	|	|	1726	|	|	|	1929	|	|	|	2129		...	...	0625	0656	0731	0756	0829	|	0928	|	|	|
Derby **123 170** d.	1643	1711**b**	1742	1816**a**	1844**b**	1909**c**	1943	2009**c**	2043	2119**a**	2146**b**		...	0556	0638	0713**c**	0744	0813**b**	0844	0916**a**	0944**b**	1016**a**	1044**b**	1116**a**
Chesterfield **170** d.	1704	|	1803	|	1903	1928	2004	|	2104	2138	2208		...	0631	0657	0732	0803	0832	0903	|	1003	|	1103	|
Sheffield **170** d.	1721	1747**b**	1821	1847	1926**d**	1956**g**	2021	2053**a**	2121	2154	2230**b**		...	0649**b**	0712	0754**d**	0822**b**	0847	0921**c**	0947	1021**c**	1047	1121**c**	1147
Doncaster **180** d.	|	|	|	1918	|	2018	|	2121	|	2231	|		...	0719	|	0825	|	0924	|	1020	|	1119	|	1219
Wakefield Westgate **180** d.	1749	1819	1850	|	1951	|	2048	|	2150	|	2301		...	|	0740	|	0847	|	0947	|	1047	|	1147	|
Leeds **190 180** d.	1808**b**	1838**c**	1908**b**	|	2008	|	2101	|	2203	|	2315		...	|	0757	|	0908**d**	|	1008**d**	|	1108**d**	|	1208**d**	|
York **190 180** a.	1831	1901	1930	1939	2030	2038	...	2141	...	2251	...		...	0743	0819	0847	0930	0945	1030	1040	1130	1139	1230	1239
York **180** d.	1833	1905	1933	1945	2032	2048	...	2146	...	...	...		...	0748	0829	0850	0932	0948	1032	1048	1132	1149	1232	1248
Darlington **180** d.	1902	1932	2003	2012	2059	2115	...	2213	...	...	...		...	0815	0857	0917	1000	1018	1100	1116	1159	1216	1300	1315
Durham **180** d.	1920	1949	2021	2029	2116	2132	...	2230	...	...	...		...	0832	0914	0934	1017	1035	1117	1133	1216	1233	1317	1332
Newcastle **180** a.	1933	2001	2034	2042	2128	2144	...	2247	...	...	...		...	0845	0927	0946	1029	1047	1129	1145	1228	1246	1329	1345
Newcastle **180** d.	1936	2003	2036	...	2135	...	...	...	...	...	..		0738	...	0935	...	1035	...	1133	...	1236	...	1335	...
Alnmouth **180** a.	2001	2027	|	...	2159	...	...	...	...	..	....		|	...	0959	...	|	...	|	...	|	...	1359	...
Berwick upon Tweed **180** a.	2025	|	2125	...	|	...	...	...	...	....	...		0823	...	1021	...	|	...	1218	...	|	...	1421	...
Edinburgh Waverley **180 220** a.	2108	2128	2213	...	2302	...	...	...	...	...	...		0907	...	1103	...	1205	...	1301	...	1405	...	1503	...
Motherwell **220** a.	2207	...	...	...	...	...	...	...	...	...	...		0956	...	1154	...	...	...	1354	...	...	...	1554	...
Glasgow Central **220** a.	2224	...	...	...	...	...	...	...	...	...	...		1015	...	1215	...	...	...	1415	...	...	...	1615	...

	⑥	⑥	⑥	⑥	⑥	⑥	⑥	⑥	⑥	⑥	⑥	⑥	⑥	⑥	⑥	⑥	⑥	⑥	⑥	⑥	⑥	⑦	⑦	⑦
			B		C		B		D															
Plymouth **120** d.	0725	...	0825	...	0925	...	1025	...	1125	...	1225	...	1325	...	1425	...	1525	...	1625	...	1725		...	...
Bristol Temple Meads **120** d.	0930	...	1030	...	1130	...	1230	...	1330	...	1430	...	1530	...	1630	...	1730	...	1830	...	1930		...	...
Southampton Central **119** d.	|	...	|	0947	|	...	|	1147	|	...	|	1347	|	...	|	1547	|	...	|	1747	|		...	...
Reading **119** d.	|	0945	|	1045	|	1145	|	1245	|	1345	|	1445	|	1545	|	1645	|	1745	|	1845	|		...	...
Birmingham New Street **123** d.	1103	1130	1203	1230	1303	1330	1403	1430	1503	1530	1603	1630	1703	1730	1803	1830	1903	1930	2003	2030	2103		...	...
Tamworth **123** d.	|	|	1219	|	|	|	1419	|	|	|	1619	|	|	|	1819	|	|	|	2019	|	2119		...	...
Burton on Trent **123** d.	1128	|	|	|	1327	|	|	|	1527	|	|	1654	1726	|	|	|	1927	|	|	|	2130		...	...
Derby **123 170** d.	1144**b**	1216**a**	1244**b**	1316**a**	1344**b**	1416**a**	1444**b**	1516**a**	1544**c**	1616**a**	1643	1716**a**	1744**b**	1816**a**	1844**c**	1916**a**	1943**c**	2016**a**	2044**c**	2127	2146		...	...
Chesterfield **170** d.	1203	|	1303	|	1403	|	1503	|	1603	|	1704	|	1803	|	1903	1935	2004	2035	2105	2147	2208		...	...
Sheffield **170** d.	1221**c**	1247	1321**c**	1347	1421	1447	1521**c**	1547	1621	1647	1721**c**	1747	1821**c**	1847	1921**c**	1956**d**	2023	2053**c**	2121	2203**c**	2230**d**		...	...
Doncaster **180** d.	|	1319	|	1419	|	1520	|	1619	|	1720**c**	|	|	|	1920	|	2022	|	2124	|	2226	2254		...	...
Wakefield Westgate **180** d.	1247	|	1347	|	1447	|	1547	|	1647	|	1748	1815	1847	|	1951	|	2051	|	2148	|	2312		...	...
Leeds **190 180** d.	1308**d**	|	1408**d**	|	1508**d**	|	1608**d**	|	1708**d**	|	1808**d**	1838**a**	1908**d**	|	2008**c**	|	2119**g**	|	2201	|	2325		...	0920
York **190 180** a.	1330	1339	1430	1439	1530	1540	1630	1639	1729	1740	1830	1901	1930	1940	2030	2042	2159	2144	...	2246	...		...	0942
York **180** d.	1332	1346	1432	1448	1532	1546	1632	1648	1730	1745	1832	1905	1936	1945	2032	2048	...	2148	...	...	...		...	0944
Darlington **180** d.	1400	1417	1500	1515	1600	1616	1700	1715	1758	1812	1902	1933	2005	2012	2059	2115	...	2215	...	...	...		...	1011
Durham **180** d.	1417	1434	1517	1532	1617	1633	1717	1732	1814	1829	1919	1950	2022	2029	2116	2133	...	2232	...	...	...		...	1028
Newcastle **180** a.	1429	1446	1529	1544	1629	[illegible]	1729	1745	1830	1841	1932	2002	2035	2042	2128	2147	...	2247	...	...	...		...	1040
Newcastle **180** d.	1433	...	1535	...	1632		[illegible]	...	1837	...	1935	...	2036	...	2132	...	...	...	...	...	...		0945	1042
Alnmouth **180** a.	|	...	1559	...	1659			...	|	...	2000	...	|	...	2156	...	...	...	...	...	...		1012	|
Berwick upon Tweed **180** a.	|	...	1621	...	|	...			1919	...	2024	...	2122	...	|	...	...	...	...	...	...		|	1124
Edinburgh Waverley **180 220** a.	1602	...	1703	...	1803	...			2005	...	2107	...	2209	...	2257	...	...	...	...	...	...		1112	1206
Motherwell **220** a.	...	...	1754	...	...	...	19[illegible]		...	...	2155	...	...	...	...	...	...	...	...	...	...		...	1259
Glasgow Central **220** a.	...	...	1811	...	...	...	201[illegible]		...	...	2220	...	...	...	...	...	...	...	...	...	...		...	1319

	⑦	⑦	⑦	⑦	⑦	⑦		⑦	⑦	⑦	⑦	⑦	⑦	⑦	⑦	⑦	⑦	⑦	⑦	⑦	⑦	⑦	⑦	⑦
								C			G	B											B	
Plymouth **120** d.	...	...	...	...	...	...	...	0925	...	1025	...	1125	...	1225	...	1325	...	1425	...	1524	...	1625	1725	1825
Bristol Temple Meads **120** d.	...	...	...	0915	1030	...	...	1130	...	1230	...	1330	...	1430	...	1530	...	1630	...	1730	...	1830	1930	2030
Southampton Central **119** d.	...	...	...	|	|	...	...	|	...	|	...	|	...	|	...	|	...	|	...	|	...	|	|	|
Reading **119** d.	...	...	...	|	|	...	...	|	...	|	1254	|	1341	|	1441	|	1541	|	1641	|	1741	|	|	|
Birmingham New Street **123** d.	...	0903	1003	1103	1203	1230	...	1303	1330	1403	1430	1503	1530	1603	1630	1703	1730	1803	1830	1903	1930	2003	2103	2203
Tamworth **123** d.	...	0919	1018	|	1219	|	...	|	|	1419	|	|	|	1619	|	|	|	1819	|	|	|	2019	2119	2219
Burton on Trent **123** d.	...	0928	1029	1125	|	|	...	1326	|	|	|	1525	|	|	|	1728	|	|	|	1926	|	|	2129	|
Derby **123 170** d.	...	0944	1044**c**	1144**d**	1244**b**	1311**a**	...	1344**d**	1411**a**	1444**b**	1511**a**	1544**d**	1611**a**	1644**b**	1712**a**	1743	1812**a**	1843**c**	1906	1942	2009**d**	2044**b**	2144	2242
Chesterfield **170** d.	...	1003	1103	1203	1303	1330	...	1403	1430	1503	|	1603	|	1703	|	1804	|	1905	|	2003	|	2103	2203	2303
Sheffield **170** d.	0921	1021**b**	1121**c**	1221	1321	1351**d**	...	1421**c**	1451**b**	1521**c**	1551**c**	1621	1651	1721**c**	1752	1821	1852**d**	1921	1952**a**	2021	2052**a**	2121**b**	2221	2319
Doncaster **180** d.	|	|	|	|	|	1417**b**	...	|	1522**a**	|	1618	|	1719**b**	|	1817	|	1920**d**	|	2018	|	2123	|	|	|
Wakefield Westgate **180** d.	0946	1046	1146	1246	1347	|	...	1446	|	1546	|	1646	|	1745	1835	1850	|	1951	|	2053	|	2148	2244	|
Leeds **190 180** d.	1008**b**	1105**b**	1205**c**	1305**b**	1405**c**	|	...	1505**b**	|	1605	|	1705**d**	|	1805	1859**d**	1908**b**	|	2008**c**	|	2108	|	2202	2259	0008
York **190 180** a.	1030	1127	1227	1327	1427	1437	...	1527	1543	1627	1638	1727	1740	1827	1921	1930	1940	2030	2039	2131	2143	...	...	...
York **180** d.	1032	1129	1229	1329	1429	1448	...	1529	1545	1629	1645	1729	1743	1829	1923	1932	1945	2032	2048	...	2149	...	...	...
Darlington **180** d.	1059	1156	1256	1358	1457	1515	...	1556	1612	1656	1712	1756	1811	1856	1950	2001	2013	2101	2115	...	2226	...	...	...
Durham **180** d.	1116	1213	1313	1415	1514	1532	...	1613	1629	1713	1730	1813	1828	1913	2007	2018	2030	2118	2133	...	2243	...	...	...
Newcastle **180** a.	1128	1225	1325	1427	1526	1544	...	1625	1642	1725	1744	1825	1841	1925	2019	2031	2042	2131	2145	...	2312	...	...	...
Newcastle **180** d.	1131	1230	1328	1431	1528	...	...	1628	...	1728	...	1828	...	1932	...	2034	2056	2134	...	...	...	...	...	...
Alnmouth **180** a.	|	|	1352	|	1553	...	...	1652	...	1755	...	|	...	1956	...	|	|	2159	...	...	...	...	...	...
Berwick upon Tweed **180** a.	1216	|	1413	|	1612	...	...	|	...	1817	...	1910	...	2018	...	2122	|	|	...	...	...	...	...	...
Edinburgh Waverley **180 220** a.	1258	1401	1457	1602	1655	...	...	1758	...	1858	...	1957	...	2100	...	2210	2218	2303	...	...	...	...	...	...
Motherwell **220** a.	1354	...	1555	...	1752	...	...	...	...	2002	...	...	...	2155	...	...	...	...	...	...	...	...	...	...
Glasgow Central **220** a.	1414	...	1612	...	1813	...	...	...	...	2019	...	...	...	2212	...	...	...	...	...	...	...	...	...	...

A – From Winchester (Table **119**).
B – From Penzance (Tables **117**/**120**).
C – To Aberdeen (Table **222**).
D – To Dundee (Table **222**).
E – From Bournemouth (Table **119**).
G – From Guildford (Table **134**).
H – From Bath Spa (Table **120**).
J – From Paignton (Table **120**).
a – Arrives 10–12 minutes earlier.
b – Arrives 5–6 minutes earlier.
c – Arrives 4 minutes earlier.
d – Arrives 7–9 minutes earlier.
g – Arrives 15–16 minutes earlier.

① – Mondays ② – Tuesdays ③ – Wednesdays ④ – Thursdays ⑤ – Fridays ⑥ – Saturdays ⑦ – Sundays Ⓑ – Not Saturdays 31

Ⓐ (Mondays to Fridays / Saturdays) — first block

Station	Times
Glasgow Central 220 d. (Ⓐ)	0601 … 0748 … 0900 … … 1100
Motherwell 220 d.	0616 … 0804 … 0915 … … 1115
Edinburgh Waverley 180 220 d.	0606 … 0700 0707 … 0810 … 0908 … 1010 … 1106 … 1208
Berwick upon Tweed 180 d.	0650 … 0741 … 0851 … 0953 … 1051 … 1151 … 1250
Alnmouth 180 d.	0711 … 0801 … … 1212
Newcastle 180 a.	0738 … 0830 0836 … 0940 … 1037 … 1136 … 1238 … 1334
Newcastle 180 d.	0625 0645 0725 0740 … 0835 0841 0935 0942 1035 1042 1135 1144 1234 1241 1335 1343 1436
Durham 180 d.	0638 0657 0738 0754 … 0848 0855 0949 0955 1048 1055 1149 1156 1247 1254 1349 1355 1448
Darlington 180 d.	0656 0715 0755 0812 … 0906 0913 1007 1013 1106 1112 1207 1214 1305 1313 1407 1413 1506
York 180 a.	0722 0741 0823 0839 … 0932 0940 1033 1040 1133 1139 1233 1239 1331 1339 1433 1439 1532
York 190 180 d.	0640 0727 0743 0826 0845 … 0935 0944 1035 1045 1135 1145 1235 1245 1335 1345 1435 1445 1535
Leeds 190 180 d.	0600 0616 0705 … 0811 … 0911 … 1011 … 1111 … 1211 … 1311 … 1411 … 1511
Wakefield Westgate 180 d.	0612 0628 0719 … 0823 … 0923 … 1023 … 1123 … 1223 … 1323 … 1423 … 1523
Doncaster 180 d.	0646 … 0756b … 0852 … 0959 … 1100 … 1159 … 1259 … 1359 … 1500 … 1559
Sheffield 170 d.	0601 0652e 0718c 0753 0821 0854 0924d 0954 1024 1054 1124 1155 1224a 1255a 1324a 1355a 1424a 1455 1524 1555 1624
Chesterfield 170 d.	0626 0706 0730 0806 0833 0907 1008 1108 1207 1307 1407 1507 1607
Derby 123 170 d.	0610 0648a 0727 0750 0828 0853 0928a 0953 1030 1053 1130 1153 1228a 1253 1328 1353 1428a 1453 1528a 1553 1628a 1653
Burton on Trent 123 d.	0620 0658 0738 0800 0838 0938
Tamworth 123 d.	0631 0709 0750 0811 0850 … 1050 … 1246 … 1447 … 1647
Birmingham New Street 123 a.	0652 0727 0808 0827 0910 0927 1008 1027 1109 … 1127 1207 1227 1304 1327 1408 1427 1508 1527 1602 1628 1708 1728
Reading 119 a.	0908 1010 1109 1208 1307 1409 1508 1611 1708 1808 1910
Southampton Central 119 a.	1117 1317 1517 1716
Bristol Temple Meads 120 a.	0839 0939 1043 1141 1242 1342 1443 1541 1643 1740 1841
Plymouth 120 a.	1042 1144 1247 1338 1443 1543 1645 1742 1849 1943 2040

Column notes above certain trains: **D**, **B**, **C B**, **G**, **B**.

Ⓐ (continued) / ⑥ (Saturdays) — second block

Station	Ⓐ times	⑥ times
Glasgow Central 220 d.	1300 … 1500 … 1700 1900	0606 0700
Motherwell 220 d.	1316 … 1516 … 1716 1916	
Edinburgh Waverley 180 220 d.	1307 1408 1508 … 1606 1707 … 1807 2003	0649 0741
Berwick upon Tweed 180 d.	1450 … 1752 … 1854 2048	
Alnmouth 180 d.	1413 … 1705 … 1914 2109	0710 0801
Newcastle 180 a.	1439 1534 1633 … 1733 1838 … 1940 2135	0737 0830
Newcastle 180 d.	1442 1505 1541 1635 1641 … 1732 1741 1835 1843 1935 1942 2136	0623 0645 0735 0741 0835
Durham 180 d.	1456 1518 1554 1648 1654 … 1748 1754 1848 1855 1950 1955 2150	0638 0657 0747 0755 0848
Darlington 180 d.	1514 1535 1613 1706 1712 … 1806 1813 1907 1913 2007 2013 2209	0655 0715 0805 0813 0906
York 180 a.	1541 1601 1639 1732 1739 … 1833 1840 1933 1939 2032 2040 2235	0721 0741 0831 0840 0932
York 190 180 d.	1545 1605 1645 1735 1745 … 1835 1845 1936 1945 2036 2045	0620 0727 0745 0835 0845 0935
Leeds 190 180 d.	1611 1640c 1711 … 1811 … 1911 … 2011 … 2111	0600 0616 0711e … 0811 … 0911
Wakefield Westgate 180 d.	1623 1652 1723 … 1823 … 1923 … 2024 … 2123	0612 0629 0723 … 0824 … 0923
Doncaster 180 d.	1759 … 1859 … 2000 … 2102	0647 … 0751 … 0859 … 0959
Sheffield 170 d.	1655a 1724 1758d 1824a 1858d … 1924a 1958d 2024 2058b 2129 2201c	0650c 0718 0756b 0820 0854 0924a 0954 1024a
Chesterfield 170 d.	1708 1810 1911 … 2010 2110 2141 2225	0704 0730 0808 0832 0907 1008
Derby 123 170 d.	1729 1753 1829 1853 1930 … 1954 2029 2054 2129 2202a 2245	0610 0648 0726 0751a 0828 0853 0931d 0953 1029 1053
Burton on Trent 123 d.	1740 … 1941 … 2140 2256	0620 0658 0737 0800 0838 0941
Tamworth 123 d.	1848 … 2047 2150 2307	0631 0709 0748 0812 0849 1049
Birmingham New Street 123 a.	1806 1827 1908 1927 2007 … 2027 2107 2129 2209 2251 2326	0650 0728 0808 0827 0908 0927 1006 1027 1108 1127
Reading 119 a.	2009 2107 … 2216	0909 1008 1110 1206 1309
Southampton Central 119 a.	2320	1117 1317
Bristol Temple Meads 120 a.	1942 2042 2136 … 2243 2339	0838 0939 1042 1139 1242
Plymouth 120 a.	2146 2245 2344	1039 1151 1240 1339 1445

---

⑥ (Saturdays continued) — third block

Column notes above certain trains: **D**, **B**, **C B**, **G**, **B**.

Station	Times
Glasgow Central 220 d.	0601 … 0748 … 0900 … … 1100 … … 1300 … 1500 … 1700
Motherwell 220 d.	0617 … 0805 … 0915 … … 1115 … 1316 … 1516 … 1716
Edinburgh Waverley 180 220 d.	0707 0806 0908 1005 1108 … 1206 1309 1405 1508 1605 1708 1808
Berwick upon Tweed 180 d.	0850 0953 1047 … 1153 … 1247 … 1447 … 1754 1853
Alnmouth 180 d.	0912 … 1213 … 1412 … 1705 … 1914
Newcastle 180 a.	0834 0939 1037 1135 1239 … 1332 1438 1535 1633 1733 1837 1940
Newcastle 180 d.	0843 0935 0942 1035 1044 1135 1142 1235 1244 1335 … 1344 1435 1444 1505 1544 1635 1644 1732 1744 1836 1844 1935 1945
Durham 180 d.	0855 0949 0956 1048 1056 1149 1155 1248 1256 1348 1356 1448 1456 1518 1556 1648 1656 1748 1756 1856 1907 1950 1957
Darlington 180 d.	0914 1007 1014 1106 1114 1206 1212 1306 1314 1406 1414 1506 1514 1535 1614 1705 1714 1806 1814 1907 1914 2007 2015
York 180 a.	0940 1033 1041 1131 1140 1232 1239 1331 1341 1432 1440 1531 1541 1606 1640 1732 1740 1831 1840 1933 1940 2033 2041
York 190 180 d.	0945 1035 1045 1135 1145 1235 1245 1335 1345 1436 1445 1535 1545 1606 1645 1735 1745 1835 1845 1936 1945 2035 2045
Leeds 190 180 d.	1011a 1111 1211 1311 1411 1511 1611 1640c 1711 1811 1911 2011 2111
Wakefield Westgate 180 d.	1024 1123 1223 1323 1423 1523 1623 1658 1723 1823 1924 2023 2123
Doncaster 180 d.	1159 1259 1359 1500 1559 … 1759 1859 2000 2059
Sheffield 170 d.	1055a 1124 1155a 1224a 1255 1324a 1355a 1424 1455a 1524 … 1555a 1624 1655a 1724a 1755a 1824 1858d 1924 1955a 2024 2055 2125 2155
Chesterfield 170 d.	1107 1209 1307 1408 1507 … 1607 1807 1910 2007 2107 2137 2207
Derby 123 170 d.	1130b 1153 1230 1328a 1353 1430 1453 1528a 1553 … 1628a 1653 1728a 1753 1829b 1853 1929 1954 2028a 2053 2128a 2156 2226
Burton on Trent 123 d.	1141 … 1338 … 1538 … 1738 … 1939 … 2138 2237
Tamworth 123 d.	1249 … 1449 … 1648 … 1847 … 2046 2149 2247
Birmingham New Street 123 a.	1208 1227 1308 1327 1402 1426 1508 1527 1602 1627 1707 1727 1807 1827 1907 1927 2006 2027 2104 2125 2206 2244 2306
Reading 119 a.	1408 1508 1609 1710 1810 1910 2008 2108 2214
Southampton Central 119 a.	1517 … 1717 … 2320
Bristol Temple Meads 120 a.	1338 1441 1538 1643 1739 1843 1939 2042 2133 2241
Plymouth 120 a.	1541 1643 1739 1851 1942 2043 2138 2250 2356

---

⑦ (Sundays) — fourth block

Column notes above certain trains: **B**, **B**, **C**, **G**.

Station	Times
Glasgow Central 220 d. (⑦)	1055 … 1202 … 1348 1455 … 1655 1900
Motherwell 220 d.	1114 … 1218 … 1403 1513 … 1713 1916
Edinburgh Waverley 180 220 d.	0908 1008 … 1104 1208 1308 1355 1408 1508 1608 1708 1806 2018
Berwick upon Tweed 180 d.	0951 … 1150 1249 … 1436 1449 … 1753 1852 2040
Alnmouth 180 d.	1107 1210 … 1411 … 1707 … 2104
Newcastle 180 a.	1035 1136 1236 1334 1437 1519 1535 1636 1736 1836 1938 2148
Newcastle 180 d.	0935 1039 1140 1240 1335 1340 1436 1441 1524 1540 1635 1640 1735 1740 1825 1840 1926 1941
Durham 180 d.	0947 1053 1152 1253 1347 1353 1448 1453 1536 1552 1647 1652 1747 1753 1837 1852 1939 1953
Darlington 180 d.	1005 1110 1210 1310 1406 1410 1506 1510 1554 1610 1705 1710 1806 1811 1855 1910 1956 2010
York 180 a.	1031 1138 1236 1336 1432 1436 1532 1537 1621 1637 1731 1738 1832 1839 1921 1936 2022 2037
York 190 180 d.	0933 1033 1141 1241 1341 1435 1441 1535 1541 1625 1641 1735 1741 1835 1841 1921 1941 2024 2041
Leeds 190 180 d.	0810 0900 1000 1100 1211b 1311d … 1411d … 1511d … 1611d … 1711d … 1811b 1911d 2011d 2111d
Wakefield Westgate 180 d.	0823 0911 1012 1112 1224 1324 … 1423 … 1523 … 1623 … 1723 … 1823 1923 2023 2123
Doncaster 180 d.	0932 1030 1130 … 1459 … 1559 … 1651 … 1759 … 1859 1954a … 2051a
Sheffield 170 d.	0854 0957 1057 1157a 1257 1357a 1422 1455b 1524 1555b 1624 1655b 1724c 1755a 1824 1855b 1924 2021b 2054a 2132 2154a
Chesterfield 170 d.	0907 1009 1109 1209 1309 1409 1432 1507 1607 1707 1807 1907 2007 2106 2132 2206
Derby 123 170 d.	0928 1033 1129 1229 1332 1429 1453 1526 1553 1627 1654 1727 1754 1826 1854 1927 1956a 2027 2054b 2126 2153 2226
Burton on Trent 123 d.	1140 … 1343 … 1537 … 1737 … 1938 … 2137 2203 2237
Tamworth 123 d.	1053 … 1248 … 1448 1646 … 1847 … 2046 2147 2214 2247
Birmingham New Street 123 a.	1018 1121 1204 1306 1409 1505 1526 1601 1626 1703 1726 1801 1826 1903 1928 2002 2027 2103 2126 2205 2231 2305
Reading 119 a.	1701 … 1810 … 1905 … 2008 … 2113 2206
Southampton Central 119 a.	
Bristol Temple Meads 120 a.	1151 1250 1331 1431 1534 1631 1731 1835 1932 2031 2130 2244 2333
Plymouth 120 a.	1352 1452 1537 1638 1742 1838 1943 2045 2141 2246 2346

A – To Winchester (Table **119**).	D – From Dundee (Table **222**).	H – To Paignton (Table **120**).	c – Arrives 9–10 minutes earlier.
B – To Penzance (Tables **117/120**).	E – To Bournemouth (Table **119**).		d – Arrives 7–8 minutes earlier.
C – From Aberdeen (Table **222**).	G – To Guildford (Table **134**).	b – Arrives 5–6 minutes earlier.	e – Arrives 12 minutes earlier.

BIRMINGHAM - WORCESTER - HEREFORD

km		Ⓐ	Ⓐ	Ⓐ	Ⓐ		Ⓐ	Ⓐ	Ⓐ	Ⓐ	Ⓐ	Ⓐ	Ⓐ	Ⓐ	Ⓐ	Ⓐ	Ⓐ	⑥	⑥		⑥	⑥	⑥	⑥	⑥
0	**Birmingham** New St. d.	0659	0719	0759	0849		1549	1619	1649	1719	1749	1819	1919	1959	2059	2200	2300	0649	0749		1749	1849	1919	2059	2210
21	Bromsgrove d.	0721	0744	0821	0910		1610	1640	1710	1740	1809	1842	1942	2019	2120	2220	2320	0710	0810		1810	1910	1940	2120	|
32	Droitwich Spa d.	0730	0754	0830	0920	and	1620	1652	1720	1752	1819	1857	1952	2029	2130	2234	2330	0720	0820	and	1820	1920	1951	2130	2235
40	**Worcester** Shrub Hill . d.	|	0807	|	|	hourly	|	1706c	1732a	1804a	1832a	1910	2012c	2036	|	2247	2339	|	|	hourly	1831	1935a	|	2147c	2243
41	**Worcester** Foregate St d.	0742	0811	0840	0932	until	1630	1709	1735	1807	1835	*1939*	2015	*2046*	2141	*2310*	...	0732	0832	until	1835	1938	2001	2150	...
54	Great Malvern 130 d.	0800a	0822	0853	0945		1643	1722	1747	1819	1849	*1952*	2027	*2059*	2154	*2323*	...	0745	0845		1848	1950	2025c	2202	...
65	Ledbury 130 d.	0813	...	0907	0959		1659	...	1800	1831	1904	*2008*	2041	*2115*	2209	...	...	0759	0859		1901	...	2039	2215	...
87	**Hereford** 130 a.	0833	...	0927	1019		1719	...	1821	1851	1923	*2027*	2101	*2133*	2228	...	...	0819	0919		1919	...	2102	2235	...

	⑦	⑦	⑦	⑦	⑦	⑦	⑦	⑦	⑦
Birmingham New St d.	1000	1200	1400	1558	1758	1900	2000	2100	2205
Bromsgrove d.	1020	1220	1420	1618	1818	1920	2020	2120	2225
Droitwich Spa d.	1030	1232	1430	1628	1828	1930	2030	2130	2236
Worcester Shrub Hill d.	1051b	1247c	1451b	1639	1839	1942a	2058b	2141a	2251a
Worcester Foregate St d.	1054	1250	1454	1642	1842	1944	2100	2144	2254
Great Malvern 130 d.	1106	1302	1506	1703c	1859a	*2033*	*2139*	2156	2307
Ledbury 130 d.	1118	1315	1518	1716	1912	*2048*	...	2209	...
Hereford 130 a.	1134	1332	1534	1734	1930	*2104*	...	2227	...

	Ⓐ	Ⓐ	Ⓐ	Ⓐ	Ⓐ	Ⓐ	Ⓐ	Ⓐ	Ⓐ		Ⓐ	Ⓐ
Hereford 130 d.	*0447*	*0528*	...	...	0709	0732	...	0845	0939		1739	1848
Ledbury 130 d.	|	*0545*	...	...	0725	0750	...	0906	0958		1758	1904
Great Malvern 130 d.	0548	*0559*	0647	0702	0737	0807a	0840	0917	1010	and	1810	1915
Worcester F'gate St d.	0602	*0614*	0658	0716	0749	0824a	0852	0930	1024	hourly	1824	1928
Worcester Shrub H d.	|	0626	0706a	0723a	0755a	|	|	0936	|	until	|	|
Droitwich Spa d.	0611	0633	0713	0733	0805	0833	0901	0943	1033		1833	1937
Bromsgrove d.	0621	0643	0723	|	|	0843	0911	0953	1043		1842	1947
Birmingham N St a.	0649	0709	0749	0809	0839	0909	0939	1019	1109		1909	2018

	Ⓐ	Ⓐ	Ⓐ	Ⓐ	⑥	⑥	⑥	⑥		⑥	⑥	⑥	⑥	⑥	⑥
Hereford 130 d.	1950	2056	2129	2259	...	...	*0617*	0739		1739	1911	1959	*2020*	*2135*	2249
Ledbury 130 d.	2009	2114	2145	2315	...	...	*0634*	0758		1758	1928	2015	*2040*	*2151*	2305
Great Malvern 130 d.	2020	2125	2156	2327	...	0622	0717	0810	and	1810	1939	2027	2130	*2203*	2317
Worcester Foregate St d.	2031	2137	2210	2340	...	0634	0728	0824	hourly	1824	1951	2040	2142	*2215*	2328
Worcester Shrub Hill d.	2037	2139	|	2347	0607	|	0735	|	until	|	|	|	2154c	2247	2336
Droitwich Spa d.	2045	...	2219	...	0615	0643	0743	0833		1833	2000	2049	2202	2255	...
Bromsgrove d.	2055	...	2229	...	|	0653	0753	0843		1843	|	2059	|	|	...
Birmingham New St a.	2120	...	2254	...	0648	0718	0818	0909		1909	2055n	2120	2255n	2336n	...

	⑦	⑦	⑦	⑦	⑦	⑦	⑦	⑦	⑦	⑦
Hereford 130 d.	...	1005	1202	1405	1609	*1634*	1809	*1830*	2005	2239
Ledbury 130 d.	...	1022	1218	1422	1625	*1652*	1825	*1848*	2022	2258
Great Malvern 130 d.	...	1034	1230	1434	1637	*1705*	1837	*1911*	2037a	2310
Worcester Foregate St d.	0901	1046	1242	1446	1649	*1724*	1849	1949	2049	2323
Worcester Shrub Hill d.	0905	1058c	1255c	1455c	1655a	1757	1855a	1955a	2055a	2327
Droitwich Spa d.	0914	1106	1303	1503	1703	1805	1903	2003	2103	...
Bromsgrove d.	0924	1115	1313	1513	1713	1815	1913	2013	2113	...
Birmingham New St a.	0948	1138	1338	1538	1738	1838	1938	2038	2138	...

a – Arrives 4–5 minutes earlier. b – Arrives 14 minutes earlier. c – Arrives 7–10 minutes earlier. n – Birmingham Snow Hill.

BIRMINGHAM - KIDDERMINSTER - WORCESTER

km		Ⓐ	⑥	Ⓐ	⑥	Ⓐ	⑥	ⒶA	Ⓐ	⑥		⚒	⚒	⚒	⚒	⚒	⚒	⚒	⚒	⚒	⚒	⚒	⚒	⑥	Ⓐ	⚒
0	**Birmingham** Moor St d.	0604	0633	0649	0701	0719	0749	0749	0834	0845	...	0909	0939	1009	1039	1109	1139	1209	1239	1309	1339	1409	1439	1509	1509	1539
1	**Birmingham** Snow Hill. d.	0607	0637	0653	0705	0723	0753	0753	0843	0853	...	0913	0943	1013	1043	1113	1143	1213	1243	1313	1343	1413	1443	1513	1513	1543
20	Stourbridge Junction d.	0636	0706	0722	0734	0752	0819	0822	0909	0922	...	0939	1009	1039	1109	1139	1209	1239	1309	1339	1409	1439	1509	1539	1539	1608
31	Kidderminster △ d.	0648	0717	0734	0745	0804	0831	0834	0920	0933	...	0947	1018	1047	1118	1147	1218	1247	1318	1347	1418	1447	1518	1547	1552	1618
45	Droitwich Spa d.	0658	0731	0747	0756	0817	0842	0847	0930	0944	...	1000	1030	1100	1130	1200	1230	1300	1330	1400	1430	1500	1530	1600	1606	1630
54	**Worcester** Shrub Hill. a.	|	0740	|	0805	0824	|	|	0940	0952	...	|	1038r	|	1138	|	1238t	|	1338r	1408t	1440	1510t	1538r	|	1614	|
54	**Worcester** Foregate St. a.	0709	...	0757	0813	0833	0851	0858	...	...	...	1009	1039t	1109	...	1209	1239r	1309	1340t	1409r	1446	1509r	1539t	1609	1625	1642

	⚒	⑥	Ⓐ	⑥	Ⓐ	Ⓐ	⑥	Ⓐ	⑥A	ⒶA	⑥	⚒	⑥	ⒶA	⑥	Ⓐ	⑥	Ⓐ	⚒	⑦	⑦A	⑦A	⑦A	⑦A	⑦A	⑦A
Birmingham Moor St d.	1609	1639	1639	1709	1709	1732	1739	1749	1819	1839	1849	1924	1953	1954	2052	2053	2152	2154	2257	0924	1015	1115	1215	1315	1415	1515
Birmingham Snow Hill d.	1613	1643	1643	1713	1713	1736	1743	1753	1823	1843	1853	1928	1956	1958	2056	2058	2156	2158	2301	0928	1022	1122	1222	1322	1422	1522
Stourbridge Junction d.	1639	1709	1710	1741	1739	1802	1809	1820	1849	1909	1923	1957	2025	2027	2125	2127	2225	2227	2330	0954	1047	1147	1247	1347	1447	1547
Kidderminster △ d.	1647	1718	1723	1751	1752	1814	1822	1832	1900	1920	1934	2009	2036	2039	2136	2139	2236	2239	2342	1003	1059	1159	1259	1357	1459	1557
Droitwich Spa d.	1700	1730	1737	1804	1804	1828	1837	1845	1914	1932	1946	2022	2048	2050	2148	2152	2250	2252	2354	1015	1111	1211	1311	1408	1511	1608
Worcester Shrub Hill a.	|	|	|	1812	1812	|	|	|	|	|	1954	2031r	2056	2059	2156	2159	2257	2259	0005	1022	1119	1219	|	|	|	|
Worcester Foregate St a.	1709	1739	1746	*1822*	...	1839	1846	1854	1923	1943	...	2031t	2101	...	...	2208	2304	2310	...	1032	1135	...	1320	1417	1520	1617

	⑦A	⑦	⑦A	⑦A	⑦A	⑦A	⑦	⑦
Birmingham Moor St d.	1615	1702	1715	1815	1915	2015	2143	2252
Birmingham Snow Hill d.	1622	1706	1722	1822	1922	2022	2146	2256
Stourbridge Junction d.	1647	1724	1747	1847	1947	2047	2210	2322
Kidderminster △ d.	1657	1733	1757	1859	1957	2057	2220	2331
Droitwich Spa d.	1708	1745	1809	1911	2009	2109	2231	2343
Worcester Shrub Hill a.	|	1752	|	1919	2017	2117	2239	2351
Worcester Foregate St a.	1717	...	1819	...	...	2124	...	...

	Ⓐ	⑥	ⒶA	⑥	Ⓐ	Ⓐ	⑥	Ⓐ	Ⓐ	⑥	Ⓐ	⑥	Ⓐ
Worcester Foregate St d.	...	...	...	...	...	...	...	0714	...	0747	0802	...	0839
Worcester Shrub Hill d.	0530	0544	0612	0625	0635	0650	0701	|	0735	|	|	0815	0845
Droitwich Spa d.	0538	0552	0620	0633	0643	0703	0709	0723	0743	0756	0811	0823	0853
Kidderminster △ d.	0548	0605	0633	0646	0656	0716	0722	0736	0754	0806	0824	0836	0906
Stourbridge Junction d.	0556	0617	0649	0701	0708	0728	0735	0748	0807	0819	0835	0848	0918
Birmingham Snow Hill a.	0627	0647	0722	0732	0738	0759	0805	0815	0835	0845	0907	0915	0945
Birmingham Moor St a.	0638	0653	0728	0740	0743	0806	0810	0820	0840	0850	0911	0920	0950

	⑥A	Ⓐ	⑥	⑥	Ⓐ	⚒	⚒	⚒	⚒	⚒	⚒	⚒		⚒	⚒	⚒	⚒	Ⓐ	⑥	Ⓐ	⑥	Ⓐ	⚒A	⑥	Ⓐ	⑥	Ⓐ
Worcester Foregate St d.	0856	0903	0916	...	...	1016	...	1116t	1151	1216	1251r	...	...	1351	1416	...	1516r	1533	1547	1613	1614	1634	1647	...	1715	1747	1756
Worcester Shrub Hill d.	|	|	|	0948	0952	|	1052	1117r	|	|	1252t	1317	...	|	|	1452	1517t	1547	|	|	|	1640	|	1715	|	|	|
Droitwich Spa d.	0905	0912	0925	0956	1000	1025	1100	1125	1200	1225	1300	1325	...	1400	1425	1500	1525	1555	1556	1622	1623	1648	1655	1723	1725	1756	1805
Kidderminster △ d.	0916	0925	0938	1006	1010	1038	1110	1138	1210	1238	1310	1338	...	1410	1438	1510	1538	1606	1610	1635	1636	1701	1706	1736	1738	1806	1815
Stourbridge Junction d.	0927	0937	0948	1014	1018	1048	1118	1148	1218	1248	1318	1348	...	1418	1448	1518	1548	1618	1618	1648	1648	1712	1718	1748	1750	1818	1825
Birmingham Snow Hill a.	0956	1004	1015	1041	1045	1115	1145	1215	1245	1315	1345	1415	...	1445	1515	1545	1615	1645	1645	1718	1715	1739	1745	1815	1817	1845	1855
Birmingham Moor St a.	1001	1010	1020	1050	1050	1120	1150	1220	1250	1320	1350	1420	...	1450	1520	1550	1620	1650	1650	1725	1720	1745	1750	1820	1825	1858	1900

	⑥	Ⓐ	⑥	Ⓐ	⑥	Ⓐ	⑥	Ⓐ	⚒	Ⓐ	⑥	⑦A	⑦A	⑦A	⑦A	⑦A	⑦A	⑦A	⑦	⑦A	⑦A	⑦	⑦	⑦	⑦	⑦
Worcester Foregate St d.	1812	...	1846	1851	1946	1951	2051	...	2142r	2217	...	0920	1026	1118	1220	1326	1426	1528	1545	1626	1727	1826	...	...	2118	2223
Worcester Shrub Hill d.	1817	1837	|	|	|	|	|	2052	2154	2227	2247	0926	|	1126	1226	|	|	|	|	|	|	|	1938	2038	2125	2229
Droitwich Spa d.	1825	1845	1855	1900	1955	2000	2100	2100	2202	2235	2255	0935	1035	1135	1235	1335	1435	1537	1554	1635	1736	1835	1946	2046	2133	2237
Kidderminster △ d.	1837	1855	1910	1913	2010	2013	2113	2113	2213	2248	2305	0945	1045	1145	1245	1345	1445	1547	1604	1645	1746	1845	1956	2056	2144	2247
Stourbridge Junction d.	1850	1906	1925	1925	2025	2025	2125	2125	2225	2259	2318	0957	1057	1157	1257	1357	1457	1557	1617	1657	1759	1855	2007	2107	2153	2257
Birmingham Snow Hill a.	1916	1934	1955	1955	2055	2055	2155	2154	2255	2328	2336	1022	1122	1222	1322	1422	1522	1623	1636	1722	1824	1921	2033	2133	2219	2325
Birmingham Moor St a.	1920	...	2000	2000	2100	2100	2200	2200	2300	2337	2340	1030	1130	1230	1330	1430	1530	1630	1645	1730	1830	1925	2037	2137	2223	...

A – To/from Stratford upon Avon (Table **127**). r – ⑥ only. t – Ⓐ only. △ – **Severn Valley Railway** (🚂 Kidderminster - Bridgnorth: *26 km*). ✆ 01299 403816. www.svr.co.uk.

STRATFORD UPON AVON - BIRMINGHAM

km		Ⓐ	ⒶA	Ⓐ	Ⓐ	Ⓐ	Ⓐ	Ⓐ	and at	Ⓐ	Ⓐ	Ⓐ	ⒶA	Ⓐ	Ⓐ	ⒶA	Ⓐ	Ⓐ	Ⓐ	Ⓐ	Ⓐ	⑥	⑥
0	**Stratford upon Avon** d.	0626	0652	0719	0743	0826	0926	1003	the same	1603	1626	1727	1755	1827	1851	1903	1926	2026	2126	2233	2330	0700	0743
13	Henley in Arden d.	0641	0707	0735	0758	0841	0941	|	minutes	|	1641	1743	1807	1843	1907	|	1941	2041	2139	2246	|	0715	0758
40	**Birmingham** Moor St d.	0724	0749	0808	0839	0918	1018	1049	past each	1649	1719	1818	1839	1919	1935	1954	2018	2118	2218	2319	0006	0755	0838
41	**Birmingham** Snow Hill a.	0726	0751	0810	0841	0920	1020	1052	hour until	1652	1721	1821	1841	1922	1937	1956	2020	2120	2220	2321	0008	0757	0840

	⑥	⑥	and at	⑥	⑥A	⑥	⑥	⑥	⑥	⑥	⑥	⑥	⑥	⑦A	⑦A	⑦A	⑦A	⑦A	⑦A	⑦A	⑦A	⑦A	⑦A	⑦A
Stratford upon Avon d.	0826	0903	the same	1703	1726	1754	1813	1848	1926	2026	2126	2233	2330	0929	1029	1129	1229	1329	1429	1529	1629	1729	1829	1929
Henley in Arden d.	0841	|	minutes	|	1741	1808	1828	1903	1941	2041	2140	2247	|	0943	1043	1143	1243	1343	1443	1543	1643	1743	1843	1943
Birmingham Moor St d.	0918	0949	past each	1749	1819	1839	1909	1944	2018	2118	2218	2319	0008	1015	1115	1215	1315	1415	1515	1615	1715	1815	1915	2015
Birmingham Snow Hill a.	0920	0952	hour until	1752	1821	1843	1911	1946	2020	2120	2220	2322	0010	1017	1117	1217	1317	1417	1517	1617	1717	1817	1917	2017

	Ⓐ	Ⓐ	Ⓐ	ⒶA	Ⓐ	Ⓐ	Ⓐ	and at	Ⓐ	Ⓐ	Ⓐ	Ⓐ	Ⓐ	ⒶA	Ⓐ	Ⓐ	Ⓐ	Ⓐ	Ⓐ	Ⓐ	⑥	⑥	⑥
Birmingham Snow Hill d.	0553	0630	0640	0725	0828	0858	0928	the same	1458	1528	1628	1703	1728	1747	1758	1828	1928	2028	2128	2228	0725	0828	0858
Birmingham Moor St d.	0556	0633	0643	0728	0831	0901	0931	minutes	1501	1531	1631	1706	1731	1750	1801	1831	1931	2031	2131	2231	0728	0831	0901
Henley in Arden d.	|	0705	0720	0806	0906	|	1006	past each	|	1606	1707	1736	1807	1828	|	1907	2007	2107	2207	2307	0806	0906	|
Stratford upon Avon a.	0648	0720	0736	0823	0923	0949	1023	hour until	1541	1623	1724	1749	1824	1843	1859	1923	2023	2123	2223	2323	0821	0923	0949

	⑥	⑥A	⑥	⑥	and at	⑥	⑥	⑥	⑥A	⑥	⑥	⑥	⑥	⑥	⑦	⑦A	⑦A	⑦A	⑦A	⑦A	⑦A	⑦A	⑦A	⑦A
Birmingham Snow Hill d.	0928	0958	1028	1058	the same	1628	1658	1707	1747	1828	1928	2028	2128	2228	0927	1027	1127	1227	1327	1427	1527	1627	1727	1827
Birmingham Moor St d.	0931	1001	1031	1101	minutes	1631	1701	1710	1750	1831	1931	2031	2131	2231	0930	1030	1130	1230	1330	1430	1530	1630	1730	1830
Henley in Arden d.	1006	|	1106	|	past each	1706	|	1748	1828	1906	2007	2107	2207	2307	1001	1101	1201	1301	1401	1501	1601	1701	1801	1901
Stratford upon Avon a.	1023	1041	1123	1141	hour until	1723	1741	1803	1843	1923	2023	2123	2223	2323	1015	1115	1215	1315	1415	1515	1615	1715	1815	1915

A – To/from Worcester Shrub Hill or Worcester Foregate Street (Table **126**).

🚂 – THE SHAKESPEARE EXPRESS – (12) ✕ (1st class only) and 🍷 Birmingham Snow Hill - Stratford upon Avon and v.v. Runs ⑦ July 15 - Sept. 2, 2018 (subject to confirmation). National Rail tickets NOT valid.
From Birmingham Snow Hill 1000 and 1356 (Birmingham Moor Street 5 minutes later). From Stratford upon Avon at 1236 and 1613. Journey time: 59–68 minutes.
To book contact Vintage Trains Ltd. ✆ 0121 708 4960. www.shakespeareexpress.com.

LONDON - BIRMINGHAM

km			②–④	①	Ⓐ	Ⓐ	Ⓐ	Ⓐ	Ⓐ	Ⓐ		Ⓐ	Ⓐ	Ⓐ	Ⓐ	Ⓐ	Ⓐ	Ⓐ	Ⓐ	Ⓐ	Ⓐ	Ⓐ	Ⓐ	Ⓐ	Ⓐ	Ⓐ
0	**London** Marylebone ◇ d.		0005	0005	...	0605	0617	0711	0748	0814	...	0837	0910	0940	1010	1040	1110	1140	1210	1240	1310	1340	1410	1440	1510	1540
45	High Wycombe ◇ d.	Ⓐ	0036	0038	...	|	0701	|	0814	|	...	|	0936	|	1036	|	1135	|	1234	|	1334	|	1434	|	1535	|
88	Bicester North ◇ d.		0105	0108	0545	0647	0733	0754	0836	|	...	0926	|	1029	|	1132	|	1227	|	1327	|	1427	|	1529	|	1627
111	Banbury **119** ◇ d.		0122	0127	0604	0703	0749	0807	0850	0908	...	0940	1008	1043	1107	1146	1207	1240	1308	1340	1410	1440	1507	1542	1609	1640
143	Leamington Spa **119** d.		...	...	0625	0721	0808	0825	0908	0926	...	0958	1025	1101	1125	1204	1226	1258	1326	1358	1427	1458	1525	1559	1626	1658
146	Warwick d.		...	...	0630	0726	0813	0829	0912	0930	...	1003	|	1105	|	1209	|	1302	|	1402	|	1502	|	1603	|	1702
147	Warwick Parkway d.		...	...	0633	0729	...	0833	0916	0934	...	1007	1032	1109	1132	1213	1232	1306	1332	1406	1433	1506	1530	1607	1632	1706
169	Solihull a.		...	...	0649	0750	...	0844	0931	0945	...	1023	1044	1124	1144	1230	1244	1321	1344	1421	1444	1521	1544	1622	1643	1721
180	**Birmingham** Moor Street **126** a.		...	...	0659	0802	...	0853	0942	0954	...	1035	1053	1133	1156	1241	1256	1333	1356	1433	1456	1533	1556	1633	1653	1736
181	**Birmingham** Snow Hill **126** a.		...	...	0707	0810		0901	...	1002	...	...	1101	1142	...	1251	...	1341	...	1441	...	1541	...	1641	1701	1744

	Ⓐ	Ⓐ	Ⓐ	Ⓐ	Ⓐ	Ⓐ	Ⓐ	Ⓐ	Ⓐ	Ⓐ	Ⓐ	Ⓐ	Ⓐ	Ⓐ	Ⓐ	Ⓐ	Ⓐ	Ⓐ			⑥	⑥	⑥	⑥	⑥	⑥
London Marylebone ◇ d.	1615	1621	1647	1715	1746	1815	1847	1824	1915	1947	2010	2037	2110	2140	2043	2210	2237	2307	...		0020	...	0700	0810	0840	0910
High Wycombe ◇ d.	|	1648	|	|	|	|	|	1902	|	|	2035	|	2136	2204	2114	2235	2302	|	...	⑥	0051	0612	0723	0834	|	0934
Bicester North ◇ d.	|	1711	1734	|	1835	|	1937	1944	2002	2034	2059	2124	2159	2228	2143	2259	2327	2350	...		0120	0645	0750	0857	0926	|
Banbury **119** ◇ d.	1708	1724	1747	1809	1848	1909	1951	2006	2016	2047	2112	2139	2214	2241	2201	2313	2341	0003	...		0135	0703	0804	0910	0940	1007
Leamington Spa **119** d.	1726	1741	1804	1827	1905	1927	2009	2026	2035	2104	2130	2157	2231	2259	2220	2331	2359	0021	...		0156	0721	0823	0928	0958	1025
Warwick d.	|	|	1808	|	1909	|	2013	|	|	2108	|	2201	|	2303	2224	|	0003	0025	...		...	0725	|	0932	1002	|
Warwick Parkway d.	1732	1747	1812	1834	1913	1934	2017	2031	2043	2112	2136	2205	2238	2307	...	2337	0007	0029	...		...	0729	0829	0935	1006	1031
Solihull a.	1744	1802	1826	1849	1928	1950	2032	...	2058	2133	2148	2220	2250	2330	...	2348	0023	0040	...		...	0747	0846	0950	1021	1043
Birmingham Moor Street **126** a.	1754	1811	1838	1859	1938	2000	2041	...	2110	2143	2158	2230	2300	2339	...	0001	0036	0052	...		...	0800	0859	1001	1033	1055
Birmingham Snow Hill **126** a.	1757	1822	...	1902	1946	2004	2049	...	...	2151	2206	2238	2304	2347	...	...	...	...	...		...	...	0907	1009	1041	...
Stourbridge Junction **126** a.	1825	...	...	1926	...	2033	...	...	...	...	2236	...	2350	...	...	...	...	...	...		...	...	...	...	...	...
Kidderminster **126** a.	1844	...	...	1941	...	2048	...	...	...	...	2250	...	...	...	...	...	...	...	...		...	...	...	...	...	...

	⑥	⑥	⑥	⑥	⑥	⑥	⑥		⑥	⑥	⑥	⑥	⑥	⑥	⑥	⑥	⑥	⑥	⑥	⑥	⑥	⑥	⑥	⑥	⑥	⑥
London Marylebone ◇ d.	0940	1010	1040	1110	1140	1210	1240	...	1310	1340	1410	1440	1510	1540	1610	1640	1710	1740	1810	1840	1910	1940	2010	2040	2110	2210
High Wycombe ◇ d.	|	1034	|	1134	|	1234	|	...	1335	|	1434	|	1534	|	1634	|	1734	|	1834	|	1934	|	2034	|	2134	2234
Bicester North ◇ d.	1024	|	1128	|	1224	|	1324	...	|	1424	|	1524	|	1624	|	1724	|	1824	|	1924	|	2024	|	2124	2157	2257
Banbury **119** ◇ d.	1037	1107	1143	1210	1237	1307	1337	...	1409	1437	1507	1537	1609	1637	1707	1737	1809	1837	1907	1937	2009	2037	2107	2137	2210	2310
Leamington Spa **119** d.	1055	1125	1201	1227	1255	1325	1355	...	1427	1455	1525	1555	1626	1655	1725	1755	1826	1855	1926	1955	2027	2055	2125	2155	2228	2328
Warwick d.	1059	|	1205	|	1259	|	1359	...	|	1459	|	1559	|	1659	|	1759	|	1859	|	1959	|	2059	|	2159	2232	2332
Warwick Parkway d.	1103	1132	1209	1234	1303	1332	1403	...	1433	1503	1532	1603	1633	1703	1732	1803	1833	1903	1933	2003	2033	2103	2132	2203	2236	2337
Solihull a.	1120	1144	1224	1245	1320	1344	1420	...	1444	1520	1544	1620	1644	1720	1744	1820	1847	1918	1946	2018	2045	2118	2144	2218	2258	2354
Birmingham Moor Street **126** a.	1133	1156	1233	1256	1333	1356	1433	...	1456	1533	1556	1633	1656	1733	1756	1833	1858	1927	1958	2027	2057	2127	2157	2227	2306	0006
Birmingham Snow Hill **126** a.	1141	...	1241	...	1341	...	1441	...	...	1541	...	1641	...	1741	...	1841	1902	1935	2002	2035	...	2130	...	2235	2314	...
Stourbridge Junction **126** a.	...	...	...	...	...	...	...	...	...	...	...	...	...	...	...	...	1927	...	2029	...	...	2156	...	...	...	...
Kidderminster **126** a.	...	...	...	...	...	...	...	...	...	...	...	...	...	...	...	...	1944	...	2045	...	...	2212	...	...	...	...

		⑦	⑦		⑦	⑦	⑦	⑦	⑦	⑦	⑦	⑦		⑦	⑦	⑦	⑦	⑦	⑦	⑦		⑦	⑦	⑦	⑦
London Marylebone ◇ d.		0815	0910	...	0940	0943	1010	1040	1110	1140	1210	1240		1710	1740	1810	1840	1910	1940	2010	...	2040	2043	2110	2208
High Wycombe ◇ d.	⑦	0845	0934	...	|	1018	1034	|	1134	|	1234	|		1734	|	1835	|	1934	|	2034	...	|	2114	2134	2234
Bicester North ◇ d.		0910	|	...	1024	1047	|	1124	|	1224	|	1326	and at	|	1826	|	1926	|	2026	|	...	2126	2143	|	2256
Banbury **119** ◇ d.		0929	1007	...	1037	1111	1107	1137	1207	1237	1307	1339	the	1807	1839	1907	1939	2007	2039	2107	...	2139	2201	2207	2309
Leamington Spa **119** d.		0947	1025	...	1055	1132	1125	1155	1225	1255	1325	1357	same	1825	1857	1925	1957	2025	2057	2125	...	2157	2220	2225	2327
Warwick d.		0951	|	...	1059	1138	|	1159	|	1259	|	1401	minutes	|	1901	|	2001	|	2101	|	...	2201	2224	2229	2331
Warwick Parkway d.		0955	1032	...	1103	...	1132	1203	1232	1303	1332	1405	past	1832	1905	1932	2005	2032	2105	2132	...	2205	...	2234	2334
Solihull a.		1016	1044	...	1118	...	1144	1218	1244	1319	1344	1420	each	1844	1920	1943	2020	2044	2128	2144	...	2220	...	2257	2349
Birmingham Moor Street **126** a.		1024	1053	...	1127	...	1156	1227	1256	1329	1356	1429	hour	1856	1929	1953	2029	2056	2137	2156	...	2229	...	2306	2358
Birmingham Snow Hill **126** a.		1032	1101	...	1135	...	...	1235	...	1337	...	1437	until	...	1937	1957	2037	...	2140	...	...	2232	...	2314	0007
Sourbridge Junction **126** a.		...	...	...	...	...	...	...	...	...	...	...		...	...	2021	...	...	2204	...	...	2256	...	...	...
Kidderminster **126** a.		...	...	...	...	...	...	...	...	...	...	...		...	...	2036	...	...	2218	...	...	2310	...	...	...

		Ⓐ	Ⓐ	Ⓐ	Ⓐ	Ⓐ	Ⓐ	Ⓐ	Ⓐ	Ⓐ	Ⓐ	Ⓐ	Ⓐ	Ⓐ	Ⓐ	Ⓐ	Ⓐ	Ⓐ	Ⓐ	Ⓐ	Ⓐ	Ⓐ	Ⓐ	Ⓐ	Ⓐ	Ⓐ
Kidderminster **126** d.		...	...	...	...	...	0609	...	...	...	0705	0730	...	0809	...	...	...	...	...	...	...	...	...	...	...	...
Stourbridge Junction **126** d.	Ⓐ	...	...	...	...	...	0618	...	0638	...	0714	0738	...	0823	...	...	...	...	...	...	...	...	...	...	...	...
Birmingham Snow Hill **126** d.		...	...	...	...	...	0650	...	0707	...	0750	0807	0822	0852	0912	...	1012	...	1112	...	1212	...	1311	...	1412	...
Birmingham Moor Street **126** d.		...	0515	0542	0610	0628	0655	...	0711	...	0754	0810	0825	0855	0915	0955	1015	1055	1115	1155	1215	1255	1315	1355	1415	1455
Solihull d.		...	0524	0551	0619	0638	0704	...	0720	...	0803	0819	0837	0907	0924	1004	1024	1104	1124	1204	1224	1304	1324	1404	1424	1504
Warwick Parkway d.		...	0536	0605	0634	0659	0718	...	0739	0800	0815	0834	0902	0919	0939	1016	1039	1117	1139	1216	1239	1317	1340	1416	1439	1516
Warwick d.		...	|	0608	|	0702	|	...	|	0803	|	0837	0906	|	0942	|	1042	|	1142	|	1242	|	1344	|	1442	|
Leamington Spa **119** d.		...	0541	0613	0641	0706	0724	...	0746	0808	0821	0843	0912	0925	0946	1022	1046	1123	1146	1222	1246	1323	1349	1422	1446	1521
Banbury **119** ◇ d.		0517	0559	0631	0659	0724	|	0750	0806	0827	0841	0902	0931	0944	1004	1040	1104	1140	1204	1240	1304	1341	1407	1440	1504	1539
Bicester North ◇ d.		0533	0611	0646	0711	0740	|	0807	|	0841	|	|	0944	|	1016	|	1116	|	1216	|	1317	|	1420	|	1516	|
High Wycombe ◇ d.		0600	0635	|	|	|	|	0831	|	0905	|	|	1008	|	|	1110	|	1213	|	1313	|	1413	|	1510	1537	1610
London Marylebone ◇ a.		0630	0703	0735	0802	0833	0834	0905	0907	0935	0938	0959	1036	1040	1108	1140	1208	1242	1309	1343	1409	1443	1508	1540	1608	1642

	Ⓐ	Ⓐ	Ⓐ	Ⓐ	Ⓐ	Ⓐ	Ⓐ	Ⓐ	Ⓐ	Ⓐ	Ⓐ	Ⓐ	Ⓐ		⑥	⑥	⑥	⑥	⑥	⑥	⑥	⑥	⑥	⑥	⑥	⑥
Kidderminster **126** d.	...	...	...	...	...	...	...	...	...	...	...	...	...		...	...	...	...	0637	0712	...	0813	...	0910	...	1011
Stourbridge Junction **126** d.	...	...	...	...	...	...	...	...	...	...	...	...	...	⑥	...	...	...	...	0645	0722	...	0824	...	0920	...	1019
Birmingham Snow Hill **126** d.	1512	...	1612	1652	1707	...	1752	1812	1840	1917	2015	2115	...		...	...	0612	0646	0712	0751	...	0853	0912	0951	1012	1052
Birmingham Moor Street **126** d.	1515	1555	1615	1655	1710	...	1755	1815	1843	1920	2018	2118	...		...	...	0615	0649	0715	0755	0815	0856	0915	0955	1015	1055
Solihull d.	1524	1604	1624	1704	1719	...	1806	1824	1852	1929	2027	2127	...		...	...	0624	0702	0724	0805	0824	0905	0924	1004	1024	1104
Warwick Parkway d.	1540	1617	1639	1716	1736	...	1822	1845	1907	1949	2042	2147	...		...	...	0644	0714	0739	0818	0839	0916	0939	1019	1039	1116
Warwick d.	1543	|	1642	1719	1739	1805	|	1848	|	1952	2045	2150	2206		...	...	0647	|	0742	|	0842	|	0942	|	1042	|
Leamington Spa **119** d.	1547	1623	1646	1723	1743	1809	1828	1853	1912	1957	2050	2155	2210		...	...	0652	0720	0746	0824	0846	0922	0946	1025	1046	1121
Banbury **119** ◇ d.	1605	1641	1704	1741	1801	1828	1846	1912	1930	2016	2113	2213	2230		0604	0624	0710	0739	0804	0844	0904	0940	1004	1044	1104	1139
Bicester North ◇ d.	1617	|	1716	|	1814	1845	1858	1928	1942	2030	2125	2225	2246		0618	0639	0722	0751	0816	|	0916	|	1016	|	1116	|
High Wycombe ◇ d.	|	1713	|	1811	1838	|	|	|	2009	2101	2145	2245	2317		0647	0703	0746	0811	|	0914	|	1014	|	1118	|	1214
London Marylebone ◇ a.	1712	1745	1813	1839	1911	1941	1944	2023	2037	2135	2212	2312	2358		0724	0736	0814	0842	0911	0941	1011	1041	1111	1146	1211	1241

	⑥	⑥	⑥	⑥	⑥	⑥	⑥	⑥	⑥	⑥		⑥	⑥	⑥	⑥	⑥	⑥	⑥	⑥	⑥	⑥	⑥	⑥		⑦	⑦
Birmingham Snow Hill **126** d.	1112	...	1212	...	1312	...	1412	...	1512	...	...	1612	...	1712	...	1812	...	1912	...	...	2012	...	2115		...	...
Birmingham Moor Street **126** d.	1115	1155	1215	1255	1315	1355	1415	1455	1515	1555	...	1615	1655	1715	1755	1815	1855	1915	1955	...	2015	2045	2118	⑦	...	...
Solihull d.	1124	1204	1224	1304	1324	1404	1424	1504	1524	1604	...	1624	1704	1724	1804	1824	1904	1924	2004	...	2024	2055	2127		...	...
Warwick Parkway d.	1139	1219	1239	1316	1339	1416	1439	1516	1539	1616	...	1639	1716	1739	1816	1839	1916	1939	2016	...	2039	2113	2149		...	...
Warwick d.	1142	|	1242	|	1342	|	1442	|	1542	|	...	1642	|	1742	|	1842	|	1942	|	...	2042	2117	2152		...	...
Leamington Spa **119** d.	1146	1225	1246	1322	1346	1422	1446	1522	1546	1622	...	1646	1722	1746	1822	1846	1922	1946	2023	...	2046	2122	2157		...	...
Banbury **119** ◇ d.	1204	1244	1304	1340	1407	1440	1504	1540	1604	1641	...	1704	1740	1804	1840	1904	1940	2004	2041	2045	2104	2140	2216		0749	0849
Bicester North ◇ d.	1216	|	1316	|	1420	|	1516	|	1616	|	...	1716	|	1816	|	1916	|	2016	|	2101	2116	2152	2232		0803	0903
High Wycombe ◇ d.	|	1314	|	1414	|	1514	|	1614	|	1714	...	|	1814	|	1914	|	2014	|	2114	2130	|	2214	2302		0833	0932
London Marylebone ◇ a.	1311	1341	1411	1441	1511	1541	1610	1646	1711	1741	...	1811	1841	1911	1941	2011	2041	2111	2141	2207	2211	2241	2348		0923	1006

	⑦	⑦		⑦	⑦	⑦	⑦	⑦	⑦	⑦	⑦	⑦	⑦	⑦		⑦	⑦	⑦	⑦	⑦	⑦	⑦	⑦	⑦	⑦
Kidderminster **126** d.	...	...	...	...	...	...	0940	...	...	1113	...	...	...	...		...	...	...	...	...	...	...	...	...	...
Stourbridge Junction **126** d.	...	...	...	...	...	...	0948	...	...	1122	...	...	...	...		...	...	...	...	...	...	...	...	...	...
Birmingham Snow Hill d.	...	...	...	0912	...	...	1012	...	1112	1149	1212	...	1312	...	and at	1712	...	1812	...	1912	...	...	2012	...	2115
Birmingham Moor Street d.	0825	0855	...	0915	...	0955	1015	1055	1115	1155	1215	1255	1315	1355	the	1715	1755	1815	1855	1915	...	1939	2015	...	2118
Solihull d.	0834	0904	...	0924	...	1004	1024	1104	1124	1204	1224	1304	1324	1404	same	1724	1804	1824	1904	1924	...	1948	2024	...	2127
Warwick Parkway d.	0849	0916	...	0939	...	1016	1039	1116	1139	1216	1239	1316	1339	1416	minutes	1739	1816	1839	1916	1939	...	|	2039	...	2144
Warwick d.	0852	|	...	0942	1001	|	1042	|	1142	|	1242	|	1342	|	past	1742	|	1842	|	1942	...	2011	2042	2103	2147
Leamington Spa **119** d.	0858	0922	...	0946	1006	1022	1046	1122	1146	1222	1246	1322	1346	1422	each	1746	1822	1846	1922	1946	...	2017	2046	2108	2152
Banbury **119** ◇ d.	0916	0940	...	1004	1024	1040	1107	1140	1204	1240	1304	1340	1404	1440	hour	1807	1840	1904	1941	2004	2013	2036	2104	2128	2215
Bicester North ◇ d.	0929	|	...	1016	1036	|	1119	|	1216	|	1316	|	1416	|	until	1819	|	1916	1953	2016	2032	2052	2116	2142	2231
High Wycombe ◇ d.	|	1013	...	|	1103	1114	|	1213	|	1313	|	1413	|	1513		|	1913	|	2016	|	2103	2116	|	2213	2301
London Marylebone ◇ a.	1018	1041	...	1109	1139	1142	1210	1240	1310	1340	1410	1440	1510	1540		1910	1940	2010	2045	2110	2141	2153	2213	2253	2342

◇ – Frequent additional services are available between these stations.

LONDON - STRATFORD UPON AVON

km			Ⓐ	Ⓐ	Ⓐ	Ⓐ	Ⓐ		Ⓐ	Ⓐ	Ⓐ	Ⓐ		⑥	⑥	⑥	⑥	⑥	⑥	⑥		⑦	⑦	⑦		⑦	⑦
0	**London** Marylebone d.	Ⓐ	...	0617	0814	1010	1140	...	1410	1621	1824	2043	⑥	0700	1010	1210	1410	1610	1810	2010	⑦	0943	1210	1410	...	1610	1810
45	High Wycombe d.		...	0701	|	1036	|	...	1434	1648	1902	2114		0723	1034	1234	1434	1634	1834	2034		1018	1234	1434	...	1634	1835
88	Bicester North d.		0545	0733	|	|	1227	...	|	1711	1944	2143		0750	|	|	|	|	|	|		1047	|	|	...	|	|
111	Banbury **119** d.		0604	0749	0908	1107	1240	...	1507	1724	2006	2201		0804	1107	1307	1507	1707	1907	2107		1111	1307	1507	...	1707	1907
143	Leamington Spa **119** a.		0624	0808	0925	1124	1257	...	1524	1741	2025	2219		0822	1124	1324	1524	1724	1924	2124		1130	1324	1524	...	1724	1924
143	Leamington Spa d.		0651	0808	0940	1132	1332	...	1532	1811	2026	2220		0830	1132	1332	1532	1732	1932	2132		1132	1332	1532	...	1732	1932
146	Warwick d.		0656	0813	0945	1137	1337	...	1537	1816	|	2224		0834	1137	1337	1537	1737	1937	2137		1138	1337	1537	...	1737	1937
165	**Stratford u. Avon** Pkwy. a.		0722	0837	1008	1157	1401	...	1601	1846	2050	2245		0901	1155	1400	1558	1805	2000	2200		1157	1356	1556	...	1756	1956
167	**Stratford upon Avon** a.		0731	0846	1017	1206	1412	...	1612	1851	2054	2256		0912	1205	1409	1608	1815	2010	2210		1207	1406	1606	...	1806	2006

		Ⓐ	Ⓐ	Ⓐ	Ⓐ	Ⓐ	Ⓐ	Ⓐ	Ⓐ	Ⓐ	Ⓐ		⑥	⑥	⑥	⑥	⑥	⑥	⑥	⑥		⑦	⑦	⑦	⑦	⑦	⑦
Stratford upon Avon d.	Ⓐ	0606	0733	0900	1037	1240	1437	1736	1912**h**	2139	2315	⑥	0756	1040	1242	1442	1641	1841	2042	2215	⑦	0938	1219	1446	1646	1846	2038
Stratford u. Avon Pkwy. d.		0610	0737	0904	1041	1244	1441	1740	1916**h**	2143	|		0800	1044	1246	1446	1645	1845	2046	|		0941	1223	1450	1650	1850	2042
Warwick d.		0640	0803	0928	1104	1304	1505	1805	1952	2206	2334		0824	1108	1309	1509	1709	1909	2109	2235		1001	1247	1511	1711	1911	2103
Leamington Spa a.		0645	0807	0937	1114	1314	1516	1809	1957	2210	2338		0828	1116	1317	1517	1717	1917	2117	2240		1005	1254	1517	1717	1917	2107
Leamington Spa **119** d.		0706	0808	0946	1123	1323	1547	1809	1958	2210	2339		0829	1146	1346	1546	1746	1946	2157	2241		1006	1322	1546	1746	1946	2108
Banbury **119** d.		0724	0827	1004	1140	1341	1605	1828	2016	2230	2357		0848	1204	1407	1604	1804	2004	2216	2302		1024	1340	1606	1807	2004	2128
Bicester North d.		0740	0841	1016	|	|	1617	1845	2030	2246	...		0903	1216	1420	1616	1816	2016	2232	...		1036	|	1618	1819	2016	2142
High Wycombe d.		|	0905	|	1213	1413	|	|	2101	2317	...		0930	|	|	|	|	|	2302	...		1103	1413	|	|	|	2213
London Marylebone a.		0833	0935	1108	1242	1443	1712	1941	2135	2358	...		1005	1311	1511	1711	1911	2111	2348	...		1139	1440	1710	1910	2110	2253

LONDON - OXFORD via High Wycombe

km			Ⓐ	Ⓐ	Ⓐ	Ⓐ	Ⓐ	Ⓐ	Ⓐ	Ⓐ	Ⓐ	Ⓐ	Ⓐ	Ⓐ	Ⓐ	Ⓐ	Ⓐ	Ⓐ	Ⓐ	Ⓐ	Ⓐ	Ⓐ	Ⓐ	Ⓐ	Ⓐ	Ⓐ
0	**London** Marylebone d.	Ⓐ	0609	0648	0714	0740	0811	0841	0900	0935	1006	1035	1107	1135	1207	1235	1306	1335	1406	1435	1505	1535	1618	1650	1718	1750
45	High Wycombe d.		0640	0717	0738	0804	|	0906	|	1000	|	1100	|	1200	|	1259	|	1359	|	1503	|	1600	|	1713	|	1814
90	Bicester Village d.		0708	0745	0802	0831	0854	0931	0952	1023	1053	1124	1154	1223	1254	1321	1354	1421	1454	1526	1555	1622	1706	1739	1805	1840
103	**Oxford** Parkway a.		0718	0752	0812	0839	0901	0938	1001	1030	1101	1132	1202	1230	1304	1330	1402	1430	1502	1535	1603	1629	1713	1748	1812	1847
108	**Oxford** **131** a.		0729	0802	0822	0848	0911	0947	1011	1038	1109	1139	1210	1238	1312	1338	1410	1438	1510	1546	1612	1638	1722	1756	1822	1855

	Ⓐ	Ⓐ	Ⓐ	Ⓐ	Ⓐ	Ⓐ	Ⓐ	Ⓐ	Ⓐ	Ⓐ	Ⓐ		⑥	⑥	⑥	⑥	⑥	⑥	⑥	⑥	⑥	⑥		⑥
London Marylebone d.	1818	1850	1921	1950	2007	2040	2102	2132	2207	2240	2310	⑥	0556	0625	0706	0740	0806	0835	0906	0935	1006	1035	and at	1835
High Wycombe d.	|	1916	1945	2014	|	2105	|	2159	|	2307	2339		0626	0652	0730	0803	|	0858	|	0958	|	1059	the same	1858
Bicester Village d.	1908	1942	2011	2039	2052	2128	2155	2226	2253	2333	0010		0655	0724	0756	0826	0854	0921	0954	1022	1054	1122	minutes past	1922
Oxford Parkway a.	1915	1949	2018	2046	2102	2135	2202	2234	2302	2341	0018		0703	0735	0803	0835	0901	0931	1001	1029	1101	1129	each hour until ♥	1929
Oxford **131** a.	1925	1957	2027	2056	2112	2145	2211	2241	2312	2350	0028		0711	0747	0812	0844	0910	0939	1010	1038	1110	1139		1937

	⑥	⑥	⑥	⑥	⑥	⑥	⑥	⑥	⑥			⑦		⑦	⑦	⑦		⑦	⑦	⑦	⑦		⑦	⑦
London Marylebone d.	1906	1935	2006	2035	2106	2135	2206	2235	2310	...	⑦	0735	...	0835	0905	0935	and at	2005	2035	2105	2135	...	2215	2315
High Wycombe d.	|	1958	|	2058	|	2159	|	2306	2336	...		0805	...	0859	|	0958	the same	|	2058	|	2159	...	|	2347
Bicester Village d.	1954	2022	2054	2122	2154	2222	2253	2331	2359	...		0834	...	0922	0953	1021	minutes past	2053	2120	2151	2222	...	2309	0018
Oxford Parkway a.	2001	2029	2101	2131	2201	2229	2301	2338	0009	...		0843	...	0929	1000	1030	each hour until ♥	2100	2128	2159	2231	...	2317	0026
Oxford **131** a.	2010	2037	2110	2139	2210	2239	2309	2346	0018	...		0851	...	0937	1009	1039		2109	2136	2208	2239	...	2326	0035

		Ⓐ	Ⓐ	Ⓐ	Ⓐ	Ⓐ	Ⓐ	Ⓐ	Ⓐ	Ⓐ	Ⓐ	Ⓐ	Ⓐ	Ⓐ	Ⓐ	Ⓐ	Ⓐ	Ⓐ		Ⓐ	Ⓐ	Ⓐ	Ⓐ	Ⓐ
Oxford **131** d.	Ⓐ	0536	0601	0625	0643	0717	0743	0801	0821	0840	0910	0936	1010	1041	1108	1142	1211	1240	and at	1611	1638	1654	1723	1737
Oxford Parkway d.		0542	0607	0631	0650	0725	0750	0808	0827	0850	0916	0945	1017	1047	1115	1148	1217	1247	the same	1617	1644	1703	1729	1746
Bicester Village d.		0552	0617	0640	0659	0735	0759	0820	0836	0859	0925	0957	1026	1056	1124	1157	1226	1256	minutes past	1626	1656	1720	1738	1758
High Wycombe d.		0625	0646	|	0727	|	0827	0851	0901	0927	0950	|	1051	|	1151	|	1251	|	each hour until ♥	1651	|	1745	1806	|
London Marylebone a.		0700	0723	0730	0757	0820	0857	0927	0930	0956	1019	1041	1118	1146	1218	1246	1318	1346		1721	1750	1826	1835	1853**r**

	Ⓐ	Ⓐ	①–④	⑤	Ⓐ	Ⓐ	Ⓐ	Ⓐ	Ⓐ	Ⓐ	Ⓐ	Ⓐ	Ⓐ		⑥	⑥	⑥	⑥	⑥	⑥	⑥	⑥		⑥
Oxford **131** d.	1803	1822	1902	1902	1927	2000	2026	2055	2115	2137	2215	2241	2315	⑥	0612	0635	0710	0736	0811	0840	0909	0942	and at	1911
Oxford Parkway d.	1810	1829	1909	1909	1936	2009	2032	2101	2121	2148	2221	2247	2321		0618	0641	0716	0744	0817	0847	0915	0948	the same	1917
Bicester Village d.	1823	1838	1918	1918	1947	2019	2041	2110	2130	2157	2230	2258	2331		0628	0650	0727	0755	0826	0858	0926	0957	minutes past	1926
High Wycombe d.	1845	1906	|	|	2013	|	2109	2138	|	2222	2300	2326	0004		0656	|	0755	|	0851	|	0951	|	each hour until ♥	1951
London Marylebone a.	1912	1933	2008	2013	2043	2110	2138	2205	2218	2252	2352	0011	...		0727	0740	0828	0854	0918	0946	1018	1048		2018

	⑥	⑥	⑥	⑥	⑥	⑥		⑦	⑦	⑦	⑦	⑦	⑦	⑦		⑦	⑦	⑦	⑦	⑦	⑦	⑦	⑦	⑦
Oxford **131** d.	1942	2011	2042	2109	2142	2209	⑦	0743	0810	0838	0901	0942	1010	1041	and at	1811	1841	1909	1941	2011	2049	2108	2148	2207
Oxford Parkway d.	1948	2017	2048	2115	2148	2215		0749	0816	0844	0907	0948	1017	1048	the same	1817	1847	1915	1948	2017	2055	2114	2154	2214
Bicester Village d.	1957	2026	2057	2126	2157	2226		0758	0825	0853	0918	0957	1026	1057	minutes past	1826	1856	1926	1957	2026	2104	2125	2203	2223
High Wycombe d.	|	2051	|	2151	2222	2252		0823	0850	|	0944	|	1051	|	each hour until ♥	1851	|	1951	|	2051	|	2150	|	2251
London Marylebone a.	2048	2118	2147	2218	2249	2328		0851	0926	0942	1011	1045	1118	1145		1918	1945	2017	2048	2118	2156	2216	2256	2316

h – Change at **Hatton** (a. 1936 / d. 1944). **r** – Arrives 1848 ①–④. ♥ – Timings may vary by up to 2 minutes.

CH 2nd class

LONDON - AYLESBURY 129

km			Ⓐ	Ⓐ	Ⓐ	Ⓐ	Ⓐ	Ⓐ	Ⓐ	Ⓐ	Ⓐ	Ⓐ	Ⓐ	Ⓐ	Ⓐ	Ⓐ	Ⓐ	Ⓐ	Ⓐ	Ⓐ	Ⓐ	Ⓐ	Ⓐ	Ⓐ	Ⓐ
0	**London** Marylebone △ d.	Ⓐ	0633	0652	0757	0857	0957	1057	1157	1257	1357	1457	1527	1612	1642	1730	1758	1832	1859	1932	1956	2057	2157	2257	2357
38	Amersham △ d.		0708	0727	0832	0932	1032	1132	1232	1332	1432	1532	1602	1647	1717	|	1829	|	1934	2008	2031	2132	2232	2332	0032
60	**Aylesbury** △ d.		0730	0756	0854	0954	1054	1154	1254	1354	1454	1554	1626	1709	1739	1824	1855	1925	2003	2031	2053	2154	2254	2354	0054
65	**Aylesbury** Vale Parkway a.		0739	0804	0903	1003	1103	1203	1303	1403	1503	1603	1634	1718	1748	1832	1904	1933	2011	2039	2102	2203	2303	0003	0103

		⑥	⑥	⑥	⑥	⑥		⑥	⑥	⑥	⑥		⑦	⑦	⑦	⑦	⑦		⑦	⑦	⑦		⑦
London Marylebone △ d.	⑥	...	0727	0757	0857	0957	and at	2057	2157	2227	2257	⑦	0757	0857	0957	1057	1157	and at	1957	2057	2127	...	2227
Amersham △ d.		0702	0802	0832	0932	1032	the same	2132	2232	2302	2332		0832	0932	1032	1132	1232	the same	2032	2132	2202	...	2302
Aylesbury △ d.		0726	0824	0854	0954	1054	minutes past each	2154	2254	2324	2354		0854	0954	1054	1154	1254	minutes past each	2054	2154	2224	...	2324
Aylesbury Vale Parkway a.		...	0833	0903	1003	1103	hour until	2203	2303	2333	0003		0903	1003	1103	1203	1303	hour until	2103	2203	2233	...	2333

		Ⓐ	Ⓐ	Ⓐ	Ⓐ	Ⓐ	Ⓐ	Ⓐ	Ⓐ	Ⓐ	Ⓐ	Ⓐ	Ⓐ	Ⓐ	Ⓐ	Ⓐ	Ⓐ	Ⓐ	Ⓐ	Ⓐ	Ⓐ		Ⓐ	Ⓐ	Ⓐ
Aylesbury Vale Parkway d.	Ⓐ	0517	0544	0619	0653	0725	0751	0812	0839	0918	1013	1113	1213	1313	1413	1513	1613	1643	1734	1806	1842	...	1943	2048	2113
Aylesbury ▽ d.		0521	0549	0624	0658	0730	0802	0817	0844	0923	1018	1118	1218	1318	1418	1518	1618	1648	1750	1820	1847	...	1948	2053	2118
Amersham ▽ d.		0543	0611	0647	0721	0753	0825	0839	0905	0944	1039	1139	1239	1339	1439	1539	1639	1709	1811	1842	1908	...	2009	2114	2139
London Marylebone ▽ a.		0616	0649	0722	0753	0826	0900	0916	0944	1023	1120	1220	1320	1420	1520	1620	1720	1748	1850	1920	1948	...	2049	2153	2219

		⑥	⑥	⑥	⑥		⑥	⑥	⑥	⑥	⑥		⑦	⑦	⑦	⑦	⑦		⑦	⑦	⑦	⑦	⑦
Aylesbury Vale Parkway d.	⑥	0613	0713	0813	0913	and at	1913	2013	2113	2213	...	⑦	0713	0813	0913	1013	1113	and at	1813	1913	2013	2113	2243
Aylesbury ▽ d.		0618	0718	0818	0918	the same	1918	2018	2118	2218	2318		0718	0818	0918	1018	1118	the same	1818	1918	2018	2118	2248
Amersham ▽ d.		0639	0739	0839	0939	minutes past each	1939	2039	2139	2239	2342		0739	0839	0939	1039	1139	minutes past each	1839	1939	2039	2139	2309
London Marylebone ▽ a.		0718	0818	0920	1020	hour until	2020	2120	2220	2320	...		0820	0920	1020	1120	1220	hour until	1920	2020	2120	2220	2348

△ – Additional trains London Marylebone - Aylesbury on Ⓐ at 0726, 0827 and hourly until 1427, 1557, 1627, 1711, 1740, 1812, 1843, 1918, 2023, 2127, 2227, 2327; on ⑥ at 0827 and hourly until 2127, 2327, 2357; on ⑦ at 1527 and hourly until 2027, 2157, 2257, 2327.

▽ – Additional trains Aylesbury - London Marylebone on Ⓐ at 0607, 0638, 0710, 0741, 0902, 0948 and hourly until 1548, 1715, 1918, 2021, 2148, 2248; on ⑥ at 0648 and hourly until 2148; on ⑦ at 0848, 0948, 1548 and hourly until 2148.

130 LONDON - WORCESTER - HEREFORD

Most trains convey 🍸 GW

Other services: London Paddington - Oxford see Table **131**; Worcester - Hereford see Table **125**.

km		Ⓐ	Ⓐ	Ⓐ	Ⓐ	Ⓐ	Ⓐ	Ⓐ	Ⓐ	Ⓐ	Ⓐ	Ⓐ	Ⓐ	Ⓐ	Ⓐ	Ⓐ	Ⓐ	Ⓐ	Ⓐ	Ⓐ	Ⓐ	Ⓐ	⑤
0	London Padd. **131 132** d.	...	0512	0547	0652	0750	0821	0921	1022	1122	1221	1322	1421	1522	1552	1622	1722	1752	1822	1922	2022	2148	2320
58	Reading **131 132** d.	...	0550	0618	0722	0823	0853	0952	1053	1153	1252	1353	1452	1553	1623	1653**u**	1752	1821	1851	1953	2053	2220	0003
103	**Oxford** **131** d.	0514	0621	0652	0801	0851	0923	1020	1125	1224	1323	1419	1523	1624	1650	1726	1817	1850	1924	2023	2124	2256	0036
148	Moreton in Marsh d.	0542	0645	0729	0841	0929	1000	1057	1202	1302	1400	1456	1600	1701	1726	1818	1854	1931	2002	2106**f**	2201	2337	0111
172	Evesham a.	0559	...	0748	0901	0944	1020	1112	1221	1321	1419	1512	1618	1720	...	1838	1914	1947	2021	2126	2220	2356	...
172	Evesham d.	0559	...	0751	0952	0944	1030	1113	1222	1318	1420	1513	1623	1721	...	1839	1915	1948	2022	2131	2221	2357	...
194	**Worcester** Shrub Hill a.	0619	...	0809	0920	0959	1048	1127	1240	1340	1438	1527	1641	1739	...	1857	1933	2006	2040	2149	2239	0015	...
195	**Worcester** Foregate St a.	0622	...	0815	0924	1003	1052	1131	1246	1344	...	1541	1644	1743	...	1911	1938	...	2044	2201	2243	...	...
208	Great Malvern **125** a.	...	...	...	0937	1015	1105	...	1259	...	...	...	...	1757	...	1926	1951	...	2058	2215	2257	...	...
219	Ledbury **125** a.	...	...	...	...	...	1120	...	1321	...	...	...	...	...	...	...	2006	...	2114	2233	...	...	...
241	**Hereford** **125** a.	...	...	...	...	...	1140	...	1347	...	...	...	...	...	...	...	2026	...	2133	2252	...	...	...

	⑥	⑥	⑥
London Padd. **131 132** d.	0518	0622	0722
Reading **131 132** d.	0554	0653	0753
Oxford **131** d.	0624	0723	0823
Moreton in Marsh d.	0701	0759	0900
Evesham a.	0721	0819	0919
Evesham d.	0724	0820	0920
Worcester Shrub Hill a.	0743	0840	0940
Worcester Foregate St a.	0748	0844	0944
Great Malvern **125** a.	0802	0900	1000
Ledbury **125** a.	...	...	...
Hereford **125** a.	...	...	...

	⑥	⑥	⑥	⑥	⑥	⑥	⑥	⑥	⑥	⑥	⑥	⑥	⑥
London Padd. **131 132** d.	0822	0922	1022	1122	1222	1322	1422	1520	1622	1722	1822	1952	2150
Reading **131 132** d.	0854	0953	1054	1153	1253	1353	1453	1554	1654	1754	1854	2023	2224
Oxford **131** d.	0924	1023	1123	1223	1323	1423	1523	1625	1723	1823	1923	2049	2253
Moreton in Marsh d.	1001	1100	1200	1300	1400	1504	1600	1659	1804	1900	2004	2126	2330
Evesham a.	1020	1119	1219	1319	...	1523	1619	1717	1823	1919	2023	2144	2347
Evesham d.	1022	1120	1227	1323	...	1524	1621	1720	1824	1920	2025	2145	2348
Worcester Shrub Hill a.	1040	1140	1246	1342	...	1544	1640	1740	1844	1940	2045	2205	0010
Worcester Foregate St. a.	1045	1147	1250	1346	...	1548	1644	1744	1856	1944	2049	2209	...
Great Malvern **125** a.	1059	...	1304	1403	...	1604	1700	1801	1910	...	2102	2225	...
Ledbury **125** a.	1121	...	1321	...	...	...	...	...	1924	...	2116	...	...
Hereford **125** a.	1140	...	1340	...	...	...	...	...	1945	...	2135	...	...

	⑦	⑦**d**	⑦**c**	⑦	⑦	⑦	⑦	⑦	⑦	⑦	⑦	⑦	⑦	⑦
London Padd. **131 132** d.	0803	0842	0842	0935	1042	1242	1342	1442	1542	1642	1742	1842	1942	2142
Reading **131 132** d.	0845	0922	0922	1013	1122	1322	1422	1522	1620	1723	1825	1924	2022	2223
Oxford **131** d.	0917	0952	0958	1048	1154	1352	1452	1551	1653	1755	1856	1956	2053	2259
Moreton in Marsh d.	0952	1025	1032	1124	1230	1430	1526	1626	1725	1832	1933	2032	2130	2335
Evesham a.	1010	1041	1048	1143	1249	1451	1544	1647	1741	1849	1954	2049	2149	2354
Evesham d.	1014	1046	1051	1149	1250	1452	1545	1649	1742	1849	1955	2051	2150	2354
Worcester Shrub Hill a.	1033	1102	1106	1207	1310	1510	1604	1708	1801	1907	2014	2111	2209	0016
Worcester Foregate St. a.	1038	1106	1110	1211	1314	1514	1607	1712	1804	1912	2018	...	2213	...
Great Malvern **125** a.	1054	1120	1123	1225	1327	1528	...	1725	...	1924	2032	...	2226	...
Ledbury **125** a.	...	1137	1138	...	1342	1542	...	1739	...	...	2046	...	...	...
Hereford **125** a.	...	1156	1157	...	1407	1601	...	1756	...	...	2104	...	...	...

	Ⓐ	Ⓐ	Ⓐ	Ⓐ	Ⓐ	Ⓐ	Ⓐ	Ⓐ	Ⓐ	Ⓐ	Ⓐ	Ⓐ	Ⓐ	Ⓐ	Ⓐ	Ⓐ	Ⓐ	Ⓐ	Ⓐ	Ⓐ	Ⓐ	Ⓐ
Hereford **125** d.	...	0447	0528	...	...	0642	...	...	...	...	...	1209	...	...	...	1514	...	...	...	...	...	2151
Ledbury **125** d.	...	0504	0545	...	...	0702	...	...	...	...	...	1227	...	...	...	1531	...	...	...	...	...	2211
Great Malvern **125** d.	...	0517	0559	...	...	0715	...	...	0954	1059	...	1240	...	...	...	1545	...	...	1834	1942	...	2224
Worcester Foregate St. d.	...	0532	0614	...	0653	0731	0825	...	1009	1115	1200	1255	1355	...	1551	1601	...	1726	1848	1957	2059	2236
Worcester Shrub Hill d.	0511	0537	0619	...	0656	0735	0839	...	1014	1122	1205	1259	1359	1522	1555	1607	...	1733	1853	2002	2103	2244
Evesham a.	0525	0553	0635	...	0712	0752	0856	...	1030	1136	1221	1316	1416	1536	1609	1623	...	1750	1910	2018	2120	2300
Evesham d.	0529	0558	0637	...	0713	0754	0902	...	1032	1137	1226	1317	1425	1537	1610	1624	...	1751	1919	2023	2121	2301
Moreton in Marsh d.	0549	0614	0656	0710	0728	0815	0922	0950	1052	1152	1246	1346**r**	1445	1553	1626	1646	1738	1811	1940	2044	2141	2322
Oxford **131** a.	0626	0651	0730	0749	0811	0853	0959	1025	1129	1230	1324	1424	1524	1629	1657	1728	1804	1900	2028	2128	2225	2359
Reading **131 132** a.	0652	0721	0755	0820	...	0918	1025	1055	1156	1255	1355	1455	1555	1656	1727	1755	1830	1926	2055	2156	2257	0039
London Padd. **131 132** a.	0727	0752	0827	0851	...	0946	1057	1130	1228	1329	1427	1527	1627	1729	1759	1829	1902	1959	2129	2231	2336**j**	0118

	⑥	⑥	⑥	⑥
Hereford **125** d.	...	0617	0713	...
Ledbury **125** d.	...	0634	0730	...
Great Malvern **125** d.	0554	0648	0744	0843
Worcester Foregate St. d.	0609	0703	0759	0858
Worcester Shrub Hill d.	0613	0708	0804	0904
Evesham a.	0630	0725	0821	0920
Evesham d.	0631	0726	0826	0922
Moreton in Marsh d.	0651	0746	0846	0942
Oxford **131** a.	0728	0827	0924	1022
Reading **131 132** a.	0754	0854	0952	1056
London Padd. **131 132** a.	0827	0928	1025	1129

	⑥		⑥	⑥	⑥	⑥	⑥	⑥	⑥	⑥	⑥	⑥	⑥
Hereford **125** d.	...	...	...	...	1213	...	1513	...	...	...	...	2020	...
Ledbury **125** d.	...	...	...	...	1230	...	1530	...	...	...	...	2041	...
Great Malvern **125** d.	0945	...	1045	...	1246	1435	1544	1635	1745	1835	...	2054	2241
Worcester Foregate St. d.	1000	...	1100	1206	1301	1457	1559	1657	1800	1848	2004	2111	2256
Worcester Shrub Hill d.	1004	...	1104	1210	1306	1502	1604	1702	1806	1902	2008	2118	2300
Evesham a.	1021	...	1121	1227	1323	1519	1621	1719	1823	1918	2026	2135	2319
Evesham d.	1025	...	1125	1228	1326	1528	1622	1725	1828	1928	2028	2136	...
Moreton in Marsh d.	1045	...	1145	1248	1345	1548	1642	1745	1848	1947	2048	2156	...
Oxford **131** a.	1122	...	1222	1325	1427	1627	1722	1822	1925	2021	2127	2234	...
Reading **131 132** a.	1154	...	1254	1352	1453	1654	1754	1854	1954	2051	2156	2308	...
London Padd. **131 132** a.	1226	...	1328	1426	1526	1726	1827	1926	2027	2125	2229	2351	...

	⑦	⑦		⑦	⑦	⑦	⑦	⑦	⑦	⑦	⑦		⑦	⑦
Hereford **125** d.	...	...	...	...	...	1332	1432	...	1634	...	1830	...	...	...
Ledbury **125** d.	...	...	...	...	...	1351	1452	...	1652	...	1849	...	...	...
Great Malvern **125** d.	...	0925	...	1114	1315	1407	1509	...	1705	...	1912	...	2015	...
Worcester Foregate St. d.	...	0937	...	1128	1328	1424	1524	1628	1724	1826	1930	...	2028	...
Worcester Shrub Hill d.	0839	0940	...	1131	1333	1429	1528	1632	1728	1830	1935	...	2031	2128
Evesham a.	0855	0956	...	1147	1349	1446	1546	1646	1747	1848	1950	...	2048	2145
Evesham d.	0857	0958	...	1155	1355	1455	1555	1655	1755	1855	1955	...	2049	2149
Moreton in Marsh d.	0916	1017	...	1213	1415	1511	1613	1713	1816	1913	2015	...	2108	2208
Oxford **131** a.	0950	1055	...	1250	1450	1549	1654	1754	1851	1953	2053	...	2148	2243
Reading **131 132** a.	1023	1124	...	1323	1522	1622	1724	1823	1924	2023	2124	...	2220	2314
London Padd. **131 132** a.	1101	1206	...	1407	1604	1706	1806	1904	2004	2100	2213	...	2301	0002

c – Until Mar. 25. d – From April 1. f – Arrives 2101. j – 2330 on ⑤. r – Arrives 1336. u – Calls to pick up only.

131 LONDON - OXFORD via Reading

GW

km		②–⑤	Ⓐ	Ⓐ	Ⓐ	Ⓐ	Ⓐ	Ⓐ	Ⓐ	Ⓐ	Ⓐ	Ⓐ	Ⓐ	Ⓐ	Ⓐ	Ⓐ	Ⓐ	Ⓐ	Ⓐ	Ⓐ	Ⓐ	Ⓐ	Ⓐ	Ⓐ	Ⓐ
0	London P ◇**130 132** d.	0025	0512	0547	0620	0652	0721	0750	0821	0851	0921	0950	1022	1052	1122	1150	1221	1250	1322	1350	1421	1450	1522	1552	1622
30	Slough **131a** d.	0043	0530	0603	0636	0708	0736	0807	0837	0907	0937	1006	1038	1108	1138	1207	1237	1306	1338	1407	1437	1507	1538	1608	1638**u**
58	Reading **130 132** d.	0103	0550	0618	0651	0722	0752	0823	0853	0922	0952	1021	1053	1123	1153	1223	1252	1321	1353	1423	1452	1522	1553	1623	1653**u**
85	Didcot Parkway **132** d.	0119	|	0634	0707	0743	|	|	|	0938	|	|	|	1139	|	|	|	1338	|	|	|	1537	|	|	|
102	**Oxford** **130 128** a.	0135	0617	0650	0722	0757	0817	0849	0919	0951	1018	1049	1123	1152	1221	1248	1321	1351	1417	1447	1521	1550	1622	1647	1724

	Ⓐ	Ⓐ	Ⓐ	Ⓐ	Ⓐ	Ⓐ	Ⓐ	Ⓐ	Ⓐ	Ⓐ	①–④	⑤	⑤	①–④	Ⓐ	⑤	①–④	⑤
London P ◇ **130 132** d.	1652	1722	1752	1822	1852	1922	1952	2022	2050	2118	2148	2150	2218	2218	2250	2320	2320	2342
Slough **131a** d.	|	|	|	|	|	1938	2008	2038	2107	2134	2204	2206	|	|	2310	2337	2340	2358
Reading **130 132** d.	1721	1752	1821	1851	1919	1953	2023	2053	2123	2149	2220	2221	2250	2259	2333	0003	0004	0023
Didcot Parkway **132** d.	|	|	|	|	|	|	|	|	|	|	|	|	|	|	|	|	|	0047
Oxford **130 128** a.	1745	1816	1849	1922	1944	2021	2053	2122	2153	2218	2254	2254	2330	2329	0001	0034	0032	0101

	⑥	⑥	⑥	⑥	⑥	⑥	⑥
London P ◇ **130 132** d.	0022	0518	0552	0622	0652	0722	0752
Slough **131a** d.	0043	0534	0608	0638	0708	0738	0809
Reading **130 132** d.	0101	0554	0623	0653	0723	0753	0825
Didcot Parkway **132** d.	0117	0610	0639	|	|	|	|
Oxford **130 128** a.	0131	0622	0652	0719	0752	0819	0851

	⑥		⑥	⑥	⑥	⑥	⑥	⑥	⑥	⑥
London P ◇ **130 132** d.	0822	and at the	1952	2022	2050	2120	2150	2220	2250	2333
Slough **131a** d.	0838	same	2008	2038	2106	2136	2206	2236	2308	2351
Reading **130 132** d.	0854	minutes past each	2023	2053	2121	2157	2224	2257	2330	0013
Didcot Parkway **132** d.	|	hour until	|	|	2138	2213	2239	2314	2347	0029
Oxford **130 128** a.	0921	♥	2046	2120	2153	2226	2250	2328	0001	0043

	⑦	⑦**d**	⑦**c**	⑦	⑦		⑦	⑦	⑦	⑦	⑦	⑦	⑦	⑦
London P ◇ **130 132** d.	0803	0842	0842	0935	1042	and	1742	1842	1942	2042	2142	2203	2233	2337
Slough **131a** d.	0823	0906	0906	0956	1106	hourly	1805	1900	2004	2106	2205	|	2256	0001
Reading **130 132** d.	0845	0922	0922	1013	1122	until	1825	1924	2022	2122	2223	2246	2316	0020
Didcot Parkway **132** d.	0901	0938	0945	1031	1138	♥	1842	1941	2037	2139	2244	2302**a**	2331**a**	0035**a**
Oxford **130 128** a.	0912	0949	0956	1044	1149		1854	1952	2050	2151	2257	*2351**	*0035**	*0115**

	②–⑤	②–⑤	Ⓐ	Ⓐ	Ⓐ	Ⓐ	Ⓐ	Ⓐ	Ⓐ	Ⓐ	Ⓐ	Ⓐ	Ⓐ	Ⓐ	Ⓐ	Ⓐ		Ⓐ	Ⓐ	Ⓐ	Ⓐ	Ⓐ	Ⓐ
Oxford **130 128** d.	0007	0027	*0454*	*0523*	...	0557	0628	0653	0731	0753	0807	0854	0901	0931	1001	1031	and at the same	1601	1631	1701	1731	1806	1831
Didcot Parkway **132** d.	0023	0047	0517	0540	0601	0614	|	0707	|	|	0821	|	0917	|	|	|	minutes past	|	|	|	|	|	|
Reading **130 132** a.	0038	0114	0543	0556	0619	0628	0653	0721	0755	0820	0835	0918	0931	0957	1025	1055	each hour until	1625	1656	1727	1755	1830	1857
Slough **131a** a.	0056	*0245*	0608	|	|	0648	|	|	|	|	|	|	|	1012	1039	1111	♥	1640	1710	1741	1809	1844	1912
London P ◇ **130 132** a.	0117	*0315*	0646	0622	0653	0706	0727	0752	0827	0851	0907	0946	0959	1031	1057	1130		1700	1729	1759	1829	1902	1930

	Ⓐ	Ⓐ	Ⓐ	Ⓐ	Ⓐ	Ⓐ	⑤	①–④	Ⓐ	Ⓐ
Oxford **130 128** d.	1902	1931	2003	2031	2101	2131	2201	2201	2231	2301
Didcot Parkway **132** d.	|	|	|	|	|	|	2214	2214	|	2317
Reading **130 132** a.	1926	1956	2027	2055	2128	2156	2232	2230	2257	2331
Slough **131a** a.	1940	2011	2041	2109	2143	2211	2250	2302	2316	2354
London P ◇ **130 132** a.	1959	2030	2059	2129	2206	2231	2309	2322	2336	0024

	⑥	⑥	⑥	⑥	⑥	⑥	⑥	⑥	⑥	⑥		⑥	⑥
Oxford **130 128** d.	0007	0027	0400	0514	*0542*	0631	0701	0731	0801	0831	and at the same	1901	1931
Didcot Parkway **132** d.	0022	0047	0413	0532	0605	|	|	|	|	|	minutes past	|	|
Reading **130 132** a.	0039	0114	0429	0557	0630	0656	0724	0754	0824	0854	each hour until	1924	1954
Slough **131a** a.	0057	...	*0501*	*0626*	0654	0711	0738	0808	0838	0910	♥	1938	2008
London P ◇ **130 132** a.	0118	...	*0532*	*0701*	0731	0730	0756	0827	0856	0928		1956	2027

	⑥	⑥	⑥	⑥	⑥	⑥	⑥	⑥
Oxford **130 128** d.	2001	2027	2101	2129	2201	2235	2301	*2310*
Didcot Parkway **132** d.	|	|	|	2143	2214	2253	2316	2334
Reading **130 132** a.	2024	2051	2124	2156	2227	2308	2330	2348
Slough **131a** a.	2038	2106	2138	2211	2242	2331	2351	|
London P ◇ **130 132** a.	2056	2125	2156	2229	2300	2351	0017	0033

	⑦	⑦	⑦	⑦	⑦	⑦	⑦	⑦	⑦	⑦	⑦	⑦	⑦	⑦	⑦	⑦	⑦
Oxford **130 128** d.	*0714**	0852	0955	1055	1200	1254	1400	1455	1555	1655	1755	1855	1955	2055	2150	2245	*2300**
Didcot Parkway **132** d.	0759	0904	1007	1109	1213	1308	1413	1508	1608	1708	1808	1909	2008	2108	2204	2258	2353
Reading **130 132** a.	0819	0918	1023	1124	1227	1323	1426	1522	1622	1724	1823	1924	2023	2125	2220	2314	0018
Slough **131a** a.	0836	0937	1039	1141	1243	1342	1443	1539	1641	1740	1839	1939	2038	2145	2237	2335	0043
London P ◇ **130 132** a.	0857	0957	1101	1206	1304	1407	1503	1604	1706	1805	1904	2004	2100	2213	2301	0002	0115

a – Arrival time. b – ②–⑤ only. c – Until Mar. 25. d – From April 1. u – Calls to pick up only. * – Connection by 🚌. ◇ – London Paddington. ♥ – Timings may vary by up to 5 minutes.

131a SLOUGH - WINDSOR

Journey time 6 minutes 2nd class GW

From Slough:
Ⓐ: 0530, 0550, 0610, 0630, 0650, 0708, 0730, 0750, 0808, 0830, 0850, 0910, 0930, 0950, 1010, 1030, 1050 and every 20 minutes until 1650; then 1710, 1730, 1751, 1810, 1830, 1850, 1910, 1930, 1950 and every 20 minutes until 2250, 2312 and 2336.
⑥: 0617 and every 30 minutes until 0947, 1011, 1030, 1050 and every 20 minutes until 1850, 1917, 1947 and every 30 minutes until 2247, 2322 and 2356.
⑦: 0822, 0852, 0922, 0952, 1012 and every 20 minutes until 1852, 1922 and every 30 minutes until 2322.

From Windsor & Eton Central:
Ⓐ: 0539, 0559, 0619, 0639, 0659, 0717, 0739, 0759, 0817, 0839, 0859, 0919, 0939, 0959, 1019, 1039 and every 20 minutes until 1659; then 1719, 1739, 1800, 1819 and every 20 minutes until 2259, 2321, 2346.
⑥: 0627 and every 30 minutes until 0957, 1021, 1039, 1059 and every 20 minutes until 1859, 1927, 1957, 2027, 2057 and every 30 minutes until 2257, 2331.
⑦: 0005, 0832, 0902, 0932, 1002, 1022 and every 20 minutes until 1902, 1932 and every 30 minutes until 2332.

For explanation of standard symbols see page 1

LONDON - BRISTOL TEMPLE MEADS - TAUNTON

km		ⒶQ	Ⓐ	Ⓐ	ⒶD	Ⓐ	Ⓐ	Ⓐ	Ⓐ	Ⓐ	Ⓐ	Ⓐ	Ⓐ	Ⓐ	Ⓐ	Ⓐ	Ⓐ	Ⓐ	Ⓐ	Ⓐ	Ⓐ	Ⓐ	Ⓐ
0	**London** Paddington 130 131 d.	0518	0630	0700	0730	0800	0830	0900	0930	1000	1030	1100	1130	1200	1230	1300	1330	1400	1430	1500	1530	1600	1630
58	Reading 130 131 d.	0555	0657	0728	0757	0827	0857	0927	0957	1027	1059	1127	1158	1227	1257	1327	1358	1427	1457	1528	1558	1627	1657
85	Didcot Parkway 131 d.	0610	0712	0744	|	0843	|	0941	|	1041	|	1141	|	1243	|	1341	1413	|	1511	|	1612	|	1713
124	Swindon 132a d.	0628	0730	0802	0824	0901	0930	0959	1026	1100	1129	1159	1230	1301	1325	1359	1431	1456	1529	1557	1630	1656	1731
151	Chippenham 132a d.	0642	0744	0817	0839	0915	0944	1014	1040	1114	1142	1214	1244	1315	1339	1414	1445	1511	1544	1611	1645	1710	1745
172	Bath a.	0655	0758	0831	0853	0929	0958	1028	1054	1128	1157	1228	1258	1329	1353	1428	1459	1527	1557	1625	1659	1724	1759
190	**Bristol** Temple M 115 120 120a a.	0710	0817	0846	0910	0943	1012	1042	1108	1142	1213	1242	1316	1343	1407	1442	1516	1541	1611	1639	1713	1738	1813
221	Weston-super-Mare 120 120a a.	...	...	...	|	...	...	...	...	...	1237	...	...	...	...	...	...	...	1650	...	1750	...	1852
262	**Taunton** 115 120 120a a.	...	...	...	0944	...	...	...	...	...	...	...	...	...	...	...	...	...	...	...	...	...	1930

	Ⓐ	Ⓐ	Ⓐ	Ⓐ	Ⓐ	①–④	⑤	Ⓐ	Ⓐ	Ⓐ	ⒶB	⑤	①–④	ⒶC	⑥	⑥	⑥D	⑥	⑥		⑥	⑥	⑥
London Paddington 130 131 d.	1700	1730	1800	1830	1900	1912	1912	1930	2000	2045	2145	2215	2215	2330	0630	0700	0730	0800	0830	...	0900	0930	1000
Reading 130 131 d.	1727	1757	1828	1857	1927	|	1939	1959	2027	2112	2213	2244	2256	0010	0658	0728	0758	0830	0858	...	0928	0958	1028
Didcot Parkway 131 d.	1742	1812	1842	1913	1942	|	1954	2013	2041	2126	2233	2301	2313	0029	0713	|	0813	|	0913	...	|	1014	|
Swindon 132a d.	1800	1830	1901	1931	2000	2010e	2012	2032	2059	2144	2251	2319	2331	0047	0731	0756	0831	0858	0931	...	0956	1032	1056
Chippenham 132a d.	1814	1845	1915	1945	2014	|	|	2046	2114	2159	2305	2334	2346	0101	0746	0810	0845	0912	0946	...	1010	1047	1110
Bath a.	1828	1859	1929	1959	2028	n	k	2100	2128	2213	2319	2348	2359	0115	0759	0823	0859	0925	0959	...	1023	1101	1123
Bristol Temple M 115 120 120a a.	1842	1913	1943	2013	2042	2048	2059	2114	2142	2227	2333	0003	0014	0129	0814	0838	0913	0940	1014	...	1039	1115	1138
Weston-super-Mare 120 120a a.	...	1950	...	2053	...	...	...	2148	...	...	0006s	...	...	...	...	...	|	...	...	...	...	...	...
Taunton 115 120 120a a.	...	2031	...	...	...	...	...	...	...	...	0035	...	...	...	...	...	0947	...	...	...	...	...	...

	⑥	⑥	⑥	⑥	⑥	⑥	⑥	⑥	⑥	⑥	⑥	⑥	⑥A	⑥	⑥	⑥	⑥	⑥	⑥	⑥	⑥B	⑥	⑥	⑥
London Paddington 130 131 d.	1030	1100	1130	1200	1230	1300	1330	1400	1430	1500	1530	1600	1630	1700	1730	1800	1830	1900	1930	2000	2030	2132	2235	2330
Reading 130 131 d.	1058	1128	1158	1229	1258	1328	1358	1428	1458	1528	1558	1628	1658	1728	1759	1828	1858	1928	1958	2028	2058	2200	2303	0005
Didcot Parkway 131 d.	1113	|	1213	|	1313	|	1413	|	1513	|	1614	|	1713	|	1812	|	1913	|	2013	2043	2113	2215	2319	0022
Swindon 132a d.	1131	1156	1232	1257	1331	1356	1432	1456	1531	1556	1632	1656	1732	1756	1831	1856	1931	1956	2031	2101	2131	2233	2338	0041
Chippenham 132a d.	1146	1210	1246	1312	1345	1410	1446	1511	1546	1610	1646	1710	1746	1810	1846	1910	1945	2010	2045	2115	2145	2247	2353	0055
Bath a.	1159	1223	1300	1325	1358	1423	1500	1527	1559	1623	1659	1723	1800	1823	1859	1923	1959	2023	2058	2128	2159	2300	0006	0108
Bristol Temple M 115 120 120a a.	1214	1240	1314	1341	1413	1438	1511	1541	1614	1638	1714	1738	1814	1841	1914	1940	2014	2040	2113	2143	2213	2315	0021	0123
Weston-super-Mare 120 120a a.	...	...	...	...	...	...	...	...	...	...	...	...	1836	...	1950	...	2036	2127	...	...	2246s	...	...	...
Taunton 115 120 120a a.	...	...	...	...	...	...	...	...	...	...	...	...	1906	...	...	...	2101	2159	...	...	2315	...	...	...

	⑦D	⑦	⑦	⑦	⑦	⑦E	⑦	⑦	⑦	⑦	⑦	⑦	⑦	⑦	⑦	⑦B	⑦	⑦	⑦	⑦	⑦	⑦	⑦
London Paddington 130 131 d.	0800	0903	1003	1103	1203	1303	1403	1503	1527	1603	1627	1703	1730	1803	1827	1903	1927	2003	2103	2203	2233	2303	2337
Reading 130 131 d.	0836	0938	1038	1138	1238	1338	1438	1538	1604	1638	1700	1738	1806	1838	1903	1938	2003	2038	2142	2246	2316	2346	0020
Didcot Parkway 131 d.	0852	0958	1053	1153	1253	1353	1453	1553	|	1653	|	1753	|	1853	|	1953	|	2053	2155	2303	2331s	0001s	0035s
Swindon 132a d.	0911	1015	1110	1210	1310	1410	1510	1610	1631	1710	1728	1810	1833	1910	1929	2010	2032	2110	2212	2322	2347s	0019s	0053s
Chippenham 132a d.	0926	1029	1125	1225	1325	1425	1525	1625	1646	1725	1741	1825	1848	1925	1944	2025	2045	2125	2227	2336	|	0033s	0106s
Bath a.	0939	1044	1139	1239	1339	1439	1539	1639	1700	1739	1757	1839	1901	1939	1959	2039	2102	2139	2241	2351	h	0049s	0123s
Bristol Temple M 115 120 120a a.	0953	1059	1154	1254	1355	1455	1555	1653	1714	1755	1813	1855	1917	1955	2013	2055	2116	2154	2257	0006	0029	0103	0139
Weston-super-Mare 120 120a a.	|	...	1231	...	1428	|	...	1724	...	...	...	...	1957	...	...	2124	...	2228	...	...	...	...	...
Taunton 115 120 120a a.	1031	...	...	...	...	1528	...	1759	...	...	...	...	...	...	...	2146	...	...	...	...	...	...	...

LONDON - BRISTOL PARKWAY - CARDIFF - SWANSEA

km		Ⓐ	Ⓐ	Ⓐ	Ⓐ	Ⓐ	Ⓐ	Ⓐ	Ⓐ	Ⓐ	Ⓐ✕	Ⓐ	Ⓐ	Ⓐ	Ⓐ	Ⓐ	Ⓐ	Ⓐ	Ⓐ	Ⓐ	Ⓐ	Ⓐ	Ⓐ
0	**London** Paddington 130 131 d.	0518	0645	0715	0745	0815	0845	0915	0945	1015	1045	1115	1145	1215	1245	1315	1345	1415	1445	1515	1545	1615	1645
58	Reading 130 131 d.	0555	0712	0742	0812	0842	0912	0942	1012	1042	1112	1142	1212	1242	1312	1342	1412	1442	1512	1542	1612	1642	1712
85	Didcot Parkway 131 d.	0610	|	0756	|	0856	|	0956	|	1056	|	1156	|	1256	|	1356	|	1456	|	1556	|	1656	|
124	Swindon d.	0628	0739	0814	0839	0914	0939	1014	1040	1114	1139	1214	1240	1314	1339	1414	1440	1514	1539	1614	1640	1714	1740
180	**Bristol** Parkway d.	0716t	0810r	0841	0906	0941	1006	1041	1107	1141	1210r	1241	1310r	1344	1409r	1441	1507	1541	1606	1641	1709	1741	1809
215	Newport 136 149 a.	0748	0831	0904	0929	1003	1032	1104	1130	1203	1231	1303	1332	1405	1431	1506	1530	1603	1629	1704	1732	1802	1830
234	**Cardiff** Central 135 136 149 a.	0803	0847	0921	0944	1021	1048	1123	1146	1221	1247	1322	1348	1421	1447	1523	1545	1622	1644	1723	1747	1822	1849
266	Bridgend 135 a.	0826	0909	...	1006	...	1110	...	1208	...	1309	...	1410	...	1509	...	1607	...	1709	...	1809	1849	1911
286	Port Talbot 135 a.	0839	0922	...	1019	...	1123	...	1221	...	1322	...	1424	...	1522	...	1620	...	1722	...	1822	1902	1924
295	Neath 135 a.	0847	0929	...	1027	...	1130	...	1228	...	1330	...	1431	...	1529	...	1628	...	1729	...	1830	1910	1932
307	**Swansea** 135 a.	0900	0943	...	1045	...	1144	...	1242	...	1343	...	1445	...	1543	...	1641	...	1743	...	1843	1923	1945

	ⒶG	Ⓐ	Ⓐ	Ⓐ	①–④	⑤	⑤	①–④	⑤	①–④	⑤	①–④	Ⓐ	⑥F	⑥	⑥	⑥	⑥	⑥	⑥	⑥	⑥	⑥
London Paddington 130 131 d.	1715	1745	1815	1845	1915	1915	2015	2015	2115	2115	2245	2245	2330	...	0745	0845	0945	1045	1145	1245	1345	1445	1545
Reading 130 131 d.	1742	1812	1842	1913	1942	1948	2042	2042	2143	2143	2313	2324r	0010	...	0812	0912	1012	1112	1212	1312	1412	1512	1612
Didcot Parkway 131 d.	1756	|	1856	|	1957	|	2056	2056	2203	2203	2330	2343	0029	...	|	|	|	|	|	|	|	|	|
Swindon d.	1814	1841	1941	1940	2015	2018	2114	2114	2221	2221	2348	0001	0047	...	0841	0940	1041	1140	1241	1340	1441	1540	1640
Bristol Parkway d.	1841	1911r	1941	2007	2042	2045	2141	2141	2248	2248	0015	0028	0136t	0710	0909r	1009r	1109r	1209r	1309r	1409r	1509r	1609r	1709r
Newport 136 149 a.	1910	1933	2004	2032	2103	2106	2204	2204	2309	2316	0036	0056	0209s	0731	0929	1030	1130	1230	1330	1430	1530	1630	1731
Cardiff Central 135 136 149 a.	1926	1949	2019	2052	2118	2122	2219	2225	2325	2337	0052	0117	0230	0747	0945	1045	1145	1245	1345	1445	1545	1644	1746
Bridgend 135 a.	1949	2011	2044	2115	2145	2145	2241	2248	2347	0001	0116	0142	...	0809	1009	1109	1209	1309	1409	1509	1609	1709	1809
Port Talbot 135 a.	2002	2025	2057	2128	2158	2158	2254	2303	2359	0013	0129	0155	...	0822	1021	1121	1221	1321	1421	1521	1621	1721	1821
Neath 135 a.	2010	2032	2105	2135	2206	2206	2302	2310	0007	0021	0137	0202	...	0830	1029	1129	1229	1329	1429	1529	1629	1729	1829
Swansea 135 a.	2023	2046	2118	2150	2220	2220	2315	2324	0021	0034	0155	0216	...	0844	1043	1143	1243	1343	1443	1543	1643	1743	1846

	⑥	⑥G	⑥	⑥	⑥	⑥	⑥	⑦a	⑦b	⑦G	⑦	⑦G	⑦	⑦G	⑦	⑦	⑦	⑦	⑦	⑦	⑦	⑦	⑦
London Paddington 130 131 d.	1645	1745	1845	1915	1945	2045	2200	0830	0837	0930	1037	1137	1237	1337	1437	1537	1637	1737	1837	1900	1937	2037	2137
Reading 130 131 d.	1712	1812	1912	1942	2012	2112	2230	0907	0917	1007	1113	1213	1313	1413	1513	1613	1713	1813	1913	1936	2013	2113	2213
Didcot Parkway 131 d.	|	|	|	1957	|	|	2248	0925	0933	|	1129	1229	1329	1429	1529	1629	1729	1829	1929	|	2029	2129	2227
Swindon d.	1741	1840	1941	2016	2041	2140	2307	0943	0951	1036	1148	1248	1348	1448	1548	1648	1748	1848	1948	2004	2048	2147	2245
Bristol Parkway d.	1809r	1908r	2009r	2043r	2109r	2212f	2333	1009	1017	1101	1214	1314	1414	1514	1614	1714	1814	1914	2014	2032	2114	2214	2314
Newport 136 149 a.	1830	1930	2030	2104	2130	2244	0001	1028	1036	1123	1235	1335	1435	1535	1635	1737	1837	1937	2037	2049	2137	2237	2334
Cardiff Central 135 136 149 a.	1847	1944	2044	2118	2148	2305	0022	1051	1058	1147	1258	1358	1458	1558	1658	1801	1901	1959	2059	2115	2159	2300	2357
Bridgend 135 a.	1909	2009	2109	2145	2210	2328	...	1114	1121	1211	1320	1420	1520	1620	1720	1822	1922	2020	2121	2136	2221	2322	0020
Port Talbot 135 a.	1921	2021	2121	2158	2222	2340	...	1127	1134	1224	1332	1432	1532	1632	1732	1836	1936	2033	2134	2149	2234	2337	0034
Neath 135 a.	1929	2029	2129	2205	2230	2348	...	1135	1142	1232	1339	1439	1539	1639	1739	1844	1944	2041	2141	2158	2241	2345	0042
Swansea 135 a.	1943	2042	2143	2220	2244	0003	...	1149	1156	1245	1355	1455	1557	1658	1755	1900	1957	2055	2155	2211	2255	0003	0057

A – To Paignton (Table **115**).
B – To Exeter St Davids (Table **115**).
C – To Cardiff Central (See lower panel).
D – To Penzance (Tables **115**/**117**).
E – To Plymouth (Table **115**).
F – From Bristol Temple Meads dep. 0645.
G – To Carmarthen (Table **135**).
Q – To Swansea (See lower panel).

a – Until Mar. 25.
b – From April 1.
e – Arrives 2003.
f – Arrives 2204.
h – Also calls Bristol Parkway (to set down only) a. 0017.
k – Also calls Bristol Parkway a. 2038 / d. 2039.
m – Also calls Bristol Parkway a. 2030 / d. 2030.
n – Also calls Bristol Parkway a. 2035 / d. 2037.

r – Arrives 4–5 minutes earlier.
s – Calls to set down only.
t – Bristol Temple Meads.
u – Calls to pick up only.

132 SWANSEA, CARDIFF and BRISTOL - LONDON

🍷 available on most services GW

TAUNTON - BRISTOL TEMPLE MEADS - LONDON

		Ⓐ	Ⓐ	Ⓐ	Ⓐ	Ⓐ	Ⓐ		Ⓐ E	Ⓐ T	Ⓐ	Ⓐ	Ⓐ	Ⓐ A	Ⓐ	Ⓐ	Ⓐ	Ⓐ	Ⓐ	Ⓐ	Ⓐ	Ⓐ	Ⓐ	Ⓐ
Taunton 115 120 120a d.		...	...	...	...	...	...	...	0657	...	0712	...	...	0907	...	...	...	...	...	...	...	...	...	...
Weston-s-Mare 120 120a d.	Ⓐ	...	...	...	...	0620	0648	...	0726	...	0743	...	...	0929	...	...	...	...	...	...	1301	...	...	...
Bristol T M 115 120 120a d.		0445	0529	0600	0633	0700	0730	...	0800	0812	0830	0900	0930	1000	1030	1100	1130	1200	1230	1300	1330	1400	1430	1500
Bath d.		b	0541	0612	0645	0712	0742	...	0814	0830	0843	0912	0942	1012	1042	1113	1142	1212	1242	1312	1342	1413	1442	1512
Chippenham 132a d.		|	0554	0625	0658	0725	0755	...	0826	0845	0855	0925	0955	1025	1055	1126	1155	1225	1255	1325	1355	1426	1455	1525
Swindon 132a d.		0522	0610	0641	0714	0741	0811	...	0842	0902	0911	0941	1011	1042	1111	1142	1211	1242	1311	1341	1411	1442	1511	1541
Didcot Parkway 131 a.		0539	0627	0658	|	0800	0828	...	0859	...	0928	|	1028	|	1128	|	1228	|	1328	|	1428	|	1528	|
Reading 130 131 a.		0554	0641	0713	0743	0816	0844	...	0915	...	0944	1008	1042	1110	1142	1209	1242	1310	1343	1407	1443	1511	1543	1608
London Paddington 130 131 a.		0622	0716	0744	0814	0844	0912	...	0943	...	1014	1039	1111	1137	1214	1238	1312	1337	1414	1436	1514	1538	1613	1640

	Ⓐ	Ⓐ	Ⓐ	Ⓐ		Ⓐ	Ⓐ	Ⓐ	Ⓐ	Ⓐ	Ⓐ D		Ⓐ		⑥	⑥ Q	⑥	⑥	⑥		⑥	⑥	⑥ B	⑥
Taunton 115 120 120a d.	...	...	...	...	...	...	...	...	...	...	2115	...	2132		...	...	...	...	...	...	0654	...	0759	...
Weston-s-Mare 120 120a d.	...	...	...	...	...	1710	...	1808	...	...	|	...	2202	⑥	...	...	...	0625	...	...	0726	...	0829	...
Bristol T M 115 120 120a d.	1530	1600	1630	1700	...	1731	1800	1830	1930	2030	2150	...	2235		0530	0600	0630	0700	0730	...	0800	0830	0900	0930
Bath d.	1542	1613	1642	1712	...	1744	1812	1842	1942	2042	2203	...	2247		0543	0613	0643	0713	0743	...	0813	0843	0913	0943
Chippenham 132a d.	1555	1626	1655	1725	...	1756	1825	1855	1955	2055	2216	...	2300		0556	0625	0655	0725	0756	...	0825	0855	0925	0956
Swindon 132a d.	1611	1642	1711	1741	...	1812	1842	1911	2011	2111	2234	...	2316		0612	0641	0711	0742	0812	...	0842	0912	0941	1012
Didcot Parkway 131 a.	1628	|	1728	1758	...	1829	|	1928	2028	2128	2251	...	2334		0629	0658	0727	0759	0829	...	0900	0929	|	1029
Reading 130 131 a.	1643	1710	1743	1813	...	1845	1910	1943	2043	2145	2307	...	2353		0643	0713	0743	0813	0844	...	0915	0943	1011	1045
London Paddington 130 131 a.	1714	1740	1813	1843	...	1912	1938	2014	2114	2213	2342	...	0033		0714	0741	0814	0844	0914	...	0944	1014	1039	1114

	⑥	⑥	⑥	⑥ A	⑥	⑥	⑥	⑥	⑥	⑥	⑥	⑥	⑥	⑥	⑥	⑥	⑥	⑥	⑥	⑥	⑥ D	⑥		⑦
Taunton 115 120 120a d.	...	...	...	1045	...	...	...	...	...	...	...	...	...	...	...	...	...	...	...	...	2114	2130		...
Weston-s-Mare 120 120a d.	...	...	...	1107	...	...	...	...	...	...	...	...	...	...	...	...	...	...	...	2010	|	2153	⑦	...
Bristol T M 115 120 120a d.	1000	1030	1100	1130	1200	1230	1300	1330	1400	1430	1500	1530	1600	1630	1700	1730	1800	1830	1930	2033	2147	2230		0745
Bath d.	1013	1043	1113	1143	1213	1243	1313	1343	1413	1443	1513	1543	1613	1643	1713	1743	1813	1843	1943	2046	2202	2246		0758
Chippenham 132a **d.**	1026	1055	1126	1155	1225	1256	1325	1355	1426	1456	1526	1556	1625	1655	1725	1755	1825	1855	1955	2058	2215	2258		0810
Swindon 132a d.	1042	1111	1142	1211	1242	1312	1341	1411	1442	1512	1542	1612	1641	1711	1742	1811	1841	1911	2011	2114	2231	2314		0826
Didcot Parkway 131 a.	|	1128	|	1228	|	1329	|	1428	|	1529	|	1629	|	1728	|	1828	|	1928	2029	2131	2248	2332		0844
Reading 130 131 a.	1109	1143	1210	1246	1310	1343	1412	1443	1508	1543	1610	1645	1708	1743	1808	1845	1908	1943	2044	2146	2304	2348		0900
London Paddington 130 131 a.	1140	1214	1238	1314	1338	1414	1440	1514	1541	1614	1638	1714	1738	1814	1837	1914	1937	2014	2114	2214	2343	0033		0939

	⑦	⑦	⑦	⑦	⑦	⑦	⑦	⑦	⑦	⑦	⑦	⑦	⑦	⑦	⑦	⑦	⑦ E	⑦ A	⑦ E	⑦	⑦	⑦	⑦	⑦ E
Taunton 115 120 120a d.	...	...	...	...	...	...	...	...	...	...	...	...	...	...	...	...	1637	1658	1746	...	...	1856	...	2129
Weston-s-Mare 120 120a d.	...	0826	...	0956	...	...	...	...	...	...	1320	...	1451	...	...	...	1700	1729	|	...	...	1925	2026	|
Bristol T M 115 120 120a d.	0815	0900	0947	1030	1105	1130	1205	1230	1305	1330	1405	1505	1530	1559	1630	1705	1730	1805	1830	1905	1930	2000	2100	2210
Bath d.	0828	0913	1000	1043	1118	1143	1218	1243	1318	1343	1418	1518	1543	1612	1643	1718	1743	1818	1843	1918	1943	2013	2113	2223
Chippenham 132a d.	0840	0925	1012	1055	1130	1155	1230	1255	1330	1355	1430	1530	1555	1624	1655	1730	1755	1830	1855	1930	1955	2025	2125	2235
Swindon 132a d.	0856	0941	1029	1111	1146	1211	1245	1311	1346	1411	1445	1546	1611	1640	1711	1745	1811	1846	1911	1946	2011	2040	2141	2252
Didcot Parkway 131 a.	|	0956	1045	1127	1203	1227	1303	1327	|	1426	|	1602	1628	|	1728	|	1828	|	1928	|	2028	2057	2156	2310
Reading 130 131 a.	0926	1019	1101	1144	1219	1244	1320	1344	1414	1444	1514	1619	1644	1708	1744	1814	1844	1914	1944	2014	2044	2114	2213	2326
London Padd 130 131 a.	1004	1058	1143	1228	1258	1321	1359	1421	1458	1521	1559	1658	1721	1758	1821	1858	1921	1958	2021	2057	2121	2158	2257	0005

SWANSEA - CARDIFF - BRISTOL PARKWAY - LONDON

		Ⓐ S	Ⓐ	Ⓐ	Ⓐ	Ⓐ ✕	Ⓐ		Ⓐ	Ⓐ	Ⓐ	Ⓐ G	Ⓐ	Ⓐ	Ⓐ	Ⓐ	Ⓐ	Ⓐ	Ⓐ	Ⓐ	Ⓐ	Ⓐ	Ⓐ	Ⓐ
Swansea 135 d.		...	0354	0458	0529	0559	0629	...	0659	0729	0759	0829	...	0929	...	1029	...	1129	...	1229	...	1329	...	1429
Neath 135 d.	Ⓐ	...	0406	0510	0541	0611	0641	...	0711	0741	0811	0841	...	0941	...	1041	...	1141	...	1241	...	1341	...	1441
Port Talbot 135 d.		...	0414	0518	0549	0619	0649	...	0719	0749	0819	0849	...	0949	...	1049	...	1149	...	1249	...	1349	...	1449
Bridgend 135 d.		...	0427	0531	0602	0632	0702	...	0732	0802	0832	0902	...	1002	...	1102	...	1202	...	1302	...	1402	...	1502
Cardiff Central 135 136 149 d.		...	0512	0555	0626	0656	0726	...	0756	0826	0856	0926	0956	1026	1056	1126	1156	1226	1256	1326	1356	1426	1456	1526
Newport 136 149 d.		...	0533	0609	0640	0710	0740	...	0810	0840	0910	0940	1010	1040	1110	1140	1210	1240	1310	1340	1410	1440	1510	1540
Bristol Parkway d.		0455	0603	0631	0702	0733	0803	...	0832	0903	0933	1003	1033	1103	1132	1203	1233	1303	1333	1403	1433	1503	1533	1603
Swindon d.		0522	0630	0658	0729	0800	0830	...	0859	0930	1000	1030	1100	1130	1159	1230	1300	1330	1400	1430	1500	1530	1600	1630
Didcot Parkway 131 a.		0539	0647	|	0746	|	|	...	|	|	1017	1047	1117	|	1216	1247	1317	|	1417	1447	1517	|	1617	1647
Reading 130 131 a.		0554	0702	0725	0802	|	0857	...	0926	1000	1032	1102	1132	1159	1231	1302	1332	1358	1432	1502	1532	1558	1632	1702
London Paddington 130 131 a.		0622	0730	0759	0832	0855	0926	...	0955	1037	1100	1132	1200	1230	1301	1332	1407	1430	1502	1530	1601	1630	1702	1731

	Ⓐ	Ⓐ	Ⓐ	Ⓐ	Ⓐ	Ⓐ	Ⓐ	Ⓐ	①–④	⑤		⑥ t	⑥	⑥	⑥	⑥	⑥	⑥	⑥	⑥	⑥	⑥ G	⑥	⑥
Swansea 135 d.	...	1529	...	1629	...	1729	1829	1929	2029	2029		0359	0459	0529	0559	0629	0659	0729	0759	0829	0929	1029	1129	1229
Neath 135 d.	...	1541	...	1641	...	1741	1841	1941	2041	2041	⑥	0411	0511	0541	0611	0641	0711	0741	0811	0841	0941	1041	1141	1241
Port Talbot 135 d.	...	1549	...	1649	...	1749	1849	1949	2049	2049		0419	0519	0549	0619	0649	0719	0749	0819	0849	0949	1049	1149	1249
Bridgend 135 d.	...	1602	...	1702	...	1802	1902	2002	2102	2102		0431	0532	0602	0632	0702	0732	0802	0832	0902	1002	1102	1202	1302
Cardiff Central 135 136 149 d.	1556	1626	1656	1726	1756	1826	1926	2026	2126	2126		0455	0556	0626	0656	0726	0756	0826	0856	0926	1026	1126	1226	1326
Newport 136 149 d.	1610	1640	1710	1740	1810	1840	1940	2040	2140	2140		0509	0610	0640	0710	0740	0810	0840	0910	0940	1040	1140	1240	1340
Bristol Parkway d.	1633	1703	1733	1803	1833	1903	2003	2103	2203	2203		0542r	0634f	0704f	0733	0804f	0833	0904f	0933	1004f	1104f	1204f	1304f	1404f
Swindon d.	1700	1730	1800	1830	1900	1930	2030	2135	2230	2230		0641	0701	0731	0800	0831	0900	0931	1000	1031	1131	1231	1331	1431
Didcot Parkway 131 a.	1717	|	1817	1847	1917	|	2047	2152	|	|		0658	|	|	0816	|	0917	|	1017	|	|	|	|	|
Reading 130 131 a.	1734	1758	1834	1902	1932	1958	2102	2209	2300	2302		0713	0728	0758	0832	0858	0932	0957	1032	1100	1158	1258	1357	1457
London Paddington 130 131 a.	1802	1831	1907	1933	2001	2031	2131	2253a	2339	2336		0741	0759	0830	0859	0930	0959	1029	1101	1131	1229	1331	1429	1529

	⑥	⑥	⑥		⑥	⑥	⑥	⑥		⑦	⑦	⑦	⑦	⑦	⑦	⑦	⑦	⑦	⑦ G	⑦	⑦ G		⑦	⑦ G
Swansea 135 d.	1329	1429	1529	...	1629	1729	1829	1929		...	0807	0928	1028	1124	1224	1324	1424	1524	1551	1651	1751	...	1851	1955
Neath 135 d.	1341	1441	1541	...	1641	1741	1841	1941	⑦	...	0819	0940	1040	1136	1236	1336	1436	1536	1603	1703	1803	...	1903	2007
Port Talbot 135 d.	1349	1449	1549	...	1649	1749	1849	1949		...	0826	0947	1047	1143	1243	1343	1443	1543	1610	1710	1810	...	1910	2014
Bridgend 135 d.	1402	1502	1602	...	1702	1802	1902	2002		...	0840	1000	1100	1156	1256	1356	1456	1556	1623	1723	1823	...	1923	2028
Cardiff Central 135 136 149 d.	1426	1526	1626	...	1726	1826	1926	2026		0804	0901	1025	1125	1220	1320	1419	1520	1619	1649	1750	1850	...	1949	2055
Newport 136 149 d.	1440	1540	1640	...	1740	1840	1940	2040		0823	0921	1044	1144	1238	1338	1438	1538	1639	1708	1809	1908	...	2009	2114
Bristol Parkway d.	1504	1604f	1704f	...	1804f	1903	2004f	2103		0852	0950	1106	1205	1301	1402	1501	1601	1701	1729	1829	1929	...	2031	2138
Swindon d.	1531	1631	1731	...	1831	1929	2031	2130		0919	1018	1133	1233	1328	1428	1528	1628	1728	1757	1856	1957	...	2056	2205
Didcot Parkway 131 a.	|	|	|	...	|	|	|	2147		|	1035	|	|	1345	1445	1545	1645	1745	1814	1915	2014	...	|	|
Reading 130 131 a.	1558	1658	1758	...	1858	1958	2057	2202		0949	1050	1200	1300	1400	1501	1601	1701	1801	1829	1930	2029	...	2125	2240
London Paddington 130 131 a.	1629	1729	1830	...	1929	2030	2128	2238		1029	1128	1243	1343	1443	1544	1643	1743	1843	1907	2007	2107	...	2203	2322

- **A** – From Paignton (Table **115**).
- **B** – From Exeter St Davids (Table **115**).
- **D** – From Penzance (Tables **115 / 117**).
- **E** – From Plymouth (Table **115**).
- **G** – From Carmarthen (Table **135**).
- **Q** – From Swansea (See lower panel).
- **S** – From Bristol Temple Meads (See upper panel).
- **T** – From Gloucester (Table **138**).

- **a** – Arrives 2239 on ⑤.
- **b** – Also calls Bristol Parkway a. 0454 / d. 0455.
- **f** – Arrives 4 minutes earlier.
- **q** – ①–④ only.
- **r** – Arrives 0536.
- **t** – Also calls Bristol Temple Meads a. 0553 / d. 0600.

GW 2nd class — SWINDON - WESTBURY — 132a

Service from Jan. 1. For service until Dec. 31 please contact National Rail Enquiries ✆ +44 (0) 3457 48 49 50.

km		Ⓐ	Ⓐ	Ⓐ	Ⓐ	Ⓐ	Ⓐ	Ⓐ	Ⓐ	Ⓐ	⑥	⑥	⑥	⑥	⑥	⑥	⑥	⑥	⑦	⑦	⑦	⑦	⑦	⑦
		A							AB									B						
	Gloucester **133 140** d.	0517	...	...	...	...	...	...	1754	...	...	...	...	...	...	...	...	2014	...	...	...	...	...	...
0	**Swindon** 133 132 d.	0610	0849	1047	1247	1329	1518	1736	1848	2006	0836	1036	1236	1436	1522	1736	1936	2106	0926	1128	1328	1528	1718	1953
27	Chippenham 132 d.	0627	0906	1104	1304	1346	1535	1753	1905	2023	0853	1053	1253	1453	1539	1753	1953	2123	0943	1145	1345	1545	1735	2010
37	Melksham d.	0636	0915	1113	1313	1357	1546	1803	1915	2032	0902	1102	1302	1502	1548	1802	2002	2132	0952	1154	1354	1554	1744	2019
46	Trowbridge 140 d.	0646	0933	1124	1323	1406	1600	1813	1924	2042	0912	1112	1312	1512	1559	1812	2012	2142	1001	1203	1403	1603	1754	2029
52	**Westbury** 140 a.	0653	0942	1131	1332	1412	1606	1819	1931	2049	0920	1120	1320	1520	1607	1820	2020	2150	1008	1210	1410	1610	1801	2036

	Ⓐ	Ⓐ	Ⓐ	Ⓐ	Ⓐ	Ⓐ	Ⓐ	Ⓐ	Ⓐ	⑥	⑥	⑥	⑥	⑥	⑥	⑥	⑥	⑦	⑦	⑦	⑦	⑦	⑦	⑦
	B								B															B
Westbury 140 d.	0704	0733	0948	1147	1220	1414	1621	1832	1932	0733	0822	0932	1132	1332	1506	1632	1832	0827	1030	1230	1435	1620	1839	1941
Trowbridge 140 d.	0710	0739	0954	1153	1226	1420	1627	1838	1938	0739	0829	0938	1138	1338	1512	1638	1838	0832	1035	1235	1440	1625	1845	1946
Melksham d.	0720	0749	1004	1203	1236	1429	1637	1848	1947	0749	0838	0948	1148	1348	1522	1648	1848	0843	1046	1246	1450	1635	1854	1957
Chippenham 132 a.	0730	0802	1014	1212	1245	1439	1646	1900	2000	0800	0848	1000	1200	1400	1531	1700	1900	0852	1100	1300	1500	1645	1904	2007
Swindon 133 132 a.	0748	0819	1032	1234	1303	1502	1704	1921	2018	0820	0907	1020	1220	1420	1550	1722	1922	0913	1120	1320	1519	1705	1922	2025
Gloucester **133 140** a.	0852	...	...	...	...	...	...	...	2123	...	...	...	...	...	...	...	...	...	...	...	...	...	...	2126

A – To Southampton Central (Table **140**).
B – From / to Cheltenham Spa (Table **133**).

GW Most London trains convey 🍷 — LONDON - CHELTENHAM — 133

Service from Jan. 1. For service until Dec. 31 please contact National Rail Enquiries ✆ +44 (0) 3457 48 49 50.

km		Ⓐ	Ⓐ	Ⓐ	Ⓐ	Ⓐ	Ⓐ	Ⓐ	Ⓐ	Ⓐ	Ⓐ	Ⓐ	Ⓐ	Ⓐ	Ⓐ	Ⓐ	Ⓐ	Ⓐ	Ⓐ	⑥	⑥	⑥	⑥
			2A		2		2		2		2		2			2A		2	2	2		2	
0	**London** Paddington 132 d.	...	...	0736	...	0936	...	1136	...	1336	...	1536	...	1736	1837	...	1948	...	...	...	0815	...	1015
58	Reading 132 d.	...	...	0803	...	1003	...	1203	...	1403	...	1603	...	|	|	...	2020	...	...	...	0842	...	1042
85	Didcot Parkway 132 d.	...	...	0817	...	1017	...	1217	...	1417	...	1617	...	1817	1917	...	2035	...	...	...	0857	...	1057
124	**Swindon** 132 d.	0640	0750	0836	0936	1033	1136	1236	1336	1436	1536	1636	1754	1837	1937	2025	2055	2154	2336	0716	0916	1014	1116
164	Stroud d.	0709	0820	0907	1005	1107	1205	1307	1405	1507	1605	1707	1823	1907	2006	2053	2124	2223	0005	0745	0945	1043	1145
183	Gloucester a.	0731	0848	0927	1028	1127	1228	1327	1428	1527	1627	1727	1847	1931	2027	2115	2145	2246	0028	0805	1006	1104	1206
194	**Cheltenham** Spa 138 a.	0747	0905	0952	1046	1152	1246	1352	1445	1552	1645	1752	1903	1949	2043	2133	2200	2302	0043t	0820	1022	1120	1222
	Worcester Shrub Hill 138 a.	...	...	...	...	...	...	...	...	...	...	...	...	...	...	...	2222	...	...	...	...	...	...

	⑥	⑥	⑥	⑥	⑥	⑥	⑥	⑥	⑥	⑥	⑥	⑦	⑦	⑦	⑦		⑦	⑦	⑦	⑦	⑦	⑦	⑦	⑦
	2		2		2		2		2		2		2				2			2		2A		2
London Paddington 132 d.	...	1215	...	1415	...	1615	...	1815	...	2015	...	0827	...	1027	1228	...	...	1430	1630	...	1830	...	2027	...
Reading 132 d.	...	1242	...	1442	...	1642	...	1842	...	2042	...	0903	...	1103	1303	...	...	1507	1703	...	1903	...	2103	...
Didcot Parkway 132 d.	...	1257	...	1457	...	1656	...	1856	...	2057	...	|	...	|	|	...	...	|	|	...	|	...	|	...
Swindon 132 d.	1214	1316	1414	1516	1614	1716	1814	1916	2000	2118	2241	0938	1044	1138	1338	...	1425	1538	1738	1843	1937	2034	2133	2257
Stroud d.	1243	1345	1443	1545	1643	1745	1843	1945	2029	2146	2310	1006	1113	1206	1406	...	1455	1606	1806	1911	2005	2103	2201	2326
Gloucester a.	1304	1406	1504	1606	1704	1806	1904	2006	2050	2207	2331	1027	1133	1227	1427	...	1516	1627	1827	1934	2027	2123	2222	2346
Cheltenham Spa 138 a.	1320	1422	1520	1622	1720	1822	1920	2022	2104	2222	...	1044	1147	1244	1445	...	1533	1645	1845	...	2045	2135	2240	0007
Worcester Shrub Hill 138 a.	...	...	...	...	...	...	...	...	...	...	...	...	...	...	...	...	...	...	...	...	...	...	...	...

	Ⓐ	Ⓐ	Ⓐ	Ⓐ	Ⓐ		Ⓐ	Ⓐ	Ⓐ	Ⓐ	Ⓐ	Ⓐ	Ⓐ		Ⓐ	Ⓐ	Ⓐ	Ⓐ	Ⓐ	Ⓐ	Ⓐ	⑥	⑥
	2B			C				2		2		2			2		2B		2	2	2	2	
Worcester Shrub Hill 138 d.	...	0528	...	...	0708	...	...	...	...	...	...	...	...	...	...	...	...	...	...	...	...	...	...
Cheltenham Spa 138 d.	...	0554	0630	...	0731	...	0831	0918	1036	1120	1236	1320	1436	...	1520	1620	1741	1834	2001	2102	2201	0530	0731
Gloucester d.	0517	0610	0646	0705	0746	...	0848	0932	1051	1134	1252	1333	1452	...	1533	1643	1754	1850	2013	2121	2213	0543	0747
Stroud d.	0537	0631	0706	|	0806	...	0908	0952	1113	1155	1314	1352	1514	...	1552	1704	1812	1911	2031	2138	2232	0601	0807
Swindon 132 d.	0607	0702	0736	0902	0836	...	0945	1023	1145	1223	1345	1422	1545	...	1622	1735	1842	1941	2102	2209	2303	0632	0837
Didcot Parkway 132 a.	...	0719	0755	...	0853	...	1002	...	1202	...	1402	...	1602	...	...	|	...	1958	...	...	...	...	0854
Reading 132 a.	...	0734	0812	...	0908	...	1016	...	1216	...	1417	...	1616	...	...	1803	...	2014	...	...	...	...	0909
London Paddington 132 a.	...	0806	0842	...	0938	...	1045	...	1244	...	1445	...	1643	...	...	1839	...	2043	...	...	...	...	0939

	⑥	⑥	⑥	⑥	⑥	⑥	⑥	⑥		⑥	⑥	⑥	⑥	⑥	⑦	⑦	⑦	⑦		⑦	⑦	⑦	⑦	⑦
		2		2		2		2			2		2A	2	2		2				2			2
Worcester Shrub Hill 138 d.	0837	...	...	...	...	...	...	...	...	...	...	...	...	...	...	...	...	...	...	...	...	...	...	...
Cheltenham Spa 138 d.	0900	1001	1100	1201	1300	1401	1500	1601	...	1700	1801	1900	2002	2120	0924	1118	1232	1346	...	1546	1632	1746	1946	2147
Gloucester d.	0915	1014	1115	1214	1316	1414	1515	1614	...	1716	1814	1916	2014	2135	0937	1134	1245	1402	...	1602	1645	1802	2001	2159
Stroud d.	0935	1032	1135	1232	1336	1432	1535	1632	...	1736	1832	1936	2032	2153	0955	1153	1303	1422	...	1622	1702	1822	2021	2217
Swindon 132 d.	1005	1104	1205	1304	1405	1504	1605	1704	...	1806	1904	2006	2103	2225	1024	1221	1332	1450	...	1652	1733	1852	2050	2247
Didcot Parkway 132 a.	1022	...	1222	...	1423	...	1622	...	...	1823	...	2023	...	...	...	|	...	|	...	|	...	|	|	...
Reading 132 a.	1037	...	1237	...	1437	...	1637	...	...	1837	...	2038	...	...	...	1251	...	1518	...	1721	...	1919	2120	...
London Paddington 132 a.	1107	...	1307	...	1507	...	1707	...	...	1906	...	2106	...	...	...	1328	...	1601	...	1801	...	2000	2200	...

A – To / from Westbury (Table **132a**).
B – To Southampton Central (Tables **132a** and **140**).
C – Via Bristol and Bath (Tables **132** and **138**).
t – On ②–⑤ mornings arrives 0040.

GW — GATWICK AIRPORT ✈ - READING — 134

Service on ⑦ is valid from Jan. 7 (for service until Dec. 31 please contact National Rail Enquiries ✆ +44 (0) 3457 48 49 50).

km		Ⓐ	Ⓐ	Ⓐ	Ⓐ	Ⓐ	Ⓐ	Ⓐ	Ⓐ	Ⓐ	Ⓐ	Ⓐ	Ⓐ		Ⓐ	Ⓐ	Ⓐ	Ⓐ	Ⓐ	Ⓐ	Ⓐ	Ⓐ	Ⓐ	Ⓐ	Ⓐ	Ⓐ	Ⓐ	Ⓐ
		A			2		2		2	🍷	2	🍷	2	and at	2	🍷	2	🍷	2		2		2			2		2
0	**Gatwick** Airport ✈ d.	...	0531	0556	...	0658	...	0758	...	0910	...	1003	...	the same	...	1503	...	1603	...	1703	...	1803	...	1913	2003	...	2103	...
10	Redhill d.	...	0543	0613	0624	0710	0728	0808	0833	0923	0934	1014	1034	minutes	1434	1514	1529	1614	1632	1713	1743	1813	1843	1927	2014	2034	2114	2135
43	Guildford d.	0602	0613	0643	0704	0743	0813r	0838	0913	0954	1014	1044	1109	past each	1509	1544	1614r	1644	1709	1744	1826	1847r	1926	1956	2044	2116	2144	2215
84	**Reading** a.	0632	0658	0729	0752	0828	0900	0917	0951	1023	1059	1119	1154	hour until	1554	1619	1700	1719	1754	1824	1915	1927	2015	2034	2119	2201	2221	2306

	Ⓐ	Ⓐ	⑥	⑥		⑥	⑥	⑥		⑥	⑥	⑥	⑥	⑦	⑦	⑦	⑦	⑦	⑦	⑦		⑦	⑦	⑦	⑦	⑦
			A				2		and at		2										and at					
																					the same					
Gatwick Airport ✈ d.	2222	2318	...	0531	...	0603	...	0703	the same	2103	...	2219	2318	0611	0711	0811	...	0918	...	1018	minutes	...	2018	2108	2218	2308
Redhill d.	2232	2334	...	0542	...	0613	0634	0713	minutes	2114	2136	2233	2329	0620	0720	0829	0852	0930	0948	1030	past each	1948	2030	2119	2230	2319
Guildford d.	2314	0002	0609	0612	...	0644	0709	0744	past each	2144	2214	2314	0002	0651	0752	0859	0927	1000	1023	1100	hour until	2023	2100	2157	2300	2359
Reading a.	0001	0040	0643	0701	...	0719	0754	0819	hour until	2219	2257	0001	0037	0726	0835	0935	1010	1035	1106	1135	△	2107	2136	2241	2337	0043

	Ⓐ	Ⓐ	Ⓐ	Ⓐ	Ⓐ	Ⓐ	Ⓐ	Ⓐ	Ⓐ	Ⓐ		Ⓐ	Ⓐ	Ⓐ	Ⓐ	Ⓐ	Ⓐ	Ⓐ	Ⓐ	Ⓐ	Ⓐ	Ⓐ	Ⓐ	Ⓐ	Ⓐ		Ⓐ	Ⓐ
			2		2	🍷	2	🍷	2	🍷	and at	🍷	2		2	🍷	2		2	A			2	2			2	
Reading d.	0434	0524	0554	0634	0704	0734	0804	0832	0904	0934	the same	1434	1504	1528	1604	1634	1704	1734	1804	1821	1834	1934	2004	2034	2134	...	2234	2334
Guildford d.	0510	0600	0643	0710	0748	0818	0848	0913	0948	1010	minutes	1510	1548	1610	1650	1710	1750	1818	1854	1859	1910	2010	2048	2110	2218	...	2318	0021
Redhill a.	0539	0629	0724	0738	0830	0846	0930	0942	1025	1038	past each	1538	1627	1640	1732	1738	1832	1847	1935	...	1942	2038	2130	2145	2248	...	2358	0049
Gatwick Airport ✈ a.	0555	0642	...	0750	...	0859	...	0957	...	1050	hour until	1551	...	1659	...	1754	...	1900	...	...	1956	2050	...	2204	2302	...	0011	0103

	⑥	⑥	⑥		⑥	⑥	⑥	⑥	⑥	⑥	⑥	⑥	⑥	⑥	⑥	⑦	⑦	⑦		⑦	⑦	⑦	⑦	⑦	⑦	⑦
			2	and at		2	A		2		2								and at					A		
Reading d.	0434	0534	0604	the same	1734	1804	1823	1834	1904	1934	2004	2034	2134	2234	2334	0603	0748	0818	the same	1848	1918	2012	2118	2214	2219	2315
Guildford d.	0510	0610	0648	minutes	1810	1848	1901	1910	1948	2010	2048	2110	2218	2318	0021	0639	0832	0854	minutes	1932	1954	2055	2201	2242	2256	2359
Redhill a.	0539	0639	0725	past each	1838	1925	...	1938	2025	2038	2126	2146	2253	2358	0049	0708	0906	0924	past each	2006	2024	2136	2235	...	2336	0030
Gatwick Airport ✈ a.	0558	0650	...	hour until	1850	...	...	1950	...	2050	...	2159	2305	0008	0100	0728	...	0935	hour until	...	2035	2148	2247	...	2347	0041

A – To / from Newcastle (Table **124**).
r – Arrives 6 – 7 minutes earlier.
△ – Additional train on ⑦ Guildford d. 1214 - Reading a. 1248 **A**.

① – Mondays ② – Tuesdays ③ – Wednesdays ④ – Thursdays ⑤ – Fridays ⑥ – Saturdays ⑦ – Sundays Ⓐ – Not Saturdays 39

135 CARDIFF - SWANSEA - SOUTH WEST WALES

2nd class AW

km			②–⑤	Ⓐ	Ⓐ	Ⓐ	Ⓐ 🍷	Ⓐ	Ⓐ 🍷	Ⓐ 🍷	Ⓐ	Ⓐ	Ⓐ	Ⓐ 🍷E	Ⓐ 🍷E	Ⓐ 🍷	Ⓐ	Ⓐ 🍷	Ⓐ 🍷	Ⓐ	Ⓐ 🍷	Ⓐ 🍷	Ⓐ	Ⓐ	Ⓐ 🍷	Ⓐ 🍷
	Manchester P **149** .. d.	Ⓐ	...	...	...	...	...	...	...	...	...	...	...	...	...	0630	...	0730	...	...	0830	0930	...	...	1030	1130
0	**Cardiff** Central ... **132** d.		...	...	...	...	...	...	...	0535	0642	...	0714	0750	0904	1004	...	1041	...	1114	1138	1240	...	1313	1340	1443
32	Bridgend .... **132** d.		...	...	...	...	...	...	...	0607	0705	...	0739	0809	0924	1023	...	1100	...	1134	1159	1259	...	1334	1404	1502
52	Port Talbot .... **132** d.		...	...	...	...	...	...	...	0623	0722	...	0758	0825	0937	1036	...	1112	...	1150	1211	1312	...	1350	1418	1515
61	Neath .... **132** d.		...	...	...	...	...	...	...	0634	0733	...	0809	0835	0944	1043	...	1119	...	1201	1218	1319	...	1401	1425	1522
73	**Swansea** .... **132** a.		...	...	...	...	...	...	...	0651	0749	...	0828	0852	0956	1055	...	1133	...	1220	1235	1334	...	1420	1435	1535
73	**Swansea** .... **146** d.		0015	...	...	...	...	...	0545	0653	0752	0814	...	0906	1002	1105	1100	1137	1200	1222	1240	1337	1400	*1435*	1437	1537
91	Llanelli .... **146** d.		0032	...	...	...	...	...	0604	0711	0810	0831	...	0925	1021	1123	1117	1153	1219	1240	1259	1356	1416	*1451*	1456	1556
124	**Carmarthen** .... a.		0107	...	...	...	...	...	0638	0743	0841	|	...	0955	1053	1149	|	1225	1248	...	1324	1430	1445	...	1522	1630
124	**Carmarthen** .... d.		...	0450	0530	0550	0558	...	0639	0746	0843	|	...	0959	*1058*	1153	|	...	1251	...	1330	...	1451	...	1528	...
147	Whitland.................. d.		...	0503	0547	0605	0613	...	0656	0800	0902	0910	...	1014	*1113*	1206	1151	...	1306	...	1345	...	1506	...	1543	...
172	Tenby.................... a.		...	|	0614	|	|	...	0724	|	0930	|	...	|	*1141*	|	|	...	1334	...	|	...	1534	...	|	...
191	**Pembroke Dock** ... a.		...	|	0654	|	|	...	0807	|	1018	|	...	|	*1223*	|	|	...	1419	...	|	...	1619	...	|	...
166	Clarbeston Road .... d.		...	0518**x**	...	0620**x**	0627**x**	0720	...	0814**x**	...	0925**x**	...	1028**x**	...	1220**x**	|	...	...	...	1359**x**	...	...	...	1557**x**	...
174	Haverfordwest.......... d.		...	0529	...	|	0635	|	...	0823	...	|	...	1036	...	1228	|	...	...	...	1408	...	...	...	1606	...
189	**Milford Haven**.......... a.		...	0552	...	|	0658	|	...	0843	...	|	...	1057	...	1253	|	...	...	...	1431	...	...	...	1625	...
191	**Fishguard** Hbr ...... a.		...	...	...	0644	...	0744	...	...	...	0950	...	...	...	...	1230	...	...	...	...	...	...	...	...	...

	Ⓐ	Ⓐ 🍷C	Ⓐ 🍷	Ⓐ 🍷B	Ⓐ 🍷	Ⓐ 🍷	Ⓐ	Ⓐ 🍷	Ⓐ	Ⓐ Aa	Ⓐ Ab	Ⓐ 🍷		①–④	⑤	Ⓐ
Manchester P **149** .. d.	...	...	1230	...	1330	1430	...	1530	...	...	...	1630	...	1830	1832	1930
Cardiff Central ....**132** d.	...	1513	1539	1604	1704	1739	1806	1904	...	1923	1929	1946	2104	2215	2208	2315
Bridgend..............**132** d.	...	1532	1601	1624	1727	1800	1830	1923	...	1944	1950	2005	2127	2241	2235	2345
Port Talbot...........**132** d.	...	1549	1614	1639	1742	1818	1847	1938	...	1957	2003	2021	2145	2254	2247	0001
Neath ....**132** d.	...	1559	1621	1646	1752	1826	1858	1948	...	2004	2010	2028	2152	|	2254	0013
Swansea.............**132** a.	...	1615	1635	1700	1807	1839	1914	2004	...	2017	2021	2042	2205	|	2307	0028
Swansea.............**146** d.	1600	1620	1640	1702	1814	1842	*1934*	2011	...	2026	2034	2048	2227	|	2311	0045
Llanelli.................**146** d.	1618	1638	1659	1724	1833	1901	*1954*	2030	...	2044	2051	2111	2245	2324	2331	0102**s**
Carmarthen .... a.	1647	...	1728	1755	1902	1928	*2029*	2058	...	2112	2123	2139	2318	2359	0007	0140
Carmarthen .... d.	1651	...	1731	1757	1905	1930	▬	*2103*	2110	...	...	2141	2320	...	...	...
Whitland .... d.	1706	...	1746	1813	1921	1946	...	*2118*	2125	...	...	2156	2335	...	...	...
Tenby...................... a.	1734	...	|	|	1955	|	Ⓐ	|	2152	...	...	|	|	...	...	...
Pembroke Dock .... a.	1819	...	|	|	*2036*	|		|	2226	...	...	|	|	...	...	...
Clarbeston Road........ d.	...	...	1800**x**	1827**x**	...	2000**x**	2005	*2133***x**	...	...	...	2210**x**	2350**x**	...	...	...
Haverfordwest............ d.	...	...	1808	|	...	2009	|	|	...	...	...	2223	2358	...	...	...
Milford Haven........... a.	...	...	1831	|	...	2032	|	|	...	...	...	2246	0021	...	...	...
Fishguard Hbr....... a.	...	...	...	1856	...	...	2029	*2202*	...	...	...	...	...	...	...	...

		⑥	⑥	⑥	⑥	⑥	⑥	⑥ 🍷	⑥	⑥
Manchester P **149** .. d.	⑥	...	...	...	...	...	...	...	...	...
Cardiff Central ....**132** d.		...	...	...	...	...	...	0533	0642	...
Bridgend..............**132** d.		...	...	...	...	...	...	0603	0703	...
Port Talbot...........**132** d.		...	...	...	...	...	...	0620	0719	...
Neath ....**132** d.		...	...	...	...	...	...	0631	0730	...
Swansea.............**132** a.		...	...	...	...	...	...	0647	0746	...
Swansea.............**146** d.		*0005*	...	...	...	...	0545	0653	0750	0815
Llanelli.................**146** d.		*0025*	...	...	...	...	0604	0711	0808	0836
Carmarthen .... a.		*0100*	...	...	...	...	0638	0743	0840	0908
Carmarthen .... d.		0450	0530	0550	0558	...	0639	0746	0843	...
Whitland .... d.		0503	0546	0606	0613	...	0656	0800	0902	...
Tenby...................... a.		|	0614	|	|	...	0724	|	0930	...
Pembroke Dock .... a.		|	0659	|	|	...	0807	|	1017	...
Clarbeston Road........ d.		0518**x**	...	0621**x**	0627**x**	0720	...	0815**x**	...	...
Haverfordwest............ d.		0530	...	|	0635	|	...	0823	...	...
Milford Haven........... a.		0553	...	|	0658	|	...	0848	...	...
Fishguard Hbr....... a.		...	...	0646	...	0744	...	...	...	...

	⑥	⑥ 🍷E	⑥ 🍷E	⑥	⑥ 🍷	⑥ 🍷	⑥	⑥ 🍷	⑥	⑥ 🍷		⑥	⑥ 🍷	⑥	⑥ 🍷	⑥ 🍷	⑥	⑥	⑥ 🍷	⑥ 🍷B	⑥	⑥ 🍷	⑥	⑥ 🍷	⑥ 🍷	⑥
Manchester P **149** .. d.	...	...	...	...	0630	...	...	0730	...	0830	...	...	0930	...	1030	1130	...	...	1230	...	...	1330	...	1430	1530	...
Cardiff Central ....**132** d.	0714	0758	0904	0914	1000	...	...	1105	1114	1204	...	...	1304	1310	1404	1504	...	1514	1540	1604	...	1704	1738	1804	1904	...
Bridgend..............**132** d.	0738	0817	0923	0934	1019	...	...	1124	1134	1223	...	...	1323	1332	1423	1523	...	1534	1559	1624	...	1725	1758	1825	1924	...
Port Talbot...........**132** d.	0754	0830	0936	0952	1031	...	...	1138	1150	1236	...	...	1336	1348	1436	1536	...	1550	1617	1640	...	1740	1814	1841	1939	...
Neath ....**132** d.	0805	0837	0943	1003	1038	...	...	1146	1201	1243	...	...	1343	1359	1443	1543	...	1601	1624	1648	...	1750	1825	1849	1949	...
Swansea.............**132** a.	0822	0851	0955	1021	1054	...	...	1159	1220	1255	...	...	1357	1418	1455	1555	...	1617	1636	1701	...	1805	1844	1901	2005	...
Swansea.............**146** d.	▬	0905	1004	▬	1104	1100	1150	1205	...	1302	...	1350	1405	...	1500	1600	1609	1623	1640	1706	1750	1809	...	1904	2013	...
Llanelli.................**146** d.	...	0924	1022	⑥	1122	1117	1211**t**	1224	...	1322	...	1406	1424	...	1520	1619	1628	1641	1659	1724	1809	1828	...	1924	2032	...
Carmarthen .... a.	⑥	0953	1051		1149	|	1240	1253	...	1347	...	1440	1453	...	1545	1653	1657	...	1728	1755	1847	1901	...	1951	2057	...
Carmarthen .... d.		0957	...	1056	1152	|	1258	...	...	1351	...	1458	...	...	1549	...	1659	...	1731	1757	...	1905	...	1956	2100	2107
Whitland .... d.	0907	1014	...	1111	1207	1151	1312	...	...	1406	...	1512	...	...	1604	...	1714	...	1746	1813	...	1921	...	2011	2115	2123
Tenby...................... a.	|	|	...	1139	|	|	1340	...	...	|	...	1540	...	...	|	...	1741	...	|	|	...	1953	...	|	2142	|
Pembroke Dock .... a.	|	|	...	1220	|	|	1419	...	...	|	...	1619	...	...	|	...	1821	...	|	|	...	2025	...	|	2218	|
Clarbeston Road........ d.	0922**x**	1028**x**	...	...	1221**x**	|	...	...	...	1420**x**	...	...	...	...	1618**x**	...	...	...	1800**x**	1827**x**	...	...	...	2026**x**	...	2137**x**
Haverfordwest............ d.	|	1036	...	...	1229	|	...	...	...	1429	...	...	...	...	1626	...	...	...	1808	|	...	...	...	2034	...	|
Milford Haven........... a.	|	1058	...	...	1252	|	...	...	...	1452	...	...	...	...	1649	...	...	...	1831	|	...	...	...	2057	...	|
Fishguard Hbr....... a.	0947	...	...	...	...	1230	...	...	...	...	...	...	...	...	...	...	...	...	...	1854	...	...	...	...	...	2202

	A	⑥ 🍷	⑥	⑥ 🍷	⑥	⑥
Manchester P **149** .. d.	...	1630	...	1830	...	...
Cardiff Central ....**132** d.	1950	2001	2104	2208	...	2235
Bridgend..............**132** d.	2010	2020	2123	2235	...	2302
Port Talbot...........**132** d.	2023	2033	2139	2247	...	2319
Neath ....**132** d.	2031	|	2146	2254	...	2331
Swansea.............**132** a.	2043	|	2157	2307	...	2347
Swansea.............**146** d.	2100	|	2225	2310	2347	2353
Llanelli.................**146** d.	2117	2106**t**	2244	2329	0004	0011**s**
Carmarthen .... a.	2151	2134	2323	0003	0035	0051
Carmarthen .... d.	...	2205	...	...	0037	...
Whitland .... d.	...	2220	...	...	0053	...
Tenby...................... a.	...	|	...	...	|	...
Pembroke Dock .... a.	...	|	...	...	|	...
Clarbeston Road........ d.	...	2234**x**	...	...	0106**x**	...
Haverfordwest............ d.	...	2242	...	...	|	...
Milford Haven........... a.	...	2305	...	...	|	...
Fishguard Hbr....... a.	...	...	...	...	0135	...

		⑦	⑦	⑦	⑦ 🍷	⑦ 🍷	⑦ F	⑦ A	⑦ 🍷	⑦	⑦ A	⑦ 🍷	⑦	⑦ A	⑦ 🍷	⑦	⑦	⑦	⑦ 🍷	⑦
Manchester P **149** .. d.	⑦	...	...	...	...	...	...	...	...	...	...	1031	...	...	1233	...	1430	...	...	...
Cardiff Central ....**132** d.		...	...	...	...	0956	1119	1149	1205	...	1400	1405	...	1600	1614	...	1810	...	2013	2230
Bridgend..............**132** d.		...	...	...	...	1025	1139	1212	1235	...	1420	1435	...	1620	1643	...	1839	...	2033	2251
Port Talbot...........**132** d.		...	...	...	...	1040	1153	1225	1251	...	1433	1452	...	1633	1659	...	1856	...	2049	2305
Neath ....**132** d.		...	...	...	...	1048	1201	1233	|	...	1440	1500	...	1640	1707	...	1904	...	2057	2313
Swansea.............**132** a.		...	...	...	...	1100	1214	1245	|	...	1455	1512	...	1658	1720	...	1917	...	2110	2325
Swansea.............**146** d.		0010	...	...	1045	1104	1216	1252	|	1402	1504	1536	1638	1707	1725	1837	1922	2050	2118	2338
Llanelli.................**146** d.		0028**s**	...	...	1102	1124	1235	1309	1321	1422	1521	1555	1658	1726	1745	1857	1941	2110	2137	2358
Carmarthen .... a.		0103	...	...	1127	1156	1308	1338	1354	1455	1549	1624	1730	1754	1815	1929	2009	2142	2206	0033
Carmarthen .... d.		...	0955	1019	1130	1206	...	...	1355	1457	...	1627	1735	...	1820	1932	2010	2147	2210	...
Whitland .... d.		...	1011	1034	1145	1222	...	...	1411	1512	...	1644	1752	...	1837	1948	2030	2203	2226	...
Tenby...................... a.		...	|	1101	|	|	...	...	|	1540	...	|	1820	...	|	|	*2102*	|	|	...
Pembroke Dock .... a.		...	|	1141	|	|	...	...	|	1617	...	|	1859	...	|	|	*2136*	|	|	...
Clarbeston Road........ d.		...	1027**x**	...	|	1239**x**	...	...	1427**x**	...	...	1700**x**	...	...	1853**x**	2004**x**	2046**x**	|	2242**x**	...
Haverfordwest............ d.		...	1035	...	|	1247	...	...	1435	...	...	1708	...	...	1901	2012	2054	|	2250	...
Milford Haven........... a.		...	1055	...	|	1307	...	...	1459	...	...	1729	...	...	1925	...	2120	|	2310	...
Fishguard Hbr....... a.		...	...	...	1226	...	...	...	...	...	...	...	...	...	...	...	...	2244	...	...

		②–⑤	Ⓐ	Ⓐ 🍷	Ⓐ 🍷	Ⓐ 🍷	Ⓐ 🍷	Ⓐ	Ⓐ 🍷	Ⓐ 🍷	Ⓐ 🍷	Ⓐ S	Ⓐ 🍷	Ⓐ 🍷	Ⓐ 🍷	Ⓐ 🍷	Ⓐ S	Ⓐ	Ⓐ 🍷	Ⓐ 🍷	Ⓐ 🍷	Ⓐ D	Ⓐ 🍷	Ⓐ 🍷	Ⓐ 🍷	
Fishguard Hbr....... d.	Ⓐ	...	...	...	...	...	...	0650	...	...	0750	...	...	...	*0954*	...	...	...	...	1250	...	...	...	...	...	...
Milford Haven........... d.		0018	...	...	...	...	0555	|	0705	...	|	...	0908	...	|	1108	...	...	...	|	1308	...	...	...	1508	...
Haverfordwest............ d.		0033	...	...	...	...	0610	|	0720	...	|	...	0923	...	|	1123	...	...	...	|	1323	...	...	...	1523	...
Clarbeston Road........ d.		0041**x**	...	...	...	...	0618**x**	0714	0728**x**	...	0811**x**	...	0931**x**	...	*1017***x**	1131**x**	...	...	...	|	1331**x**	...	...	...	1531**x**	...
Pembroke Dock .... d.		|	...	...	...	...	|	▬	|	0659	|	...	|	0909	|	|	...	1109	...	|	|	...	1309	...	|	...
Tenby...................... d.		|	...	...	...	...	|	...	|	0729	|	...	|	0938	|	|	...	1143	...	|	|	...	1341	...	|	...
Whitland .... d.		0054	...	...	...	...	0631	Ⓐ	0741	0753	0824	...	0944	1007	*1032*	1144	...	1211	...	1324	1344	...	1409	...	1544	...
Carmarthen .... a.		0116	...	...	...	...	0647	A	0755	0812	0843	...	1003	1024	*1049*	1200	...	1229	...	1340	1400	...	1430	...	1600	...
Carmarthen .... d.		...	0303	0503	0546	0615	0650	0730	0801	0815	0900	...	1006	1031	1103	1205	...	1233	1302	1347	1405	...	1438	1503	1605	...
Llanelli.................**146** d.		...	0325	0528	0615	0644	0719	0805	0830	0841	0925	0939	1032	1056	1131	1230	1242	1259	1330	1409	1430	...	1503	1532	1630	...
Swansea.............**146** a.		...	0346	|	0635	0704	0738	0821	0849	0901	0951	1002	1049	1123	1150	1249	1301	1322	1351	|	1449	...	1523	1551	1649	...
Swansea.............**132** d.		...	*0352*	|	0638	0706	0742	0829	0853	*0910*	0955	1006	1055	...	1155	1254	1307	...	1355	|	1455	1510	...	1555	1655	...
Neath ....**132** d.		...	*0404*	|	0653	0717	0753	0841	0904	*0925*	1006	|	1106	...	1206	1305	1322	...	1406	|	1506	1525	...	1606	1706	...
Port Talbot...........**132** d.		...	*0412*	0601	0704	0724	0800	0849	0911	*0936*	1013	|	1113	...	1213	1312	1333	...	1413	|	1513	1536	...	1613	1713	...
Bridgend..............**132** d.		...	*0425*	0616	0720	0740	0815	0902	0924	*0953*	1026	|	1126	...	1226	1325	1352	...	1426	|	1526	1553	...	1626	1726	...
Cardiff Central ....**132** a.		...	*0512*	0645	0749	0803	0838	0923	0945	*1018*	1048	1110	1148	...	1248	1348	1413	...	1447	1519	1547	1614	...	1647	1746	...
Manchester P **149** .. a.		...	...	1015	...	1115	1215	...	1315	...	1415	...	1515	...	1615	1715	...	...	1815	...	1915	...	...	2019	2106	...

A – From / to London (operated by GW, see Table **132**). Conveys [12] and 🍷.
B – From Gloucester (Table **121**).
C – From Holyhead (Tables **149** and **160**).
D – To Chester (Tables **149** and **160**).
E – From Crewe (Table **149**).
F – From Hereford (Table **149**).
S – From Shrewsbury (Table **146**).

a – From Jan. 1.
b – Until Dec. 29.
s – Calls to set down only.
t – Arrives 4 – 5 minutes earlier.
x – Calls on request.

	Ⓐ	Ⓐ	Ⓐ	Ⓐ	Ⓐ	Ⓐ	Ⓐ	Ⓐ C	Ⓐ	Ⓐ	Ⓐ	Ⓐ	⑥	⑥ 🍷	⑥ 🍷	⑥ 🍷	⑥ 🍷	⑥	⑥ 🍷	⑥	⑥ S	⑥ 🍷	⑥ A	⑥ 🍷	⑥
Fishguard Hbr d.	...	...	...	1908	...	...	...	...	...	2214	...	...	...	...	...	...	...	0650	...	...	...	0750	...	...	...
Milford Haven d.	1711	...	...	|	1912	...	2036	...	...	|	...	2318	0018	...	...	...	0555	|	0705	...	...	|	...	0908	...
Haverfordwest d.	1726	...	...	|	1927	...	2051	...	...	|	...	2333	0033	...	...	...	0610	|	0720	...	...	|	...	0923	...
Clarbeston Road d.	1734**x**	...	...	1930**x**	1937**x**	...	2059**x**	...	...	2236**x**	...	2341**x**	0041**x**	...	...	...	0618**x**	0714	0728**x**	...	...	0811**x**	...	0931**x**	...
Pembroke Dock d.	|	1709	...	|	|	*1919*	|	...	2109	|	2228	|	|	...	...	...	|	...	|	0659	...	|	...	|	...
Tenby d.	|	1738	...	|	|	1957	|	...	2153	|	2255	|	|	...	...	...	|	...	|	0729	...	|	...	|	...
Whitland d.	1775	1807	...	1942	1950	2027	2112	...	2221	2250	2325	2354	0054	...	...	...	0631	...	0741	0753	...	0824	...	0944	...
Carmarthen a.	1803	1824	...	2000	2006	2045	2134	...	2243	2308	2344	0016	0116	...	...	...	0647	...	0755	0811	...	0843	...	1002	...
Carmarthen d.	1808	1831	1850	...	2011	2047	...	...	...	2310	...	...	*0244*	0504	0555	0620	0650	...	0801	0814	...	0900	0938	1004	...
Llanelli 146 d.	1836	1857	1921	...	2035	2117	...	2201	...	2340	...	...	*0306*	0529	0624	0648	0719	...	0830	0842	0855	0928	1006	1031	...
Swansea 146 a.	1856	1922	1943	...	2055	2142	...	2222	...	0008	...	...	*0329*	|	0643	0708	0738	...	0849	0900	0922	0950	1022	1048	...
Swansea 132 d.	1900	...	1951	...	2058	2145	...	2232	...	...	...	...	...	|	0647	0711	0744	...	0854	*0910*	0933	0954	1029	1055	1110
Neath 132 d.	1914	...	2002	...	2109	2200	...	2247	...	...	...	...	...	|	0658	0726	0755	...	0906	*0925*	0945	1006	1041	1106	1125
Port Talbot 132 d.	1925	...	2009	...	2116	2211	...	2258	...	...	...	...	...	0602	0705	0737	0802	...	0913	*0936*	0952	1013	1049	1113	1136
Bridgend 132 d.	1940	...	2023	...	2131	2227	...	2315	...	...	...	...	...	0617	0720	0753	0817	...	0928	*0953*	1009	1028	1102	1128	1152
Cardiff Central 132 a.	2003	...	2045	...	2203	2255	...	2340	...	...	...	...	...	0644	0743	0836	0844	...	0953	*1018*	1033	1048	1122	1148	1215
Manchester P **149** a.	...	...	...	...	...	...	...	...	...	...	...	...	...	1016	1115	...	1215	...	1315	...	...	1415	...	1515	...

	⑥	⑥	⑥ 🍷	⑥ 🍷	⑥ 🍷 S	⑥	⑥ 🍷	⑥ 🍷	⑥ 🍷	⑥	⑥	⑥ 🍷	⑥ 🍷	⑥	⑥	⑥ 🍷	⑥	⑥	⑥	⑥	⑥	⑥	⑥	⑥	⑥	⑥
Fishguard Hbr d.	...	0953	...	...	...	...	...	1243	...	...	...	...	...	...	...	...	...	...	...	1900	...	...	...	2100	...	...
Milford Haven d.	...	|	...	1108	...	...	...	|	1308	...	...	...	1508	...	...	...	1708	...	...	|	1908	...	...	|	2116	...
Haverfordwest d.	...	|	...	1123	...	...	...	|	1323	...	...	...	1523	...	...	...	1723	...	...	|	1923	...	...	|	2131	...
Clarbeston Road d.	...	1014**x**	...	1131**x**	...	...	...	|	1331**x**	...	...	...	1531**x**	...	...	...	1731**x**	...	...	1922**x**	1931**x**	...	...	2122**x**	2139**x**	...
Pembroke Dock d.	0909	|	...	|	...	1109	...	|	|	...	1309	...	|	...	1509	...	|	1712	...	|	|	1909	...	|	|	2109
Tenby d.	0937	|	...	|	...	1141	...	|	|	...	1342	...	|	...	1544	...	|	1743	...	|	|	1951	...	|	|	2142
Whitland d.	1005	1029	...	1144	...	1209	...	1317	1344	...	1411	...	1544	...	1612	...	1745	1811	...	1934	1944	2021	...	2136	2152	2211
Carmarthen a.	1023	1046	...	1200	...	1227	...	1332	1400	...	1428	...	1600	...	1630	...	1803	1829	...	1952	2004	2039	...	2159	2214	2232
Carmarthen d.	1027	...	1109	1205	...	1233	1302	1337	1405	...	1433	1503	1605	...	1632	1702	1807	1833	1854	...	2007	2047	...	...	...	...
Llanelli 146 d.	1053	...	1137	1230	1242	1259	1330	1406	1430	...	1458	1532	1630	1647	1658	1730	1836	1859	1925	...	2031	2117	*2138*	...	...	...
Swansea 146 a.	1119	...	1156	1249	1301	1319	1349	|	1449	...	1520	1551	1649	1704	1720	1749	1856	1921	1947	...	2051	2142	*2206*	...	...	...
Swansea 132 d.	...	...	1200	1253	1307	...	1400	|	1455	1510	...	1555	1658	1710	...	1754	1900	...	1952	...	2055	2143	2220	...	...	...
Neath 132 d.	...	...	1211	1304	1322	...	1411	|	1506	1525	...	1606	1709	1725	...	1805	1911	...	2003	...	2106	2159	2235	...	...	...
Port Talbot 132 d.	...	...	1218	1311	1333	...	1418	1438	1513	1536	...	1613	1716	1736	...	1812	1919	...	2010	...	2113	2210	2246	...	...	...
Bridgend 132 d.	...	...	1231	1326	1352	...	1431	|	1526	1553	...	1628	1731	1752	...	1827	1933	...	2024	...	2126	2226	2302	...	...	...
Cardiff Central 132 a.	...	...	1252	1348	1413	...	1452	1518	1551	1616	...	1649	1752	1820	...	1847	1956	...	2047	...	2147	2250	2326	...	...	...
Manchester P **149** a.	...	...	1615	1714	...	...	1815	...	1915	...	...	2015	2115	...	...	2214	*2349*	...	...	...	...	...	...	...	...	...

	⑥	⑥	⑥	⑦	⑦ 🍷	⑦	⑦ 🍷	⑦	⑦	⑦ 🍷	⑦ A	⑦	⑦ 🍷 k	⑦ A k	⑦ k	⑦ k	⑦ A	⑦ S	⑦ k	⑦ k	⑦	⑦	⑦ k	⑦	⑦ k
Fishguard Hbr d.	2214	...	...	...	...	...	...	...	1240	...	...	...	...	...	...	...	...	...	...	...	...	...	...	2303	...
Milford Haven d.	|	...	2318	...	...	...	1123	...	|	1318	...	...	1513	...	...	1732	...	...	...	1938	...	2135	...	|	2315
Haverfordwest d.	|	...	2333	...	...	...	1138	...	|	1331	...	...	1528	...	...	1747	...	...	...	1953	...	2151	...	|	2330
Clarbeston Road d.	2236**x**	...	2341**x**	...	...	...	1147**x**	...	|	1340**x**	...	...	1537**x**	...	...	1755**x**	...	...	...	2001**x**	...	2159**x**	...	2325**x**	2339**x**
Pembroke Dock d.	|	2218	|	...	...	...	|	1200	|	|	...	...	|	...	1625	|	...	...	1901	|	...	|	2146	|	|
Tenby d.	|	2245	|	...	...	...	|	1228	|	|	...	...	|	...	1653	|	...	...	1929	|	...	|	2214	|	|
Whitland d.	2250	2315	2354	...	...	...	1203	1300	1314	1357	...	...	1554	...	1724	1810	...	...	2000	2017	...	2214	2245	2338	2353
Carmarthen a.	2308	2334	0016	...	...	...	1221	1317	1330	1415	...	...	1611	...	1742	1829	...	...	2017	2036	...	2231	2306	2357	0014
Carmarthen d.	2310	...	...	0943	1030	1053	1224	1320	1340	1425	1458	1540	1616	1655	1747	...	1905	...	2021	...	2115	2234	...	2357	...
Llanelli 146 d.	2341	...	...	1013	1056	1123	1250	1350	1402	1451	1527	1610	1649	1722	1818	...	1932	2004	2052	...	2141	2304	...	|	...
Swansea 146 a.	0003	...	...	1036	1118	1147	1313	1416	|	1513	1543	1635	1715	1739	1846	...	1949	2025	2119	...	2204	2327	...	0037	...
Swansea 132 d.	...	...	...	...	1131	*1224*	1343	...	|	1534	1551	...	1730	1751	*1851*	...	1955	2040	...	...	2210	2331	...	...	...
Neath 132 d.	...	...	...	...	1142	*1236*	1354	...	|	1545	1603	...	1741	1803	*1903*	...	2007	2051	...	...	2221	2343	...	...	...
Port Talbot 132 d.	...	...	...	...	1149	*1243*	1401	...	|	1552	1610	...	1748	1810	*1910*	...	2014	2058	...	...	2228	2350	...	...	...
Bridgend 132 d.	...	...	...	...	1204	*1256*	1417	...	|	1607	1623	...	1803	1823	*1923*	...	2028	2114	...	...	2245	0006	...	...	...
Cardiff Central 132 a.	...	...	...	...	1233	*1317*	1448	...	1509	1637	1645	...	1832	1846	*1946*	...	2049	2137	...	...	2310	0035	...	...	...
Manchester P **149** a.	...	...	...	...	1614	...	1818	...	...	2016	...	...	2219	...	...	...	...	...	...	...	...	...	...	...	...

A – To London (operated by GW, see Table **132**). Conveys 12 and 🍷.
C – From Crewe (Tables **146** and **149**).
S – From Shrewsbury (Table **146**).
x – Calls on request.

Service from Jan. 1 (for service until Dec. 31 please contact National Rail Enquiries ✆ +44 (0) 3457 48 49 50).

km		Ⓐ A	Ⓐ B	Ⓐ A	Ⓐ P	Ⓐ A	Ⓐ G	Ⓐ A		Ⓐ A	Ⓐ G	Ⓐ A	Ⓐ D	Ⓐ	⑤	Ⓐ	Ⓐ	Ⓐ	⑥ E	⑥ A	⑥ B	⑥ A	⑥ G
0	**Cardiff** Central ‡ d.	0630	0700	0730	0800	0830	0900	0930	and at the same	1930	2000	2030	2100	2130	2204	2204	2236	2327	0455	0630	0700	0730	0800
19	Newport ‡ d.	0644	0714	0744	0815	0844	0915	0944	minutes past each hour until	1944	2016	2044	2115	2144	2218	2218	2251	2345	0509	0644	0715	0744	0815
61	**Bristol** T Meads a.	0720	0751	0818	0851	0919	0954	1019	▲ H	2017	2052	2117	2151	2221	2259	2306	2337**r**	0033	0553	0718	0752	0818	0854

		⑥ G	⑥ A	⑥	⑥ A	⑥ D	⑥	⑦ A	⑦ A	⑦ A	⑦ A	⑦ A	⑦ A	⑦ A	⑦ A	⑦ A	⑦ J	⑦ A	⑦ A	⑦ A	⑦ A	⑦ A	⑦	⑦ K
Cardiff Central ‡ d.	and at the same	1900	1930	1954	2030	2100	2200	0810	0908	1008	1108	1208	1308	1408	1508	1608	1635	1708	1740	1808	1908	2019	2118	2210
Newport ‡ d.	minutes past each hour until	1915	1944	2010	2044	2115	2215	0828	0926	1029	1129	1228	1328	1425	1529	1627	1653	1728	1758	1826	1929	2033	2137	2229
Bristol T Meads a.	▽	1952	2018	2049	2117	2154	2300	0909	1012	1103	1203	1304	1402	1503	1604	1703	1728	1802	1839	1904	2007	2113	2221	2313

	②–⑤ E	Ⓐ	Ⓐ	Ⓐ D	Ⓐ E	Ⓐ G	Ⓐ M	Ⓐ	Ⓐ A	Ⓐ G		Ⓐ G	Ⓐ A	Ⓐ B	Ⓐ A	Ⓐ	Ⓐ A	Ⓐ A	⑥ E	⑥	⑥	⑥	⑥
Bristol T Meads d.	0136	0554	0620	0651	0717	0721	0753	0824	0854	0921	and at the same	1921	1954	2015	2054	2119	2154	2254	0136	0651	0723	0755	0823
Newport ‡ a.	0209**s**	0636	0659	0726	0748	0803	0826	0905	0924	0958	minutes past each hour until	1959	2025	2047	2125	2159	2235**a**	2334**f**	0209**s**	0727	0758	0825	0901
Cardiff Central ‡ a.	0230	0651	0715	0741	0803	0821	0842	0926	0940	1014	▽ L	2014	2041	2103	2141	2214	2257**a**	2357**f**	0230	0744	0817	0842	0923

	⑥ A	⑥		⑥ G	⑥ A	⑥ B	⑥ A	⑥ G	⑥ A	⑥ A	⑦	⑦	⑦ M	⑦ A	⑦	⑦ A	⑦	⑦ J	⑦ A	⑦	⑦ A		⑦ A	⑦ A
Bristol T Meads d.	0855	0922	and at the same	1919	1954	2010	2054	2129	2157	2255	0848	0948	1048	1147	1248	1348	1416	1448	1548	1612	1648	and	2145	2248
Newport ‡ a.	0925	0958	minutes past each hour until	1955	2023	2044	2123	2209	2237	2335	0925	1019	1121	1221	1319	1419	1447	1520	1619	1644	1722	hourly until	2220	2320
Cardiff Central ‡ a.	0942	1018	▽ N	2013	2042	2100	2142	2232	2300	2356	0944	1040	1143	1241	1340	1441	1508	1540	1641	1705	1744	▲	2248	2341

A – To/from Portsmouth Harbour (Table **140**).
B – To/from Manchester Piccadilly (Tables **121/122**).
D – To/from Westbury (Table **140**).
E – To/from London Paddington (Table **132**).
G – To/from Taunton (Table **120a**).
H – 0900 from Cardiff extended to Penzance (Tables **115/117**); 1300 from Cardiff extended to Exeter St Davids (Table **115**).
J – To/from Brighton (Table **140**).
K – To Warminster (Table **140**).
L – 1121 from Bristol starts from Penzance (Tables **115/117**); 1521 from Bristol starts from Paignton (Table **115**).
M – From Frome (Table **140**).
N – 0921 from Bristol starts from Weston-super-Mare d. 0839; all other xx21 services from Bristol start from Taunton (Table **134**).
P – To Paignton (Table **115**).
a – On ⑤ arrives Newport 2229, Cardiff 2244.
f – On ⑤ arrives Newport 2328, Cardiff 2355.
r – On ⑤ arrives 2326.
s – Calls to set down only.
▽ – Timings may vary by up to 6 minutes.
▲ – Timings may vary by up to 3 minutes.
‡ – For additional services see Tables **121, 132** and **149**.

138 WORCESTER - GLOUCESTER - BRISTOL

2nd class GW

km		Ⓐ	ⒶA	ⒶB	ⒶC	ⒶB	ⒶB	ⒶB	ⒶB	ⒶB	ⒶB	ⒶB	ⒶB	ⒶB	ⒶB	ⒶB	Ⓐ	Ⓐ	Ⓐ	Ⓐ	Ⓐ	⑥A	⑥
	Great Malvern d.	...	...	...	...	...	...	0850	...	1048	...	1251	...	1450	...	1648	...	1850	...	2136	...	...	...
0	**Worcester** Shrub Hill d.	0528	...	...	...	0649	*0708*	0906	...	1106	...	1306	...	1506	...	1706	...	1907	...	2152	2228	...	...
24	Ashchurch for Tewkesbury d.	0544	...	...	*0627*	0705	|	0924	...	1124	...	1324	...	1524	...	1724	...	1924	...	2208	2251	...	...
36	Cheltenham Spa ◧ d.	0554	...	0624	*0643*	0716	*0731*	0933	...	1133	...	1333	...	1533	...	1733	...	1934	2120	2218	2305	...	0648
46	**Gloucester** ◧ a.	0603	...	0634	*0653*	0726	*0740*	0942	...	1142	...	1344	...	1544	...	1742	...	1943	2129	2228	2317	...	0658
46	**Gloucester** d.	...	0616	0642	0705	0741	0841	0944	1041	1147	1242	1346	1441	1546	1640	1746	1842	1945	2135	2232	...	0621	0702
97	**Bristol** Parkway d.	...	0657	0724	0749	0820	0919	1022	1120	1223	1319	1423	1520	1624	1720	1823	1919	2027	2211	2304	...	0701	0743
108	**Bristol** Temple Meads a.	...	0713	0740	0800	0836	0935	1039	1135	1235	1336	1439	1538	1639	1735	1838	1934	2038	2224	2314	...	0713	0755

	⑥	⑥B	⑥B	⑥B	⑥B	⑥	⑥B	⑥B	⑥B	⑥B	⑥B	⑥B	⑥B	⑥	⑥	⑥	⑥	⑦A	⑦	⑦	⑦	⑦	⑦	⑦
Great Malvern d.	...	...	...	...	...	1045	...	...	...	1450	...	1650	...	1850	...	2115	...	...	...	...	...	...	...	...
Worcester Shrub Hill d.	...	0649	...	0910	...	1113	...	1254	...	1507	...	1708	...	1908	...	2132	2225	...	1138	1436	1640	1840	2038	...
Ashchurch for Tewkesbury d.	*0633*	0705	...	0927	...	1129	...	1311	...	1524	...	1724	...	1924	...	2151	2241	...	1153	1451	1656	1856	2054	...
Cheltenham Spa ◧ d.	0648	0716	...	0936	...	1138	...	1320	...	1534	...	1734	...	1934	2102	2202	2251	1004	1203	1501	1706	1906	2103	2201
Gloucester ◧ a.	0658	0725	...	0946	...	1147	...	1335	...	1543	...	1744	...	1944	2112	2212	2301	1014	1214	1512	1716	1916	2113	2211
Gloucester d.	0702	0741	0841	0947	1041	1150	1242	1342	1441	1547	1642	1747	1841	1947	2114	...	...	1016	1218	1513	1719	1919	2115	...
Bristol Parkway d.	0743	0820	0919	1024	1120	1225	1319	1420	1519	1624	1720	1825	1920	2026	2152	...	...	1055	1258	1556	1757	1958	2155	...
Bristol Temple Meads a.	0755	0834	0935	1040	1135	1238	1334	1437	1534	1639	1736	1839	1935	2039	2206	...	...	1107	1309	1608	1809	2010	2207	...

	Ⓐ	Ⓐ	ⒶB	ⒶB	Ⓐ	Ⓐ	ⒶB	ⒶB	ⒶB	ⒶB	ⒶB	ⒶB	ⒶB	ⒶB	ⒶB	Ⓐ	Ⓐ	ⒶA	Ⓐ	⑥	⑥	⑥B	⑥B
Bristol Temple Meads d.	...	...	0734	0841	0941	1041	1141	1241	1341	1441	1541	1641	1741	1836	1941	2041	...	2141	2242	...	...	0741	0841
Bristol Parkway d.	...	...	0749	0855	0952	1053	1152	1252	1352	1453	1552	1652	1753	1847	1952	2052	...	2153	2253	...	...	0753	0853
Gloucester a.	...	...	0832	0933	1032	1132	1231	1331	1431	1532	1631	1732	1833	1926	2032	2132	...	2233	2338	...	...	0832	0930
Gloucester ◧ d.	0600	0714	...	0938	...	1137	...	1337	...	1537	...	1737	...	1934	2038	2133	2151	*2247*	...	0600	0715	...	0938
Cheltenham Spa ◧ a.	0611	0724	...	0946	...	1146	...	1345	...	1546	...	1746	...	1944	2048	2144	2200	*2256*	...	0610	0724	...	0946
Ashchurch for Tewkesbury a.	0619	0733	...	0955	...	1156	...	1355	...	1556	...	1756	...	1953	...	2153	|	...	...	0619	0733	...	0955
Worcester Shrub Hill a.	0639	0753	...	1014	...	1213	...	1412	...	1614	...	1816	...	2018	...	2211	2222	...	...	0640	0753	...	1014
Great Malvern a.	...	0809	...	1031	...	1230	...	1430	...	1629	...	1835	...	2035	...	...	...	...	...	...	...	...	1033

	⑥B	⑥B	⑥B	⑥B	⑥B	⑥B	⑥B	⑥B	⑥B	⑥B	⑥B	⑥	⑥		⑦	⑦		⑦	⑦	⑦	⑦		⑦	⑦
Bristol Temple Meads d.	0941	1041	1141	1241	1341	1441	1541	1641	1741	1841	1941	2041	2211	...	0920	1211	...	1441	1641	1837	2041	...	2230	...
Bristol Parkway d.	0952	1052	1152	1255	1352	1453	1552	1652	1752	1852	1952	2052	2223	...	0929	1222	...	1451	1651	1846	2050	...	2239	...
Gloucester a.	1033	1132	1231	1332	1434	1533	1633	1733	1832	1932	2032	2132	2303	...	1010	1303	...	1532	1732	1930	2132	...	2321	...
Gloucester ◧ d.	...	1137	...	1337	...	1537	...	1737	...	1938	2038	2138	...	...	1012	1305	...	1534	1735	1937	2136	...	...	2356
Cheltenham Spa ◧ a.	...	1146	...	1346	...	1547	...	1747	...	1947	2048	2148	...	...	1021	1316	...	1544	1745	1946	2145	...	...	0007
Ashchurch for Tewkesbury a.	...	1156	...	1355	...	1556	...	1756	...	1956	...	2157	...	...	1030	1325	...	1554	1755	1956	...	...	...	...
Worcester Shrub Hill a.	...	1213	...	1413	...	1614	...	1816	...	2014	...	2218	...	...	1051	1344	...	1611	1815	2022	...	...	...	...
Great Malvern a.	...	...	...	1432	...	1632	...	1836	...	2035	...	...	...	...	...	...	...	...	...	...	...	...	...	...

A – To/from Taunton (Table **120a**). B – To/from Weymouth, Westbury or Frome (see Table **140**). C – To Swindon (Table **132**). ◧ – See also Tables **121** and **133.**

140 BRISTOL - WESTBURY - SOUTHAMPTON, PORTSMOUTH and WEYMOUTH

GW, SW

km		⚒	Ⓐ	⑥	ⒶP	Ⓐ	⑥	⚒	⚒C	⚒	⚒	⚒	⑥A	ⒶA	⚒W	⚒	⚒A	⚒	⚒A	⚒	⚒A	⚒	ⒶA	⑥A	⚒W	⚒	⚒A
	Cardiff Central **136** d.	...	...	...	...	...	...	...	...	0630	...	0730	...	...	...	0830	...	0930	...	1030	...	1130	...	...	...	1230	...
0	**Bristol** Temple M d.	...	...	...	0515	0544	0549	...	...	0722	0747	0822	0839	0841	0851	0922	0946	1022	1048	1122	1149	1222	1239	1243	1249	1322	1344**g**
19	Bath Spa d.	...	...	...	|	0603	0607	...	...	0736	0807	0836	0857	0859	0907	0935	1005	1035	1107	1135	1207	1235	1256	1301	1307	1335	1402**g**
34	Bradford on Avon d.	...	...	...	0539	0619	0623	...	...	0748	0823	0847	0913	0915	0921	0947	1020	1047	1123	1147	1223	1247	1312	1313	1319	1347	1418**g**
39	Trowbridge **132a** d.	...	...	...	0546	0626	0629	...	0646**t**	0754	0829	0854	0919	0921	0927	0954	1027	1053	1129	1153	1229	1253	1318	1319	1327	1353	1424**g**
46	**Westbury** **132a** a.	...	...	...	0554	0633	0636	...	0653**t**	0804**c**	0836	0901	0926	0928	0935	1001	1034**d**	1101	1136	1201	1236	1301	1325	1326	1334	1401	1431**g**
46	**Westbury** d.	0524	0549	0602	...	0640	0643	0654	0701	0805**c**	...	0902	0933	0933	0939	1001	1035**d**	1101	...	1201	1239	1301	1330	1329	1339	1401	1435**g**
	Frome d.	|	|	|	...	|	|	0703	|	|	...	|	0942	0942	|	|	1044	|	...	|	1248	|	|	|	|	|	1453**j**
	Castle Cary d.	|	|	|	...	|	|	0721	|	|	...	|	1000	1000	|	|	1101	|	...	|	1305	|	|	|	|	|	...
	Yeovil Pen Mill d.	|	|	|	...	|	|	0735	|	|	...	|	1015	1014	|	|	1115	|	...	|	1319	|	|	|	|	|	...
	Dorchester West d.	|	|	|	...	|	|	0809	|	|	...	|	1054	1048	|	|	1149**a**	|	...	|	1356	|	|	|	|	|	...
	Weymouth a.	|	|	|	...	|	|	0824	|	|	...	|	1109	1103	|	|	1209	|	...	|	1410	|	|	|	|	|	...
53	Warminster d.	0532	0557	0610	...	0648	0651	...	0712	0810	...	0910	...	...	0946	1010	...	1109	...	1209	...	1309	1339	1338	1346	1409	...
85	**Salisbury** d.	0555	0619	0632	...	0711	0724**b**	...	0736	0833	...	0932	...	...	1009	1032	...	1132	...	1232	...	1331	1402	1402	1412	1432	...
112	Romsey d.	...	0638	0651	...	0730	0743	...	0754	0852	...	0950	...	...	...	1050	...	1150	...	1250	...	1350	1421	1421	...	1450	...
123	**Southampton** Cent a.	...	0649	0702	...	0740	0754	...	0809	0904	...	1004	...	...	...	1104	...	1203	...	1304	...	1404	1432	1432	...	1504	...
147	Fareham a.	...	0715	0727	...	0805	0823	...	...	0927	...	1027	...	...	...	1127	...	1227	...	1327	...	1427	1458	1455	...	1527	...
164	**Portsmouth** & S'sea a.	...	0738	0746	...	0824	0845	...	...	0946	...	1046	...	...	...	1146	...	1246	...	1346	...	1446	**B**	**B**	...	1546	...
165	**Portsmouth** Harbour a.	...	0742	0752	...	0828	0851	...	...	0952	...	1052	...	...	...	1152	...	1252	...	1352	...	1452	...	...	...	1552	...

	ⒶE	⚒	⚒A	⚒	⚒A	⚒W	⚒	⚒A	ⒶG	Ⓐ	⑥	⚒A	⚒	⑥	ⒶD	⚒A	⑥	Ⓐ	ⒶG	⚒	⑥	Ⓐ	⚒	⚒	ⒶG	⚒	⚒	⑥
Cardiff Central **136** d.	...	1330	...	1430	...	...	1530	...	**W**	1630	1630	...	1730	...	...	...	1830	1830	...	...	1930	1930	...	2030	...	2100	...	...
Bristol Temple M d.	...	1422	1448	1522	1544	1551	1622	1648	...	1723	1722	1749	1822	...	...	1849	1922	1923	...	1949	2022	2022	2049	2122	...	2201	2223	2310
Bath Spa d.	...	1435	1506	1535	1602	1607	1635	1706	...	1737	1726	1807	1836	...	...	1907	1936	1937	...	2007	2036	2036	2107	2136	...	2219	2236	2328
Bradford on Avon d.	...	1447	1522	1547	1618	1624	1647	1723	...	1750	1748	1823	1848	...	...	1923	1948	1950	...	2023	2048	2047	2123	2148	...	2235	2247	2344
Trowbridge **132a** d.	...	1453	1528	1554	1624	1630	1653	1729	...	1757	1754	1829	1854	...	1924	1929	1954	1957	...	2029	2054	2053	2129	2154	...	2241	2253	2350
Westbury **132a** a.	...	1501	1536	1601	1633	1637	1701	1736	...	1806	1801	1836	1903**e**	...	1931	1939	2001	2006	...	2036	2101	2100	2136	2203**t**	...	2250	2300	2357
Westbury d.	1457	1501	1538	1601	...	1639	1701	1738	1745	1807	1802	1840	1904**e**	1920	1940	...	2002	2009	2011	2037	2102	2101	2140	2203**t**	2218	...	2305	2358
Frome d.	1507	|	1547	|	...	|	|	1747	|	|	|	1849	|	|	|	...	|	|	|	2048	|	|	2150	|	|	...	|	0009
Castle Cary d.	1524	|	1609**j**	|	...	|	|	1805	|	|	|	1906	|	|	|	...	|	|	|	...	|	|	2208	|	|	...	|	...
Yeovil Pen Mill d.	1539	|	1624	|	...	|	|	1820	|	|	|	1919	|	|	|	...	|	|	|	...	|	|	2223	|	|	...	|	...
Dorchester West d.	...	|	1658	|	...	|	|	1855	|	|	|	1954	|	|	|	...	|	|	|	...	|	|	2258	|	|	...	|	...
Weymouth a.	...	|	1710	|	...	|	|	1912	|	|	|	2010	|	|	|	...	|	|	|	...	|	|	2314	|	|	...	|	...
Warminster d.	...	1509	...	1609	...	1647	1709	...	1752	1815	1810	...	1910	1930	1950	...	2010	2017	2019	...	2110	2109	...	2211	2226	...	2312	...
Salisbury d.	...	1532	...	1632	...	1709	1732	...	1817	1837	1833	...	1933	1952	2011	...	2033	2039	2042	...	2133	2132	...	2232	2246	...	2338	...
Romsey d.	...	1550	...	1650	...	...	1750	...	...	1855	1851	...	1951	2011	2030	...	2051	2057	...	...	2151	2150	...	2253	...	...	...	...
Southampton Cent a.	...	1604	...	1704	...	...	1804	...	...	1905	1903	...	2003	2022	2044	...	2103	2107	...	...	2202	2202	...	2304	...	...	...	...
Fareham a.	...	1627	...	1727	...	...	1827	...	...	1927	1927	...	2027	...	...	...	2127	2129	...	...	2226	2242	...	2327	...	...	...	...
Portsmouth & S'sea a.	...	1646	...	1746	...	...	1852**r**	...	...	1947	1946	...	2048	...	...	...	2146	2147	...	...	2245	2258	...	2348	...	...	...	...
Portsmouth Harbour a.	...	1652	...	1752	...	...	1858**r**	...	...	1951	1952	...	2053	...	...	...	2152	2151	...	...	2252	2303	...	2352	...	...	...	...

	Ⓐ	⑦	⑦	⑦	⑦	⑦B	⑦	⑦B	⑦	⑦		⑦	⑦W	⑦	⑦	⑦W	⑦B	⑦	⑦	⑦	⑦	⑦	⑦	⑦	⑦	⑦	⑦
Cardiff Central **136** d.	...	...	0810	...	0908	1008	1108	1208	...	1308	...	1408	...	1508	1608	...	1635	...	1708	1740	1808	1908	...	2019	...	...	2210
Bristol Temple M d.	2320	0823	0911	0925	1015	1110	1210	1310	...	1410	...	1510	1604	1615	1710	...	1740	1743	1810	1847	1910	2015	2048	2125	2135	2215	2315
Bath Spa d.	2338	0842	0930	0944	1027	1126	1227	1327	...	1428	...	1527	1620	1627	1728	...	1752	1801	1827	1901	1926	2027	2106	2139	2149	2233	2329
Bradford on Avon d.	2354	0855	0943	1000	1044	1139	1244	1340	...	1444	...	1540	1631	1644	1740	...	1805	1816	1839	1913	1938	2044	2123	2151	2200	2250	2341
Trowbridge **132a** d.	2359	0902	0949	1007	1050	1147	1250	1348	...	1451	...	1547	1637	1650	1747	...	1812	1824	1847	1919	1946	2053	2130	2157	2206	2256	2347
Westbury **132a** a.	0007	0908	0957	1013	1058	1154	1256	1354	...	1457	...	1554	1644	1658	1754	...	1819	1831	1854	1928	1953	2100	2137	2204	2213	2303	2354
Westbury d.	0008	0912	1000	1018	1101	1201	1301	1400	1425	1500	...	1603	1646	1701	1801	1816	1820	1831	1901	1930	1959	2104	2138	2205	2215	...	2355
Frome d.	0017	0923	|	1031	|	|	|	|	1433	|	...	|	|	|	|	1804**f**	|	1839	|	|	|	|	2148	|	|	...	0004
Castle Cary d.	...	0940	|	1049	|	|	|	|	1450	|	...	|	|	|	|	|	|	1858	|	|	|	|	2205	|	|	...	...
Yeovil Pen Mill d.	...	0954	|	1104	|	|	|	|	1505	|	...	|	|	|	|	|	|	1912	|	|	|	|	2221	|	|	...	...
Dorchester West d.	...	1029	|	1141	|	|	|	|	1540	|	...	|	|	|	|	|	|	1947	|	|	|	|	2255	|	|	...	...
Weymouth a.	...	1042	|	1154	|	|	|	|	1554	|	...	|	|	|	|	|	|	2003	|	|	|	|	2307	|	|	...	...
Warminster d.	...	...	1009	...	1108	1210	1308	1410	▬	1507	...	1612	1653	1710	1808	1823	1829	...	1908	1937	2008	2111	...	2213	2222	...	...
Salisbury d.	...	...	1033	...	1132	1232	1332	1435	...	1530	...	1632	1716	1732	1832	1843	1856	...	1932	2000	2032	2132	...	2236	2246	...	...
Romsey d.	...	...	1051	...	1150	1250	1350	1454	...	1550	...	1650	...	1750	1850	...	1914	...	1950	2019	2050	2150	...	2256	...	...	...
Southampton Cent a.	...	...	1104	...	1203	1303	1403	1502	⑦	1603	...	1703	...	1803	1903	...	1925	...	2003	2028	2103	2203	...	2306	...	...	...
Fareham a.	...	...	1127	...	1226	1329	1426	1527	1544	1625	...	1726	...	1826	1924	...	1949	...	2024	2053	2124	2228	...	2330	...	...	...
Portsmouth & S'sea a.	...	...	1145	...	1244	*1408*	1444	**B**	1608	1644	...	1744	...	1844	1944	...	**B**	...	2044	2114	2143	2245	...	2348	...	...	...
Portsmouth Harbour a.	...	...	1153	...	1252	*1413*	1452	...	1613	1651	...	1752	...	1853	1952	...	...	...	2052	2125	2151	2252	...	2356	...	...	...

A – From Gloucester, Cheltenham Spa, Worcester or Great Malvern (see Table **138**).
B – To Brighton (journey time from Fareham: 1 hr 16 m - 1 hr 29 m), also calling at Havant, Chichester, Worthing and Hove.
C – From Gloucester on Ⓐ (Table **132a**).
D – From Cheltenham Spa (Table **132a**).
E – From London Waterloo (see other direction of table).
G – From Yeovil (see other direction of table).
P – To London Paddington (Table **115**).
W – To London Waterloo (Table **113**).
a – Departs 1154 on ⑥.
b – Arrives 0712.
c – Arr. 0801/dep. 0802 on ⑥.
d – Arr. 1036/dep. 1037 on ⑥.
e – Arr. 1901/dep. 1902 on ⑥.
f – Calls at Frome before Westbury.
g – 5 minutes later on Ⓐ.
h – Arrives 1604.
j – Arrives 4 – 5 minutes earlier on Ⓐ.
r – Arrives 6 minutes earlier on ⑥.
t – Arr. 2201/dep. 2202 on ⑥.

PORTSMOUTH, SOUTHAMPTON and WEYMOUTH - WESTBURY - BRISTOL 140

km			Ⓐ	⚒A	Ⓐ	⚒	Ⓐ	⚒A	Ⓐ	⑥	⚒	⑥A	ⒶA	Ⓐ	⑥	ⒶA	⑥A	⚒	⚒A	⚒	⚒W	ⒶA	⑥A	⚒	⚒A	⑥A	⚒	ⒶA	⑥A
	Portsmouth Hbr ....d.	⚒	...	a	...	...	...	...	0600	0608	...	...	...	0705	0723	...	...	0823	...	0923	...	...	...	1023	...	...	1123	...	...
	Portsmouth & S....d.		...	...	...	...	...	...	0604	0612	...	...	...	0709	0727	...	...	0827	...	0927	...	B	B	1027	...	...	1127	...	...
	Fareham ....d.		...	...	...	...	...	...	0624	0632	...	...	...	0729	0747	...	...	0847	...	0947	...	1013	1015	1047	...	...	1147	...	...
	Southampton C ....d.		...	...	...	...	...	...	0646	0657	...	...	...	0753	0810	0823	0830	0910	...	1010	...	1042	1042	1110	...	...	1210	1227	1227
	Romsey ....d.		...	...	...	...	...	...	0700	0711	...	...	...	0811	0821	0835	0841	0921	...	1021	...	1054	1054	1121	...	...	1221	1239	1238
	Salisbury ....d.		...	0607	...	0640	...	...	0719	0730	...	...	...	0830	0840	0903	0905	0940	...	1040	1052	1113	1113	1140	...	...	1240	1307	1303r
	Warminster ....d.		...	0628	...	0700	...	0723	0739	0750	...	...	...	0852	0901	0925	0927	1001	...	1101	1112	1132	1133	1201	...	...	1301	1334	1325
0	**Weymouth** ....d.		...	|	...	|	0533	|	|	|	0644	...	...	|	|	|	|	|	0853	|	|	|	|	|	1110	1114	|	|	|
11	Dorchester West.d.		...	|	...	|	0546	|	|	|	0657	...	...	|	|	|	|	|	0906	|	|	|	|	|	1123	1127	|	|	|
44	Yeovil Pen Mill....d.		...	|	...	|	0621	|	|	|	0734	...	...	|	|	|	|	|	0941	|	|	|	|	|	1203	1206	|	|	|
63	Castle Cary ....d.		...	|	...	|	0635	|	|	|	0748	...	...	|	|	|	|	|	0955	|	|	|	|	|	1218	1220	|	|	|
86	Frome ....d.		...	|	0645	|	0656	|	|	|	0807	...	...	|	|	|	|	|	1015	|	|	|	|	|	1237	1238	|	|	|
95	**Westbury** ....a.		...	0637	0654	0708	0708	0732	0749	0800	0816	...	...	0901	0909	0935	0937	1009	1024	1109	1120	1140	1142	1209	1246	1247	1309	1342	1334
95	**Westbury** ..... **132a** d.		0558	0638	0655	0709	0717	0738	0754	0806	0817	0838	0845	0910	0910	0938	0938	1010	1038	1110	1121	1141	1144	1210	1247	1248	1310	1344	1338
105	Trowbridge.... **132a** d.		0604	0644	0702	0715	0723	0744	0800	0812	0824	0844	0851	0916	0916	0944	0945	1016	1044	1116	1127	1148	1151	1216	1253	1255	1316	1350	1344
110	Bradford on Avon...d.		0610	0650	0708	0721	0729	0750	0806	0818	0830	0850	0857	0922	0922	0950	0951	1022	1050	1122	1133	1154	1157	1222	1259	1301	1322	1356	1350
125	Bath Spa ....a.		0626	0706	0724	0733	0745	0807	0821	0830	0846	0905	0913	0934	0934	1006	1006	1034	1106	1134	1147	1210	1213	1234	1316	1317	1334	1412	1406
144	**Bristol** Temple M ..a.		0646	0727	0747	0752	0806	0829	0842	0844	0906	0927	0933	0951	0948	1028	1028	1048	1128	1148	1206	1229	1235	1248	1336	1337	1349	1435	1427
	Cardiff Cent **136** .a.		0741	...	0842	...	...	...	0940	0942	...	...	...	1040	1040	...	...	1142	...	1242	...	...	...	1342	...	...	1441	...	...

	⚒	⚒W	ⒶA	⑥A	ⒶD	⚒	⚒A	⚒	⚒A	⚒	ⒶC	ⒶA	⑥A	⚒	⚒A	⚒	⑥	Ⓐ	Ⓐ	⑥	ⒶW	⚒	⚒	⚒	⚒W	Ⓐ	⑥	⚒	ⒶW
Portsmouth Hbr.....d.	1223	...	...	...	W	1323	...	1423	...	1523	...	...	...	1623	...	1723	...	...	...	...	s	1823	...	1923	...	...	...	2023	s
Portsmouth & S ....d.	1227	...	...	...	...	1327	...	1427	...	1527	...	...	...	1627	...	1727	...	...	B	B	...	1827	...	1927	...	...	...	2027	...
Fareham..................d.	1247	...	...	...	...	1347	...	1447	...	1547	...	...	...	1647	...	1747	...	...	1814	1815	...	1847	...	1947	...	...	...	2047	...
Southampton C.....d.	1309	...	...	...	...	1410	...	1510	...	1610	...	...	...	1710	...	1810	...	...	1842	1845	...	1910	...	2010	...	...	...	2110	...
Romsey....................d.	1320	...	...	...	...	1421	...	1521	...	1621	...	...	...	1721	...	1821	...	...	1853	1856	...	1921	...	2021	...	...	...	2121	...
Salisbury ....d.	1339	1352	...	...	1424	1440	...	1540	...	1640	...	...	...	1740	1818	1840	...	...	1913	1915	1823	1940	...	2040	2057	...	...	2140	2025
Warminster ....d.	1400	1412	...	...	1444	1501	1528	1601	...	1701	...	1728	1728	1801	|	1859	...	...	1932	1935	|	2001	...	2101	2117	...	...	2201	|
Weymouth..........d.	|	|	1322	1322	|	|	|	|	1508	|	...	|	|	|	|	|	1730	1730	|	|	|	|	...	|	|	2021	2021	|	|
Dorchester West..d.	|	|	1335	1335	|	|	|	|	1521	|	...	|	|	|	|	|	1743	1743	|	|	|	|	...	|	|	2034	2034	|	|
Yeovil Pen Mill ....d.	|	|	1410	1410	|	|	|	|	1556	|	1653	|	|	|	|	|	1820	1823	|	|	1927	|	...	|	|	2106	2109	|	2127r
Castle Cary ....d.	|	|	1424	1427r	|	|	|	|	1610	|	1707	|	|	|	|	|	1840r	1837	|	|	1940	|	...	|	|	2118	2123	|	2141
Frome ....d.	|	|	1442	1445	|	|	|	|	1629	|	1724	|	|	|	|	|	1858	1856	|	|	1957	|	...	|	|	2137	2142	|	2158
Westbury ....a.	1409	1420	1451	1455	1451	1509	1537	1609	1638	1709	1733	1736	1737	1809	1826	1907c	1907	1904	1940	1944	2006	2010	...	2109	2125	2146	2152	2209	2212
Westbury ...... **132a** d.	1410	1421	1452	1456	...	1510	1538	1610	1639	1710	...	1738	1748	1810	1838	1908c	1921	1921	1941	1945	...	2010	2038	2110	2125	2155	2155	2210	...
Trowbridge .... **132a** d.	1416	1427	1459	1503	...	1516	1544	1616	1646	1716	...	1744	1754	1816	1844	1916	1927	1927	1948	1951	...	2016	2044	2116	2131	2202	2202	2216	...
Bradford on Avon....d.	1422	1433	1505	1509	...	1522	1550	1622	1652	1722	...	1750	1800	1822	1850	1922	1933	1933	1954	1957	...	2022	2050	2122	2137	2208	2208	2222	...
Bath Spa ....a.	1434	1446	1521	1521	...	1534	1606	1634	1709	1734	...	1806	1816	1835	1906	1934	1949	1949	2008	2009	...	2036	2106	2135	2150	2224	2224	2234	...
Bristol Temple M ...a.	1448	1505	1535	1536	...	1548	1629	1648	1731	1748	...	1828	1836	1849	1929	1948	2009	2009	2027	2028	...	2050	2129	2149	2206	2243	2245	2250	...
Cardiff Cent **136**..a.	1541	...	...	...	...	1642	...	1742	...	1849j	...	...	...	1942	...	2042	...	...	...	...	...	2142	...	2300t	...	...	...	2356t	...

	Ⓐ	⑥	Ⓐ		⑦	⑦	⑦	⑦	⑦	⑦	⑦	⑦W	⑦	⑦	⑦	⑦	⑦	⑦	⑦	⑦	⑦	⑦	⑦	⑦W	⑦	⑦	⑦	⑦	⑦
Portsmouth Hbr.....d.	...	...	2123	⑦	...	...	0908	...	...	1108	...	...	1308	...	1408	1508	...	...	1608	...	1708	...	1808	...	...	1908	...	2008	2205
Portsmouth & S ....d.	...	...	2127		...	...	0912	...	...	1112	B	...	1312	...	1412	1512	...	...	1612	B	1712	...	1812	...	B	1912	...	2012	2212
Fareham..................d.	...	...	2148		...	...	0932	...	...	1132	1232	...	1332	...	1432	1532	...	...	1632	1703	1732	...	1832	...	1905	1932	...	2032	2232
Southampton C.....d.	2120	2132	2222		...	...	0954	...	...	1154	1254	...	1354	...	1454	1554	...	...	1654	1726	1754	...	1854	...	1928	1954	...	2054	2257
Romsey....................d.	2131	2143	2234		...	...	1006	...	...	1206	1306	...	1406	...	1506	1606	...	...	1706	1739	1806	...	1906	...	1940	2006	...	2106	2308
Salisbury ....d.	2153	2204	2300		...	...	1025	...	...	1225	1325	1355	1425	...	1525	1625	...	1710	1725	1758	1825	...	1925	1955	2001	2025	...	2125	2328
Warminster ....d.	2215	2226	2320		...	...	1049	...	...	1244	1344	1415	1444	...	1544	1644	...	1736	1744	1818	1844	...	1944	2015	2021	2044	...	2144	2350
Weymouth..........d.	|	|	|		...	...	|	...	1105	|	|	|	|	1415	|	|	1610	|	|	|	|	1756	|	|	|	|	2009	|	|
Dorchester West..d.	|	|	|		...	...	|	...	1118	|	|	|	|	1428	|	|	1623	|	|	|	|	1809	|	|	|	|	2022	|	|
Yeovil Pen Mill ....d.	|	|	|		...	...	|	...	1154	|	|	|	|	1504	|	|	1658	|	|	|	|	1844	|	|	|	|	2057	|	|
Castle Cary ....d.	|	|	|		...	...	|	...	1208	|	|	|	|	1519	|	|	1713	|	|	|	|	1859	|	|	|	|	2110	|	|
Frome ....d.	|	|	|		...	0935	|	1140	1227	|	|	|	|	1537	|	|	1731	1757f	|	|	|	1918	|	|	|	|	2129	|	|
Westbury ....a.	2230	2235	2329		...	0944	1058	1149	1236	1254	1356	1423	1456	1546	1556	1656	1740	1744	1756	1826	1856	1927	1957	2023	2030	2056	2139	2156	2359
Westbury ...... **132a** d.	*2235*	2240	...		0848	0953	1058	1150	...	1256	1356	1424	1500	1547	1604	1700	1741	...	1800	1829	1901	1930	2000	2023	2039	2100	2149	2200	...
Trowbridge .... **132a** d.	*2241*	2246	...		0854	0959	1105	1156	...	1302	1402	1430	1506	1553	1610	1706	1748	...	1806	1835	1906	1936	2006	2029	2045	2106	2155	2206	...
Bradford on Avon....d.	*2247*	2252	...		0900	1005	1111	1202	...	1308	1408	1436	1512	1559	1616	1712	1754	...	1812	1841	1912	1944	2012	2035	2051	2112	2201	2212	...
Bath Spa ....a.	*2303*	2308	...		0917	1021	1124	1219	...	1322	1424	1450	1524	1615	1628	1724	1806	...	1829	1852	1925	2003	2025	2049	2108	2125	2218	2225	...
Bristol Temple M ...a.	*2325*	2328	...		0936	1040	1144	1238	...	1341	1444	1506	1540	1636	1641	1744	1831	...	1843	1914	1939	2025	2039	2105	2127	2140	2237	2240	...
Cardiff Cent **136**..a.	...	...	...		...	1143	1241	...	...	1441	1540	...	1641	...	1744	1841	...	...	1941	...	2043	...	2138	...	...	2248	...	2341	...

A – To Gloucester, Cheltenham Spa, Worcester or Great Malvern (see Table **138**).
B – From Brighton (journey time to Fareham 1hr 14m - 1hr 22m), also calling at Hove, Worthing, Chichester and Havant.
C – From Yeovil Junction (dep.1646). To London (see other direction of table).
D – To Yeovil (see other direction of table).
W – From London Waterloo (Table **113**).
a – Runs 3 minutes later on Ⓐ.
c – On ⑥ Westbury a. 1909 / d. 1910.
f – Arrival time. Calls after Westbury.
j – Arrives 1842 on ⑥.
r – Arrives 4 – 6 minutes earlier.
s – To Salisbury (see other direction of table).
t – Arrives 13 – 16 minutes earlier on ⑤.

EAST CROYDON - MILTON KEYNES 141

km			Ⓐ	Ⓐ	Ⓐ	Ⓐ	Ⓐ	Ⓐ	Ⓐ	Ⓐ	Ⓐ	Ⓐ		Ⓐ	Ⓐ	Ⓐ	Ⓐ	Ⓐ	Ⓐ			⑥	⑥
0	**East Croydon** ....d.	Ⓐ	...	...	...	...	...	...	0750	0808	0910	1010		1711	1811	1912	...	...	...	...	⑥	...	...
12	Clapham Junction .... ▶ d.		0503	0530	0555	0620	0638	0739	0819	0839	0939	1039	and at	1739	1839	1939	2039	2139	2239	...		0508	0538
18	Kensington Olympia ⊙ ...... ▶ d.		0514	0544	0607	0630	0649	0750	0831	0850	0950	1050	the same	1750	1850	1950	2050	2150	2250	...		0519	0549
27	Wembley Central ....d.		|	0602	0624	0647	0707	0808	0847	0908	1008	1109	minutes	1809	1909	2009	2108	|	|	...		|	0607
40	Watford Junction............ **142** d.		0540	0614	0636	0657	0719	0820	0901	0920	1020	1121	past each	1821	1921	2021	2120	2223	2332	...		0547	0620
76	Leighton Buzzard........... **142** d.		...	0642	...	...	0751	0848	...	0948	1048	1148	hour until	1848	1948	2048	2150	...	...	...		...	0647
87	Bletchley......................... **142** d.		...	0649	...	...	0758	0855	..	0955	1057	1155		1855	1955	2055	2158	...	...	...		...	0655
92	**Milton Keynes** .... **142** a.		...	0656	...	...	0803	0901	...	1001	1102	1200		1900	2000	2100	2205	...	...	...		...	0700

	⑥	⑥	⑥		⑥	⑥	⑥	⑥	⑥	⑥		⑦	⑦	⑦	⑦	⑦	⑦		⑦	⑦	⑦	⑦
East Croydon ....d.	...	0610	0710		1710	1810	1910	...	...	...	⑦	...	...	...	...	...	...		...	...	...	...
Clapham Junction .... ▶ d.	0609	0636	0739	and at	1739	1839	1938	2025	2150	2241		0815	0915	1015	1115	1205	1305	and at	1905	2005	2115	2215
Kensington Olympia ⊙ ...... ▶ d.	0620	0647	0750	the same	1750	1852	1948	2036	2201	2251		0826	0926	1026	1126	1216	1316	the same	1916	2016	2125	2226
Wembley Central ....d.	0638	0709	0809	minutes	1809	1909	|	|	|	|		|	|	|	|	|	|	minutes	|	|	|	|
Watford Junction............ **142** d.	0650	0721	0821	past each	1821	1921	2015	2109	2230	2319		0855	0957	1055	1154	1242	1342	past each	1942	2042	2153	2256
Leighton Buzzard........... **142** d.	...	0748	0848	hour until	1848	...	...	...	...	...		...	...	...	...	...	...	hour until	...	...	...	...
Bletchley......................... **142** d.	...	0755	0855		1855	...	...	...	...	...		...	...	...	...	...	...		...	...	...	...
Milton Keynes .... **142** a.	...	0800	0900		1900	...	...	...	...	...		...	...	...	...	...	...		...	...	...	...

		Ⓐ	Ⓐ	Ⓐ	Ⓐ	Ⓐ	Ⓐ	Ⓐ	Ⓐ		Ⓐ	Ⓐ	Ⓐ	Ⓐ	Ⓐ	Ⓐ	Ⓐ	Ⓐ			⑥	⑥	
Milton Keynes .... **142** d.	Ⓐ	...	...	...	0701	0813	...	0913	1013		1713	1813	1915	2013	2113	...	2211	...	...	⑥	...	...	...
Bletchley......................... **142** d.		...	...	...	0706	0817	...	0917	1017	and at	1717	1817	1920	2017	2117	...	2215	...	...		...	...	...
Leighton Buzzard........... **142** d.		...	...	...	0713	0824	...	0924	1024	the same	1724	1824	1927	2024	2124	...	2222	...	...		...	...	...
Watford Junction............ **142** d.		0554	0653	0725	0738	0852	0915	0952	1052	minutes	1752	1851	1954	2051	2151	2227	2253	2336	...		0552	0655	...
Wembley Central ....d.		0605	0705	0737	0750	0904	0927	1004	1103	past each	1804	1905	2006	2104	|	|	|	|	...		0603	0706	...
Kensington Olympia ⊡ ...... ▶ d.		0622	0722	0758	0807	0922	0947	1022	1122	hour until	1822	1920	2023	2122	2222	2251	2323	0007	...		0623	0724	...
Clapham Junction .... ▶ a.		0632	0732	0809	0817	0932	0957	1032	1132		1832	1930	2033	2132	2233	2301	2334	0017	...		0633	0734	...
East Croydon ....a.		...	...	...	0904	1001	...	1101	1201		1903	...	...	...	...	...	2359	...	...		0656	0801	...

	⑥		⑥	⑥	⑥	⑥	⑥	⑥	⑥	⑥		⑦	⑦	⑦	⑦	⑦		⑦	⑦	⑦	⑦	⑦
Milton Keynes .... **142** d.	0713		1713	1813	...	1914	...	...	...	...	⑦	...	...	...	...	...		...	...	...	...	...
Bletchley......................... **142** d.	0717	and at	1717	1817	...	1918	...	...	...	...		...	...	...	...	...	and at	...	...	...	...	...
Leighton Buzzard........... **142** d.	0724	the same	1724	1824	...	1925	...	...	...	...		...	...	...	...	...	the same	...	...	...	...	...
Watford Junction............ **142** d.	0752	minutes	1752	1851	1931	1951	2043	2144	2248	2325		0917	1017	1122	1222	1322	minutes	1922	2022	2117	2217	2317
Wembley Central ....d.	0804	past each	1804	1903	1942	|	|	|	|	|		|	|	|	|	|	past each	|	|	|	|	|
Kensington Olympia ⊡ ...... ▶ d.	0822	hour until	1822	1921	2001	2022	2111	2212	2316	2353		0947	1047	1149	1250	1349	hour until	1950	2049	2147	2247	2347
Clapham Junction .... ▶ a.	0832		1832	1931	2010	2032	2121	2221	2326	0002		0958	1058	1159	1259	1400		1959	2059	2200	2257	2357
East Croydon ....a.	0901		1901	2001	...	2101	...	...	...	...		...	...	...	...	...		...	...	...	...	0023

⊙ – All trains call at Shepherd's Bush, 2 – 3 minutes after Kensington Olympia.
⊡ – All trains call at Shepherd's Bush, 2 – 3 minutes before Kensington Olympia.
▶ – Additional local services run between Clapham Junction and Shepherd's Bush.

km	Ⓐ	Ⓐ	Ⓐ	Ⓐ	Ⓐ	Ⓐ	Ⓐ	Ⓐ A	Ⓐ	Ⓐ	Ⓐ	Ⓐ	Ⓐ	Ⓐ	Ⓐ	Ⓐ		Ⓐ	Ⓐ	Ⓐ	Ⓐ	Ⓐ	Ⓐ	Ⓐ	Ⓐ
0	**London** Euston 143 ‡ d.	0004	0034	...	...	0534	...	0624	0634	0713	0749	0754	0813	0849	0854	0913	and	1449	1454	1513	1549	1554	1613	1650	1713
28	Watford Junction 143 ‡ d.	0025	0057	...	...	0555	...	0641	0654	|	0803	0811	|	0903	0911	|	at	1503	1511	|	1603	1611	|	|	|
64	Leighton Buzzard d.	0053	0131	...	...	0628	...	0709	0725	0742	|	0836	0842	|	0936	0942	the	|	1536	1542	|	1636	1642	1720	|
75	Bletchley d.	0100	0138	...	...	0635	...	0716	0732	0750	|	0843	0850	0924y	0943	0950	same	|	1543	1550	|	1643	1650	1727	|
80	Milton Keynes 143 ‡ d.	0109	0146	0537	...	0640	...	0724	0737	0754	0825	0849	0854	0929y	0949	0954	minutes	1525	1549	1554	1625	1649	1654	1732	1748
106	**Northampton** 143 a.	0126	0203	0553	...	0656	...	0740	0753	0810	0840	0905	0911	0944y	1006	1010	past	1544	1606	1610	1640	1706	1713	1748	1810
106	**Northampton** 143 d.	...	*0516*	0555	0616	0658	0715	0745	0755	0813	0855	0916	*0925*	0955	...	1016	each	1555	...	1616	1655	1716	...	1755	1819
136	Rugby 143 ‡ d.	...	*0538*	0617	0638	0720	0737	0804	0817	0835	0917	0938	*0947*	1017	...	1038	hour	1617	...	1638	1717	1738	...	1817	1841
154	Coventry ‡ d.	...	*0550*	0630	0650	0732	0749	...	0830	0850	0930	0950	*1011*r	1030	...	1050	until	1630	...	1650	1730	1750	...	1830	1853
171	**Birmingham** Int'l ✈ ‡ d.	...	*0605*	0646	0705	0748	0805	...	0846	0905	0946	1005	*1029*	1046	...	1105	△	1646	...	1705	1746	1805	...	1846	1908
185	**Birmingham** New St ‡ a.	...	*0617*	0701	0717	0805	0817	...	0902	0918	1001	1017	*1042*	1101	...	1117		1702	...	1717	1801	1817	...	1901	1920

	Ⓐ	Ⓐ	Ⓐ	Ⓐ	Ⓐ	Ⓐ A	Ⓐ	Ⓐ	Ⓐ	Ⓐ	Ⓐ	Ⓐ A	Ⓐ	Ⓐ	Ⓐ	Ⓐ	Ⓐ	Ⓐ	Ⓐ	⑥	⑥	⑥	⑥	⑥	⑥	⑥
London Euston 143 ‡ d.	1724	1749	1752	1813	1816	1849	1852	1913	1949	1954	2013	2049	2054	2113	2149	2154	2224	2304	2324	0004	0034	...	...	0534	...	...
Watford Junction 143 ‡ d.	1743	|	1811	|	|	|	|	|	|	2011	|	|	2112	|	|	2215	2241	2328	2341	0025	0058	...	...	0553	...	...
Leighton Buzzard d.	1809	1820	|	|	1844	|	1920	1942	2018	2036	2042	2118	2137	2144	2218	2247	2307	0001	0007	0053	0130	...	...	0625	...	...
Bletchley d.	1816	|	1841	|	|	|	1927	|	|	2043	2049	|	2144	2152	|	2254	2314	0008	0014	0100	0137	0522	...	0632	...	...
Milton Keynes 143 ‡ d.	1822	1831	1846	1846	1854	1923	1932	1956	2029	2049	2054	2129	2150	2157	2232	2302	2323	0017	0022	0109	0146	0537	...	0637	...	...
Northampton 143 a.	1838	1848	1905	1900	1918	1938	1953	2011	2045	2106	2111	2146	2209	2215	2250	2320	2340	0034	0040	0126	0203	0553	...	0653	...	...
Northampton 143 d.	1839	1857	...	1920	1931	1947	1955	2019	2055	...	2116	2155	...	2219	2255	...	...	...	...	...	...	0555	0616	0655	0716	0737
Rugby 143 ‡ d.	1901	1919	...	1942	1956	2006	2017	2041	2117	...	2138	2217	...	2241	2317	...	...	...	...	...	...	0617	0638	0717	0738	0759
Coventry ‡ d.	1911	1932	...	1954	2011	...	2030	2053	2130	...	2150	2230	...	2253	2330	...	...	...	...	...	...	0630	0650	0730	0750	0811
Birmingham Int'l ✈ ‡ d.	1929	1948	...	2009	2029	...	2046	2108	2146	...	2205	2246	...	2311	2348	...	...	...	...	...	...	0646	0705	0746	0805	0829
Birmingham New St ‡ a.	1942	2003	...	2020	2042	...	2102	2120	2202	...	2218	2302	...	2322	0004	...	...	...	...	...	...	0701	0717	0801	0817	0842

	⑥	⑥	⑥	⑥	⑥	⑥	⑥	⑥	⑥	⑥		⑥	⑥	⑥	⑥	⑥	⑥	⑥	⑥	⑥	⑥	⑥	⑥	⑥	⑥	⑥
London Euston 143 ‡ d.	0624	...	0705	0749	0754	...	0849	0854	0913	0949	and	1754	1813	1849	1854	1913	...	1946	2034	2040	2107	2128	2154	2234	2304	2340
Watford Junction 143 ‡ d.	0641	...	0726	0803	0811	...	0903	0911	|	1003	at	1811	|	1903	1911	|	...	2002	2050	2101	2124	2144	2214	2250	2324	2359
Leighton Buzzard d.	0709	...	0759	|	0836	...	|	0936	0942	|	the	1836	1844	|	1936	1942	...	2034	2118	|	2150	2208	2247	2316	2356	0032
Bletchley d.	0719	...	0806	|	0843	...	0924	0943	0950	1024x	same	1843	1852	|	1943	1950	...	2041	2125	2131	2157	2215	2254	2323	0003	0039
Milton Keynes 143 ‡ d.	0724	...	0811	0825	0849	...	0929	0949	0954	1029x	minutes	1849	1856	1925	1949	1954	...	2049	2133	2140	2206	2224	2303	2331	0011	0047
Northampton 143 a.	0741	...	0828	0840	0905	...	0944	1006	1013	1045x	past	1906	1913	1944	2006	2011	...	2106	2150	2156	2223	2243	2320	2348	0028	0104
Northampton 143 d.	*0755*	0816	0837	0855	0916	0937	0955	...	1016	1055	each	...	1916	1955	...	2022	2055	2116	2159	2216	...	2255	...	...	...	...
Rugby 143 ‡ d.	*0817*	0838	0859	0917	0938	0959	1017	...	1038	1117	hour	...	1938	2017	...	2044	2117	2138	2221	2238	...	2317	...	...	...	...
Coventry ‡ d.	*0830*	0850	0911	0930	0950	1011	1030	...	1050	1130	until	...	1950	2030	...	2056	2130	2150	2233	2250	...	2330	...	...	...	...
Birmingham Int'l ✈ ‡ d.	*0846*	0905	0929	0946	1005	1029	1046	...	1105	1146	△	...	2005	2046	...	2114	2146	2205	2249	2305	...	2348	...	...	...	...
Birmingham New St ‡ a.	*0901*	0917	0942	1001	1017	1042	1101	...	1117	1201		...	2017	2102	...	2125	2201	2217	2304	2317	...	0004	...	...	...	...

⑦	⑦	⑦	⑦	⑦	⑦	⑦	⑦	⑦ A	⑦	⑦ A	⑦	⑦	⑦	⑦	⑦	⑦ A		⑦ A	⑦	⑦	⑦	⑦	⑦	⑦	⑦
London Euston 143 ‡ d.	0015	0654	0724	0752	0824	0855	0924	0954	1001	1024	1028	1054	1124	1154	1234	1250	and	1950	2034	2106	2130	2200	2228	2258	2334
Watford Junction 143 ‡ d.	0035	0713	0745	0810	0845	0914	0945	1010	1019	1040	1046	1114	1142	1214	1250	1306	at	2006	2050	2123	2150	2219	2249	2318	2355
Leighton Buzzard d.	0106	0741	0814	0839	0914	0941	1014	1035	1047	1105	1115	1143	1212	1243	1315	1327	the	2027	2115	2149	2219	2247	2318	2351	0028
Bletchley d.	0113	0748	0821	0845	0921	0948	1021	1042	|	1112	|	1150	1219	1250	1322	|	same	|	2122	2156	2226	2254	2325	2358	0035
Milton Keynes 143 ‡ d.	0119	0758	0830	0851	0927	0957	1027	1050	1058	1120	1128	1158	1228	1258	1328	1337	minutes	2037	2129	2204	2234	2303	2333	0006	0043
Northampton 143 a.	0136	0815	0847	0909	0944	1014	1044	1106	1116	1138	1145	1215	1244	1315	1344	1351	past	2054	2146	2221	2250	2319	2350	0024	0100
Northampton 143 d.	...	...	...	0926	1000	...	1100	1108	...	1140	1158	...	1255	...	1355	1402	each	2106	2155	...	2252	2332	...	...	...
Rugby 143 ‡ d.	...	...	...	0948	1022	...	1122	1130	...	1202	1220	...	1317	...	1417	1424	hour	2128	2217	...	2314	2354	...	...	...
Coventry ‡ d.	...	...	...	1000	1034	...	1134	...	...	...	1232	...	1330	...	1430	...	until	...	2230	...	2338	0007	...	...	...
Birmingham Int'l ✈ ‡ d.	...	...	...	1009	1052	...	1152	...	...	...	1250	...	1348	...	1448	...	△	...	2248	...	2356	...	...	...	...
Birmingham New St ‡ a.	...	...	...	1026	1103	...	1203	...	...	...	1301	...	1359	...	1459	...		...	2259	...	0007	...	...	...	...

Ⓐ	Ⓐ	Ⓐ	Ⓐ	Ⓐ	Ⓐ	Ⓐ	Ⓐ	Ⓐ	Ⓐ A	Ⓐ	Ⓐ	Ⓐ	Ⓐ	Ⓐ	Ⓐ	Ⓐ	Ⓐ A	Ⓐ	Ⓐ	Ⓐ	Ⓐ	Ⓐ	Ⓐ		Ⓐ
Birmingham New St ‡ d.	...	...	...	...	...	0545	...	...	...	0553	0633	...	0614	0654	0714	0733	0754	*0814*	0833	0854	0914	0933	0954	and	1554
Birmingham Int'l ✈ ‡ d.	...	...	...	...	...	0555	...	...	...	0605	0645	...	0630	0705	0730	0745	0805	*0830*	0845	0905	0930	0945	1005	at	1605
Coventry ‡ d.	...	...	...	...	...	0606	0557	...	...	0621	0700	...	0648	0721	0742	0804	0821	*0848*	0900	0925	0948	1000	1021	the	1621
Rugby 143 ‡ d.	...	...	...	0516	...	0620	0612	...	0647	0632	0712	...	0659	0732	0753	0815	0839	*0859*	0912	0938	0959	1012	1032	same	1632
Northampton 143 a.	...	...	...	0537	...	0640	0633	...	0709	0654	0735	...	0724	0754	0816	0837	0900	*0920*	0933	0959	1020	1033	1054	minutes	1657
Northampton 143 d.	0415	0448	0505	0546	0618	0641	0638	0700	0716	0710	0742	0732	0738	0805	0825	0847	0905	0925	0950	1005	1025	1050	1105	past	1705
Milton Keynes 143 ‡ d.	0430	0504	0521	0603	0635	|	0655	0718	|	0731	|	0747	0755	0822	0841	0905	0922	0941	1007	1022	1041	1107	1122	each	1722
Bletchley d.	0435	0509	0526	0608	0640	|	0700	|	|	|	|	0752	0800	0827	0846	|	0927	0946	|	1027	1046	|	1127	hour	1727
Leighton Buzzard d.	0442	0515	0533	0615	0647	|	0707	0727	|	0740	|	0759	0807	0833	0853	|	0934	0953	|	1034	1053	|	1134	until	1733
Watford Junction 143 ‡ d.	0513	0550	0602	0635	0705	|	|	|	|	|	|	0827	|	|	|	0928	0959	|	1031	1059	|	1131	1159	△	1759
London Euston 143 ‡ a.	0537	0611	0620	0651	0722	0729	0739	0802	0808	0812	0828	0848	0839	0910	0927	0946	1019	1023	1046	1119	1127	1146	1218		1818

	Ⓐ	Ⓐ	Ⓐ	Ⓐ	Ⓐ	Ⓐ	Ⓐ	Ⓐ	Ⓐ	Ⓐ	Ⓐ	Ⓐ	Ⓐ	Ⓐ	Ⓐ	Ⓐ	Ⓐ	Ⓐ	Ⓐ	⑥	⑥	⑥	⑥		⑥	⑥
Birmingham New St ‡ d.	...	1633	1654	1714	1733	1754	1814	1833	1854	1914	1933	1954	2033	2054	2134	2154	...	2254	2310	...	...	...	0614	...	0654	0714
Birmingham Int'l ✈ ‡ d.	...	1645	1705	1727	1745	1805	1830	1845	1905	1930	1945	2005	2045	2105	2145	2205	...	2305	2320	...	...	...	0630	...	0705	0730
Coventry ‡ d.	...	1700	1721	1742	1800	1821	1848	1900	1921	1948	2000	2021	2100	2121	2200	2221	...	2321	2331	...	...	...	0648	...	0721	0748
Rugby 143 ‡ d.	...	1716	1732	1756	1812	1832	1859	1918	1932	1959	2015	2032	2114	2132	2212	2232	...	2332	2344	...	...	...	0659	...	0732	0759
Northampton 143 a.	...	1738	1756	1817	1837	1853	1921	1941	1954	2023	2038	2053	2135	2154	2235	2253	...	2355	0005s	...	...	...	0720	...	0754	0820
Northampton 143 d.	1725	1750	1805	1825	1850	1905	1925	1950	2005	2025	...	2105	2137	2205	...	2255	2335	...	|	0515	0605	0705	0735	...	0805	0825
Milton Keynes 143 ‡ d.	1741	1807	1822	1841	1907	1922	1941	2007	2025	2041	...	2122	2153	2222	...	2313	2351	...	0024	0532	0622	0722	0752	...	0822	0841
Bletchley d.	1746	|	1827	1846	|	1927	1946	|	2030	2046	...	2127	2158	2227	...	2318	2356	...	|	0537	0627	0727	0757	...	0827	0846
Leighton Buzzard d.	1753	|	1833	1853	|	1933	1953	|	2037	2053	...	2134	2204	2233	...	2324	0003	...	|	0544	0633	0733	0803	...	0833	0853
Watford Junction 143 ‡ d.	|	1831	1859	|	1931	1959	|	2031	2101	|	...	2159	2233	2303	...	2359	0035	...	0052s	0617	0701	0759	0828	...	0859	|
London Euston 143 ‡ a.	1827	1846	1920	1928	1947	2020	2027	2048	2120	2128	...	2222	2252	2321	...	0021	0058	...	0113	0639	0720	0818	0846	...	0919	0927

	⑥	⑥	⑥	⑥	⑥		⑥	⑥	⑥	⑥	⑥	⑥	⑥	⑥	⑥	⑥	⑥	⑥	⑥	⑥ A	⑥	⑥	⑥	⑥	⑥	⑥
Birmingham New St ‡ d.	0733	0754	0814	0833	0854	and	1554	1614	1633	1654	1714	1733	1754	1814	1833	1854	1914	1933	1954	...	2033	2054	2134	2154	2214	2254
Birmingham Int'l ✈ ‡ d.	0745	0805	0830	0845	0905	at	1605	1630	1645	1705	1731	1745	1805	1830	1845	1905	1930	1945	2005	...	2045	2105	2145	2205	2230	2305
Coventry ‡ d.	0800	0821	0848	0900	0921	the	1621	1648	1700	1721	1749	1800	1821	1848	1900	1921	1948	2000	2021	...	2100	2121	2200	2221	2248	2321
Rugby 143 ‡ d.	0812	0832	0859	0912	0932	same	1632	1659	1712	1732	1759	1812	1832	1859	1912	1932	1959	2012	2032	2047	2112	2132	2212	2232	2259	2332
Northampton 143 a.	0836	0857	0920	0934	0954	minutes	1654	1720	1734	1753	1821	1834	1854	1920	1934	1953	2020	2035	2053	2106	2135	2153	2233	2253	2321	2355
Northampton 143 d.	0850	0905	0925	0950	1005	past	1705	1725	1750	1805	1831	1850	1905	1931	...	2002	2032	...	2102	2121	...	2205	2243	...	2330	...
Milton Keynes 143 ‡ d.	0907	0922	0941	1007	1022	each	1722	1741	1807	1822	1847	1907	1922	1947	...	2018	2047	...	2118	2135	...	2221	2259	...	2346	...
Bletchley d.	|	0927	0946	|	1027	hour	1727	1746	|	1827	1852	|	1927	1952	...	2023	|	...	|	2140	...	2226	2304	...	2351	...
Leighton Buzzard d.	|	0934	0953	|	1034	until	1734	1753	|	1834	1859	|	1934	1959	...	2030	2056	...	|	2147	...	2232	2311	...	2358	...
Watford Junction 143 ‡ d.	0934	0959	|	1031	1059	△	1759	|	1831	1859	1927	1931	1959	2027	...	2052	2126	...	2152	2220	...	2307	2346	...	0020	...
London Euston 143 ‡ a.	0949	1019	1027	1046	1119		1819	1827	1846	1919	1946	1946	2019	2046	...	2112	2146	...	2212	2238	...	2327	0006	...	0040	...

⑦	⑦	⑦	⑦	⑦		⑦	⑦	⑦	⑦	⑦	⑦	⑦ A	⑦		⑦	⑦	⑦ A	⑦	⑦	⑦ A		⑦	⑦	⑦	⑦
Birmingham New St ‡ d.	...	...	...	...	...	...	...	...	0914	...	1014	...	1114	and	...	1914	...	...	2014	...	...	2114	...	2214	2300
Birmingham Int'l ✈ ‡ d.	...	...	...	...	...	...	...	...	0925	...	1025	...	1125	at	...	1925	...	...	2025	...	...	2125	...	2225	2310
Coventry ‡ d.	...	...	...	...	...	...	...	...	0944	...	1044	...	1144	the	...	1944	...	...	2044	...	...	2144	...	2244	2321
Rugby 143 ‡ d.	...	...	...	...	...	...	...	...	0955	...	1055	1120	1155	same	1920	1955	2017	...	2055	2120	...	2155	...	2255	2335
Northampton 143 a.	...	...	...	...	...	...	...	...	1017	...	1117	1141	1217	minutes	1941	2017	2038	...	2117	2141	...	2217	...	2319	2354s
Northampton 143 d.	...	0615*	0753	0823	...	0853	0930	1008	1037	1106	1126	1150	1226	past	1950	2025	2051	...	2129	2155	...	2226	2300	...	|
Milton Keynes 143 ‡ d.	0642	0711	0809	0839	...	0909	0946	1025	1055	1123	1142	1207	1242	each	2007	2041	2107	2115	2145	2211	...	2242	2316	...	0013s
Bletchley d.	0647	0716	0814	0844	...	0914	0951	1030	1100	1128	1147	|	1247	hour	|	2046	|	2120	2150	2216	...	2246	2321	...	|
Leighton Buzzard d.	0653	0723	0821	0851	...	0921	0958	1037	1106	1135	1154	1215	1253	until	2016	2052	2115	2126	2156	2223	...	2253	2328	...	|
Watford Junction 143 ‡ d.	0725	0754	0853	0922	...	0952	1029	1105	1137	1206	1218	1240	1318	△	2035	2122	2140	2156	2226	2254	...	2323	2359	...	0043s
London Euston 143 ‡ a.	0745	0814	0913	0945	...	1013	1051	1126	1159	1226	1238	1301	1338		2054	2142	2158	2219	2248	2317	...	2343	0022	...	0103

A – To/from Crewe (Table **143**).

r – Arrives 0958.

s – Stops to set down only.

x – Trains 11xx and hourly to 17xx do not call at Bletchley and then run 4 minutes earlier to Northampton.

y – Trains 11xx and hourly to 14xx do not call at Bletchley and then run 4 minutes earlier to Northampton.

* – Connection by 🚌.

△ – Timings may vary by up to 3 minutes.

‡ – For faster journeys between these stations see Table **150**.

LM — LONDON - CREWE via Stoke-on-Trent — 143

km		⚒ ⑥	Ⓐ	Ⓐ	⑥	⚒	⚒		⚒	Ⓐ	⑥	⑥	Ⓐ	⑥	Ⓐ	⑥	Ⓐ	Ⓐ	Ⓐ	⑦ ⑦	⑦	⑦
0	**London** Euston **142 150/2/3** d.	...	...	...	...	0624	0746		1546	1646	1646	1746	1746	1846	1849	...	1946	2046	2049	...	0954	1024
27	Watford Junction ..... **142 150** d.	...	...	...	...	0641	|	and	|	|	|	|	|	|	|	...	|	|	|	...	1010	1040
78	Milton Keynes ... **142 150 152** d.	...	...	...	...	0724	0819	at	1619	1719	1719	1819	1819	1919	1923	...	2019	2119	2129	...	1050	1120
104	Northampton .... **142** d.	0541	0545	0635	0638	0745	|	the	|	|	|	|	|	|	1947	...	|	|	2155	0940	1108	1140
135	Rugby .... **142 150** d.	0602	0606	0659	0658	0804	0842	same	1642	1747	1742	1842	1847	1942	2006	...	2042	2145	2217	1003	1130	1203
158	Nuneaton .... d.	0616	0620	0712	0712	0816	0854	minutes	1654	1800	1754	1854	1900	1958	2019	...	2100	2200	|	1016	1143	1216
178	Tamworth (Low Level) .... d.	0629	0635	0729	0729	0829	0909	past	1709	1815	1809	1909	1915	2014	2032	...	2115	2215	|	1030	1157	1230
188	Lichfield Trent Valley .... d.	0635	0641	0735	0735	0835	0917	each	1717	1822	1817	1917	1922	2021	2038	...	2122	2222	|	1037	1204	1237
217	Stafford .... **153** d.	0658	0700	0755	0755	0855	0942	hour	1742	1842	1844	1942	1942	2044	2055	2110	2142	|	2353	1100	1221	1300
231	Stone .... d.	0707	0709	0804	0804	0904	0951	until	1751	|	1853	1951	|	|	2104	2119	2151	|	|	1109	1230	1309
243	Stoke on Trent .... **152** d.	0715	0721	0812	0815	0912	1002		1802	1907	1902	2002	2002	2102	2112	2127	2202	2251	|	1117	1241	1317
268	**Crewe** .... **152 153** a.	0737	0743	0834	0837	0937	1024		1824	1926	1927	2024	2025	2122	2134	2149	2224	2310	0022	1141	1303	1341

	⑦	⑦	⑦	⑦	⑦		⑦	⑦	⑦	⑦
London Euston **142 150/2/3** d.	1124	1250	1350	1450	1550	...	1650	1750	1850	1950
Watford Junction ..... **142 150** d.	1142	1306	1406	1506	1606	...	1706	1806	1906	2006
Milton Keynes ... **142 150 152** d.	1228	1337	1437	1537	1637	...	1737	1837	1937	2037
Northampton .... **142** d.	1302	1402	1502	1602	1702	...	1802	1902	2002	2106
Rugby .... **142 150** d.	1326	1426	1526	1626	1726	...	1826	1926	2026	2130
Nuneaton .... d.	1340	1440	1540	1640	1740	...	1840	1940	2040	2143
Tamworth (Low Level) .... d.	1355	1455	1555	1655	1755	...	1855	1955	2055	2158
Lichfield Trent Valley .... d.	1401	1501	1601	1701	1801	...	1901	2001	2101	2204
Stafford .... **153** d.	1421	1521	1621	1721	1821	...	1921	2021	2121	2223
Stone .... d.	1430	1530	1630	1730	1830	...	1930	2030	2130	2232
Stoke on Trent .... **152** d.	1440	1541	1641	1741	1841	...	1941	2041	2141	2241
Crewe .... **152 153** a.	1503	1603	1703	1803	1906	...	2006	2106	2206	2303

	⚒ Ⓐ	⑥	Ⓐ	⑥	⑥	Ⓐ	Ⓐ	⑥
Crewe .... **152 153** d.	0521	0601	0652	0700	0718	0649	0755	0802
Stoke on Trent .... **152** d.	|	0624	0717	0722	0738	|	0817	0828
Stone .... d.	|	|	|	0731	|	|	0825	0836
Stafford .... **153** d.	|	0648	0739	0748	0808	0710	0837	0855
Lichfield Trent Valley .... d.	0608	0705	0757	0805	0825	|	0854	0913
Tamworth (Low Level) .... d.	0615	0711	0803	0811	0831	|	0901	0920
Nuneaton .... d.	0631	0727	0819	0827	0847	|	0916	0936
Rugby .... **142 150** d.	0646	0743	0834	0843	0903	0839	0932	0953
Northampton .... d.	0716	|	|	|	|	0905	|	|
Milton Keynes .... **142 150 152** d.	|	0805	0900	0915	0925	0922	0954	1015
Watford Junction .... **142 150** d.	|	|	|	|	|	0959	|	|
London Euston .... **142 150/2/3** a.	0808	0840	0937	0952	1000	1019	1029	1050

	⚒		⚒	⚒	⑥	Ⓐ	Ⓐ	⑥		Ⓐ	⑦ ⑦	⑦	⑦	⑦	⑦		⑦	⑦	⑦	⑦	⑦	⑦	⑦
Crewe .... **152 153** d.	0902		1602	1702	1802	1802	1902	1902	...	2010	0932	1037	1137	1237	1337	...	1432	1537	1637	1737	1837	1937	2042
Stoke on Trent .... **152** d.	0928	and	1628	1728	1828	1828	1928	1928	...	2033	0953	1059	1159	1259	1359	...	1453	1559	1659	1759	1859	1959	2107
Stone .... d.	0936	at	1636	1736	1836	1836	1936	1936	...	2041	1001	1107	1207	1307	1407	...	1501	1607	1707	1807	1907	2007	2115
Stafford .... **153** d.	0955	the	1655	1755	1855	1855	1950	1951	...	2100	1019	1119	1219	1319	1419	...	1519	1619	1719	1819	1922	2019	2127
Lichfield Trent Valley .... d.	1013	same	1713	1813	1913	1913	2008	2008	...	2118	1036	1136	1236	1336	1436	...	1536	1636	1736	1836	1939	2036	2144
Tamworth (Low Level) .... d.	1020	minutes	1720	1820	1920	1920	2015	2015	...	2125	1043	1143	1243	1343	1443	...	1543	1643	1743	1843	1946	2043	2151
Nuneaton .... d.	1036	past	1736	1836	1936	1936	2030	2031	...	2140	1058	1158	1258	1358	1458	...	1558	1658	1758	1858	2001	2058	2206
Rugby .... **142 150** d.	1053	each	1753	1853	1952	1953	2047	2047	...	2158	1120	1220	1320	1420	1520	...	1620	1720	1820	1920	2017	2120	2222
Northampton .... d.	|	hour	|	|	2012	|	2107	2121	...	2217	1150	1250	1350	1450	1550	...	1650	1750	1850	1950	2051	2155	2244
Milton Keynes ... **142 150 152** d.	1115	until	1815	1915	...	2015	...	2135	...	...	1207	1307	1407	1507	1607	...	1707	1807	1907	2007	2107	2211	...
Watford Junction ..... **142 150** d.	|		|	|	...	|	...	2220	...	...	1240	1335	1435	1535	1635	...	1735	1835	1935	2035	2140	2254	...
London Euston **142 150/2/3** a.	1150		1852	1950	...	2051	...	2238	...	...	1301	1353	1453	1553	1653	...	1753	1853	1953	2054	2158	2317	...

LM — 2nd class only — NUNEATON - COVENTRY — Journey 22 minutes — *16 km* — 143a

From Nuneaton:

Ⓐ: 0633, 0737, 0833, 1014, 1114, 1214, 1314, 1413, 1514 and hourly until 2114, 2220.

⑥: 0644, 0814, 0914, 1014 and hourly until 1814, 1944, 2114, 2220.

⑦: 1236, 1411, 1511, 1611, 1711, 1811, 2011, 2200.

From Coventry:

Ⓐ: 0604, 0704, 0804, 0904, 1042 and hourly until 1842, 1942, 2042, 2142.

⑥: 0615, 0715, 0842, 0942, 1042 and hourly until 1742, 1842, 2015, 2142.

⑦: 1146, 1339, 1439, 1539, 1639, 1739, 1939, 2132.

LM — BEDFORD - BLETCHLEY — 143b

		Ⓐ	⑥	⚒	⚒	⚒	⚒	⚒	⚒		⚒	⚒	⚒	Ⓐ	⑥	Ⓐ		⑥	Ⓐ	⑥	Ⓐ	⑥	⚒	⚒
0	**Bedford** .... d.	0610	0629	0729	0829	0929	1055	1155	1255	...	1355	1455	1555	1640	1700	1740	...	1755	1826	1839	1929	1936	2100	2200
20	Woburn Sands .... d.	0642	0701	0801	0901	1001	1126	1226	1326	...	1426	1526	1626	1712	1731	1812	...	1826	1857	1910	2001	2007	2131	2232
27	**Bletchley** .... a.	0653	0712	0812	0912	1012	1138	1238	1338	...	1438	1538	1638	1722	1743	1822	...	1838	1909	1922	2012	2019	2143	2243
	Milton Keynes **142** .... a.	*0722*	*0724*	*0824*	*0924*	*1021*	*1148*	*1248*	*1348*	...	*1448*	*1548*	*1648*	*1732*	*1753*	*1846*	...	*1848*	*1924*	*1948*	*2024*	*2034*	*2205*f	*2302*

	Ⓐ	⑥	Ⓐ	⑥	⚒	Ⓐ	⑥	⚒	⚒	⚒	⚒	⚒	⚒	Ⓐ	⑥	Ⓐ	⑥	Ⓐ	⑥	Ⓐ	⑥	Ⓐ	⑥	⚒
Milton Keynes **142** .... d.	*0504*	*0435*	*0603*	*0622*	*0722*	*0813*	*0822*	*0947*	*1047*	*1147*	*1247*	*1347*	*1447*	*1541*	*1547*	*1641*	*1647*	*1722*	*1741*	*1822*	*1822*	*1947*	*1947*	*2047*r
Bletchley .... d.	0516	0534	0624	0634	0731	0822	0834	1001	1101	1201	1301	1401	1501	1551	1601	1651	1701	1736	1750	1831	1847	2001	2004	2101
Woburn Sands .... d.	0527	0545	0636	0645	0742	0834	0845	1012	1112	1212	1312	1412	1512	1602	1612	1702	1712	1748	1801	1842	1858	2012	2015	2112
Bedford .... a.	0600	0618	0708	0718	0815	0906	0918	1045	1145	1245	1345	1445	1545	1635	1645	1735	1745	1820	1834	1915	1931	2045	2048	2145

f – Arrives 2156 on Ⓐ.

r – Departs 2050 on ⑥.

LM — BIRMINGHAM - CREWE - LIVERPOOL — 144

km		Ⓐ Ⓐ	Ⓐ	Ⓐ	Ⓐ	Ⓐ	Ⓐ	Ⓐ		Ⓐ	Ⓐ	Ⓐ	Ⓐ	Ⓐ	Ⓐ	Ⓐ	Ⓐ	Ⓐ	Ⓐ	⑥ ⑥	⑥	⑥	⑥
0	**Birmingham** New St **122** d.	...	...	...	0601	0636	0701	0736	and at	1701	1736	1801	1836	1901	1936	2036	2136	2239	2309	...	...	...	0601
19	Wolverhampton .... **122** d.	...	...	...	0621	0654	0720	0754	the same	1720	1754	1820	1854	1920	1954	2054	2154	2305	2336	...	...	...	0620
43	Stafford .... **122 143 153** d.	...	...	...	0637	0710	0736	0810	minutes	1736	1810	1836	1910	1945	2010	2110	2210	2321	2353	...	...	...	0636
82	**Crewe** .... **143 153** d.	0540	0603	0633	0659	0733	0759	0832	past each	1757	1832	1859	1933	2032	2033	2133	2236	2358	0022	0548	0614	0633	0659
118	Runcorn .... **153** d.	0601	0630	0700	0725	0800	0825	0852	hour until	1825	1857	1922	1956	...	2056	2156	2301	...	...	0607	0633	0700	0725
131	**Liverpool** SP ‡ .... a.	0608	0638	0708	0733	0808	0832	0901	★	1832	1905	1930	2005	...	2105	2204	2308	...	...	0616	0642	0709	0732
140	**Liverpool** Lime St .... **153** a.	0621	0651	0721	0746	0821	0844	0911		1844	1917	1942	2017	...	2118	2216	2320	...	...	0626	0654	0721	0744

	⑥	⑥	⑥	⑥	⑥		⑥	⑥	⑥	⑥	⑥	⑥	⑥	⑥	⑥	⑦ ⑦	⑦	⑦	⑦		⑦	⑦	⑦
Birmingham New St **122** d.	0636	0701	0736	0801	0836	and at	1701	1736	1801	1836	1901	2001	2036	2136	2239	0942	1042	1142	1235	and at	1835	1935	2142
Wolverhampton .... **122** d.	0654	0720	0754	0820	0854	the same	1720	1754	1820	1854	1920	2022	2054	2159	2306	1000	1100	1200	1253	the same	1853	1953	2200
Stafford .... **122 143 153** d.	0710	0736	0810	0836	0910	minutes	1736	1810	1836	1910	1936	2038	2110	2216	2322	1017	1117	1217	1309	minutes	1909	2009	2217
Crewe .... **143 153** d.	0733	0759	0832	0857	0932	past each	1757	1832	1857	1930	1957	2059	2149	2236	2342	1038	1138	1238	1331	past each	1931	2031	2238
Runcorn .... **153** d.	0800	0825	0852	0922	0952	hour until	1825	1852	1922	...	2025	2121	*2224*	...	...	1101	1201	1301	1354	hour until	1954	2054	2300
Liverpool SP ‡ .... a.	0808	0832	0901	0930	1001	★	1832	1901	1930	...	2033	2129	|	...	...	1109	1209	1310	1403		2003	2103	2310
Liverpool Lime St .... **153** a.	0821	0844	0911	0942	1011		1844	1911	1942	...	2044	2140	*2242*	...	...	1121	1221	1321	1414		2014	2114	2324

	Ⓐ Ⓐ	Ⓐ	Ⓐ	Ⓐ	Ⓐ	Ⓐ	Ⓐ		Ⓐ	Ⓐ	Ⓐ	Ⓐ	Ⓐ	Ⓐ	Ⓐ	Ⓐ	Ⓐ	Ⓐ	Ⓐ	⑥ ⑥	⑥	⑥	⑥
Liverpool Lime St .... **153** d.	...	...	0630	0704	0734	0804	0834	and at	1704	1734	1804	1834	1912	1934	2004	2034	2134	2234	2334	...	...	0632	0704
Liverpool SP ‡ .... d.	...	...	0640	0715	0744	0815	0844	the same	1716	1744	1815	1844	1922	1944	2015	2044	2144	2246	2346	...	...	0642	0715
Runcorn .... **153** d.	...	...	0648	0723	0752	0823	0852	minutes	1725	1752	1825	1852	1930	1952	2025	2052	2152	2255	2355	...	...	0650	0723
Crewe .... **143 153** d.	0619	0649	0717	0749	0817	0849	0919	past each	1749	1819	1849	1919	1955	2019	2047	2119	2219	2324	0026	0611	0649	0719**b**	0749
Stafford .... **122 143 153** d.	0640	0710	0740	0810	0840	0910	0940	hour until	1810	1840	1910	1940	2016	2040	2110	2140	2240	...	...	0631	0710	0740	0810
Wolverhampton .... **122** a.	0657	0726	0758	0827	0858	0927	0957	★	1827	1859	1928	1957	2032	2057	2127	2157	2259	...	...	0647	0727	0757	0827
Birmingham New St **122** a.	0720	0750	0818	0848	0918	0948	1018		1848	1918	1948	2018	2050	2118	2148	2218	2326	...	...	0715	0750	0818	0848

	⑥	⑥	⑥		⑥	⑥	⑥	⑥	⑥	⑥	⑥	⑥		⑥		⑦ ⑦	⑦	⑦		⑦	⑦	⑦	⑦
Liverpool Lime St .... **153** d.	0734	0804	0834	and at	1704	1734	1804	1834	1904	1934	2034	2134	...	2204	...	...	1134	1234	and at	1934	2034	2134	2330
Liverpool SP ‡ .... d.	0744	0815	0844	the same	1716	1744	1815	1844	1915	1944	2044	2144	...	2215	...	...	1144	1244	the same	1944	2044	2144	2342
Runcorn .... **153** d.	0752	0825	0852	minutes	1725	1752	1824	1852	1925	1952	2052	2152	...	2223	...	...	1152	1252	minutes	1952	2052	2152	2352
Crewe .... **143 153** d.	0819	0849	0919	past each	1749	1819	1849	1919	1951	2019	2119	2219	...	2247	...	1021	1219	1319	past each	2019	2119	2219	0020
Stafford .... **122 143 153** d.	0840	0910	0940	hour until	1810	1840	1910	1940	2010	2040	2140	2240	...	...	...	1042	1240	1340	hour until	2040	2140	2240	...
Wolverhampton .... **122** a.	0858	0927	0958	★	1828	1857	1928	1958	2029	2057	2158	2258	...	...	...	1101	1256	1357		2057	2157	2257	...
Birmingham New St **122** a.	0918	0948	1018		1848	1918	1948	2018	2048	2118	2218	2318	...		...	1119	1315	1415		2115	2215	2316	...

b – Arrives 0715.

‡ – Liverpool South Parkway. 🚌 connections available to / from Liverpool John Lennon Airport.

★ – Timings may vary by ± 3 minutes.

km		⚒	⑥	Ⓐ	⚒A	⑥🍷	ⒶB	Ⓐ	⑥🍷	Ⓐ🍷	⚒	Ⓐ🍷	⑥🍷	⑥🍷	Ⓐ🍷	⚒	⑥🍷	Ⓐ🍷	⚒	⚒🍷	⚒🍷	ⒶC	⚒	⚒🍷	⑥C	Ⓐ🍷	⑥🍷
	London Euston **150** d.		...	...	...	M	...	...	...	L	...	L	...	...	...	...	...	...	...	...	...	1023	...	...	1123	...	...
0	**Birmingham** Int'l ✈ d.		...	...	...	...	...	...	...	...	...	0709	0709	...	...	0809	0910	0910	1009	...	1110	1133	1209	...	1233	1308	1310
13	**Birmingham** New St. d.		...	...	0530	...	...	...	...	...	0625	0723	0724	...	...	0825	0925	0925	1025	...	1125	1153	1225	...	1253	1325	1325
34	Wolverhampton d.		...	...	0548	...	...	...	...	...	0643	0742	0742	...	...	0843	0943	0943	1043	...	1142	1211	1243	...	1311	1343	1342
59	Telford Central d.		...	...	|	...	...	...	...	...	0659	0759	0759	...	...	0900	1000	0959	1059	...	1159	1228	1259	...	1328	1400	1359
65	Wellington d.		...	...	|	...	...	...	...	...	0706	0805	0805	...	...	0907	1006	1005	1106	...	1205	1235	1306	...	1335	1406	1406
81	**Shrewsbury** a.		...	...	|	...	...	...	...	...	0722	0819	0820	...	...	0920	1018	1021	1119	...	1221	1251	1320	...	1354	1420	1419
	Aberystwyth **147** a.		...	...	|	...	...	...	...	...	0923	|	|	...	...	1120	|	|	1320	...	|	...	1520	...	...	|	|
	Cardiff Central **149** d.		...	...	|	...	...	...	0520	0508	...	|	|	0721	0721	...	|	|	...	0921	|	...	...	1121	...	|	|
81	**Shrewsbury** d.		0520	0520	|	0610	*0610*	0700	0722	0724	...	0821	0822	0925	0924	...	1022	1023	...	1125	1225	...	...	1325	...	1425	1422
110	Gobowen d.		0539	0539	|	0630	*0630*	0720	0743	0743	...	0840	0841	0944	0943	...	1042	1044	...	1144	1243	...	...	1344	...	1445	1442
122	Ruabon d.		0551	0551	|	0642	*0642*	0732	0754	0754	...	0852	0853	0955	0954	...	1054	1056	...	1155	1255	...	...	1355	...	1457	1454
129	Wrexham General d.		0558	0604**b**	|	0650	0700	0740	0801	0802	...	0900	0901	1002	1002	...	1101	1102	...	1202	1301	...	...	1402	...	1503	1500
149	**Chester** 160 a.		0617	0625	0643	0710	0716	...	0819	0821	...	0919	0918	1020	1020	...	1120	1121	...	1220	1322	...	...	1420	...	1521	1521
	Holyhead **160** a.		...	...	0820	...	...	...	1014	...	...	...	1105	1209	1222	...	1312	1317	...	1414	1510	...	...	1614	...	1716	1714

	⚒	⚒🍷	Ⓐ🍷	⑥🍷	⚒	⚒🍷	ⒶE	Ⓐ🍷	⑥🍷	Ⓐ✕	⚒	⑥	Ⓐ	Ⓐ🍷	⚒🍷	⚒C	⑥	Ⓐ	Ⓐ	⑥J	ⒶM	⑥	⑥	Ⓐ	⑥G
London Euston **150** d.	...	...	...	...	...	...	...	L	...	...	...	...	...	F	...	1823	...	...	...	...	...	...	...	...	...
Birmingham International ✈ d.	1409	...	1509	1509	1609	...	...	1709	1709	...	1809	...	...	...	1904**e**	1933	2009	2004	...	...	2104	2109	...	...	...
Birmingham New Street d.	1425	...	1525	1525	1625	...	...	1725	1725	...	1825	...	...	...	1925	1950	2025	2025	...	...	2125	2125	...	2214	2235
Wolverhampton d.	1443	...	1542	1543	1643	...	...	1742	1743	...	1843	...	...	...	1943	2019	2043	2043	...	...	2142	2143	...	2244	2253
Telford Central d.	1459	...	1558	1600	1659	...	...	1801	1800	...	1859	...	...	...	2000	2036	2059	2059	...	...	2158	2200	...	2310	2309
Wellington d.	1506	...	1605	1607	1706	...	...	1806	1807	...	1906	...	...	...	2006	2043	2106	2105	...	...	2206	2206	...	2318	2316
Shrewsbury a.	1520	...	1619	1620	1720	...	...	1820	1820	...	1919	...	...	...	2020	2055	2120	2118	...	...	2218	2223	...	2330	2328
Aberystwyth **147** a.	1720	...	|	|	1922	...	...	|	|	...	2123	...	...	...	|	...	2330	2337	...	...	|	|	...	...	...
Cardiff Central **149** d.	...	1321	|	|	...	1521	1621	|	|	1716	▬	1721	...	1821	|	...	...	...	1934	1934	|	|	2055	...	...
Shrewsbury d.	...	1526	1624	1625	...	1724	1810	1825	1822	1909	...	1924	1924	2013	2024	...	...	...	2139	2137	2224	2225	2306	...	...
Gobowen d.	...	1545	1644	1645	...	1743	|	1844	1842	|	...	1943	1943	|	2043	...	...	...	2158	2156	2243	2244	|	...	...
Ruabon d.	...	1556	1656	1657	...	1754	**a**	1856	1854	|	⑥	1954	1955	**a**	2055	...	...	...	2209	2207	2255	2256	**a**	...	...
Wrexham General d.	...	1604	1703	1704	...	1802	|	1905	1902	1943	1946	2002	2002	|	2102	...	...	...	2214	2213	2301	2303	|	...	...
Chester 160 a.	...	1624	1721	1720	...	1822	1905	1924	1921	2002	2006	2022	2024	2108	2121	...	...	...	2234	2232	2319	2322	0022	...	...
Holyhead **160** a.	...	1821	1917	1913	...	2020	...	...	2131	2145	...	2225	...	...	...	...	...	...	0048	...	...	...	...	...	...

	Ⓐ	Ⓐ	⑥	Ⓐ	⑦	⑦🍷	⑦	⑦	⑦🍷	⑦🍷	⑦🍷	⑦🍷	⑦🍷	⑦🍷	⑦	⑦🍷	⑦🍷	⑦🍷	⑦	⑦C	⑦	⑦	⑦	⑦	⑦
London Euston **150** d.	...	...	...	...		...	...	...	...	...	...	...	...	...	...	...	...	...	...	1900	...	...	...	...	...
Birmingham International ✈ d.	...	...	...	...		...	0951	1048	1207	1307	...	1407	1507	1607	...	1707	1807	1907	2008	2013	2108	...	2211	2240	2308
Birmingham New Street d.	...	2332	2335	2252		...	1004	1105	1224	1324	...	1424	1524	1624	...	1724	1824	1924	2024	2027	2124	...	2224	2255	2324
Wolverhampton d.	...	0002	2354	2327		...	1022	1127	1242	1342	...	1443	1543	1643	...	1743	1843	1943	2043	2056	2143	...	2242	2315	2346
Telford Central d.	...	0029	0022	|		...	1049	1154	1259	1358	...	1459	1559	1659	...	1759	1859	1959	2059	2113	2210	...	2309	|	0013
Wellington d.	...	0036	0030	|		...	1057	1201	1305	1404	...	1506	1606	1706	...	1805	1906	2006	2106	2120	2217	...	2316	|	0020
Shrewsbury a.	...	0052	0045	|		...	1110	1215	1324	1418	...	1519	1622	1719	...	1819	1919	2019	2119	2135	2230	...	2332	|	0036
Aberystwyth **147** a.	...	▬	▬	|		...	1320	|	1523	|	...	1721	|	1922	...	|	2120	|	2315	...	|	...	...	|	...
Cardiff Central **149** d.	2117	⑥	Ⓐ	|		...	...	|	...	|	1313	...	|	...	1513	|	...	|	▬	...	|	2101	...	|	...
Shrewsbury d.	2318	2333	2337	|		1016	...	1217	...	1420	1524	...	1624	...	1730	1820	...	2023	...	...	2232	2319	...	|	...
Gobowen d.	|	2352	2357	|		1035	...	1237	...	1439	1544	...	1643	...	1749	1840	...	2043	...	...	|	|	...	|	...
Ruabon d.	**a**	0004	0009	|		1047	...	1249	...	1451	1556	...	1655	...	1801	1851	...	2055	⑦	...	**a**	**a**	...	|	...
Wrexham General d.	|	0014	0015	|		1054	...	1256	...	1458	1602	...	1706	...	1808	1858	...	2102	2235	...	|	|	...	|	...
Chester 160 a.	0031	0033	0035	0037		1114	...	1320	...	1518	1622	...	1726	...	1825	1922	...	2120	2255	...	2331	0033	...	0022	...
Holyhead **160** a.	...	...	...	0215		...	...	...	...	...	1837	...	...	...	2018	2134	...	...	...	...	...	...	...	0220	...

	⚒	⑥	Ⓐ	Ⓐ	⑥	Ⓐ	⑥	Ⓐ	⑥🍷	Ⓐ🍷	⚒	⑥C	⑥🍷	Ⓐ✕	Ⓐ🍷	Ⓐ🍷	⑥🍷	⚒	⑥🍷	Ⓐ🍷	Ⓐ🍷	Ⓐ🍷	⑥🍷	⚒	⚒🍷
Holyhead **160** d.		...	...	...	...	...	...	...	0425	0425	...	...	0522	0533	...	0628	0635	...	0715	L	...	0805	0820	...	0923
Chester 160 d.		0422	0422	...	...	0530	0537	0545	0620	0618	...	...	0721	0714	...	0819	0819	...	0930	0926	...	1020	1019	...	1130
Wrexham General d.		|	|	...	...	0546	0555	0603	0636	0635	...	...	0737	0732	0747	0834	0834	...	0946	0942	...	1036	1035	...	1145
Ruabon d.		|	|	...	...	0553	▬	▬	0643	0642	...	...	0744	|	0755	0841	0841	...	0953	0949	...	1042	1042	...	1153
Gobowen d.		|	|	...	...	0605	...	...	0655	0655	...	...	0756	|	0807	0853	0853	...	1005	1001	...	1054	1054	...	1205
Shrewsbury a.		|	|	...	...	0627	...	...	0715	0715	...	...	0820	0807	0828	0913	0913	...	1029	1022	...	1114	1114	...	1229
Cardiff Central **149** a.		|	|	...	...	|	...	...	0920	0919	...	...	|	0958	Ⓐ🍷	1115	1120	...	|	1210	...	1321	1317	...	|
Aberystwyth **147** d.		|	|	...	...	|	⑥	ⒶC	...	...	0530	...	|	...	G	...	...	0730	|	...	...	...	...	0930	|
Shrewsbury d.		|	|	0518	0522	0633	0633	0639	...	...	0733	0818	0833	...	0832	...	...	0933	1033	...	1032	...	...	1133	1233
Wellington d.		|	|	0531	0535	0646	0646	0653	...	...	0746	0832	0846	...	0845	...	...	0946	1046	...	1046	...	...	1146	1246
Telford Central d.		|	|	0538	0542	0653	0653	0700	...	...	0753	0839	0853	...	0852	...	...	0953	1053	...	1052	...	...	1153	1253
Wolverhampton a.		0539	0539	0558	0601	0711	0711	0717	...	...	0811	0900	0911	...	0910	...	...	1010	1111	...	1109	...	...	1212	1310
Birmingham New Street a.		0558	0610	0615	0619	0730	0730	0747	...	...	0829	0921	0927	...	0929	...	...	1030	1128	...	1130	...	...	1232	1329
Birmingham International ✈ a.		...	...	0649	0649	0749	0749	0759	...	...	0849	0939	0950	...	0949	...	...	1050	1150	...	1149	...	...	1250	1350
London Euston a.		...	...	...	...	...	...	0913	...	...	...	1056	...	...	...	...	...	...	...	...	...	...	...	...	...

	⑥🍷	Ⓐ🍷F	⚒	⑥🍷	Ⓐ🍷	Ⓐ🍷	⑥🍷	⚒C	⚒	Ⓐ🍷	⑥🍷	⑥🍷	Ⓐ🍷	⚒	⑥🍷	Ⓐ🍷	⚒🍷	⚒	Ⓐ🍷	⑥🍷	ⒶB	⑥	⑥	Ⓐ	ⒶD
Holyhead **160** d.	1033	1040	...	1123	1127	1232	1238	...	...	1324	1328	1425	1434	...	1523	1544	1650	...	1730	1730	...	...	...	...	...
Chester 160 d.	1219	1219	...	1330	1330	1419	1419	...	...	1530	1530	1619	1619	...	1728	1730	1828	...	1916	1928	2022	2026	...	...	2135
Wrexham General d.	1234	1234	...	1346	1346	1434	1434	...	...	1546	1546	1635	1635	...	1744	1748	1845	...	1932	1944	2038	2042	...	...	|
Ruabon d.	1241	1241	...	1353	1353	1441	1441	...	...	1553	1553	1642	1642	...	1751	1754	1851	...	1939	1951	*2056*	2049	...	...	|
Gobowen d.	1253	1253	...	1405	1405	1453	1453	...	...	1605	1605	1654	1654	...	1803	1806	1903	...	1950	2002	*2107*	2101	...	...	|
Shrewsbury a.	1313	1314	...	1428	1427	1513	1513	...	...	1629	1629	1714	1714	...	1824	1827	1924	...	2014	2026	*2128*	2121	...	...	|
Cardiff Central **149** a.	1524	1510	...	|	|	1716	1708	...	...	|	|	1915	1920	...	|	|	2138**h**	...	...	...	...	...	...	...	|
Aberystwyth **147** d.	...	...	1130	|	|	...	...	...	1330	|	|	...	...	1530	|	|	...	1730	...	⑥	...	...	1930	1930	|
Shrewsbury d.	...	...	1334	1433	1433	...	...	1524	1533	1633	1633	...	...	1733	1833	1833	...	1932	...	2047	...	...	2133	2133	|
Wellington d.	...	...	1348	1446	1446	...	...	1538	1546	1647	1647	...	...	1746	1846	1846	...	1946	...	2100	...	...	2146	2147	|
Telford Central d.	...	...	1354	1453	1453	...	...	1544	1553	1654	1653	...	...	1753	1853	1853	...	1953	...	2108	...	...	2153	2153	|
Wolverhampton a.	...	...	1412	1511	1511	...	...	1601	1610	1709	1708	...	...	1811	1911	1911	...	2011	...	2136	...	...	2209	2211	2227
Birmingham New Street a.	...	...	1432	1528	1530	...	...	1622	1630	1730	1728	...	...	1830	1928	1930	...	2029	...	2156	...	...	2231	2231	2248
Birmingham International ✈ a.	...	...	1449	1550	1549	...	...	1639	1649	1749	1750	...	...	1849	1949	1949	...	2049	...	...	...	...	...	...	...
London Euston a.	...	...	...	...	...	...	...	1756	...	...	...	...	...	...	...	...	...	...	...	...	...	...	...	...	...

	Ⓐ	⑥	⚒	⑦	⑦	⑦	⑦	⑦	⑦🍷	⑦	⑦🍷	⑦	⑦C	⑦🍷	⑦🍷	⑦🍷	⑦	⑦	⑦🍷	⑦	⑦🍷	⑦	⑦	⑦	⑦
Holyhead **160** d.	1921	1921	...		...	...	...	...	...	1020	...	...	...	...	...	...	...	1625	...	...	1825	...	...	...	...
Chester 160 d.	2121	2120	2228		0808	...	0922	...	1131	1221	...	1331	...	...	1531	...	1731	1824	...	1926	2027	...	2126	2204	2300
Wrexham General d.	2137	2137	2242		0828	...	0938	...	1148	1238	...	1348	...	...	1548	...	1748	1841	...	1942	|	...	2144	2223	|
Ruabon d.	2144	2143	2249		▬	...	0945	...	1154	1245	...	1354	...	...	1554	...	1754	1847	...	1949	|	...	2150	...	|
Gobowen d.	2155	2156	2300		...	...	0957	...	1206	1257	...	1406	...	...	1606	...	1806	1859	...	2000	|	...	2202	...	|
Shrewsbury a.	2216	2217	2323		...	...	1018	...	1227	1318	...	1427	...	...	1627	...	1827	1920	...	2021	|	...	2222	...	0014
Cardiff Central **149** a.	|	|	|		...	...	|	...	|	1537	...	|	...	...	|	...	|	2137	...	|	|	...	|	...	...
Aberystwyth **147** d.	|	|	|		⑦	...	|	0930	|	...	1130	|	...	1330	|	1530	|	...	1730	|	|	1930	|	...	...
Shrewsbury d.	2218	2231	2324		0810	0909	1020	1140	1231	...	1331	1431	1524	1533	1640	1733	1831	...	1931	2023	|	2131	2223	...	...
Wellington d.	2232	2245	2338		0824	0923	1034	1154	1245	...	1345	1445	1538	1547	1654	1747	1845	...	1945	2037	|	2145	2237	...	...
Telford Central d.	2238	2251	2345		0831	0930	1040	1200	1251	...	1351	1451	1544	1553	1700	1753	1851	...	1951	2044	|	2151	2245	...	...
Wolverhampton a.	2255	2308	0017		0859	0958	1056	1216	1307	...	1407	1507	1601	1609	1715	1809	1907	...	2007	2111	2129	2207	2314	...	...
Birmingham New Street a.	2328	2330	...		0915	1014	1113	1233	1323	...	1423	1524	1620	1625	1737	1827	1926	...	2025	2129	2153	2227	...	...	...
Birmingham International ✈ a.	...	...	...		0932	1032	1131	1302	1357	...	1500	1557	1639	1700	1757	1900	1957	...	2101	2157	2208	2301	...	...	...
London Euston a.	...	...	...		...	...	...	...	...	...	...	...	1757	...	...	...	...	...	...	...	...	...	...	...	...

A – 12 and 🍷 Birmingham New Street - Crewe - Holyhead (Table **151**).
B – 12 and 🍷 Wrexham - London Euston and v.v. (Table **151**).
C – 12 and 🍷 Shrewsbury - London Euston and v.v. (Table **150**).
D – 12 and 🍷 Bangor - Crewe - Birmingham New Street (Table **151**).
E – From Swansea (Table **135**).
F – To / from Llanelli (Table **135**).
G – To / from Crewe (Table **149**).
J – To / from Llandudno Junction (Table **165**).
L – To / from Llandudno (Table **165**).
M – To / from Manchester Piccadilly (Table **160**).

a – Via Crewe (Table **149**).
b – Arrives 0557.
e – Departs 1909 on ⑥.
h – Arrives 2135 on ⑥.

AW 2nd class — SHREWSBURY - SWANSEA — 146

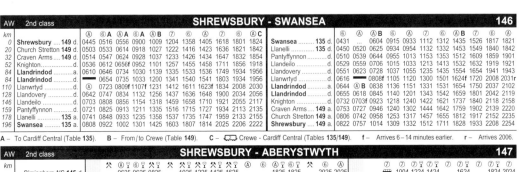

km		Ⓐ	⑥ A	Ⓐ A	⑥ A	Ⓐ B	⑦	⑥	Ⓐ	⑦	⑥	Ⓐ C
0	**Shrewsbury** .... **149** d.	0445	0516	0556	0900	1009	1204	1358	1405	1618	1801	1824
20	Church Stretton **149** d.	0503	0533	0614	0918	1027	1222	1416	1423	1636	1821	1842
32	Craven Arms .... **149** d.	0514	0547	0624	0928	1037	1233	1426	1434	1647	1832	1854
52	Knighton ....d.	0536	0612	0656**f**	0952	1101	1257	1455	1458	1711	1856	1918
84	**Llandrindod** ....a.	0610	0646	0734	1030	1139	1335	1533	1536	1749	1934	1956
84	**Llandrindod** ....d.	▬	0654	0735	1033	1200	1341	1540	1541	1803	1934	1956
110	Llanwrtyd ....d.	Ⓐ	0723	0809**f**	1107**f**	1231	1412	1611	1623**f**	1834	2008	2030
128	Llandovery ....d.	0642	0747	0834	1132	1256	1437	1636	1648	1900	2034	2056
146	Llandeilo ....d.	0703	0808	0856	1154	1318	1459	1658	1710	1921	2055	2117
159	Pantyffynnon ....d.	0721	0825	0913	1211	1335	1516	1715	1727	1934	2113	2135
178	Llanelli .... **135** a.	0741	0848	0933	1235	1358	1537	1735	1747	1959	2133	2155
196	**Swansea** .... **135** a.	0808	0922	1002	1301	1425	1603	1807	1814	2025	2206	2222

	⑥	Ⓐ	Ⓐ B	⑥	Ⓐ	⑦	⑥	Ⓐ B	⑦	⑥	Ⓐ
Swansea .... **135** d.	0431	...	0604	0915	0933	1112	1312	1435	1526	1817	1821
Llanelli .... **135** d.	0450	0520	0625	0934	0954	1132	1332	1453	1549	1840	1842
Pantyffynnon ....d.	0510	0539	0644	0955	1013	1153	1353	1512	1609	1859	1901
Llandeilo ....d.	0529	0559	0706	1015	1033	1213	1413	1532	1632	1919	1921
Llandovery ....d.	0551	0623	0728	1037	1055	1235	1435	1554	1654	1941	1943
Llanwrtyd ....d.	0616	▬	0808**f**	1105	1120	1300	1501	1624**f**	1720	2008	2031**r**
Llandrindod ....a.	0644	Ⓐ B	0838	1136	1151	1331	1531	1654	1750	2037	2102
Llandrindod ....d.	0655	0618	0845	1140	1201	1343	1542	1659	1801	2042	2119
Knighton ....d.	0732	0703**f**	0923	1218	1240	1422	1621	1737	1840	2118	2158
Craven Arms .... **149** a.	0753	0727	0946	1240	1302	1444	1642	1759	1902	2139	2220
Church Stretton **149** a.	0806	0742	0958	1253	1317	1457	1655	1812	1917	2152	2235
Shrewsbury .... **149** a.	0822	0757	1014	1309	1332	1512	1711	1828	1933	2208	2254

A – To Cardiff Central (Table **135**). B – From / to Crewe (Table **149**). C – (2) Crewe - Cardiff Central (Tables **135/149**). f – Arrives 6 – 14 minutes earlier. r – Arrives 2006.

AW 2nd class — SHREWSBURY - ABERYSTWYTH — 147

km			⚒	Ⓐ🍷	⑥🍷	⚒🍷	⚒	⚒🍷	⚒🍷	⚒🍷	⚒🍷	Ⓐ	⑥	Ⓐ🍷	⑥🍷	⚒	⑥	Ⓐ			⑦	⑦	⑦🍷	⑦🍷	⑦	⑦🍷	⑦	⑦🍷	⑦
	B'mingham NS **145** d.		...	0625	0625	0825	...	1025	1225	1425	1625	...	...	1825	1825	...	2025	2025		...	🚌	1004	1224	1424	...	1624	...	1824	2024
0	**Shrewsbury** .... d.	⚒	0625	0727	0729	0930	1029	1127	1329	1530	1727	1831	1827	1930	1930	2032	2143	2150	⑦	...	0830	1128	1328	1527	1629	1727	1828	1927	2127
32	Welshpool .... d.		0648	0749	0752	0952	1051	1149	1351	1552	1749	1853	1849	1952	1952	2053	2205	2212		...	0905	1150	1350	1551	1651	1749	1850	1949	2149
54	Newtown .... d.		0703	0803	0806	1006	1106	1203	1405	1606	1803	1907	1903	2006	2006	2108	2220	2227		...	0930	1204	1404	1605	1705	1803	1904	2003	2203
63	Caersws .... d.		0710	0810	0813	1013	1113	1210	1412	1613	1810	1914	1910	2013	2013	2115	2227	2234		...	0945	1211	1412	1612	1712	1811	1911	2010	2210
98	**Machynlleth** .... a.		0742	0841	0844	1045	1141	1243	1443	1644	1841	1945	1942	2047	2047	2143	2255	2302		...	1025	1245	1443	1643	1742	1842	1940	2041	2239
98	**Machynlleth** .... **148** d.		0746	0848	0849	1050	1141**r**	1247	1449	1650	1849	1948	1946	2049	2052	2149	2302	2307		...	1025	1250	1448	1648	1745	1848	1942	2047	2245
104	Dovey Junction ... **148** d.		0755	0855	0856	1056	1154	1254**r**	1455	1656	1858	1957	1955	2057	2100	2157	2308	2313		...	|	1258	1458	1655	1755	1856	1956	2055	2252
118	Borth .... d.		0805	0905	0906	1106	1204	1304**r**	1505	1706	1908	2007	2005	2107	2110	2207	2318	2323		...	1050	1308	1508	1705	1805	1906	2006	2105	2302
131	**Aberystwyth** .... a.		0820	0922	0923	1120	1220	1320	1520	1720	1922	2020	2020	2120	2123	2223	2330	2337		...	1110	1320	1523	1721	1821	1922	2021	2120	2315

		⚒🍷	⚒	Ⓐ🍷	⑥🍷	Ⓐ	⑥	⚒🍷	Ⓐ🍷	⑥🍷	⚒	⚒🍷	⚒🍷	⑥🍷	Ⓐ🍷	Ⓐ	⑥	⑥	Ⓐ		⑦	⑦🍷	⑦🍷	⑦	⑦	⑦🍷		⑦🍷	⑦
Aberystwyth ....d.	⚒	0530	0630	0730	0730	0830	0830	0930	1130	1130	1230	1330	1530	1730	1730	1832	1833	1930	1930	⑦	0930	1030	1130	1330	1434	1530	...	1730	1930
Borth ....d.		0543	0643	0743	0743	0843	0843	0943	1143	1143	1243	1343	1543	1743	1743	1845	1845	1943	1943		0943	1043	1143	1343	1447	1543	...	1743	1943
Dovey Junction .... **148** d.		0553	0653	0753	0754	0858	0859	0953	1153	1155	1257	1353	1553	1753	1753	1856	1856	1959	1959		0953	1056	1153	1356	1457	1553	...	1753	1953
Machynlleth .... **148** a.		0601	0701	0800	0801	0905	0906	1000	1201	1200	1305	1400	1600	1800	1800	1903	1903	2004	2006		1000	1103	1200	1403	1504	1600	...	1800	2000
Machynlleth ....d.		0601	0703	0805	0808	0906	0908	1008	1204	1207	1306	1407	1608	1805	1805	1909	1905	2011	2011		1008	1105	1206	1406	1508	1605	...	1805	2005
Caersws ....d.		0628	0730	0828	0831	0933	0935	1035	1232	1234	1333	1434	1631	1828	1830	1932	1928	2034	2034		1031	1128	1229	1429	1531	1630	...	1828	2028
Newtown ....d.		0635	0737	0839	0842	0940	0942	1042	1239	1241	1340	1441	1642	1839	1841	1943	1939	2044	2044		1041	1138	1240	1440	1541	1641	...	1839	2039
Welshpool ....d.		0650	0752	0854	0856	0955	0956	1056	1254	1255	1354	1455	1656	1853	1856	1957	2000	2102	2059		1057	1154	1254	1455	1556	1655	...	1854	2053
Shrewsbury ....a.		0713	0814	0916	0918	1017	1018	1118	1316	1317	1418	1519	1720	1915	1918	2022	2022	2124	2121		1119	1217	1316	1517	1620	1717	...	1916	2116
B'mingham NS **145** .a.		0829	...	1030	1030	...	...	1232	1430	1432	...	1630	1830	2029	2029	...	...	2231	2231		1233	...	1423	1625	...	1827	...	2025	2227

r – On ⑥ departs 3 minutes later.

▷ – Additional journeys Machynlleth - Aberystwyth and v.v. :
From Machynlleth at 0453 ⚒, 0545 Ⓐ, 0547 ⑥, 0647 ⚒, 0850 ⑦, 0947 ⑦, 1049 ⑦, 1349 ⑦, 1801 ⚒.
From Aberystwyth at 1830 ⑦, 2030 Ⓑ, 2036 ⑥, 2130 Ⓑ, 2135 ⑥, 2230 ⚒, 2320 ⑦, 2335 ⑥, 2340 Ⓐ.

AW 2nd class — MACHYNLLETH - PWLLHELI — 148

km			Ⓐ	Ⓐ	Ⓐ	Ⓐ	Ⓐ		Ⓐ	Ⓐ	Ⓐ	Ⓐ		⑥	⑥	⑥	⑥		⑥	⑥	⑥	⑥	⑥			⑦
	Birmingham New Str. **145** .. d.		...	...	*0625*	0825	*1025*	...	1225	1425	1625	*1825*		...	...	*0625*	*0825*	...	*1025*	1225	1425	*1625*	*1825*		...	1624
	Shrewsbury **147** .... d.	Ⓐ	...	...	*0727*	0930	*1127*	...	1329	1530	1729	*1930*	⑥	...	...	*0729*	*0931*	...	*1129*	1329	1530	*1727*	*1930*	⑦	...	1727
0	**Machynlleth** .... **147** d.		0507	0643	0852	1055	1251	...	1456	1655	1904	2147		0507	0643	0853	1055	...	1252	1456	1655	1904	2147		...	1855
6	Dovey Junction .... **147** d.		0513	0649	0858	1101	1257	...	1502	1701	1910	2153		0513	0649	0859	1101	...	1258	1502	1701	1910	2153		...	1901
16	Aberdovey ....d.		0526	0702	0911	1114	1310	...	1515	1714	1923	2206		0526	0702	0912	1114	...	1311	1515	1714	1923	2206		...	1914
22	Tywyn .... a.		0533	0711	0920	1123	1319	...	1524	1724	1932	2215		0533	0711	0921	1123	...	1319	1524	1724	1932	2215		...	1920
22	Tywyn .... d.		0533	0716	0929	1130	1325	...	1526	1729	1933	2216		0533	0714	0929	1132	...	1324	1525	1729	1933	2217		...	1925
37	Fairbourne ....d.		0552	0734	0948	1149	1344	...	1545	1747	1951	2235		0552	0732	0948	1150	...	1343	1544	1747	1951	2235		...	1944
41	**Barmouth** ....a.		0604	0745	0959	1159	1355	...	1556	1758	2003	2246		0604	0745	0959	1201	...	1354	1555	1758	2002	2246		...	1952
41	**Barmouth** ....d.		...	0747	1001	1201	1357	...	1558	1800	2004	2247		...	0747	1001	1202	...	1356	1557	1800	2004	2248		...	1954
58	Harlech ....a.		...	0811	1025	1225	1421	...	1622	1824	2030	2312		...	0811	1025	1226	...	1420	1621	1824	2030	2312		...	2020
58	Harlech ....d.		...	0825	1027	1227	1431	...	1629	1833	2030	2313		...	0825	1027	1229	...	1431	1629	1833	2030	2314		...	2022
67	Penrhyndeudraeth ....d.		...	0838	1040	1240	1444	...	1642	1846	2043	2326		...	0838	1040	1242	...	1444	1642	1846	2043	2327		...	2036
69	Minffordd .... **160** d.		...	0842	1044	1244	1448	...	1645	1849	2047	2330		...	0842	1044	1245	...	1448	1645	1849	2047	2330		...	2039
72	**Porthmadog** .... **160** d.		...	0850	1052	1252	1456	...	1653	1857	2055	2338		...	0850	1052	1253	...	1456	1653	1857	2055	2338		...	2045
80	Criccieth ....d.		...	0857	1059	1259	1503	...	1700	1904	2103	2346		...	0857	1059	1301	...	1503	1700	1904	2103	2346		...	2053
93	**Pwllheli** ....a.		...	0912	1114	1315	1520	...	1718	1920	2118	0001		...	0913	1114	1316	...	1520	1716	1919	2118	0001		...	2112

		Ⓐ	Ⓐ	Ⓐ	Ⓐ		Ⓐ	Ⓐ		Ⓐ	Ⓐ	Ⓐ		⑥	⑥	⑥	⑥		⑥	⑥	⑥	⑥	⑥		⑦	
Pwllheli ....d.		...	0629	0724	0934	...	1137	1338	...	1537	1742	2026		...	0629	0724	0934	...	1137	1338	1537	1742	2026		1348	...
Criccieth ....d.	Ⓐ	...	0643	0738	0948	...	1151	1352	...	1551	1756	2040	⑥	...	0643	0738	0948	...	1151	1352	1551	1756	2040	⑦	1402	...
Porthmadog .... **160** d.		...	0653	0747	0957	...	1201	1402	...	1601	1806	2055**b**		...	0653	0747	0958	...	1201	1402	1601	1806	2056**b**		1412	...
Minffordd .... **160** d.		...	0657	0752	1001	...	1205	1406	...	1605	1810	2059		...	0657	0752	1002	...	1205	1406	1605	1810	2101		1416	...
Penrhyndeudraeth ....d.		...	0701	0756	1005	...	1209	1410	...	1609	1814	2103		...	0701	0756	1006	...	1209	1410	1609	1814	2104		1420	...
Harlech ....a.		...	0715	0809	1020	...	1224	1425	...	1624	1827	2117		...	0715	0809	1021	...	1224	1425	1624	1827	2118		1432	...
Harlech ....d.		...	0717	0821	1029	...	1228	1428	...	1629	1830	2119		...	0717	0821	1028	...	1228	1428	1629	1830	2120		1434	...
Barmouth ....a.		...	0742	0845	1054	...	1253	1453	...	1654	1855	2144		...	0742	0845	1053	...	1253	1453	1654	1855	2145		1459	...
Barmouth ....d.		0645	0746	0852	1059	...	1255	1455	...	1656	1857	2146		0645	0746	0852	1101	...	1255	1455	1656	1857	2147		1501	...
Fairbourne ....d.		0653	0754	0900	1107	...	1303	1503	...	1704	1905	2154		0653	0754	0900	1109	...	1303	1503	1704	1905	2155		1509	...
Tywyn ....a.		0713	0812	0920	1127	...	1323	1524	...	1724	1925	2214		0713	0812	0920	1129	...	1323	1524	1724	1925	2215		1527	...
Tywyn ....d.		0714	0816	0927	1130	...	1325	1526	...	1727	1934	2217		0714	0816	0927	1130	...	1325	1526	1727	1935	2217		1528	...
Aberdovey ....d.		0720	0822	0933	1136	...	1331	1532	...	1733	1940	2223		0720	0822	0933	1136	...	1331	1532	1733	1941	2223		1535	...
Dovey Junction .... **147** d.		0735	0838	0947	1149	...	1345	1546	...	1747	1956	2238		0735	0838	0947	1151	...	1345	1546	1747	1956	2238		1549	...
Machynlleth .... **147** a.		0743	0845	0954	1157	...	1352	1554	...	1755	2004	2245		0743	0845	0955	1158	...	1353	1555	1755	2003	2245		1559	...
Shrewsbury **147** ....a.		0916	*1017*	1118	1316	...	1519	1720	...	*1918*	2121**c**	...		0918	*1018*	1118	1317	...	1517	1719	*1915*	*2124*	...		1717	...
Birmingham New Str. **145** ...a.		1030	...	1230	1430	...	1630	1830	...	*2029*	2231**c**	...		1030	...	1232	1432	...	1630	1830	*2029*	*2231*	...		1827	...

b – Arrives 2048. c – On ⑤ change at Machynlleth. f – Arrives 1148.

AW 2nd class Most trains convey 🍷 — CARDIFF - HEREFORD - CREWE - MANCHESTER — 149

Most Manchester trains continue to / from destinations on Table **135**

km			Ⓐ	Ⓐ J	Ⓐ	Ⓐ R	Ⓐ	Ⓐ	Ⓐ	Ⓐ S	Ⓐ	Ⓐ	Ⓐ	Ⓐ	Ⓐ		Ⓐ	Ⓐ	Ⓐ	Ⓐ	Ⓐ	Ⓐ	Ⓐ	Ⓐ	Ⓐ T	Ⓐ	Ⓐ ✕
0	**Cardiff** Central ..... **132** d.	Ⓐ	0435	0508	0538	...	0650	0721	0805	...	0850	0921	1005	1050	1121	...	1205	1250	1321	1405	1450	1521	1550	1621	...	1650	1716
19	Newport .... **132** d.		0453	0527	0557	...	0704	0736	0819	...	0905	0935	1019	1104	1136	...	1219	1304	1335	1419	1504	1536	1604	1635	...	1704	1731
30	Cwmbrân ....d.		0505	0539	0608	...	0714	0746	0829	...	0915	0946	1029	1114	1146	...	1229	1314	1346	1429	1514	1546	1614	1644	...	1714	1742
35	Pontypool & New Inn ..d.		0511	0545	0614	...	|	0752	|	...	|	0951	|	|	1152	...	|	|	1351	|	|	1552	1619	|	...	|	1749
50	Abergavenny ....d.		0522	0554	0623	...	0727	0801	0842	...	0928	1001	1042	1127	1201	...	1242	1326	1401	1443	1527	1601	1629	1657	...	1727	1800
89	**Hereford** ....d.		0547	0625**g**	0649	...	0753	0827	0908	...	0954	1027	1108	1153	1227	...	1308	1355	1425	1508	1553	1628	1654	1724	...	1753	1825
109	Leominster ....d.		0600	0638	0702	...	0806	|	0921	...	1007	|	1121	1206	|	...	1321	1408	|	1521	1606	1641	1707	|	...	1806	|
127	Ludlow ....d.		0611	0649	0713	...	0817	0848	0932	...	1018	1048	1132	1217	1248	...	1332	1419	1446	1532	1617	1652	1718	|	...	1817	|
138	Craven Arms .... **146** d.		0620	0657	0721	0728	0825	0856	|	0947	1026	1057	|	1225	1256	...	|	1427	1455	|	1625	1700	1727	|	1800	1825	|
150	Church Stretton .... **146** d.		0629	0708	0730	0742	0834	0905	|	0959	1039	1106	|	1238	1305	...	|	1436	1504	|	|	1709	1736	|	1813	1841	|
170	**Shrewsbury** .... **146** a.		0643	0722	0744	0757	0848	0919	0958	1014	1052	1121	1158	1252	1321	...	1358	1450	1523	1558	1648	1724	1750	1809	1828	1855	1908
170	**Shrewsbury** ....¶ d.		0644	0724	0746	0800	0851	0924	1000	1018	1054	1125	1159	1254	1325	...	1359	1452	1526	1559	1650	1725	1753	1810	1830	1856	1909
200	Whitchurch ....¶ d.		0704	|	0806	0828	0908	|	|	1046	1112	|	|	1310	|	...	|	1509	|	|	1710	|	1809	|	1857	1913	|
223	**Crewe** ....¶ a.		0724	|	0824	0853	0927	|	1028	1110	1128	|	1228	1328	|	...	1428	1528	|	1628	1727	|	1827	1843	1920	1933	|
	Chester **145, 160** ......a.		|	0821	|	...	|	1020	|	...	|	1220	|	|	1420	...	|	|	1624	|	|	1821	|	1905	...	|	2002
	Holyhead **145, 160** ...a.		|	...	|	...	|	1222	|	...	|	1414	|	|	1614	...	|	|	1821	|	|	2020	|	...	...	|	2145
263	Stockport ....a.		0753	...	0859	...	0957	...	1058	...	1158	...	1258	1358	...	...	1458	1558	...	1659	1758	...	1858	...	...	2003	...
273	**Manchester** Piccadilly .a.		0808	...	0915	...	1015	...	1115	...	1215	...	1315	1415	...	...	1515	1615	...	1715	1815	...	1915	...	...	2019	...

J – To / from Llandudno (Tables **145 / 160**). L – To Llandudno Junction (Tables **145 / 160**).

For continuation of Table and additional footnotes see next page ▶ ▶ ▶

① – Mondays ② – Tuesdays ③ – Wednesdays ④ – Thursdays ⑤ – Fridays ⑥ – Saturdays ⑦ – Sundays Ⓑ – Not Saturdays 47

149 CARDIFF - HEREFORD - CREWE - MANCHESTER

Most trains convey 🍷 2nd class AW

Most Manchester trains continue to / from destinations on Table **135**

	Ⓐ	Ⓐ	Ⓐ	Ⓐ	Ⓐ	Ⓐ	Ⓐ	⑥	⑥	⑥	⑥	⑥	⑥	⑥	⑥	⑥	⑥	⑥	⑥	⑥	⑥	⑥	⑥	⑥	⑥	⑥
Cardiff Central ... **132** d.	1750	1821	1855	1934	2017	2117	2155	0435	0520	0537	0650	0721	0750	0850	0921	0955	1055	1121	1155	1255	1321	1355	1455	1521	1555	1618
Newport ... **132** d.	1804	1835	1909	1948	2031	2132	2212	0452	0535	0556	0704	0736	0804	0904	0935	1009	1109	1135	1209	1309	1336	1409	1509	1536	1609	1634
Cwmbrân ... d.	1815	1845	1919	1958	2041	2143	2224	0503	0545	0608	0714	0746	0814	0914	0946	1019	1119	1146	1219	1319	1346	1419	1519	1546	1619	1644
Pontypool & New Inn . d.	1820	|	1924	2003	2047	|	2230	0509	0551	0613	|	0751	|	|	0952	|	|	1150	|	|	1350	|	|	1552	1624	1650
Abergavenny ... d.	1829	1859	1934	2012	2056	2156	2240	0518	0600	0623	0727	0801	0827	0927	1001	1032	1132	1200	1232	1332	1401	1432	1532	1601	1634	1702
Hereford ... d.	1855	1924	1959	2039	2122	2221	2308	0547	0625	0649	0753	0827	0853	0953	1026	1058	1158	1228	1258	1358	1427	1458	1558	1629**d**	1700	...
Leominster ... d.	1908	|	2012	2052	2135	2234	2321	0600	0638	0702	0806	|	0906	1006	|	1111	1211	|	1311	1411	|	1511	1611	1642	1713	...
Ludlow ... d.	1919	1945	2023	2103	2146	2245	2332	0611	0649	0713	0817	0848	0917	1017	1048	1122	1222	1249	1322	1422	1448	1522	1622	1654	1724	...
Craven Arms ... **146** d.	1927	|	2032	2112	2154	2254	2342	0620	0657	0721	0825	0856	|	1025	1057	|	1230	1257	|	1430	1456	|	1630	|	|	...
Church Stretton .. **146** d.	1936	|	2041	2121	2204	2303	2351	0629	0706	0730	0834	0905	|	1034	1107	|	1239	1306	|	1440	1505	|	1639	1708	|	...
Shrewsbury ... **146** a.	1950	2011	2055	2137	2218	2317	0007	0643	0722	0744	0851	0923	0943	1048	1123	1148	1252	1320	1348	1453	1524	1548	1653	1722	1750	...
Shrewsbury ... **145**¶ d.	1952	2013	2056	2139	2220	2318	0012	0646	0722	0746	0852	0925	0947	1050	1125	1149	1254	1325	1349	1455	1528	1549	1655	1724	1752	...
Whitchurch ... ¶ d.	|	|	2113	|	2243	2344	0038	0706	|	0806	0909	|	1004	1107	|	1206	|	|	1406	|	|	1606	|	|	1808	...
Crewe ... ¶ a.	2022	2043	2133	|	2304	0005	0103	0725	|	0824	0927	|	1023	1125	|	1224	1326	|	1424	1525	|	1624	1726	|	1827	...
Chester **145, 160** ... a.	|	2108	|	2234	|	0031	...	|	0819	|	|	1020	|	|	1219	|	|	1419	|	|	1624	|	|	1822	|	...
Holyhead **145, 160** .. a.	|	...	|	0048	|	...	...	|	1014	|	|	1209	|	|	1413	|	|	1613	|	|	1819	|	|	2018	|	...
Stockport ... a.	2050	...	2201	...	2332	...	...	0754	...	0858	0958	...	1058	1158	...	1258	1358	...	1458	1558	...	1659	1758	...	1858	...
Manchester P'dilly ... a.	2106	...	2215	...	2350	...	...	0810	...	0915	1016	...	1115	1215	...	1315	1415	...	1515	1615	...	1714	1815	...	1915	...

	⑥	⑥	⑥	⑥	⑥ L	⑥	⑥	⑥	⑦	⑦	⑦	⑦	⑦	⑦	⑦	⑦	⑦	⑦	⑦		⑦	⑦	⑦	⑦	⑦	⑦
Cardiff Central ... **132** d.	1655	1721	1755	1850	1934	2010	2055	2154	...	0830	0917	1034	1135	1236	1313	1340	1456	1513	1556	...	1640	1735	1836	1940	2101	2315
Newport ... **132** d.	1709	1735	1809	1904	1948	2026	2110	2212	...	0849	0940	1054	1154	1254	1335	1358	1514	1533	1614	...	1658	1753	1858	1959	2119	2338
Cwmbrân ... d.	1719	1746	1820	1915	1958	2037	2121	2224	...	0900	0951	1105	1207	1309	1347	1409	1524	1544	1624	...	1709	1804	1909	2010	2130	2348
Pontypool & New Inn . d.	|	1752	1825	1920	2003	2042	|	2229	...	0906	0957	1111	1213	1315	|	|	|	1550	|	...	1715	1810	|	2016	2136	2354
Abergavenny ... d.	1732	1801	1835	1930	2012	2052	2134	2239	...	0915	1008	1121	1224	1325	1400	1422	1538	1559	1637	...	1725	1820	1922	2026	2146	0004
Hereford ... d.	1758	1827	1900	1955	2039	2120	2200	2306	...	0941	1036	1150	1254**d**	1355**d**	1426	1448	1604	1628**d**	1704	...	1753**d**	1849**d**	1949	2054	2214	0035
Leominster ... d.	1811	|	1913	2008	2052	2133	2214	—	...	0955	1050	1203	1308	1408	|	1501	|	1641	|	...	1807	1903	2003	2108	2227	...
Ludlow ... d.	1822	1848	1924	2019	2103	2144	2225	...	...	1006	1101	1214	1319	1419	1448	1512	1625	1652	1726	...	1818	1914	2014	2119	2238	...
Craven Arms ... **146** d.	1830	1856	|	2028	2112	2154	2233	...	...	1014	|	1224	|	1428	|	|	|	1700	|	...	1826	|	2022	2129	2248	...
Church Stretton .. **146** d.	1839	1905	|	2037	2121	2203	2242	⑥	...	1023	|	1233	|	1437	|	|	|	1709	|	...	1835	|	2031	2138	2257	...
Shrewsbury ... **146** a.	1853	1919	1950	2053	2135	2217	2257	**V**	...	1037	1130	1248	1348	1451	1521	1538	1651	1723	1752	...	1849	1941	2045	2156	2314	...
Shrewsbury ... **145**¶ d.	1855	1924	1952	2057	2137	2219	2306	2330	0955	1039	1131	1251	1350	1453	1524	1540	1653	1730	1754	...	1854	1942	2048	*2232*	2319	...
Whitchurch ... ¶ d.	|	|	2008	|	|	2244	2332	2355	|	1100	1158	|	|	|	|	1606	|	|	|	...	|	2007	|	|	2346	...
Crewe ... ¶ a.	1926	|	2027	2128	|	2304	2354	0016	1025	1122	1222	1326	1425	1525	|	1627	1725	|	1825	...	1924	2028	2121	*2303*	0009	...
Chester **145, 160** ... a.	|	2022	|	|	2232	|	0022	...	|	|	*1320*t	|	*1518*t	|	1622	*1726*t	|	1825	*1922*t	...	|	*2120*t	|	*2331*	0033	...
Holyhead **145, 160** .. a.	|	2225	|	|	...	|	...	...	|	|	|	|	|	|	1837	|	|	2018	*2134*t	...	|	|	|	...	...	...
Stockport ... a.	1958	...	2059	2158	...	2332	...	...	1058	|	1258	1359	1500	1558	...	1658	1758	...	1858	...	1958	2057	2158	...	...	...
Manchester P'dilly ... a.	2015	...	2115	2214	...	2349	...	...	1117	1203	1313	1416	1515	1614	...	1714	1818	...	1915	...	2016	2115	2219	...	...	...

	Ⓐ R	Ⓐ	Ⓐ	Ⓐ	Ⓐ	Ⓐ	Ⓐ ✕	Ⓐ	Ⓐ	Ⓐ	Ⓐ S	Ⓐ J	Ⓐ	Ⓐ	Ⓐ	Ⓐ	Ⓐ	Ⓐ	Ⓐ	Ⓐ	Ⓐ	Ⓐ	Ⓐ	Ⓐ	Ⓐ T	Ⓐ
Manchester P'dilly ... d.	...	...	...	...	...	0630	...	0730	...	0830	...	...	0930	...	1030	1130	...	1230	1330	...	1430	1530	...	1630	...	1730
Stockport ... d.	...	...	...	...	...	0639	...	0739	...	0839	...	...	0939	...	1040	1140	...	1240	1340	...	1440	1540	...	1640	...	1740
Holyhead **145, 160** .. d.	...	...	...	...	0425	|	0533	|	0628	|	...	...	|	0805	|	|	1040	|	|	1232	|	|	1434	|	...	|
Chester **145, 160** ... d.	...	...	...	...	0618	|	0714	|	0819	|	...	0926	|	1020	|	|	1219	|	|	1419	|	|	1619	|	...	|
Crewe ... ¶ d.	...	0449	...	0558	|	0708	|	0808	|	0908	0914	|	1008	|	1108	1208	|	1308	1408	|	1508	1608	|	1708	1720	1809
Whitchurch ... ¶ d.	...	0508	...	0619	|	|	|	|	|	|	0937	|	|	|	|	|	|	|	1428	|	|	1628	|	|	1743	1829
Shrewsbury ... **145**¶ a.	...	0528	...	0645	0715	0742	0807	0837	0913	0937	1006	1022	1037	1114	1137	1237	1314	1337	1445	1513	1537	1647	1714	1737	1812	1848
Shrewsbury ... **146** d.	0445	0530	0610	0647	0718	0744	0810	0840	0914	0940	1009	1024	1039	1116	1139	1239	1315	1340	1450	1515	1540	1650	1716	1740	1824	1850
Church Stretton .. **146** d.	0503	0545	0626	0702	|	0759	|	|	0930	|	1027	|	1054	|	1154	|	1330	|	1505	1530	|	1706	1731	|	1842	1905
Craven Arms ... **146** d.	0513	0553	0634	0710	|	0807	|	|	0938	|	1037	|	|	1137	|	|	1338	|	1513	1538	|	1714	1739	|	1854	1913
Ludlow ... d.	—	0601	0643	0717	0744	0815	|	0906	0945	1006	...	|	1108	1144	1208	1305	1345	1406	1520	1546	1606	1721	1746	1806	...	1920
Leominster ... d.	Ⓐ	0611	0654	0728	0754	0826	|	0916	|	1016	...	|	1118	|	1218	1315	|	1416	1531	|	1616	1732	1757	1816	...	1931
Hereford ... d.	0526	0641**e**	0710	0745	0811	0842	0858	0933	1010	1033	...	|	1135	1208	1235	1332	1411	1433	1551	1611	1633	1751	1814	1833	...	1948
Abergavenny ... d.	0551	0704	0734	0808	0834	0905	|	0958	1033	1056	...	|	1158	1231	1258	1355	1433	1456	1614	1634	1656	1814	1837	1856	...	2011
Pontypool & New Inn . d.	0602	0714	0745	0818	0844	|	|	|	1043	|	...	|	|	1242	|	1405	|	|	1623	1644	|	1824	|	|	...	2021
Cwmbrân ... d.	0607	0719	0750	0823	0849	0917	|	1011	1048	1109	...	|	1211	1247	1311	1410	|	1509	1628	1649	1709	1829	1849	1909	...	2026
Newport ... **132** a.	0619	0729	0800	0837	0900	0934	0940	1022	1101	1120	...	1153	1222	1256	1322	1420	1454	1521	1639	1659	1721	1839	1900	1922	...	2037
Cardiff Central ... **132** a.	0642	0749	0818	0855	0919	0959	0958	1038	1115	1138	...	1210	1237	1321	1340	1437	1510	1539	1657	1716	1738	1855	1920	1943	...	2103

	Ⓐ	Ⓐ	Ⓐ	Ⓐ	Ⓐ	Ⓐ	Ⓐ	⑥ S	⑥	⑥	⑥	⑥	⑥	⑥	⑥	⑥	⑥	⑥	⑥	⑥	⑥	⑥	⑥	⑥	⑥	⑥
Manchester P'dilly ... d.	...	1830	1930	2030	2136	...	2236	...	...	...	...	...	0630	0730	...	0830	0930	...	1030	1130	...	1230	1330	...	1430	1530
Stockport ... d.	...	1839	1939	2040	2145	...	2244	...	...	...	...	...	0639	0739	...	0839	0940	...	1039	1140	...	1240	1340	...	1440	1540
Holyhead **145, 160** .. d.	1650	|	|	|	|	...	|	...	...	...	...	0425	|	|	0635	|	|	0820	|	|	1033	|	|	1238	|	|
Chester **145, 160** ... d.	1828	|	|	|	|	...	|	...	...	...	...	0620	|	|	0819	|	|	1019	|	|	1219	|	|	1419	|	|
Crewe ... ¶ d.	|	1908	2010	2121	2212	...	2314	...	0454	...	0555	|	0708	0808	|	0908	1008	|	1108	1208	|	1308	1408	|	1509	1608
Whitchurch ... ¶ d.	|	1929	2029	2142	2233	...	2334	...	0513	...	0616	|	0728	0827	|	|	|	|	|	1228	|	|	1427	|	|	1627
Shrewsbury ... **145**¶ a.	1924	1955	2048	2208	2301	...	0004	...	0533	...	0642	0715	0747	0845	0913	0937	1036	1114	1137	1245	1313	1337	1445	1513	1538	1645
Shrewsbury ... **146** d.	1925	1956	2050	2209	...	2308	...	0516	0540	0613	0644	0718	0750	0850	0915	0940	1038	1115	1140	1250	1315	1340	1446	1515	1540	1646
Church Stretton .. **146** d.	1940	2011	2105	2224	...	2324	...	0533	0555	0628	0659	|	0805	0905	|	0955	1054	|	1155	1305	1330	|	1501	|	1555	1701
Craven Arms ... **146** d.	1948	2019	2113	2232	...	2332	...	0547	0603	0636	0707	|	0813	0913	|	1003	1102	|	1203	1313	1338	|	1509	|	1603	1709
Ludlow ... d.	1956	2027	2120	2240	...	2341	...	—	0610	0644	0714	0744	0820	0920	0944	1010	1109	1141	1210	1320	1344	1406	1517	1541	1610	1717
Leominster ... d.	|	2037	2131	2250	...	2352	...	⑥	0621	0655	0725	0754	0831	0931	|	1021	1120	|	1221	1331	|	1416	1527	|	1621	1727
Hereford ... d.	2022	2054	2150**d**	2311	...	0009	...	0542	0642**d**	0711	0744**d**	0811	0851	0950	1009	1038	1140**d**	1206	1238	1351	1410	1433	1546	1606	1638	1746
Abergavenny ... d.	2045	2122	2216	2334	...	0033	...	0607	0705	0734	0807	0834	0914	1013	1032	1101	1203	1229	1301	1414	1432	1456	1609	1629	1701	1809
Pontypool & New Inn . d.	|	2132	|	2343	...	|	...	0618	0715	0744	0817	0844	|	|	1042	|	|	1239	|	|	1443	|	|	1639	|	|
Cwmbrân ... d.	2057	2137	2228	2348	...	0046	...	0623	0720	0749	0822	0849	0926	1025	1047	1113	1215	1244	1313	1426	1448	1509	1621	1644	1713	1821
Newport ... **132** a.	2115	2151	2240	2359	...	0057	...	0634	0737	0800	0831	0900	0937	1036	1057	1127	1227	1254	1328	1436	1504	1521	1635	1654	1733	1835
Cardiff Central ... **132** a.	2138	2211**f**	2300	0023	...	0121	...	0654	0754	0819	0850	0920	0959	1102	1120	1157	1257	1317	1353	1453	1524	1537	1654	1708	1753	1855

	⑥	⑥	⑥	⑥	⑥	⑥	⑥	⑥	⑥	⑦ 🚌	⑦	⑦	⑦	⑦	⑦	⑦	⑦	⑦	⑦	⑦	⑦	⑦	⑦	⑦	⑦	⑦
Manchester P'dilly ... d.	...	1630	1730	...	1830	1930	2030	2133	2235	...	...	0930	1031	1124	...	1233	1330	1430	1530	1630	1730	...	1830	1930	2030	...
Stockport ... d.	...	1640	1740	...	1839	1939	2039	2143	2244	...	...	0940	1040	1140	...	1243	1340	1440	1539	1639	1739	...	1839	1939	2039	...
Holyhead **145, 160** .. d.	1425	|	|	1650	|	|	|	|	|	...	...	|	|	|	1020	|	|	|	|	|	|	1625	|	|	|	...
Chester **145, 160** ... d.	1619	|	|	1829	|	|	|	|	|	...	...	*0922*t	|	*1131*t	1221	|	*1331*t	|	*1531*t	|	*1731*t	1824	|	*1926*t	|	2300
Crewe ... ¶ d.	|	1708	1809	|	1910	2009	2109	2212	2314	...	...	1013	1111	1213	|	1313	1413	1510	1613	1713	1813	|	1913	2010	2113	2323
Whitchurch ... ¶ d.	|	1727	1828	|	1931	2028	2130	2233	2334	...	...	1035	|	|	|	1334	|	|	|	1734	|	|	1934	|	2135	2345
Shrewsbury ... **145**¶ a.	1714	1744	1846	1924	1956	2047	2153	2301	0005	...	...	1101	1141	1243	1318	1359	1443	1544	1643	1800	1843	1920	2000	2044	2203	0014
Shrewsbury ... **146** d.	1716	1746	1850	1926	1958	2048	2155	...	—	0750	...	1103	1145	1244	1319	1401	1444	1547	1644	1801	1844	1921	2001	2045	2204	...
Church Stretton .. **146** d.	|	1801	1905	1941	2013	2103	2210	...	...	0815	...	1119	|	|	1335	|	1500	|	1700	|	|	1937	|	2101	2220	...
Craven Arms ... **146** d.	|	1809	1913	1949	2021	2111	2218	...	...	0835	...	1127	|	|	1343	|	1508	|	1708	|	|	1945	|	2110	2229	...
Ludlow ... d.	1742	1816	1920	1955	2028	2119	2226	...	⑥	0855	...	1136	1213	1313	1351	1428	1516	1617	1716	1829	1912	1953	2029	2118	2237	...
Leominster ... d.	|	1827	1931	|	2039	2129	2237	...		0920	...	1147	1223	1324	1402	1439	1526	1628	1726	1839	|	2004	2039	2130	2249	...
Hereford ... d.	1807	1844	1951	2021	2056	2146	2253	...	2315	0950	1007	1203	1239	1340	1419	1456	1543	1644	1743	1857	1936	2021	2055	2146	2305	...
Abergavenny ... d.	1830	1907	2014	2044	2119	2209	2316	...	2338	...	1031	1227	1302	1403	1442	1519	1606	1708	1806	1920	1959	2046	2118	2210	2329	...
Pontypool & New Inn . d.	1840	|	2023	|	2128	|	2326	...	|	...	1041	|	1312	|	1452	|	1616	|	1816	|	|	2056	|	2221	2339	...
Cwmbrân ... d.	1845	1919	2028	2057	2133	2222	2331	...	2350	...	1046	1240	1317	1416	1457	1531	1621	1721	1821	1933	2011	2101	2131	2226	2344	...
Newport ... **132** a.	1855	1934	2040	2113	2144	2233	2344	...	0007	...	1057	1253	1329	1426	1510	1546	1632	1735	1834	1943	2026	2110	2144	2235	2354	...
Cardiff Central ... **132** a.	1915	1958	2100	2135	2205	2301	0010	...	0034	...	1118	1318	1355	1449	1537	1611	1656	1756	1857	2008	2051	2137	2210	2258	0018	...

◄◄◄ For additional notes see previous page.

R – To / from Llandrindod (Table **146**).
S – To / from Swansea (Table **146**).
T – To / from Cardiff Central (Tables **146** / **135**).
V – To / from Birmingham (Table **145**).

d – Arrives 4 – 6 minutes earlier.
e – Arrives 0630.
f – Arrives 2205 on ⑤.
g – Arrives 0618.
t – Change at Shrewsbury.

¶ – Additional journeys Shrewsbury - Whitchurch - Crewe and v.v.:
From Shrewsbury at 0012②–⑥, 0531Ⓐ, 0544⑥, 0757⑥, 1018⑥, 1224✕, 1424✕, 1624✕, 1825⑥, 2032✕, 2330⑥.
From Crewe at 0640Ⓐ, 0720⑥, 0734Ⓐ**V**, 0920⑥, 1120✕, 1320✕, 1520⑥, 1522Ⓐ, 1720⑥.

LONDON - BIRMINGHAM - WOLVERHAMPTON — 150

VT Most trains convey 🍸

Certain services continue to / from destinations in Table **154**. For trains via Northampton see Table **142**.

km		Ⓐ	Ⓐ	Ⓐ	Ⓐ	Ⓐ	Ⓐ	C	Ⓐ	Ⓐ	Ⓐ	Ⓐ	Ⓐ D		Ⓐ	Ⓐ	Ⓐ	Ⓐ	Ⓐ	Ⓐ		Ⓐ	Ⓐ	Ⓐ
0	**London** Euston **143 151/2/3** d.		0620	0643	0703	0723	0743	and	1703	1723	1743	1803	1823	...	1843	1903	1923	1943	2003	2023	...	2043	2103	2143
28	Watford Junction △ d.		0634	|	|	0737	|	at the	|	1737	|	|	1837	...	|	|	1937	|	|	2037	...	|	|	2158
80	Milton Keynes **143 151/2/3** d.		|	0713	|	|	0813	same	|	|	1813**u**	|	|	...	1913	|	|	2013	|	|	...	2113	2135	2217
133	Rugby a.		0712	|	0751	|	|	minutes	1751	|	|	1851	|	...	|	1951	|	|	2051	|	...	|	2156	|
151	Coventry **119** a.		0722	0742	0802	0822	0842	past	1802	1822	1842	1902	1922	...	1942	2002	2022	2042	2102	2124	...	2142	2207	2246
168	Birmingham Int'l ✈ **119** a.		0733	0753	0813	0833	0853	each	1813	1833	1853	1913	1933	...	1953	2013	2033	2053	2113	2134	...	2153	2218	2300
182	**Birmingham** NS **119 122** a.		0745	0809	0826	0845	0905	hour	1826	1845	1905	1926	1945	...	2008	2026	2045	2104	2126	2146	...	2205	2230	2316
190	Sandwell & Dudley a.		...	0824	...	...	0924	until	...	...	1924	|	1958	...	2024	...	2058	2124	|	2159	...	2216	2241	2333
202	**Wolverhampton** **122** a.		...	0837	...	...	0937		...	...	1937	1959	2011	...	2037	...	2110	2137	2157	2210	...	2228	2253	2346

	Ⓐ	①–④	⑤	⑥	⑥	⑥	⑥	⑥	⑥	⑥	⑥	E	⑥	⑥	⑥	⑥	⑥ D	⑥	⑥	⑥	⑥	⑥	⑥	⑥
London Euston **143 151/2/3** d.	2230	2330	2330		0623	0703	0723	0743	0803	0823	0843	and	1703	1723	1743	1803	1823	1843	1903	1923	1943	2025	2103	2143
Watford Junction △ d.	2245	|	|		0637	|	0737	|	|	0837	|	at the	|	1737	|	|	1837	|	|	1937	|	2040	2118	2158
Milton Keynes **143 151/2/3** d.	2329	0029	0028		|	|	|	0813	|	|	0913	same	|	|	1813	|	|	1913	|	|	2020	|	2150	2230
Rugby a.	2358	0100	0105		|	0751	|	|	0851	|	|	minutes	1751	|	|	1852	|	|	1951	|	|	|	2211	2252
Coventry **119** a.	0010	0113	0118		0722	0802	0822	0842	0902	0922	0942	past	1802	1822	1842	1903	1922	1942	2002	2022	2050	2136	2222	2302
Birmingham Int'l ✈ **119** a.	0021	0124	0129		0733	0813	0833	0853	0913	0933	0953	each	1813	1833	1853	1913	1933	1953	2013	2033	2101	2150	2233	2313
Birmingham NS **119 122** a.	0033	0136	0141		0745	0826	0845	0904	0926	0945	1004	hour	1826	1845	1905	1926	1945	2008	2024	2045	2113	2204	2245	2325
Sandwell & Dudley a.	|	|	|		...	...	...	0924	...	...	1024	until	...	1858	1924	1943	1958	2024	2053	2058	|	2224	2256	2336
Wolverhampton **122** a.	0102	0205	0210		...	...	...	0937	...	...	1037		...	1910	1937	1955	2011	2037	2108	2112	2137	2237	2308	2348

	⑦	⑦	⑦	⑦	⑦	⑦	⑦	⑦	⑦		⑦	⑦	⑦	⑦	⑦ D	⑦	⑦	⑦	⑦	⑦	⑦	⑦	⑦	⑦
London Euston **143 151/2/3** d.		0850	0950	1050	1150	1220	1240	1300	1320	and	1740	1800	1820	1840	1900	1920	1940	2000	2018	2038	2054	2155	2225	2325
Watford Junction △ d.		0907	1005	1105	1205	1234	|	|	1334	at the	|	|	1834	|	|	1934	|	|	2032	|	2110	2209	2239	2339
Milton Keynes **143 151/2/3** d.		0939	1038	1138	1230	|	1313	|	|	same	1813	|	|	1913	|	|	2013	|	|	2116	2143	2245	2312	0012
Rugby a.		1013	1113	1213	1249	|	|	1351	|	minutes	|	1851	|	|	1952	|	|	2051	|	|	2205	2322	2346	0046**s**
Coventry **119** a.		1024	1123	1223	1259	1322	1342	1402	1422	past	1844	1902	1922	1942	2003	2022	2042	2103	2120	2146	2216	2333	2357	0058**s**
Birmingham Int'l ✈ **119** a.		1035	1134	1234	1310	1333	1353	1413	1433	each	1854	1913	1933	1953	2013	2033	2053	2113	2131	2157	2227	2344	0008	0109**s**
Birmingham NS **119 122** a.		1047	1147	1247	1322	1345	1404	1424	1445	hour	1905	1924	1945	2004	2024	2045	2105	2124	2145	2209	2239	2356	0021	0122**s**
Sandwell & Dudley a.		1058	1158	1258	...	1356	1425	...	...	until	1925	1948	...	2024	2035	2056	2124	...	2156	2224	2251	|	|	|
Wolverhampton **122** a.		1111	1211	1310	...	1408	1437	...	...	☆	1937	2000	...	2037	2047	2111	2137	...	2208	2236	2303	0015	0041	0142

	Ⓐ	Ⓐ	Ⓐ	Ⓐ	Ⓐ	Ⓐ	Ⓐ	Ⓐ	Ⓐ	Ⓐ D	Ⓐ K	Ⓐ	Ⓐ	Ⓐ	Ⓐ	F	Ⓐ	Ⓐ	Ⓐ	Ⓐ	Ⓐ	Ⓐ	Ⓐ	Ⓐ
Wolverhampton **122** d.		0500	0524	0545	0604	0627	0645	0705	...	0724	0745	...	...	0845	...	and	...	1845	...	1945	...	2047	2145	2245
Sandwell & Dudley d.		|	0534	0555	0615	0638	0656	0715	...	|	0757	...	...	0855	...	at the	...	1855	...	1955	...	2057	2155	2255
Birmingham NS **119 122** d.		0529	0550	0610	0630	0650	0710	0730	...	0750	0810	0830	0850	0910	0930	same	1850	1910	1930	2010	2050	2110	2210	2310
Birmingham Int'l ✈ **119** d.		0540	0600	0620	0640	0700	0720	|	0741	0800	0821	0840	0900	0920	0940	minutes	1900	1920	1940	2020	2100	2120	2220	2320
Coventry **119** d.		0551	0611	0631	0651	0711	0731	|	0752	0811	0831	0851	0911	0931	0951	past	1911	1931	1951	2031	2111	2131	2231	2331
Rugby d.		0603	|	|	|	|	|	|	|	0823	|	|	0923	|	|	each	1923	|	2003	|	2123	|	2245	2344
Milton Keynes **143 151/2/3** d.		0626	0638	0659	|	0740**s**	|	|	|	|	|	0920	|	1000	|	hour	|	2000	|	2100	|	2159	2308	0024
Watford Junction ▽ a.		0647	|	|	0737	|	|	|	|	|	0916	|	|	|	1039	until	|	|	2041	2119	|	2220	2339	0052
London Euston **143 151/2/3** a.		0705	0713	0734	0753	0815	0831	0843	0850	0913	0933	0953	1013	1032	1056	☆	2015	2032	2057	2137	2213	2241	0004	0113

	⑥	⑥	⑥	⑥	⑥	⑥	⑥	⑥	⑥		⑥	⑥	⑥	⑥ D	⑥	⑥	⑥	F	⑥	⑥	⑥	⑥	⑥	⑥
Wolverhampton **122** d.		...	0545	0606	0627	0645	0705	0725	0745	...	...	...	...	0905	...	0945	...	and	...	...	1845	1945	2045	2109
Sandwell & Dudley d.		...	0555	0617	0637	0656	0715	|	0755	...	...	...	...	|	...	0955	...	at the	...	...	1855	1955	2055	2119
Birmingham NS **119 122** d.		0550	0609	0630	0650	0710	0730	0750	0810	...	0830	0850	0910	0930	0950	1010	1030	same	1830	1850	1910	2010	2110	2130
Birmingham Int'l ✈ **119** d.		0600	0620	0640	0700	0720	0740	0800	0820	...	0840	0900	0920	0940	1000	1020	1040	minutes	1840	1900	1920	2020	2120	2140
Coventry **119** d.		0611	0630	0651	0711	0731	0751	0811	0831	...	0851	0911	0931	0951	1011	1031	1051	past	1851	1911	1931	2031	2131	2151
Rugby d.		0624	|	|	0723	|	|	0823	|	...	|	0923	|	|	1023	|	|	each	|	1923	1943	2043	2143	2203
Milton Keynes **143 151/2/3** d.		|	0659	|	|	0759	|	|	0859	...	|	|	0959	|	|	1059	|	hour	|	|	2007	2105	2205	2226
Watford Junction ▽ a.		|	0719	0737	|	|	0837	|	|	...	0939	|	|	1039	|	|	1139	until	1939	|	2034	2135	2234	2312
London Euston **143 151/2/3** a.		0715	0736	0753	0817	0833	0854	0913	0934	...	0957	1015	1033	1056	1114	1133	1155	☆	1955	2023	2055	2156	2253	2333

	⑦	⑦	⑦	⑦	⑦	⑦	⑦	⑦	F	⑦	⑦	⑦	⑦	⑦	⑦	⑦	⑦	⑦	⑦	⑦		⑦	⑦	⑦
Wolverhampton **122** d.		0805	0905	1005	1105	...	1145	...	and	...	1645	...	...	1745	...	...	1845	...	1945	...	...	2105	2205	2237
Sandwell & Dudley d.		0815	0915	1015	1115	...	1155	...	at the	...	1655	...	...	1755	...	...	1855	...	1955	...	...	2117	2216	2248
Birmingham NS **119 122** d.		0830	0930	1030	1130	1150	1210	1230	same	1650	1710	1730	1750	1810	1830	1850	1910	1930	2010	2030	...	2130	2230	2300
Birmingham Int'l ✈ **119** d.		0840	0940	1040	1140	1200	1220	1240	minutes	1700	1720	1740	1800	1820	1840	1900	1920	1940	2020	2040	...	2140	2240	2310
Coventry **119** d.		0851	0951	1051	1151	1211	1231	1251	past	1711	1730	1751	1811	1831	1851	1911	1931	1951	2031	2051	...	2151	2251	2321
Rugby d.		0904	1004	1104	1205	1225	|	|	each	1725	|	|	1825	|	|	1926	|	|	|	2105	...	2204	2304	2335
Milton Keynes **143 151/2/3** d.		0939	1039	1139	1227	|	1301	|	hour	|	1759	|	|	1859	|	|	2000	|	2101	2128	...	2237	2337	0013**s**
Watford Junction ▽ a.		1007	1111	1208	|	|	|	1338	until	|	|	1838	|	|	1938	|	|	2039	|	2202	...	2305	0006	0043
London Euston **143 151/2/3** a.		1025	1131	1225	1304	1318	1338	1357	☆	1818	1836	1857	1917	1937	1957	2018	2037	2057	2146	2222	...	2323	0025	0103

C – The 1023 from London continues to Shrewsbury (Table **145**) calling at Wolverhampton (a. 1210).
D – To / from Shrewsbury (Table **145**).
E – The 1123 from London continues to Shrewsbury (Table **145**) calling at Wolverhampton (a. 1310).
F – The 1630 from Birmingham New Street starts from Shrewsbury (Table **145**) calling at Wolverhampton (d. 1604).
K – From Manchester Piccadilly (Table **152**).
s – Calls to set down only.
u – Calls to pick up only.
☆ – Timings may vary by up to 3 minutes.
△ – Trains call here to pick up only.
▽ – Trains call here to set down only.

LONDON - CHESTER (- HOLYHEAD) — 151

VT Most trains convey 🍸

km		Ⓐ	Ⓐ A	Ⓐ	Ⓐ	Ⓐ		Ⓐ	Ⓐ	Ⓐ	Ⓐ	Ⓐ	Ⓐ	Ⓐ		Ⓐ	Ⓐ G	Ⓐ	Ⓐ		⑥	⑥ A	⑥
0	**London** Euston **143 150/2/3/4** d.		...	0710	0810	0910	...	1010	1110	1210	1310	1410	1510	1610	...	1710	1810	1910	2010	...		...	0810
80	Milton Keynes **143 150/2/3/4** d.		...	0741	0843	0941	...	1041	1141	1241	1341	1441	1541	1641**u**	...	1741**u**	1841**u**	1941	2041	...		...	0841
254	Crewe **143 152/3/4 160** d.		0623	0849	0953	1049	...	1149	1249	1352	1449	1549	1649	1749	...	1857	1956	2055	2149	...		0623	0949
288	**Chester** **160** a.		0643	0911	1013	1113	...	1211	1311	1413	1510	1610	1711	1808	...	1916	2015	2120	2213	...		0643	1010
	Bangor **160** a.		0749	*1051*	1124	1216	...	*1330*	*1435*	*1530*	*1642*	*1738*	*1846*	1918	...	2028	2125	2229	*0013*	...		0749	*1135*
	Holyhead **160** a.		0820	*1120*	1155	1247	...	*1414*	*1508*	*1614*	*1716*	*1821*	*1917*	*2020*	...	2058	2156	2300	*0048*	...		0820	*1209*

	⑥	⑥	⑥	⑥	⑥	⑥	⑥	⑥	⑥	⑥		⑦	⑦	⑦	⑦	⑦	⑦	⑦	⑦	⑦	⑦		⑦
London Euston **143 150/2/3/4** d.	0910	1010	1110	1210	1310	1410	1510	1610	1710	1810	...		*0815*	*0945*	*1115*	*1337*	*1437*	1508	1608	1708	1808	...	1908
Milton Keynes **143 150/2/3/4** d.	0941	1041	1141	1241	1341	1441	1541	1641	1740	1841	...		|	*1033*	*1204*	|	|	1542	1642	1742	1842	...	1942
Crewe **143 152/3/4 160** d.	1049	1156	1249	1352	1449	1549	1649	1749	1852	1949	...		1042	1227	1327	1527	1627	1652	1752	1901	1952	...	2055
Chester **160** a.	1113	1217	1311	1415	1509	1610	1711	1810	1911	2009	...		1102	1252	1351	1549	1649	1711	1812	1920	2013	...	2113
Bangor **160** a.	1216	*1332*	*1438*	*1532*	*1636*	1717	*1841*	1921	2023	*2142*	...		1209	1417	1512	1712	1817	*1914*	*1947*	2034	2123	...	2222
Holyhead **160** a.	1247	*1413*	*1510*	*1613*	*1714*	1748	*1913*	1952	2054	*2225*	...		1240	1453	1555	1757	1854	*1954*	*2018*	2103	2154	...	2253

	Ⓐ	Ⓐ H	Ⓐ	Ⓐ G	Ⓐ	Ⓐ		Ⓐ	Ⓐ	Ⓐ	Ⓐ	Ⓐ	Ⓐ	Ⓐ	Ⓐ	Ⓐ	Ⓐ B	⑥	⑥ H	⑥	⑥	⑥	⑥
Holyhead **160** d.		...	0448	0551	0655	*0715*	...	0855	*0923*	*1040*	*1127*	1252	1358	*1434*	*1544*	*1730*	*1921*		...	*0425*	0652	0755	0855
Bangor **160** d.		...	0514	0618	0722	*0802*	...	0922	*1002*	*1107*	*1200*	1320	1425	*1504*	*1623*	*1809*	2020		...	*0457*	0720	0822	0922
Chester **160** d.		0422	0626	0735	0835	0935	...	1035	1135	1235	1335	1435	1535	1635	1735	1935	2135		0422	0717	0835	0935	1035
Crewe **143 152/3/4 160** a.		0444	0647	0754	0854	0954	...	1054	1154	1254	1354	1454	1554	1654	1754	1954	2154		0443	0736	0854	0954	1054
Milton Keynes **143 150/2/3/4** a.		*0651*	|	|	1002	1102	...	1202	1302	1402	1502	1602	1702	1802	1901	2104	...		*0711*	0852	1002	1102	1202
London Euston **143 150/2/3/4** a.		*0726*	0834	0941	1037	1137	...	1237	1337	1439	1536	1637	1737	1839	1938	2140	...		*0750*	0930	1036	1136	1236

	⑥	⑥	⑥		⑥	⑥	⑥		⑥	⑥		⑦	⑦	⑦	⑦	⑦	⑦	⑦		⑦	⑦	⑦	⑦
Holyhead **160** d.	*0923*	*1033*	*1123*	...	*1238*	1358	*1425*	...	*1523*	*1823*	...		0845	*0845*	1055	1150	1250	1355	...	*1530*	*1625*	*1730*	*1825*
Bangor **160** d.	*1002*	*1105*	*1202*	...	*1307*	1425	*1453*	...	*1602*	*1903*	...		0913	*0913*	1122	1217	1318	1422	...	*1558*	*1704*	*1759*	*1904*
Chester **160** d.	1135	1235	1335	...	1435	1535	1635	...	1735	2035	...		1039	1128	1233	1330	1433	1533	...	1735	1835	1935	2037
Crewe **143 152/3/4 160** a.	1154	1254	1354	...	1454	1554	1654	...	1754	2054	...		1103	1147	1253	1350	1454	1552	...	1753	1853	1956	2056
Milton Keynes **143 150/2/3/4** a.	1302	1402	1502	...	1602	1702	1802	...	|	...	...		|	1304	1403	1503	1603	1703	...	1904	2003	*2136*	*2304*
London Euston **143 150/2/3/4** a.	1336	1436	1536	...	1636	1736	1837	...	*2002*	...	...		*1310*	1343	1441	1542	1641	1741	...	1942	2041	*2225*	*2352*

A – From Birmingham New Street (d. 0530), Wolverhampton (d. 0548) and Stafford (d. 0601).
B – To Wolverhampton (a. 2227) and Birmingham New Street (a. 2250).
G – Conveys 🚌12 London Euston - Wrexham and v.v. (Table **145**).
H – To Stafford (a. 0524), Wolverhampton (a. 0539) and Birmingham New Street (a. 0558 ⑥, 0610 Ⓐ).
u – Calls to pick up only.

① – Mondays ② – Tuesdays ③ – Wednesdays ④ – Thursdays ⑤ – Fridays ⑥ – Saturdays ⑦ – Sundays Ⓑ – Not Saturdays **49**

152 LONDON - MANCHESTER

VT

km			Ⓐ	Ⓐ	Ⓐ	Ⓐ	Ⓐ	Ⓐ	Ⓐ	Ⓐ	Ⓐ	Ⓐ	Ⓐ		Ⓐ	Ⓐ	Ⓐ	④⑤2	Ⓐ		Ⓐ	Ⓐ	Ⓐ	Ⓐ
0	**London** Euston 150/1/3/4 d.	Ⓐ	0616	0636	0655	0720	0735	0800	0820	0840	0900	0920	0940	and at	1800	1820	1840	1857	1900	...	1920	1940	2000	2040
80	Milton Keynes 150/1/4 d.		0646	│	0727	0750	0806	│	0850	│	│	0950	│	the same	│	1850**u**	│	│	│	...	1950	│	│	│
235	Stoke on Trent 122 d.		0745	│	0825	0848	│	0925	0948	│	1025	1048	│	minutes	1925	1948	│	│	2025	...	2050	│	2126	│
267	Macclesfield 122 d.		0802	│	0841	│	│	0941	│	│	1041	│	│	past each	1941	│	│	│	│	...	2107	│	2142	│
	Crewe 154 d.		│	0811	│	│	0911	│	│	1011	│	│	1111	hour until	│	│	2018	2033**s**	│	...	│	2123	│	2213
	Wilmslow d.		│	0827	│	│	0927	│	│	1027	│	│	1127		│	│	2033	│	│	...	│	2138	│	2229
287	Stockport 122 d.		0817	0837	0856	0917	0937	0955	1017	1037	1056	1117	1137	♡	1956	2017	2043	│	2053	...	2120	│	2155	2239
296	**Manchester** Piccadilly 122 a.		0825	0846	0904	0925	0945	1004	1028	1046	1104	1128	1146		2005	2028	2052	2110	2104	...	2128	2154	2204	2248

	Ⓐ	Ⓐ		Ⓐ	Ⓐ		⑥	⑥	⑥	⑥	⑥		⑥	⑥	⑥	⑥	⑥		⑥	⑥	⑥	⑥		⑥
London Euston 150/1/3/4 d.	2100	2140	...	2200	2300	⑥	0636	0655	0720	0735	0800	...	0820	0840	0900	0920	0940	and at	1900	1920	1940	2020	...	2100
Milton Keynes 150/1/4 d.	2131	│	...	2240	│		│	0727	0750	0806	│	...	0850	│	│	0950		the same	│	1950	│	2105	...	2145
Stoke on Trent 122 d.	2228	2308	...	│	0118**s**		│	0825	0848	│	0925	...	0948	│	1025	1048		minutes	2025	2048	│	2205	...	│
Macclesfield 122 d.	2244	2324	...	│	0134**s**		│	0841	│	│	0941	...	│	│	1041	│		past each	2041	│	│	2221	...	│
Crewe 154 d.	│	│	...	0017	│		0811	│	│	0911	│	...	│	1011	│	│	1111	hour until	│	│	2119	│	...	2259
Wilmslow d.	│	│	...	...	│		0827	│	│	0927	│	...	│	1027	│	│	1127		│	│	2134	│	...	2315
Stockport 122 d.	2259	2339	...	...	0148**s**		0837	0856	0917	0937	0955	...	1017	1037	1056	1117	1137	☆	2056	2120	2145	2236	...	2327
Manchester Piccadilly 122 a.	2308	2349	...	...	0159		0846	0904	0928	0945	1004	...	1028	1046	1104	1128	1146		2104	2130	2153	2250	...	2339

		⑦	⑦	⑦	⑦		⑦	⑦	⑦	⑦	⑦	⑦	⑦		⑦	⑦	⑦	⑦	⑦	⑦	⑦	⑦	⑦	⑦
London Euston 150/1/3/4 d.	⑦	0810	0820	0920	1020	...	1120	1217	1237	1257	1317	1337	1357	and at	1817	1837	1857	1917	1937	1957	2015	2035	2125	2151
Milton Keynes 150/1/4 d.		0856	0906	1007	1107	...	1208	1250	│	│	1350	│	│	the same	1850	│	│	1950	│	│	2048	│	2214	2239
Stoke on Trent 122 d.		│	1021	1123	1225	...	1311	1350	│	1426	1450	│	1526	minutes	1950	│	2026	2050	│	2126	2150	│	2329	│
Macclesfield 122 d.		│	1038	1139	1242	...	1328	│	│	1442	│	│	1542	past each	│	│	2042	│	│	2142	│	│	2346	│
Crewe 154 d.		1019	│	│	│	...	│	│	1413	│	│	1513	│	until	│	2013	│	│	2113	│	│	2221	│	0016**s**
Wilmslow d.		1034	│	│	│	...	│	│	1429	│	│	1529	│		│	2029	│	│	2129	│	│	2236	│	│
Stockport 122 d.		1044	1052	1153	1256	...	1342	1421	1439	1456	1520	1539	1556	☆	2021	2039	2057	2119	2139	2159	2220	2246	0001	0038**s**
Manchester Piccadilly 122 a.		1054	1102	1204	1305	...	1350	1431	1448	1506	1531	1548	1605		2030	2048	2106	2131	2149	2209	2229	2254	0009	0048

km			Ⓐ	Ⓐ	Ⓐ	Ⓐ	Ⓐ	Ⓐ	Ⓐ	Ⓐ	Ⓐ	Ⓐ	Ⓐ	Ⓐ	Ⓐ	Ⓐ	Ⓐ	Ⓐ		Ⓐ	Ⓐ	Ⓐ	Ⓐ	Ⓐ
0	**Manchester** Piccadilly 122 d.	Ⓐ	0505	0555	0610	0635	0643	0700	0715	0627	0735	0755	0815	0835	0855	0915	0935	0955	and at	1655	1715	1735	1755	1815
9	Stockport 122 d.		0513	0603	0618	0643	0651	0707**u**	0723	0635	0743	0804	0823	0843	0904	0923	0943	1004	the same	1704	1723	1743	1804	1823
30	Wilmslow d.		│	0611	│	│	0659	│	│	│	│	0811	│	│	0911	│	│	1011	minutes	1711	│	│	1811	│
50	Crewe 154 d.		0536	0628	│	│	0717	│	│	│	│	0829	│	│	0930	│	│	1029	past each	1729	│	│	1829	│
	Macclesfield 122 d.		│	│	0631	0656	│	│	│	0648	0756	│	│	0856	│	│	0956	│	until	│	│	1756	│	│
	Stoke on Trent 122 d.		│	│	0648	0712	│	│	0750	0706	0812	│	0850	0912	│	0950	1012	│		│	1750	1812	│	1850
	Milton Keynes 150/1/4 a.		0651	│	│	│	│	│	0846	**b**	│	│	0949	│	│	1046	│	│	♧	│	1848	│	1933	1946
304	**London** Euston 150/1/3/4 a.		0726	0808	0820	0846	0854	0900	0921	0933	0949	1016	1026	1051	1108	1121	1141	1202		1906	1924	1941	2008	2021

	Ⓐ	Ⓐ	Ⓐ	Ⓐ	Ⓐ	Ⓐ		⑥	⑥	⑥	⑥	⑥	⑥	⑥	⑥	⑥	⑥	⑥	⑥	⑥	⑥		⑥	⑥
Manchester Piccadilly 122 d.	1835	1855	1915	1955	2015	2115	⑥	0525	0555	0610	0635	0655	0715	0735	0755	0815	0835	0855	0915	0935	0955	and at	1715	1735
Stockport 122 d.	1843	1903	1923	2004	2023	2123		0534	0603	0618	0643	0704	0723	0743	0804	0823	0843	0904	0923	0943	1004	the same	1723	1743
Wilmslow d.	│	1911	│	2011	│	│		0541	0611	│	│	0711	│	│	0811	│	│	0911	│	│	1011	minutes	│	│
Crewe 154 d.	│	1929	│	2029	│	│		0600	0629	│	│	0729	│	│	0829	│	│	0930	│	│	1029	past each	│	│
Macclesfield 122 d.	1856	│	1936	│	2036	2136		│	│	0631	0656	│	│	0756	│	│	0856	│	│	0956	│	until	│	1756
Stoke on Trent 122 d.	1912	│	1952	│	2052	2153		│	│	0648	0712	│	0750	0812	│	0850	0912	│	0950	1012	│		1750	1812
Milton Keynes 150/1/4 a.	│	2031	2048	2135	2151	2300		0711	0731	│	│	│	0846	│	│	0946	│	│	1046	│	│	♧	1848	│
London Euston 150/1/3/4 a.	2039	2106	2123	2210	2228	2348		0750	0807	0825	0845	0902	0921	0940	1008	1021	1041	1107	1121	1142	1203		1922	1939

	⑥	⑥	⑥	⑥	⑥	⑥		⑦	⑦	⑦	⑦	⑦	⑦	⑦	⑦	⑦		⑦	⑦	⑦	⑦	⑦	⑦	⑦
Manchester Piccadilly 122 d.	1755	1815	1835	1855	1935	2035	⑦	0805	0820	0920	1020	1035	1115	1135	1155	1215	and at	1815	1835	1855	1915	1935	2021	2055
Stockport 122 d.	1804	1823	1843	1904	1943	2043		0814	0828	0928	1029	1046	1124	1144	1205	1223	the same	1822	1842	1904	1922	1941	2027	2103
Wilmslow d.	1811	│	│	1911	│	│		0822	│	│	1037	│	│	│	1212	│	minutes	│	│	1911	│	│	│	│
Crewe 154 d.	1829	│	│	1929	│	│		0843	│	│	1055	│	│	│	1230	│	past each	│	│	1929	│	│	│	│
Macclesfield 122 d.	│	│	1856	│	1956	2056		│	0841	0940	│	1057	│	1157	│	│	until	│	1855	│	│	1954	2040	2116
Stoke on Trent 122 d.	│	1849	1912	│	2012	2112		│	0857	1000	│	1115	1152	1214	│	1251		1850	1912	│	1950	2011	2057	2133
Milton Keynes 150/1/4 a.	│	1945	│	│	2110	2210		│	│	1116	│	1221	1250	│	│	1347	☆	1948	│	│	2046	│	2203	2246
London Euston 150/1/3/4 a.	2002	2034	2057	2120	2159	2259		1055	1059	1206	1254	1257	1328	1348	1410	1428		2027	2045	2108	2131	2201	2256	2346

b – Via Birmingham New Street (Table **150**).
s – Calls to set down only.

☆ – Timings may vary by up to 3 minutes.
♡ – The 1720 Ⓐ from London calls at Milton Keynes to pick up only.

♧ – The 1255 from Manchester Piccadilly arrives London Euston 1507⑥,1509Ⓐ; the 1315 from Manchester Piccadilly arrives London Euston 1528⚒; the 1415 from Manchester Piccadilly arrives London Euston 1621⑥,1624Ⓐ.

153 LONDON - LIVERPOOL

🍷 conveyed on most services VT

km			Ⓐ	⚒	⑥	Ⓐ	Ⓐ	⑥	⚒	⚒		⚒	⚒	⚒	⚒	⚒	⑥	Ⓐ	⑥	Ⓐ	⚒	⑥	Ⓐ
0	**London** Euston 142/3 150/1/2/4 d.	⚒	0527	0707	0807	0807	0907	0907	1007	1107	...	1207	1307	1407	1507	1607	1633	1707	1707	1733	1807	1833	1833
80	Milton Keynes 142/3 150/1/2/4 d.		0615	│	│	0838	│	│	│	│	...	│	│	│	│	│	│	│	│	│	│	│	│
135	Rugby 142/3 150 d.		│	│	│	│	│	│	│	│	...	│	│	│	│	│	│	│	│	1823	│	│	1923
155	Nuneaton 143 d.		0645	│	│	│	│	│	│	│	...	│	│	│	│	│	│	│	1803	│	│	│	│
215	Stafford 143 144 d.		0708	0823	0924	0927	1024	1026	1124	1224	...	1324	1424	1524	1624	1724	1759	1824	1827	1856	1924	1959	1954
254	Crewe 143 144 151 152 154 d.		0728	0843	0943	│	1043	1046	1143	1243	...	1343	1443	1543	1643	1743	│	1844	1847	1916	1943	│	2016
290	Runcorn 144 a.		0745	0900	1000	1001	1100	1103	1200	1300	...	1400	1501	1600	1701	1800	1832	1900	1904	1933	2000	2031	2033
312	**Liverpool** Lime Street 144 a.		0803	0920	1019	1019	1119	1120	1219	1319	...	1420	1519	1620	1720	1819	1852	1920	1922	1952	2020	2051	2053

	Ⓐ	⑥	Ⓐ	⑥	Ⓐ		⑦	⑦	⑦	⑦		⑦	⑦	⑦	⑦	⑦	⑦		⑦	⑦	⑦	⑦	⑦
London Euston 142/3 150/1/2/4 d.	1907	1907	2007	2011	2107	⑦	0815	0914	1015	1115	...	1205	1305	1405	1505	1605	1705	...	1805	1905	2005	2008	2121
Milton Keynes 142/3 150/1/2/4 d.	│	│	│	│	2139		│	│	│	1204	...	│	│	│	│	│	│	...	│	│	│	2041	│
Rugby 142 143 150 d.	│	│	│	2115	│		│	│	│	│	...	│	│	│	│	│	│	...	│	│	│	│	│
Nuneaton 143 d.	│	2003	2103	│	2208		0944	1045	1147	│	...	│	│	│	│	│	1804	...	│	2004	2104	│	2253
Stafford 143 144 d.	│	2027	2127	2146	│		1008	1114	1214	1253	...	1325	1425	1525	1625	1726	│	...	1925	2029	│	2133	2318
Crewe 143 144 151 152 154 d.	│	2047	2148	2206	2251		1030	1136	1234	1315	...	1345	1445	1545	1645	1746	1846	...	1945	2049	2146	2155	2344
Runcorn 144 a.	2050	2105	2205	2224	2309		1047	1153	1251	1332	...	1402	1502	1602	1702	1802	1902	...	2002	2106	2203	2212	0004
Liverpool Lime Street 144 a.	2108	2123	2222	2242	2334		1105	1211	1308	1351	...	1420	1520	1623	1721	1821	1921	...	2020	2123	2220	2229	0027

		Ⓐ	⑥	Ⓐ	⑥	Ⓐ	⑥	Ⓐ	⑥	Ⓐ	⑥	⚒	⚒	⚒	⑥	Ⓐ	⚒	⚒	⚒	Ⓐ	⑥	⑥	Ⓐ
Liverpool Lime Street 144 d.	⚒	0526	0547	0605	0645	0700	0720	0747	0747	0847	0847	0947	1047	1147	1247	1247	1347	1447	1547	1647	1647	1747	1747
Runcorn 144 d.		0543	0603	0621	0701	0715**u**	0737	0803	0803	0903	0903	1003	1103	1203	1303	1303	1403	1503	1603	1703	1703	1803	1803
Crewe 143 144 151 152 154 d.		0602	│	│	0720	│	0757	0823	0822	0925	0924	1022	1122	1222	1324	1325	1422	1522	1622	│	1723	│	1824
Stafford 143 144 d.		0622	0636	0654	0739	│	0816	0843	0842	0944	0943	1042	1142	1242	1343	1344	1442	1542	1642	1736	1743	1836	1843
Nuneaton 143 d.		│	0659	│	│	│	│	│	0905	│	│	│	│	│	│	│	│	│	│	│	│	│	│
Rugby 142 143 150 d.		0654	│	│	│	│	│	│	│	│	│	│	│	│	│	│	│	│	│	│	│	│	│
Milton Keynes 142/3 150/1/2/4 d.		0714	│	│	│	│	│	│	│	│	│	│	│	│	│	│	│	│	│	1824	│	│	│
London Euston 142/3 150/1/2/4 a.		0750	0802	0823	0857	0904	0944	1000	1004	1102	1102	1159	1259	1400	1500	1504	1559	1659	1759	1903	1907	1959	2004

	Ⓐ	⑥	Ⓐ	⑥	Ⓐ		⑦	⑦	⑦		⑦	⑦	⑦	⑦	⑦	⑦	⑦		⑦	⑦	⑦	⑦	⑦
Liverpool Lime Street 144 d.	1847	1847	1947	1948	2048	⑦	0818	0838	0938	...	1038	1147	1247	1347	1447	1547	1618	...	1647	1747	1847	1947	2047
Runcorn 144 d.	1903	1903	2003	2004	2104		0835	0854	0954	...	1054	1203	1303	1403	1503	1603	1634	...	1703	1803	1903	2003	2103
Crewe 143 144 151 152 154 d.	1922	1923	2024	2023	2124		0853	0913	1014	...	1114	1223	1323	1423	1523	1623	1654	...	1723	1823	1923	2024	2124
Stafford 143 144 d.	1942	1942	│	2043	2144		│	0933	1034	...	1136	1244	1344	1444	1544	1644	│	...	1744	1844	1944	2043	2144
Nuneaton 143 d.	│	│	2103	│	2218		│	0956	1057	...	1159	│	│	│	│	│	│	...	│	│	│	│	2219
Rugby 142 143 150 d.	│	│	│	│	2232		│	│	│	...	│	│	│	│	│	│	│	...	│	│	│	│	2233
Milton Keynes 142/3 150/1/2/4 d.	│	│	│	│	2255		1021	│	1147	...	│	│	│	│	│	│	1805	...	│	│	│	2137	2306
London Euston 142/3 150/1/2/4 a.	2102	2117	2206	2215	2343		1105	1134	1229	...	1310	1403	1503	1603	1704	1803	1841	...	1903	2004	2103	2225	2352

u – Calls to pick up only.

km		Ⓐ	⚒	⚒	⚒	⚒	Ⓐ	⚒	⑥	Ⓐ	⑥	⑥ W	⚒	Ⓐ ◐	⑥	Ⓐ	⑥	⚒	Ⓐ Ba	⚒ ◐	⚒	⚒	⚒ ◐	⚒
0	**London Euston** ... **143 150/1/2/3** d.	...	...	...	...	...	0531	...	0605	...	...	...	0730	0643	...	...	...	0830	...	0743	...	0930	0843	...
80	Milton Keynes .... **143 150/1/2/3** d.	...	...	...	...	...	0623	...	0641	...	...	...	|	0713	...	...	...	|	...	0813	...	|	0913	...
	Birmingham New St ... **144 150** d.	...	...	...	0615	...	|	...	|	0715	0715	...	|	0815	0815	...	...	|	...	0915	...	|	1015	...
	Wolverhampton .... **144 150** d.	...	...	...	0637	...	|	...	|	0737	0737	...	|	0837	0837	...	...	|	...	0937	...	|	1037	...
253	Crewe .... **143 144 151 152 153** d.	...	0557	...	0709	...	0732	...	0755	0809	0809	...	|	0909	0909	...	...	|	...	1009	...	|	1109	...
291	Warrington Bank Quay .... d.	...	0615	...	0727	...	0749	...	0812	0827	0827	...	0914	0927	0927	...	...	1014	...	1027	...	1114	1127	...
	Manchester Airport ✈ .. **156 157** d.	...	|	0558	|	0700	|	0729	|	|	|	0829	|	|	|	0900	0900	|	0929	|	1000	|	|	1100
	Manchester Piccadilly .. **156 157** d.	0457	|	0614	|	0715	|	0744	|	|	|	0845	|	|	|	0915	0915	|	0945	|	1015	|	|	1115
310	Wigan North Western .... d.	|	0625	0643**t**	0738	0743**t**	0800	0811**t**	0823	0838	0838	|	0925	0938	0938	0944**t**	|	1025	|	1037	1043**t**	1125	1138	1143**t**
334	**Preston** .... **156 157 158** d.	0540**r**	0640	0658	0753	0758	0815	0825	0837	0853	0853	0932	0941	0954	0953	0958	0957	1041	1048	1053	1058	1141	1153	1158
368	Lancaster .... **157 158** d.	0556	0654	0714	0808	0815	0829	0841	0852	0908	0909	0948	0955	1008	1008	1015	1014	1055	1105	1108	1115	1155	1208	1215
398	Oxenholme .... **158** d.	0611	0709	0728	0822	|	0842	0855	0906	|	|	1004	|	1022	1022	1029	1029	1108	...	|	|	|	1221	1229
450	Penrith .... d.	|	0734	0753	|	0852	|	0920	0932	0944	0946	...	1031	|	|	1054	1053	|	...	1145	|	1230	|	|
478	Carlisle .... **214** d.	0652	0751	0810	0901	0910	0921	0937	0948	1002	1001	...	1047	1101	1101	1111	1110	1147	...	1202	1207	1247	1301	1308
519	Lockerbie .... d.	0711	0810	0829	|	0928	|	0956	|	|	|	...	|	|	|	1130	1129	|	...	|	|	|	|	|
	Haymarket .... a.	|	|	0930**s**	1013	|	|	1057**s**	|	|	|	...	|	1216	1217	|	|	|	...	|	1321**s**	|	1412	|
641	**Edinburgh** Waverley .... a.	|	|	0936	1018	|	|	1103	|	|	|	...	|	1222	1222	|	|	|	...	|	1326	|	1417	|
643	**Glasgow** Central .... **214** a.	0819	0912	...	...	1029	1038	...	1059	1115	1115	...	1159	...	...	1229	1230	1259	...	1315	...	1359	...	1430

	Ⓐ	⑥	⑥ W	⚒ ◐	⑥	Ⓐ	⚒	⚒ ◐	Ⓐ	⑥	⚒		⚒ ◐	⚒	Ⓐ	⑥	⚒ ◐	Ⓐ	⑥	⑥	Ⓐ	⑥ ◐	Ⓐ ◐	⚒	⚒
London Euston .... **143 150/1/2/3** d.	1030	1030	...	0943	...	...	1130	1043	...	...	1230	...	1143	...	1330	1330	1243	...	...	1430	1430	1343	1343	...	1530
Milton Keynes .... **143 150/1/2/3** d.	|	|	...	1013	...	...	|	1113	...	...	|	...	1213	...	|	|	1313	...	...	|	|	1413	1413	...	|
Birmingham New St ... **144 150** d.	|	|	...	1115	...	...	|	1215	...	...	|	...	1315	...	|	|	1415	...	...	|	|	1515	1515	...	|
Wolverhampton .... **144 150** d.	|	|	...	1137	...	...	|	1237	...	...	|	...	1337	...	|	|	1437	...	...	|	|	1537	1537	...	|
Crewe .... **143 144 151 152 153** d	|	|	...	1209	...	...	|	1309	...	...	|	...	1409	...	|	|	1509	...	...	|	|	1609	1609	...	|
Warrington Bank Quay .... d.	1214	1213	...	1227	...	...	1314	1327	...	...	1414	...	1427	...	1514	1514	1527	...	...	1614	1614	1627	1627	...	1714
Manchester Airport ✈ .. **156 157** d.	|	|	1129	|	1200	1200	|	|	1300	1300	|	...	|	1400	|	|	|	1500	1500	|	|	|	|	1600	|
Manchester Piccadilly ... **156 157** d.	|	|	1146	|	1215	1215	|	|	1315	1315	|	...	|	1415	|	|	|	1515	1515	|	|	|	|	1615	|
Wigan North Western .... d.	1225	1224	|	1238	1243**t**	1244**t**	1325	1338	1343**t**	1343**t**	1425	...	1438	1443**t**	1525	1525	1538	1543**t**	1543**t**	1625	1625	1638	1638	1643**t**	1725
Preston .... **156 157 158** d.	1241	1241	1248**c**	1253	1258	1258	1341	1353	1358	1402	1441	...	1453	1458	1541	1540	1553	1558	1558	1641	1641	1653	1653	1658	1741
Lancaster .... **157 158** d.	|	1255	1303	1308	1315	1316	1355	1408	1415	|	1455	...	1508	1515	|	1554	1608	1615	1614	1655	1655	1708	1708	1715	1755
Oxenholme .... **158** d.	|	1308	1320	1322	1329	1329	1408	|	|	|	|	...	1522	1529	1606	1610	|	1629	1629	|	1709	1722	1722	1729	1808
Penrith .... d.	1328	|	...	|	1354	1354	|	1443	1451	|	1530	...	|	1555	1631	|	1644	|	1654	1730	1735	|	1747	1754	|
Carlisle .... **214** d.	1345	1347	...	1400	1412	1411	1447	1459	1508	1508	1546	...	1602	1611	1648	1648	1701	1711	1711	1747	1751	1802	1805	1810	1847
Lockerbie .... d.	|	|	...	|	1430	1430	|	|	1528	1528	|	...	|	1630	|	|	|	1730	1730	|	|	|	|	1829	|
Haymarket .... a.	|	|	...	|	1528**s**	1534**s**	|	1616	|	|	|	...	|	1730**s**	|	|	1814	|	|	|	|	|	|	1931**s**	|
Edinburgh Waverley .... a.	|	|	...	|	1535	1539	|	1622	|	|	|	...	|	1737	|	|	1822	|	|	|	|	|	|	1941**d**	|
Glasgow Central .... **214** a.	1459	1459	...	1515	...	...	1559	...	1629	1629	1659	...	1715	...	1759	1759	...	1828	1829	1859	1915	1915	1923	...	1959

	⚒ ◐	Ⓐ	⑥	Ⓐ	⑥	⚒ ◐	⚒	Ⓐ A	Ⓐ	Ⓐ	⑥	Ⓐ ◐	⑥ ◐	Ⓐ	Ⓐ	⚒	Ⓐ ◐	⑥ ◐	⑥ B	Ⓐ t	⑤	Ⓐ	⑥	⚒ ◐	Ⓐ
London Euston .... **143 150/1/2/3** d.	1443	...	...	1630	1630	1543	...	1633	1657	1730	1730	1643	1643	...	1757	1830	1743	1743	...	...	1846	1930	1930	1843	2030
Milton Keynes .... **143 150/1/2/3** d.	1513	...	...	|	|	1613	...	|	|	|	|	1713	1713	...	|	|	1813**u**	1813	...	...	1919	|	|	1913	|
Birmingham New St ... **144 150** d.	1615	...	...	|	|	1715	...	|	|	|	|	1815	1815	...	|	|	1915	1915	...	...	|	|	|	2015	|
Wolverhampton .... **144 150** d.	1637	...	...	|	|	1737	...	|	|	|	|	1837	1837	...	|	|	1937	1937	...	...	|	|	|	2037	|
Crewe .... **143 144 151 152 153** d	1709	...	...	|	|	1809	...	1820	|	|	|	1909	1909	...	|	|	2009	2009	...	...	2042**s**	|	2105	2115**d**	2219
Warrington Bank Quay .... d.	1727	...	...	1815	1814	1827	...	1837	1850	1914	1914	1927	1927	...	1950	2014	2027	2027	...	...	2101**s**	2116	2123	...	2236
Manchester Airport ✈ .. **156 157** d.	|	1700	1700	|	|	|	1800	|	|	|	|	|	|	1858**b**	|	|	|	|	2000	2000	|	|	|	...	|
Manchester Piccadilly ... **156 157** d.	|	1715	1715	|	|	|	1815	|	|	|	|	|	|	1916**b**	|	|	|	|	2016	2016	|	|	|	...	|
Wigan North Western .... d.	1738	|	1743**t**	1826	1825	1838	1843**t**	1848	1901	1925	1925	1938	1938	|	2001	2025	2038	2038	|	2044	2112**s**	2127	2133	...	2247
Preston .... **156 157 158** d.	1753	1758	1758	1843	1841	1853	1858	1902	1915	1941	1941	1953	1954	1958	2015	2041	2053	2052	2058	2058	2131	2142	2147	...	2300
Lancaster .... **157 158** d.	1808	1816	1814	1858	1855	1908	1915	...	1930	1955	1955	2008	...	2015	2030	2055	2108	...	2114	2115	...	2157	...	...	...
Oxenholme .... **158** d.	1823	1829	1830	|	1908	1921	1929	...	1945	2008	2008	|	...	2029	...	2110	2123	...	...	2129	...	2210	...	...	...
Penrith .... d.	1848	1854	1855	1932	1934	|	1954	...	2010	|	2034	2045	...	|	...	2135	|	...	...	2154	...	2235	...	...	...
Carlisle .... **214** d.	1904	1910	1911	1948	1951	2001	2011	...	2025	2047	2050	2102	...	2108	...	2150	2202	...	...	2212	...	2251	...	...	...
Lockerbie .... d.	|	1930	1930	|	|	|	|	...	2044	|	|	|	...	2129	...	2209	|	...	...	2230	...	|	...	...	...
Haymarket .... a.	2014	|	|	|	|	|	2131**s**	...	|	|	|	2213	...	|	...	|	|	...	...	2328**s**	...	|	...	...	...
Edinburgh Waverley .... a.	2023	|	|	|	|	|	2139**d**	...	|	|	|	2221	...	|	...	|	|	...	...	2334	...	|	...	...	...
Glasgow Central .... **214** a.	...	2034	2034	2059	2102	2115	...	...	2144	2202	2201	...	...	2233	...	2309	2317	...	...	...	...	0005	...	...	...

	Ⓐ ◐	⑥	Ⓐ B	Ⓐ	⑦	⑦	⑦ g	⑦ n	⑦	⑦	⑦	⑦	⑦		⑦	⑦	⑦	⑦	⑦	⑦	⑦	⑦	⑦	⑦	⑦	⑦
London Euston .... **143 150/1/2/3** d.	1943	2031	...	2110		...	...	...	...	...	...	...	0845	...	...	...	0945	...	...	1045	...	...	1228	...	...
Milton Keynes .... **143 150/1/2/3** d.	2013	|	...	|		...	...	...	...	...	...	...	0933	...	...	...	1033	...	...	1133	...	...	|	...	...
Birmingham New St ... **144 150** d.	2115	|	...	|		...	...	...	0845	0920	...	...	|	...	1020	...	|	1120	...	|	1220	...	|	1320	...
Wolverhampton .... **144 150** d.	2137	|	...	|		...	...	...	0904	0937	...	...	|	...	1037	...	|	1137	...	|	1237	...	|	1337	...
Crewe .... **143 144 151 152 153** d	2216	2231	...	2259		...	...	...	0937	1009	...	1027	1057	...	1109	...	1157	1209	...	1258	1309	...	|	1409	...
Warrington Bank Quay .... d.	...	2248	...	2321		...	...	...	0954	1027	...	1043	1113	...	1127	...	1214	1227	...	1315	1327	...	1416	1427	...
Manchester Airport ✈ .. **156 157** d.	...	|	2200	|		0825**n**	0900	...	|	|	1000	|	|	...	|	1100	|	|	1200	|	|	1300	|	|	1400
Manchester Piccadilly ... **156 157** d.	...	|	2215	|		0842	0915	0940	|	|	1016	|	|	...	|	1116	|	|	1216	|	|	1315**b**	|	|	1415**b**
Wigan North Western .... d.	...	2302	2254	2332		|	0944	1011**t**	1006	1038	1043**t**	1054	1124	...	1138	1143**t**	1225	1238	1243**t**	1326	1338	1343**t**	1427	1438	1443**t**
Preston .... **156 157 158** d.	...	2317	2314	2350		0925	0959	1025	1019	1102**e**	1107**e**	1119**f**	1139	...	1153	1156	1240	1253	1258	1341	1353	1357	1442	1453	1457
Lancaster .... **157 158** d.	...	...	2330	...		0941	1015	1042	...	1118	1124	1136	1154	...	1208	1212	1255	1308	1315	1356	1408	1413	1458	1509	1514
Oxenholme .... **158** d.	...	...	...	...		0955	1029	1056	...	1133	1138	...	1208	...	1224	1227	1308	1322	1329	1409	|	1429	|	1524	1528
Penrith .... d.	...	...	...	...		|	1054	1121	...	|	1203	...	1234	...	|	|	1334	|	1354	1435	1445	1453	1532	|	1553
Carlisle .... **214** d.	...	...	...	...		1036	1111	1138	...	1212	1221	...	1249	...	1303	1308	1350	1402	1411	1451	1503	1510	1548	1603	1611
Lockerbie .... d.	...	...	...	...		|	1130	|	...	|	|	...	|	...	|	|	|	|	1430	|	|	|	|	|	1629
Haymarket .... a.	...	...	...	...		1159	|	|	...	|	1342**s**	...	|	...	1415	|	|	|	1529**s**	|	1614	|	|	|	1727**s**
Edinburgh Waverley .... a.	...	...	...	...		1206	|	|	...	|	1347	...	|	...	1420	|	|	|	1534	|	1620	|	|	|	1733
Glasgow Central .... **214** a.	...	...	...	...		...	1237	1301	...	1327	...	...	1404	...	...	1427	1504	1516	...	1605	...	1626	1702	1715	...

	⑦	⑦ ◐	⑦	⑦	⑦ ◐	⑦	⑦	⑦ B	⑦ ◐	⑦	⑦	⑦ ◐	⑦	⑦	⑦ ◐	⑦	⑦		⑦ ◐	⑦	⑦ B	⑦ ◐	⑦	⑦ ◐	⑦
London Euston .... **143 150/1/2/3** d.	1328	1240	...	1428	1340	...	1528	...	1440	...	1628	1540	...	1728	1640	...	1828	...	1740	1928	...	1840	2025	1940	2050
Milton Keynes .... **143 150/1/2/3** d.	|	1313	...	|	1413	...	|	...	1513	...	|	1613	...	|	1713	...	|	...	1813	|	...	1913	|	2013	2137
Birmingham New St ... **144 150** d.	|	1415	...	|	1515	...	|	...	1615	...	|	1715	...	|	1815	...	|	...	1915	|	...	2015	|	2115	|
Wolverhampton .... **144 150** d.	|	1437	...	|	1537	...	|	...	1637	...	|	1737	...	|	1837	...	|	...	1937	|	...	2037	|	2137	|
Crewe .... **143 144 151 152 153** d	|	1509	...	|	1609	...	|	...	1709	...	|	1809	...	|	1909	...	|	...	2009	|	...	2110	2213	2217	2251
Warrington Bank Quay .... d.	1516	1527	...	1616	1627	...	1716	...	1727	...	1816	1827	...	1917	1927	...	2016	...	2027	2116	...	...	2230	2236	2308
Manchester Airport ✈ .. **156 157** d.	|	|	1500	|	|	1600	|	1629	|	1700	|	|	1800	|	|	1858**b**	|	...	|	|	2029	...	|	|	|
Manchester Piccadilly ... **156 157** d.	|	|	1514**b**	|	|	1615	|	1646	|	1716	|	|	1815**b**	|	|	1915	|	...	|	|	2045	...	|	|	|
Wigan North Western .... d.	1527	1538	1543**t**	1627	1638	1643**t**	1727	|	1738	1743**t**	1827	1838	1843**t**	1928	1938	1943**t**	2027	...	2038	2127	|	...	2241	2247	2319
Preston .... **156 157 158** d.	1542	1553	1558	1642	1652	1656	1742	1747**p**	1753	1758	1842	1853	1857	1942	1953	1958	2042	...	2053	2142	2147**p**	...	2255	2301	2338
Lancaster .... **157 158** d.	1558	1608	1615	1657	1707	1713	1757	1803	1809	1815	1857	1908	1914	1957	2008	2015	2057	...	2108	2157	2203	...	...	...	...
Oxenholme .... **158** d.	1611	|	1629	|	1722	1727	1811	...	1823	1829	1911	1922	1928	2012	|	2029	2111	...	2123	2211	...	...	...	...	...
Penrith .... d.	|	1645	|	1732	|	1752	|	...	1848	1854	1936	|	1953	2037	2045	2054	2136	...	|	2236	...	...	...	...	...
Carlisle .... **214** d.	1649	1702	1708	1748	1802	1809	1849	...	1904	1917**f**	1953	2001	2011	2051	2102	2112	2152	...	2202	2252	...	...	...	...	...
Lockerbie .... d.	|	|	1727	|	|	1828	|	...	|	1937	|	|	2030	|	|	2131	|	...	2221	|	...	...	...	...	...
Haymarket .... a.	|	1811	|	|	|	1930**s**	|	...	2014	|	|	|	2128**s**	|	2214	|	|	...	|	|	...	...	...	...	...
Edinburgh Waverley .... a.	|	1818	|	|	|	1935	|	...	2020	|	|	|	2133	|	2219	|	|	...	|	|	...	...	...	...	...
Glasgow Central .... **214** a.	1802	...	1826	1902	1913	...	2002	...	...	2038	2104	2112	...	2203	...	2233	2328	...	2321	0029	...	...	...	...	...

A – To Blackpool North (a. 1931). Until Mar. 23 operated by 🚌 Preston - Blackpool (a. 2005).
B – To Barrow-in-Furness (Table **157**).
W – To Windermere (Table **158**).

a – Until Mar. 23.
b – Departs 4 minutes later from Feb. 12.
c – Arrives 1234.
d – Arrives 4 minutes earlier on ⑥.
e – Arrives 10 – 11 minutes earlier.

f – Arrives 6 – 7 minutes earlier.
g – Until Dec. 31.
n – From Jan. 7.
p – Arrives 15 minutes earlier.
r – Arrives 0536.

s – Calls to set down only.
t – Until Feb. 11.
◐ – Via Table **150**.

154 GLASGOW and EDINBURGH - PRESTON - MANCHESTER, BIRMINGHAM and LONDON

TP, VT

km		Ⓐ	⑥	Ⓐ B	Ⓐ	Ⓐ C	⑥ C	Ⓐ	⑥	⑥ ◐	⚒	Ⓐ	⑥	Ⓐ ◐	⑥ ◐	Ⓐ C	⑥ ◐	Ⓐ ◐	⚒	⚒	⚒ ◐	⚒ d	⑥	Ⓐ
	Glasgow Central 214 d.	...	...	...	...	...	...	0428	0426	...	0422	0540	0540	...	...	...	0550	0549	...	0630	...	0710	0735	0737
	Edinburgh Waverley d.	...	...	...	...	...	...	│	│	...	│	│	│	...	...	...	│	│	0615	│	0652	│	│	│
	Haymarket d.	...	...	...	...	...	...	│	│	...	│	│	│	...	...	...	│	│	0619u	│	0656	│	│	│
	Lockerbie d.	...	...	...	...	...	...	│	│	...	0550	│	│	...	...	...	│	│	│	0726	│	0810	│	│
	Carlisle 214 d.	...	...	...	...	...	...	0544	0544	...	0621c	0650	0649	...	...	...	0702	0703	0733	0746	0807	0833	0849	0850
	Penrith d.	...	...	...	...	...	...	0558	0558	...	0642	│	│	...	...	...	0717	0718	0748	0800	0822	0848	│	│
	Oxenholme 158 d.	...	...	...	...	...	...	0621	0621	...	0708	0725	0724	...	...	...	0741	0742	0812	0823	│	0912	0923	0924
	Lancaster 157 158 d.	0513	0538	...	...	0615	0624	0636	0636	...	0723	0739	0738	0658	0658	0748	0756	0757	0827	0838	0857	0927	0938	0939
0	**Preston** 156 157 158 d.	0533	0558	0600	0617	0640	0644	0657	0657	0617	0743	0759	0758	0717	0717	│	0817	0817	0847	0859	0917	0947	0959	1000
24	Wigan North Western d.	0545	0609	0611	0628	│	│	0709	0709	0628	0755t	0810	0809	0728	0728	│	0828	0828	0859t	0910	0928	0959t	1010	1011
57	**Manchester** Piccadilly 156 157 a.	│	│	│	│	0728	0728	│	│	│	0827	│	│	│	│	0857	│	│	0928	│	│	1029	│	│
73	**Manchester** Airport ✈ 156 157 a.	│	│	│	│	0747	0747	│	│	│	0844	│	│	│	│	0917	│	│	0944	│	│	1044	│	│
—	Warrington Bank Quay d.	0556	0620	0622	0639	...	...	0719	0719	0639	...	0821	0820	0739	0739	...	0839	0839	...	0920	0939	...	1021	1020
0	Crewe 144 151 152 153 a.	│	│	0642	0659	...	...	│	│	0657	...	│	│	0757	0757	...	0857	0857	...	│	0958	...	│	│
63	Wolverhampton 144 150 a.	│	│	│	0735	...	...	│	│	0732	...	│	│	0833	0833	...	0933	0932	...	│	1033	...	│	│
82	**Birmingham** New St 144 150 a.	│	│	│	0756	...	...	│	│	0805	...	│	│	0905	0905	...	1005	1005	...	│	1105	...	│	│
	Milton Keynes 150/1/2/3 a.	│	0738	│	...	...	...	│	│	0858	...	│	│	0958	...	...	1058	1058	...	│	1158	...	│	│
	London Euston 150/1/2/3 a.	0758	0814	0834	...	...	...	0907	0908	0934	...	1009	1011	1032	...	...	1133	1134	...	1111	1233	...	1208	1210

	⑤2	⚒ ◐	⚒	⚒	⚒ ◐	⑥ W	⑥	Ⓐ	Ⓐ W	⚒	⚒ ◐	⚒	⚒	⚒ ◐	Ⓐ	⑥ W	⑥	⚒	Ⓐ ◐	⑥ ◐	Ⓐ	⑥	⑥ C	⚒	⚒ ◐
Glasgow Central 214 d.	...	0800	...	0840	...	...	0906	0906	...	0940	1000	...	1040	...	1110	...	1110	1140	1200	1200	...	...	...	1240	...
Edinburgh Waverley d.	...	│	0812	│	0851	...	│	│	...	│	│	1011	│	1052	│	...	│	│	│	│	1212	1212	...	│	1252
Haymarket d.	..	│	0816u	│	0857	...	│	│	...	│	│	1015u	│	1057	│	...	│	│	│	│	1216u	1216u	...	│	1257
Lockerbie d.	...	│	0910	│	│	...	1008	1008	...	│	│	1110	│	│	1208	...	1208	│	│	│	1311	1310	...	│	│
Carlisle 214 d.	...	0911	0933	0949	1008	...	1031	1033	...	1049	1111	1133	1149	1208	1231	...	1231	1249	1311	1313	1333	1333	...	1349	1408
Penrith d.	...	│	0948	1003	│	...	1046	1048	...	│	1125	1148	│	│	1247	...	1247	1303	│	│	│	1348	...	│	1422
Oxenholme 158 d.	...	│	1012	│	1042	1101	1110	│	1114	1123	│	1212	1223	1243	1312	1312	│	│	│	│	1410	1412	...	1424	│
Lancaster 157 158 d.	...	0956	1027	1038	1057	1117	1125	1124	1132	1138	│	1227	1238	1257	1327	1343	1327	1338	1357	1400	1425	1427	1434	1439	1457
Preston 156 157 158 d.	0952	1017	1047	1058	1116	1137	1147	1147	1207e	1158	1217	1247	1258	1317	1347	1406	1347	1358	1417	1420	1447	1447	1509g	1458	1517
Wigan North Western d.	1004	1028	1059t	1109	1128	...	│	1159t	│	1209	1228	1259t	1309	1328	1359t	...	1359t	1409	1429	1432	1459t	1459t	│	1509	1528
Manchester Piccadilly 156 157 a.	│	│	1129	│	│	...	1228	1228	1256	│	│	1328	│	│	1429	...	1428	│	│	│	1528	1528	1556	│	│
Manchester Airport ✈ 156 157 a.	│	│	1144	│	│	...	1244	1244	1323	│	│	1344	│	│	1444	...	1444	│	│	│	1544	1544	1623	│	│
Warrington Bank Quay d.	1016	1039	...	1120	1139	...	...	...	...	1220	1239	...	1320	1339	...	...	...	1420	1440	1443	...	...	...	1520	1539
Crewe 144 151 152 153 a.	1038	1058	...	│	1157	...	...	...	...	│	1259	...	│	1357	...	...	...	│	1457	1459	...	...	...	│	1557
Wolverhampton 144 150 a.	│	1133	...	│	1233	...	...	...	...	│	1333	...	│	1433	...	...	...	│	1533	1533	...	...	...	│	1633
Birmingham New St 144 150 a.	│	1205	...	│	1305	...	...	...	...	│	1405	...	│	1505	...	...	...	│	1605	1605	...	...	...	│	1705
Milton Keynes 150/1/2/3 a.	│	1258	...	│	1358	...	...	...	...	│	1458	...	│	1558	...	...	...	│	1658	1658	...	...	...	│	1758
London Euston 150/1/2/3 a.	1230	1334	...	1310	1433	...	...	...	...	1410	1534	...	1513	1634	...	...	...	1609	1733	1733	...	...	...	1711	1834

	⚒	⚒	⚒ ◐	⚒	⚒	Ⓐ ◐	⑥ ◐	Ⓐ	⑥	⚒	Ⓐ ◐	⑥ ◐	⚒	Ⓐ	⑥	⑥ W	Ⓐ W	Ⓐ ◐	⑥ ◐	⚒	Ⓐ	⑥	Ⓐ	⑥	⚒
Glasgow Central 214 d.	1310	1340	1400	...	1440	...	...	1510	1510	1540	1600	1600	...	1640	1640	...	...	...	...	1710	1730	1740	1740	1800	...
Edinburgh Waverley d.	│	│	│	1418	│	1452	1452	│	│	│	│	│	1612	│	│	...	...	1652	1652	│	│	│	│	│	1813
Haymarket d.	│	│	│	1422u	│	1458	1457	│	│	│	│	│	1616u	│	│	...	...	1657	1658	│	│	│	│	│	1817u
Lockerbie d.	1409	│	│	1518	│	│	│	1609	1609	│	│	│	1710	│	│	...	...	│	│	1809	│	1833	1833	│	1912
Carlisle 214 d.	1430	1449	1511	1540	1549	1608	1608	1631	1630	1649	1711	1711	1733	1753	1752	...	...	1808	1807	1831	1846	1853	1857	1911	1934
Penrith d.	1445	│	│	│	│	1621	1622	1645	1645	1703	│	│	1748	1807	│	...	...	│	│	1846	1901	1907	│	│	1949
Oxenholme 158 d.	1509	1523	1545	1616	1624	│	│	1714	1709	│	1745	1745	1812	1831	1826	1831	1834	1842	1843	1910	1925	1929	1933	│	2013
Lancaster 157 158 d.	1525	1538	│	1630	1638	1657	1657	1729	1725	1737	│	│	1827	1845	1841	1847	1903a	1859	1858	1926	1939	1944	1947	1958	2028
Preston 156 157 158 d.	1547	1558	1617	1650	1658	1717	1717	1748	1746	1758	1817b	1819	1847	1905	1902	1910f	1926	1917	1918	1947	1959	2004	2008	2017	2048
Wigan North Western d.	1559t	1609	1628	│	1709	1728	1728	1800t	1759t	1809	1828	1830	1859t	1916	1913	│	...	1931	1929	1959t	2010	2015	2019	2028	2100t
Manchester Piccadilly 156 157 a.	1628	│	│	1731	│	│	│	1829	1829	│	│	│	1930	│	│	1957	...	│	│	2029	│	│	│	│	2131
Manchester Airport ✈ 156 157 a.	1645	│	│	1747	│	│	│	1844	1845	│	│	│	1945	│	│	2019	...	│	│	2047h	│	│	│	│	2146
Warrington Bank Quay d.	...	1620	1639	...	1720	1739	1739	...	...	1820	1839	1841	...	1927	1924	...	...	1941	1940	...	2021	2026	2032	2039	...
Crewe 144 151 152 153 a.	...	│	1657	...	│	1757	1757	...	...	│	1857	1900	...	│	│	...	...	2000	1959	...	2040	2045	2051	2059	...
Wolverhampton 144 150 a.	...	│	1733	...	│	1833	1832	...	...	│	1933	1934	...	│	│	...	...	2038	2034	...	│	│	2130	2132	...
Birmingham New St 144 150 a.	...	│	1805	...	│	1905	1905	...	...	│	2005	2005	...	│	│	...	...	2105	2105	...	│	│	2154	2151	...
Milton Keynes 150/1/2/3 a.	...	│	1858	...	│	1958	2005	...	...	│	2058	2104	...	2045	2042	...	...	2158	2204	...	2149	2151	...	...	...
London Euston 150/1/2/3 a.	...	1810	1933	...	1910	2032	2055	...	...	2015	2137	2156	...	2120	2133	...	...	2241	2253	...	2226	2242	...	...	...

	Ⓐ	⑥	Ⓐ	⑥	Ⓐ	Ⓐ	Ⓐ	⑦	⑦	⑦	⑦	⑦	⑦ k	⑦	⑦ C	⑦ k	⑦ m	⑦	⑦ ◐	⑦	⑦	⑦ ◐	⑦	⑦	⑦ ◐
Glasgow Central 214 d.	1840	1840	...	...	1847	2010	...		...	...	...	...	0825	...	...	...	0924	0938	...	...	1038	...	1116	1138	1155
Edinburgh Waverley d.	│	│	1852	1852	│	│	2014		...	...	...	...	│	...	...	0915	│	│	...	1012	│	1051	│	│	│
Haymarket d.	│	│	1856	1856	│	│	2018u		...	...	...	...	│	...	...	0919	│	│	...	1016u	│	1055	│	│	│
Lockerbie d.	│	│	│	│	2003	2106	2113		...	...	...	...	│	...	...	1014	│	│	...	1110	│	│	│	│	│
Carlisle 214 d.	1949	1949	2007	2009	2029	2126	2135		...	...	...	...	0948	...	...	1035	1044	1051	...	1133	1153	1207	1235	1249	1307
Penrith d.	│	2003	│	2023	2044	2139	│		...	...	...	...	1003	...	...	1051	│	1105	...	1148	1207	│	1250	│	│
Oxenholme 158 d.	2024	2026	2042	2047	2109	2203	2212		...	...	...	...	1027	...	...	1115	1123	1128	...	1212	1231	1243	1314	1323	│
Lancaster 157 158 d.	2038	2041	2056	2102	2124	2218	2227		...	...	...	...	1042	...	1124	1130	1138	1143	1158	1227	1245	1257	1329	1338	1354
Preston 156 157 158 d.	2058	2101	2117	2122	2144	2240b	2247		0900	1000	1017	1058	1103	1117	1147b	1149	1158	1203	1217	1247	1305	1317	1349	1358	1417
Wigan North Western d.	2109	2112	2128	2133	215t	2252	2259t		0911	1012	1028	1109	│	1128	│	│	│	1214	1228	1259t	1316	1328	│	1409	1428
Manchester Piccadilly 156 157 a.	│	│	│	│	2236	│	2328		│	│	│	│	1148n	│	1227	1226p	1236p	│	│	1329	│	│	1428	│	│
Manchester Airport ✈ 156 157 a.	│	│	│	│	2254	│	2344		│	│	│	│	...	│	1247	...	...	│	│	1344	│	│	1445	│	│
Warrington Bank Quay d.	2120	2123	2139	2144	...	2303	...		0922	1022	1039	1120	...	1139	...	...	...	1225	1239	...	1327	1339	...	1420	1439
Crewe 144 151 152 153 a.	│	2142	2159	2204	...	2326	...		0941	1041	1059	│	...	1159	...	...	...	│	1259	...	│	1359	...	│	1458
Wolverhampton 144 150 a.	│	2222	2232	2239	...	...	...		│	│	1131	│	...	1232	...	...	...	│	1332	...	│	1432	...	│	1534
Birmingham New St 144 150 a.	│	2248	2252	2258	...	...	...		│	│	1150	│	...	1250	...	...	...	│	1406	...	│	1506	...	│	1606
Milton Keynes 150/1/2/3 a.	2240	...	...	...	...	...	...		1107	1207	...	│	...	...	...	...	...	│	1458	...	│	1558	...	│	1658
London Euston 150/1/2/3 a.	2334	...	...	...	...	...	...		1203	1244	...	1321	...	...	...	...	...	1415	1537	...	1518	1637	...	1612	1736

	⑦	⑦	⑦ C	⑦ ◐	⑦	⑦	⑦ ◐	⑦	⑦	⑦ ◐	⑦	⑦	⑦ ◐	⑦	⑦ W	⑦	⑦	⑦	⑦	⑦	⑦	⑦	⑦ W	⑦	⑦
Glasgow Central 214 d.	...	1238	...	...	1316	1338	1355	...	1438	...	1516	1538	1557	...	...	1638	...	1716	1738	...	1837	...	...	...	2008
Edinburgh Waverley d.	1212	│	...	1251	│	│	│	1412	│	1451	│	│	│	1612	...	│	1651	│	│	1812	│	1851	...	1957	│
Haymarket d.	1216u	│	...	1255	│	│	│	1416u	│	1456	│	│	│	1616u	...	│	1655	│	│	1816u	│	1856	...	2001u	│
Lockerbie d.	1311	│	...	│	│	│	│	1510	│	│	1615	│	│	1710	...	│	│	│	1832	1910	│	│	...	2056	2104
Carlisle 214 d.	1333	1349	...	1407	1436	1449	1511	1533	1549	1607b	1636	1649	1710	1733	...	1751	1807	1833	1852	1933	1948	2007b	...	2118	2125
Penrith d.	1348	│	...	1422	│	│	│	1548	│	1622	│	1703	│	1748	...	1805	│	1848	1906	1948	│	2022	...	│	2140
Oxenholme 158 d.	1412	1423	...	│	1512	1523	1545	1612	1623	│	1712	│	1744	1812	1823	1828	1842	1912	1929	2012	2023	│	2112	2155	2204
Lancaster 157 158 d.	1427	1438	1445	1457	1527	1538	│	1627	1638	1657	1727	1738	│	1827	1838	1843	1857	1927	1944	2027	2037	2057	2131	2210	2219
Preston 156 157 158 d.	1447	1458	1508b	1517	1547	1558	1617	1647	1658	1717	1747	1758	1817b	1847	1908q	1903	1917	1947	2004	2047	2057	2117	2154	2230	2239
Wigan North Western d.	1459t	1509	│	1528	1600t	1609	1629	│	1709	1729	1801t	1809	1828	1859t	│	1914	1928	2002t	2015	2059t	2108	2129	...	│	2253
Manchester Piccadilly 156 157 a.	1529	│	1556	│	1629	│	│	1726	│	│	1830	│	│	1928	1956	│	│	2030	│	2128	│	│	...	2309	│
Manchester Airport ✈ 156 157 a.	1544	│	1615	│	1645	│	│	1741	│	│	1845	│	│	1945	2015	│	│	2045	│	2144	│	│	...	2326	│
Warrington Bank Quay d.	...	1520	...	1539	...	1620	1640	...	1720	1740	...	1820	1839	...	...	1925	1939	...	2026	...	2119	2139	...	...	2304
Crewe 144 151 152 153 a.	...	│	...	1559	...	│	1659	...	│	1759	...	│	1858	...	...	│	1959	...	2045	...	2139	2159	...	...	2322
Wolverhampton 144 150 a.	...	│	...	1632	...	│	1732	...	│	1833	...	│	1934	...	...	│	2033	...	│	...	2214	2232	...	...	...
Birmingham New St 144 150 a.	...	│	...	1706	...	│	1805	...	│	1906	...	│	2006	...	...	│	2051	...	│	...	2233	2255	...	...	...
Milton Keynes 150/1/2/3 a.	...	│	...	1758	...	│	1858	...	│	1958	...	│	2059	...	...	│	...	...	2152	...	...	...	...	...	...
London Euston 150/1/2/3 a.	...	1711	...	1836	...	1813	1937	...	1910	2037	...	2012	2146	...	...	2119	...	...	2253	...	...	...	...	...	...

B – From Blackpool North d. 0525 (until Mar. 25 connection d. 0457, by 🚌).
C – From Barrow-in-Furness.
W – From Windermere (Table **158**).
a – Arrives 9 minutes earlier.
b – Arrives 4–5 minutes earlier.
c – Arrives 0613.
d – Does not run on ① from April 3.
e – Arrives 1151.
f – Arrives 1905.
g – Arrives 1451.
h – Arrives 2043 on ⑥.
k – Dec. 10 - Dec. 31; Feb. 18 - Mar. 25.
m – Jan. 7 - Feb. 11 and from April 1.
n – Manchester Victoria.
p – Manchester Oxford Road.
q – Arrives 1858.
t – Until Feb. 11.
u – Calls to pick up only.
◐ – Via Table **150**.

EM 2nd class — CREWE - STOKE - DERBY — 155

km		Ⓐ	Ⓐ	Ⓐ	Ⓐ		Ⓐ	Ⓐ		⑥	⑥	⑥		⑥	⑥		⑦	⑦	⑦	⑦	⑦	⑦	⑦	⑦
0	**Crewe** 143 d.	Ⓐ	0607	0658	0807	and at	1907	2045	...	⑥	0607	0707	0807	and at	1907	2045	...	⑦	1404	1505	1608	1708	1808	1908	2015	2116
24	Stoke on Trent 143 d.		0633	0724	0833	the same	1933	2118	...		0633	0733	0833	the same	1933	2119	...		1429	1532	1635	1735	1835	1935	2040	2142
33	Blythe Bridge d.		0646	0736	0845	minutes	1945	2130	...		0645	0745	0845	minutes	1945	2131	...		1441	1544	1647	1747	1847	1947	2052	2154
51	Uttoxeter d.		0658	0749	0858	past each	1958	2142	...		0658	0758	0858	past each	1958	2144	...		1454	1557	1659	1759	1859	1959	2105	2206
82	**Derby** a.		0725	0816	0926	hour until	2025	2208	...		0724	0826	0926	hour until	2022	2210	...		1519	1624	1727	1828	1928	2028	2134	2236

		Ⓐ	Ⓐ	Ⓐ		Ⓐ	Ⓐ			⑥	⑥	⑥		⑥	⑥			⑦	⑦	⑦	⑦	⑦	⑦	⑦
Derby d.	Ⓐ	0640	0740	0842	and at	1942	2042	...	⑥	0640	0740	0842	and at	1942	2042	...	⑦	1438	1538	1638	1741	1841	1941	2040
Uttoxeter d.		0705	0807	0907	the same	2007	2107	...		0707	0807	0907	the same	2007	2107	...		1503	1603	1703	1806	1905	2006	2105
Blythe Bridge d.		0719	0821	0921	minutes	2021	2121	...		0721	0821	0921	minutes	2021	2121	...		1517	1617	1717	1820	1919	2020	2119
Stoke on Trent 143 a.		0732	0832	0933	past each	2033	2133	...		0734	0832	0933	past each	2033	2133	...		1530	1631	1730	1833	1933	2034	2133
Crewe 143 a.		0759	0859	1001	hour until	2101	2159	...		0759	0859	1001	hour until	2101	2201	...		1600	1700	1802	1901	2002	2100	2200

NT 2nd Class only — MANCHESTER - PRESTON - BLACKPOOL — 156

For other trains Manchester - Preston and v.v. see Tables **154** and **157**

Service to March 25, 2018 – For service from March 26 please contact National Rail Enquiries ✆ +44 (0) 3457 48 49 50.

Until March 25, 2018, the line between Preston and Blackpool North will be temporarily closed to allow electrification and other route improvement work to take place. A replacement 🚌 service will operate every 15 minutes from 0630 to 2359 on ⚒ and from 0930 to 2345 on ⑦. Journey time: 50 minutes.

km			Ⓐ	Ⓐ	Ⓐ	Ⓐ	Ⓐ	Ⓐ	Ⓐ		Ⓐ	Ⓐ	Ⓐ	Ⓐ	Ⓐ		⑤	①-④	⑤	①-④	①-④	⑤	①-④		⑥	⑥	⑥
0	**Manchester** Airport d.	Ⓐ	0527	0618	0757	0825	0929	1029	1129	and at	1629	1729	1829	1929	2029	...	2129	2129	2229	2229	2330	2330	🚌	⑥	0527	0629	0757
16	**Manchester** Piccadilly d.		0543	0633	0816	0846	0945	1045	1146	the same	1645	1745	1846	1946	2045	...	2146	2146	2246	2246	2345	2345	2355		0544	0646	0815
34	Bolton d.		0603	0652	0833	0907	1006	1107	1207	minutes	1706	1808	1906	2006	2106	...	2207	2207	2308	|	|	2359s	0020s		0603	0706	0834
66	**Preston** a.		0636	0724	0905	0946	1032	1137	1237	past each	1735	1839	1939	2037	2138	...	2236	2244	2338	2337	0034	0027	0055		0632	0740	0900
66	**Preston** d.		0645*	0745*	0915*	1000*	1045*	1145*	1245*	hour until	1745*	1900*	2000*	2045*	2200*	...	2245*	2300*	2400*	2345*	...	...	0055		0645*	0800*	0915*
94	**Blackpool** North a.		0735*	0835*	1005*	1050*	1135*	1235*	1335*	♧	1835*	1950*	2050*	2135*	2250*	...	2335*	2350*	0050*	0035*	...	...	0135		0735*	0850*	1005*

	⑥	⑥		⑥	⑥	⑥	⑥	⑥		⑥	⑥		⑦🚌	⑦🚌	⑦	⑦	⑦	⑦	⑦		⑦	⑦	⑦		⑦	⑦
Manchester Airport d.	0829	0929	and at	1629	1729	1829	1929	2029	...	2129	2229	⑦	0005	0530	0845	0929	1029	1129	1229	and at	1929	2029	2129	...	2229	2330
Manchester Piccadilly d.	0845	0946	the same	1646	1746	1846	1945	2046	...	2147	2246		0030	0555	0904	0947	1046	1146	1246	the same	1946	2045	2146	...	2246	2346
Bolton d.	0907	1007	minutes	1707	1809	1907	2006	2107	...	2207	2307		0055s	0620s	0924	1007	1106	1207	1307	minutes	2007	2104	2206	...	|	|
Preston a.	0930	1036	past each	1735	1844	1936	2035	2134	...	2237	2337		0130s	0655s	0952	1037	1135	1236	1338	past each	2037	2132	2244	...	2336	0035
Preston d.	0945*	1045*	hour until	1745*	1900*	1945*	2045*	2145*	...	2245*	2345*		|	|	1000*	1045*	1145*	1245*	1345*	hour until	2045*	2145*	2300*	...	2345*	...
Blackpool North a.	1035*	1135*	♣	1835*	1950*	2035*	2135*	2235*	...	2335*	0035*		0210	0735	1050*	1135*	1235*	1335*	1435*	♧	2135*	2235*	0050*	...	0135*	...

		Ⓐ	Ⓐ🚌	Ⓐ	Ⓐ	Ⓐ	Ⓐ	Ⓐ		Ⓐ	Ⓐ	Ⓐ	Ⓐ	Ⓐ	Ⓐ	Ⓐ	Ⓐ	Ⓐ		⑥	⑥	⑥	⑥	⑥	⑥	⑥	⑥
Blackpool North d.	Ⓐ	...	0337	...	...	...	0715*	0800*	and at	1500*	1600*	1630*	1715*	1800*	1900*	2000*	2100*	2200*	⑥	...	...	...	0700*	0800*	0900*	1000*	1100*
Preston a.		...	|	...	...	...	0805*	0850*	the same	1550*	1650*	1720*	1805*	1850*	1950*	2050*	2150*	2250*		...	...	...	0750*	0850*	0950*	1050*	1150*
Preston d.		0402	0417u	0504	0640	0705	0820	0905	minutes	1609	1705	1743	1821	1910	2010	2105	2205	2310		0415	0510	0706	0809	0905	1007	1105	1205
Bolton d.		|	0452u	|	0708	0734	0856	0936	past each	1635	1735	1813	1856	1935	2037	2135	2235	2339		0435u	0539	0735	0836	0935	1034	1135	1235
Manchester Piccadilly a.		0447	0517	0551	0728	0756	0918	0957	hour until	1656	1756	1837	1921	1956	2059	2157	2258	2357		0457	0559	0757	0857	0957	1057	1157	1257
Manchester Airport a.		0503	...	0606	0747	0815	0944	1021	♧	1717	1815	1855	1945	2022	2119	2214	2314	0021		0514	0614	0817	0921	1021	1120	1221	1321

	⑥	⑥	⑥	⑥	⑥	⑥	⑥	⑥	⑥	⑥	⑥		⑦🚌	⑦🚌	⑦	⑦	⑦	⑦	⑦	⑦	⑦	⑦	⑦		⑦	⑦	⑦
Blackpool North d.	1200*	1300*	1400	1500*	1600*	1700*	1800*	1900*	2000*	2100*	2200*	⑦	0320	0520	...	...	1000*	1100*	1200*	1300*	1400*	1500*	1600*	and at	2000*	2100*	2230*
Preston a.	1250*	1350*	1450*	1550*	1650*	1750*	1850*	1950*	2050*	2150*	2250*		|	|	...	...	1050*	1150*	1250*	1350*	1450*	1550*	1650*	the same	2050*	2150*	2320*
Preston d.	1304	1411	1509	1605	1705	1805	1910	2007	2108	2205	2310		0400u	0600u	0905	1005	1106	1206	1304	1405	1508	1605	1705	minutes	2105	2205	2343
Bolton d.	1334	1435	1535	1635	1735	1835	1935	2036	2135	2235	2339		0435u	0635u	0935	1035	1136	1235	1336	1435	1535	1635	1735	past each	2135	|	|
Manchester Piccadilly a.	1357	1457	1556	1657	1757	1858	1957	2057	2156	2259	2358		0500u	0700u	0957	1057	1158	1257	1357	1457	1556	1657	1757	hour until	2157	2257	0027
Manchester Airport a.	1421	1521	1623	1723	1823	1922	2019	2116	2215	2315	0023		0525	0725	1019	1115	1215	1316	1415	1516	1615	1715	1813	♣	2214	2315	0044

b – ⑤ only.
s – Calls to set down only.
u – Calls to pick up only.
♧ – Timings may vary by up to 5 minutes.
* – Connection by 🚌.
♣ – Timings may vary by up to 3 minutes.

NT — MANCHESTER - PRESTON - BARROW IN FURNESS — 157

For other trains Manchester - Preston / Lancaster and v.v. see Tables **154** and **156**.

km			Ⓐ2	Ⓐ2	Ⓐ2D	Ⓐ2	Ⓐ2	Ⓐ	Ⓐ2A	Ⓐ	Ⓐ2	Ⓐ2A	Ⓐ	Ⓐ2	Ⓐ2	Ⓐ2	Ⓐ2	Ⓐ	Ⓐ2	Ⓐ2	Ⓐ	Ⓐ		⑥	⑥2A	⑥
0	**Manchester** Airport ✈ d.	Ⓐ	...	...	...	...	...	0929a	...	...	...	...	...	...	...	1603	1629g	1729a	...	...	...	2200	⑥	...	...	...
16	**Manchester** Piccadilly d.		...	...	...	0824f	...	0945a	...	...	...	...	...	...	...	1627	1645g	1745a	...	...	...	2215		...	...	...
34	Bolton d.		...	...	...	0841	...	1006a	...	...	...	...		...	...	1650	1731	1808a	...	...	...	|		...	...	...
66	**Preston** d.		0519	...	...	0925	1004	1048j	...	...	...	...	1546	...	...	1728	1805	1847t	2006	2109	2147	2314		...	0842	0945
100	Lancaster d.		0542	0734	0848	0945	1025	1105	1219	1320	1437	1533	1602	1648	1720	1748	1826	1903	2026	2129	2203	2330		0733	0902	1001
110	Carnforth d.		0552	0743	0857	0955	1035	1113	1229	1328	1447	1543	1610	1658	1730	1758	1838	1911	2038	2139	2211	2338		0742	0912	1009
119	Arnside d.		0602	0753	0908	1006	1047	1123	1239	1338	1457	1554	1620	1709	1741	1809	1848	1921	2048	2150	2221	2348		0752	0922	1019
124	Grange over Sands d.		0608	0759	0914	1012	1053	1129	1245	1344	1503	1600	1626	1715	1747	1815	1854	1927	2054	2156	2227	2353		0758	0928	1025
140	Ulverston d.		0625	0816	0931	1028	1112	1143	1302	1400	1520	1615	1642	1732	1803	1831	1911	1943	2111	2212	2243	0010		0815	0944	1041
156	**Barrow in Furness** a.		0646	0839	0950	1052	1133	1203	1323	1423	1542	1637	1705	1756	1825	1853	1934	2006	2132	2236	2306	0032		0838	1006	1104

	⑥2A	⑥	⑥2A	⑥	⑥2	⑥	⑥2E	⑥2	⑥	⑥	⑥2E	⑥		⑥		⑦		⑦	⑦2	⑦2	⑦2		⑦	⑦2	⑦2	⑦
Manchester Airport ✈ d.	...	...	...	...	...	...	...	...	1629	...	...	2000	...	...	⑦	...	...	...	...	...	...	...	1629	...	...	2029
Manchester Piccadilly d.	...	...	...	...	...	...	...	...	1646	...	...	2016	...	...		...	...	...	...	...	...	...	1646	...	...	2045
Bolton d.	...	...	...	...	...	...	...	...	1707	...	...	2034	...	...		...	...	...	...	...	...	...	1705	...	...	2104
Preston d.	...	...	...	1407	...	1546	...	...	1745r	1908	2003	2058	...	...		1014	...	1204	1402	1604	...	...	1747n	2004	...	2147e
Lancaster d.	1125	1223	1332	1423	1520	1602	1700	1731	1801	1929	2023	2114	...	2314		1034	...	1220	1422	1625	1720	...	1803	2024	2103	2203
Carnforth d.	1134	1231	1341	1431	1530	1610	1710	1741	1810	1939	2033	2122	...	2322		1044	...	1228	1432	1635	1730	...	1811	2034	2128	2211
Arnside d.	1145	1241	1352	1440	1540	1620	1721	1753	1820	1949	2044	2132	...	2334		1055	...	1238	1443	1651	1741	...	1821	2044	2138	2221
Grange over Sands d.	1151	1247	1358	1445	1546	1626	1727	1759	1826	1955	2050	2138	...	2339		1101	...	1244	1449	1708	1747	...	1827	2050	2144	2227
Ulverston d.	1207	1303	1414	1458	1603	1642	1744	1816	1842	2012	2106	2154	...	2355		1117	...	1300	1505	1711	1802	...	1843	2107	2200	2243
Barrow in Furness a.	1229	1326	1436	1518	1624	1705	1806	1840	1904	2035	2128	2217	...	0017		1141	...	1323	1528	1731	1826	...	1906	2130	2224	2306

		Ⓐ	Ⓐ2	Ⓐ2	Ⓐ		Ⓐ2	Ⓐ2A	Ⓐ	Ⓐ2	Ⓐ2	Ⓐ2	Ⓐ2A	Ⓐ2	Ⓐ2A		Ⓐ2	ⒶB	Ⓐ2	Ⓐ	Ⓐ2			⑥2	⑥	⑥
Barrow in Furness d.	Ⓐ	0434	0522	0615	0648	...	0712	0806	0849	1009	1112	1213	1331	1441	1524	...	1610	1720	1803	2015	2143	...	⑥	0435	0532	0615
Ulverston d.		0450	0538	0634	0707	...	0730	0827	0907	1028	1132	1232	1349	1457	1543	...	1628	1737	1821	2034	2201	...		0451	0547	0634
Grange over Sands d.		0502	0550	0650	0723	...	0744	0845	0923	1044	1148	1247	1405	1509	1559	...	1644	1752	1837	2050	2217	...		0503	0600	0650
Arnside d.		0508	0556	0656	0729	...	0750	0851	0929	1050	1154	1253	1411	1515	1605	...	1650	1758	1843	2056	2223	...		0509	0606	0656
Carnforth d.		0518	0607	0707	0740	...	0802	0905	0941	1108	1206	1305	1423	1525	1617	...	1702	1809	1856	2107	2236	...		0519	0616	0707
Lancaster a.		0530	0615	0718	0748	...	0814	0913	0950h	1119	1215	1314	1433	1533	1628	...	1714	1818	1904	2115	2245	...		0531	0623	0718
Preston a.		...	0638	...	0806	...	...	0937	1022	...	1240	...	...	1553b	...	...	...	...	1932	2135	2311	...		...	0642	...
Bolton a.		...	0707	...	0835	...	...	...	...	...	...	...	...	1635	...	...	...	...	...	...	...	...		...	0708	...
Manchester Piccadilly a.		...	0728	...	0857	...	...	...	...	...	...	...	...	1656	...	...	...	...	...	...	...	...		...	0728	...
Manchester Airport ✈ a.		...	0747	...	0917	...	...	...	...	...	...	...	...	1717	...	...	...	...	...	...	...	...		...	0747	...

	⑥2	⑥2	⑥	⑥2C	⑥	⑥2A		⑥	⑥2A	⑥	⑥2	⑥🍸B	⑥2A	⑥	⑥2			⑦		⑦	⑦2	⑦2	⑦	⑦2	⑦2	⑦2D
Barrow in Furness d.	0707	0808	0850	1009	1120	1211	...	1333	1455	1525	1629	1720	1803	1917	2135	...	⑦	0922	...	1023	1218	1310	1348	1612	1815	1911
Ulverston d.	0726	0826	0907	1028	1137	1229	...	1352	1515	1541	1647	1737	1821	1936	2153	...		0941	...	1042	1237	1329	1405	1631	1834	1929
Grange over Sands d.	0742	0842	0922	1044	1152	1245	...	1408	1532	1553	1703	1752	1837	1952	2209	...		0957	...	1058	1253	1345	1419	1647	1850	1945
Arnside d.	0748	0848	0928	1050	1158	1251	...	1414	1539	1559	1709	1758	1843	1958	2215	...		1003	...	1104	1259	1351	1425	1653	1856	1951
Carnforth d.	0800	0900	0939	1102	1209	1303	...	1425	1556	1609	1723	1809	1856	2009	2228	...		1014	...	1115	1311	1403	1437	1706	1909	2004
Lancaster a.	0808h	0909	0947	1111	1219	1315	...	1433	1609	1617	1736	1819	1905	2017	2240	...		1022	...	1123	1320	1412	1444	1714	1917	2014
Preston a.	0841	...	1006	...	...	...	...	1451c	...	1637	...	...	1931	2037	...	...		1039	...	1143	1343	...	1504	1738	1942	...
Bolton a.	...	...	1034	...	...	...	...	1534	...	...	...	...	...	...	...	...		...	...	1208	...	...	1535	...	...	...
Manchester Piccadilly a.	...	...	1057	...	...	...	...	1556	...	...	...	...	...	...	...	...		...	...	1227	...	...	1556	...	...	...
Manchester Airport ✈ a.	...	...	1120	...	...	...	...	1623	...	...	...	...	...	...	...	...		...	...	1247	...	...	1615	...	...	...

A – From / to Carlisle (Table **159**).
B – To Windermere (Table **158**).
C – From Sellafield (Table **159**).
D – To / from Morcambe (Table **174**).
E – To Millom (Table **159**).
a – From Mar. 26 change at Preston.
b – Departs 1609.
c – Departs 1509.
e – Arrives 2132.
f – Manchester **Victoria**.
g – Change at Manchester **Oxford Road** (a. 1649 / d. 1719).
h – Departs 10 minutes later.
j – Arrives 1032.
n – Arrives 1732.
r – Arrives 1735.
t – Arrives 1839.

① – Mondays ② – Tuesdays ③ – Wednesdays ④ – Thursdays ⑤ – Fridays ⑥ – Saturdays ⑦ – Sundays Ⓐ – Not Saturdays 53

158 PRESTON - OXENHOLME - WINDERMERE — 2nd Class — NT

km		ⒶB	Ⓐ	Ⓐ	Ⓐ	Ⓐ	Ⓐ	Ⓐ	Ⓐ	Ⓐ	Ⓐ	Ⓐ	Ⓐ	Ⓐ	Ⓐ	Ⓐ	Ⓐ	Ⓐ		⑥	⑥	⑥	⑥	⑥	⑥
			2	2	2	2	2	2	2	2	2 ♈B								2	2	2	2	M2	2
	Preston 154 d.		…	…	…	1029	…	…	…	…	…	…								…	…	…	…	0932	1044
	Lancaster 154 d.	0546	…	…	…	1100	…	…	…	…	1821								0602	…	…	…	…	0948		
0	Oxenholme 154 d.	0623	0733	0826	0911	1033	1120	1226	1333	1422	1534	1622	1734	1838	1934	2022	2115	2218		0622	0721	0826	0911	1004	1120
4	Kendal d.	0628	0737	0830	0915	1037	1125	1230	1337	1426	1538	1626	1738	1843	1938	2026	2119	2222		0627	0725	0830	0915	1009	1125
16	Windermere a.	0641	0752	0846	0931	1050	1142	1243	1354	1443	1555	1643	1755	1858	1953	2041	2132	2237		0641	0742	0846	0931	1025	1142

	⑥	⑥	⑥	⑥	⑥	⑥	⑥	⑥	⑥		⑥		⑦	⑦	⑦	⑦	⑦	⑦	⑦	⑦	⑦	⑦	⑦
	2	M		2	2		2				♈B			2								2	2	2
Preston 154 d.	…	1247		1430			1704				…		1020									…	…	…
Lancaster 154 d.	…	1303		1500			1720	1825			…		1036									…	…	…
Oxenholme 154 d.	1226	1320	1417	1519	1634	1740	1842	1934	2022		2120		1052		1136		1227	1335	1421	1535	1621	1733	1841	1927	2016
Kendal d.	1230	1324	1421	1524	1638	1744	1846	1938	2026		2130		1056		1140		1231	1339	1425	1539	1625	1737	1845	1931	2020
Windermere a.	1243	1340	1436	1541	1655	1759	1901	1953	2041		2205		1110		1155		1246	1354	1440	1554	1640	1752	1901	1944	2036

	ⒶM	Ⓐ	Ⓐ	Ⓐ	Ⓐ	Ⓐ	Ⓐ	Ⓐ	Ⓐ	Ⓐ	Ⓐ	Ⓐ	Ⓐ	Ⓐ	Ⓐ	Ⓐ		⑥	⑥	⑥	⑥	⑥	⑥
					M	2	2	2	2	2	2							2	2	2	2	2	2
Windermere d.	0645	0756	0850	0947	1056	1147	1247	1358	1458	1600	1649	1803	1906	1958	2050	2140	2245		0657	0747	0850	0937	1040	1147
Kendal d.	0659	0811	0902	1001	1108	1202	1302	1413	1513	1613	1704	1818	1918	2012	2104	2154	2259		0712	0802	0902	0952	1054	1202
Oxenholme 154 a.	0704	0816	0907	1006	1113	1207	1307	1418	1518	1618	1709	1823	1923	2017	2109	2159	2304		0717	0807	0907	0957	1059	1207
Lancaster 154 a.					1131							1854				2322						1117	…
Preston 154 a.					1151							1926				2342						1039	1137	…

	⑥	⑥	⑥	⑥	⑥	⑥	⑥	⑥		⑥		⑥		⑦	⑦	⑦	⑦	⑦	⑦	⑦	⑦	⑦	⑦	⑦
	2			2	2	M					🚌									M	2	2	2
Windermere d.	1251	1345	1441	1550	1707	1803	1906	1958		2045		2140			1114	1206	1250	1358	1447	1558	1648	1802	1905	1948	2040
Kendal d.	1306	1359	1455	1605	1722	1817	1918	2012		2056		2215			1126	1220	1302	1412	1501	1612	1702	1816	1918	2002	2055
Oxenholme 154 a.	1311	1404	1500	1610	1727	1822	1923	2017		2101		2225			1131	1225	1307	1417	1506	1617	1707	1821	1923	2007	2100
Lancaster 154 a.	1333		1517		1748	1846				2118		2310										1838			2131
Preston 154 a.	1406		1537		1811	1905						2350										1858			2154

B – From Barrow in Furness (Table 157).   M – From / to Manchester Airport (Table 154).

159 BARROW - WHITEHAVEN - CARLISLE — 2nd class — NT

km		Ⓐ	Ⓐ	Ⓐ	Ⓐ	Ⓐ	Ⓐ	Ⓐ	Ⓐ	Ⓐ	Ⓐ	Ⓐ	Ⓐ	Ⓐ	Ⓐ	Ⓐ	Ⓐ	Ⓐ	Ⓐ		⑥	⑥
	Lancaster 154 157 d.	…	…	…	…	…	…	…	1219	…	1533	…	…	…	…	…	…	…	…			…
0	Barrow in Furness 157 d.	…	0546	0651	0744	…	0920	1010	1140	1236	1331	1437	1643	1731	1830	1940	…	2134	…			0546
26	Millom d.	…	0621	0719	0812	…	0948	1038	1214	1304	1359	1512	1711	1805	1858	2010	…	2204	…			0621
47	Ravenglass for Eskdale 🚂 d.	…	0642	0737	0829	…	1005	1055	1235	1321	1416	1533	1728	1826	1915	…	…	…	…			0642
56	Sellafield d.	…	0656	0751	0840	…	1019	1108	1248	1336	1428	1547	1740	1840	1925	…	…	…	…			0656
74	Whitehaven d.	0624	0718	0812	…	0904	1037	1128	1310	1356	1454a	1612	1800	1915	1946	…	2030	…	2151	…		0622	0718
85	Workington d.	0642	0739	0831	…	0922	1055	1146	1332	1414	1513	1634	1818	1936	2004	…	2048	…	2211	…		0640	0739
92	Maryport d.	0650	0749	0839	…	0930	1104	1154	1342	1422	1522	1644	1826	1946	2013	…	2056	…	…	…		0648	0749
119	Wigton d.	0711	0812	0900	…	0951	1126	1216	1405	1443	1544	1707	1847	2010	2034	…	2117	…	…	…		0709	0812
138	Carlisle a.	0733	0833	0925	…	1013	1149	1238	1426	1506	1604	1728	1910	2031	2055	…	2139	…	…	…		0731	0833

	⑥	⑥	⑥	⑥	⑥B	⑥	⑥	⑥	⑥	⑥	⑥	⑥	⑥	⑥	⑥B		⑦	⑦	⑦	⑦
Lancaster 154 157 d.	…	…	…	…	0902	…	1125	…	1332	…	1700	…	…	2023						
Barrow in Furness 157 d.	0655	0741	…	0845	1010	1138	1239	1350	1452	1533	1732	1810	…	1940	2130					
Millom d.	0724	0809	…	0919	1038	1212	1307	1418	1520	1601	1806	1840	…	2010	2200					
Ravenglass for Eskdale 🚂 d.	0742	0826	…	0940	1055	1233	1324	1435	1537	1618	1827	…	…	…	…					
Sellafield d.	0756	0839	…	0954	1108	1246	1336	1447	1550	1630	1841	…	…	…	…					
Whitehaven d.	0816	…	0906	1019	1128	1308	1355	1507	1612	1656	1913	…	1943	2030	…		1233	1433	1633	1933
Workington d.	0834	…	0924	1040	1146	1329	1413	1525	1630	1714	1934	…	2001	2048	…		1251	1451	1651	1951
Maryport d.	0842	…	0932	1051	1154	1340	1421	1533	1638	1722	1944	…	2009	2056	…		1259	1459	1659	1959
Wigton d.	0904	…	0953	1114	1216	1403	1442	1555	1659	1744	2008	…	2030	2117	…		1318	1518	1718	2018
Carlisle a.	0926	…	1015	1137	1238	1426	1505	1617	1719	1806	2029	…	2053	2139	…		1341	1541	1741	2041

	Ⓐ	ⒶB	Ⓐ	Ⓐ	Ⓐ	Ⓐ	Ⓐ	Ⓐ	Ⓐ	Ⓐ	Ⓐ	Ⓐ	Ⓐ	Ⓐ	ⒶA	Ⓐ	Ⓐ	Ⓐ	Ⓐ		⑥
Carlisle d.	…	0515	…	0737	…	0842	0938	1054	1208	1252	1435	1513	1631	1737	1814	…	1915	2037	…	2200	…
Wigton d.	…	0534	…	0755	…	0901	0956	1112	1226	1310	1454	1531	1649	1756	1832	…	1933	2055	…	2218	…
Maryport d.	…	0558	0646	0816	…	0925	1017	1133	1247	1331	1517	1552	1710	1820	1853	…	1954	2116	…	2239	…
Workington d.	…	0609	0704	0827	…	0935	1028	1144	1258	1342	1528	1604	1721	1831	1904	…	2005	2127	…	2250	…
Whitehaven d.	…	0631	0724	0847	…	0956	1048	1205	1318	1403	1549	1623	1741	1852	1925	…	2025	2147	…	2310	…
Sellafield d.	…	0652	0742	…	0900	1018	1108	1225	1335	1424	1611	1644	1804	1917	…	…	…	…	…	…	…
Ravenglass for Eskdale 🚂 d.	…	0706	0753	…	0910	1031	1118	1235	1345	1431	1624	1655	1814	1930	…	…	…	…	…	…	…
Millom d.	0609	0727	0812	…	0929	1052	1136	1254	1404	1450	1645	1715	1835	1951	…	2016	…	…	2209	…	0609
Barrow in Furness 157 a.	0642	0803	0845	…	1000	1130	1208	1326	1436	1522	1723	1749	1910	2031	…	2049	…	…	2242	…	0641
Lancaster 154 157 a.	…	0913	…	…	…	…	1433	…	1628	…	…	…	…	…	…	…	…	…	…		

	⑥	⑥	⑥	⑥	⑥	⑥	⑥	⑥	⑥B	⑥	⑥	⑥A	⑥	⑥	⑥	⑥		⑦	⑦	⑦	⑦
Carlisle d.	0515	0735	…	0842	0938	1054	1156	1252	1433	1525	1636	1740	1814	1900	…	2015	…	2145	…	1410	1710	1910	2110
Wigton d.	0534	0753	…	0901	0956	1112	1215	1310	1452	1543	1654	1758	1832	1918	…	2032	…	2203	…	1427	1727	1927	2127
Maryport d.	0557	0814	…	0925	1017	1133	1239	1331	1515	1604	1715	1819	1853	1939	…	2052	…	2224	…	1447	1747	1947	2147
Workington d.	0608	0825	…	0935	1028	1144	1251	1342	1526	1616	1726	1830	1904	1950	…	2104	…	2235	…	1459	1759	1959	2159
Whitehaven d.	0630	0845	…	0956	1048	1204	1315	1402	1547	1636	1748	1850	1925	2010	…	2125	…	2255	…	1520	1820	2020	2220
Sellafield d.	0651	…	0905	1018	1108	1222	1336	1419	1612	1656	1808	1911	…	…	…	…	…	…	…				
Ravenglass for Eskdale 🚂 d.	0705	…	0915	1031	1118	1232	1350	1429	1625	1706	1818	1921	…	…	…	…	…	…	…				
Millom d.	0725	…	0934	1052	1136	1251	1411	1448	1646	1725	1837	1939	…	…	2016	…	2208	…					
Barrow in Furness 157 a.	0803	…	1005	1130	1208	1325	1449	1520	1723	1757	1911	2013	…	…	2049	…	2241	…					
Lancaster 154 157 a.	…	1111	…	1315	…	1609	…	1905	…														

A – From Newcastle (Table 213).   a – Arrives 1448.   🚂 – Ravenglass and Eskdale Railway. ✆ 01229 717171. www.ravenglass-railway.co.uk
B – To / from Preston (Table 157).

km	Ⓐ	Ⓐ	Ⓐ	Ⓐ	Ⓐ 🍷C	Ⓐ 🍷A	Ⓐ	Ⓐ 🍷	Ⓐ ✕C	Ⓐ✕ AW	Ⓐ	Ⓐ	Ⓐ 🍷C	Ⓐ ✕A	Ⓐ 🍷	Ⓐ 🍷	Ⓐ 🍷C	Ⓐ 🍷	Ⓐ 🍷C	Ⓐ ✕A	Ⓐ 🍷	Ⓐ 🍷M	Ⓐ 🍷	Ⓐ 🍷C	Ⓐ 🍷	Ⓐ 🍷M
0	**Holyhead** d.	...	...	...	0425	0448	...	0514	0533	0551	...	...	0628	0655	...	0715	...	...	0805	0855	...	0923	...	1040	...	1127
40	Bangor d.	...	...	...	0457	0514	...	0544	0601	0618	...	...	0706	0722	...	0802d	...	...	0902c	0922	...	1002	...	1107	...	1200
	Llandudno ‡ d.	...	...	...	|	|	...	|	|	|	...	0646	|	|	0745	|	0830	...	|	|	0945	|	1044	|	1144	|
64	Llandudno Junction ‡ d.	...	0438	...	0515	0532	0546	0607	0619	0636	...	0656	0725	0740	0754	0825	0839	0854	0925	0940	0954	1025	1053	1125	1153	1223
71	Colwyn Bay d.	...	0444	...	0521	0538	0552	0613	0627	0642	...	0702	0731	0747	0800	0831	0845	0900	0931	0947	1000	1031	1059	1131	1159	1229
88	Rhyl d.	...	0457	...	0531	0549	0602	0626	0638	0653	...	0715	0741	0758	0813	0841	0856	0913	0941	0958	1013	1041	1112	1141	1212	1240
94	Prestatyn d.	...	0502	...	0537	|	0608	0631	|	0658	...	0721	0747	0804	0819	0847	|	0919	0947	1004	1019	1047	1118	1147	1218	1245
116	Flint d.	...	0516	...	0550	|	0621	0645	0655	0712	...	0735	0800	0817	0832	0900	|	0932	1000	1017	1032	1100	1131	1200	1231	1259
136	**Chester** a.	...	0534	...	0605	0617	0638	0702	0709	0726	...	0753	0815	0831	0850	0914	0923	0950	1015	1031	1050	1115	1149	1214	1249	1313
136	**Chester 151** ♥ d.	0334	0537	0538	...	0626	0640	0712	...	0735	0738	0755	...	0835	0852	0916	...	0952	...	1035	1052	...	1152	...	1252	...
170	**Crewe 151** ♥ a.	|	0558	|	...	0647	|	|	...	0754	|	0818	...	0854	|	0937	...	|	...	1054	|	...	|	...	|	...
165	Warrington Bank Quay a.	|	...	0605	...	...	0709	0739	...	...	0808	...	...	...	0918	...	...	1018	...	...	1118	...	1220	...	1318	...
201	**Manchester** Piccadilly a.	0442	...	0643	...	...	0751	0814	...	...	0853	...	...	...	0952	...	...	1052	...	...	1152	...	1252	...	1352	...
217	**Manchester** Airport a.	0504	...	...	...	...	...	...	...	...	...	...	...	...	1020	...	...	1120	...	...	1220	...	1320	...	1420	...

	Ⓐ 🍷	Ⓐ 🍷C	Ⓐ 🍷A	Ⓐ 🍷	Ⓐ 🍷M	Ⓐ 🍷A	Ⓐ 🍷	Ⓐ 🍷	Ⓐ 🍷C	Ⓐ	Ⓐ 🍷	Ⓐ 🍷M	Ⓐ 🍷	Ⓐ 🍷C	Ⓐ	Ⓐ 🍷D	Ⓐ	Ⓐ	Ⓐ	Ⓐ	Ⓐ	Ⓐ B	Ⓐ 🍷B	Ⓐ	Ⓐ	Ⓐ	Ⓐ M
Holyhead d.	...	1232	1252	1305	1324	1358	...	...	1434	...	...	1544	...	1650	...	1730	...	...	1823	...	...	1921	...	...	2032	...	...
Bangor d.	...	1307	1320	1332	1404	1425	...	...	1504	...	...	1623	...	1718	...	1809	...	...	1902	...	...	2000	2020	...	2101	...	...
Llandudno ‡ d.	...	|	|	|	|	|	1440	1508	|	...	1607	|	1705	|	...	|	...	1844	|	1934	...	|	|	2043	|	2145	...
Llandudno Junction ‡ d.	1253	1325	1339	1350	1429	1443	1449	1517	1527	1618	1625	1646	1715	1737	...	1832	1839	1853	1926	1946	...	2023	2038	2052	2128	2155	...
Colwyn Bay d.	1259	1331	1345	1358	1435	1450	1455	1523	1533	1624	1631	|	1721	1743	...	|	1845	1859	1932	1954	...	2029	2044	2058	2134	2201	...
Rhyl d.	1312	1341	1356	1412	1445	1500	1508	1536	1544	1634	1644	|	1733	1753	...	|	1855	1912	1942	2009	...	2039	2055	2111	2147	2216	...
Prestatyn d.	1318	1347	1401	1418	1451	|	1514	1542	1549	1640	1649	|	1739	1759	...	|	1901	1918	1948	2016	...	2045	2101	2117	2152	2222	...
Flint d.	1331	1400	1415	1431	1504	|	1527	1555	1603	1653	1703	|	1752	1812	...	|	1914	1931	2001	2030	...	2058	2114	2130	2206	2237	...
Chester a.	1349	1415	1428	1445	1525	1528	1544	1613	1617	1707	1720	1726	1811	1826	...	1911	1930	1949	2016	2044	...	2116	2128	2147	2222	2255	...
Chester 151 ♥ d.	1350	...	1435	1447	...	1535	1549	1622	...	...	1722	...	1816	...	1850	...	...	1952	2018	2046	2052	...	2135	2151	2224	2301	2322
Crewe 151 ♥ a.	|	...	1454	|	...	1554	|	|	...	...	|	...	|	...	|	...	...	|	2041	2106	|	...	2154	|	2252	2326	|
Warrington Bank Quay a.	1418	...	...	1517	...	...	1618	1651	...	...	1749	...	1845	...	1918	...	...	2018	...	...	2119	...	...	2217	...	...	2351
Manchester Piccadilly a.	1452	...	...	1554	...	...	1654	1727	...	...	1825	...	1927	...	1952	...	...	2052	...	...	2153	...	...	2255	...	...	0025
Manchester Airport a.	1520	...	...	...	...	...	...	...	...	...	...	...	...	...	2020	...	...	2121	...	...	...	...	...	...	...	...	...

⑥	⑥	⑥ B	⑥	⑥	⑥ 🍷C	⑥	⑥	⑥ 🍷D	⑥ 🍷M	⑥ 🍷	⑥ 🍷C	⑥ 🍷A	⑥ 🍷	⑥ 🍷M	⑥ 🍷A	⑥ 🍷	⑥ C🍷	⑥ 🍷A	⑥ 🍷	⑥ 🍷M	⑥ 🍷	⑥ 🍷C	⑥ 🍷	⑥ 🍷M	⑥ 🍷	⑥ 🍷C
Holyhead d.	...	...	...	...	0425	...	...	...	0522	...	0635	0652	...	0715	0755	...	0820	0855	...	0923	...	1033	...	1123	...	1238
Bangor d.	...	...	...	...	0457	...	...	...	0601	...	0707	0720	...	0802	0822	...	0902	0922	...	1002	...	1105	...	1202	...	1307
Llandudno ‡ d.	...	...	...	...	|	...	...	...	|	0634	|	|	0745	|	|	0845	|	|	0945	|	1044	|	1144	|	1240	|
Llandudno Junction ‡ d.	...	...	0438	...	0515	...	0537	...	0624	0644	0725	0738	0754	0825	0840	0854	0925	0940	0954	1025	1053	1125	1153	1225	1253e	1325
Colwyn Bay d.	...	...	0444	...	0521	...	0543	...	0630	0650	0731	0744	0800	0831	0847	0900	0931	0947	1000	1031	1059	1131	1159	1231	1259	1331
Rhyl d.	...	...	0457	...	0531	...	0556	...	0640	0703	0741	0755	0813	0841	0858	0913	0941	0958	1013	1041	1112	1141	1212	1241	1312	1341
Prestatyn d.	...	...	0502	...	0537	...	0601	...	0646	0708	0747	0801	0819	0847	0904	0919	0947	1003	1019	1047	1118	1147	1218	1247	1318	1347
Flint d.	...	...	0516	...	0550	...	0615	...	0659	0721	0800	0815	0832	0900	0917	0932	1000	|	1032	1100	1131	1200	1231	1300	1331	1400
Chester a.	...	...	0533	...	0604	...	0633	...	0715	0738	0815	0828	0850	0915	0931	0950	1014	1028	1050	1116	1149	1216	1249	1315	1349	1414
Chester 151 ♥ d.	0336	0422	0537	0538	...	0613	0635	0712	...	0740	...	0835	0852	...	0935	0952	...	1035	1052	...	1152	...	1251	...	1352	...
Crewe 151 ♥ a.	|	0443	0558	|	...	|	0659	|	...	|	...	0854	|	...	0954	|	...	1054	|	...	|	...	|	...	|	...
Warrington Bank Quay a.	|	...	...	0605	...	0639	...	0738	...	0806	...	...	0918	...	...	1018	...	...	1118	...	1220	...	1318	...	1420	...
Manchester Piccadilly a.	0441	...	...	0643	...	0717	...	0818	...	0852	...	...	0952	...	...	1052	...	...	1152	...	1252	...	1352	...	1452	...
Manchester Airport a.	0504	...	...	...	...	...	...	...	...	0920	...	...	1020	...	...	1120	...	...	1220	...	1320	...	1420	...	1520	...

	⑥ 🍷	⑥ 🍷M	⑥ 🍷A	⑥ 🍷	⑥ 🍷C	⑥ 🍷	⑥ 🍷M	⑥ 🍷	⑥ 🍷C	⑥ 🍷	⑥ 🍷D	⑥	⑥	⑥	⑥ B	⑥	⑥	⑥	⑥	⑥	⑦	⑦	⑦	⑦ 🍷	⑦ 🍷A	⑦ 🍷
Holyhead d.	...	1328	1358	...	1425	...	1523	...	1650	...	1730	...	1823	...	1921	...	...	2037	...	...	...	...	0845	...	...	...
Bangor d.	1333	1407	1425	...	1453	...	1602	...	1718	...	1809	...	1903	...	2000	...	...	2106	...	...	...	...	0913	...	...	...
Llandudno ‡ d.	|	|	|	1442	|	1544	|	1644	|	1744	|	1844	|	1942	|	2043	...	|	2145	...	...	...	|	...	...	...
Llandudno Junction ‡ d.	1356	1425	1443	1451	1516	1553	1625	1653	1736	1753	1832	1853	1926	1951	2023	2052	...	2129	2155	...	...	...	0935	...	...	...
Colwyn Bay d.	1402	1431	1450	1457	1522	1559	1631	1659	1742	1759	1838	1859	1932	1957	2029	2058	...	2135	2201	...	...	...	0941	...	...	...
Rhyl d.	1415	1441	1500	1510	1533	1612	1641	1712	1752	1812	1848	1912	1942	2010	2039	2111	...	2148	2216	...	...	...	0954	...	...	...
Prestatyn d.	1421	1447	|	1516	1538	1618	1647	1718	1758	1818	1854	1918	1948	2016	2045	2117	...	2154	2222	...	...	...	0959	...	...	...
Flint d.	1434	1500	|	1529	1552	1631	1700	1731	1811	1831	1907	1931	2001	2029	2058	2130	...	2207	2237	...	...	...	1013	...	...	...
Chester a.	1452	1517	1527	1546	1605	1648	1715	1749	1825	1849	1924	1949	2016	2047	2113	2148	...	2223	2255	...	...	...	1030	...	...	...
Chester 151 ♥ d.	1453	...	1535	1548	...	1652	...	1750	...	1852	...	1950	2018	2050	...	...	2153	2226	2301	2322	0839	0942	1039	1036	1128	1136
Crewe 151 ♥ a.	|	...	1554	|	...	|	...	|	...	|	...	|	2041	|	...	...	|	2250	2326	|	|	|	1103	|	1147	|
Warrington Bank Quay a.	1520	...	...	1617	...	1719	...	1818	...	1920	...	2018	...	2119	...	...	2220	...	...	2350	0907	1009	...	1103	...	1203
Manchester Piccadilly a.	1552	...	...	1652	...	1752	...	1852	...	1952	...	2056	...	2156	...	...	2255	...	...	0022	0945	1048	...	1141	...	1241
Manchester Airport a.	1620	...	...	1720	...	1821	...	...	...	2019	...	...	...	...	...	...	...	...	...	...	...	...	...	...	...	...

	⑦ 🍷C	⑦ 🍷A	⑦ 🍷	⑦ 🍷A	⑦ 🍷	⑦ 🍷A	⑦ 🍷	⑦ 🍷A	⑦		⑦ 🍷	⑦	⑦	⑦ 🍷A	⑦	⑦ 🍷C	⑦ 🍷A	⑦	⑦	⑦	⑦ 🍷M	⑦	⑦	⑦	⑦	⑦	⑦
Holyhead d.	1020	1055	...	1150	...	1250	...	1355	...	...	1430	...	1530	...	...	1625	...	...	1730	...	1825	...	1940	...	...	2035	2140
Bangor d.	1059	1122	...	1217	...	1318	...	1422	...	...	1508	...	1558	...	...	1704	...	...	1759	...	1904	...	2009	...	...	2114	2209
Llandudno ‡ d.	|	|	...	|	...	|	...	|	...	...	|	...	|	...	...	|	...	...	|	...	|	...	|	...	...	|	|
Llandudno Junction ‡ d.	1122	1140	...	1235	...	1336	...	1440	...	...	1526	...	1625	...	...	1725	...	...	1824	...	1924	...	2037	...	...	2137	2227
Colwyn Bay d.	1128	1146	...	1242	...	1342	...			...	1532	...	1631	...	...	1731	...	...	1830	...	1930	...	2043	...	...	2143	2233
Rhyl d.	1141	1157	...	1253	...	1353	...			...	1545	...	1644	...	...	1744	...	...	1843	...	1943	...	2056	...	...	2156	2243
Prestatyn d.	1146	1203	...	1259	...	1359	...			...	1551	...	1649	...	...	1749	...	...	1848	...	1948	...	2102	...	...	2201	2249
Flint d.	1200	1216	...	|	...	1413	...	|			1604	...	1703	...	...	1803	...	...	1902	...	2002	...	2116	...	...	2215	2302
Chester a.	1218	1230	...	1324	...	1426	...	1531			1622	...	1720	...	...	1821	...	...	1921	...	2019	...	2133	...	...	2232	2316
Chester 151 ♥ d.	...	1233	1236	1330	1336	1433	1436	1533	[illegible]		1636	1627	1722	1735	1736	...	1835	1836	1924	1936	2027	2036	2135	2143	2206	2235	...
Crewe 151 ♥ a.	...	1253	|	1350	|	1454	|	1552	|		|	1651	1744	1753	|	...	1853	|	1948	|	2048	|	2159	|	|	2300	...
Warrington Bank Quay a.	...	...	1303	...	1403	...	1503	...	1603	...	1703	...	...	...	1803	...	...	1903	...	2003	...	2103	...	2210	2233	...	...
Manchester Piccadilly a.	...	...	1340	...	1441	...	1540	...	1640	...	1740	...	...	...	1840	...	...	1940	...	2041	...	2140	..	2249	2310	...	...
Manchester Airport a.	...	...	...	...	...	...	...	...	...	...	...	...	...	...	...	...	...	...	...	...	...	...	...	...	...	...	...

CAERNARFON - PORTHMADOG - BLAENAU FFESTINIOG △ § (Service shown is provisional and subject to confirmation)

km		🚂 H	🚂 G	🚂 EF JK	🚂 H	🚂 JK	🚂 G	🚂 FJ K	🚂 H	🚂 EF	🚂 JK	🚂 JK	🚂 FJ K
0	**Blaenau Ffestiniog** d.	...	...	1135	...	1220	...	1340	...	1505	1525	1605	1720
19	Minffordd d.	...	...	1230	...	1315	...	1435	...	1555	1625	1700	1815
22	**Porthmadog** Hbr d.	0940	1050	1245	1255	1330	1415	1455	1540	1615	1640	1710	1830
35	Beddgelert d.	1025	1130	...	1335	...	1455	...	1615	...	...	...	...
42	Rhyd Ddu d.	1100	1200	...	1400	...	1520	...	1645	...	...	...	...
50	Waunfawr d.	1125	1225	...	1430	...	1550	...	1715	...	...	...	...
61	**Caernarfon** a.	1205	1305	...	1510	...	1625	...	1750	...	...	...	...

	🚂 EF KL	🚂 JK	🚂 FJ	🚂 K	🚂 GH	🚂 EF KL	🚂 JK	🚂 H	🚂 FJ K	🚂 G	🚂 H
Caernarfon d.	...	...	...	...	1000	...	...	1300	...	1420	1545
Waunfawr d.	...	...	...	...	1030	...	...	1330	...	1450	1615
Rhyd Ddu d.	...	...	...	...	1055	...	...	1400	...	1520	1645
Beddgelert d.	...	...	...	...	1130	...	...	1425	...	1550	1710
Porthmadog Hbr d.	1005	1040	1125	1150	1215	1335	1430	1515	1550	1635	1755
Minffordd d.	1015	1050	1135	1200	...	1345	1435	...	1600	...	...
Blaenau Ffestiniog d.	1120	1155	1235	1315	...	1445	1540	...	1705	...	...

A – Conveys (12) to / from London Euston (Table **151**).
B – To / from Birmingham New Street (Table **145** or **151**).
C – To / from Cardiff Central (Tables **145** and **149**).
D – To Shrewsbury (Table **145**).
E – FR Pink service: Mar. 24, 25, Apr, 14, 16, 20 – 23, 27 – 30, May 4, 11, 14, 18, 21, 25.
F – FR Blue service: Mar. 26 – 30, Apr. 3 – 13, 15, 17, 18, 19, 24, 25, 26, May 1, 2, 3, 5 – 10, 12, 13, 15, 16, 17, 19, 20, 22, 23, 24, 26, 27.
G – WHR Yellow service: Mar. 24 – 29, Apr. 4 – 15, 18, 18, 19, 21, 22, 24, 25, 26, 28, 29, May 1, 2, 3, 8, 9, 10, 12, 13, 15, 16, 17, 20 – 27.
H – WHR Red service: Mar. 30, 31, Apr. 1, 2, 3, May 5, 6, 7, 18, 19, 28 – 31.
J – FR Yellow service: Mar. 31, Apr 1, 2.
K – FR Red service: May 29, 30, 31.
L – To Wolverhampton (Table **145**).
M – To / from Birmingham International (Table **145**).

W – Conveys (12) London - Chester - Wrexham and v.v. (Tables **145** and **151**).
b – Runs 15 minutes later on certain dates (check with operator for details).
c – Arrives 20 minutes earlier.
d – Arrives 10 minutes earlier.
e – Arrives 6 minutes earlier.
f – Arrives 7 – 8 minutes earlier.
g – Departs 15 – 19 minutes later.
h – Departs 6 – 10 minutes later.
* – Connection by 🚌.
‡ – For full service Llandudno - Llandudno Junction and v.v. see next page.
♥ – For full service Chester - Crewe and v.v. see next page.
§ – Additional trains operate May 29, 30 and 31 at 0840 and 1805 from Porthmadog returning at 1010 and 1940 from Blaenau Ffestiniog.
△ – Operators: Ffestiniog Railway and Welsh Highland Railway. www.festrail.co.uk Ffestiniog Railway and Welsh Highland Railway ✆ 01766 516024.

① – Mondays ② – Tuesdays ③ – Wednesdays ④ – Thursdays ⑤ – Fridays ⑥ – Saturdays ⑦ – Sundays Ⓐ – Not Saturdays 55

Ⓐ	①	②–⑤	Ⓐ	Ⓐ	Ⓐ	Ⓐ	Ⓐ	Ⓐ	Ⓐ	Ⓐ	Ⓐ	Ⓐ	Ⓐ	Ⓐ	Ⓐ	Ⓐ	Ⓐ	Ⓐ	Ⓐ	Ⓐ	Ⓐ	Ⓐ	Ⓐ	Ⓐ	Ⓐ
	M	B	🍸B	🍸	🍸	🍸	🍸C	🍸	🍸M	🍸	🍸	🍸A	🍸C	🍸	🍸A	🍸M	🍸	🍸C	🍸	🍸M	🍸	🍸C	🍸	🍸M	🍸
Manchester Airport d.	...	...	...	0533	...	...	...	...	...	...	...	...	...	...	...	...	1036	...	1136	...	1236	...	1336	...	1436
Manchester Piccadilly d.	...	...	...	0547	...	0650	...	0750	...	0850	...	...	...	0950	...	...	1052	...	1152	...	1252	...	1352	...	1452
Warrington Bank Quay d.	...	...	...	0621	...	0725	...	0824	...	0926	...	...	...	1027	...	...	1126	...	1227	...	1326	...	1426	...	1526
Crewe 151 ♥ d.	0001	0015	0623	|	0654	|	...	|	...	|	...	0953	...	|	1049	...	|	...	|	...	|	...	|	...	|
Chester 151 ♥ a.	0022	0037	0643	0649	0717	0752	...	0853	...	0953	...	1013	...	1058	1113	...	1153	...	1255	...	1353	...	1454	...	1553
Chester d.	0038	0040	0644	0655	0719	0755	0822	0855	0923	0958	1002	1016	1024	1100	1116	1125	1155	1224	1256	1324	1355	1424	1455	1525	1555
Flint d.	0051	0053	0657	0708	0734	0810	0838	0908	0938	|	1018	1029	1039	|	|	1138	1210	1237	1311	1337	1410	1437	1510	1538	1610
Prestatyn d.	0104	0106	0710	0721	0747	0823	0852	0921	0951	|	1031	1042	1053	1124	|	1151	1223	1250	1325	1350	1423	1450	1524	1552	1623
Rhyl d.	0110	0112	0716	0727	0753	0829	0858	0927	0957	|	1037	1048	1059	1131	1143	1157	1229	1256	1331	1356	1429	1456	1530	1558	1629
Colwyn Bay d.	0121	0123	0727	0738	0807	0843	0912	0938	1011	|	1051	1059	1109	|	1154	1211	1243	1307	1345	1407	1443	1507	1544	1608	1643
Llandudno Junction ‡ d.	0128	0129	0733	0744	0816	0851	0918	0944	1018	1036	1058	1106	1116	1146	1201	1218	1250	1313	1352	1413	1450	1513	1550	1620	1650
Llandudno ‡ a.	|	|	|	0756	|	...	0927	|	1031	|	1109	|	|	|	|	|	...	|	1404	|	1501	|	1602	|	1702
Bangor d.	0144	0146	0750	...	0838	...	...	1008	...	1053	...	1125	1139	1202	1217	1236	...	1331	...	1437	...	1531	...	1644	...
Holyhead ▽ a.	0220	0215	0820	...	0922	...	...	1036	...	1120	...	1155	1222	1239	1247	1317	...	1414	...	1508	...	1614	...	1716	...

	Ⓐ	Ⓐ	Ⓐ	Ⓐ	Ⓐ	Ⓐ	Ⓐ	Ⓐ		Ⓐ	Ⓐ	Ⓐ	Ⓐ	Ⓐ🍸	Ⓐ	Ⓐ	Ⓐ	Ⓐ	Ⓐ	Ⓐ	Ⓐ	Ⓐ	Ⓐ	⑥	⑥	⑥
	🍸C	🍸	🍸M	🍸	🍸A	🍸C	🍸	🍸		🍸A	🍸M		C✕	AW			🍸A				C				B	🍸B
Manchester Airport d.	...	1536	...	...	...	...	...	...	...	...	...	...	...	...	...	...	...	2032	...	2132	...	...	...	⑥	...	...
Manchester Piccadilly d.	...	1552	...	1650	...	...	1719	1750	...	...	...	1850	...	...	...	1950	...	2050	...	2150	...	2212	2314		...	...
Warrington Bank Quay d.	...	1626	...	1728	...	...	1752	1824	...	...	...	1922	...	...	...	2026	...	2126	...	2224	...	2257	2348		...	...
Crewe 151 ♥ d.	...	|	...	|	1749	...	|	|	...	1857	...	|	...	1956	...	|	2055	|	2136	|	...	|	|		0015	0623
Chester 151 ♥ a.	...	1654	...	1801	1808	...	1822	1853	...	1916	...	1950	...	2015	...	2053	2120	2155	2159	2251	...	2325	0015		0037	0643
Chester d.	1627	1655	1725	1803	1810	1824	...	1855	...	1923	1932	...	2006	2026	2034	...	2124	...	2204	...	2256	...	...		0040	0644
Flint d.	1640	1710	1740	|	1823	1839	...	1910	...	1936	1947	...	2018	|	2049	...	2137	...	2219	...	2311	...	...		0053	0657
Prestatyn d.	1654	1723	1753	1826	1836	1853	...	1923	...	1949	2000	...	|	|	2102	...	2150	...	2232	...	2324	...	...		0106	0710
Rhyl d.	1700	1729	1759	1833	1842	1859	...	1929	...	1955	2006	...	2035	2053	2108	...	2157	...	2238	...	2330	...	...		0112	0716
Colwyn Bay d.	1710	1743	1813	1845	1853	1913	...	1940	...	2006	2020	...	2047	2104	2122	...	2208	...	2252	...	2344	...	...		0123	0727
Llandudno Junction ‡ d.	1716	1750	1825	1852	1900	1919	...	1950e	...	2013	2030e	...	2054	2110	2129	...	2214	...	2259	...	2352	...	...		0129	0733
Llandudno ‡ a.	|	1802	|	1904	|	|	...	|	...	|	2042	...	|	|	|	...	|	...	|	...	|	...	...		|	|
Bangor d.	1739	...	1847	...	1918	1935	...	2015	...	2029	...	...	2111	2127	2152	...	2231	...	2322	...	0014	...	...		0146	0750
Holyhead ▽ a.	1821	...	1917	...	...	2020	...	2045	...	2058	...	...	2145	2156	2235	...	2300	...	0005	...	0048	...	...		0215	0820

	⑥	⑥	⑥	⑥	⑥	⑥	⑥	⑥	⑥	⑥	⑥	⑥	⑥	⑥	⑥	⑥	⑥	⑥	⑥	⑥	⑥	⑥	⑥	⑥	⑥	⑥
	🍸	🍸	🍸	🍸C	🍸	🍸M	🍸	🍸C	🍸	🍸A	🍸M	🍸		🍸C	🍸	🍸M	🍸	🍸C	🍸	🍸M	🍸	🍸A	🍸C	🍸	🍸M	🍸
Manchester Airport d.	0533	...	...	...	...	...	...	...	0936	...	...	1036	...	...	1136	...	1236	...	1336	...	1436	...	...	1536	...	1636
Manchester Piccadilly d.	0548	...	0650	...	0750	...	0850	...	0952	...	...	1052	...	...	1152	...	1252	...	1352	...	1452	...	...	1552	...	1652
Warrington Bank Quay d.	0621	...	0723	...	0825	...	0926	...	1026	...	...	1126	...	...	1227	...	1326	...	1426	...	1527	...	...	1626	...	1726
Crewe 151 ♥ d.	|	0703	|	...	|	...	|	...	|	1049	...	|	...	...	|	...	|	...	|	...	|	1549	...	|	...	|
Chester 151 ♥ a.	0649	0723	0750	...	0854	...	0953	...	1053	1113	...	1153	...	...	1255	...	1353	...	1453	...	1554	1610	...	1654	...	1753
Chester d.	0655	0725	0755	0822	0856	0924	0955	1023	1055	1116	1124	1155	...	1223	1256	1326	1355	1423	1455	1522	1556	1612	1627	1655	1724	1755
Flint d.	0710	0739	0810	0836	0911	0937	1010	1036	1110	|	1139	1210	...	1236	1311	1339	1410	1436	1510	1537	1611	1625	1642	1710	1739	1810
Prestatyn d.	0723	0752	0823	0849	0924	0950	1023	1050	1123	|	1152	1223	...	1250	1325	1352	1423	1450	1523	1550	1624	1638	1655	1724	1752	1823
Rhyl d.	0729	0758	0829	0855	0930	0956	1029	1056	1129	1143	1158	1229	...	1257	1331	1358	1429	1457	1529	1556	1630	1645	1701	1730	1758	1829
Colwyn Bay d.	0743	0809	0843	0906	0944	1007	1043	1106	1143	1154	1209	1243	...	1309	1345	1409	1443	1509	1543	1607	1644	1656	1712	1744	1812	1843
Llandudno Junction ‡ d.	0750	0815	0850	0912	0951	1013	1050	1113	1150	1201	1215	1250	1257	1315	1351	1415	1450	1515	1550	1614	1651	1702	1717	1750	1819	1850
Llandudno ‡ a.	0802	|	0902	|	1003	|	1102	|	1202	|	|	|	1307	|	1402	|	1502	|	1602	|	1702	|	|	1803	|	1902
Bangor d.	...	0838	...	0936	...	1031	...	1136	...	1217	1233	1315	...	1333	...	1440	...	1532	...	1637	...	1719	1741	...	1843	...
Holyhead ▽ a.	...	0921	...	1014	...	1105	...	1209	...	1247	1312	...	...	1413	...	1510	...	1613	...	1714	...	1748	1819	...	1913	...

	⑥	⑥	⑥	⑥	⑥	⑥	⑥	⑥	⑥	⑥	⑥	⑥	⑥	⑥	⑥	⑦	⑦	⑦	⑦	⑦	⑦	⑦	⑦	⑦	⑦	⑦
	🍸A	🍸C	🍸	🍸A	🍸M		C				C	🚌					🚌			🍸			🍸	🍸	🍸	🍸
Manchester Airport d.	...	...	1736	...	...	1836	...	...	...	2032	...	...	...	...	...	⑦	...	...	...	...	...	...	...	...	...	...
Manchester Piccadilly d.	...	...	1752	...	...	1852	...	1951	...	2050	...	...	2151	2226	2314		0718	...	0956	...	1056	...	1156	...	1256	...
Warrington Bank Quay d.	...	...	1826	...	...	1926	...	2030	...	|	...	...	2224	2256	2348		0838	...	1028	...	1127	...	1227	...	1329	...
Crewe 151 ♥ d.	1749	...	|	1852	...	|	...	|	2100	2128	...	...	|	|	|		|	0925	|	1042	|	1127	|	1227	|	1327
Chester 151 ♥ a.	1810	...	1853	1911	...	1954	...	2057	2121	2158	...	...	2254	2325	0015		0938	0947	1058	1102	1155	1150	1255	1252	1357	1351
Chester d.	1816	1824	1855	1918	1932	...	2032	...	2126	...	2236	...	...	...	...		...	0948	...	1107	...	1203	...	1302	...	1402
Flint d.	1829	1839	1910	1931	1947	...	2047	...	2141	...	2251	...	...	...	...		...	1003	...	|	...	1218	...	1317	...	1417
Prestatyn d.	1842	1852	1923	1944	2000	...	2100	...	2154	...	2305	...	...	...	...		...	1017	...	1130	...	1231	...	1330	...	1430
Rhyl d.	1849	1858	1929	1951	2006	...	2106	...	2200	...	2311	...	...	...	...		...	1023	...	1137	...	1237	...	1336	...	1436
Colwyn Bay d.	1900	1909	1943	2002	2020	...	2119	...	2214	...	2325	...	...	...	...		...	1037	...	1148	...	1248	...	1350	...	1450
Llandudno Junction ‡ d.	1906	1916	1950	2008	2027	...	2126	...	2221	...	2338	2348	...	...	...		...	1043	...	1154	...	1254	...	1357	...	1457
Llandudno ‡ a.	|	|	2002	|	|	...	|	...	|	...	|	...	...	...	...		...	|	...	|	...	|	...	|	...	|
Bangor d.	1923	1933	...	2025	2048	...	2143	...	2245	...	...	0013	...	...	...		...	1106	...	1211	...	1311	...	1419	...	1514
Holyhead ▽ a.	1952	2018	...	2054	2131	...	2225	...	2318	...	...	0048	...	...	...		...	1149	...	1240	...	1340	...	1453	...	1555

	⑦	⑦	⑦	⑦	⑦	⑦	⑦	⑦	⑦	⑦	⑦	⑦	⑦	⑦	⑦	⑦	⑦	⑦	⑦	⑦	⑦	⑦	⑦	⑦	⑦	⑦
	🍸	🍸	🍸		🍸C	🍸		🍸A			🍸A	🍸C		🍸	🍸A	🍸M		🍸A		🍸A						
Manchester Airport d.	...	...	...	...	...	...	...	...	...	...	...	...	...	...	...	...	...	...	...	...	...	...	...	...	...	...
Manchester Piccadilly d.	1356	...	1456	...	...	1556	...	...	1656	...	...	...	...	1756	...	...	1856	...	1956	...	2056	...	2156	...	2256	2325
Warrington Bank Quay d.	1427	...	1528	...	...	1627	...	...	1727	...	...	...	...	1827	...	...	1930	...	2031	...	2128	...	2226	...	2330	2354
Crewe 151 ♥ d.	|	1427	|	1527	...	|	1627	1652	|	1727	1752	...	1827	|	1901	...	|	1952	|	2055	|	2128	|	2229	|	|
Chester 151 ♥ a.	1455	1451	1556	1549	...	1655	1649	1711	1755	1749	1812	...	1849	1855	1920	...	1958	2013	2059	2113	2156	2151	2254	2252	2357	0024
Chester d.	...	1502	...	1602	1636	...	1702	...	...	1802	...	1829	1852	...	1929	1938	...	2018	...	2117	...	2201	...	2302	...	...
Flint d.	...	1517	...	1617	1651	...	1717	...	...	1817	...	1844	1907	...	1942	1955	...	2031	...	2130	...	2216	...	2317	...	...
Prestatyn d.	...	1530	...	1630	1704	...	1730	...	...	1830	...	1857	1921	...	1955	2011	...	2044	...	2143	...	2229	...	2330	...	...
Rhyl d.	...	1536	...	1636	1710	...	1736	...	...	1836	...	1903	1927	...	2002	2017	...	2051	...	2150	...	2235	...	2336	...	...
Colwyn Bay d.	...	1550	...	1650	1724	...	1750	...	...	1850	...	1917	1941	...	2013	2031	...	2102	...	2201	...	2249	...	2347	...	...
Llandudno Junction ‡ d.	...	1557	...	1657	1731	...	1757	...	...	1857	...	1924	1947	...	2019	2037	...	2108	...	2207	...	2256	...	2353	...	...
Llandudno ‡ a.	...	|	...	|	|	...	|	...	...	|	...	|	|	...	|	|	...	|	...	|	...	|	...	|	...	...
Bangor d.	...	1619	...	1714	1754	...	1819	...	...	1914	...	1948	2009	...	2036	2059	...	2125	...	2224	...	2313	...	0016	...	...
Holyhead ▽ a.	...	1653	...	1757	1837	...	1854	...	...	1954	...	2018	2044	...	2103	2134	...	2154	...	2253	...	2355	...	0051	...	...

LLANDUDNO - BLAENAU FFESTINIOG

km		⚒	⚒	Ⓐ	⑥	⚒	⚒		⑥	Ⓐ	
0	**Llandudno** d.	...	*0708*	1008	1022	1308	1620	...	1903	1905	...
5	**Llandudno** Junction d.	0530	0726	1028**d**	1034	1330**d**	1633	...	1919**f**	1923**d**	...
18	Llanrwst d.	0548	0749	1050	1056	1352	1655	...	1941	1945	...
24	Betws y Coed d.	0554	0755	1056	1102	1358	1701	...	1947	1951	...
44	**Blaenau Ffestiniog** d.	0624	0829	1130	1136	1432	1735	...	2021	2023	...

	⚒	Ⓐ	⑥	⚒	⑥	Ⓐ	Ⓐ	⑥	⚒	
Blaenau Ffestiniog d.	0624	0835	0846	1135	1457	1457	1736	1737	2023	...
Betws y Coed d.	0650	0902	0913	1202	1524	1524	1803	1804	2050	...
Llanrwst d.	0656	0908	0919	1208	1530	1530	1809	1810	2056	...
Llandudno Junction a.	0720	0933**g**	0944**g**	1233	1555	1555**h**	1834**h**	1835**h**	2121**h**	...
Llandudno a.	*0741*	0956	1013	1245	1609	1617	1853	1853	2144	...

♥ – All trains **Chester** - **Crewe**. Journey time ± 23 minutes:
On ⚒: 0422, 0455, 0537, 0551, 0626Ⓐ, 0635⑥, 0645Ⓐ, 0717⑥, 0735Ⓐ, 0755, 0835, 0855, 0916Ⓐ, 0935, 0955, 1035, 1055 and at the same minutes past each hour until 1735, 1755, 1855, 1935Ⓐ, 1955, 2018, 2035⑥, 2046Ⓐ, 2055, 2135Ⓐ, 2224Ⓐ, 2226⑥, 2301.
On ⑦: 0840, 0939, 1039, 1128, 1221, 1233, 1320, 1330, 1423, 1433, 1533, 1600, 1627, 1722, 1735, 1835, 1859, 1924, 1935, 1950, 2027, 2037, 2050, 2135, 2150, 2235, 2300.

♥ – All trains **Crewe** - **Chester**. Journey time ± 23 minutes:
On ⚒: 0001①, 0007②–⑥, 0010① 0015②–⑥, 0623, 0654Ⓐ, 0703⑥, 0711Ⓐ, 0723⑥, 0823, 0849Ⓐ, 0923, 0940Ⓐ, 0949⑥, 0953Ⓐ, 1023, 1049, 1123, 1149Ⓐ,1156⑥, 1223, 1249 and at the same minutes past each hour until 1823, 1845Ⓐ, 1852⑥, 1857Ⓐ, 1923, 1949⑥, 1956Ⓐ, 2023, 2048Ⓐ, 2055Ⓐ, 2100⑥, 2136, 2149Ⓐ, 2223, 2321⑥, 2330Ⓐ, 2357⑥.
On ⑦: 0925, 1007, 1042, 1105, 1127, 1155, 1227, 1254, 1327, 1357, 1427, 1457, 1527, 1627, 1652, 1727, 1752, 1827, 1901, 1924, 1952, 2027, 2055, 2128, 2203, 2229, 2306, 2338.

‡ – All trains **Llandudno Junction** - **Llandudno**. Journey time ± 10 minutes:
On ⚒: 0540Ⓐ, 0613, 0651, 0731, 0744Ⓐ, 0750⑥, 0817Ⓐ, 0828⑥, 0850⑥, 0918Ⓐ, 0928⑥, 0948Ⓐ, 0951⑥, 1003⑥, 1018Ⓐ, 1028⑥, 1050⑥, 1058Ⓐ, 1126⑥, 1128Ⓐ, 1150⑥, 1224⑥, 1235, 1257, 1351, 1428, 1450, 1530⑥, 1550, 1559⑥, 1605Ⓐ, 1626⑥, 1650, 1728⑥, 1750, 1826, 1841, 1850⑥, 1852Ⓐ, 1928⑥, 1950⑥, 1955Ⓐ, 2030, 2058Ⓐ, 2132.
On ⑦ from April 1: 1100, 1200, 1258, 1400, 1504, 1600, 1700.

‡ – All trains **Llandudno** - **Llandudno Junction**. Journey time ± 10 minutes:
On ⚒: 0554Ⓐ, 0634⑥, 0646Ⓐ, 0708, 0745, 0802Ⓐ, 0808⑥, 0830Ⓐ, 0845⑥, 0908⑥, 0945, 1008, 1022⑥, 1044, 1108⑥, 1112Ⓐ, 1144, 1208⑥, 1240⑥, 1246, 1308, 1408, 1440Ⓐ, 1442⑥, 1508, 1544⑥, 1607, 1620, 1644⑥, 1705Ⓐ, 1708⑥, 1744⑥, 1808, 1844, 1903⑥, 1905Ⓐ, 1913⑥, 1934Ⓐ, 1942⑥, 2008, 2043, 2111Ⓐ, 2145.
On ⑦ from April 1: 1119, 1218, 1319, 1419, 1515, 1612, 1712.

← FOR OTHER NOTES SEE PREVIOUS PAGE

CS — 🛏 Sleeper trains LONDON - SCOTLAND 🛏 — 161

All trains in this table convey 🛏 1, 2 cl., [2] (reservation compulsory) 🍴 and 🍸. Only available for overnight journeys.

	⑦	⑦	⑦	Ⓐ	Ⓐ	Ⓐ	⑦	⑦	Ⓐ	Ⓐ
							◐a	◐a	◐	◐
London Euston **151/2/3** d.	2057	2057	2057	2115	2115	2115	2328	2328	2353	2353
Watford Junction d.	2117	2117	2117	2133	2133	2133	2349	2349	0013	0013
Crewe **151 152 153 154** d.	2336	2336	2336	2354	2354	2354	|	|	|	|
Preston **154** d.	0035	0035	0035	0100	0100	0100	|	|	|	|
Carlisle **154** a.	|	|	|	|	|	|	0445	0445	0513	0513
Motherwell a.	|	|	|	|	|	|	|	0655	|	0655
Glasgow Central **154** ◧ a.	|	|	|	|	|	|	|	0720	|	0720
Edinburgh Waverley **154** ◧ a.	|	|	|	|	|	|	0721	...	0721	...
Dundee **222** a.	0608	|	|	0607	|	|	...	...	...	...
Aberdeen **222** ◧ a.	0735	|	|	0735	|	|	...	...	...	...
Perth **223** a.	...	0538	|	...	0538	|	...	...	...	...
Inverness **223** a.	...	0839	|	...	0839	|	...	...	...	...
Fort William **218** a.	...	...	0955	...	...	0955	...	...	...	...

	⑦	⑦	Ⓐ	Ⓐ	Ⓐ	Ⓐ	Ⓐ	⑦	⑦	⑦
	a	a								
Fort William **218** d.	...	...	...	...	1950	...	...	1900	...	...
Inverness **223** d.	...	...	...	...	|	2045	...	|	2026	...
Perth **223** d.	...	...	...	...	|	2330	...	|	2306	...
Aberdeen **222** d.	...	...	...	...	|	|	2143	|	|	2143
Dundee **222** d.	...	...	...	...	|	|	2307	|	|	2307
Edinburgh Waverley **154** d.	2315	...	2340	...	|	|	|	|	|	|
Glasgow Central **154** d.	|	2315	|	2340	|	|	|	|	|	|
Motherwell d.	|	2330	|	2357	|	|	|	|	|	|
Carlisle **154** d.	0143	0143	0145	0145	|	|	|	|	|	|
Preston **154** a.	|	|	|	|	0433	0433	0433	0432	0432	0432
Crewe **151 152 153 154** a.	|	|	|	|	0536	0536	0536	0536	0536	0536
Watford Junction a.	0642	0642	0643	0643	|	|	|	|	|	|
London Euston **151/2/3** ◧ a.	0707	0707	0707	0707	0747	0747	0747	0747	0747	0747

a – Service subject to alteration from April 1.

◐ – Sleeping-car passengers may occupy their cabins from 2200.

◧ – Sleeping-car passengers may occupy their cabins until 0800 following arrival at these stations.

NT 2nd class — PRESTON - LIVERPOOL — 162

km			⚒	⚒	⑥	Ⓐ	⚒		⚒	⚒	⚒	⚒		⚒	⚒	⚒		⑦	⑦	⑦		⑦	⑦	⑦
0	**Preston** d.	⚒	0729	0831	0930	0930	1030	and	1630	1730	1829	1930	...	2030	2140	2242	⑦	0834	0927	1027	and	2127	2227	2310
24	Wigan North Western d.		0748	0850	0949	0949	1049	hourly	1649	1749	1850	1949	...	2048	2201	2304		0853	0947	1046	hourly	2147	2247	2330
38	St Helens Central d.		0804	0903	1004	1002	1102	until	1702	1802	1903	2002	...	2101	2217	2319		0909	1003	1103	until	2203	2303	2346
57	**Liverpool** Lime Street a.		0831	0926	1026	1028	1127	★	1727	1826	1926	2026	...	2126	2247	2350		0937	1032	1131	★	2231	2331	0014

		⚒	⚒	⚒	⚒		⚒	⚒	⚒	⚒	⚒	⚒	⑥	Ⓐ	⚒		⑦	⑦	⑦		⑦	⑦	⑦
Liverpool Lime Street d.	⚒	0658	0756	0826	0928	and	1629	1717	1731	1801	1930	2030	2147	2147	2302	⑦	0847	0947	1047	and	2047	2147	2247
St Helens Central d.		0717	0814	0848	0948	hourly	1647	1742	1759	1828	1948	2048	2214	2214	2329		0913	1013	1113	hourly	2113	2213	2313
Wigan North Western d.		0730	0830	0902	1003	until	1701	1759	1817	1851c	2002	2102	2231	2239	2345		0929	1030	1131	until	2131	2229	2328
Preston a.		0753	0857	0923	1025	★	1723	1823	1840a	1916c	2027	2132b	2254	2301	0011		0952	1052	1154	★	2154	2253	2351

a – On ⑥ arrives 1843. **b** – On ⑥ arrives 2123. **c** – On ⑥ arrives 4–6 minutes earlier. ★ – Timings may vary by up to 3 minutes.

ME, NT 2nd class — MANCHESTER and LIVERPOOL local services — 163

MANCHESTER - CLITHEROE
Journey time: ± 76–80 minutes *57 km* NT

From Manchester Victoria:

Ⓐ: Trains call at Bolton ± 19 and Blackburn ± 48 minutes later: 0555, 0700, 0752**p**, 0902, 1003, 1102, 1201, 1300, 1402, 1502, 1602, 1635, 1702, 1802, 1903, 2000, 2103, 2202.

⑥: Trains call at Bolton ± 19 and Blackburn ± 48 minutes later: 0555, 0700, 0753**p**, 0903, 1003, 1102, 1202, 1302, 1403, 1503, 1602, 1635, 1703, 1803, 1903, 2003, 2103, 2203.

⑦: Trains call at Bolton ± 19 and Blackburn ± 48 minutes later: 0803, 0903 and hourly until 2103.

From Clitheroe:

Ⓐ: Trains call at Blackburn ± 23 and Bolton ± 54 minutes later: 0645, 0705, 0745, 0825, 0946, 1046, 1146, 1246, 1346, 1446, 1528, 1646, 1745, 1810, 1846, 1946, 2046, 2144, 2244⑤.

⑥: Trains call at Blackburn ± 24 and Bolton ± 51 minutes later: 0705, 0745, 0825, 0946, 1046, 1146, 1246, 1346, 1446, 1528, 1645, 1745, 1803, 1845, 1946, 2045, 2144, 2248.

⑦: Trains call at Blackburn ± 24 and Bolton ± 53 minutes later: 0946, 1046 and hourly until 1646, 1744, 1846, 1946, 2044.

MANCHESTER - BUXTON
Journey time: ± 60–70 minutes *41 km* NT

From Manchester Piccadilly:

Trains call at Stockport ± 11, Hazel Grove ± 22 and New Mills Newtown ± 38 minutes later.

Ⓐ: 0649, 0749, 0849, 0949, 1049, 1149, 1249, 1349, 1449, 1549, 1621, 1649, 1722, 1749, 1821, 1849, 1949, 2049, 2149, 2310.

⑥: 0649, 0749, 0849, and hourly until 1649, 1721, 1749, 1849, 1949, 2049, 2154, 2310.

⑦: 0856, 0950, 1051, 1149 and hourly until 1949, 2049, 2149, 2249.

From Buxton:

Trains call at New Mills Newtown ± 21, Hazel Grove ± 34 and at Stockport ± 46 minutes later.

Ⓐ: 0602, 0623, 0653, 0724, 0748, 0826, 0972, 1094, 1129, 1229, 1329, 1429, 1529, 1629, 1702, 1728, 1802, 1829, 1929, 2029, 2129, 2257.

⑥: 0602, 0627, 0725, 0803, 0827, 0927, 1029 and hourly until 1629, 1728, 1829, 1929, 2029, 2129, 2257.

⑦: 0823, 0920, 1027, 1127 and hourly until 1927, 2027, 2129, 2227.

MANCHESTER - NORTHWICH - CHESTER
Journey time: ± 90–95 minutes *73 km* NT

From Manchester Piccadilly:

Trains call at Stockport ± 13, Altrincham ± 29 and Northwich ± 57 minutes later.

⚒: 0618, 0717, 0817Ⓐ, 0818⑥, 0917, 1017, 1117, 1217, 1317, 1417, 1517, 1617, 1709Ⓐ,1717⑥, 1817, 1917, 2017, 2117⑥, 2122Ⓐ, 2217, 2317.

⑦: 0923, 1122, 1321, 1523, 1721, 1921, 2122.

From Chester:

Trains call at Northwich ± 30, Altrincham ± 55 and Stockport ± 74 minutes later.

⚒: 0602, 0659, 0804, 0859, 0959, 1059, 1159, 1259, 1359, 1459, 1559, 1659, 1804, 1904, 2004, 2133, 2248.

⑦: 0902, 1104, 1304, 1504, 1704, 1904, 2104.

MANCHESTER - ST HELENS - LIVERPOOL
Journey time: ± 63 minutes *51 km* NT

From Manchester Victoria:

Trains call at St Helens Junction ± 30 minutes later.

⚒: 0539, 0600Ⓐ, 0602⑥, 0702, 0738, 0802, 0838, 0902, 1002, 1102, 1202, 1302, 1359Ⓐ, 1402⑥, 1502, 1559Ⓐ, 1602⑥, 1702, 1738, 1802, 1900Ⓐ, 1902⑥, 2002Ⓐ, 2006⑥, 2109, 2209, 2309.

⑦: 0859**p**, 1001**p**, 1100**p**, and hourly (note **p** applies to all trains) until 2301**p**.

From Liverpool Lime Street:

Trains call at St Helens Junction ± 28 minutes later.

⚒: 0520⑥, 0525Ⓐ, 0620, 0720, 0744, 0820 and hourly until 1619, 1645, 1719, 1740, 1820, 1918Ⓐ, 1920⑥, 2020⑥, 2022Ⓐ, 2120⑥, 2122Ⓐ, 2220, 2320.

⑦: 0816**p** 0916**p**, and hourly (note **p** applies to all trains) until 2216**p**, 2315**p**.

MANCHESTER - WIGAN - SOUTHPORT
Journey time: ± 75 minutes *62 km* NT

From Manchester Piccadilly:

Trains call at Wigan Wallgate ± 35 minutes later.

Ⓐ: 0641**v**, 0704**v**, 0738**v**, 0810**v**, 0823, 0922 and hourly until 1823, 1924, 2022, 2122, 2238.

⑥: 0641**v**, 0703**v**, 0823, 0922 and hourly until 1723, 1822, 1923, 2020, 2120, 2237.

⑦: 0835, 0935, 1031, 1133, 1232, 1335 and hourly until 2035.

From Southport:

Trains call at Wigan Wallgate ± 30 minutes later.

Ⓐ: 0621, 0652**v**, 0719, 0757**v**, 0823 and hourly until 1623, 1732, 1815, 1920, 2020, 2218.

⑥: 0621, 0719, 0822, 0923 and hourly until 1623, 1732, 1815, 1920, 2020, 2122**v**, 2218.

⑦: 0910, 1005 and hourly until 2205.

MANCHESTER AIRPORT - CREWE
Journey time: ± 33 minutes *37 km* NT

From Manchester Airport:

⚒: 0547, 0711, 0811, 0911, 1011, 1111 and hourly until 1611, 1711⑥, 1713Ⓐ, 1811. Additional later services (and all day on ⑦) available by changing at Wilmslow.

From Crewe:

⚒: 0634, 0730⑥, 0831, 0934 and hourly until 1434, 1533, 1634, 1733, 1834. Additional later services (and all day on ⑦) available by changing at Wilmslow.

LIVERPOOL - BIRKENHEAD - CHESTER
Journey time: ± 42 minutes *29 km* ME

From Liverpool Lime Street (Low Level):

Trains call at Liverpool Central ± 2 minutes and Birkenhead Central ± 9 minutes later.

⚒: 0538, 0608, 0643, 0713, 0743, 0755Ⓐ, 0813, 0821Ⓐ, 0843, 0858⑥, 0913, 0928, 0943, 0958 and every 15 minutes until 1858, 1913 and every 30 minutes until 2343.

⑦: 0813, 0843 and every 30 minutes until 2313, 2343.

From Chester:

Trains call at Birkenhead Central ± 33 minutes and Liverpool Central ± 44* minutes later.

⚒: 0555, 0630, 0700, 0722Ⓐ, 0730⑥, 0737Ⓐ, 0752Ⓐ, 0800⑥, 0807Ⓐ, 0815⑥, 0831, 0845 and every 15 minutes until 1830, 1900 and every 30 minutes until 2300.

⑦: 0800, 0830 and every 30 minutes until 2300.

LIVERPOOL - SOUTHPORT
Journey time: ± 44 minutes *30 km* ME

From Liverpool Central:

⚒: 0608, 0623, 0638, 0653, 0708 and every 15 minutes until 2308, 2323, 2338.

⑦: 0807, 0823, 0853, 0923, 0953, 1023 and every 30 minutes hour until 2253, 2323, 2338.

From Southport:

⚒: 0538, 0553, 0608, 0623, 0643, 0658, 0713, 0728, 0738Ⓐ, 0743⑥, 0748Ⓐ, 0758, 0803Ⓐ, 0813 and every 15 minutes until 2258, 2316.

⑦: 0758, 0828, 0858, 0928, 0958, 1028, 1058 and every 15 minutes until 2258, 2316.

p – Starts/terminates at Manchester **Piccadilly**, not Victoria.
v – Starts/terminates at Manchester **Victoria**, not Piccadilly.

* – Trains FROM Chester call at Liverpool Lime Street, then Liverpool Central.

km		⚒	②–⑥	⚒	Ⓐ	⑥	Ⓐ	⑥S	⚒	Ⓐ	⑥	Ⓐ	⑥	⑥	Ⓐ	⚒	Ⓐ	⚒	⚒	⚒		⚒	⚒	⚒	ⒶF	⚒	⚒
0	**London** St Pancras ..d.		0015	...	0545	0545	0632	0637	...	0652	0652	0655	0701	...	0724	0729	...	0757	0801	0815	...	0826	0829	0856	...	0900	0915
47	Luton ✈ Parkway......d.		0043	...	|	|	|	|	...	0713	0713	|	|	...	|	0749	...	|	|	|	...	|	0849	|	...	|	|
49	Luton ....d.		0047	...	0612	0612	0654	0659	...	|	|	0718	0722	...	|	|	...	|	0822	|	...	|	|	|	...	0922	|
80	Bedford ....d.		0111	...	0627	0627	0709	|	...	|	|	0733	0736	...	|	0804	...	|	0837	|	...	|	0904	|	...	0937	|
105	Wellingborough ....d.		0131	...	0639	0639	0721	|	...	|	|	0746	0748	...	|	0817	...	|	0849	|	...	|	0917	|	...	0949	|
116	Kettering ....d.		0143	...	0647	0647	0729	0727	0738	|	|	0756	0758	...	|	0823	0832	|	0900	|	...	|	0923	|	...	1000	|
128	**Corby** ....a.		|	...	|	|	|	|	0747	|	|	|	|	...	|	|	0841	|	0911	|	...	|	|	|	0926	1011	|
133	Market Harborough ...d.		0155	...	0657	0657	0739	0737	...	|	|	0807	0808	...	0816	0834	...	|	...	0910	...	|	0934	|	|	...	1010
159	**Leicester** ....d.		0210	...	0712	0712	0752	0753	...	0758	0800	0823	0823	0830	0830	0848	...	0901	...	0925	...	0930	0948	1001	|	...	1025
180	Loughborough ....d.		▬	...	0722	0723	0802	0803	...	0808	0809	0834	0833	0840	0840	0858	...	|	...	|	...	0940	0958	|	|	...	|
191	E. Midlands Parkway.d.		...	...	0729	|	|	0811	...	0816	0818	0842	0841	0848	0848	|	...	|	...	0942	...	0948	|	|	1031	...	1042
204	**Nottingham** ....a.		⚒	...	|	|	|	|	...	0832	0831	0854	0854	|	|	0918	...	|	...	0955	...	|	1018	|	|	...	1055
207	**Derby** ....a.		0627	0721	0745	0743	0817	0823	...	...	...	...	...	0903	0903	...	...	0923	...	...	...	1003	...	1023	1045	...	...
246	Chesterfield ....d.		0646	0743	0810	0810	0838	0844	...	...	...	...	...	0927	0927	...	...	0943	...	...	...	1027	...	1043	...	...	...
265	**Sheffield** ....a.		0713	0800	0827	0826	0855	0858	...	...	...	...	...	0940	0941	...	...	0958	...	...	...	1041	...	1100	...	...	...

	⚒	⚒	⚒	⚒	⚒	⚒	⚒	⚒	⚒	⚒	⚒	⚒		⚒	⚒	⚒	⚒	⚒	⚒	⚒	⚒	⚒	⚒	⚒	⚒	⚒	⚒
London St Pancras.. d.	0926	0929	0958	1001	1015	1026	1029	1058	1101	1115	1126	1129	...	1158	1201	1215	1226	1229	1258	1301	1315	1326	1329	1358	1401	1415	1426
Luton ✈ Parkway ..... d.	|	0949	|	|	|	|	1049	|	|	|	|	1149	...	|	|	|	|	1249	|	|	|	|	1349	|	|	|	|
Luton .... d.	|	|	|	1022	|	|	|	|	1122	|	|	|	...	|	1222	|	|	|	|	1322	|	|	|	|	1422	|	|
Bedford...................... d.	|	1004	|	1037	|	|	1104	|	1137	|	|	1204	...	|	1237	|	|	1304	|	1337	|	|	1404	|	1437	|	|
Wellingborough......... d.	|	1017	|	1049	|	|	1117	|	1149	|	|	1217	...	|	1249	|	|	1317	|	1349	|	|	1417	|	1449	|	|
Kettering.................. d.	|	1023	|	1100	|	|	1123	|	1200	|	|	1223	...	|	1300	|	|	1323	|	1400	|	|	1423	|	1500	|	|
Corby .... a.	|	|	|	1111	|	|	|	|	1212	|	|	|	...	|	1311	|	|	|	|	1412	|	|	|	|	1512	|	|
Market Harborough ... d.	|	1034	|	...	1110	|	1134	|	...	1210	|	1234	...	|	...	1310	|	1334	|	...	1410	|	1434	|	...	1510	|
Leicester................. d.	1030	1048	1101	...	1125	1130	1148	1201	...	1225	1230	1248	...	1301	...	1325	1330	1348	1401	...	1425	1430	1448	1501	...	1525	1530
Loughborough........... d.	1040	1058	|	...	|	1140	1158	|	...	|	1240	1258	...	|	...	|	1340	1358	|	...	|	1440	1458	|	...	|	1540
E. Midlands Parkway d.	1048	|	|	...	1142	1148	|	|	...	1242	1248	|	...	|	...	1342	1348	|	|	...	1442	1448	|	|	...	1542	1548
Nottingham .... a.	|	1118	|	...	1155	|	1218	|	...	1255	|	1318	...	|	...	1355	|	1418	|	...	1455	|	1518	|	...	1555	|
Derby....................... a.	1103	...	1123	...	...	1203	...	1223	...	...	1303	...	...	1323	...	...	1403	...	1423	...	...	1503	...	1523	...	...	1603
Chesterfield .... d.	1127	...	1143	...	...	1227	...	1243	...	...	1327	...	...	1343	...	...	1427	...	1443	...	...	1527	...	1543	...	...	1627
Sheffield .... a.	1141	...	1159	...	...	1241	...	1259	...	...	1341	...	...	1402	...	...	1441	...	1500	...	...	1541	...	1559	...	...	1641

	⚒	⚒	⚒	⚒	⑥	Ⓐ	⚒	⚒	⚒	⚒	⚒	⑥	Ⓐ	⚒	⑥	Ⓐ	Ⓐ	⑥	Ⓐ	⑥	⑥B	Ⓐ	⚒	Ⓐ	⑥	ⒶC	⑥
London St Pancras.. d.	1429	1458	1501	1515	1526	1526	1529	1558	1601	1615	1626	1629	1629	1657	1701	1700	1700	1715	1715	1726	1729	1730	1757	1745	1801	1800	1826
Luton ✈ Parkway ..... d.	1449	|	|	|	|	|	1549	|	|	|	|	1649	1649	|	|	|	|	|	|	|	1749	|	|	1808	|	|	|
Luton .... d.	|	|	1522	|	|	|	|	|	1622	|	|	|	1653	|	1722	|	|	|	1740	|	|	|	|	|	1822	1822	|
Bedford...................... d.	1504	|	1537	|	|	|	1604	|	1637	|	|	1704	1707	|	1737	1737	1737	|	|	|	1804	1804	|	|	1837	1837	|
Wellingborough......... d.	1517	|	1549	|	|	|	1617	|	1649	|	|	1717	1719	|	1749	1749	1749	|	|	|	1817	1817	|	1832	1849	1849	|
Kettering.................. d.	1523	|	1600	|	|	|	1623	|	1700	|	|	1723	1726	|	1800	1806**g**	1814**g**	|	|	|	1823	1823	|	1844	1900	1906	|
Corby .... a.	|	|	1611	|	|	|	|	|	1711	|	|	|	|	|	1811	1815	|	|	|	|	|	|	|	|	1911	1916	|
Market Harborough ... d.	1534	|	...	1610	|	|	1634	|	...	1710	|	1734	1736	|	...	...	|	1810	1816	|	1834	1834	|	1856	...	...	|
Leicester................. d.	1548	1601	...	1625	1630	1630	1648	1701	...	1725	1730	1748	1751	1801	...	...	1837	1825	1832	1830	1848	1848	1901	1914	...	...	1930
Loughborough........... d.	1558	|	...	|	1640	1640	1658	|	...	|	1740	1758	1801	|	...	...	1847	|	|	1840	1858	1858	|	1926	...	...	1940
E. Midlands Parkway d.	|	|	...	1642	1648	1648	|	|	...	1742	1748	|	|	|	...	...	1856	1842	1850	1848	|	1905	|	1934	...	...	1948
Nottingham .... a.	1618	|	...	1655	|	|	1718	|	...	1755	|	1818	1821	|	...	...	|	1855	1909	|	1918	1920	|	1947**c**	...	...	|
Derby....................... a.	...	1623	...	...	1703	1703**r**	...	1723	...	...	1803	...	...	1823	...	...	1913	...	...	1903	...	...	1923	2031	...	...	2003
Chesterfield .... d.	...	1643	...	...	1727	1734	...	1743	...	...	1827	...	...	1843	...	...	1934	...	...	1927	...	...	1943	...	...	...	2027
Sheffield .... a.	...	1659	...	...	1742	1748	...	1800	...	...	1841	...	...	1900	...	...	1950	...	...	1941	...	...	1959	...	...	...	2041

	Ⓐ	⑥L	ⒶL	⑥	ⒶB	⑥	Ⓐ	⑥	Ⓐ	Ⓐ	⑥	⑥	Ⓐ	⑥	ⒶL	⑥L	ⒶL	Ⓐ	⑥	Ⓐ	⑥	⚒	Ⓐ	⑥	⑥	Ⓐ	Ⓐ
London St Pancras.. d.	1825	1815	1815	1829	1830	1858	1857	1901	1900	1915	1915	1926	1928	1929	1955	1958	1932	2000	2001	2015	2015	2026	2030	2030	2056	2055	2100
Luton ✈ Parkway ..... d.	|	|	|	1849	1850	|	|	|	|	|	|	|	|	1949	|	|	1953	|	|	|	|	|	2049	2050	|	|	|
Luton .... d.	1850	|	|	|	|	|	|	1922	1924	|	|	|	|	|	|	|	|	2022	2025	|	|	|	|	|	|	|	2123
Bedford...................... d.	|	|	|	1904	1907	|	|	1937	1940	|	|	|	|	2004	|	|	2009	2037	2039	|	|	|	2104	2104	|	|	2138
Wellingborough......... d.	|	|	1903	1917	1920	|	|	1949	1954	|	|	|	|	2017	|	|	2022	2049	2051	|	|	|	2118	2117	|	|	2150
Kettering.................. d.	|	|	1911	1923	1926	|	|	2000	2006	|	|	|	2019	2023	|	|	|	2101	2100	|	|	|	2123	2124	|	|	2157
Corby .... a.	|	|	|	|	|	|	|	2011	2017	|	|	|	|	|	|	|	|	2112	2111	|	|	|	|	|	|	|	|
Market Harborough ... d.	1927	1910	|	1934	|	|	1949	...	...	2010	2010	|	2029	2034	|	|	2038	...	...	2109	2110	|	2134	2134	|	|	2207
Leicester................. d.	1942	1925	1934	1948	1952	2001	2002	...	...	2025	2025	2030	2045	2048	2102	2105	2053	...	...	2122	2125	2130	2148	2148	2201	2203	2222
Loughborough........... d.	1953	|	1945	1958	|	|	2013	...	...	|	|	2040	2055	2058	|	|	2103	...	...	|	|	2140	2158	2158	|	|	2232
E. Midlands Parkway d.	|	1942	1954	|	2009	|	2021	...	...	2038	2042	2051	2102	|	|	|	|	...	...	2136	2138	2148	|	2207	|	|	2239
Nottingham .... a.	|	1955**c**	2008**a**	2018	2023	|	|	...	...	2051	2055	|	|	2118	|	|	2128**b**	...	...	2149	2150	|	2218	2221	|	|	|
Derby....................... a.	2015	|	|	...	...	2023	2034	...	...	...	...	2108	2119	...	2129	2131**d**	|	...	...	...	...	2205	...	...	2223	2225	2254
Chesterfield .... d.	2039	2052	2109	...	...	2043	2054	...	...	...	...	...	...	...	2153	2203	2222	...	...	...	...	...	...	...	2247	2245	...
Sheffield .... a.	2055	2105	2123	...	...	2059	2109	...	...	...	...	...	...	...	2208	2217	2236	...	...	...	...	...	...	...	2300	2301	...

	⑥	⑥	Ⓐ	⚒	⚒	⚒	⑥	Ⓐ	⑥	Ⓐ	Ⓐ
London St Pancras.. d.	2101	...	...	2125	2130	2200	...	...	2226	2225	2315
Luton ✈ Parkway ..... d.	|	...	...	|	2151	|	...	...	2247	2248	|
Luton .... d.	2124	...	...	|	|	2224	...	...	|	|	2346
Bedford...................... d.	2139	...	...	|	2205	2239	...	...	2303	2303	0012
Wellingborough......... d.	2152	...	...	|	2218	2252	...	...	2315	2317	0024
Kettering.................. d.	2202	2206	2211	|	2225	2300	2305	2311	2322	2326	0042
Corby .... a.	|	2221	2226	|	|	|	2319	2326	|	|	|
Market Harborough ... d.	2213	...	...	2218	2235	2311	...	...	2332	2337	0052
Leicester................. d.	2229	...	...	2233	2249	2327	...	...	2346	2353	0107
Loughborough........... d.	|	...	...	2243	2259	2338	...	...	2356	0004	0119
E. Midlands Parkway d.	2245	...	...	2250	2307	2347	...	...	0004	0012	0130
Nottingham .... a.	|	...	...	2304	|	0006	...	...	|	|	0145
Derby....................... a.	2259	...	...	...	2325	...	...	...	0019	0026	0210
Chesterfield .... d.	...	...	...	...	...	...	...	...	...	0048	...
Sheffield .... a.	...	...	...	...	...	...	...	...	...	0104	...

⑦ ❖	⑦Y	⑦	⑦	⑦	⑦	⑦	⑦	⑦	⑦	⑦	⑦	⑦	⑦	⑦	⑦
London St Pancras.. d.	...	0900	0930	1000	1030	1100	1130	1210	1237	1250	1310	1337	1355	1410	1440
Luton ✈ Parkway ..... d.	...	0928	|	1029	|	1129	1159	1231	1258	|	1331	1358	|	1431	|
Luton .... d.	...	|	0959	|	1102	1133	1203	1234	1300	|	1334	1400	|	|	1502
Bedford...................... d.	...	0950	1019	1054	1125	1154	1223	1249	1316	|	1349	1416	|	1446	1516
Wellingborough......... d.	...	1003	1031	1108	1136	1207	1235	1302	1328	|	1402	1428	|	1459	1528
Kettering.................. d.	...	1010	1038	1116	1143	1215	1242	1309	1340	1339	1409	1437	|	1506	1540
Corby .... a.	...	|	|	|	|	|	|	|	1350	|	|	1447	|	|	1550
Market Harborough ... d.	...	1020	1049	1127	1153	1225	1252	1319	...	1350	1419	...	1451	1516	...
Leicester................. d.	1020	1036	1105	1145	1210	1241	1309	1336	...	1408	1436	...	1509	1533	...
Loughborough........... d.	1030	1046	1115	1156	1220	1251	1319	1346	...	1419	1446	...	1520	1543	...
E. Midlands Parkway d.	1037	1053	1123	1205	1227	1259	1326	1353	...	1428	1453	...	1528	1550	...
Nottingham .... a.	|	1108	|	1216	|	1312	|	1407	...	|	1507	...	|	1605	...
Derby....................... a.	1054	...	1143**t**	...	1243**t**	...	1342**t**	...	...	1444	...	...	1545	...	...
Chesterfield .... d.	1114	...	1210	...	1312	...	1411	...	...	1509	...	...	1609	...	...
Sheffield .... a.	1128	...	1228	...	1328	...	1427	...	...	1529	...	...	1628	...	...

	⑦L	⑦	⑦	⑦	⑦	⑦	⑦	⑦	⑦	⑦	⑦	⑦	⑦	⑦L	⑦	⑦	⑦	⑦	⑦	⑦	⑦	⑦	⑦L	⑦	⑦	⑦	⑦
London St Pancras.. d.	1455	1510	1540	1555	1610	1635	1640	1705	1710	1735	1740	1805	1810	1835	1840	1905	1910	1935	1940	2000	2010	2035	2040	2110	2130	2230	2300
Luton ✈ Parkway ..... d.	|	1533	|	|	1631	|	|	|	1731	|	|	|	1831	|	|	|	1931	|	|	|	2031	|	|	2131	|	2251	2327
Luton .... d.	|	|	1602	|	|	|	1702	|	|	|	1802	|	|	|	1902	|	|	|	2002	|	|	|	2104	|	2152	|	|
Bedford...................... d.	|	1548	1616	|	1646	|	1716	|	1746	|	1816	|	1846	|	1916	|	1946	|	2016	|	2047	|	2120	2146	2206	2313	2351
Wellingborough......... d.	|	1602	1629	|	1659	|	1729	|	1758	|	1829	|	1858	|	1929	|	1958	|	2029	|	2058	|	2133	2159	2219	2326	0004
Kettering.................. d.	|	1611	1637	|	1706	|	1737	|	1806	|	1837	|	1905	|	1937	|	2005	|	2037	|	2106	|	2141	2206	2227	2333	0012
Corby .... a.	|	|	|	|	|	|	|	|	|	|	|	|	|	|	|	|	|	|	|	|	|	|	|	|	|	|	|
Market Harborough ... d.	1551	1622	|	1651	1716	|	1747	|	1815	|	1847	|	1915	|	1947	|	2015	|	2047	|	2116	|	2152	2216	2237	2343	0022
Leicester................. d.	1608	1638	1702	1709	1733	1744	1803	1811	1833	1841	1903	1910	1932	1945	2003	2022	2033	2041	2103	2110	2133	2141	2210	2233	2254	0004	0042
Loughborough........... d.	1619	1651	1712	|	1743	|	1813	|	1843	|	1913	|	1942	|	2013	|	2043	|	2113	2121	2143	2151	|	2247	2304	0014	0052
E. Midlands Parkway d.	1627	1659	1719	1725	1750	1800	1821	1825	1850	1855	1921	1925	1949	2001	2021	2039	2050	2055	2121	2129	2150	2159	2226	2258	2316	0026	0104
Nottingham .... a.	|	1714	|	|	1805	|	|	1836	1905	|	|	1936	2005	|	|	2051	2105	|	|	2145	2205	|	|	2311	|	0042	|
Derby....................... a.	1647	...	1737	1743	...	1814	1836	...	...	1908**t**	1937	...	...	2013	2037	...	...	2107	2136	...	...	2211	2240**t**	...	2335	...	0119
Chesterfield .... d.	1714	...	...	1809	...	1837	...	...	...	1934	...	...	...	2037	...	...	...	2129	...	...	...	...	2309	...	2355	...	...
Sheffield .... a.	1728	...	...	1825	...	1851	...	...	...	1950	...	...	...	2051	...	...	...	2143	...	...	...	...	2323	...	0008	...	...

B – To/from Lincoln (Table **186**).
C – To/from Melton Mowbray (see panel on page 137).
D – To/from London St. Pancras (Table **170**).
E – 🚌12 Derby - Corby - London St Pancras.
F – Via Melton Mowbray (see panel on page 137).
L – To/from Leeds (Table **171**).
R – From York (d. 1750) and Doncaster (d. 1813).
S – To Doncaster (a. 0953) and York (a. 1017).
V – From York (d. 1750) and Doncaster (d. 1813⑦, 1819⑥).

Y – To Doncaster (a. 1152) and York (a. 1215).
a – Departs 2033.
b – Departs 2146.
c – Departs 18–21 minutes later.
d – Departs 2142.
e – Arrives 1121.
f – Arrives Kettering 9 minutes after Corby.
g – Arrives 1800.
h – Also calls at Doncaster (d. 0557).

j – Arrives 1821.
k – Arrives 7–9 minutes earlier.
n – Arrives 0919.
p – On Ⓐ Chesterfield d. 0002, Nottingham a. 0040.
r – Departs 1715.
t – Departs 7–10 minutes later.
❖ – For additional Kettering - Corby services on ⑦, see next page.

	⚒	Ⓐ	⑥	Ⓐ	Ⓐ	⑥	⑥	Ⓐ	Ⓐ C	⑥	Ⓐ	⑥	⚒	⑥	Ⓐ	Ⓐ	⑥	Ⓐ	Ⓐ L h	⑥	⑥	Ⓐ	Ⓐ	Ⓐ	⑥	Ⓐ	⑥
Sheffield d.		...	...	...	...	...	0529	...	...	...	0530	...	...	...	...	0600	0629	...	0629	...	...	...	...	0649	...	...	...
Chesterfield d.		...	...	...	...	...	0541	...	...	...	0542	...	...	...	...	0613	0641	...	0640	...	...	...	...	0701	...	...	...
Derby d.		...	...	0500	0519	0521	0601	...	...	...	0604	...	...	0621	...	0633	0701	...	0705	...	0721	...	...	0722	...	...	...
Nottingham d.		...	...	|	|	|	|	0532	...	0605	|	0632	...	|	0630	|	|	0652	|	0705	|	0710	...	|	0730	0755	...
E. Midlands Parkway d.		...	...	0511	|	0535	|	0543	...	|	0617	0643	...	0635	0642	|	|	0704	|	|	0735	0725	...	0733	0743	0804	...
Loughborough d.		...	...	0518	|	0542	|	0552	...	0621	0626	|	...	0642	|	0653	|	|	0722	0721	0742	|	...	0741	|	|	...
Leicester d.		0445	0445	0529	0543	0553	0624	0604	...	0632	0639	0700	...	0653	0659	0706	0724	0719	0736	0732	0753	0742	...	0756	0801	0819	...
Market Harborough d.		|	|	0543	0558	0607	|	0620	...	0646	0654	0714	...	|	0713	|	|	0733	|	0746	|	0757	...	|	0815	|	...
Corby d.		|	|	|	|	|	|	|	0635	|	|	|	0706	|	|	|	|	|	|	|	|	|	0802	|	|	|	0816
Kettering d.		0505	0505	0554	0608	0617	|	0631	0645	0656	0706	|	0717	0726	0724	0730	|	0743	0759	0756	|	0809	0811	0817	|	|	0826
Wellingborough d.		0517	0517	0602	0616	0624	|	0640	0654	0703	0714	|	...	0734	0732	0738	|	0751	0807	0803	|	|	...	0825	|	|	0834
Bedford d.		0538	0544	|	0630	0638	|	|	0709	0717	|	|	...	0747	|	0755	|	|	|	0817	|	0829	...	|	|	|	0847
Luton d.		|	|	0625	|	0653	|	|	0724	|	|	|	...	0803	0757	|	|	0815	|	|	|	|	...	|	|	|	0903
Luton ✈ Parkway d.		0556	0601	|	|	|	|	0704	|	0732	0739	|	...	|	|	0811	|	|	|	0832	|	|	...	|	|	|	|
London St Pancras a.		0619	0628	0649	0708	0718	0729	0731	0748	0756	0807	0814	...	0827	0823	0839	0831	0842	0856	0856	0900	0906	...	0910	0914	0926	0926

	⚒	Ⓐ	⚒ B	⑥	Ⓐ	Ⓐ L	⑥ L	⚒	⚒	⚒	⚒	Ⓐ	⑥ L	⚒	⚒	⚒		⚒	⚒	⚒	⚒	⚒	⚒	⚒	⚒	⚒	⚒
Sheffield d.	0729	...	...	...	0746	0724	0737	...	0829	...	0849	...	0834	...	0929	...	...	0949	...	...	1029	...	1049	...	...	1129	...
Chesterfield d.	0741	...	...	...	0759	0737	0750	...	0841	...	0901	...	0847	...	0941	...	...	1001	...	...	1041	...	1101	...	...	1141	...
Derby d.	0801	0736	...	0821	0819	|	|	...	0901	...	0921	...	|	...	1001	...	...	1021	...	...	1101	...	1121	...	...	1201	...
Nottingham d.	|	|	0805	|	|	0832k	0832k	...	|	0905	|	0932	0932n	...	|	1005	...	|	1032	...	|	1105	|	1132	...	|	1205
E. Midlands Parkway d.	|	|	|	0835	0835	0843	0843	...	|	|	0935	0943	0943	...	|	|	...	1035	1043	...	|	|	1135	1143	...	|	|
Loughborough d.	|	0754	0821	0842	0842	|	|	...	|	0921	0942	|	|	...	|	1021	...	1042	|	...	|	1121	1142	|	...	|	1221
Leicester d.	0824	0805	0832	0853	0856	0900	0900	...	0924	0932	0953	1000	1000	...	1024	1032	...	1053	1100	...	1124	1132	1153	1200	...	1224	1232
Market Harborough d.	|	0819	0846	|	|	0914	0914	...	|	0946	|	1014	1014	...	|	1046	...	|	1114	...	|	1146	|	1214	...	|	1246
Corby d.	|	|	|	|	|	|	|	0916	|	|	|	|	|	1016	|	|	...	|	|	1116	|	|	|	|	1216	|	|
Kettering d.	|	0829	0856	|	|	|	|	0926	|	0956	|	|	|	1026	|	1056	...	|	|	1126	|	1156	|	|	1226	|	1256
Wellingborough d.	|	0842	0903	|	|	|	|	0934	|	1003	|	|	|	1034	|	1103	...	|	|	1134	|	1203	|	|	1234	|	1303
Bedford d.	|	0905	0917	|	|	|	|	0947	|	1017	|	|	|	1047	|	1117	...	|	|	1147	|	1217	|	|	1247	|	1317
Luton d.	|	0919	|	|	|	|	|	1003	|	|	|	|	|	1103	|	|	...	|	|	1203	|	|	|	|	1303	|	|
Luton ✈ Parkway d.	|	|	0932	|	|	|	|	|	|	1032	|	|	|	|	|	1132	...	|	|	|	|	1232	|	|	|	|	1332
London St Pancras a.	0933	0945	0956	0959	1006	1017	1014	1026	1030	1056	1100	1114	1114	1126	1130	1156	...	1201	1214	1226	1231	1256	1300	1314	1326	1331	1357

	⚒	⚒	⚒	⚒	⚒	⚒	⚒	⚒	⚒	⚒	⚒	⚒	⚒	⚒	⚒	⚒	⚒	⚒	⚒	⚒	⑥	Ⓐ	⑥	Ⓐ	⚒	⑥	Ⓐ
Sheffield d.	1149	...	...	1229	...	1249	...	...	1329	...	1349	...	...	1429	...	1449	...	...	1529	...	1549	1549	...	...	...	1629	1629
Chesterfield d.	1201	...	...	1241	...	1301	...	...	1341	...	1401	...	...	1441	...	1501	...	...	1541	...	1601	1601	...	...	...	1641	1641
Derby d.	1221	...	...	1301	...	1321	...	...	1401	...	1421	...	...	1501	...	1521	...	...	1601	...	1621	1621	...	...	...	1701	1701
Nottingham d.	|	1232	...	|	1305	|	1332	...	|	1405	|	1432	...	|	1505	|	1532	...	|	1605	|	|	1632	1630	...	|	|
E. Midlands Parkway d.	1235	1243	...	|	|	1335	1343	...	|	|	1435	1443	...	|	|	1535	1543	...	|	|	1635	1635	1643	1641	...	|	|
Loughborough d.	1242	|	...	|	1321	1342	|	...	|	1421	1442	|	...	|	1521	1542	|	...	|	1621	1642	1642	|	|	...	|	|
Leicester d.	1253	1300	...	1324	1332	1353	1400	...	1424	1432	1453	1500	...	1524	1532	1553	1600	...	1624	1632	1653	1653	1700	1658	...	1726	1724
Market Harborough d.	|	1314	...	|	1346	|	1414	...	|	1446	|	1514	...	|	1546	|	1614	...	|	1646	|	|	1714	1712	...	|	|
Corby d.	|	|	1316	|	|	|	|	1416	|	|	|	|	1516	|	|	|	|	1616	|	|	|	|	|	|	1716	|	|
Kettering d.	|	|	1326	|	1356	|	|	1426	|	1456	|	|	1526	|	1556	|	|	1626	|	1656	|	1714	|	|	1726	|	|
Wellingborough d.	|	|	1334	|	1403	|	|	1434	|	1503	|	|	1534	|	1603	|	|	1634	|	1703	|	|	|	|	1734	|	|
Bedford d.	|	|	1347	|	1417	|	|	1447	|	1517	|	|	1547	|	1617	|	|	1647	|	1717	|	|	|	|	1747	|	|
Luton d.	|	|	1403	|	|	|	|	1503	|	|	|	|	1603	|	|	|	|	1703	|	|	|	|	|	1749	1803	|	1811
Luton ✈ Parkway d.	|	|	|	|	1431	|	|	|	|	1532	|	|	|	|	1632	|	|	|	|	1732	|	|	|	|	|	|	|
London St Pancras a.	1400	1414	1427	1430	1456	1459	1514	1527	1531	1556	1559	1614	1627	1632	1656	1700	1715	1726	1730	1756	1800	1807	1814	1815	1826	1829	1836

	⚒	⑥	Ⓐ	⚒	Ⓐ E	⑥	⚒	⚒	Ⓐ	⑥		⚒	Ⓐ	⑥	⚒	⚒	Ⓐ	⑥	⑥ V	⚒	Ⓐ	⚒	⑥	⑥	Ⓐ	Ⓐ	Ⓐ
Sheffield d.	...	1649	1649	...	...	...	1729	...	1738	1749	...	...	...	...	1829	...	1849	...	1849	...	...	1929	...	...	...	...	...
Chesterfield d.	...	1701	1701	...	...	...	1741	...	1754	1801	...	...	...	...	1841	...	1901	...	1901	...	...	1941	...	...	...	...	...
Derby d.	...	1721	1721	...	1636	...	1801	...	1821	1821	...	...	...	...	1901	...	1921	...	1921	...	...	2001	...	...	...	...	...
Nottingham d.	1705	|	|	1732	|	...	|	1805	|	|	...	1832	...	...	|	1905	|	...	|	1932	...	|	...	2005	2002	...	2102
E. Midlands Parkway d.	|	1735	1735	1743	1648	...	|	|	1835	1835	...	1843	...	...	|	|	1935	...	1935	1943	...	|	...	2017	2015	...	2114
Loughborough d.	1721	1742	1742	|	|	...	|	1821	1842	1842	...	|	...	...	|	1921	1942	...	1942	|	...	|	...	2025	2022	...	2122
Leicester d.	1732	1753	1753	1800	|	...	1824	1832	1853	1853	...	1900	...	...	1924	1932	1953	...	1953	2000	...	2024	...	2036	2033	...	2133
Market Harborough d.	1746	|	|	1814	|	...	|	1846	|	|	...	1914	...	...	|	1946	|	...	|	2014	...	|	...	2049	2047	...	2147
Corby d.	|	|	|	|	1751	1816	|	|	|	|	...	|	1856	1916	|	|	|	1950	|	|	1953	|	2043	|	|	2051	|
Kettering d.	1756	|	1814	|	1823f	1826	|	1856	|	|	...	|	1926f	1926	|	1956	|	2026f	2014	|	2026f	|	2126f	2058	2057	2118f	2157
Wellingborough d.	1803	|	|	|	1834	1834	|	1903	|	|	...	|	1934	1934	|	2003	|	2034	|	|	2034	|	2134	2107	2104	2127	2204
Bedford d.	1817	|	|	|	1847	1847	|	1917	|	|	...	|	1947	1947	|	2017	|	2047	|	|	2047	|	2147	2121	2118	2143	2218
Luton d.	|	|	|	|	1903	1903	|	|	|	|	...	|	2003	2003	|	|	|	2103	|	|	2103	|	2203	|	|	2200	2235
Luton ✈ Parkway d.	1832	|	|	|	|	|	|	1932	|	|	...	|	|	|	|	2032	|	|	|	|	|	|	|	2136	2132	|	2239
London St Pancras a.	1856	1900	1903	1915	1926	1926	1933	1958	2002	2000	...	2016	2027	2027	2033	2056	2101	2126	2103	2116	2126	2134	2226	2159	2157	2225	2305

	⑥	⑥	Ⓐ	⑥	⑥	Ⓐ	⚒	Ⓐ	⑥	⑥	Ⓐ	⚒	⑦	⑦	⑦	⑦	⑦	⑦	⑦	⑦	⑦	⑦	⑦ L	⑦ L	⑦	⑦	⑦
Sheffield d.	2029	...	2049	...	...	...	2137	2202	2242	2320	2321	2337	⑦	...	...	...	...	0818	...	0925	...	1025	1035	1143	...	...	1249
Chesterfield d.	2040	...	2101	...	...	...	2155	2214	2256	2332	2345	2353p		...	...	...	...	0831	...	0938	...	1037	1048	1155	...	...	1301
Derby d.	2100	...	2121	...	...	...	|	2235	|	0006	0005	|		0650	...	0751	...	0851	...	0959	...	1057	|	1217	...	...	1322
Nottingham d.	|	...	|	2105	2132	2132	2234	▬	2328	...	...	0030p	✣	|	0729	|	0822	|	0920	|	1030	|	1139e	|	...	1249	|
E. Midlands Parkway d.	2113	...	2135	2117	|	|	*2323*	...	...	...	...	...		0702	0739	0805	0835	0905	0931	1013	1045	1111	1150	1234	...	1303	1336
Loughborough d.	2120	...	2142	2125	2147	2147	*2331*	...	...	...	...	...		|	|	0813	0843	0912	0940	1020	1053	1119	1159	1242	...	1312	1344
Leicester d.	2131	...	2153	2137	2158	2158	*2356*	...	...	...	...	...		0720	0755	0825	0855	0924	0954	1032	1108	1130	1213	1256	...	1326	1355
Market Harborough d.	...	...	|	2150	2212	2212	...	⚒	...	...	...	...		0738	0811	0841	0911	0940	1011	1045	1122	1143	1227	1310	...	1340	1408
Corby d.	...	2143	|	|	|	|	...	2243	...	...	...	...		|	|	|	|	|	|	|	|	|	|	|	1310	|	|
Kettering d.	...	2152	|	2158	2223	2223	...	2252	...	...	...	...		0749	0821	0851	0921	0950	1022	1055	1133	1153	1238	|	1320	1351	|
Wellingborough d.	...	...	|	2207	2230	2230	...	...	...	...	...	...		0801	0832	0902	0932	1002	1030	1102	1141	1201	1246	|	1329	1359	|
Bedford d.	...	...	|	2221	2243	2245	...	...	...	...	...	...		0815	0845	0915	0945	1015	1045	1116	1157	1215	1302	|	1341	1415	|
Luton d.	...	...	|	2236	2301	2302	...	...	...	...	...	...		0834	|	0935	|	1035	|	1136	|	1230	|	|	1357	|	|
Luton ✈ Parkway d.	...	...	|	2240	|	|	...	...	...	...	...	...		|	0907	|	1007	|	1106	|	1213	|	1318	|	|	1431	|
London St Pancras a.	...	...	2301	2315	2340	2338	...	...	...	...	...	...		0915	0945	1015	1048	1117	1148	1214	1241	1254	1344	1409	1421	1459	1504

	⑦	⑦	⑦	⑦	⑦	⑦	⑦	⑦	⑦ L	⑦	⑦	⑦	⑦	⑦	⑦	⑦	⑦	⑦	⑦	⑦	⑦ V	⑦	⑦	⑦	⑦	⑦	⑦
Sheffield d.	...	...	1343	...	...	1449	...	...	1529	1550	...	...	...	1649	...	...	...	1750	...	...	1847	...	1928	2026	...	2236	2330
Chesterfield d.	...	...	1356	...	...	1501	...	...	1542	1602	...	...	...	1700	...	...	...	1802	...	...	1900	...	1941	2039	...	2248	2344
Derby d.	...	...	1417	...	...	1522	...	...	1602	1626	...	...	1657	1723	...	...	1806	1826j	...	...	1919	...	2003	2101	...	2323	|
Nottingham d.	...	1349	|	...	1452	|	1543	1552	|	|	1645	1650	|	|	1745	1752	|	|	1845	1852	|	1951	|	|	2121	...	0023
E. Midlands Parkway d.	...	1403	1431	...	1504	1536	1553	1605	1616	1637	1655	1703	1711	1736	1755	1804	1820	1837	1855	1905	1934	2004	2018	2113	2131	...	...
Loughborough d.	...	1412	1439	...	1512	1543	|	1612	1625	|	|	1711	1719	|	|	1812	1828	|	1902	1912	1942	2011	2027	|	2139	...	...
Leicester d.	...	1426	1455	...	1524	1555	1612	1624	1639	1655	1710	1723	1731	1754	1814	1825	1840	1854	1914	1925	1955	2023	2041	2132	2154	...	...
Market Harborough d.	...	1440	1508	...	1537	|	|	1637	1653	|	|	1736	1744	|	|	1838	1853	|	1927	1938	2008	2036	2055	2146	2208	...	...
Corby d.	1410	|	|	1510	|	|	|	|	|	|	|	|	|	|	|	|	|	|	|	|	|	|	|	|	|	...	...
Kettering d.	1420	1451	|	1520	1547	|	|	1647	1703	|	|	1746	1755	|	|	1848	1905	|	1937	1948	2015	2046	2106	2157	2218	...	...
Wellingborough d.	1428	1459	|	1528	1554	|	|	1655	1712	|	|	1754	1802	|	|	1855	1912	|	1945	1955	2025	2053	2114	2205	2225	...	...
Bedford d.	1443	1515	|	1543	1609	|	|	1709	1728	|	|	1808	1817	|	|	1909	1928	|	1959	2009	2040	2109	2131	2221	2239	...	...
Luton d.	1457	|	|	1557	|	1642	|	|	1745	|	|	|	1831	|	|	|	1944	|	2015	|	2054	2123	2146	2237	2254	...	...
Luton ✈ Parkway d.	|	1531	|	|	1624	|	|	1725	|	|	|	1824	|	|	|	1924	|	|	|	2024	2058	|	|	|	|	...	...
London St Pancras a.	1521	1557	1605	1621	1648	1709	1723	1748	1810	1802	1817	1847	1855	1909	1925	1948	2007	2000	2039	2049	2121	2148	2213	2303	2324	...	...

✣ – **Kettering - Corby** and v.v. additional trains on ⑦. Journey time: 10 minutes.
From Kettering at 0955, 1055, 1155, 1250, 1650, 1750, 1855, 1950, 2050, 2155.
From Corby at 0930, 1025, 1125, 1220, 1620, 1720, 1820, 1920, 2020, 2125.

← FOR OTHER NOTES SEE PREVIOUS PAGE

CORBY - MELTON MOWBRAY - DERBY

km		Ⓐ	Ⓐ D			Ⓐ D	Ⓐ E	
0	**Corby** d.	0926	1916	...	**Derby** d.	...	1636	...
23	Oakham d.	0947	1936	...	East Mids Parkway d.	...	1648	...
43	**Melton Mowbray** d.	1000	1948	...	**Melton Mowbray** d.	0600	1714	...
81	East Mids Parkway d.	1031	...	...	Oakham d.	0612	1727	...
97	**Derby** a.	1045	...	...	**Corby** a.	0635	1751	...

NOTTINGHAM - SHEFFIELD - HUDDERSFIELD and LEEDS

2nd class NT

NOTTINGHAM - SHEFFIELD - LEEDS

km			Ⓐ	⚒	⚒	Ⓐ	⚒	Ⓐ	⚒	Ⓐ	⑥	⚒	⚒	⚒	⚒		⚒	⚒	⑥	Ⓐ	Ⓐ	⑥	⚒	⚒	⚒	⑥A
0	**Nottingham** . 170 206 d.	⚒	...	...	0520	...	...	0621	*0639*	0712	0711	*0746*	0817	*0847*	0917	and	1644	1717	*1744*	*1747*	1817	1817	*1847*	1917	...	2016
18	Langley Mill d.		...	...	|	...	...	0640	|	0731	0730	|	0836	|	0936	at	|	1736	*1800*	*1803*	1836	1836	|	1936	...	2033
29	Alfreton 206 d.		...	...	|	...	...	0648	*0700*	0739	0738	*0809*	0844	*0908*	0944	the	*1705*	1744	*1808*	*1811*	1844	1844	*1908*	1944	...	2041
45	Chesterfield.. 170 206 d.		...	...	0549	0626	...	0658	*0710*	0749	0748	*0820*	0855	*0920*	0955	same	*1715*	1755	*1818*	*1820*	1855	1855	*1920*	1956	...	2052
64	**Sheffield** 170 206 a.		...	...	0615	0646	...	0716	*0728*	0804	0811	*0837*	0914	*0937*	1014	minutes	*1737*	1814	*1834*	*1838*	1914	1914	*1937*	2014	...	2105
64	**Sheffield** 192 193 d.		0550	0606	...	0649	0706	0718	0751	0818	0818	0850	0918	0950	1018	past	1750	1818	1850	1850	1922	1916	1952	2018	2106	2126
70	Meadowhall.. 192 193 d.		0556	0612	...	0655	0712	0724	0757	0825	0825	0856	0924	0956	1024	each	1756	1824	1856	1856	1927	1922	1958	2024	2112	|
90	Barnsley d.		0610	0634	...	0712	0734	0741	0812	0842	0842	0912	0942	1012	1042	hour	1813	1842	1915	1915	1943	1943	2013	2043	2134	|
107	Wakefield Kirkgate d.		0628	0651	...	0728	0751	0758	0828	0858	0858	0928	0958	1028	1058	until	1828	1858	1932	1931	1959	1959	2028	2059	2152	2202e
130	**Leeds** a.		0649	0729	...	0751	0826	0819	0849	0919	0919	0949	1017	1049	1118	◇	1851	1926	1951	1952	2019	2018	2049	2120	2228	2218

	ⒶA	⚒A	Ⓐ	⑥	⚒	Ⓐ	ⒶA		⑦	⑦B	⑦	⑦	⑦	⑦	⑦	⑦	⑦	⑦	⑦A	⑦	⑦	⑦	⑦A	⑦	⑦	⑦	⑦A
Nottingham.. 170 206 d.	2033	...	...	2117	...	2114	2146	⑦	...	...	...	1008	1117	1217	1317	1417	1512	1617	...	1717	1817	1917	*1943*	...	*2015*	2133	...
Langley Mill d.	2050	...	...	2136	...	2141	2203		...	...	...	1032	1136	1236	1336	1436	1536	1636	...	1736	1836	1936	|	...	*2034*	2157	...
Alfreton 206 d.	2058	...	...	2144	...	2149	2211		...	...	...	1040	1144	1244	1344	1444	1544	1644	...	1744	1844	1944	*2004*	...	*2042*	2205	...
Chesterfield .. 170 206 d.	2109	...	...	2155	...	2201	2222		...	...	...	1051	1154	1254	1354	1454	1556	1654	...	1754	1854	1954	*2014*	...	*2052*	2216	...
Sheffield 170 206 a.	2123	...	...	2214	...	2220	2236		...	...	...	1110	1215	1315	1415	1515	1615	1715	...	1815	1915	2015	*2031*	...	*2117*	2236	...
Sheffield 192 193 d.	2126	2217	2206	...	2224	...	2253		0839	1017	1039	1117	1217	1317	1417	1517	1617	1717	1734	1817	1917	2017	2103	2039	2136	2239	2326
Meadowhall .. 192 193 d.	|	|	2212	...	2231	...	|		0845	1023	1045	1123	1223	1323	1423	1523	1623	1723	|	1823	1923	2023	|	2045	2142	2245	|
Barnsley d.	|	|	2234	...	|	...	|		0910	1037	1110	1137	1237	1337	1437	1537	1637	1737	|	1837	1937	2037	|	2110	|	2310	|
Wakefield Kirkgate d.	2201e	2247e	2255	...	2318e	...	2323e		0930	1056	1130	1156	1259	1356	1456	1556	1656	1756	1806e	1856	1956	2056	2129e	2130	2228e	2330	2352e
Leeds a.	2218	2305	2330	...	2340	...	2342		1005	1116	1205	1216	1318	1416	1516	1616	1716	1816	1822	1916	2016	2116	2145	2205	2247	0005	0007

		Ⓐ	⑥	Ⓐ	⚒	ⒶA	Ⓐ	⑥	Ⓐ	ⒶA	⑥A	⚒	⚒	⑥A	⚒	⚒	⚒		⚒	⚒	⚒	⑥	Ⓐ	⚒	⚒	⚒
Leeds d.	⚒	...	...	...	...	0525	...	...	0605	0634	0634	0638	0705	0738	0740	0805	0840	and	1706	1740	1806	1840	1840	1906	1945	2030
Wakefield Kirkgate d.		...	...	...	...	0538e	0604	...	0622	0647e	0646e	0709	0725	0751e	0758	0825	0858	at	1725	1758	1825	1858	1858	1925	2002	2049
Barnsley d.		...	...	*0523*	0551	|	0622	0622	0638	|	|	0727	0742	|	0814	0840	0914	the	1740	1814	1840	1914	1918	1940	2019	2105
Meadowhall .. 192 193 d.		...	...	*0545*	0613	|	0643	0643	0652	|	|	0749	0755	|	0830	0854	0930	same	1754	1829	1854	1932	1935	1954	2036	2122
Sheffield 192 193 a.		...	...	*0554*	0626	0620	0653	0652	0700	0722	0722	0758	0805	0822	0840	0902	0937	minutes	1803	1838	1903	1939	1942	2002	2045	2130
Sheffield 170 206 d.		0505	0554	0603	...	...	...	0703	0703	0724	0737	...	0808	0834	...	0905	...	past	1805	...	1905	...	...	2005	...	*2137*
Chesterfield .. 170 206 d.		0520	0619	0619	...	...	...	0719	0720	0737	0750	...	0824	0847	...	0922	...	each	1822	...	1922	...	...	2022	...	*2154*
Alfreton 206 d.		|	0629	0630	...	...	...	0729	0731	0748	0801	...	0834	0857	...	0932	...	hour	1832	...	1932	...	...	2033	...	*2205*
Langley Mill d.		|	0637	0637	...	...	...	0737	0739	0757	0809	...	0842	|	...	0940	...	until	1840	...	1940	...	...	2040	...	*2213*
Nottingham.. 170 206 a.		0607	0702	0701	...	...	...	0755	0757	0823	0825	...	0902	0919	...	1000	...	◇	1900	...	2000	...	...	2100	...	*2234*

	⚒	⚒	Ⓐ	⑥	Ⓐ	⑥		⑦	⑦	⑦	⑦A	⑦	⑦A	⑦	⑦		⑦	⑦	⑦A	⑦	⑦	⑦	⑦B	⑦	⑦	⑦	⑦
Leeds d.	2037	2137	*2148*	*2148*	2237	2244	⑦	...	0832	0905	0950	1002	1050	1105	1205	...	1305	1405	1434	1505	1605	1705	1803	1905	2022	2145	2217
Wakefield Kirkgate d.	2108	2208	*2206e*	*2204e*	2308	2300e		...	0903	0922	1003e	1019	1103e	1121	1222	...	1322	1422	1447e	1522	1622	1722	1822	1922	2052	2200e	2248
Barnsley d.	2126	2229	|	|	2331	|		...	0924	0941	|	1038	|	1141	1241	...	1341	1441	|	1541	1641	1741	1841	1941	2113	|	2312
Meadowhall .. 192 193 d.	2148	2250	*2254*	*2251*	2352	2344		...	0945	0957	|	1053	|	1156	1254	...	1356	1457	|	1557	1657	1758	1857	1954	2136	2245	2336
Sheffield 192 193 a.	2157	2301	*2304*	*2303*	0002	2353		...	0955	1004	1030	1102	1131	1203	1304	...	1405	1506	1517	1605	1705	1805	1904	2004	2143	2256	2343
Sheffield 170 206 d.	...	...	2337	2338	...	...		0905	...	1007	1035	1103	...	1207	1306	...	1407	1507	...	1607	1707	1807	1907	2007	...	*2330*	...
Chesterfield .. 170 206 d.	...	...	0002	2353	...	...		0921	...	1023	1048	1120	...	1223	1323	...	1423	1523	...	1623	1723	1823	1923	2023	...	*2344*	...
Alfreton 206 d.	...	...	|	|	...	...		0932	...	1033	|	1130	...	1233	1333	...	1433	1533	...	1633	1733	1833	1933	2033	...	*2355*	...
Langley Mill d.	...	...	|	|	...	...		0940	...	1041	|	1138	...	1241	1341	...	1441	1541	...	1641	1741	1841	1941	2041	...	*0002*	...
Nottingham.. 170 206 a.	...	...	0040	0030	...	...		1000	...	1101	1121	1158	...	1301	1401	...	1501	1601	...	1701	1801	1901	1959	2101	...	*0023*	...

SHEFFIELD - HUDDERSFIELD *'The Penistone Line'*

km			Ⓐ	⚒	⚒	and at	⚒	Ⓐ	⑥	⑥	Ⓐ	⚒	⚒	⚒	⚒	⚒		⑦	⑦	⑦	⑦	⑦	⑦	⑦	⑦
0	**Sheffield** 192 193 d.	⚒	0536	0636	0736	the same	1536	1633	1636	1737	1737	1836	1937	2042	2140	2241	⑦	0939	1149	1236	1339	1539	1654	1740	1939
6	Meadowhall... 192 193 d.		0542	0642	0742	minutes	1542	1639	1642	1743	1743	1842	1943	2048	2146	2247		0945	1155	1242	1345	1545	1700	1747	1945
26	Barnsley d.		0601	0701	0801	past each	1601	1700	1703	1804	1804	1903	2008	2108	2208	2308		1006	1216	1306	1406	1606	1715	1810	2006
38	Penistone d.		0618	0718	0818	hour until	1618	1717	1720	1821	1824	1920	2025	2125	2225	2325		1023	1233	1323	1423	1623	1732	1827	2023
59	**Huddersfield** a.		0648	0749	0849	◇	1649	1747	1750	1851	1855	1953	2055	2156	2256	2355		1054	1303	1353	1453	1654	1803	1858	2053

		⚒	⚒	⚒	⚒	and at	⚒	Ⓐ	⑥	Ⓐ	⚒	⚒	⚒	⚒			⑦	⑦	⑦	⑦	⑦	⑦	⑦	⑦
Huddersfield d.	⚒	0610	0710	0808	0913	the same	1713	1751	1813	1818	1918	2018	2118	2218	...	⑦	0919	1015	1119	1319	1415	1519	1723	1919
Penistone d.		0642	0742	0842	0944	minutes	1744	1831	1844	1849	1950	2052	2149	2249	...		0950	1046	1150	1350	1446	1550	1755	1950
Barnsley d.		0658	0758	0858	1001	past each	1801	1848	1901	1906	2007	2112	2206	2306	...		1012	1103	1207	1412	1503	1612	1812	2012
Meadowhall 192 193 d.		0722	0822	0921	1021	hour until	1822	1906	1920	1925	2028	2131	2225	2327	...		1035	1121	1230	1435	1521	1636	1836	2035
Sheffield 192 193 a.		0729	0829	0928	1029	◇	1831	1914	1930	1933	2036	2140	2236	2336	...		1044	1128	1238	1443	1528	1644	1844	2043

A – From / to London St. Pancras (Table **170**).
B – To / from Carlisle (Table **173**).
e – Wakefield Westgate.
◇ – Timings may vary by up to 2 minutes.

172 NOTTINGHAM - WORKSOP and MATLOCK

2nd class EM

NOTTINGHAM - WORKSOP *'The Robin Hood Line'*

km			⚒	⑥	Ⓐ	⑥	Ⓐ	⚒	⚒		⚒	⚒	⚒	⚒	⚒	⚒	⑥		⑦	⑦	⑦	⑦	⑦	⑦	⑦	⑦
0	**Nottingham** d.	⚒	0540	0605	0605	0703	0701	0826	0926	and	1726	1755	1855	1955	2055	2205	2305	⑦	0807	0942	1128	1328	1525	1653	1829	2025
28	Mansfield d.		0613	0638	0638	0740	0740	0900	0957	hourly	1803	1836	1929	2036	2136	2242	2343		0840	1016	1202	1401	1558	1726	1902	2058
50	**Worksop** a.		0649	0719	0723	0814	0818	0933	1033	until	1837	1908	2005	2109	2208	2314	...		...	...	...	...	...	...	...	...

		⚒	⚒	⚒	⚒	⚒		⚒	⚒	⚒	⚒	⚒	⚒	⚒	⚒			⑦	⑦	⑦	⑦	⑦	⑦	⑦	⑦
Worksop d.	⚒	0550	0656	0738	0838	0938	and	1538	1642	1746	1841	1922	2022	2122	2222	...	⑦	...	...	...	...	...	...	...	...
Mansfield d.		0621	0729	0810	0910	1010	hourly	1610	1714	1818	1913	1953	2053	2153	2253	...		0855	1033	1217	1415	1612	1739	1921	2110
Nottingham a.		0656	0805	0845	0943	1043	until	1643	1746	1852	1948	2030	2125	2226	2326	...		0931	1107	1251	1450	1646	1813	1955	2144

NOTTINGHAM - DERBY - MATLOCK

km			⚒	Ⓐ	⑥	⚒	⚒	⚒		⚒	⚒	Ⓐ	⑥		⑦	⑦	⑦	⑦	⑦	⑦	⑦	⑦	⑦
0	**Nottingham** 123 d.	⚒	...	0617	0620	0720	0820	0920		1920	2020	*2139*	*2139*	⑦	...	0926	1127	1323	1528	1623	1722	1922	2124
26	**Derby** 123 a.		...	0650	0650	0750	0850	0950	and	1950	2050	*2208*	*2208*		...	0954	1155	1351	1556	1651	1751	1950	2152
26	**Derby** d.		0542	0651	0652	0752	0852	0952	hourly	1952	2052	2215	2216		0756	0956	1156	1356	1558	1656	1756	1952	2155
34	Duffield ◧ d.		0549	0658	0659	0759	0859	0959	until	1959	2059	2222	2223		0803	1003	1204	1403	1605	1704	1803	1959	2202
46	Whatstandwell ◧ d.		0604	0713	0714	0814	0914	1014		2014	2114	2237	2239		0818	1018	1219	1418	1620	1719	1818	2014	2217
50	Cromford d.		0610	0719	0720	0820	0920	1020	★	2020	2120	2243	2245		0824	1024	1224	1424	1626	1724	1824	2020	2223
52	Matlock Bath ◧ d.		0612	0721	0722	0822	0922	1022		2022	2122	2245	2247		0826	1026	1227	1426	1628	1727	1826	2022	2225
53	**Matlock** ◧ a.		0615	0725	0726	0826	0926	1026		2026	2126	2249	2250		0830	1030	1230	1430	1632	1730	1830	2026	2229

		⚒	⚒	⚒	⚒	⚒		⚒	⑥	Ⓐ	⚒	⚒	⚒		⑦	⑦	⑦	⑦	⑦	⑦	⑦	⑦	⑦
Matlock ◧ d.	⚒	0620	0737	0837	0937	1037		1837	1937	1937	2037	2141	2254	⑦	0838	1038	1238	1441	1638	1742	1838	2038	2244
Matlock Bath ◧ d.		0622	0739	0839	0939	1039	and	1839	1939	1939	2039	2143	2256		0840	1040	1240	1443	1640	1744	1840	2040	2246
Cromford d.		0625	0742	0842	0942	1042	hourly	1842	1942	1942	2042	2146	2259		0843	1043	1243	1446	1643	1747	1843	2043	2249
Whatstandwell ◧ d.		0630	0747	0847	0947	1047	until	1847	1947	1947	2047	2151	2304		0848	1048	1248	1451	1648	1752	1848	2048	2254
Duffield ◧ d.		0646	0803	0903	1003	1103		1903	2003	2003	2103	2207	2321		0905	1105	1305	1507	1705	1809	1905	2105	2311
Derby d.		0655	0811	0911	1011	1111	★	1911	2011	2011	2111	2216	2328		0912	1112	1312	1515	1712	1816	1912	2112	2318
Derby 123 d.		*0708*	0813	0913	1013	1113		1913	2013	2016	2114	*2259*	2330		0914	1114	1314	1516	1714	1818	1914	2114	...
Nottingham 123 a.		*0738*	0846	0942	1041	1141		1941	2043	2043	2141	*2327*	0002		0941	1141	1341	1543	1744	1845	1944	2141	...

★ – Timings may vary by up to 2 minutes.

◧ – Visitor attractions near these stations:
Duffield: Ecclesbourne Valley Railway (shares National Rail station). ✆ 01629 823076.
Whatstandwell: Crich National Tramway Museum (1.6 km walk). ✆ 01773 854321.
Matlock Bath: Heights of Abraham (short walk to cable car). ✆ 01629 582365.
Matlock: Peak Rail (shares National Rail station). ✆ 01629 580381.

NT 2nd class — LEEDS - SETTLE - CARLISLE — 173

km			Ⓐ		⑥	⚒	⑦		⚒	⚒	⑦C		⚒	⑦		⚒	⑦	⑥	Ⓐ	⚒		⚒A		⑦A
	London Kings Cross **180** ....d.	...	...	...	...	...	...	...	...	...	...	...	...	...	...	...	...	...	...	...	...	1803	...	1835f
0	**Leeds** ..... **174 176** d.	...	0529	...	0619	0849	0900	...	0947	1049	1120	...	1249	1357	...	1449	1741	1750	1806	1919	...	2039	...	2058
27	Keighley ..... **174 176** d.	...	0556	...	0642	0912	0929	...	1012	1112	1142	...	1312	1421	...	1512	1802	1813	1829	1942	...	2058s	...	2117s
42	Skipton ..... **174 176** d.	...	0615	...	0656	0926	0948	...	1026	1126	1155	...	1326	1435	...	1526	1815	1835	1846	2000	...	2113	...	2132
58	Hellifield ..... **174 191** d.	...	0627	...	0708	0940	1002	...	|	1137	|	...	1340	1449	...	1537	1828	1849	1900	2015	...	...	...	...
66	**Settle** ..... d.	...	0636	...	0715	0950	1011	...	1044	1146	1214	...	1348	1458	...	1545	1835	1857	1908	2024	...	...	...	...
76	Horton in Ribblesdale ..... d.	...	|	...	0724	0958	1020	...	|	1154	|	...	1357	1507	...	1553	1844	1906	1917	2032	...	...	...	...
84	Ribblehead ..... d.	...	0651	...	0732	1006	1028	...	|	1202	|	...	1405	1515	...	1601	1851	1914	1925	2042	...	...	...	...
93	Dent ..... d.	...	|	...	0741	1016	1038	...	|	1212	|	...	1414	1525	...	1611	1901	1923	1934	...	...	...	...	...
99	Garsdale ..... d.	...	0706	...	0747	1021	1043	...	|	1217	|	...	1420	1530	...	1616	1907	1929	1940	...	...	...	...	...
115	Kirkby Stephen ..... d.	...	0718	...	0759	1034	1056	...	1122	1230	1251	...	1432	1543	...	1629	1919	1941	1952	...	...	...	...	...
132	Appleby ..... d.	...	0732	...	0812	1047	1110	...	1136	1243	1305	...	1445	1556	...	1641	1931	1954	2005	...	...	...	...	...
149	Langwathby ..... d.	...	0746	...	0826	1101	1124	...	|	1257	|	...	1459	1610	...	1655	1945	2008	2019	...	...	...	...	...
166	Armathwaite ..... d.	...	0759	...	0839	1115	1138	...	|	1311	|	...	1512	1624	...	1709	1959	2021	2032	...	...	...	...	...
182	**Carlisle** ..... a.	...	0817	...	0858	1134	1155	...	1217	1329	1347	...	1530t	1643	...	1728	2014	2040	2052	...	...	...	...	...

	⑥A	ⒶA	⑥	Ⓐ	⑥	Ⓐ	⑦	⑥	⑥	Ⓐ	⑦	Ⓐ		⑥	Ⓐ	⑦D	⑥	⚒	⑦		⑥	Ⓐ	Ⓐ	⑥
Carlisle ..... d.	...	...	...	0550	0752	0853	0925	0924	1148	1155	1259	1404	...	1421	1506	1520	1547	1615	1723	...	1807	1814	...	...
Armathwaite ..... d.	...	...	...	0604	0806	0907	0939	0938	1203	1209	1313	1418	...	1435	|	|	|	1631	1737	...	1821	1828	...	...
Langwathby ..... d.	...	...	...	0618	0819	0920	0953	0951	1217	1222	1327	1431	...	1448	|	|	|	1645	1751	...	1834	1841	...	...
Appleby ..... d.	...	...	...	0632	0834	0935	1007	1006	1232	1236	1341	1447	...	1504	1543	1557	1626	1701	1806	...	1849	1856	...	...
Kirkby Stephen ..... d.	...	...	...	0646	0847	0948	1021	1019	1246	1250	1355	1500	...	1517	1556	1610	1639	1714	1820	...	1902	1909	...	...
Garsdale ..... d.	...	...	...	0659	0900	1002	1034	1033	1259	1302	1408	1513	...	1530	|	|	|	1727	1833	...	1915	1922	...	...
Dent ..... d.	...	...	...	|	0905	1007	1040	1038	1304	1308	1414	1518	...	1535	|	|	|	1732	1839	...	1920	1927	...	...
Ribblehead ..... d.	...	...	0714	0714	0915	1017	1049	1047	1314	1317	1423	1529	...	1545	|	|	|	1742	1848	...	1930	1937	2100	2100
Horton in Ribblesdale ..... d.	...	...	0720	0720	0921	1024	1056	1054	1320	1324	1430	1536	...	1551	|	|	|	1748	1855	...	1936	1943	2106	2106
Settle ..... d.	...	...	0728	0728	0929	1032	1104	1102	1328	1332	1438	1545	...	1559	1634	1646	1716	1757	1904	...	1944	1951	2114	2114
Hellifield ..... **191** d.	...	...	0737	0737	0937	1039	1113	1109	1337	1339	1447	1553	...	1607	|	|	|	1806	1812	...	1952	1959	2123	2123
Skipton ..... **174 176** a.	0655	0655	0753	0753	0952	1054	1129	1124	1355	1356	1504	1608	...	1622	1654	1707	1738	1823	1927	...	2007	2014	2138d	2140
Keighley ..... **174 176** a.	0709u	0707u	0808	0807	1008	1107	1140	1137	1407	1407	1516	1622	...	1637	1707	1720	1751	1837	1938	...	2018	2025	2202	*2203*
Leeds ..... **174 176** a.	0733	0731	0837	0838	1035	1136	1205	1207	1436	1437	1545	1653	...	1707	1738	1746	1817	1907	2007	...	2045	2050	2234	*2234*
London Kings Cross **180** ....a.	0951	0956	...	...	...	...	...	...	...	...	...	...	...	...	...	...	...	...	...	...	...	...	...	...

A – (12) and 🍷 London Kings Cross - Skipton and v.v. (Table **180**).
C – From Sheffield (Table **171**).
D – To Nottingham (Table **171**).
d – Departs 2146
f – Departs 1815 Feb. 18 - Mar. 25.
s – Calls to set down only.
t – On ⑥ arrives 1527.
u – Calls to pick up only.

NT 2nd class — LEEDS - LANCASTER - HEYSHAM — 174

km	km		Ⓐ	⑥		⑥	Ⓐ		⑦	Ⓐ		⑥	⑦		Ⓐ	⑥		⑦	⑥		Ⓐ	⑦		
0	0	**Leeds** ..... **173 176** d.	...	0554	...	0819	0818	...	0840	1017	...	1019	1059	...	1316	1350	...	1459	1646	...	1645	1720	...	...
27	27	Keighley ..... **173 176** d.	...	0621	...	0843	0841	...	0907	1043	...	1042	1123	...	1340	1413	...	1522	1710	...	1709	1747	...	...
42	42	Skipton ..... **173 176** d.	0541	0638	...	0900	0855	...	0926	1100	...	1100	1140	...	1401	1433	...	1538	1725	...	1725	1803	...	...
58	58	Hellifield ..... **173** d.	0556	0652	...	0914	0910	...	0940	1114	...	1114	1154	...	1415	1448	...	1552	1740	...	1739	1818	...	...
66	66	Giggleswick ..... d.	0607	0703	...	0925	0920	...	0952	1124	...	1125	1204	...	1425	1459	...	1602	1750	...	1750	1828	...	...
82	82	Bentham ..... d.	0621	0717	...	0939	0934	...	1006	1139	...	1139	1218	...	1440	1513	...	1617	1805	...	1804	1842	...	...
103	103	Carnforth ..... d.	0643	0739	...	1002	0956	...	1029	1202	...	1202	1242	...	1502	1536	...	1638	1826	...	1827	1904	...	...
113		**Lancaster** ..... a.	0652	0750	...	1013	1008	...	1038	1211	...	1211	1252	...	1516	1545	...	1647	1838	...	1838	1912	...	...
120	112	Morecambe ..... a.	*0736*	*0838*	...	1031	1032	...	1055	1243	...	1236	1312	...	1535	1602	...	1714	1858	...	1901	1935	...	...
127	119	**Heysham** Port ..... a.	...	...	...	...	...	...	...	1301	...	1254	...	...	...	...	...	...	...	...	...	...	...	...

		Ⓐ	⑥		⑥	Ⓐ		⑦	⑥		Ⓐ	⑦		Ⓐ	⑥		⑦	Ⓐ		⑥	⑦		
Heysham Port ..... d.	...	...	...	...	...	...	...	...	1315	...	1317	...	...	...	...	...	...	...	...	...	...	...	...
Morecambe ..... d.	...	*0610*	*0736*	...	1034	1034	...	1222	1331	...	1333	1446d	...	1619d	1616	...	1723	1908	...	1909	1946	...	...
Lancaster ..... d.	...	0707	0823	...	1049	1049	...	1248	1348	...	1349	1429d	...	1605d	1640	...	1737	1924	...	1925	2002	...	...
Carnforth ..... d.	...	0718	0833	...	1107	1107	...	1258	1358	...	1359	1500	...	1632	1650	...	1754	1934	...	1935	2012	...	...
Bentham ..... d.	...	0737	0852	...	1126	1126	...	1317	1418	...	1418	1520	...	1652	1709	...	1813	1953	...	1954	2032	...	...
Giggleswick ..... d.	...	0752	0907	...	1142	1142	...	1332	1433	...	1434	1535	...	1708	1725	...	1832	2009	...	2010	2047	...	...
Hellifield ..... **173** d.	...	0803	0919	...	1153	1153	...	1344	1446	...	1444	1546	...	1720	1736	...	1842	2020	...	2020	2058	...	...
Skipton ..... **173 176** a.	...	0821	0936	...	1210	1210	...	1401	1503	...	1503	1603	...	1737	1753	...	1859	2038	...	2037	2115	...	...
Keighley ..... **173 176** a.	...	0837	0951	...	1222	1223	...	1416	1520	...	1520	1617	...	1750	1807	...	1912	2050	...	2048	2126	...	...
Leeds ..... **173 176** a.	...	0905	1020	...	1250	1249	...	1444	1548	...	1547	1646	...	1815	1835	...	1944	2115	...	2116	2154	...	...

d – Calls at Lancaster, then Morecambe.

NT 2nd class — LEEDS - HARROGATE - YORK — 175

km		⚒	Ⓐ	⑥	Ⓐ	⑥	⑥	Ⓐ	Ⓐa	⑥	Ⓐ	⑥	Ⓐ	⚒a	⚒	⚒a	⚒	and at	⚒	⚒a	⚒	⚒a	Ⓐ	⑥	⚒a	⚒
0	**Leeds** .... **124 188** d.		0609	0610	0631	0636	0713	0714	0736	0741	0743	0755	0801	0814	0829	0844	0859	the same	1529	1544	1559	1616	1629	1629	1643	1659
29	**Harrogate** ..... d.		0646	0647	0711	0713	0749	0751	0804	0818	0820	0832	0838	0843	0906	0914	0936	minutes	1606	1612	1636	1644	1707	1706	1715	1737
36	Knaresborough .... d.		0654	0657	0721	0723	0759	0759	...	0826	0829	0842	0848	...	0915	...	0947	past each	1615	...	1647	...	1715	1714	...	1746
62	**York** ...... **124 188** a.		0725	0726	0750	0750	0827	0832	...	0859	0858	...	...	...	0946	...	...	hour until	1645	...	...	...	1745	1744	...	...

	⚒	⚒	Ⓐ	⚒	⑥a	Ⓐa	⚒		⑥a	Ⓐa	Ⓐ	⚒	⚒	⑥	Ⓐ	⑦	⑦	⑦	⑦	⑦	⑦	and at	⑦	⑦	⑦	⑦
Leeds ..... **124 188** d.	1713	1729	1743	1759	1813	1817	1829	...	1845	1849	1859	1930	2029	2120	2129		0905	0935	1005	1036	1103	the same	1936	2005	2105	2131
Harrogate ..... d.	1750	1806	1820	1836	1844	1849	1907	...	1914	1916	1936	2007	2106	2157	2206		0942	1012	1042	1213	1140	minutes	2013	2042	2142	2208
Knaresborough .... d.	1801	1814	1837t	1847	...	...	1916	...	...	...	1947	2016	2115	2208	2216		0953	1023	1052	1224	1150	past each	2024	2052	2152	2219
York ..... **124 188** a.	...	1846	1904	...	...	...	1945	...	...	...	...	2045	2145	...	...		1020	...	1120	...	1225	hour until	...	2120	2220	...

	⚒	⑥	Ⓐ	Ⓐa	⑥	Ⓐ	Ⓐ	⑥	Ⓐ	Ⓐ	⑥	⚒a	⑥	Ⓐ	⑥	Ⓐ	Ⓐa	⚒	⚒a	⚒	⚒a	and at	⚒a	⚒	⚒a	⚒
York ..... **124 188** d.		...	...	...	0652	0649	...	...	...	0754	0756	...	...	...	0843	0847	...	0911	...	...	...	the same	...	1511	...	...
Knaresborough ... d.		0647	0657	...	0720b	0716	0742	0750	0757	0819	0821	...	0850	0855	0908	0911	...	0936	...	1005	...	minutes	...	1536	...	1605
Harrogate ..... d.		0656	0707	0720	0729	0740s	0751	0759	0806	0829	0830	0851	0859	0904	0918	0921	0932	0945	1002	1014	1032	past each	1530	1545	1600	1614
Leeds ..... **124 188** a.		0733	0746	0748	0806	0816	0830	0836	0840	0908	0907	0922	0936	0937	0955	0957	1004	1022	1031	1052	1101	hour until	1604	1622	1633	1652

	⚒	⚒a	⚒	⚒	⚒	⑥	Ⓐ	Ⓐ	⑥	Ⓐ	⚒	⚒	⚒	⑥	Ⓐ	⑦	⑦	⑦	⑦	⑦	⑦	⑦	and at	⑦	⑦	⑦
York ..... **124 188** d.	1611	...	...	1704	1727	...	...	1805	1812	...	1913	2011	2112	2157	2211		...	1045	...	1147	...	1244	the same	...	2044	2146
Knaresborough ... d.	1636	...	1706	1734	1756	1808	1810	1834	1837	1906	1938	2036	2137	2222	2237		1042	1112	1142	1212	1242	1311	minutes	2042	2109	2211
Harrogate ..... d.	1645	1702	1715	1744	1805	1817	1824t	1843	1846	1915	1947	2045	2146	2236	2248		1051	1122	1151	1222	1251	1321	past each	2051	2119	2221
Leeds ..... **124 188** a.	1722	1735c	1752	1822	1843	1854	1901	1924	1923	1952	2024	2123	2223	2313	2326		1128	1159	1228	1259	1328	1359	hour until	2128	2156	2258

Additional trains	ⒶA	⑥A	⑦A	⑦	Ⓐ	⑥	⑥	⑦	Ⓐ
Leeds ..... d.	1959	2059	2031	2226	2238	2233	2322	2323	2332
Harrogate .... a.	2023	2123	2055	2305	2317	2311	0001	0002	0012

Additional trains	Ⓐ	⑥	Ⓐ	Ⓐ	ⒶA	⑥A	Ⓐ	⑦	⑦	⑦A	⚒a	⚒a	⑥a	Ⓐa	Ⓐa	⑦
Harrogate .... d.	0602	0605	0625	0659	0734	0735	0815	0922	1022	1707	1731	1900	1924	1928	2018	2312
Leeds ..... a.	0640	0643	0701	0734	0803	0807	0852	0959	1059	1733	1804	1934	1952	2001	2046	2350

A – (12) and 🍷 Harrogate - Leeds - London Kings Cross and v.v. (Table **180**).
a – From Mar. 26.
b – Arrives 0716.
c – Arrives 1730 on ⑥.
r – Arrives 1031.
s – Arrives 0726.
t – Arrives 6 – 8 minutes earlier.

NT 2nd class — WEST YORKSHIRE LOCAL SERVICES — 176

BRADFORD FORSTER SQUARE - SKIPTON

Journey: ± 38 minutes *30 km*

From Bradford Forster Square: Trains call at **Keighley** ± 22 minutes later.

Ⓐ: 0603, 0638, 0715, 0741, 0811, 0841, 0911 and every 30 minutes until 1541, 1612, 1638, 1711, 1738, 1816, 1841, 1908, 1936, 2009, 2109, 2209, 2309.

⑥: 0609, 0709, 0811, 0842, 0911 and every 30 minutes until 1541, 1612, 1638, 1711, 1738, 1811, 1841, 1908, 1936, 2009, 2112, 2202, 2309.

⑦: 0948, 1048, 1148, 1248, 1348, 1448, 1548, 1648, 1748, 1848, 1948, 2048, 2148, 2248.

From Skipton: Trains call at **Keighley** ± 14 minutes later.

Ⓐ: 0556, 0626, 0700, 0724, 0800, 0831, 0900 and every 30 minutes until 1330, 1402, 1430, 1458, 1530, 1558, 1630, 1700, 1724, 1800, 1830, 1900, 1931, 1954, 2054, 2154.

⑥: 0600, 0704, 0730, 0800, 0831, 0900 and every 30 minutes until 1330, 1401, 1430, 1458, 1530, 1600, 1630, 1700, 1728, 1800, 1830, 1900, 1930, 1954, 2057, 2155.

⑦: 0842, 0942, 1042, 1142, 1242, 1342, 1442, 1542, 1645, 1742, 1842, 1942, 2038, 2140.

Table continues on next page ▶ ▶ ▶

Stopping trains. For faster trains see Table 180.   **LEEDS - DONCASTER**   Journey: ± 50 minutes   48 km

From Leeds:
Ⓐ: 0620, 0721, 0821 and hourly until 1621, 1657, 1721, 1821, 1921, 2022, 2121, 2240.
Ⓖ: 0621, 0721, 0821 and hourly until 1921, 2022, 2121, 2219.
Ⓦ: 1021, 1221, 1421, 1621, 1821, 2021, 2121.

From Doncaster:
Ⓐ: 0626, 0708, 0726, 0756, 0826 and hourly until 1826, 1922, 2026, 2127, 2227.
Ⓖ: 0626, 0726, 0827, 0926 and hourly until 1626, 1727, 1826, 1922, 2026, 2122, 2226.
Ⓦ: 0912, 1112, 1312, 1512, 1712, 1927, 2152.

See also Tables 173/174   **LEEDS - SKIPTON**   Journey: ± 45 minutes   42 km

From Leeds: Trains call at **Keighley** ± 24 minutes later.
Ⓐ: 0529, 0616, 0657, 0725, 0749, 0825, 0855, 0926, 0956 and every 30 minutes until 1726, 1740, 1756, 1826, 1856, 1926, 1956, 2022, 2055, 2126, 2156, 2226, 2256, 2319.
Ⓖ: 0554, 0650, 0750, 0825, 0855, 0926, 0956 and every 30 minutes until 1956, 2026, 2101, 2126, 2204, 2226, 2256, 2319.
Ⓦ: 0840, 0900, 1016, 1126, 1216 and hourly until 2116, 2220, 2320.

From Skipton: Trains call at **Keighley** ± 13 minutes later.
Ⓐ: 0545, 0614, 0640, 0706, 0716, 0730, 0745, 0813, 0837, 0917, 0947 and every 30 minutes until 1617, 1647, 1715, 1747, 1817, 1847, 1915, 1947, 2022, 2045, 2117, 2217.
Ⓖ: 0545, 0644, 0745, 0816, 0847, 0917, 0947, and every 30 minutes until 1917, 1947, 2022, 2050, 2117, 2149, 2217.
Ⓦ: 0832, 0912, 1012 and hourly until 1612, 1714, 1812, 1912, 2012, 2122, 2212, 2312.

For Leeds - Bradford Interchange see Table 190   **LEEDS - BRADFORD FORSTER SQUARE**   Journey: ± 21 minutes   22 km

From Leeds:
Ⓐ: 0645, 0739, 0810, 0832, 0841, 0910, 0941, 1012, 1040, and every 30 minutes until 1540, 1606, 1638, 1709, 1736, 1810, 1837, 1908, 2101.
Ⓖ: 0710, 0810, 0841, 0910, 0939, 1010, 1040, and every 30 minutes until 1540, 1607, 1638, 1708, 1736, 1809, 1837, 1908, 2158.
Ⓦ: 0831, 0941 and hourly until 1641, 1745, 1841, 1942, 2041, 2141, 2241.

From Bradford Forster Square:
Ⓐ: 0558, 0630, 0654, 0757, 0826, 0902, 0930, 1000 and every 30 minutes until 1600, 1630, 1701, 1730, 1800, 1830, 1900, 1930.
Ⓖ: 0600, 0630, 0658, 0758, 0826, 0901, 0930, 1000 and every 30 minutes until 1600, 1630, 1701, 1730, 1800, 1831, 1900, 1930.
Ⓦ: 0913, 1013, 1113, 1213, 1312, 1413, 1513, 1613, 1713, 1814, 1913, 2013, 2113, 2213, 2313.

LEEDS - ILKLEY   Journey: ± 30 minutes   26 km

From Leeds:
Ⓐ: 0600, 0634, 0704, 0729, 0733, 0758, 0835, 0902 and every 30 minutes until 1602, 1632, 1702, 1716, 1732, 1746, 1802, 1832, 1902, 1933, 2007, 2107, 2207, 2315.
Ⓖ: 0602, 0702, 0758, 0832, 0902, 0932, 1004, 1032 and every 30 minutes until 1832, 1903, 1933, 2007, 2107, 2208, 2315.
Ⓦ: 0912 and hourly until 2112, 2213, 2316.

From Ilkley:
Ⓐ: 0602, 0633, 0710, 0737, 0756, 0805, 0816, 0838, 0910, 0938 and at the same minutes past each hour until 1438, 1510, 1536, 1612, 1638, 1712, 1743, 1804, 1812, 1842, 1910, 1938, 2028, 2118, 2218, 2318.
Ⓖ: 0610, 0710, 0810, 0838, 0910, 0940, 1010, 1038 and at the same minutes past each hour until 1538, 1612, 1638, 1712, 1738, 1812, 1842, 1910, 1938, 2028, 2118, 2224, 2318.
Ⓦ: 0832, 0921 and hourly until 2021, 2120, 2221, 2321.

HUDDERSFIELD - WAKEFIELD WESTGATE   Journey: ± 38 minutes   25 km

From Huddersfield: Trains call at **Wakefield Kirkgate** ± 30 minutes later.
Ⓐ: 0531, 0631, 0735, 0831, 0931 and hourly until 1931, 2031, 2135.
Ⓖ: 0640, 0735, 0831, 0931 and hourly until 1931, 2031, 2135.

From Wakefield Westgate: Trains call at **Wakefield Kirkgate** ± 5 minutes later.
Ⓐ: 0643, 0744, 0844, and hourly until 1844, 1946, 2050, 2142, 2248.
Ⓖ: 0744, 0844, 0944, and hourly until 1844, 1944, 2050, 2144, 2248.

BRADFORD FORSTER SQUARE - ILKLEY   Journey: ± 31 minutes   22 km

From Bradford Forster Square:
Ⓐ: 0615, 0642, 0711, 0745, 0816, 0846 and every 30 minutes until 1246, 1315, 1346, 1416, 1446, 1516, 1546, 1616, 1643, 1716, 1748, 1811, 1846, 1941, 2038, 2140, 2240, 2326.
Ⓖ: 0615, 0716, 0816, 0846 and every 30 minutes until 1716, 1743, 1816, 1846, 1946, 2038, 2140, 2240, 2320.
Ⓦ: 0938, 1038, 1138 and hourly until 2138, 2238.

From Ilkley:
Ⓐ: 0617, 0652, 0720, 0748, 0824, 0852, 0921, 0951 and every 30 minutes until 1651, 1720, 1751, 1821, 1851, 1921, 2009, 2043, 2143, 2243.
Ⓖ: 0621, 0721, 0821, 0852, 0921, 0951 and every 30 minutes until 1851, 1921, 2009, 2048, 2143, 2243.
Ⓦ: 0854, 0953, 1053 and hourly until 2053, 2153.

---

177   **HULL - BRIDLINGTON - SCARBOROUGH**   2nd class   NT

km			✕	✕	✕Ⓐ		✕Ⓐ	✕	⑥Ⓐ		ⓐⒶ	✕	ⓐⒶ	⑥Ⓐ			⑦	⑦Ⓐ	⑦Ⓐ	⑦Ⓐ		⑦Ⓐ	⑦Ⓐ	⑦Ⓐ
0	Hull .... △ d.	⚒	0653	0814	0947	1114	...	1314	1444	1614	...	1618	1738	1915	1922	...	⑦	0925	1025	1205	1405	...	1605	1800	1859
13	Beverley..................... △ d.		0707	0828	1001	1128	...	1328	1458	1628	...	1632	1752	1929	1936	...		0939	1039	1219	1419	...	1619	1814	1913
31	Driffield .... △ d.		0724	0842	1015	1140	...	1340	1512	1643	...	1647	1809	1943	1951	...		0956	1054	1234	1434	...	1634	1826	1928
50	Bridlington .... △ a.		0739	0857	1030	1154	...	1354	1527	1658	...	1702	1825	1958	2006	...		1011	1109	1249	1449	...	1649	1839	1946
50	Bridlington .... d.		0741	0900	1038	1206	...	1406	1535	1704	...	1704	1835	2003	2019	...		1014	1111	1255	1455	...	1655	1844	...
71	Filey............................ d.		0803	0922	1100	1228	...	1428	1557	1726	...	1726	1857	2025	2041	...		1036	1133	1317	1517	...	1717	1906	...
87	Scarborough .... a.		0821	0940	1118	1246	...	1446	1615	1744	...	1744	1915	2043	2059	...		1054	1151	1335	1535	...	1735	1924	...

		✕B	✕	✕	✕Ⓐ		✕Ⓐ	✕B	✕Ⓐ		✕		⑥	Ⓐ		⑦Ⓐ	⑦Ⓐ	⑦Ⓐ	⑦Ⓐ	⑦Ⓐ	⑦Ⓐ	⑦Ⓐ	⑦
Scarborough .... d.	⚒	0650	0902	1000	1128	...	1328	1457	1625	...	1757	...	1940	2004	⑦	...	1111	1206	1406	1606	...	1806	1937
Filey .... d.		0705	0917	1015	1143	...	1343	1512	1640	...	1812	...	1955	2019		...	1126	1221	1421	1621	...	1821	1952
Bridlington .... a.		0727	0939	1037	1205	...	1405	1534	1702	...	1834	...	2017	2041		...	1148	1243	1443	1643	...	1843	2014
Bridlington .... △ d.		0730	0941	1041	1211	...	1411	1536	1705	...	1841	...	2023	2044		0951	1206	1246	1446	1646	1746	1856	2016
Driffield .... △ d.		0747	0957	1057	1224	...	1424	1552	1719	...	1857	...	2039	2100		1007	1206	1259	1459	1659	1759	1912	2029
Beverley .... △ d.		0806	1012	1112	1237	...	1437	1607	1731	...	1912	...	2054	2115		1022	1221	1312	1512	1712	1812	1929	2042
Hull .... △ a.		0822	1028	1128	1253	...	1454	1623	1748	...	1930	...	2110	2131		1038	1237	1328	1528	1728	1828	1945	2058

A – From/to Sheffield (Table 192).   B – From/to Doncaster (Table 192).
△ – All trains Hull - Bridlington and v.v.:
    From Hull on ✕ at 0556, 0620, 0653, 0714, 0752, 0814, 0916 A, 0947, 1013 A, 1044, 1114 A, 1144, 1214 A, 1244, 1314 A, 1344, 1412 A, 1444, 1514 A, 1544, 1614 ⑥A, 1618 ⓐⒶ, 1644, 1714 A, 1738, 1814 A, 1915 ⓐⒶ, 1922 ⑥A, 2014 A, 2147 A; on ⑦ at 0900, 0925, 1025 A, 1125 B, 1205 A, 1255, 1405 A, 1500 A, 1605 A, 1655 A, 1715, 1800 A, 1859 A.
    From Bridlington on ✕ at 0644, 0712 A, 0730, 0808 A, 0905 A, 0941, 1011 A, 1041 and at the same minutes past each hour until 1511 A, 1536, 1611 A, 1641, 1705 ⑥A, 1706 ⓐⒶ, 1736, 1815, 1841, 1908 ⓐⒶ, 1911 ⑥A, 2023 ⑥, 2044 ⓐ, 2128 ⑥, 2128 ⓐ, 2242; on ⑦ at 0951 A, 1150 A, 1246 A, 1346 A, 1446 A, 1545 A, 1646 A, 1720, 1746 A, 1816, 1856 A, 1956, 2016.

---

178   **HULL - YORK**   2nd class   NT

km		✕	⑦	Ⓐ	⑥	✕	⑥	⑦	✕	⑥	Ⓐ	⑦	Ⓐ	Ⓐ	⑥	Ⓐ	⑥	Ⓐ	⑥	⑥	⑥	⑦	✕	⑥	Ⓐ	⑦
0	Hull .... **181 189** d.	0707	0854	0902	0902	1011	1107	1146	1204	1307	1315	1317	1414	1419	1422	1503	1503	1606	1610	1610	1711	1716	1725	1918	1925	2030	2102
50	Selby .. **181 189** d.	0749	0929	0939	0939	1048	1142	1221	1239	1349	1358	1352	1449	1454	1458	1538	1541	1641	1649	1649	1801	1804	1800	1955	2000	2105	2138
84	York .... a.	0823	0951	1011	1008	1120	1205	1253	1304	1422	1426	1418	1520	1525	1526	1601	1606	1704	1713	1713	1824	1828	1826	2024	2025	2127	2200

	Ⓐ	⑥	✕	⑥	⑦	⑥	⑦	✕	⑦	✕	⑦	⑥	⑦	Ⓐ	⑥	Ⓐ	⑦	Ⓐ	⑥	✕	⑥	Ⓐ	⑦	⑥	⑦	⑥
York .... d.	0730	0740	0841	0951	1018	1040	1047	1145	1205	1247	1344	1354	1447	1452	1502	1606	1606	1611	1714	1725	1809	1840	1916	1950	2150	2212	2229
Selby.. **181 189** d.	0749	0800	0908	1010	1039	1059	1107	1205	1225	1307	1410	1425	1507	1512	1522	1637	1634	1639	1734	1751	1840	1912	1936	2009	2210	2231	2248
Hull .... **181 189** a.	0843	0856	0946	1052	1120	1135	1151	1251	1303	1351	1451	1504	1551	1549	1559	1714	1722	1725	1811	1831	1926	1957	2013	2045	2247	2315	2331

179 LINCOLN - SHEFFIELD

NT 2nd class

km		⚒	⚒	Ⓐg	⑥	Ⓐh	⚒g	⚒h	⚒g	⚒h	⚒g	Ⓐh	⑥h	⚒g	Ⓐh	⑥h	⑥	⚒g	⚒h	⚒g	Ⓐh	⑥h	⚒g	Ⓐh	⑥h	⚒g	Ⓐh	⑥h	⑥
0	**Lincoln** d.	...	...	0700	0700	0707	0825	0832	0925	0929	1025	1032	1036	1125	1132	1138	...	1227	1232	1326	1332	1336	1425	1432	1436	1523	1532	1536	...
26	Gainsborough ‡ d.	...	...	0721	0721	0728	0846	0853	0946	0950	1046	1053	1057	1146	1153	1159	1211f	1248	1253	1347	1353	1357	1446	1453	1457	1546	1553	1557	1617f
40	Retford ▽ d.	...	0701	0740	0740	0745	0901	0908	1001	1007	1101	1108	1112	1201	1208	1214	1231	1303	1308	1402	1408	1412	1501	1508	1512	1601	1608	1612	1636
52	Worksop ▽ d.	0630	0713	0751	0752	0757	0913	0920	1013	1020	1113	1115	1124	1213	1220	1226	1243	1315	1320r	1414	1420	1424	1513	1520	1524	1613	1620	1624	1648
78	**Sheffield** ▽ a.	0702	0749	0825	0825	0825	0948	0948	1048	1048	1148	1148	1148	1249	1247	1250	1317	1348	1350	1448	1448	1448	1550	1545	1549	1649	1645	1649	1723

	Ⓐ	⑥	⚒	⚒	⑥	Ⓐ	⑥	⚒	⚒	⚒	⚒	⚒	⚒	⑦	⑦	⑦	⑦	⑦	⑦	⑦	⑦	⑦	⑦	⑦	⑦	⑦	⑦	⑦	⑦	⑦
Lincoln d.	1632	1636	1721	...	1825	1825	...	1941	2027	...	2127	...	...		...	1005	1113	1214	1313	...	1413	1515	1609	1715	1820	1915	2018	2108	...	2150
Gainsborough ‡ d.	1653	1657	1741	...	1844	1846	1932f	2003	2048	...	2148	...	...		...	1026	1135	1235	1334	...	1434	1536	1632	1736	1841	1936	2040	2129	...	2211
Retford ▽ d.	1708	1712	1756	1814	1900	1903	1954	2018	2103	...	2203	2245	...		0915	1041	1150	1251	1349	1425	1449	1551	1645	1751	1856	1951	2054	2144	2201	2227
Worksop ▽ d.	1720	1724	1809	1825	1912	1915	2005	2030	2115	2131	2215	2258	2328		0929	1053	1202	1303	1401	1437	1501	1603	1658	1803	1909	2003	2106	2156	2213	2239
Sheffield ▽ a.	1745	1748	1834	1858	1946	1953	2040	2104	2145	2204	2249	2331	0002		1002	1125	1235	1335	1435	1510	1535	1635	1731	1835	1937	2035	2135	2222	2245	2312

	⚒	⚒	⚒	⚒	⑥	⚒h		⚒g	⚒h	⚒g	⚒h	⚒g	⑥h		⚒g	Ⓐh	⑥	⚒h	⚒g	⚒h		⚒g	Ⓐh	⑥h	⚒g		⑥h	Ⓐh	⚒g
Sheffield ▽ d.	0539	0546	0644	0730	0803	0844	...	0844	0944	0944	1044	1044	1144	...	1144	1159	1203	1244	1244	1344	...	1344	1444	1444	1444	...	1544	1544	1544
Worksop ▽ d.	0603	0623	0715	0801	0834	0907	...	0915	1007	1015	1108	1115	1208	...	1215	1223	1237	1307	1315	1407	...	1415	1507	1507	1515	...	1607	1615	1615
Retford ▽ d.	0613	0636	0725	0811	0845	0917	...	0925	1017	1025	1118	1125	1218	...	1225	1236	1247	1317	1325	1417	...	1425	1517	1518	1525	...	1617	1625	1625
Gainsborough ‡ d.	0628	...	0740	0825	0902f	0932	...	0943	1032	1040	1133	1140	1233	...	1240	1250	1304f	1335	1340	1432	...	1440	1532	1537	1540	...	1632	1640	1640
Lincoln a.	0653	...	0805	0851	...	0957	...	1006	1057	1104	1158	1204	1258	...	1304	1315	...	1400	1404	1457	...	1504	1557	1602	1604	...	1657	1704	1704

	⑥	⚒h	⚒g	⚒	⚒		⚒	⚒	⚒	⑦	⑦	⑦		⑦	⑦	⑦	⑦	⑦		⑦	⑦	⑦		⑦	⑦	⑦		⑦	⑦
Sheffield ▽ d.	1601	1644	1644	1722	1744	...	1844	1949	2142	0842	0942	1044	...	1141	1242	1314	1342	1442	...	1543	1642	1743	...	1843	1932	2024	...	2106	2124
Worksop ▽ d.	1637	1710	1715	1753	1815	...	1915	2020	2215	0906	1013	1110	...	1212	1308	1345	1402	1508	...	1614	1708	1814	...	1914	2003	2055	...	2137	2148
Retford ▽ d.	1646	1720	1725	1807	1825	...	1925	2030	2228	0916	1023	1120	...	1222	1318	1356	1412	1518	...	1624	1718	1824	...	1924	2013	2105	...	2148	2158
Gainsborough ‡ d.	1702f	1735	1740	...	1840	...	1940	2045	...	0931	1037	1134	...	1237	1332	...	1426	1532	...	1639	1732	1839	...	1939	2028	2119	...	...	2212
Lincoln a.	...	1800	1804	...	1905	...	2006	2110	...	0955	1101	1200	...	1301	1356	...	1452	1557	...	1703	1759	1903	...	2007	2051	2144	...	...	2240

f – Gainsborough Central.
g – Until Mar. 24.
h – From Mar. 26.
r – Departs 1325 on ⑥.

▽ – Additional trains Retford - Worksop - Sheffield and v.v. from Mar. 26:
From **Retford** on ⚒ at 0831, 0931, 1031, 1131, 1331, 1431, 1531, 1629 Ⓐ, 1729, 1929.
From **Sheffield** on ⚒ at 0828, 0927Ⓐ, 0930⑥, 1028, 1144Ⓐ, 1227, 1328⑥, 1429, 1527Ⓐ, 1630, 1826.

180 LONDON - LEEDS, YORK, NEWCASTLE and EDINBURGH

GR Most services convey 🍷

For additional services see Tables **124, 181, 182, 183, 184** and **188**.

km		⑥	Ⓐ	⑥	Ⓐ	Ⓐ A	⑥ A	⚒	⚒	⚒	Ⓐ	⑥	⚒	⑥	Ⓐ	⚒	⚒	⚒	⚒	Ⓐ	⑥	⚒	Ⓐ	⑥	⚒	⚒
0	**London** Kings Cross d.	...	...	...	...	...	...	0550	0615	0630	0700	0700	0705	0710	0708	0730	0735	0800	0806	0830	0830	0833	0900	0900	0903	0908
44	Stevenage d.	...	...	...	...	...	...	0611	0636	0651	|	|	|	|	0728	|	0756	|	|	|	|	0854	|	|	|	0929
123	Peterborough d.	...	...	...	...	...	...	0642	0707	0722	0747	0747	0752	|	0800	0817	|	|	0853	0917	0917	|	0947	0947	0951	1001
170	Grantham d.	...	...	...	...	...	...	0702	0726	0741	|	|	|	|	0819	|	0840	|	|	|	|	0940	|	|	|	1021
193	Newark North Gate d.	...	...	...	...	...	...	0715	0739	|	|	|	|	0824	0832	0845	|	|	|	0945	0945	|	|	|	|	1034
223	Retford d.	...	...	...	...	...	...	0730	0754	|	|	|	|	0838	0846	|	|	|	|	|	|	|	|	|	|	1049
251	Doncaster d.	...	...	0610	0615	...	...	0746	0810	0814	|	|	0842	0852	0902	0910	0914	|	0942	1010	1010	1014	|	|	1042	1105
283	Wakefield Westgate a.	...	...	|	|	...	...	0802	|	0831	|	|	0900	|	|	|	0933	|	0959	|	|	1031	|	|	1059	|
299	**Leeds** a.	...	...	|	|	0710	0710	0818	|	0848	|	|	0917	|	|	|	0947	|	1015	|	|	1049	|	|	1116	|
303	**York** d.	...	...	0635	0639	0737	0735	...	0835	...	0855	0900	...	0914	0925	0935	...	0953	...	1035	1036	...	1053	1053	...	1130
351	Northallerton d.	...	...	0655	|	|	|	...	0854	...	|	|	...	...	...	|	...	|	...	1055	1055	...	|	|	...	...
374	Darlington d.	...	...	0709	0708	0806	0805	...	0908	...	0924	0929	...	...	...	1005	...	1022	...	1109	1109	...	1122	1122	...	...
409	Durham d.	...	...	0726	0726	0824	0823	...	0926	...	|	|	...	...	...	1022	...	|	...	1126	1127	...	|	|	...	...
432	**Newcastle** a.	0620	0622	0739	0739	0838	0837	...	0939	...	0951	0955	...	...	...	1036	...	1052	...	1141	1140	...	1150	1150	...	...
488	Alnmouth a.	0650	0653	0809	0808	|	|	...	|	...	|	|	...	...	...	1107	...	|	...	...	|	...	|	|	...	...
540	Berwick upon Tweed a.	0715	0717	0832	0830	0928	0927	...	|	...	1036	1040	...	...	...	|	...	1137	...	...	|	...	1234	1238	...	...
632	**Edinburgh** Waverley a.	0804	0807	0918	0921	1020	1024	...	1112a	...	1119	1125	...	...	...	1208	...	1224b	...	...	1308	...	1316	1324	...	...

	⚒	⚒	⚒ A	⚒	⚒	⚒	⚒	⚒	Ⓐ	⑥	⑥	Ⓐ	⚒	⚒	⚒ B	⑥	⚒	Ⓐ	⚒	⑥	Ⓐ	Ⓐ	⑥	⚒	⑥	Ⓐ	⑥
London Kings Cross d.	0930	0935	1000	1003	1006	1030	1035	1100	1105	1105	1108	1108	1130	1135	1200	1203	1203	1208	1230	1235	1235	1300	1300	1304	1307	1308	1330
Stevenage d.	|	0956	|	|	1028	|	1056	|	|	|	1130	1129	|	1156	|	|	|	1229	|	1256	1256	|	|	|	|	1329	|
Peterborough d.	1017	|	|	1051	1059	1117	|	|	1153	1154	1200	1200	1217	|	|	1251	1251	1300	1317	|	|	1347	1347	1352	1356	1401	1417
Grantham d.	|	1040	|	|	1119	|	1140	|	|	|	1219	1219	|	1240	|	|	|	1320	|	1340	1340	|	|	|	1416	1421	|
Newark North Gate d.	1045	|	|	|	1135	1145	|	|	|	|	|	1232	1245	|	|	|	|	1334	1345	|	|	|	|	|	|	1434	1446
Retford d.	|	|	|	|	...	|	|	|	|	|	1247	1247	|	|	|	|	|	...	|	|	|	|	|	|	1445	1449	|
Doncaster d.	1111	1117	|	1142	...	1210	1214	|	1242	1248	1303	1305	1311	1315	|	1340	1343	...	1410	1414	1417	|	|	1441	1501	1505	1510
Wakefield Westgate a.	|	1135	|	1159	...	|	1233	|	1259	1304	|	|	|	1332	|	1359	1359	...	|	1431	1433	|	|	1459	|	|	|
Leeds a.	|	1150	|	1216	...	|	1248	|	1316	1319	|	|	|	1348	|	1414	1416	...	|	1446	1449	|	|	1516	|	|	|
York d.	1135	...	1154	...	...	1235	...	1252	...	...	1324	1328	1335	...	1354	...	...	...	1435	...	...	1454	1453	...	1524	1530	1536
Northallerton d.	|	...	|	...	...	1255	...	|	...	...	...	...	|	...	|	...	...	...	1455	...	...	|	|	...	...	...	|
Darlington d.	1205	...	1223	...	...	1309	...	1321	...	...	...	...	1406	...	1423	...	...	...	1509	...	...	1523	1522	...	...	...	1606
Durham d.	1222	...	|	...	...	1326	...	|	...	...	...	...	1423	...	|	...	...	...	1526	...	...	|	|	...	...	...	1624
Newcastle a.	1238	...	1250	...	...	1339	...	1349	...	...	...	...	1439	...	1451	...	...	...	1540	...	...	1549	1549	...	...	...	1637
Alnmouth a.	1311c	...	|	...	...	|	...	|	...	...	...	...	1509c	...	|	...	...	...	...	...	...	|	|	...	...	...	1707
Berwick upon Tweed a.	|	...	1339	...	...	|	...	1434	...	...	...	...	|	...	1539	...	...	...	...	...	...	1634	1641	...	...	...	|
Edinburgh Waverley a.	1413	...	1425d	...	...	1514e	...	1526	...	...	...	...	1613e	...	1624d	...	...	...	...	...	...	1718	1726	...	...	...	1808

	Ⓐ	⑥	Ⓐ	⚒ A	⚒	⚒	Ⓐ	⑥	⚒	Ⓐ K	⑥	⚒	⑥	Ⓐ	⚒ C	⚒	Ⓐ A	⑥	⑥	Ⓐ	⚒	⚒	⑥	Ⓐ	⚒	⚒	⑥ D
London Kings Cross d.	1330	1335	1335	1400	1405	1408	1430	1430	1435	1500	1500	1505	1508	1508	1530	1535	1600	1600	1605	1606	1608	1628	1633	1633	1700	1703	1710
Stevenage d.	|	1357	1356	|	|	1429	|	|	1456	|	|	|	1529	1529	|	1556	|	|	|	|	1630	|	|	1654	|	|	|
Peterborough d.	1417	|	|	|	1452	1501	1517	1517	|	|	|	1552	1600	1601	1617	|	|	|	1652	1654	1701	1716	1720	|	|	1750	1758
Grantham d.	|	1441	1440	|	|	1520	|	|	1540	|	|	|	1619	1621	|	1640	|	|	|	|	1721	|	1739	1740	|	|	1819
Newark North Gate d.	1445	|	|	|	|	1534	1545	1545	|	|	|	|	1632	1634	1645	|	|	|	|	|	1736	1745	|	|	|	|	1832
Retford d.	|	|	|	|	|	...	|	|	|	|	|	|	1646	1649	|	|	|	|	|	|	...	|	|	1803	|	|	|
Doncaster d.	1511	1514	1517	|	1541	...	1610	1610	1614	|	|	1643	1702	1705	1711	1714	|	|	1742	1746	...	1810	1816	1819	|	1841	1855
Wakefield Westgate a.	|	1530	1533	|	1600	...	|	|	1632	|	|	1700	|	|	|	1734	|	|	1800	1805	...	|	1832	1835	|	1900	...
Leeds a.	|	1544	1550	|	1617	...	|	|	1648	|	|	1716	|	|	|	1748	|	|	1815	1820	...	|	1847	1851	|	1917	...
York d.	1535	...	...	1554	...	...	1635	1635	...	1654	1654	...	1723	1729	1734	...	1754	1750	...	...	...	1835	...	...	1853	...	...
Northallerton d.	1555	...	...	|	...	...	1655	1654	...	|	|	...	...	...	1754	...	|	|	...	...	...	1857	...	...	|	...	...
Darlington d.	1609	...	...	1622	...	...	1709	1708	...	1723	1723	...	...	...	1808	...	1823	1819	...	...	...	1911	...	...	1922	...	...
Durham d.	1626	...	...	|	...	...	1726	1726	...	|	|	...	...	...	1825	...	|	|	...	...	...	1928	...	...	|	...	...
Newcastle a.	1639	...	...	1650	...	...	1739	1739	...	1749	1749	...	...	...	1840	...	1851	1845	...	...	...	1943	...	...	1949	...	...
Alnmouth a.	1710	...	...	|	...	...	...	|	...	|	|	...	...	...	1909	...	|	|	...	...	...	|	...	...	|	...	...
Berwick upon Tweed a.	|	...	...	1740	...	...	...	|	...	1835	1843	...	...	...	|	...	1937	1935	...	...	...	|	...	...	2037	...	...
Edinburgh Waverley a.	1813	...	...	1825	...	...	...	1926	...	1918	1926	...	...	...	2013	...	2020	2019	...	...	...	2112	...	...	2121	...	...

A – To/from Aberdeen (Table **222**).
B – To/from Inverness (Table **223**).
C – On Ⓐ to Glasgow Central (Table **220**).
D – To/from Hull (Table **181**).
E – To/from Harrogate (Table **175**).
F – To/from Skipton (Table **173**).
G – To/from Bradford Forster Square (Table **182**).
H – To/from Lincoln (Table **186**).
J – To/from Sunderland (Table **210**).
K – To/from Stirling (Table **222**).

L – From Glasgow Central (Table **220**).

a – Arrives 1107 on ⑥.
b – Arrives 1218 on Ⓐ.
c – Arrives 4 minutes earlier on ⑥.
d – Arrives 4 minutes earlier on Ⓐ.
e – Arrives 6–7 minutes earlier on ⑥.
f – ⑤ only.
g – Departs 1923 on Ⓐ.
h – Until Feb. 11.
j – Arrives 8–9 minutes earlier.

k – From April 1.
m – Feb. 18 - Mar. 25.
n – Arrives 4–6 minutes earlier.
s – Calls to set down only.
u – Calls to pick up only.

★ – On ⑦ Feb. 18 - Mar. 25 service subject to alteration with extended journey times. For further details please contact National Rail Enquiries ✆ +44 (0) 3457 48 49 50.

For additional services see Tables **124, 181, 182, 183, 184** and **188**.

	Ⓐ D	⑥	Ⓐ	Ⓐ E	⑥		Ⓐ	Ⓐ	⑥	⚒ F		Ⓐ	⑥	Ⓐ	⑥	⑥ E	Ⓐ G	Ⓐ	⑥	Ⓐ	⑥		Ⓐ H	⑥ H	⚒	⚒	Ⓐ J
London Kings Cross .. d.	1719	1730	1730	1733	1735	...	1749	1800	1800	1803	...	1819	1821	1830	1830	1833	1833	1900	1900	1903	1903	...	1906	1906	1930	1933	2000
Stevenage d.	│	│	│	1756	1755	...	│	│	│	│	...	│	│	│	│	1854	1854	│	│	│	│	...	1929	│	│	1954	│
Peterborough d.	1808	1818	1817	│	│	...	1838	│	│	1852	...	1908	1911	1918	1917	│	│	│	│	1951	1951	...	2000	1958	2017	│	│
Grantham d.	1828	│	│	1842	1842	...	1906	│	│	│	...	1927	1931	│	│	1941	1941	│	│	│	│	...	2020	2022	│	2040	│
Newark North Gate d.	1841	1847	1846	│	│	...	│	│	│	1919g	...	│	│	1946	1948	│	│	│	│	│	│	...	2033	2035	2045	│	│
Retford d.	│	│	│	│	│	...	1929	│	│	│	...	│	1954	│	│	│	2004	│	│	│	│	...	...	...	│	│	│
Doncaster d.	1906	│	│	1916	1918	...	1944	│	│	1950	...	│	2010	2011	2014	2020	2021	│	│	2040	2044	...	...	...	2110	2114	│
Wakefield Westgate a.	...	│	│	1932	1934	...	2002	│	│	2006	...	│	2026	│	│	2037	2037	│	│	2059	2100	...	...	...	│	2131	│
Leeds a.	...	│	│	1947	1948	...	2020	│	│	2021	...	│	2041	│	│	2051	2052	│	│	2117	2118	...	...	...	│	2149	│
York d.	...	1930	1929	...	...	...	...	1950	1953	...	...	2020	...	2036	2037	...	...	2053	2054	...	...	...	...	...	2133	...	2153
Northallerton d.	...	│	│	...	...	...	...	│	│	...	...	2039	...	│	2056	...	...	│	│	...	...	...	...	...	2152	...	│
Darlington d.	...	1959	1958	...	...	...	...	2019	2022	...	...	2053	...	2105	2110	...	...	2122	2123	...	...	...	...	...	2206	...	2222
Durham d.	...	2017	2015	...	...	...	...	│	│	...	...	2111	...	2122	2128	...	...	│	│	...	...	...	...	...	2224	...	2240
Newcastle a.	...	2030	2028	...	...	...	...	2046	2049	...	...	2124	...	2135	2141	...	...	2149	2150	...	...	...	...	...	2237	...	2254
Alnmouth a.	...	│	2058	...	...	...	...	│	2122	...	...	...	...	2209	...	...	...	│	...	...	...	...	...	...	2309f	...	...
Berwick upon Tweed a.	...	│	│	...	...	...	...	2134	2146	...	...	...	...	│	...	...	...	2237	...	...	...	...	...	...	2333f	...	...
Edinburgh Waverley .. a.	...	2156	2208	...	...	...	...	2219	2235	...	...	...	...	2315	...	...	...	2329	...	...	...	...	...	...	0026f	...	...

	⑥	⚒	⑥	Ⓐ		⑥	Ⓐ	Ⓐ	⑥	Ⓐ	Ⓐ	Ⓐ		⑦	⑦	⑦	⑦	⑦		⑦	⑦	⑦	⑦ A	⑦	⑦	⑦	
London Kings Cross .. d.	2000	2005	2030	2035	...	2100	2100	2135	2200	2200	2257	2330	⑦	...	...	...	...	0845	...	0900	0903	0930	1000	1003	1010	1030	...
Stevenage d.	│	│	│	2056	...	│	2121	2157	│	│	│	│		...	...	...	...	│	...	│	0924	│	│	│	│	│	...
Peterborough d.	2048	2052	2118	2127	...	2148	2152	2228	2247	2249	2345s	0015s		...	...	...	...	│	...	│	0955	1017	│	1051	1057	1117	...
Grantham d.	│	│	2138	2146	...	│	│	2249	2306	2309	0006s	0043s	★	...	...	...	...	│	...	│	1014	│	│	│	1116	│	...
Newark North Gate d.	2116	2120	2151	2159	...	│	2220	2302	2319	2323	0018s	0056s		...	...	...	...	│	...	│	1027	│	│	│	1129	1145	...
Retford d.	│	│	2207	│	...	│	│	2318	2334	│	│	│		...	...	...	...	│	...	│	│	1055	│	│	│	│	...
Doncaster d.	2140	2147	2223	2223	...	│	2247	2336	2350	2352	0053s	0124s		...	...	...	0937	│	...	│	1051	1111	│	1139	1155	1210	...
Wakefield Westgate a.	│	2207	2239	2239	...	│	│	2352	0006	│	│	│		...	...	...	│	│	...	│	1107	│	│	│	1211	│	...
Leeds a.	│	2223	2254	2257	...	│	│	0008	0020	│	│	0233		...	...	0830	│	│	...	│	1124	│	│	│	1226	│	...
York d.	2205	...	...	...	...	2257	2312	...	...	0041	0130	...		...	...	0900	1000	1037	...	1048	...	1134	1150	1208j	...	1235	...
Northallerton d.	│	...	...	...	...	2318	2343	...	...	0109s	...	...		...	...	0921	│	│	...	│	...	│	│	│	...	1255	...
Darlington d.	2234	...	...	...	...	2332	2357	...	...	0123s	...	...		...	...	0936	1029	1106	...	1117	...	1203	1221	1239	...	1307	...
Durham a.	2251	...	...	...	...	2350	0014	...	...	0142s	...	...		...	...	0954	1046	1124	...	│	...	1220	│	1256	...	1326	...
Newcastle a.	2304	...	...	...	...	0003	0041	...	...	0213	...	...		0845	0915	1007	1059	1137	...	1144	...	1233	1247	1310	...	1339	...
Alnmouth a.	...	...	...	...	...	...	...	...	...	...	...	...		0914	│	1042	│	│	...	│	...	1303	│	│	...	│	...
Berwick upon Tweed a.	...	...	...	...	...	...	...	...	...	...	...	...		0938	0957	1106	1144	│	...	1233	...	│	1333	│	...	│	...
Edinburgh Waverley .. a.	...	...	...	...	...	...	...	...	...	...	...	...		1026	1040	1156	1227	1306	...	1316	...	1416	1419	1434	...	1503	...

	⑦	⑦	⑦	⑦	⑦ B	⑦	⑦	⑦	⑦	⑦		⑦	⑦	⑦ A	⑦	⑦	⑦		⑦	⑦	⑦	⑦	⑦ C	⑦	⑦	⑦	
London Kings Cross .. d.	1100	1103	1120	1130	1200	1203	1220	1230	1233	1300	...	1303	1330	1400	1403	1430	1500	...	1503	1530	1600	1605	1630	1635	1700	1705	...
Stevenage d.	│	1124	│	│	│	│	│	│	1256	│	...	1324	│	│	│	│	│	...	1525	│	│	│	│	1656	│	│	...
Peterborough d.	│	1155	│	1217	│	1251	1310	1317	│	│	...	1355	1417	│	1452	1517	│	...	1555	1618	│	1653	1717	│	│	1752	...
Grantham d.	│	1214	1224	│	│	1310	│	│	1342	│	...	1414	│	│	1511	│	│	...	1614	1638	│	1712	│	1740	│	│	...
Newark North Gate d.	│	1227	│	│	│	1323	│	1345	│	│	...	1427	│	│	1524	1545	│	...	1627	│	│	1725	1745	│	│	1820	...
Retford d.	│	│	│	1255	│	│	│	│	│	│	...	│	1455	│	│	│	│	...	1642	│	│	│	│	1803	│	│	...
Doncaster d.	│	1251	│	1311	│	1347	1359	1410	1420	│	...	1451	1511	│	1550	1610	│	...	1658	1712	│	1752	1810	1820	│	1845	...
Wakefield Westgate a.	│	1307	│	│	│	1403	│	│	1436	│	...	1507	│	│	1606	│	│	...	1714	│	│	1810	│	1839	│	1901	...
Leeds a.	│	1323	│	│	│	1418	│	│	1451	│	...	1523	│	│	1623	│	│	...	1728	│	│	1826	│	1854	│	1915	...
York d.	1251	...	1317	1334	1350	...	1422	1433	...	1453	...	...	1534	1552	...	1633	1652	...	...	1735	1749	...	1835	...	1850	...	...
Northallerton d.	│	...	1337	│	│	...	│	1453	...	│	...	...	│	│	...	1653	│	...	...	│	│	...	1855	...	│	...	...
Darlington d.	1320	...	1351	1403	1419	...	1451	1507	...	1522	...	...	1603	1622	...	1707	1721	...	...	1804	1818	...	1909	...	1919	...	...
Durham d.	│	...	1409	1420	│	...	1508	1524	...	│	...	...	1620	│	...	1724	│	...	...	1822	│	...	1926	...	│	...	...
Newcastle a.	1346	...	1422	1433	1446	...	1521	1537	...	1549	...	...	1633	1648	...	1739	1747	...	...	1835	1845	...	1939	...	1946	...	...
Alnmouth a.	│	...	│	1506	│	...	...	│	...	│	...	...	1703	│	...	│	│	...	...	1904	│	...	│	...	│	...	...
Berwick upon Tweed a.	1431	...	│	│	1534	...	...	│	...	1634	...	...	│	1734	...	│	1833	...	...	│	1932	...	│	...	2034	...	...
Edinburgh Waverley .. a.	1514	...	1556	1609	1617	...	...	1705	...	1717	...	...	1806	1817	...	1906	1916	...	...	2007	2015	...	2112	...	2117	...	...

	⑦ D	⑦	⑦	⑦	⑦ E	⑦	⑦		⑦ F	⑦	⑦	⑦ H	⑦	⑦	⑦	⑦		⑦	⑦	⑦	⑦	⑦	⑦ m	⑦ h	⑦ k	⑦	
London Kings Cross .. d.	1720	1730	1735	1800	1803	1827	1830	...	1835	1900	1903	1908	1930	1935	2000	2005	...	2035	2100	2105	2135	2200	2145	2204	2204	2235	...
Stevenage d.	│	│	1756	│	│	│	│	...	1856	│	│	1930	│	1956	│	│	...	2056	│	│	2157	│	│	│	│	│	...
Peterborough d.	│	1817	│	1847	1850	│	│	...	│	│	1951	2001	2018	2027	2047	2053	...	2127	2147	2153	2228	2248	2253	2253	2253	2324s	...
Grantham d.	1825	1837	1843	│	│	│	│	...	1941	│	│	2022	│	2046	│	│	...	2146	│	│	2248	│	2315	2315	2316	2344s	...
Newark North Gate d.	1838	│	│	│	1921	│	1946	...	│	│	2019	2036	2048	│	│	│	...	2159	│	2221	2301	│	2327	2327	2330	2356s	...
Retford d.	│	│	│	│	│	│	│	...	2004	│	│	...	│	│	│	2132	...	│	│	│	2316	│	│	│	│	│	...
Doncaster d.	1903	1912	1918	│	1950	│	2010	...	2020	│	2044	...	2114	2119	│	2148	...	2223	│	2252	2339	2345	2357	2357	0009	0026s	...
Wakefield Westgate a.	...	│	1934	│	2006	│	│	...	2036	│	2100	...	│	2135	│	2205	...	2239	│	2308	2357	│	│	│	│	│	...
Leeds a.	...	│	1949	│	2023	│	│	...	2051	│	2116	...	│	2149	│	2219	...	2255	│	2327	0012	│	│	│	│	0130	...
York d.	...	1938	...	1957	...	2027j	2036	...	...	2052	...	...	2138	...	2156	...	...	...	2301	...	...	0012	0023	0023	0034	...	...
Northallerton d.	...	│	...	│	...	│	2056	...	...	│	...	...	│	...	2230	...	...	...	2337	...	...	0045s	...	...	...	...	...
Darlington d.	...	2007	...	2026	...	2056	2110	...	...	2122	...	...	2219	...	2243	...	...	...	2348	...	...	0059s	...	...	...	...	...
Durham d.	...	2025	...	│	...	2113	2127	...	...	│	...	...	2237	...	2301	...	...	...	0007	...	...	0117s	...	...	...	...	...
Newcastle a.	...	2038	...	2052	...	2126	2140	...	...	2150	...	...	2306	...	2330	...	...	...	0036	...	...	0148	...	...	...	...	...
Alnmouth a.	...	2110	...	│	...	...	│	...	...	2223	...	...	...	...	...	...	...	...	...	...	...	...	...	...	...	...	...
Berwick upon Tweed a.	...	│	...	2143	...	...	2227	...	...	2247	...	...	...	...	...	...	...	...	...	...	...	...	...	...	...	...	...
Edinburgh Waverley .. a.	...	2214	...	2225	...	...	2310	...	...	2336	...	...	...	...	...	...	...	...	...	...	...	...	...	...	...	...	...

		⑥	Ⓐ	⚒	⚒	⚒	⚒	⚒	⑥	Ⓐ	⚒ G	Ⓐ J	⑥	Ⓐ H	⑥ H	⚒	Ⓐ	⑥	Ⓐ	Ⓐ	⑥ F	Ⓐ D	Ⓐ F	Ⓐ	⚒ E	⑥	Ⓐ
Edinburgh Waverley .. d.	⚒	...	...	...	...	...	...	...	...	...	...	...	...	...	...	...	...	...	...	0540	...	...	...	...	...	0548	0548
Berwick upon Tweed d.		...	...	...	...	...	...	...	...	...	...	...	...	...	...	...	...	...	0600	│	...	...	...	...	...	0634	0634
Alnmouth d.		...	...	...	...	...	...	...	...	...	...	...	...	...	...	...	...	...	0621	│	...	...	...	...	...	0655	0655
Newcastle d.		...	...	...	...	0445	...	0526	...	...	...	0559	0559	...	...	...	0630	0630	0655	0705	...	...	...	...	...	0727	0729
Durham d.		...	...	...	...	0500	...	0539	...	...	...	0612	0612	...	...	...	0644	0643	0708	│	...	...	...	←	...	0740	0742
Darlington d.		...	...	...	...	0518	...	0558	...	...	...	0632	0632	...	...	...	0703	0702	0732n	│	...	...	...	0732	...	0759	0801
Northallerton d.		...	...	...	...	0529	...	0609	...	...	...	│	│	...	...	...	0715	0714	→	│	...	...	...	│	...	│	│
York d.		0438	0440	...	...	0600	...	0631	...	...	...	0701	0701	...	...	...	0737	0736	...	│	...	...	...	0802	...	0830	0831
Leeds d.		│	│	0505	0530	│	0605	│	0640	0640	0700	│	│	...	...	0715	│	│	...	│	0738	...	0740	│	0815	│	│
Wakefield Westgate d.		│	│	0518	0543	│	0618	│	0623	0653	0713	│	│	...	...	0728	│	│	...	│	│	...	0753	│	0830	│	│
Doncaster d.		0505	0507	0537	0602	0623	0636	0654	0712	0713	│	│	│	...	...	0746	│	│	...	│	0810	0757	0814	│	0849	0853	0856
Retford d.		│	│	0551	│	│	0651	│	│	│	│	│	│	...	...	│	│	│	...	│	│	│	│	0836	│	│	│
Newark North Gate d.		0533	0536	0606	0625	0647	0707	│	│	0736	│	│	│	0757	0801	│	│	│	...	│	0833	0823	0839	│	│	0918	0920
Grantham d.		0545	0547	0618	0639	0659	0720	0726	│	│	│	│	│	│	│	0818	│	│	...	│	│	0835	│	│	0920	│	│
Peterborough d.		0607	0610	0639	0701	0722	0742	0750	│	│	│	0811	0815	0828	0832	│	0844	0851j	...	│	0903	0903	0907	│	│	0952j	0950
Stevenage d.		│	│	│	│	│	│	│	│	│	│	│	│	0858	0902	0904	│	│	...	│	│	│	│	│	1009	│	│
London Kings Cross .. a.		0654	0700	0729	0752	0812	0833	0843	0843	0850	0859	0906	0910	0924	0925	0929	0937	0940	...	0940	0951	0955	0956	1002	1035	1039	1041

← FOR NOTES SEE PREVIOUS PAGE

180a PETERBOROUGH - KINGS LYNN First Excel service X1

From **Peterborough** railway station : Journey 75 minutes. Buses call at **Wisbech** bus station ± 39 minutes later.

Ⓐ: 0704, 0734, 0809 and every 30 minutes until 1109, 1149, 1219 and every 30 minutes until 1449, 1520, 1550, 1620, 1650, 1720, 1755, 1833, 1903, 1933, 2033, 2233.

⑥: 0739, 0809 and every 30 minutes until 1109, 1149, 1219 and every 30 minutes until 1719, 1754, 1833, 1903, 1933, 2033, 2233.

⑦: 0909, 1009 and hourly until 2009.

Table **180a** continues on the next page.

For additional services see Tables **124, 181, 182, 183, 184** and **188**.

	⑥	Ⓐ	⚒	⚒	Ⓐ	⑥	⚒	⑥	Ⓐ	Ⓐ	⑥	Ⓐ	⑥	⚒	⚒	⚒	⚒	⚒	⚒	⚒	⚒	⚒	⚒	⚒	⚒	⚒	⚒
		K												L											A		
Edinburgh Waverley ..d.	0626	0626	...	...	0655	0655	0730	...	...	...	...	...	...	0800	0830	...	...	...	0900	0930	...	...	...	1000	1030	...	...
Berwick upon Tweed...d.	0709	0710	...	...	|	|	0812	...	...	...	...	...	...	|	0912	...	...	...	|	1012	...	...	...	|	1112	...	...
Alnmouth ....d.	|	|	...	...	|	|	|	...	...	...	...	...	...	0900	|	...	...	...	|	|	...	...	...	1100	|	...	...
Newcastle ....d.	0756	0758	...	...	0825	0825	0858	...	...	...	...	...	...	0929	0958	...	...	...	1025	1058	...	...	...	1129	1158	...	...
Durham ....d.	|	|	...	...	0838	0838	|	...	...	...	...	...	...	0942	|	...	...	...	1038	|	...	...	...	1142	|	...	...
Darlington ....d.	0825	0828	...	...	0857	0857	0927	...	...	...	...	...	...	1001	1028	...	...	...	1057	1127	...	...	...	1201	1228	...	...
Northallerton ....d.	|	|	...	...	0908	0908	|	...	...	...	...	...	...	|	|	...	...	...	1108	|	...	...	...	|	|	...	...
York ....d.	0855	0858	...	...	0930	0930	0958	...	...	1003	1003	...	...	1031	1058	...	...	...	1130	1158	...	1202	...	1231	1257	...	...
Leeds ....d.	|	|	0845	0916	|	|	|	0945	0945	|	|	1015	1015	|	|	1045	...	1115	|	|	1145	|	1215	|	|	1245	...
Wakefield Westgate.d.	|	|	0858	0929	|	|	|	0958	0958	|	|	1029	1028	|	|	1058	...	1128	|	|	1158	|	1228	|	|	1258	...
Doncaster ....d.	|	|	0917	0948	0953	0956	|	|	1018	1026	1031	1048	1047	1058	|	1119	...	1147	1154	|	1218	1225	1247	1255	|	1318	...
Retford ....d.	|	|	|	|	|	|	|	|	|	1040	1046	|	|	|	|	|	...	|	|	|	|	1240	|	|	|	|	...
Newark North Gate .....d.	|	|	|	|	1017	1020	|	|	|	1055	1101	|	|	1121	|	|	1154	|	1217	|	|	1255	|	1319	|	|	1354
Grantham ....d.	|	|	|	1019	|	|	|	|	|	1107	1113	1119	1121	|	|	|	1206	1219	|	|	|	1307	1319	|	|	|	1406
Peterborough..............d.	|	|	1009	|	1050**n**	1053**n**	|	1102	1109	1128	1134	|	|	1152	|	1210	1228	|	1250**n**	|	1308	1329	|	1351**n**	|	1408	1428
Stevenage ....d.	|	|	|	1103	|	|	|	|	|	1157	1203	1203	1208	|	|	|	1257	1303	|	|	|	1359	1403	|	|	|	1457
London Kings Cross ..a.	1050	1051	1059	1128	1142	1140	1151	1151	1158	1222	1226	1228	1233	1241	1251	1300	1323	1327	1341	1349	1358	1424	1427	1443	1451	1458	1524

	⚒	⑥	Ⓐ	Ⓐ	⚒	Ⓐ	⚒	⑥	⚒	⚒	Ⓐ	⑥	⚒	⚒	⑥	Ⓐ	⑥	Ⓐ	⚒	⑥	Ⓐ	Ⓐ	⑥	⚒	⑥	Ⓐ	Ⓐ
				B						A																	
Edinburgh Waverley ..d.	...	1100	...	1130	...	...	...	...	1200	1230	...	...	...	...	1300	1300	1330	1330	...	...	...	...	...	1400	1430	1430	...
Berwick upon Tweed...d.	...	|	...	|	...	...	...	...	|	1312	...	...	...	...	|	|	1411	1412	...	...	...	...	...	|	1511	1512	...
Alnmouth ....d.	...	|	...	|	...	...	...	...	1300	|	...	...	...	...	|	|	|	|	...	...	...	...	...	1500	|	|	...
Newcastle ....d.	...	1226	1225	1256	...	...	...	...	1329	1359	...	...	...	...	1425	1425	1459	1459	...	...	...	...	...	1532	1557	1559	...
Durham ....d.	...	1239	1238	|	...	...	...	...	1342	|	...	...	...	...	1438	1438	|	|	...	...	...	...	...	1545	|	|	...
Darlington ....d.	...	1258	1257	1325	...	...	...	...	1401	1428	...	...	...	...	1457	1457	1527	1527	...	...	...	...	...	1604	1626	1628	...
Northallerton ....d.	...	1309	1308	|	...	...	...	...	|	|	...	...	...	...	1508	1508	|	|	...	...	...	...	...	|	|	|	...
York ....d.	...	1331	1330	1358**n**	...	1402	...	1405	1431	1458	...	...	...	...	1530	1530	1557	1558	...	1602	1602	...	...	1634	1657	1657	...
Leeds ....d.	1315	|	|	|	1345	|	1415	|	|	|	1445	1445	...	1515	|	|	|	|	1545	|	|	1615	1615	|	|	|	1645
Wakefield Westgate.d.	1328	|	|	|	1358	|	1428	|	|	|	1458	1458	...	1528	|	|	|	|	1558	|	|	1628	1629	|	|	|	1658
Doncaster ....d.	1347	1354	1355	|	1418	1426	1447	1430	1454	|	1519	1519	...	1547	1554	1556	|	|	1618	1628	1625	1647	1648	1657	|	|	1718
Retford ....d.	|	|	|	|	|	1442	|	1446	|	|	|	|	...	|	|	|	|	|	|	1643	1641	|	|	|	|	|	|
Newark North Gate .....d.	|	1418	1419	|	|	1457	|	1501	1518	|	|	|	1552	|	1617	1622	|	|	|	1658	1656	|	|	1720	|	|	|
Grantham ....d.	1419	|	|	|	|	1509	1518	1513	|	|	|	|	1604	1619	|	|	|	|	|	1710	1708	1719	1722	|	|	|	|
Peterborough..............d.	|	1450**n**	1452	|	1509	1530	|	1538**n**	1551**n**	|	1609	1613	1625	|	1652**n**	1653	|	|	1709	1732	1730	|	|	1751	|	|	1808
Stevenage ....d.	1503	|	|	|	|	1559	1602	1609	|	|	|	|	1655	1703	|	|	|	|	|	1802	1800	1805	1808	|	|	|	|
London Kings Cross ..a.	1528	1539	1541	1551	1600	1625	1628	1632	1640	1652	1658	1703	1722	1727	1739	1742	1745	1753	1759	1825	1827	1830	1833	1844**c**	1846	1850	1902

	⑥	⚒	⚒	⑥	Ⓐ	⚒	⚒	⚒	⚒	⚒	⚒	Ⓐ	⑥	⚒	⚒	⚒	⚒	⑥	⑥	Ⓐ	⑥	Ⓐ	⑥	Ⓐ	⑤		⑦
																	A							A			
Edinburgh Waverley ..d.	...	...	...	1500	...	1530	...	...	...	1600	1630	...	...	...	1700	...	1731	...	1830	1830	1900	1935	2000	2100	2200	⑦	...
Berwick upon Tweed...d.	...	...	...	|	...	1612	...	...	...	|	1712	...	...	...	|	...	1818	...	1912	1918	1945	2016	2046	2148	2246		...
Alnmouth ....d.	...	...	...	|	...	|	...	...	...	|	|	...	...	...	1800	...	|	...	|	1941	2008	2039	2109	2211	2308		...
Newcastle ....d.	...	...	...	1625	1625	1659	...	...	...	1725	1758	...	...	...	1829	...	1904	...	1955	2016	2043	2114	2140	2245	2354		...
Durham ....d.	...	...	...	1638	1638	|	...	...	...	1738	|	...	...	...	1842	...	|	...	▬	2029	2056	2127	...	2259	...	★	...
Darlington ....d.	...	...	...	1657	1657	1727	...	...	...	1757	1826	...	...	...	1901	...	1934	...	...	2048	2115	2146	...	2320	...		...
Northallerton ....d.	...	...	...	1709	1709	|	...	...	...	1809	|	...	...	...	|	...	|	...	...	|	2128	2158	...	2346**s**	...		...
York ....d.	...	...	...	1731	1731	1757	...	1802	...	1831	1856	...	...	...	1931	...	2003	...	Ⓐ	2118	2151	2220	...	0016	...		0800
Leeds ....d.	1645	...	1715	|	|	|	1745	|	1815	|	|	1845	1845	1915	|	1945	|	2015	2045	|	|	|	...	0043	...		|
Wakefield Westgate.d.	1658	...	1728	|	|	|	1758	|	1828	|	|	1858	1859	1928	|	1958	|	2028	2058	|	|	|	...	...	...		|
Doncaster ....d.	1724	...	1747	1755	1756	|	1818	1825	1847	1855	|	1917	1923	1948	1954	2017	2027	2047	2116	2141	2213	2243	...	...	...		0823
Retford ....d.	|	...	1801	|	|	|	|	1839	|	|	|	|	|	|	|	|	|	2101	2131	|	...	|	...	...	...		|
Newark North Gate .....d.	|	1754	|	1820	1820	|	|	1854	|	1919	|	|	|	|	2017	|	|	2116	|	2204	...	2307	...	...	...		|
Grantham ....d.	|	1806	1824	|	|	|	|	1906	1918	|	|	|	|	2019	|	|	|	2128	2157	2216	...	2319	...	...	...		|
Peterborough..............d.	1815	1828	|	1853	1849	|	1908	1928	|	1951	|	2008	2013	|	2049	2105	2118	2153	2218	2238	...	2346	...	...	...		0911
Stevenage ....d.	|	1858	1908	|	|	|	|	1957	2003	2020	2024	|	|	2103	2118	|	2148	|	2247	2307	...	0027**s**	...	...	...		0940
London Kings Cross ...a	1903	1925	1934	1941	1943	1950**c**	1959**c**	2024	2028	2044	2052	2059	2103	2128	2142	2157**c**	2214	2240	2312	2330	...	0101	...	...	...		1004

	⑦	⑦	⑦	⑦	⑦	⑦	⑦	⑦	⑦	⑦	⑦	⑦	⑦	⑦	⑦	⑦	⑦	⑦	⑦	⑦	⑦	⑦	⑦	⑦	⑦	⑦	⑦
																								A			
Edinburgh Waverley ..d.	...	...	...	...	...	...	...	...	...	...	0900	0930	...	1000	1030	...	1100	1120	1130	...	...	1200	1220	1230	...	...	1300
Berwick upon Tweed...d.	...	...	...	...	...	...	...	...	...	...	|	1013	...	|	1112	...	|	|	1212	...	...	|	|	1313	...	...	1343
Alnmouth ....d.	...	...	...	...	...	...	...	...	...	...	|	|	...	1100	|	...	|	|	|	...	...	1300	|	|	...	...	|
Newcastle ....d.	...	0755	...	...	0855	...	...	0925	1000	...	1028	1059	...	1129	1159	...	1225	1251	1301	...	1315	1329	1350	1359	...	1420	1431
Durham ....d.	...	0809	...	...	0908	...	...	0938	|	...	1041	|	...	1142	|	...	1238	1305	|	...	1328	1342	1404	|	...	1433	|
Darlington ....d.	...	0828	...	...	0928	...	...	0957	1028	...	1100	1128	...	1201	1229	...	1257	1324	1330	...	1348	1401	|	1430	...	1452	1500
Northallerton ....d.	...	|	...	...	|	...	...	1008	|	...	1112	|	...	|	|	...	1309	|	|	...	1401	|	|	|	...	|	|
York ....d.	...	0858	...	...	0957	...	...	1030	1058	...	1134	1158	...	1231	1258	...	1332	1356	1400	...	1424	1431	1449	1459	...	1523	1530
Leeds ....d.	0805	|	0843	0905	|	0940	1005	|	|	1106	|	|	1205	|	|	1305	|	|	|	1405	|	|	|	|	1505	|	|
Wakefield Westgate.d.	0818	|	0856	0918	|	0953	1018	|	|	1119	|	|	1218	|	|	1318	|	|	|	1418	|	|	|	|	1518	|	|
Doncaster ....d.	0837	|	0920	0939	|	|	1037	1053	|	1139	1157	|	1237	1254	|	1336	1355	|	|	1437	1448	1454	|	|	1537	1546	1553
Retford ....d.	0851	|	|	|	|	1020	1052	|	|	|	1211	|	|	|	|	|	1409	|	|	|	|	|	|	|	|	|	1608
Newark North Gate .....d.	0906	|	|	1002	|	1040**n**	1107	1117	|	1203	|	|	1300	1317	|	1400	|	|	|	1500	|	1518	|	|	1600	1609	|
Grantham ....d.	0918	|	|	1014	|	|	1120	|	|	1215	|	|	1312	|	|	1412	|	|	|	1512	|	|	1540	|	1612	|	|
Peterborough..............d.	0942	1005	1011	1036	1104	1109	1142	1151	1204	1237	1251	|	1334	1351**n**	|	1435	1451	|	|	1534	1541	1551	|	|	1636	1642	1650
Stevenage ....d.	|	|	|	1105	|	|	|	|	|	1308	|	|	|	|	|	1506	|	|	|	|	|	|	|	|	1706	|	|
London Kings Cross ..a.	1032	1053	1106	1131	1152	1156	1231	1238	1251	1331	1338	1347	1421	1438	1447	1530	1538	1545	1549	1621	1631	1638	1642	1648	1730	1733	1740

	⑦	⑦	⑦	⑦	⑦	⑦	⑦	⑦	⑦	⑦	⑦	⑦	⑦	⑦	⑦	⑦	⑦	⑦	⑦	⑦	⑦	⑦	⑦	⑦	⑦	⑦	⑦
		B			A							E				A											
Edinburgh Waverley ..d.	1319	1330	...	1400	1430	...	...	1447	...	1500	1530	...	...	1600	1620	1630	...	...	1700	1730	...	1800	...	1830	1900	2000	2100
Berwick upon Tweed...d.	|	1413	...	|	|	...	...	1531	...	|	1612	...	...	|	|	1713	...	...	|	1816	...	|	...	1913	1946	2047	2147
Alnmouth ....d.	|	|	...	1500	|	...	...	|	...	|	|	...	...	1700	|	|	...	...	|	|	...	1900	...	|	|	2110	2209
Newcastle ....d.	1445	1459	...	1531	1556	...	1600	1617	...	1627	1701	...	...	1729	1749	1800	...	...	1829	1902	...	1930	...	2001	2033	2144	2236
Durham ....d.	1458	|	...	1544	|	...	1613	1630	...	1640	|	...	...	1742	|	|	...	...	1842	|	...	1944	...	|	2046	2158	...
Darlington ....d.	1518	1528	...	1603	|	...	1632	1649	...	1659	1729	...	...	1801	1817	1830	...	...	1901	1930	...	2003	...	2029	2105	2217	...
Northallerton ....d.	1532	|	...	|	|	...	1644	|	...	|	|	...	...	|	1829	|	...	...	1913	|	...	|	...	|	|	2231	...
York ....d.	1557	1601	...	1632	1659	...	1707	1722**n**	...	1730	1759	...	...	1831	1854**n**	1859	...	...	1935	2000	...	2032	...	2100	2135	2307	...
Leeds ....d.	|	|	1616	|	|	1645	|	|	1716	|	|	1745	1815	|	|	|	1845	1916	|	|	1945	|	2045	|	|	2333	...
Wakefield Westgate.d.	|	|	1629	|	|	1658	|	|	1729	|	|	1759	1828	|	|	|	1859	1929	|	|	1958	|	2058	|	|	...	...
Doncaster ....d.	|	|	1647	1656	|	1719	1735	|	1748	1757**n**	|	1818	1847	1855	|	|	1920	1948	1958	|	2020	2055	2117	2126	2158	...	...
Retford ....d.	|	|	|	|	|	|	|	|	1802	|	|	|	|	|	|	|	|	2002	|	|	|	|	2131	|	|	...	...
Newark North Gate .....d.	|	|	|	1720	|	1744	|	1803	|	|	|	1844	|	1919	|	|	1945	|	2021	|	2045	2123	|	2150	2221	...	...
Grantham ....d.	|	|	1719	|	|	|	1808	|	1825	1830	|	|	1918	|	1943	|	|	2025	|	2049	|	|	2154	2202	2233	...	...
Peterborough..............d.	|	|	|	1751	|	1814	|	1833	|	1852	|	1914	|	1951	|	|	2014	|	2051	2110	2114	2152	2216	2223	2255	...	...
Stevenage ....d.	|	|	1803	|	|	|	|	|	1909	|	|	|	2002	|	|	|	|	2109	|	|	|	|	2245	2252	2333**s**	...	...
London Kings Cross ..a.	1746	1751	1827	1838	1848	1905	1915	1920	1932	1940	1945	2005	2025	2038	2045	2050	2105	2131	2138	2157	2205	2240	2308	2315	2357	...	...

FOR NOTES SEE PAGE 143

First Excel service **X1** 🚌 KINGS LYNN - PETERBOROUGH 🚌 180a

From **Kings Lynn** bus station: Journey 80 minutes. Buses call at **Wisbech** bus station ± 32 minutes later.

Ⓐ: 0534, 0604, 0634, 0704, 0734, 0805, 0835, 0905, 0935, 1015 and every 30 minutes until 1615, 1655, 1725, 1755, 1900, 2110.

⑥: 0604, 0634, 0704, 0734, 0805, 0835, 0905, 0935, 1015 and every 30 minutes until 1615, 1655, 1725, 1755, 1900, 2110.

⑦: 0740 and hourly until 1840.

Table **180a** continues on the previous page.

181 LONDON - HULL

All trains 🍷 HT

km		Ⓐ	Ⓐ	Ⓐ	Ⓐ	Ⓐ	Ⓐ	Ⓐ	Ⓐ
							△		
0	**London** K X. **180** d.	0722	0948	1148	1348	1548	1719	1850	2030
170	Grantham **180** d.	0825	1049	1249	1449	1649	1828	1952	2131
223	Retford **180** d.	0851	1110	1311	1511	1711	|	2014	2153
251	Doncaster **180** a.	0905	1124	1324	1525	1724	1906	2027	2206
280	Selby a.	0923	1139	1341	1541	1741	1926	2049	2223
330	**Hull** a.	1001	1214	1416	1616	1818	2004	2123	2300
330	**Hull** **177** d.	...	...	...	...	...	...	2135	...
343	Beverley **177** a.	...	...	...	...	...	...	2147	...

km		⑥	⑥	⑥	⑥	⑥	⑥	⑥
						△		
0	**London** K X. **180** d.	0713	0948	1148	1448	1710	1748	1948
170	Grantham **180** d.	0820	1049	1249	1549	1819	1849	2050
223	Retford **180** d.	0843	1111	1311	1611	|	1911	2112
251	Doncaster **180** a.	0857	1124	1324	1624	1855	1924	2126
280	Selby a.	0914	1141	1341	1641	1916	1941	2143
330	**Hull** a.	1000	1218	1416	1725	1952	2018	2218
330	**Hull** **177** d.	...	...	...	...	...	2027	...
343	Beverley **177** a.	...	...	...	...	...	2040	...

km		⑦	⑦	⑦	⑦	⑦	⑦	⑦	⑦	⑦	⑦	⑦	⑦
		a	**b**	**a**	**b**	**a**	**b**	△**a**	△**b**	**a**	**b**	**a**	**b**
0	**London** K X. **180** d.	1048	1056	1248	1256	1448	1458	1720		1744	1744	1950	1957
170	Grantham **180** d.	1147	1221	1347	1421	1548	1620	1825		1848	1901	2051	2117
223	Retford **180** d.	1208	1246	1408	1444	1610	1648	|		1910	1929	2113	2139
251	Doncaster **180** a.	1222	1301	1422	1457	1624	1701	1903		1923	1942	2127	2153
280	Selby a.	1243	1318	1444	1518	1645	1719	1922		1945	1959	2143	2215
330	**Hull** a.	1321	1400	1521	1600	1722	1754	2000		2020	2034	2218	2302
330	**Hull** **177** d.	...	...	...	...	...	...	...		2030	...	...	...
343	Beverley **177** a.	...	...	...	...	...	...	...		2043	...	...	...

	Ⓐ	Ⓐ	Ⓐ	Ⓐ		Ⓐ	Ⓐ	Ⓐ	Ⓐ
		△							
Beverley **177** d.	0558	...	...	...	...	...	...	...	...
Hull **177** a.	0613	...	...	...	...	...	...	...	...
Hull d.	0626	0700	0823	1030	...	1233	1512	1710	1911
Selby d.	0700	0734	0857	1106	...	1307	1546	1745	1945
Doncaster **180** d.	0721	0757	0925	1125	...	1325	1604	1803	2003
Retford **180** d.	0740	|	0939	1139	...	1339	1618	1817	2017
Grantham **180** d.	0802	0835	1001	1200	...	1400	1639	1838	2039
London Kings X **180** a.	0914	0955	1105	1305	...	1507	1745	1945	2146

	⑥	⑥	⑥	⑥	⑥	⑥	⑥
		△					
Beverley **177** d.	0559	...	...	...	...	...	...
Hull **177** a.	0614	...	...	...	...	...	...
Hull d.	0622	0700	0823	1031	1331	1530	1836
Selby d.	0657	0734	0858	1106	1405	1605	1910
Doncaster **180** d.	0716	0758	0925	1125	1425	1624	1929
Retford **180** d.	|	|	0939	1139	1439	1638	1943
Grantham **180** d.	0747	0836	1001	1201	1501	1700	2006
London Kings X **180** a.	0852	0947	1108	1311	1607	1804	2114

	⑦	⑦	⑦	⑦	⑦		⑦	⑦	⑦	⑦	⑦
	a	**b**	**a**	**b**	**a**		**b**	**a**	**b**	**a**	**b**
Beverley **177** d.	...	...	1051	1109	...	...	...	...	...	...	...
Hull **177** a.	...	...	1104	1123	...	...	...	...	...	...	...
Hull d.	0906	0906	1112	1130	1436	...	1436	1632	1632	1847	1847
Selby d.	0939	0939	1145	1203	1510	...	1509	1706	1706	1921	1921
Doncaster **180** d.	1000	1000	1204	1227	1528	...	1528	1727	1727	1940	1940
Retford **180** d.	1014	1014	1218	1241	1542	...	1542	1741	1741	1954	1954
Grantham **180** d.	1035	1035	1239	1303	1606	...	1606	1802	1802	2016	2016
London Kings X **180** a.	1140	1159	1342	1423	1714	...	1728	1913	1921	2119	2129

a – Until Feb. 11 and from April 1.
b – Feb. 18 - Mar. 25.
△ – Operated by GR (Table **180**).

182 LONDON - BRADFORD

All trains 🍷 GC

km		Ⓐ	Ⓐ	Ⓐ	Ⓐ	Ⓐ	Ⓐ
					△		
0	**London** Kings Cross **180** d.	1048	1448	1603	1833	1952	2152
123	Peterborough d.	|	|	|	|	|	2245
251	Doncaster **180** a.	1222	1622	1735	2020	2120	2340
278	Pontefract Monkhill a.	1247	1647	|	|	|	|
292	Wakefield Kirkgate a.	1305	1705	1804	2037**e**	2146	0003
	Mirfield a.	1317	1717	1820	|	2159	...
313	Brighouse a.	1325	1725	1828	|	2207	...
322	Halifax **190** a.	1339	1739	1840	|	2223	...
335	**Bradford** Interchange **190** a.	1354	1754	1855	2123**f**	2239	...

km		⑥	⑥	⑥	⑥	⑥
						△
0	**London** Kings Cross **180** d.	1048	1548	1636	1923	1933
123	Peterborough d.	|	|	|	|	|
251	Doncaster **180** a.	1219	1720	1819	2049	2112
278	Pontefract Monkhill a.	|	|	|	2112	|
292	Wakefield Kirkgate a.	1246	1745	1845	2130	2131**e**
	Mirfield a.	1258	1758	1857	2141	|
313	Brighouse a.	1308	1809	1910	2150	|
322	Halifax **190** a.	1320	1821	1922	2203	|
335	**Bradford** Interchange **190** a.	1336	1838	1938	2219	2218**f**

km		⑦	⑦	⑦	⑦	⑦	⑦	⑦	⑦	⑦	⑦
		a	**b**	**a**	**b**	**a**	**a**	**b**	**b**	**a**	**b**
0	**London** Kings Cross **180** d.	1150	1153	1550	1558	1845	1922	1942	2012	2226	2226
123	Peterborough d.	|	|	|	|	|	|	|	|	2325	2339
251	Doncaster **180** a.	1319	1333	1717	1752	2024	2058	2124	2157	0016	0029
278	Pontefract Monkhill a.	|	|	|	|	|	|	|	|	|	|
292	Wakefield Kirkgate a.	1346	1359	1746	1821	2054	2122	2149	2232	0038	0052
	Mirfield a.	1359	1412	1759	1842	2112	2137	2203	2246	...	...
313	Brighouse a.	1408	1420	1807	1849	2123	2145	2211	2254	...	...
322	Halifax **190** a.	1420	1432	1819	1900	2136	2157	2221	2306	...	...
335	**Bradford** Interchange **190** a.	1436	1448	1835	1915	2152	2213	2237	2322	...	...

	Ⓐ	Ⓐ	Ⓐ	Ⓐ		Ⓐ	Ⓐ
		△					
Bradford Interchange **190** d.	...	0630**f**	0655	0754	...	1020	1433
Halifax **190** d.	...	|	0708	0807	...	1034	1448
Brighouse d.	...	|	0719	0818	...	1048	1504
Mirfield d.	...	|	0726	0826	...	1056	1512
Wakefield Kirkgate d.	0504	0713**e**	0744	0855	...	1113	1535
Pontefract Monkhill d.	|	|	0801	|	...	1136	1554
Doncaster **180** d.	0531	|	0831	0931	...	1207	1621
Peterborough d.	0620	|	|	|	...	|	|
London Kings Cross **180** a.	0716	0858	1010	1114	...	1343	1807

	⑥	⑥	⑥	⑥	⑥	⑥
		△				
Bradford Interchange **190** d.	...	0630**f**	0655	0851	1021	1521
Halifax **190** d.	...	|	0709	0905	1035	1535
Brighouse d.	...	|	0720	0916	1049	1549
Mirfield d.	...	|	0728	0924	1057	1557
Wakefield Kirkgate d.	0505	0713**e**	0743	0940	1114	1614
Pontefract Monkhill d.	|	|	0800	0957	1132	1635
Doncaster **180** d.	0533	|	0832	1025	1206	1709
Peterborough d.	0633	|	|	|	|	|
London Kings Cross **180** a.	0721	0859	1002	1154	1343	1843

	⑦	⑦	⑦		⑦	⑦	⑦	⑦	⑦
	a	**b**	**a**		**b**	**a**	**b**	**a**	**b**
Bradford Interchange **190** d.	0755	0810	1205	...	1205	1505	1505	1559	1559
Halifax **190** d.	0810	|	1219	...	1219	1520	1520	1613	1613
Brighouse d.	0821	|	1230	...	1230	1535	1535	1624	1624
Mirfield d.	0829	|	1237	...	1237	1543	1542	1631	1631
Wakefield Kirkgate d.	0846	0846	1255	...	1255	1602	1602	1648	1648
Pontefract Monkhill d.	|	|	|	...	|	|	|	|	|
Doncaster **180** d.	0911	0911	1321	...	1321	1627	1627	1713	1713
Peterborough d.	|	|	|	...	|	|	|	|	|
London Kings Cross **180** a.	1040	1100	1453	...	1507	1757	1814	1845	1904

a – Until Feb. 11 and from April 1.
b – Feb. 18 - Mar. 25.
e – Wakefield Westgate.
f – Bradford Forster Square.
△ – Operated by GR (Table **180**).

183 LONDON - YORK - SUNDERLAND

All trains 🍷 GC

km		Ⓐ	Ⓐ	Ⓐ	Ⓐ	Ⓐ	
0	**London** Kings Cross **180** d.	0803	1121	1253	1650	1918	...
123	Peterborough d.	0850	|	|	|	|	
303	**York** **180** d.	0958	1321	1451	1841	2119	...
339	Thirsk d.	1015	1337	1514	1858	2136	...
351	Northallerton **180** d.	1024	1346	1524	1907	2146	...
375	Eaglescliffe a.	1042	1403	1541	1924	2203	...
399	Hartlepool a.	1108	1423	1607	1944	2223	...
428	**Sunderland** a.	1138	1451	1638	2021	2251	...

km		⑥	⑥	⑥	⑥	⑥	
0	**London** Kings Cross **180** d.	0811	1121	1321	1647	1911	...
123	Peterborough d.	0859	|	|	|	|	
303	**York** **180** d.	1018	1319	1519	1842	2101	...
339	Thirsk d.	1036	1335	1536	1858	2118	...
351	Northallerton **180** d.	1045	1345	1546	1907	2128	...
375	Eaglescliffe a.	1104	1403	1604	1922	2146	...
399	Hartlepool a.	1123	1423	1623	1945	2206	...
428	**Sunderland** a.	1150	1450	1650	2021	2236	...

km		⑦	⑦	⑦	⑦	⑦	⑦	⑦	⑦
		a	**b**	**a**	**b**	**a**	**b**	**a**	**b**
0	**London** Kings Cross **180** d.	0947	0954	1348	1354	1647	1658	1822	1853
123	Peterborough d.	1034	1054	|	|	|	|	|	|
303	**York** **180** d.	1141	1216**c**	1539	1556	1842	1911	2014	2055
339	Thirsk d.	1157	1232	1556	1613	1901	1928	2030	2112
351	Northallerton **180** d.	1205	1241	1606	1621	1912	1937	2040	2121
375	Eaglescliffe a.	1224	1300	1624	1639	1930	1956	2100	2138
399	Hartlepool a.	1243	1320	1652	1704	1952	2017	2120	2158
428	**Sunderland** a.	1309	1351	1720	1735	2020	2050	2151	2225

	Ⓐ	Ⓐ	Ⓐ	Ⓐ	Ⓐ	
Sunderland d.	0645	0842	1228	1530	1731	...
Hartlepool d.	0710	0908	1252	1555	1757	...
Eaglescliffe d.	0729	0927	1311	1616	1821	...
Northallerton **180** d.	0753	0947	1331	1640	1842	...
Thirsk d.	0801	0959	1344	1649	1851	...
York **180** d.	0821	1027**d**	1406	1708	1911	...
Peterborough d.	|	|	|	|	2014	
London Kings Cross **180** a.	1020	1231	1605	1905	2105	...

	⑥	⑥	⑥	⑥	⑥	
Sunderland d.	0643	0830	1218	1529	1729	...
Hartlepool d.	0710	0855	1242	1553	1754	...
Eaglescliffe d.	0729	0914	1301	1611	1812	...
Northallerton **180** d.	0752	0943	1320	1631	1832	...
Thirsk d.	0801	0952	1330	1643	1843	...
York **180** d.	0820	1012	1352	1702	1902	...
Peterborough d.	|	|	|	|	2009	
London Kings Cross **180** a.	1014	1206	1543	1851	2056	...

	⑦	⑦	⑦	⑦	⑦	⑦	⑦	⑦
	a	**b**	**a**	**b**	**a**	**b**	**a**	**b**
Sunderland d.	0920	0920	1212	1212	1412	1412	1812	1812
Hartlepool d.	0945	0945	1236	1236	1438	1440	1840	1840
Eaglescliffe d.	1005	1003	1258	1258	1457	1458	1859	1859
Northallerton **180** d.	1024	1024	1324	1324	1524	1524	1924	1924
Thirsk d.	1033	1033	1333	1333	1533	1533	1933	1933
York **180** d.	1052	1052	1352	1352	1552	1552	1953	1953
Peterborough d.	|	|	|	|	|	|	2058	2059
London Kings Cross **180** a.	1243	1305	1541	1604	1744	1803	2144	2159

a – Until Feb. 11 and from April 1.
b – Feb. 18 - Mar. 25.
c – Arrives 1204.
d – Arrives 1018.

184 LONDON - PETERBOROUGH

TL

km		Ⓐ	Ⓐ	Ⓐ	Ⓐ	Ⓐ	Ⓐ	Ⓐ	Ⓐ	Ⓐ	Ⓐ	and at	Ⓐ	Ⓐ	Ⓐ	Ⓐ	Ⓐ	Ⓐ	Ⓐ	Ⓐ	Ⓐ	Ⓐ	Ⓐ	Ⓐ
0	**London** Kings Cross **180** d.	0034	0134	0522	0622	0634	0722	0734	0809	0822	0834	the same	1522	1534	1622	1640	1650	1707	1712	1737	1742	1807	1812	1837
4	Finsbury Park d.	0040	0140	0528	0628	0640	0728	0740	|	0828	0840	minutes	1528	1540	1628	|	1656	|	1719	|	1749	|	1819	|
44	Stevenage **180** d.	0113	0222	0559	0648	0712	0748	0812	|	0847	0912	past each	1547	1613	1650	|	1718	|	1741	|	1810	|	1840	|
95	Huntingdon d.	0152**s**	0256**s**	0639	0724	0751	0824	0851	0855	0923	0951	hour until	1624	1651	1732	1728	1756	1801	1819	1830	1847	1859	1917	1928
123	**Peterborough** **180** a.	0212	0316	0654	0739	0806	0839	0908	0912	0938	1006	▽	1639	1706	...	1743	1811	1819	1834	1853	1903	1921	1932	1943

	Ⓐ	Ⓐ	Ⓐ	Ⓐ	Ⓐ	Ⓐ	Ⓐ	Ⓐ	Ⓐ	Ⓐ	Ⓐ	Ⓐ	⑥	⑥	⑥	⑥	⑥	⑥	⑥	⑥	⑥	⑥	and at
London Kings Cross **180** d.	1842	1910	1922	1952	2010	2022	2107	2122	2207	2222	2301	2322	0001	0034	0134	0522	0622	0634	0722	0734	0822	0834	the same
Finsbury Park d.	1849	|	1928	1958	|	2028	|	2128	|	2228	|	2328	|	0040	0140	0528	0628	0640	0728	0740	0828	0840	minutes
Stevenage **180** d.	1910	|	1948	2020	|	2048	|	2147	|	2248	|	2348	0022	0113	0222	0600	0648	0713	0748	0812	0848	0912	past each
Huntingdon d.	1948	2001	2025	2058	2054	2124	2155	2224	2255	2324	2349	0024	0055**s**	0152**s**	0256**s**	0639	0724	0751	0824	0851	0924	0951	hour until
Peterborough **180** a.	2003	2019	2041	2114	2111	2139	2210	2240	2310	2343	0014	0042	0113	0212	0316	0654	0739	0807	0839	0906	0939	1006	▽

	⑥	⑥	⑥	⑥	⑥	⑥	⑥	⑥	⑥	⑥	⑥	⑥	⑥	⑥	⑥	⑥	⑥	⑥	⑥**w**	⑦**r**	⑦**r**	⑦**v**	⑦**y**	⑦**v**
London Kings Cross **180** d.	1622	1634	1640	1722	1734	1740	1822	1834	1840	1922	1934	2022	2034	2122	2134	2222	2252	2322	2352	0022	0054	0704	0808	0822
Finsbury Park d.	1628	1640	|	1728	1740	|	1828	1840	|	1928	1940	2028	2040	2128	2140	2228	2258	2328	2358	0028	0100	0710	0814	0828
Stevenage **180** d.	1648	1713	|	1748	1813	|	1848	1913	|	1948	2013	2048	2113	2148	2213	2248	2318	2348	0024	0057	0134	0750	0841	0848
Huntingdon d.	1724	1751	1728	1824	1851	1828	1924	1951	1928	2024	2051	2124	2151	2223	2251	2324	2354	0024	0103**s**	0135**s**	0212**s**	0828	0918	0924
Peterborough **180** a.	1739	1806	1743	1839	1906	1844	1939	2006	1943	2039	2106	2139	2206	2238	2306	2341	0011	0041	0124	0156	0232	0843	0933	0939

	and at	⑦**y**	⑦**v**	⑦**y**	⑦**y**	⑦**v**	⑦**v**	⑦**y**	⑦**y**	⑦**y**	⑦**v**	⑦**v**	⑦**v**	⑦**y**	⑦**v**	⑦**y**	⑦**v**	⑦**y**	⑦**v**	⑦**v**	⑦**y**	⑦**v**	⑦**v**	⑦**y**
London Kings Cross **180** d.	the same	1608	1622	*1638*	1708	1710	1722	*1738*	1800	1808	1810	1822	1840	1908	1922	2008	2022	2108	2122	2222	2222	2233	2322	2322
Finsbury Park d.	minutes	1614	1628	*1644*	1714	|	1728	*1744*	|	1814	|	1828	|	1914	1928	2014	2028	2114	2128	2228	2228	2239	2328	2328
Stevenage **180** d.	past each	1641	1648	1714	1741	|	1748	1817	|	1841	|	1848	|	1941	1948	2041	2048	2141	2148	2248	2255	2313	2348	2354
Huntingdon d.	hour until	1718	1724	1751	1818	1758	1824	1854	1858	1918	1856	1924	1933	2018	2024	2118	2124	2218	2224	2324	2332	2347	0024	0031
Peterborough **180** a.	▽	1733	1739	1806	1833	1819	1839	1909	1913	1933	1913	1939	1953	2036	2040	2133	2139	2233	2239	2343	2350	0007	0043	0051

f – Runs 6 minutes earlier until Feb. 11 and from April 1.
p – Runs 10 minutes earlier Feb. 18 - Mar. 25.
q – Runs 6 minutes earlier Jan. 7 - Feb. 11.
r – Until Dec. 31 and from April 1.
s – Calls to set down only.
t – Connection by 🚌; change at Hitchin.
v – Until Feb. 11 and from April 1.

For return service and other footnotes see next page ▷ ▷ ▷

		Ⓐ	Ⓐ	Ⓐ	Ⓐ	Ⓐ	Ⓐ	Ⓐ	Ⓐ	Ⓐ	Ⓐ	Ⓐ	Ⓐ	Ⓐ	Ⓐ	Ⓐ	Ⓐ	Ⓐ	Ⓐ	Ⓐ	Ⓐ	and at	Ⓐ	Ⓐ	Ⓐ	Ⓐ
Peterborough ... **180** d.	Ⓐ	0325	0410	0510	0540	0547	0615	0632	0656	0715	0707	0726	0733	0747	0816	0847	0919	0930	0946	1018	1046	the same	1619	1646	1722	...
Huntingdon .... d.		0339	0425	0524	0555	0601	0629	0646	0710	0733	0722	0740	0748	0802	0830	0901	0934	0944	1000	1034	1100	minutes	1634	1700	1737	1803
Stevenage .... **180** d.		0415	0504	0603	|	0639	0658	0724	0736	0758	0801	|	0827	0832	0907	0937	1003	1021	1036	1111	1136	past each	1713	1736	1815	1837
Finsbury Park .... d.		0452**s**	0537	0623	|	0706	|	0744	|	|	0821	|	0848	|	0928	1000	|	|	1056	1143	1156	hour until	1743	1756	1851	1857
London Kings X 180 a.		0501	0546	0629	0642	0712	0722	0750	0800	0821	0829	0828	0855	0855	0934	1006	1027	1047	1103	1149	1202	▽	1749	1802	1857	1904

	Ⓐ	Ⓐ	Ⓐ	Ⓐ	Ⓐ	Ⓐ	Ⓐ	Ⓐ	Ⓐ	Ⓐ	Ⓐ		⑥	⑥	⑥	⑥	⑥	⑥	⑥	⑥	⑥	⑥	⑥	⑥	⑥	⑥	⑥
Peterborough ... **180** d.	1754	1822	1846	1916	1946	2016	2044	2121	2146	2222	2244	⑥	0325	0419	0519	0546	0619	0646	0719	0746	0806	0819	0846	0908	...	0946	1013
Huntingdon .... d.	1812	1840	1901	1936	2000	2033	2058	2136	2200	2236	2258		0339	0434	0534	0600	0634	0700	0734	0800	0821	0834	0900	0923	0934	1000	1027
Stevenage .... **180** d.	1850	1918	1936	2014	2036	2111	2136	2213	2236	2317	2336		0415	0511	0611	0636	0711	0736	0811	0838	|	0911	0936	|	1011	1036	|
Finsbury Park .... d.	1910	1950	1956	2045	2056	2144	2156	2244	2256	2348	2356		0453**s**	0543	0643	0656	0743	0756	0844	0900	|	0945	0956	|	1044	1056	|
London Kings X 180 a.	1919	1956	2002	2051	2103	2149	2202	2250	2302	2354	0003		0459	0549	0649	0702	0749	0802	0850	0906	0913	0951	1002	1012	1050	1102	1116

	⑥	⑥	and at	⑥	⑥	⑥	⑥	⑥	⑥	⑥	⑥	⑥	⑥	⑥	⑥		⑦z	⑦r	⑦z	⑦r	⑦z	⑦r	⑦v	⑦y	⑦v	⑦y
Peterborough ... **180** d.	1019	1046	the same	1719	1747	1819	1846	1916	1946	2020	2046	2116	2147	2219	2246	⑦	*0405*t	0546	*0505*t	0646	*0605*t	0746	0846	0846	0915	0915
Huntingdon .... d.	1033	1101	minutes	1734	1800	1834	1900	1934	2000	2034	2100	2134	2201	2234	2300		*0445*t	0600	*0545*t	0700	*0645*t	0800	0900	0900	0930	0930
Stevenage .... **180** d.	1112	1137	past each	1811	1837	1912	1936	2011	2036	2111	2136	2211	2237	2311	2336		0637	0641	0738	0739	0836	0836	0936	0936	|	|
Finsbury Park .... d.	1144	1158	hour until	1845	1857	1945	1956	2043	2057	2143	2156	2243	2257	2343	2359**s**		0714**p**	0714	0802	0802	0906**q**	0900	0956	1003	|	|
London Kings X 180 a.	1151	1204	▽	1851	1903	1951	2002	2049	2103	2149	2202	2249	2303	2349	0009		0723**p**	0723	0814	0810	0912**q**	0906	1002	1009	1017	1026

	⑦y	⑦v	⑦v	⑦y	⑦y	⑦v	⑦v	⑦y	⑦v	⑦y	⑦	⑦v	⑦y	⑦v	⑦y	⑦v	⑦y	⑦v	⑦y	⑦v	⑦y	⑦	⑦v	⑦y	⑦	⑦	⑦
Peterborough ... **180** d.	0944	0946	1015	1015	1044	1046	1115	1115	1146	1146	1246	1346	1346	1446	1446	1546	1546	1646	1646	1746	1746	1846	1946	1946	2046	2146	2301
Huntingdon .... d.	0958	1000	1030	1030	1058	1100	1130	1130	1200	1201	1300	1400	1400	1500	1500	1600	1600	1700	1700	1800	1800	1900	2000	2000	2100	2200	2315
Stevenage .... **180** d.	1035	1036	|	|	1135	1136	|	|	1236	1240	1336	1436	1440	1536	1538	1636	1637	1736	1739	1836	1838	1936	2036	2039	2136	2236	2352
Finsbury Park .... d.	1101	1057	|	|	1201	1157	|	|	1257	1306	1403**f**	1456	1507	1557	1605	1656	1703	1756	1807	1857	1904	2003**f**	2057	2105	2203**f**	2303**f**	0020**s**
London Kings X 180 a.	1107	1103	1116	1126	1207	1203	1216	1226	1303	1312	1409**f**	1502	1513	1603	1611	1702	1709	1802	1813	1903	1910	2009**f**	2103	2111	2209**f**	2309**f**	0029

◀◀◀ For additional notes see previous page. w – From Mar. 31. y – Feb. 18 - Mar. 25. z – Jan. 7 - Mar. 25. ▽ – Timings may vary by up to 2 minutes.

EM 2nd class PETERBOROUGH - LINCOLN - DONCASTER 185

km		⑥	Ⓐ	⚒T	⚒	⚒	ⒶD	Ⓐ	⑥	⑥	Ⓐ	Ⓐ	ⒶD	⑥	⚒	Ⓐ	⚒	⚒	⑥	ⒶD	⚒	⚒D	⚒	Ⓐ	⑥	⚒
0	**Peterborough** .... d.	...	...	0630	...	0730	...	0833	0833	0932	0935	1040	1150	1152	1241	1341	1511	1625	...	...	1732	...	1836	...	...	2030
27	Spalding..................... d.	...	...	0653	...	0753	...	0854	0854	0953	0956	1101	1213	1213	1302	1404	1532	1646	...	...	1755	...	1859	...	...	2053
57	Sleaford..................... d.	0650	0653	...	0743	...	0840	0918	0919	1020	1021	1125	1242	1241	1326	1429	1614**t**	1718	1754	1756	...	1900	...	2005	2010	...
91	**Lincoln**..................... a.	0722	0726	...	0815	...	0913	0953	0956	1053	1053	1201	1314	1314	1403	1503	1647	1751	1827	1829	...	1932	...	2039	2044	...

	Ⓐ	⚒	Ⓐ	⑥	⚒	⚒N	Ⓐ	Ⓐ	⑥	⚒	Ⓐ	ⒶR	⑥R	⚒	Ⓐ	ⒶR	⑥R	⚒	⑥	Ⓐ	⚒	⚒	⑥	Ⓐ	⚒L	⑥T	ⒶT
Lincoln .... d.	0617	...	...	...	0705	0800	0910	1018	1018	1110	1210	1330	1330	1441	1512	1600	1601	...	1715	1718	1810	...	1905	1915	2048	...	...
Sleaford .... d.	0645	...	...	...	0737	0834	0942	1051	1051	1142	1242	1403	1403	1516	1544	1634	1634	...	1747	1753	1842	...	1937	1947	2120	...	...
Spalding .... d.	...	0700	0800	0805	...	0900	1006	1113	1119	1204	1307	1425	1427	1538	...	1656	1657	1808	...	...	...	1959	...	...	...	2103	2105
Peterborough .... a.	...	0722	0822	0827	...	0924	1030	1134	1143	1228	1330	1446	1451	1602	...	1718	1723	1831	...	...	...	2022	...	...	...	2125	2127

km		Ⓐ	ⒶS	⑥	⚒	ⒶP	⑥	⑥	ⒶS	⚒S
0	**Lincoln** .... d.	0700	0915	0915	1154	1315	1410	1510	1831	1932
26	Gainsborough Lea Road .... d.	0721	0935	0935	1215	1335	1430	1530	1855	1952
60	**Doncaster** .... a.	*0808*r	1002	1005	1245	1407	1458	1600	1925	2023

	⑥	Ⓐ	Ⓐ	⑥	Ⓐ	⑥	⑥	Ⓐ	⚒
Doncaster .... d.	1024	1024	1301	1305	1427	1507	1627	1937	2033
Gainsborough Lea Road .... d.	1048	1053	1329	1329	1452	1531	1652	2001	2056
Lincoln .... a.	1110	1116	1352	1354	1515	1557	1719	2023	2125

D – To/from Doncaster (lower panel).
L – To Boston (Table **194**).
N – From Nottingham (Table **186**).
P – To/from Peterborough (upper panel).
R – From Newark North Gate (Table **186**).
S – To/from Sleaford (upper panel).
T – From/to Nottingham (Table **206**).
r – Change trains at Retford (a. 0743, d. 0754).
t – Arrives 1556.

EM 2nd class GRIMSBY - LINCOLN - NOTTINGHAM 186

km			Ⓐ	Ⓐ	Ⓐ	ⒶA	ⒶB	Ⓐ	Ⓐ	Ⓐ	Ⓐ	Ⓐ	Ⓐ	Ⓐ	Ⓐ	Ⓐ	Ⓐ	Ⓐ	Ⓐ	Ⓐ	Ⓐ	Ⓐ	Ⓐ	Ⓐ	Ⓐ	Ⓐ	Ⓐ
0	**Grimsby** Town......... d.	Ⓐ	...	...	0556	...	...	...	0703	...	...	...	0920	...	...	...	1128	...	...	...	1349	...	...	...	1545	...	...
47	Market Rasen........... d.		...	...	0632	...	...	...	0739	...	...	...	0955	...	...	...	1203	...	...	...	1425	...	...	...	1621	...	...
71	**Lincoln**.................... a.		...	...	0651	...	...	...	0757	...	...	...	1014	...	...	...	1222	...	...	...	1444	...	...	...	1640	...	...
71	**Lincoln**.................... d.		0526	0646	0654	0704	0730	0736	0759	0836	0907	0937	1016	1036	1135	1140	1223	1234	1337	1436	1446	1536	1542	1634	1643	1726	1818
97	Newark North Gate a.		0556	|	0722	|	0755	|	0824	|	0932	|	1040	|	1200	|	1250	|	|	|	1511	|	1611	|	1711	|	1846
98	Newark Castle......♧ d.		0609	0714	...	0729	...	0806	...	0907	...	1007	...	1107	...	1207	...	1305	1407	1506	...	1608	...	1705	...	1756	...
126	**Nottingham** ....♧ a.		0647	0740	...	0756	...	0833	...	0930	...	1030	...	1130	...	1230	...	1330	1430	1530	...	1630	...	1730	..	1830	...

	Ⓐ	Ⓐ	Ⓐ	Ⓐ	Ⓐ		⑥	⑥A	⑥	⑥B	⑥	⑥	⑥		⑥	⑥	⑥	⑥	⑥	⑥	⑥	⑥	⑥	⑥	⑥	⑥	⑥
Grimsby Town .... d.	...	1828	...	...	2124	⑥	...	...	...	...	0650	...	...	...	...	0920	...	...	...	1128	...	...	...	1349	...	...	1600
Market Rasen .... d.	...	1904	...	...	2200		...	...	...	...	0726	...	...	...	...	0955	...	...	...	1203	...	...	...	1425	...	...	1635
Lincoln .... a.	...	1923	...	...	2219		...	...	...	...	0744	...	...	...	...	1014	...	...	...	1222	...	...	...	1444	...	...	1653
Lincoln .... d.	1835	1925	2031	2140	*2226*		0526	0704	0726	0733	0746	0835	0901	...	0936	1015	1036	1135	1140	1223	1236	1337	1432	1446	1526	1635	1655
Newark North Gate a.	|	1953	|	|	|		0556	|	|	0800	0812	|	0925	...	|	1044	|	1158	|	1252	|	|	|	1511	|	|	1722
Newark Castle ......♧ d.	1903	...	2058	2207	*2255*		0610	0729	0756	...	...	0904	...	...	1007	...	1104	...	1204	...	1306	1405	1504	...	1559	1705	...
Nottingham.........♧ a.	1930	...	2127	2239	*2328*		0647	0757	0823	...	...	0931	...	...	1030	...	1131	...	1227	...	1329	1429	1530	...	1627	1730	...

	⑥	⑥	⑥	⑥	⑥		⑦	⑦	⑦	⑦	⑦	⑦	⑦	⑦	⑦	⑦	⑦	⑦	⑦	⑦	⑦	⑦	⑦	⑦		⑦	⑦
Grimsby Town .... d.	...	...	1828	...	1945	⑦	...	...	...	...	...	...	...	...	...	...	...	...	...	...	...	...	...	...	...	...	...
Market Rasen .... d.	...	...	1902	...	2020		...	...	...	...	...	...	...	...	...	...	...	...	...	...	...	...	...	...	...	...	...
Lincoln .... a.	...	...	1921	...	2039		...	...	...	...	...	...	...	...	...	...	...	...	...	...	...	...	...	...	...	...	...
Lincoln .... d.	1725	1830	1924	1939	*2045*		0847	0959	1105	1110	1156	1245	1300	1417	1508	1544	1615	1656	1709	1805	1903	1922	2005	2100	...	2126	2210
Newark North Gate a.	|	|	1953	|	|		0919	|	1130	|	|	1310	|	|	1536	1609	|	|	1734	|	|	1946	|	2127	...	2155	|
Newark Castle ......♧ d.	1755	1859	...	2004	*2110*		0929	1024	...	1142	1224	...	1329	1449	1551	...	1646	1724	...	1834	1933	...	2036	2140	...	...	2239
Nottingham.........♧ a.	1830	1924	...	2031	*2137*		1008	1053	...	1221	1257	...	1357	1528	1620	...	1726	1754	...	1911	2005	...	2103	2209	...	...	2316

		Ⓐ	Ⓐ	ⒶP	Ⓐ	Ⓐ	Ⓐ	Ⓐ	Ⓐ	Ⓐ	Ⓐ	Ⓐ	Ⓐ	Ⓐ	ⒶP	Ⓐ	Ⓐ	Ⓐ	ⒶP	Ⓐ	Ⓐ	Ⓐ	Ⓐ	Ⓐ	Ⓐ	Ⓐ	Ⓐ
Nottingham.........♧ d.	Ⓐ	...	0554	0653	...	...	0812	0925	...	...	1029	1129	...	1229	...	1329	...	1429	...	1529	...	1627	...	1721	1750	1817	...
Newark Castle ......♧ d.		...	0630	0727	...	...	0840	0952	...	...	1051	1153	...	1253	...	1352	...	1453	...	1553	...	1653	...	1752	1818	1853	...
Newark North Gate d.		...	|	|	0742	0831	|	|	0957	1050	|	|	1206	|	1302	|	...	|	1528	|	1646	|	1728	|	|	|	1935
Lincoln .... a.		...	0704	0756	0812	0902	0908	1017	1023	1114	1126	1221	1236	1323	1330	1423	...	1522	1555	1623	1713	1717	1800	1824	1849	1922	2001
Lincoln .... d.		0557	...	...	0815	...	...	...	1025	...	...	...	1237	...	...	...	1437	...	...	...	1722	...	...	...	...	...	2002
Market Rasen .... d.		0613	...	...	0832	...	...	...	1042	...	...	...	1254	...	...	...	1454	...	...	...	1739	...	...	...	...	...	2019
Grimsby Town .... a.		0655	...	...	0912	...	...	...	1122	...	...	...	1335	...	...	...	1534	...	...	...	1818	...	...	...	...	...	2056

	Ⓐ	Ⓐ	ⒶB	ⒶA	Ⓐ	Ⓐ		⑥	⑥	⑥P	⑥	⑥	⑥	⑥	⑥	⑥	⑥	⑥	⑥	⑥P	⑥	⑥	⑥P	⑥	⑥	⑥	⑥
Nottingham.........♧ d.	1919	...	...	2030	2120	2226	⑥	...	0555	0653	...	0811	...	0922	...	1029	1129	...	1229	...	1329	1419	...	1528	1621	1729	...
Newark Castle ......♧ d.	1954	...	...	2054	2155	2257		...	0630	0726	...	0842	...	0951	...	1051	1155	...	1253	...	1351	1442	...	1554	1643	1750	...
Newark North Gate d.	|	2003	2035	|	|	2310		...	|	|	0820	|	0935	|	1049	|	|	1205	|	1302	|	|	1529	|	|	|	1807
Lincoln .... a.	2021	2027	2101	2122	2222	2340		...	0703	0758	0855	0909	0959	1019	1117	1125	1226	1236	1322	1330	1424	1511	1556	1625	1708	1823	1834
Lincoln .... d.	...	...	...	...	...	...		0538	...	*0808*	...	...	1006	...	...	...	...	1236	...	...	*1452*	...	...	...	*1722*	...	1835
Market Rasen .... d.	...	...	...	...	...	...		0554	...	*0825*	...	...	1023	...	...	...	...	1254	...	...	*1510*	...	...	...	*1738*	...	1852
Grimsby Town .... a.	...	...	...	...	...	...		0636	...	*0912*	...	...	1102	...	...	...	...	1334	...	...	*1550*	...	...	...	*1818*	...	1934

	⑥	⑥A	⑥	⑥B	⑥	⑥		⑦	⑦	⑦	⑦	⑦	⑦	⑦	⑦	⑦	⑦	⑦	⑦	⑦	⑦	⑦	⑦B	⑦B	⑦	⑦	⑦
Nottingham.........♧ d.	1819	1929	...	...	2030	2124	⑦	0930	1030	...	1130	1230	...	1330	1435	1530	...	1633	...	1727	1836	1935	**b**	**c**	2039	...	2228
Newark Castle ......♧ d.	1843	1953	...	...	2104	2157		1006	1055	...	1206	1254	...	1354	1513	1556	...	1659	...	1801	1859	1958	...	...	2103	...	2303
Newark North Gate d.	|	|	2032	2039	|	2209		|	|	1140	|	|	1335	|	|	|	1645	|	1755	|	1928**a**	|	2037	2055	|	2210	2317
Lincoln .... a.	1923	2026	2056	2103	2132	2240		1040	1123	1207	1240	1325	1402	1423	1550	1626	1716	1731	1820	1833	1957	2030	2101	2120	2135	2237	2348
Lincoln .... d.	...	...	2057	...	...	...		...	...	...	...	...	...	...	...	...	...	...	...	...	...	...	...	...	...	...	...
Market Rasen .... d.	...	...	2115	...	...	...		...	...	...	...	...	...	...	...	...	...	...	...	...	...	...	...	...	...	...	...
Grimsby Town .... a.	...	...	...	...	...	...		...	...	...	...	...	...	...	...	...	...	...	...	...	...	...	...	...	...	...	...

A – (12) 🍷 Lincoln - London St Pancras and v.v. (Table **170**).
B – (12) 🍷 Lincoln - London Kings Cross and v.v. (Table **180**).
P – To Peterborough (Table **185**).
a – Arrives 1909.
b – Not Feb. 18 - Mar. 25.
c – Feb. 18 - Mar. 25.

♧ – Additional journeys Newark Castle - Nottingham and v.v. Journey time: 28–36 minutes. **From Newark Castle** at 0642Ⓐ, 0739Ⓐ, 0741⑥, 0841Ⓐ, 0843⑥, 0938⚒, 1047⚒, 1139⚒, 1247⚒, 1347Ⓐ, 1349⑥, 1439⚒, 1547⚒, 1638⚒, 1739⚒, 1847⑥, 1947⚒. **From Nottingham** at 0756Ⓐ, 0758⑥, 0854⚒, 0949Ⓐ, 0951⑥, 1049Ⓐ, 1052⑥, 1153⚒, 1249⚒, 1349⚒, 1452⚒, 1549⚒, 1649⚒, 1748⑥, 1852Ⓐ, 1857⑥.

① – Mondays ② – Tuesdays ③ – Wednesdays ④ – Thursdays ⑤ – Fridays ⑥ – Saturdays ⑦ – Sundays Ⓐ – Not Saturdays 67

188 THE NORTH EAST and YORKSHIRE - MANCHESTER and LIVERPOOL TP

⚒

km		②–⑤	①	⑥	②–⑤	①	⑥	②–⑥	①	Ⓐ	⚒	⚒	⚒	Ⓐ	⚒	⚒	⑥	Ⓐ	⚒	⚒	⚒	⚒	⚒	⚒	⚒	⚒	⚒	Ⓐ
0	**Newcastle** d.	...	...	...	...	...	...	...	...	...	...	...	...	...	...	...	...	0533	...	...	0602	...	...	...	...	0706	...	...
23	Durham d.	...	...	...	...	...	...	...	...	...	...	...	...	...	...	...	...	0546	...	...	0620	...	...	...	...	0719	...	...
34	**Middlesbrough** d.	...	...	...	...	...	...	...	...	...	...	...	...	...	...	...	...	|	0554	...	|	...	0631	...	...	|	0715	...
58	Darlington d.	...	...	...	...	...	...	...	...	...	...	...	...	...	...	...	...	0603	|	...	0637	...	|	...	...	0736	|	...
81	Northallerton d.	...	...	...	...	...	...	...	...	...	...	...	...	...	...	...	...	|	0622	...	0649	...	0659	...	...	|	0742	...
93	Thirsk d.	...	...	...	...	...	...	...	...	...	...	...	...	...	...	...	...	|	0630	...	|	...	0710	...	...	|	0755	...
◧	**Scarborough** d.	...	...	...	...	...	...	...	...	...	...	...	...	...	...	...	...	|	|	...	|	0630	|	0700	...	|	|	0738
◧	Malton d.	...	...	...	...	...	...	...	...	...	...	...	...	...	...	...	...	|	|	...	|	0653	|	0723	...	|	|	0801
129	**York** a.	...	...	...	...	...	...	...	...	...	...	...	...	...	...	...	...	0636	0648	...	0712	0718	0728	0747	...	0810	0813	0826
129	**York** d.	0138	0138	0138	0252	0252	0252	0400	0420	...	0521	...	0555	...	0616	...	0640	0645	0651	...	0714	0723	0737	0750	...	0814	0823	0840
◧	**Hull** d.	|	|	|	|	|	|	|	|	...	|	...	|	...	|	0548	|	|	|	0637	|	|	|	|	0735	|	|	|
◧	Selby d.	|	|	|	|	|	|	|	|	...	|	...	|	...	|	0623	|	|	|	0709	|	|	|	|	0808	|	|	|
170	**Leeds** a.	0220	0204	0219	0333	0318	0333	0441	0446	...	0547	...	0618	...	0640	0647	0705	0707	0717	0733	0740	0750	0805	0820	0832	0840	0851	0904
170	**Leeds** d.	0220	0205	0220	0335	0320	0335	0449	0449	...	0550	...	0620	0635	0644	0652	0710	0710	0720	0735	0744	0753	0809	0824	0836	0844	0854	0909
185	Dewsbury d.	|	|	|	|	|	|	|	|	...	0601	...	0631	0646	|	|	0721	0721	|	0746	|	|	0820	|	0847	|	|	0920
198	Huddersfield d.	0243	0243	0256	0358	0358	0411	0526	0526	...	0611	...	0640	0655	0702	0710	0731	0731	0739	0756	0802	0811	0830	0842	0856	0902	0912	0930
227	Stalybridge d.	|	|	|	|	|	|	|	|	...	0630	...	0659	0714	|	0728	0750	0750	0759	0817	|	|	0850	|	0915	|	|	0950
	Manchester Victoria d.	|	|	|	|	|	|	|	|	...	|	...	|	|	0735	|	|	|	|	|	0835	|	|	|	|	0935	|	|
239	**Manchester** Piccadilly a.	0343	0343	0329	0458	0458	0443	0557	0557	0607	0645	0707	0715	0730	|	0743	0805	0805	0816	0833	|	0845	0905	0913	0932	|	0945	1005
255	**Manchester** Airport ✈ a.	0358	0358	0347	0513	0513	0503	0619	0619	|	0710	|	0742	...	|	0810	|	|	0839	...	|	0910	|	0939	...	|	1010	|
265	Warrington Central a.	...	...	...	...	...	...	...	...	0628	...	0728	...	...	|	...	0830	0830	...	...	|	...	0930	...	...	|	...	1030
286	**Liverpool** South Parkway a.	...	...	...	...	...	...	...	...	|	...	|	...	...	|	...	0847	0847	...	...	|	...	0947	...	...	|	...	1047
295	**Liverpool** Lime Street a.	...	...	...	...	...	...	...	...	0656	...	0753	...	...	0808	...	0859	0859	...	...	0909	...	0959	...	...	1008	...	1059

	⑥	⚒	⚒	⚒	⚒	⚒	⚒	⚒	⚒	⚒	⚒	⚒	⚒	⚒	⚒	⚒	⚒	⚒	Ⓐ	⑥	⚒	⚒	⚒	⚒	⚒	⚒	⚒	⚒	⚒
Newcastle d.	...	0748r	...	0806	...	...	...	...	0910	...	...	...	...	1003g	...	...	1048t	...	1106	1110	...	...	...	...	1206	...	...	1248t	...
Durham d.	...	0801r	...	0822	...	...	...	...	0923	...	...	...	...	1020	...	...	1101r	...	1119	1123	...	...	...	...	1222	...	...	1301r	...
Middlesbrough d.	...	|	...	|	0827	...	...	...	|	0927	...	...	...	|	1027	...	|	...	|	|	1127	...	...	...	|	1227	...	|	...
Darlington d.	...	0818r	...	0839	|	...	...	...	0940	|	...	...	...	1037	|	...	1118	...	1136	1140	|	...	...	...	1239	|	...	1318	...
Northallerton d.	...	|	...	0850	0856	...	...	...	0951	0956	...	...	...	1049	1056	...	|	...	1147	1151	1156	...	...	...	1250	1256	...	|	...
Thirsk d.	...	|	...	|	0904	...	...	...	|	1004	...	...	...	|	1104	...	|	...	|	|	1204	...	...	...	|	1304	...	|	...
Scarborough d.	0750	|	...	|	|	0850	...	...	|	|	0950	...	...	|	|	1050	|	...	|	|	|	1150	...	...	|	|	1250	|	...
Malton d.	0813	|	...	|	|	0913	...	...	|	|	1013	...	...	|	|	1113	|	...	|	|	|	1213	...	...	|	|	1313	|	...
York a.	0838	0850r	...	0915	0922	0938	...	...	1014	1022	1038	...	...	1113	1122	1138	1151	...	1210	1214	1222	1238	...	...	1313	1322	1338	1351	...
York d.	0840	0853	...	0915	0923	0940	0953	...	1015	1023	1040	1053	...	1115	1123	1140	1153	...	1215	1215	1223	1240	1253	...	1315	1323	1340	1353	...
Hull d.	|	|	0838	|	|	|	|	0938	|	|	|	|	1038	|	|	|	|	1138	|	|	|	|	|	1238	|	|	|	|	1338
Selby d.	|	|	0910	|	|	|	|	1010	|	|	|	|	1111	|	|	|	|	1210	|	|	|	|	|	1310	|	|	|	|	1410
Leeds a.	0904	0916	0934	0940	0949	1004	1017	1034	1040	1050	1104	1116	1134	1139	1150	1204	1216	1234	1239	1239	1249	1304	1316	1334	1339	1349	1404	1416	1434
Leeds d.	0909	0920	0936	0944	0953	1009	1020	1036	1044	1053	1109	1120	1136	1144	1153	1209	1220	1236	1244	1244	1253	1309	1320	1336	1344	1351	1409	1420	1436
Dewsbury d.	0920	|	0947	|	|	1020	|	1047	|	|	1120	|	1147	|	|	1220	|	1247	|	|	|	1320	|	1347	|	|	1420	|	1447
Huddersfield d.	0930	0940	0956	1002	1011	1030	1040	1056	1102	1111	1130	1140	1156	1202	1211	1230	1240	1256	1302	1302	1311	1330	1340	1356	1402	1409	1430	1440	1456
Stalybridge d.	0950	|	1015	|	|	1050	|	1115	|	|	1150	|	1215	|	|	1250	|	1315	|	|	|	1350	|	1415	|	|	1450	|	1515
Manchester Victoria d.	|	|	|	1035	|	|	|	|	1135	|	|	|	|	1235	|	|	|	|	1335	1335	|	|	|	|	1435	|	|	|	|
Manchester Piccadilly a.	1005	1013	1032	|	1045	1105	1113	1132	|	1145	1205	1213	1232	|	1245	1305	1313	1332	|	|	1344	1405	1413	1432	|	1444	1505	1513	1532
Manchester Airport ✈ a.	|	1039	...	|	1110	|	1139	...	|	1210	|	1239	...	|	1310	|	1339	...	|	|	1410	|	1439	...	|	1510	|	1539	...
Warrington Central a.	1030	...	...	|	...	1130	...	...	|	...	1230	...	...	|	...	1330	...	...	|	|	...	1430	...	...	|	...	1530	...	...
Liverpool South Parkway a.	1046	...	...	|	...	1147	...	...	|	...	1247	...	...	|	...	1347	...	...	|	|	...	1447	...	...	|	...	1547	...	...
Liverpool Lime Street a.	1058	...	...	1108	...	1159	...	...	1208	...	1259	...	...	1308	...	1359	...	...	1408	1408	...	1459	...	...	1508	...	1559	...	...

	⚒	⚒	⚒	⑥	Ⓐ	⚒	Ⓐ	⑥	⚒	⚒	Ⓐ	⑥	⚒	⚒	⚒	⚒	⚒	⚒	⚒	⚒	⚒	⑥	Ⓐ	⚒	Ⓐ	⑥	⚒	⚒	⚒
Newcastle d.	1310	...	...	...	...	...	1403	1406	...	...	1447	1452	...	1508	...	...	...	...	1606	...	...	1651	...	...	1703	1706	...	...	...
Durham d.	1323	...	...	...	...	...	1420	1422	...	...	1501	|	...	1523	...	...	...	...	1622	...	...	|	...	...	1719	1722	...	...	...
Middlesbrough d.	|	1327	...	...	...	...	|	|	1427	...	|	|	...	|	1527	...	...	...	|	1626	...	|	...	...	|	|	1726	...	...
Darlington d.	1340	|	...	...	...	...	1437	1439	|	...	1518	1519	...	1540	|	...	...	...	1639	|	...	1718	...	...	1736	1739	|	...	...
Northallerton d.	1351	1356	...	...	...	...	1448	1450	1456	...	|	|	...	1551	1556	...	...	...	1650	1654	...	|	...	...	1747	1750	1754	...	...
Thirsk d.	|	1404	...	...	...	...	|	|	1504	...	|	|	...	|	1604	...	...	...	|	1702	...	|	...	...	|	|	1802	...	...
Scarborough d.	|	|	1350	...	...	...	|	|	|	1450	|	|	...	|	|	1550	...	...	|	|	1650	|	...	...	|	|	|	1750	...
Malton d.	|	|	1413	...	...	...	|	|	|	1513	|	|	...	|	|	1613	...	...	|	|	1713	|	...	...	|	|	|	1813	...
York a.	1415	1422	1438	...	...	...	1511	1513	1522	1538	1550	1551	...	1615	1622	1638	...	...	1713	1720	1738	1751	...	...	1810	1815	1820	1838	...
York d.	1415	1423	1440	1453	1453	...	1515	1515	1523	1540	1553	1553	...	1615	1623	1640	1653	...	1715	1722	1740	1753	1753	...	1815	1815	1822	1840	1853
Hull d.	|	|	|	|	|	1438	|	|	|	|	|	|	1538	|	|	|	|	1638	|	|	|	|	|	1738	|	|	|	|	|
Selby d.	|	|	|	|	|	1510	|	|	|	|	|	|	1611	|	|	|	|	1710	|	|	|	|	|	1810	|	|	|	|	|
Leeds a.	1440	1449	1504	1516	1516	1534	1540	1539	1549	1606	1616	1616	1634	1639	1649	1706	1716	1735	1740	1749	1804	1816	1816	1834	1840	1840	1849	1904	1916
Leeds d.	1444	1453	1509	1517	1520	1536	1544	1544	1553	1609	1620	1620	1636	1644	1653	1709	1720	1737	1744	1753	1809	1820	1820	1836	1844	1844	1853	1909	1920
Dewsbury d.	|	|	1520	|	|	1547	|	|	|	1620	|	|	1647	|	|	1720	1731	1748	|	|	1820	|	|	1847	|	|	|	1920	|
Huddersfield d.	1502	1511	1530	1535	1540	1556	1602	1602	1611	1630	1640	1640	1656	1702	1711	1730	1740	1757	1802	1811	1830	1840	1840	1856	1902	1902	1911	1930	1940
Stalybridge d.	|	|	1550	|	|	1615	|	|	|	1650	|	|	1715	|	|	1750	|	1816	|	|	1850	|	|	1915	|	|	|	1950	|
Manchester Victoria d.	1535	|	|	|	|	|	1635	1635	|	|	|	|	|	1735	|	|	|	|	1836	|	|	|	|	|	1935	1935	|	|	|
Manchester Piccadilly a.	|	1542	1605	1613	1613	1634	|	|	1645	1705	1716	1713	1732	|	1742	1805	1818	1833	|	1842	1905	1914	1916	1932	|	|	1943	2005	2014
Manchester Airport ✈ a.	|	1610	|	1639	1639	...	|	|	1712	|	...	1739	...	|	1810	|	1839	...	|	1916	|	1939	...	...	|	|	2010	|	...
Warrington Central a.	|	...	1630	...	...	...	|	|	...	1730	...	...	...	|	...	1830	...	...	|	...	1930	...	...	...	|	|	...	2030	...
Liverpool South Parkway a.	|	...	1647	...	...	...	|	|	...	1747	...	...	...	|	...	1847	...	...	|	...	1947	...	...	...	|	|	...	2047	...
Liverpool Lime Street a.	1608	...	1659	...	...	...	1708	1708	...	1759	...	...	...	1808	...	1859	...	...	1909	...	1959	...	...	...	2011	2011	...	2059	...

	⚒	⚒	⚒	⚒	⚒	⚒	⚒	⚒	⚒	Ⓐ	Ⓐ	⑥	Ⓐ	⑥	⚒	⚒	⚒	⚒	⑥ a	⑥ b	①–④	⑤	⑦	⑦d 🚌	⑦ e	⑦d 🚌	⑦ e	⑦ e	⑦d 🚌
Newcastle d.	1804	...	...	...	1910	...	...	...	...	...	2027	...	...	...	...	...	...	...	2155	2155	2155	2155		...	...	...	...	...	...
Durham d.	1822	...	...	...	1923	...	...	...	...	...	2045	...	...	...	...	...	...	...	2210	2210	2210	2210		...	...	...	...	...	...
Middlesbrough d.	|	...	1827	...	|	...	1930	...	...	...	|	...	2052	2052	...	...	...	2150	|	|	|	|		...	...	...	...	...	...
Darlington d.	1839	...	|	...	1940	...	|	...	...	...	2102	...	|	|	...	...	...	2219	2227	2227	2227	2227		...	...	...	...	...	...
Northallerton d.	1850	...	1856	...	1951	...	1958	...	...	...	2113	...	2120	2120	...	...	...	2230	2238	2238	2238	2238		...	...	...	...	...	...
Thirsk d.	|	...	1904	...	|	...	2006	...	...	...	|	...	2128	2128	...	...	...	2238	|	|	|	|		...	...	...	...	...	...
Scarborough d.	|	...	|	1850	|	...	|	1950	...	2045	|	2050	|	|	...	...	2207	|	|	|	|	|		...	...	...	...	...	...
Malton d.	|	...	|	1913	|	...	|	2013	...	2109	|	2113	|	|	...	...	2230	|	|	|	|	|		...	...	...	...	...	...
York a.	1913	...	1922	1938	2014	...	2025	2038	...	2133	2136	2138	2147	2152	...	...	2255	2256	2302	2302	2302	2302		...	...	...	...	...	...
York d.	1915	...	1923	1940	2016	...	...	2040	2116	...	2141	2140	2149	...	...	2228	...	...	2305	2305	2305	2305		0130	0218f	0330	0348f	0512f	0455
Hull d.	|	1849	|	|	|	1959	...	|	|	...	|	|	|	...	2138	|	...	...	|	|	|	|		|	|	|	|	|	|
Selby d.	|	1920	|	|	|	2030	...	|	|	...	|	|	|	...	2212	|	...	...	|	|	|	|		|	|	|	|	|	|
Leeds a.	1938	1943	1951	2004	2040	2059	...	2104	2139	...	2205	2205	2214	...	2240	2305	...	...	2332	2332	2332	2332		0220	0256	0420	0426	0538	0545
Leeds d.	1941	...	1953	2009	2041	...	...	2109	2141	...	2209	2209	...	...	2241	2309	...	...	2335	2335	2335	2335		0220	0300	0420	0430	0540	0545
Dewsbury d.	1952	...	|	2020	2052	...	...	2120	2152	...	2220	2220	...	...	2252	2320	...	...	2346	2346	2346	2346		|	|	|	|	|	0610
Huddersfield d.	2002	...	2011	2030	2102	...	...	2130	2202	...	2230	2230	...	...	2302	2330	...	...	2355	2359	2355	2355		0255	0318	0455	0448	0558	0635
Stalybridge d.	|	...	|	2050	|	...	...	2150	|	...	2250	2250	...	...	|	|	...	...	|	|	|	|		|	|	|	|	|	0720
Manchester Victoria d.	2035	...	|	|	|	...	...	|	|	...	|	|	...	...	|	|	...	...	|	|	|	|		|	|	|	|	|	|
Manchester Piccadilly a.	|	...	2042	2105	2135	...	...	2205	2233	...	2305	2305	...	...	2337	0004	...	...	0027	0030	0028	0041		0355	0349	0555	0519	0630	0745
Manchester Airport ✈ a.	|	...	2113	|	2156	...	...	|	2257	...	|	|	...	...	...	...	...	...	0044	...	0050	0056		0420	0406	0620	0536	0647	0810
Warrington Central a.	|	...	...	2130	...	...	...	2230	...	...	2330	2330	...	...	...	...	...	...	...	...	...	...		...	...	...	...	...	...
Liverpool South Parkway a.	|	...	...	2147	...	...	...	2245	...	...	2345	2345	...	...	...	...	...	...	...	...	...	...		...	...	...	...	...	...
Liverpool Lime Street a.	2114n	...	...	2159	...	...	...	2256	...	...	2356	2356	...	...	...	...	...	...	...	...	...	...		...	...	...	...	...	...

a – Until Feb. 10 and from Mar. 31.
b – Feb. 17 - Mar. 24.
d – Feb. 11 - Mar. 25.
e – Until Feb. 11 and from April 1.
f – Departs 12 minutes later from April 1.
g – Departs 3 minutes later on ⑥.
n – Arrives 2108 on ⑥.
r – ⑥ only.
t – Departs 3 minutes later on Ⓐ.
◧ – Distances: York (*0 km*) - Malton (*33 km*) - Scarborough (*67 km*).
Hull (*0 km*) - Selby (*34 km*) - Leeds (*83 km*).

For explanation of standard symbols see page 1

	⑦	⑦d	⑦	⑦	⑦d	⑦	⑦	⑦	⑦	⑦	⑦	⑦	⑦	⑦	⑦	⑦	⑦	⑦	⑦	⑦	⑦	⑦	⑦	⑦	⑦	⑦	⑦	⑦	⑦	⑦
	j	🚌	j		🚌																									
Newcastle d.	...	...	...	...	...	...	...	0800	...	...	...	...	0906	...	...	1004	...	...	...	1110	1120	...	...	1206	...	...	...	1306	1310	...
Durham d.	...	...	...	...	...	...	...	0813	...	...	...	...	0919	...	...	1020	...	...	...	1123	1133	...	...	1222	...	...	...	1319	|	...
Middlesbrough d.	...	...	...	...	...	...	...	|	...	...	...	...	|	...	...	|	1027	...	...	|	|	...	...	|	1227	...	...	|	|	...
Darlington d.	...	...	...	...	...	...	...	0831	...	...	...	...	0936	...	...	1037	|	...	...	1140	1150	...	...	1240	|	...	...	1336	1341	...
Northallerton d.	...	...	...	...	...	...	...	0842	...	...	...	...	0947	...	...	1050	1056	...	...	1151	|	...	...	1251	1256	...	...	|	1353	...
Thirsk d.	...	...	...	...	...	...	...	0850	...	...	...	...	|	...	...	|	1104	...	...	|	|	...	...	|	1304	...	...	|	|	...
Scarborough d.	...	...	...	...	...	...	...	|	...	...	0853	...	|	...	...	|	|	1053	...	|	|	1153	...	|	|	1253	...	|	|	1353
Malton d.	...	...	...	...	...	...	...	|	...	...	0916	...	|	...	...	|	|	1116	...	|	|	1216	...	|	|	1316	...	|	|	1416
York a.	...	...	...	...	...	...	...	0909	...	...	0941	...	1010	...	...	1113	1122	1141	...	1214	1222	1241	...	1314	1322	1341	...	1408	1416	1441
York d.	0600**f**	0555	0700**f**	...	0655	0809	0850	0911	...	0928	0944	...	1012	1028	1045	1115	1123	1145	...	1215	1223	1245	...	1315	1323	1345	...	1415	1423	1445
Hull d.	|	|	|	...	|	|	|	|	0835	|	|	0934	|	|	|	|	|	|	1137	|	|	|	1237	|	|	|	1339	|	|	|
Selby d.	|	|	|	...	|	|	|	|	0910	|	|	1006	|	|	|	|	|	|	1208	|	|	|	1308	|	|	|	1410	|	|	|
Leeds a.	0638	0645	0738	...	0745	0835	0912	0934	0938	0953	1008	1032	1036	1051	1108	1138	1148	1208	1234	1240	1247	1308	1334	1339	1348	1408	1434	1439	1447	1508
Leeds d.	0640	0645	0740	...	0745	0838**j**	0916	0944	...	0953	1010	1036	1044	1053	1110	1144	1153	1210	1236	1244	1253	1310	1336	1344	1353	1410	1436	1444	1453	1510
Dewsbury d.	0651	0710	0751	...	0810	|	0927	|	...	|	1021	1047	|	|	1121	|	|	1221	1247	|	|	1321	1347	|	|	1421	1447	|	|	1521
Huddersfield d.	0701	0735	0801	...	0835	0859**j**	0936	1002	...	1011	1030	1056	1102	1111	1130	1202	1211	1230	1256	1302	1311	1330	1356	1402	1411	1430	1456	1502	1511	1530
Stalybridge d.	0719	0820	0819	...	0920**s**	0919**j**	0955	|	...	|	1050	1115	|	|	1150	|	|	1250	1315	|	|	1350	1415	|	|	1450	1515	|	|	1550
Manchester Victoria d.	|	|	|	...	|	|	|	1035	...	|	|	|	1135	|	|	1235	|	|	|	1335	|	|	|	1435	|	|	|	1535	|	|
Manchester Piccadilly a.	0734	0845**s**	0834	0912	0945	0935**j**	1010	|	...	1047	1106	1131	|	1142	1206	|	1242	1306	1331	|	1344	1406	1431	|	1443	1506	1531	|	1542	1606
Manchester Airp't ✈ a.	0751	0910	0855	|	...	0953**j**	|	|	...	1118	|	...	|	1209	|	|	1311	|	...	|	1405	|	...	|	1508	|	...	|	1605	|
Warrington Central d.	...	...	...	0933	...	...	1033	|	...	...	1130	...	|	...	1230	|	...	1330	...	|	...	1430	...	|	...	1530	...	|	...	1630
Liverpool South P'way a.	...	...	...	0949	...	...	1049	|	...	...	1147	...	|	...	1247	|	...	1347	...	|	...	1447	...	|	...	1547	...	|	...	1647
Liverpool Lime Street a.	...	...	...	1002	...	...	1101	1108	...	...	1159	...	1208	...	1258	1308	...	1359	...	1408	...	1458	...	1508	...	1559	...	1608	...	1658

	⑦	⑦	⑦	⑦	⑦	⑦	⑦	⑦	⑦	⑦	⑦	⑦	⑦	⑦	⑦	⑦	⑦	⑦	⑦	⑦	⑦	⑦	⑦	⑦	⑦	⑦	⑦	⑦	⑦	⑦
Newcastle d.	...	1405	...	...	...	1510	1517	...	...	1604	...	1643	...	...	1710	1719	...	1804	...	...	...	1910	...	2010	...	...	...	...	...	2200
Durham d.	...	1421	...	...	...	1523	1530	...	...	1620	...	1657	...	...	1723	|	...	1822	...	...	...	1923	...	2023	...	...	...	...	...	2214
Middlesbrough d.	...	|	1423	...	...	|	|	...	...	|	1623	|	...	...	|	|	...	|	...	1819	...	|	...	|	...	2041	...	...	2208	|
Darlington d.	...	1438	|	...	...	1540	1547	...	...	1638	|	|	...	...	1741	1746	...	1840	...	|	...	1940	...	2040	...	|	...	...	|	2231
Northallerton d.	...	|	1452	...	...	1551	|	...	...	|	1652	|	...	...	1753	1758	...	|	...	1847	...	1951	...	2051	...	2109	...	...	2237	2243
Thirsk d.	...	|	1500	...	...	|	|	...	...	|	1700	|	...	...	|	|	...	|	...	1859	...	|	...	|	...	2117	...	...	2245	|
Scarborough d.	...	|	|	1453	...	|	|	1553	...	|	|	|	1703	...	|	|	1753	|	...	|	1853	|	1953	|	...	|	2138	...	|	|
Malton d.	...	|	|	1516	...	|	|	1616	...	|	|	|	1727	...	|	|	1816	|	...	|	1916	|	2016	|	...	|	2201	...	|	|
York a.	...	1512	1522	1541	...	1614	1619	1641	...	1711	1722	1744	1751	...	1815	1821	1841	1913	...	1917	1941	2014	2041	2114	...	2141	2226	...	2307	2315
York d.	...	1515	1523	1544	...	1616	1623	1645	...	1715	1723	1745	1753	...	1815	1823	1845	1915	...	1923	1945	2015	2045	2115	...	2145	2228	...	...	2317
Hull d.	1429	|	|	|	1539	|	|	|	1643	|	|	|	|	1739	|	|	|	|	1842	|	|	|	|	|	2049	|	|	2207	...	|
Selby d.	1500	|	|	|	1610	|	|	|	1714	|	|	|	|	1810	|	|	|	|	1914	|	|	|	|	|	2120	|	|	2238	...	|
Leeds a.	1527	1539	1549	1608	1634	1640	1647	1708	1738	1742	1747	1808	1816	1834	1839	1848	1908	1938	1942	1947	2008	2039	2108	2139	2147	2208	2251	2303	...	2343
Leeds d.	1536	1544	1553	1611	1636	1644	1653	1710	1738	1744	1753	1810	...	1836	1844	1853	1910	1941	...	1953	2010	2041	2110	2141	...	2210	2253	...	...	2345
Dewsbury d.	1547	|	|	1622	1647	|	|	1721	|	|	|	1821	...	1847	|	|	1921	1952	...	|	2021	2052	2121	2152	...	2221	2304	...	...	2356
Huddersfield d.	1556	1602	1611	1631	1656	1702	1711	1730	1756	1802	1811	1830	...	1856	1902	1911	1930	2002	...	2011	2030	2102	2130	2202	...	2230	2313	...	...	0005
Stalybridge d.	1615	|	|	1651	1715	|	|	1750	|	|	|	1850	...	1915	|	|	1950	|	...	|	2050	|	2150	|	...	2250	2332	...	...	|
Manchester Victoria d.	|	1635	|	|	|	1735	|	|	|	1835	|	|	...	|	1935	|	|	2035	...	|	|	|	|	|	...	|	|	...	...	|
Manchester Piccadilly a.	1631	|	1644	1707	1731	|	1746	1806	1831	|	1843	1906	...	1931	|	1944	2006	|	...	2045	2106	2135	2206	2233	...	2305	2349	...	...	0037
Manchester Airp't ✈ a.	...	|	1708	|	...	|	1807	|	...	|	1909	|	...	...	|	2006	|	|	...	2108	|	...	|	2253	...	|	...	...	...	0056
Warrington Central d.	...	|	...	1731	...	|	...	1830	...	|	...	1930	...	...	|	...	2030	|	...	...	2130	...	2230	...	...	2330	...	...	...	...
Liverpool South P'way a.	...	|	...	1749	...	|	...	1847	...	|	...	1947	...	...	|	...	2047	|	...	...	2147	...	2246	...	...	2346	...	...	...	...
Liverpool Lime Street a.	...	1708	...	1759	...	1808	...	1859	...	1908	...	1958	...	...	2008	...	2059	2108	...	...	2159	...	2259	...	...	2359	...	...	...	...

		②–⑤	⑥	①	⚒	⚒	⚒	⚒	⚒	⚒	⚒	⚒	⚒	⚒	⚒	⚒	⚒	⚒	⚒	Ⓐ	⑥	⚒	⚒	⚒	⚒	⚒	⚒	⚒	⚒	⚒
Liverpool Lime Street d.	⚒	...	...	...	...	...	...	...	...	...	0612	...	0622	...	...	0712	...	0715	...	...	...	0813	...	0822	...	...	0912	...	0922
Liverpool South P'way d.		...	...	...	...	...	...	...	...	...	...	|	...	0632	...	...	|	...	0725	...	...	...	|	...	0832	...	...	|	...	0932
Warrington Central d.		...	...	...	...	...	...	...	...	...	...	|	...	0645	...	...	|	...	0741	...	...	...	|	...	0845	...	...	|	...	0945
Manchester Airp't ✈ d.		0038	0038	0045	...	0422	...	0530	...	...	...	|	0634	|	0706	...	|	0732	|	0806	0806	...	|	0832	|	0906	...	|	0932	|
Manchester Piccadilly d.		0053	0055	0100	...	0437	...	0547	...	0615	0626	|	0657	0712	0726	0740	|	0757	0811	0826	0826	0841	|	0857	0911	0926	0941	|	0957	1011
Manchester Victoria d.		|	|	|	...	|	...	|	...	|	|	0646	|	|	|	|	0751	|	|	|	|	|	0851	|	|	|	|	0951	|	|
Stalybridge d.		|	|	|	...	|	...	0600	...	0627	|	0658	|	0725	|	0753	|	|	0825	|	|	0854	|	|	0925	|	0954	|	|	1025
Huddersfield d.		|	0125	|	...	0540	...	0618	...	0646	0655	0717	0727	0746	0755	0812	0821	0827	0846	0855	0855	0913	0921	0927	0946	0956	1013	1021	1027	1046
Dewsbury d.		|	|	|	...	|	...	0627	...	0655	0705	0726	|	0755	0804	0823	|	|	0855	|	|	0923	|	|	0955	|	1023	|	|	1055
Leeds a.		0159	0202	0209	...	0559	...	0642	...	0708	0718	0739	0747	0812	0817	0836	0840	0846	0909	0915	0915	0936	0940	0946	1008	1015	1036	1040	1046	1108
Leeds d.		0205	0205	0215	...	0601	...	0644	...	0714	0722	0743	0749	0812	0820	0838	0843	0848	0912	0917	0917	0938	0943	0948	1012	1017	1038	1043	1048	1112
Selby d.		|	|	|	...	|	...	|	...	|	0742	|	|	|	|	0858	|	|	|	|	|	0958	|	|	|	|	1058	|	|	|
Hull a.		|	|	|	...	|	...	|	...	|	0820	|	|	|	|	0931	|	|	|	|	|	1035	|	|	|	|	1135	|	|	|
York a.		0244	0244	0244	...	0623	...	0706	...	0737	...	0806	0812	0838	0843	...	0906	0914	0936	0940	0940	...	1006	1013	1035	1041	...	1106	1113	1136
York d.		...	...	...	0600	0628	0640	0708	0718	0740	...	0808	0815	0840	...	...	0908	0915	0940	0942	0942	...	1008	1015	1040	...	...	1108	1115	1140
Malton d.		...	...	...	|	|	0704	|	|	0804	...	|	|	0904	...	...	|	|	1004	|	|	...	|	|	1104	...	...	|	|	1204
Scarborough a.		...	...	...	|	|	0729	|	|	0829	...	|	|	0930	...	...	|	|	1029	|	|	...	|	|	1129	...	...	|	|	1229
Thirsk d.		...	...	...	0616	|	...	0725	0734	...	...	|	0831	...	...	...	|	0931	...	|	|	...	|	1031	...	...	...	|	1131	...
Northallerton d.		...	...	...	0624	0649	...	0733	0742	...	...	0829	0840	...	...	...	0929	0940	...	|	|	...	1029	1040	...	...	...	1129	1140	...
Darlington d.		...	...	...	0640	0701	...	0745	|	...	...	0841	|	...	...	...	0941	|	...	|	1012	...	1041	|	...	...	...	1141	|	...
Middlesbrough a.		...	...	...	0707	|	...	|	0817	...	...	|	0912	...	...	...	|	1012	...	|	|	...	|	1112	...	...	...	|	1212	...
Durham d.		...	...	...	...	0717	...	0801	...	...	...	0857	...	...	...	...	0957	...	...	1027	1029	...	1057	...	...	...	...	1157	...	...
Newcastle a.		...	...	...	...	0735	...	0819	...	...	...	0914	...	...	...	...	1015	...	...	1042	1044	...	1114	...	...	...	...	1215	...	...

	⚒	⚒	⚒	⚒	⚒	⚒	⚒	⚒	⚒	⚒	⚒	⚒	⚒	⚒	⚒	⚒	⚒	⚒	⚒	⚒	Ⓐ	⑥	⚒	⚒	⚒	⚒	⚒	⚒	⚒	⚒
Liverpool Lime Street d.	...	...	1012	...	1022	...	...	1111	...	1122	...	...	1212	...	1222	...	...	1312	...	1322	...	...	...	1412	...	1422	...	...	1510	...
Liverpool South P'way d.	...	...	|	...	1032	...	...	|	...	1132	...	...	|	...	1232	...	...	|	...	1332	...	...	...	|	...	1432	...	...	|	...
Warrington Central d.	...	...	|	...	1045	...	...	|	...	1145	...	...	|	...	1245	...	...	|	...	1345	...	...	...	|	...	1445	...	...	|	...
Manchester Airp't ✈ d.	1006	...	|	1032	|	1106	...	|	1132	|	1206	...	|	1232	|	1306	...	|	1332	|	1406	1406	...	|	1432	|	1506	...	|	1532
Manchester Piccadilly d.	1026	1041	|	1056	1111	1126	1141	|	1157	1211	1226	1241	|	1257	1311	1326	1341	|	1357	1411	1426	1426	1441	|	1457	1511	1526	1541	|	1557
Manchester Victoria d.	|	|	1051	|	|	|	|	1151	|	|	|	|	1251	|	|	|	|	1351	|	|	|	|	|	1451	|	|	|	|	1551	|
Stalybridge d.	|	1054	|	|	1125	|	1154	|	|	1225	|	1254	|	|	1325	|	1354	|	|	1425	|	|	1454	|	|	1525	|	1554	|	|
Huddersfield d.	1055	1113	1121	1126	1146	1155	1213	1221	1227	1246	1255	1313	1321	1327	1346	1355	1413	1421	1427	1446	1455	1454	1513	1521	1527	1546	1555	1613	1621	1627
Dewsbury d.	|	1123	|	|	1155	|	1223	|	|	1255	|	1323	|	|	1355	|	1423	|	|	1455	|	|	1523	|	|	1555	|	1623	|	|
Leeds a.	1115	1136	1140	1146	1208	1215	1236	1240	1246	1308	1315	1336	1340	1346	1408	1415	1436	1440	1446	1508	1515	1515	1536	1540	1546	1608	1615	1636	1640	1646
Leeds d.	1116	1138	1143	1148	1212	1217	1238	1243	1248	1312	1317	1338	1343	1348	1412	1417	1438	1443	1448	1512	1517	1517	1538	1543	1548	1612	1617	1638	1643	1648
Selby d.	|	1158	|	|	|	|	1258	|	|	|	|	1358	|	|	|	|	1458	|	|	|	|	|	1558	|	|	|	|	1658	|	|
Hull a.	|	1235	|	|	|	|	1335	|	|	|	|	1435	|	|	|	|	1535	|	|	|	|	|	1635	|	|	|	|	1735	|	|
York a.	1140	...	1206	1213	1236	1240	...	1306	1313	1336	1340	...	1406	1413	1436	1441	...	1506	1513	1536	1540	1540	...	1606	1613	1636	1641	...	1706	1713
York d.	1141	...	1208	1215	1240	...	...	1308	1315	1340	1342	...	1408	1415	1440	...	...	1508	1515	1540	...	1542	...	1608	1615	1640	...	...	1708	1715
Malton d.	|	...	|	|	1304	...	...	|	|	1404	|	...	|	|	1504	...	...	|	|	1604	...	|	...	|	|	1704	...	...	|	|
Scarborough a.	|	...	|	|	1329	...	...	|	|	1429	|	...	|	|	1529	...	...	|	|	1629	...	|	...	|	|	1729	...	...	|	|
Thirsk a.	|	...	|	1231	...	...	...	|	1331	...	|	...	|	1431	...	...	...	|	1531	...	...	|	...	|	1631	...	...	...	|	1731
Northallerton a.	|	...	1229	1240	...	...	...	1329	1340	...	|	...	1429	1440	...	...	...	1529	1540	...	...	|	...	1629	1640	...	...	...	1729	1740
Darlington a.	|	...	1241	|	...	...	...	1341	|	...	|	...	1441	|	...	...	...	1541	|	...	...	|	...	1641	|	...	...	...	1741	|
Middlesbrough a.	|	...	|	1312	...	...	...	|	1412	...	|	...	|	1512	...	...	...	|	1612	...	...	|	...	|	1712	...	...	...	|	1812
Durham a.	1227	...	1257	...	...	...	...	1357	...	...	1427	...	1457	...	...	...	...	1557	...	...	...	1628	...	1657	...	...	...	...	1757	...
Newcastle a.	1241	...	1316	...	...	...	...	1415	...	...	1442	...	1512	...	...	...	...	1615	...	...	...	1642	...	1712	...	...	...	...	1815	...

d – Feb. 18 - Mar. 25. **f** – Departs 12 minutes later from April 1. **j** – Until Feb. 11 and from April 1.

	⚒	⚒	⚒	⚒	⚒	⚒	Ⓐ	⑥	⚒	⚒	⚒	⚒	⑥	Ⓐ	⚒	⚒	⚒	⚒	Ⓐ	⚒	⚒	⑥	⑥	Ⓐ	Ⓐ	Ⓐ	⑥	⑥
Liverpool Lime Street d.	1522	...	...	1612	...	1622	...	...	...	1710	...	1722	...	...	...	1812	...	1822	...	...	1912	...	1922	1922	...	...	...	...
Liverpool South P'way d.	1532	...	...	|	...	1632	...	...	...	|	...	1732	...	...	...	|	...	1832	...	...	|	...	1932	1932	...	...	...	...
Warrington Central d.	1545	...	...	|	...	1645	...	...	...	|	...	1745	...	...	...	|	...	1845	...	...	|	...	1945	1945	...	...	...	...
Manchester Airp't ✈ d.	|	1606	...	|	1633	|	1703	1706	...	|	1732	|	1806	...	...	|	1833	|	...	1924	|	...	|	|	...	2024	2024	...
Manchester Piccadilly d.	1611	1626	1641	|	1656	1711	1725	1726	1741	|	1754	1811	1826	1826	1841	|	1857	1911	1926	1942	|	...	2011	2011	...	2042	2042	...
Manchester Victoria d.	|	|	|	1651	|	|	|	|	|	1751	|	|	|	|	|	1851	|	|	|	|	1951	...	|	|	...	|	|	...
Stalybridge d.	1625	|	1654	|	|	1725	1738	1738	1756	|	|	1825	|	|	1854	|	|	1925	|	|	|	...	2025	2025	...	|	|	...
Huddersfield d.	1646	1655	1713	1721	1727	1746	1757	1757	1816	1821	1827	1846	1855	1855	1914	1921	1927	1946	1956	2012	2021	...	2046	2046	...	2112	2112	...
Dewsbury d.	1655	|	1723	|	|	1755	|	|	1825	|	|	1855	|	|	1924	|	|	1956	|	|	|	...	2055	2055	...	|	|	...
Leeds a.	1708	1716	1736	1742	1746	1808	1817	1817	1838	1842	1846	1909	1916	1916	1937	1942	1946	2009	2017	2031	2043	...	2108	2108	...	2131	2131	...
Leeds d.	1712	1717	1740	1744	1749	1812	1819	1819	1841	1845	1849	1912	1917	1917	1939	1943	1949	2012	2020	2033	2043	2105	2112	2112	2121	2133	2133	...
Selby d.	|	|	1801	|	|	|	|	|	1904	|	|	|	|	|	2001	|	|	|	2057	|	|	2128	|	|	2145	|	|	...
Hull a.	|	|	1838	|	|	|	|	|	1939	|	|	|	|	|	2041	|	|	|	2135	|	|	2207	|	|	2223	|	|	...
York a.	1736	1744	...	1807	1814	1836	1845	1845	...	1908	1913	1936	1940	1940	...	2006	2012	2035	...	2058	2107	...	2137	2137	...	2157	2158	...
York d.	1740	...	...	1809	1816	1840	1856	1856	...	1910	1916	1940	...	...	...	2008	2016	2040	...	...	2109	...	...	2137	...	2200	...	2212
Malton d.	1804	...	...	|	|	1904	|	|	...	|	|	2004	...	...	...	|	|	2104	...	...	|	...	...	|	...	2224	...	2236
Scarborough a.	1829	...	...	|	|	1929	|	|	...	|	|	2029	...	...	...	|	|	2129	...	...	|	...	...	|	...	2249	...	2301
Thirsk a.	...	...	...	|	1832	...	|	|	...	|	1933	...	...	...	...	|	2035	...	...	...	2126	...	...	|	...	...	...	...
Northallerton a.	...	...	...	1830	1840	...	|	|	...	1931	1941	...	...	...	...	2029	2043	...	...	...	2134	...	...	2159	...	...	...	...
Darlington a.	...	...	...	1842	|	...	|	1929	...	1943	|	...	...	...	...	2041	|	...	...	...	2146	...	...	|	...	...	...	...
Middlesbrough a.	...	...	...	|	1914	...	|	|	...	|	2014	...	...	...	...	|	2115	...	...	...	|	...	...	2232	...	...	...	...
Durham a.	...	...	...	1858	...	...	1943	1945	...	2001	...	...	...	...	...	2057	...	...	...	...	2202	...	...	...	...	...	...	...
Newcastle a.	...	...	...	1914	...	...	1957	1959	...	2019	...	...	...	...	...	2113	...	...	...	...	2220	...	...	...	...	...	...	...

	Ⓐ	Ⓐ	⑥	⚒	⚒	⚒	⚒	⑥ a	Ⓐ	⑥ b	⑦c 🚌	⑥ d	⑤	⑥ e	⑥b 🚌	①-④		⑦ g	⑦c 🚌	⑦c 🚌	⑦ g	⑦c 🚌	⑦c 🚌	⑦ g	⑦	⑦ g	⑦ c	⑦ h
Liverpool Lime Street d.	2022	...	2022	...	...	2130	...	2230	2230	2230	...	...	...	...	...	...	⑦	...	...	...	...	...	...	...	...	...	...	...
Liverpool South P'way d.	2032	...	2032	...	...	2140	...	2240	2240	2240	...	...	...	...	...	...		...	...	...	...	...	...	...	...	...	...	...
Warrington Central d.	2045	...	2045	...	...	2153	...	2253	2253	2253	...	...	...	...	...	...		...	...	...	...	...	...	...	...	...	...	...
Manchester Airp't ✈ d.	|	...	|	...	2124	|	2224	|	|	|	...	2320	2320	2320	2325	2320		0100	0100	0330	0425	0530	0605	0630	...	0729	...	...
Manchester Piccadilly d.	2111	...	2111	...	2142	2219	2242	2321	2321	2321	...	2334	2335	2334	2350	2334		0117	0125	0355	0442	0555	0630	0647	...	0747	...	...
Manchester Victoria d.	|	...	|	...	|	|	|	|	|	|	...	2350	2350	2350	|	2350		|	|	|	|	|	|	|	...	|	...	...
Stalybridge d.	2125	...	2125	...	|	2231	2254	2334	2334	2334	...	|	|	|	|	|		|	|	|	|	|	0655	0700	...	0800	...	...
Huddersfield d.	2146	...	2146	...	2211	2250	2313	2352	2352	2352	0005	0021	0019	0021	0050	0052		0147	0225	0455	0512	0655	0740	0718	...	0818	...	...
Dewsbury d.	2155	...	2155	...	|	2259	2322	|	|	...	0030	0030s	0029s	0030s	|	0102s		|	|	|	|	0720	0805	0727	...	0827	...	...
Leeds a.	2208	...	2208	...	2230	2312	2335	0011	0031	...	0055	0044	0042	0044	0140	0115		0206	0300	0530	0531	0745	0830	0740	...	0840	...	...
Leeds d.	2211	...	2211	2221	2233	2316	2336	0015	0034	...	0055	0045	0046	0047	0140	0123		0208	0300	0530	0533	0745	...	0743	...	0843	0843	0915
Selby d.	|	...	|	2243	|	|	|	|	|	...	|	|	|	|	|	|		|	|	|	|	|	...	|	...	|	|	|
Hull a.	|	...	|	2319	|	|	|	|	|	...	|	|	|	|	|	|		|	|	|	|	|	...	|	...	|	|	|
York a.	2234	...	2236	...	2258	2342	0003	0043	0113	...	0145	0113	0125	0129	0230	0207		0252f	0350	0620	0617f	0835	...	0827f	...	0906	0906	0938
York d.	2235	2242	...	...	...	...	...	...	...	...	...	...	...	...	...	...		...	...	...	...	...	...	...	0847	0908	0908	0942
Malton d.	|	2306	...	...	...	...	...	...	...	...	...	...	...	...	...	...		...	...	...	...	...	...	...	|	|	|	1005
Scarborough a.	|	2331	...	...	...	...	...	...	...	...	...	...	...	...	...	...		...	...	...	...	...	...	...	|	|	|	1031
Thirsk a.	2258	...	...	...	...	...	...	...	...	...	...	...	...	...	...	...		...	...	...	...	...	...	...	0903	|	|	...
Northallerton a.	2306	...	...	...	...	...	...	...	...	...	...	...	...	...	...	...		...	...	...	...	...	...	...	0911	0929	0929	...
Darlington a.	2318	...	...	...	...	...	...	...	...	...	...	...	...	...	...	...		...	...	...	...	...	...	...	0925	0943	0943	...
Middlesbrough a.	|	...	...	...	...	...	...	...	...	...	...	...	...	...	...	...		...	...	...	...	...	...	...	0952	|	|	...
Durham a.	2334	...	...	...	...	...	...	...	...	...	...	...	...	...	...	...		...	...	...	...	...	...	...	...	0959	0959	...
Newcastle a.	0008	...	...	...	...	...	...	...	...	...	...	...	...	...	...	...		...	...	...	...	...	...	...	...	1017	1017	...

	⑦ k	⑦ c	⑦ m	⑦ k	⑦	⑦	⑦	⑦	⑦	⑦	⑦	⑦	⑦	⑦	⑦	⑦	⑦	⑦	⑦	⑦	⑦	⑦	⑦	⑦	⑦	⑦	⑦	⑦
Liverpool Lime Street d.	...	...	...	...	...	0822	...	0912	...	0922	1010	...	1022	...	1112	...	1122	1122	1210	...	1222	...	1312	...	1322	1405	...	...
Liverpool South P'way d.	...	...	...	...	...	0832	...	|	...	0932	|	...	1032	...	|	...	1132	1132	|	...	1232	...	|	...	1332	|	...	...
Warrington Central d.	...	...	...	...	...	0844	...	|	...	0944	|	...	1044	...	|	...	1145	1145	|	...	1245	...	|	...	1345	|	...	...
Manchester Airp't ✈ d.	0758	...	0822	...	...	|	...	|	0935	|	|	1033	|	...	|	1133	|	|	|	1233	|	...	|	1333	|	|	...	1433
Manchester Piccadilly d.	0820	0847	0847	...	...	0911	0928	|	1003	1011	|	1057	1111	1143	|	1157	1210	1210	|	1257	1311	1343	|	1357	1411	|	1443	1457
Manchester Victoria d.	|	|	|	...	...	|	|	0951	|	|	1045	|	|	|	1151	|	|	|	1245	|	|	|	1351	|	|	1440	|	|
Stalybridge d.	0833	0900	0900	...	...	0924	|	|	|	1025	|	|	1125	1155	|	|	1224	1224	|	|	1325	1355	|	|	1425	|	1455	|
Huddersfield d.	0852	0918	0918	...	...	0946	1005	1021	1032	1046	1113	1127	1146	1213	1221	1227	1246	1246	1313	1327	1346	1413	1421	1427	1446	1509	1515	1527
Dewsbury d.	0901	0927	0927	...	...	0955	1015	|	|	1055	|	|	1155	1223	|	|	1255	1255	|	|	1355	1423	|	|	1455	|	1525	|
Leeds a.	0914	0940	0940	...	...	1008	1030	1040	1051	1109	1134	1146	1209	1236	1240	1246	1309	1309	1333	1346	1409	1436	1440	1446	1509	1528	1538	1546
Leeds d.	0915	0943	0943	0943	...	1012	1038	1043	1053	1112	1138	1148	1212	1238	1243	1248	1312	1312	1338	1348	1412	1438	1443	1449	1512	1536	1540	1548
Selby d.	|	|	|	|	0952	|	1105	|	|	|	|	|	|	1301	|	|	|	|	|	|	|	1458	|	|	|	|	1603	|
Hull a.	|	|	|	|	1014	|	1140	|	|	|	|	|	|	1336	|	|	|	|	|	|	|	1532	|	|	|	|	1637	|
York a.	0914	1006	1006	1006	1049	1038	...	1106	1116	1135	1201	1211	1235	...	1306	1311	1334	1334	1402	1411	1439	...	1506	1511	1540	1603	...	1611
York d.	0915	1008	1008	1008	...	1042	...	1108	1117	1142	1203	1212	1242	...	1308	1314	1339	1342	1404	1413	1442	...	1508	1514	1542	1607	...	1613
Malton d.	1006	|	|	|	...	1106	...	|	|	1206	|	|	1306	...	|	|	|	1406	|	|	1506	...	|	|	1606	|	...	|
Scarborough a.	1031	|	|	|	...	1131	...	|	|	1231	|	|	1331	...	|	|	|	1431	|	|	1531	...	|	|	1631	|	...	|
Thirsk a.	...	|	|	|	...	...	...	|	1134	...	|	|	...	...	|	1331	|	...	|	|	...	...	|	1531	...	|	...	|
Northallerton a.	...	1029	1029	1029	...	...	...	1129	1142	...	|	1233	...	...	1329	1340	|	...	1425	|	...	...	1529	1540	...	|	...	1634
Darlington a.	...	1041	1041	1041	...	...	...	1141	|	...	|	1245	...	...	1341	|	1409	...	1436	1443	...	...	1541	|	...	1637	...	1646
Middlesbrough a.	...	|	|	|	...	...	...	|	1214	...	|	|	...	...	|	1412	|	...	|	|	...	...	|	1612	...	|	...	|
Durham a.	...	1057	1057	1057	...	...	...	1157	...	...	|	1302	...	...	1357	...	1426	...	|	1500	...	...	1557	...	...	1654	...	1702
Newcastle a.	...	1114	1114	1114	...	...	...	1215	...	...	1300	1317	...	...	1416	...	1442	...	1506	1515	...	...	1615	...	...	1709	...	1717

	⑦	⑦	⑦	⑦	⑦	⑦	⑦		⑦	⑦	⑦	⑦	⑦	⑦	⑦	⑦	⑦	⑦	⑦	⑦	⑦	⑦	⑦	⑦	⑦	⑦	⑦	⑦
Liverpool Lime Street d.	1422	...	1512	...	1522	...	1612	...	...	1622	...	1712	...	1722	1812	...	1822	...	...	1912	1922	...	2012	2022	...	...	2152	...
Liverpool South P'way d.	1432	...	|	...	1532	...	|	...	...	1632	...	|	...	1732	|	...	1832	...	...	|	1932	...	|	2032	...	...	2202	...
Warrington Central d.	1445	...	|	...	1545	...	|	...	...	1645	...	|	...	1745	|	...	1845	...	...	|	1945	...	|	2045	...	...	2215	...
Manchester Airp't ✈ d.	|	...	|	1533	|	...	|	...	1633	|	...	|	1733	|	|	1833	|	...	1920	|	|	2020	|	|	...	2120	|	2320
Manchester Piccadilly d.	1511	1543	|	1557	1611	1643	|	...	1657	1711	1743	|	1757	1811	|	1857	1911	...	1942	|	2012	2042	|	2112	...	2142	2242	2346
Manchester Victoria d.	|	|	1551	|	|	|	1651	...	|	|	|	1751	|	|	1851	|	|	...	|	1951	|	|	2051	|	...	|	|	|
Stalybridge d.	1525	1555	|	|	1625	1655	|	...	|	1725	1755	|	|	1825	|	|	1925	...	|	|	2025	|	|	2125	...	|	2255	|
Huddersfield d.	1546	1613	1621	1630	1646	1713	1721	...	1727	1746	1813	1821	1827	1846	1921	1927	1946	...	2011	2021	2046	2112	2121	2146	...	2211	2313	0021
Dewsbury d.	1555	1623	|	|	1655	1723	|	...	|	1755	1823	|	|	1855	|	|	1955	...	|	|	2055	|	|	2155	...	2220	2322	0030
Leeds a.	1609	1636	1640	1649	1709	1736	1741	...	1746	1808	1836	1840	1846	1909	1940	1946	2008	...	2030	2040	2108	2133	2140	2208	...	2233	2335	0043
Leeds d.	1612	1637	1643	1650	1712	1738	1744	...	1748	1812	1838	1843	1849	1912	1943	1951	2012	2018	2033	2043	2112	2138	2143	2211	2221	2236	2341	0045
Selby d.	|	1657	|	|	|	1800	|	...	|	|	1901	|	|	|	|	|	|	2051	|	|	|	2201	|	|	2243	|	|	|
Hull a.	|	1732	|	|	|	1835	|	...	|	|	1936	|	|	|	|	|	|	2127	|	|	|	2237	|	|	2319	|	|	|
York a.	1635	...	1706	1713	1737	...	1807	...	1811	1835	...	1906	1912	1936	2006	2016	2035	...	2056	2106	2137	...	2206	2234	...	2304	0022	0113
York d.	1642	...	1708	1715	1742	...	1809	...	1813	1842	...	1908	1915	1942	2008	...	2042	...	2100	2108	...	...	2208	2235	...	...	...	...
Malton d.	1706	...	|	|	1806	...	|	...	|	1906	...	|	|	2006	|	...	2106	...	|	|	...	...	2232	|	...	...	...	...
Scarborough a.	1731	...	|	|	1831	...	|	...	|	1931	...	|	|	2031	|	...	2131	...	|	|	...	...	2257	|	...	...	...	...
Thirsk a.	...	...	|	1731	...	...	|	...	|	...	...	|	1933	...	|	...	...	...	2116	|	...	...	...	2258	...	...	...	...
Northallerton a.	...	...	1729	1740	...	...	|	...	1834	...	...	1930	1944	...	2029	...	...	...	2125	2129	...	...	...	2306	...	...	...	...
Darlington a.	...	...	1741	|	...	...	1839	...	1846	...	...	1942	|	...	2041	...	...	...	|	2141	...	...	...	2318	...	...	...	...
Middlesbrough a.	...	...	|	1812	...	...	|	...	|	...	...	|	2016	...	|	...	...	...	2158	|	...	...	...	|	...	...	...	...
Durham a.	...	...	1757	...	...	...	1856	...	1902	...	...	1958	...	...	2057	...	...	...	...	2157	...	...	...	2334	...	...	...	...
Newcastle a.	...	...	1815	...	...	...	1913	...	1917	...	...	2015	...	...	2114	...	...	...	...	2214	...	...	...	0007	...	...	...	...

a – Until Feb. 10 and from Mar. 31.
b – Feb. 17 - Mar. 24.
c – Feb. 18 - Mar. 25.
d – From Mar. 31.
e – Until Feb. 10.
f – Arrives 16 minutes earlier from April 1.
g – Until Feb. 11 and from April 1.
h – Until Mar. 25.
k – From April 1.
m – Until Feb. 11.

YORK - LEEDS - HALIFAX - BLACKPOOL and MANCHESTER 190

LEEDS - HALIFAX - MANCHESTER

km			Ⓐ	⑥	Ⓐ	⑥	Ⓐ	⚒	⚒	⚒	⚒	⚒	⚒	⚒	and	⚒	⚒	⚒	⚒	⚒	⚒	⚒	⚒		⑦	⑦
0	**Leeds** 124 188 d.	⚒	0508	0535	0608	0618	0623	0651	0718	0723	0751	0818	0826	0851	at the	1818	1823	1851	1919	1951	2035	2135	2235	⑦	0818	0908
15	Bradford Interchange d.		0531	0558	0631	0641	│	0714	0741	│	0814	0841	│	0914	same	1841	│	1914	1942	2014	2058	2158	2258		0841	0933
28	**Halifax** d.		0544	0611	0644	0654	│	0727	0754	│	0827	0854	│	0927	minutes	1854	│	1927	1955	2027	2111	2211	2311		0854	0945
	Dewsbury d.		│	│	│	│	0639	│	│	0739	│	│	0842	│	past	│	1841	│	│	│	│	│	│		│	│
	Brighouse d.		│	│	│	│	0659	│	│	0758	│	│	0859	│	each	│	1859	│	│	│	│	│	│		│	│
42	Hebden Bridge d.		0559	0627	0659	0710	0717	0742	0805	0817	0842	0906	0918	0942	hour	1906	1917	1942	2011	2042	2127	2226	2326		0909	1001
49	Todmorden d.		0607	0634	0707	0717	0724	0750	0813	0824	0850	0913	0925	0950	until	1913	1925	1950	2018	2050	2134	2234	2334		0917	1009
63	Rochdale d.		0623	0651	0720	0734	0741	0804	0825	0841	0900	0924	0942	1000		1924	1941	2000	2035	2100	2150	2250	2350		0929	1021
81	**Manchester** Victoria a.		0647	0717	0736	0758	0803	0824	0848	0904	0917	0941	1004	1017	✣	1942	2007	2017	2100	2117	2215	2315g	0008		0946	1039

	⑦	⑦	⑦	⑦	and	⑦	⑦	⑦	⑦	⑦
Leeds 124 188 d.	1008	1109	1151	1251	at the	1951	2052	2135	2208	2235
Bradford Interchange d.	1033	1133	1215	1314	same	2014	2115	2158	2231	2259
Halifax d.	1045	1145	1228	1327	minutes	2027	2128	2211	2246	2314
Dewsbury d.	│	│	│	│	past	│	│	│	│	│
Brighouse d.	│	│	│	│	each	│	│	│	2257	2324
Hebden Bridge d.	1101	1201	1244	1342	hour	2042	2144	2226	...	...
Todmorden d.	1109	1209	1251	1350	until	2050	2152	2234	...	...
Rochdale d.	1121	1221	1304	1403		2103	2222	2250	...	...
Manchester Victoria a.	1139	1239	1320	1420	✣	2120	*2245*	2313	...	...

		⚒	⑥	Ⓐ	⚒	⚒.	⚒	⚒	⚒	⚒	⚒
Manchester Victoria d.	⚒	0547	0608	0612	0636	...	0711	0726	0748	0816	0826
Rochdale d.		0602	0627	0626	0653	...	0726	0747	0802	0830	0847
Todmorden d.		0612	0644	0643	0710	...	0743	0804	0813	0841	0904
Hebden Bridge d.		0619	0651	0650	0717	0739	0750	0811	0820	0847	0911
Brighouse d.		│	│	│	│	0756	│	0829	│	│	0929
Dewsbury d.		│	│	│	│	0811	│	0842	│	│	0941
Halifax d.		0637	0709	0707	0734	│	0807	│	0833	0906	│
Bradford Interchange d.		0652	0724	0723	0750	│	0823	│	0849	0921	│
Leeds 124 188 a		0716	0746	0746	0812	0834	0844	0904	0910	0944	1003

	⚒	and	⚒	⚒	⚒	⚒	⚒	⚒	⚒	⚒	⚒	...	⚒	Ⓐ	⑥	Ⓐ		⑦	⑦	⑦	and	⑦	⑦	⑦	⑦
Manchester Victoria d.	0847	at the	1708	1725	1745	1810	1826	1848	1916	1926	2026	...	2126	2226	2254	2321	⑦	0914	1015	1115	at the	1915	2015	2115	2210
Rochdale d.	0901	same	1727	1747	1803	1827	1847	1902	1931	1947	2047	...	2147	2247	2308	2342		0928	1029	1129	same	1929	2029	2129	2231
Todmorden d.	0913	minutes	1743	1804	1816	1841	1904	1913	1942	2004	2104	...	2204	2304	2325	2359		0942	1042	1142	minutes	1942	2042	2142	2248
Hebden Bridge d.	0920	past	1750	1811	1822	1848	1911	1920	1949	2011	2111	...	2211	2311	2331	0006		0949	1049	1149	past	1949	2049	2149	2255
Brighouse d.	│	each	│	1829	│	│	1929	│	│	2029	│	...	│	│	│	│		│	│	│	each	│	│	│	│
Dewsbury d.	│	hour	│	1841	│	│	1941	│	│	2041	│	...	│	│	│	│		│	│	│	hour	│	│	│	│
Halifax d.	0933	until	1807	│	1835	1906	│	1934	2007	│	2129	...	2229	2329	2349	0024		1007	1107	1207	until	2007	2107	2207	2313
Bradford Interchange d.	0949		1824	│	1852	1922	│	1949	2022	│	2144	...	2244	2345	0004	0039		1023	1123	1223		2023	2123	2223	2331
Leeds 124 188 a.	1012	✣	1844	1903	1915	1944	2003	2011	2047	2103	2208	...	2309	0006	0026	0057		1044	1144	1244	✣	2042	2144	2244	2352

YORK - LEEDS - HALIFAX - BLACKPOOL

Until March 25, 2018, the line between Preston and Blackpool North will be temporarily closed to allow electrification and other route improvement work to take place. A replacement 🚌 service will operate every 15 minutes from 0630 to 2359 on ⚒ and from 0930 to 2345 on ⑦. Journey time: 50 minutes.

km			⚒	⚒	⚒		⚒	⚒		⚒	⚒		⑦	⑦		⑦	⑦		⑦	⑦	⑦
0	**York** 124 188 d.	⚒	...	0620	0718a	and	1718	1827	...	1918	...	⑦	0812	0905	...	1015	1118a	and	1827	1918	2027
41	**Leeds** 124 188 d.		0557	0708	0805	at the	1805	1905	...	2005	2108		0853	0953	...	1053	1208	at the	1908	2008	2108
56	Bradford Interchange d.		0617	0728	0826	same	1826	1926	...	2026	2128		0913	1014	...	1113	1228	same	1928	2028	2128
69	**Halifax** d.		0629	0740	0839	minutes	1838	1939	...	2039	2140		0926	1026	...	1126	1240	minutes	1940	2040	2140
83	Hebden Bridge d.		0646	0752	0852	past	1852	1952	...	2052	2154		0940	1041	...	1140	1252	past	1952	2052	2152
103	Burnley Manchester Road d.		0705	0812	0912	each	1912	2012	...	2112	2214		1001	1101	...	1201	1312	each	2012	2112	2212
113	Accrington d.		0714	0821	0921	hour	1921	2021	...	2121	2223		1010	1110	...	1210	1321	hour	2021	2121	2221
123	Blackburn 191 d.		0723	0829	0930	until	1930	2030	...	2130	2231		1019	1120	...	1220	1330	until	2030	2130	2230
142	Preston 156 191 a.		0747	0858	0948		1950	2048	...	2149	2252		1040	1144v	...	1239	1348		2048	2148	2248
171	**Blackpool** North 156 191 a.		0815t	0918t	1015t	✣	2017t	2115t	...	2216r	2320f		1105t	1209t	...	1303t	1415t	✣	...	2215t	...

		⚒	⚒	⚒	⚒		⚒	⚒	⚒	⚒	⚒		⑦	⑦	⑦		⑦	⑦		⑦	⑦
Blackpool North 156 191 d.	⚒	0511y	0611t	0711t	0811t	and	1611t	1656t	1811t	1911t	2029t	⑦	...	...	1111t	and	1811t	1911t	...	2011t	2111t
Preston 156 191 d.		0536	0637	0737	0836	at the	1638	1725	1837	1937	2056		0937	1037	1137	at the	1837	1937	...	2037	2138
Blackburn 191 d.		0555	0655	0755	0855	same	1655	1753	1856	1955	2124		0955	1055	1155	same	1855	1955	...	2055	2155
Accrington d.		0603	0703	0803	0903	minutes	1703	1801	1904	2003	2132		1003	1103	1203	minutes	1903	2003	...	2103	2203
Burnley Manchester Road d.		0612	0712	0812	0912	past	1712	1812	1913	2012	2141		1012	1112	1212	past	1912	2012	...	2112	2212
Hebden Bridge d.		0634	0734	0834	0934	each	1734	1834	1935	2034	2203		1034	1134	1234	each	1934	2034	...	2134	2234
Halifax d.		0648	0748	0848	0947	hour	1747	1847	1949	2049	2218		1047	1147	1247	hour	1947	2049	...	2149	2249
Bradford Interchange d.		0705	0804	0904	1002	until	1803	1904	2004	2104	2233		1103	1203	1303	until	2003	2105	...	2205	2305
Leeds 124 188 a.		0722	0822	0923	1023		1822	1924	2026	2126	2253		1122	1224	1322		2022	2122	...	2226	2324
York 124 188 a.		0803	0904	1000	1103	✣	1900	2004	...	2228d	2340		1158	1303	1400	✣	...	2203	...	...	...

a – Departs xx27 on the even hours except on ⑥ when departs 0818, 0918, 1027.
d – On ⑥ arrives 2218.
f – ⑤ from Mar. 30.
g – Arrives 2307 on ⑥.
r – Ⓐ from Mar. 26.
t – From Mar. 26.
v – 1139 from Apr. 1.
y – ⑥ from Mar. 30.
✣ – Timings may vary by ± 5 minutes.

BLACKPOOL - PRESTON - CLITHEROE - HELLIFIELD 191

km			⑦		⑦a		⑦	
0	**Blackpool North** 156 190 d.	...	*0730**	...	*0755**	...	*1215**	...
29	**Preston** 156 190 d.	...	0839	...	0901	...	1319	...
48	Blackburn 163 190 d.	...	0904	...	0927	...	1341	...
63	Clitheroe 163 d.	...	0927	...	0951	...	1404	...
85	Hellifield a.	...	0952	...	1014	...	1429	...
	Carlisle 173 a.	...	*1155*	...	1217	...	*1643*	...

		⑦		⑦b	⑦c		⑦a
Carlisle 173 d.	...	...	...	*1259*	*1259*	...	1757
Hellifield d.	...	1030	...	1455	1455	...	1948
Clitheroe 163 a.	...	1053	...	1516	1516	...	2013
Blackburn 163 190 a.	...	1125	...	1543	1543	...	2040
Preston 156 190 a.	...	1148	...	1604	1605	...	2101
Blackpool North 156 190 a.	...	*1250**	...	*1705**	1632	...	2130

a – May 20 - Sept. 9.
b – Until Mar. 25.
c – From April 1.
* – Connection by 🚌.

HULL - DONCASTER - SHEFFIELD 192

km			Ⓐ	Ⓐ	ⒶA	ⒶA	ⒶA	ⒶA	ⒶA	ⒶB	ⒶA	ⒶB	ⒶA	ⒶA	Ⓐ	ⒶB	Ⓐ	ⒶA	Ⓐ	Ⓐ		⑥	⑥	⑥A	⑥A	⑥A
0	**Hull** 181 d.	Ⓐ	0520	0640	0803	0857	0957	1057	1156	1257	1357	1457	1557	1656	1742	1757	1857	2002	2057	2220	⑥	0520	0640	0803	0857	0957
38	Goole d.		0547	0716	0830	0924	1024	1124	1225	1324	1424	1524	1624	1724	1820	│	1924	2036	2124	2254		0547	0716	0830	0924	1024
66	**Doncaster** 181 a.		0618	0747	0854	0949	1049	1149	1248	1349	1447	1549	1648	1747	1850	1848	1949	2106	2147	2324		0618	0748	0857	0949	1047
66	**Doncaster** 193 d.		0628	0749	0856	0950	1050	1149	1249	1349	1449	1549	1649	1749	1902	1850	1950	2107	2149	2325		0629	0754	0902	0950	1049
90	Meadowhall 193 d.		0657	0825	0916	1010	1110	1210	1308	1410	1510	1610	1710	1810	1929	1910	2010	2135	2212	2355		0658	0825	0924	1010	1110
96	**Sheffield** 193 a.		0707	0833	0925	1019	1121	1219	1318	1420	1519	1620	1721	1820	1936	1917	2017	2142	2221	0004		0707	0832	0931	1019	1120

	⑥A	⑥A	⑥B	⑥A	⑥B	⑥A	⑥A	⑥	⑥B	⑥	⑥A	⑥	⑥A		⑦	⑦	⑦A	⑦B	⑦B	⑦A	⑦B	⑦A	⑦B	⑦A	⑦B	⑦
Hull 181 d.	1058	1157	1258	1357	1457	1557	1656	1743	1755	1857	2002	2057	2216	⑦	0840	0943	1050	1240	1330	1441	1532	1637	1732	1835	2000	2140
Goole d.	1125	1224	1325	1426	1524	1624	1724	1821	│	1924	2036	2124	2250		0909	1017	1118	1314	1402	1509	1602	1708	1803	1903	2034	2208
Doncaster 181 a.	1148	1249	1349	1447	1547	1649	1750	1856	1848	1948	2106	2147	2319		0931	1047	1147	1337	1426	1532	1627	1731	1826	1934	2059	2238
Doncaster 193 d.	1150	1250	1350	1449	1549	1650	1750	1902	1850	1950	2109	2149	2321		0939	*1130*	1149	1339	1429	1533	1629	1732	1834	1936	2101	2240
Meadowhall 193 d.	1210	1310	1410	1510	1610	1710	1810	1929	1909	2010	2137	2211	2350		1001	│	1207	1359	1452	1554	1654	1754	1853	1957	2130	2309
Sheffield 193 a.	1220	1320	1420	1521	1617	1720	1817	1939	1919	2017	2145	2221	2358		1008	*1153*	1218	1408	1503	1601	1701	1801	1904	2006	2139	2316

		Ⓐ	ⒶA	ⒶA	ⒶB	ⒶA	ⒶB	ⒶA	ⒶA	ⒶB	ⒶA	ⒶA	ⒶB	Ⓐ	ⒶA	Ⓐ	ⒶA	Ⓐ	Ⓐ		⑥	⑥A	⑥A	⑥B	⑥A	⑥B
Sheffield 193 d.	Ⓐ	0529	0741	0841	0941	1041	1141	1241	1341	1441	1541	1641	1741	1753	1841	1946	2000	2115	2234	⑥	0529	0741	0841	0941	1041	1141
Meadowhall 193 d.		0535	0747	0847	0947	1047	1147	1247	1347	1447	1547	1647	1747	1759	1847	1953	2006	2121	2240		0535	0748	0847	0947	1047	1147
Doncaster 193 a.		0606	0819	0915	1015	1113	1215	1316	1412	1515	1615	1716	1812	1835	1911	2013	2037	2154	2312		0607	0819	0912	1015	1113	1214
Doncaster 181 d.		0610	0824	0919	1019	1119	1219	1319	1419	1519	1619	1719	1819	1839	1919	2017	2044	2156	2315		0612	0824	0919	1019	1119	1219
Goole d.		0636	0844	0939	1038	1138	1238	1338	1438	1538	1638	1741	1838	1911t	1938	2036	│	2222	2342		0638	0844	0938	1038	1138	1238
Hull 181 a.		0719	0913	1010	1110	1209	1308	1409	1511	1608	1709	1811	1908	1948	2010	2106	2145	2256	...		0721	0915	1009	1110	1209	1309

	⑥A	⑥A	⑥B	⑥A	⑥A	⑥B	⑥	⑥A	⑥	⑥A	⑥	⑥		⑦B	⑦A	⑦B	⑦B	⑦A	⑦B	⑦A	⑦B	⑦A	⑦	⑦	⑦	⑦
Sheffield 193 d.	1241	1341	1441	1541	1641	1741	1753	1841	1946	2000	2115	2233	⑦	0845	...	1026	1228	1324	1428	1529	1628	1728	1828	2002	2128	2214
Meadowhall 193 d.	1247	1347	1447	1547	1647	1747	1759	1848	1953	2006	2121	2240		0851	...	1032	1235	1330	1434	1535	1634	1734	1835	2008	2134	2220
Doncaster 193 a.	1312	1418	1518	1612	1712	1813	1837	1912	2016	2040	2154	2311		0922	...	1052	1256	1403	1456	1556	1656	1755	1855	2030	2204	2240
Doncaster 181 d.	1319	1419	1519	1619	1716	1820	1841	1914	2017	2043	2156	2312		0926	1019	1057	1258	1405	1500	1558	1656	1758	1856	2030	2206	2245
Goole d.	1338	1438	1538	1638	1740	1839	1911	1933	2036	│	2222	2339		0947	1040	1116	1317	1425	1519	1619	1715	1817	1923	2049	2225	2306
Hull 181 a.	1409	1508	1609	1710	1810	1911	1948	2004	2106	2144	2257	...		1021	1118	1150	1355	1457	1557	1652	1747	1851	1955	2121	2257	2339

A – From / to Bridlington (Table **177**).
B – From / to Scarborough (Table **177**).
t – Arrives 1905.

193 CLEETHORPES - DONCASTER - SHEFFIELD - MANCHESTER TP

km		⚒	①	②-⑥	⚒	⚒	⚒	⚒	⚒	⚒	⚒	⚒	⚒	⚒	Ⓐ	⑥	⚒	⚒	⑥	Ⓐ	⑥	⚒	⚒
0	**Cleethorpes** d.		...	...	...	...	0507	0620	0726	0826	0926	1026	1126	1226	1326	1326	1426	1526	1526	1626	1626	1726	1826
5	Grimsby Town d.		...	...	...	...	0515	0628	0734	0834	0934	1034	1134	1234	1334	1334	1434	1534	1534	1634	1634	1734	1834
48	Scunthorpe d.		...	...	...	...	0546	0703	0808	0908	1008	1108	1208	1308	1408	1408	1508	1608	1608	1708	1708	1808	1908
85	**Doncaster** a.		...	...	...	...	0623	0731	0838	0938	1038	1138	1240	1338	1438	1438	1538	1638	1638	1738	1738	1838	1938
85	**Doncaster** 192 d.		...	...	...	0538	0625	0734	0842	0942	1042	1142	1242	1342	1442	1442	1542	1642	1642	1742	1742	1840	1942
109	Meadowhall 192 d.		...	...	...	0559	0646	0752	0902	1002	1102	1202	1302	1402	1502	1502	1602	1702	1702	1802	1802	1902	2002
115	**Sheffield** 192 a.		...	...	...	0607	0655	0800	0908	1009	1108	1208	1308	1408	1508	1508	1608	1708	1708	1808	1808	1910	2008
115	**Sheffield** 206 d.		0325	0325	0511	0609	0708	0804	0911	1011	1111	1211	1311	1411	1511	1511	1611	1711	1711	1811	1811	1911	2011
175	Stockport 206 a.		|	|	|	0653	0752	0852	0952	1052	1152	1252	1352	1452	1553	1552	1652	1752	1752	1852	1852	1953	2052
184	**Manchester** Piccadilly 206 a.		0417	0451	0603	0702	0802	0903	1003	1103	1203	1303	1403	1503	1603	1603	1703	1803	1803	1903	1903	2003	2103
200	**Manchester** Airport a.		0440	0511	0628	0727	0824	0927	1027	1127	1227	1333	1427	1527	1624	1633	1728	1823	1827	1922	1928	2037	2131

	⚒	Ⓐ	⑥		⑦	⑦	⑦	⑦		⑦		⑦	⑦		⑦	⑦	⑦	⑦	⑦	⑦	⑦	⑦	⑦
Cleethorpes d.	1926	2026	2026	...		...	...	...	...	0926	...	1026	1126	...	1212	1326	1426	1526	1626	1726	1826	1926	2026
Grimsby Town d.	1934	2034	2034	...		...	...	...	...	0934	...	1034	1134	...	1220	1334	1434	1534	1634	1734	1834	1934	2034
Scunthorpe d.	2008	2108	2108	...		...	...	...	...	1008	...	1108	1208	...	1254	1408	1508	1608	1708	1808	1908	2008	2111
Doncaster a.	2040	2140	2140	...		...	...	...	...	1040	...	1140	1240	...	1332	1439	1536	1634	1738	1839	1938	2040	2141
Doncaster 192 d.	2042	2142	2142	...		...	...	0942	...	1042	...	1142	1242	...	1342	1442	1542	1642	1742	1842	1942	2042	2142
Meadowhall 192 d.	2109	2200	2200	...		...	...	1000	...	1100	...	1200	1300	...	1400	1500	1600	1700	1800	1900	2000	2100	2207
Sheffield 192 a.	2120	2208	2207	...		...	...	1010	...	1108	...	1211	1308	...	1408	1508	1608	1708	1808	1908	2009	2108	2214
Sheffield 206 d.	...	2211	*2224*	...		0751	0911	1011	...	1110	...	1211	1310	...	1411	1511	1611	1711	1811	1911	2011	2111	2215
Stockport 206 a.	...	2252	*2322*	...		0831	0952	|	...	1153	...	1251	1352	...	1452	1552	1652	1752	1852	1952	2052	2152	2259
Manchester Piccadilly 206 a.	...	2302	*2337*	...		0841	1004	1103	...	1206	...	1303	1403	...	1503	1602	1702	1802	1903	2003	2103	2203	2311
Manchester Airport a.	...	2321	...	...		0905	1024	1125	...	1227	...	1327	1427	...	1527	1627	1728	1827	1927	2028	2128	2228	...

	⚒	Ⓐ	⑥	Ⓐ	⚒	⚒	⚒	⚒	⚒	⚒	⚒	⚒	⚒	⑥	Ⓐ	⑥	Ⓐ	⚒	Ⓐ	⑥	⚒	Ⓐ	⚒
Manchester Airport d.		...	0550	0550	0655	0753	0855	0955	1055	1155	1255	1355	1455	1555	1555	1655	1655	1755	1855	1855	1955	...	...
Manchester Piccadilly 206 d.		...	0613	0613	0720	0820	0920	1020	1120	1220	1320	1420	1520	1620	1620	1720	1718	1820	1918	1918	2020	...	2043
Stockport 206 d.		...	0621	0621	0728	0828	0928	1027	1128	1228	1328	1428	1528	1628	1628	1728	1726	1828	1926	1926	2028	...	2054
Sheffield 206 a.		...	0702	0702	0810	0908	1008	1109	1208	1308	1408	1508	1608	1709	1709	1810	1810	1910	2009	2009	2112	...	2135
Sheffield 192 d.		...	0709	0712	0812	0910	1010	1110	1210	1310	1410	1510	1610	1710	1710	1812	1812	1912	2011	2027	...	2134	...
Meadowhall 192 d.		...	0715	0718	0818	0916	1016	1116	1216	1316	1416	1516	1616	1716	1716	1818	1818	1918	2017	2033	...	2140	...
Doncaster 192 a.		...	0739	0738	0837	0935	1035	1135	1235	1335	1435	1535	1635	1739	1737	1845	1845	1942	2044	2101	...	2202	...
Doncaster d.		0530	0743	0739	0839	0937	1037	1137	1237	1337	1437	1537	1637	1739	1747	1847	1847	1948	2046	2107	...	2205	...
Scunthorpe d.		0600	0809	0805	0905	1003	1103	1203	1303	1403	1503	1603	1703	1806	1813	1915	1915	2015	2112	2133	...	2231	...
Grimsby Town a.		0643	0847	0846	0940	1039	1137	1240	1337	1439	1537	1639	1737	1843	1849	1947	1948	2048	2148	2209	...	2309	...
Cleethorpes a.		0654	0856	0855	0951	1051	1149	1251	1349	1451	1549	1651	1750	1856	1859	2000	2000	2101	2200	2221	...	2320	...

	⑥	Ⓐ	⑥	⚒	Ⓐ	⑦	⑦	⑦	⑦	⑦	⑦	⑦	⑦	⑦	⑦	⑦	⑦	⑦	⑦	⑦		⑦	
Manchester Airport d.	...	2047	2047	2147	2327		0751b	0848	0955	1054	1155	1255	1355	1455	1555	1655	1755	1855	1955	2055	...	2155	...
Manchester Piccadilly 206 d.	...	2120	2120	2222	2350		0817	0914	1014	1118	1218	1320	1420	1520	1620	1720	1820	1920	2018	2120	...	2216	...
Stockport 206 d.	...	2128	2128	|	|		0826	0923	1023	1127	1228	1328	1428	1528	1628	1727	1828	1928	2027	2128	...	2224	...
Sheffield 206 a.	...	2210	2211	2315	0125		0908	1008	1103	1207	1308	1408	1509	1609	1708	1808	1908	2008	2108	2211	...	2307	...
Sheffield 192 d.	2152	2211	...	...	...		0910	1010	1110	1210	1310	1410	1510	1610	1710	1810	1910	2010	2110	2231	...	...	...
Meadowhall 192 d.	2158	2217	...	...	...		0916	1016	1116	1216	1316	1416	1516	1616	1716	1816	1916	2016	2116	2237	...	...	...
Doncaster 192 a.	2218	2243	...	...	...		0938	1036	1135	1235	1335	1435	1535	1635	1735	1835	1935	2035	2135	2256	...	...	...
Doncaster d.	2225	2245	...	...	...		0940	1037	1137	1237	1337	1437	1537	1637	1737	1837	1937	2037	2137	2258	...	...	...
Scunthorpe d.	2259	2319	...	...	...		1006	1103	1203	1303	1403	1503	1603	1703	1803	1903	2003	2103	2203	2324	...	...	...
Grimsby Town a.	2335	2357	...	...	...		1041	1142	1238	1337	1439	1538	1639	1737	1839	1937	2037	2139	2239	2358	...	...	...
Cleethorpes a.	2347	0010	...	...	...		1052	1153	1249	1349	1450	1549	1651	1749	1851	1949	2049	2151	2251	0010	...	...	...

km	NT 2nd class only	⚒	⚒	⚒	⑥	⚒	⚒	⑥	⚒	⑥	⚒	⑥	⚒	Ⓐ	⑥	⚒	⚒	⚒	⑥	Ⓐ	⑦	⑦	⑦	⑦	⑦	⑦	⑦	⑦
0	**Sheffield** ⊙ d.		0618	0712	0814	0914	1014	1114	1214	1314	1414	1514	1614	1714	1714	1814	1914	2035	2224	2248		0914	1114	1314	1514	1714	1914	2214
16	Grindleford d.		0634	0730	0828	0928	1028	1129	1228	1328	1429	1528	1628	1728	1728	1829	1928	2051	2238	2302		0929	1129	1329	1529	1729	1930	2229
18	Hathersage d.		0639	0733	0832	0932	1032	1132	1232	1332	1433	1532	1632	1732	1732	1832	1932	2055	2242	2306		0933	1133	1333	1533	1733	1934	2233
24	Hope d.		0647	0741	0839	0939	1039	1140	1239	1339	1440	1539	1639	1739	1739	1840	1939	2102	2249	2313		0940	1140	1340	1540	1740	1941	2240
32	Edale d.		0654	0749	0847	0947	1047	1148	1247	1347	1448	1547	1647	1747	1747	1848	1947	2110	2256	2322		0948	1148	1348	1548	1748	1949	2248
41	Chinley d.		0702	0757	0855	0955	1055	1156	1255	1355	1456	1555	1655	1755	1755	1856	1955	2118	2304	2330		0956	1156	1356	1556	1756	1957	2256
67	**Manchester** P'dilly ⊙ a.		0734	0835	0933	1033	1133	1233	1334	1434	1534	1634	1734	1830	1836	1935	2035	2205	2337	2359		1033	1233	1434	1634	1833	2034	2329

NT 2nd class only	⚒	⚒	⑥	Ⓐ	⑥	⚒	⑥	⚒	⑥	⚒	⑥	⚒	⚒	⚒	⚒	⚒	Ⓐ	⑥	⚒	⑦	⑦	⑦	⑦	⑦	⑦	⑦	⑦	⑦
Manchester P'dilly ⊙ d.		0546	0635	0708	0749	0849	0949	1049	1149	1249	1349	1449	1549	1649	1749	1849	2045	2049	2228		0744	0922	1140	1340	1540	1740	1940	2211
Chinley d.		0614	0714	0748	0823	0923	1025	1123	1225	1323	1425	1523	1623	1723	1823	1923	2119	2123	2253		0823	0959	1217	1417	1617	1817	2017	2243
Edale d.		0623	0723	0758	0833	0933	1034	1133	1234	1333	1434	1533	1633	1733	1833	1933	2129	2133	2301		0833	1008	1227	1427	1627	1827	2027	2251
Hope d.		0630	0730	0804	0839	0939	1040	1139	1240	1339	1440	1539	1639	1739	1839	1939	2135	2139	2307		0839	1015	1233	1433	1633	1833	2033	2257
Hathersage d.		0637	0737	0811	0846	0946	1047	1146	1247	1346	1447	1546	1646	1746	1846	1946	2142	2146	2315		0846	1021	1240	1440	1640	1840	2040	2303
Grindleford d.		0641	0741	0815	0850	0950	1050	1150	1250	1350	1450	1550	1650	1750	1850	1950	2146	2150	2319		0849	1025	1244	1444	1644	1844	2044	2312
Sheffield ⊙ a.		0658	0758	0833	0907	1006	1107	1207	1306	1407	1507	1607	1707	1808	1909	2008	2202	2208	2335		0907	1043	1300	1459	1700	1900	2100	2326

b – Until Feb. 11 and from April 1.

⊙ – Additional journeys on ⑦: From **Sheffield** at 1019, 1215, 1414, 1614, 1815. From **Manchester Piccadilly** at 0823, 1040, 1240, 1440, 1645.

194 SKEGNESS - NOTTINGHAM 2nd class EM

km		Ⓐ	Ⓐ	Ⓐ	Ⓐ	Ⓐ	Ⓐ	Ⓐ		Ⓐ	Ⓐ	Ⓐ	Ⓐ	Ⓐ	Ⓐ	Ⓐ	Ⓐ	Ⓐ	Ⓐ	Ⓐ	⑥	⑥	⑥	⑥
0	**Skegness** d.		...	...	0709	0810	0906	1015	...	1115	1215	1315	1415	1509	1611	1730	1814	1914	2015	2102		...	...	0709
8	Wainfleet d.		...	...	0719	0818	0914	1023	...	1123	1223	1323	1423	1517	1621	1738	1822	1922	2023	2110		...	...	0719
38	Boston d.		...	0613	0746	0845	0941	1050	...	1150	1250	1350	1450	1544	1648	1805	1848	1949	2050	2137		...	0613	0746
66	Sleaford d.		...	0635	0811	0907	1003	1112	...	1212	1313	1413	1512	1610	1713	1827	1913	2013	2118	2200		...	0635	0811
89	Grantham a.		...	0704	0842	0939	1031	1141	...	1241	1342	1442	1541	1641	1742	|	1941	2040	2145	|		...	0707	0842
89	Grantham 206 d.		0610	0710	0845	0945	1036	1145	...	1245	1348	1445	1545	1645	1745	|	1945	2044	2149	|		0610	0710	0845
126	**Nottingham** 206 a.		0654	0753	0920	1021	1114	1222	...	1323	1422	1523	1622	1720	1822	1922	2025	2120	2226	2253		0654	0752	0920

	⑥	⑥	⑥	⑥	⑥	⑥	⑥	⑥	⑥	⑥	⑥	⑥	⑥	⑥	⑦	⑦	⑦	⑦	⑦	⑦	⑦	⑦	⑦	⑦
Skegness d.	0815	0915	1015	1115	1215	1315	1415	1509	1611	1724	1814	1919	2015	2102		...	...	...	...	...	1410	1610	1807	1915
Wainfleet d.	0823	0923	1023	1123	1223	1323	1423	1517	1621	1732	1822	1927	2023	2110		...	...	...	...	...	1418	1618	1815	1923
Boston d.	0850	0950	1050	1150	1250	1350	1450	1544	1648	1759	1849	1954	2050	2137		...	...	...	1213	...	1445	1650	1842	1950
Sleaford d.	0912	1014	1112	1212	1312	1413	1512	1610	1713	1821	1913	2018	2112	2200		...	...	...	1235	...	1507	1712	1904	2012
Grantham a.	0941	1043	1141	1241	1341	1442	1541	1641	1742	|	1941	2045	2143	|		...	...	...	1304	...	1535	1741	1933	2041
Grantham 206 d.	0945	1046	1145	1245	1346	1445	1545	1645	1745	|	1945	2048	2147	|		0900	1045	1201	...	1509	1540	1745	1937	2045
Nottingham 206 a.	1021	1123	1222	1323	1423	1523	1622	1720	1822	1922	2024	2125	2225	2254		0933	1120	1236	...	1539	1617	1820	2012	2120

	Ⓐ	Ⓐ	Ⓐ	Ⓐ	Ⓐ		Ⓐ	Ⓐ	Ⓐ	Ⓐ	Ⓐ	Ⓐ	Ⓐ	Ⓐ	Ⓐ	Ⓐ	Ⓐ	Ⓐ A	Ⓐ	⑥	⑥	⑥	⑥	⑥
Nottingham 206 d.		0507	0550	0641	0735	...	0845	0955	1045	1145	1245	1345	1445	1545	1645	1744	1844	...	2051		0507	...	0550	0641
Grantham 206 a.		0546	0627	0719	0812	...	0926	|	1123	1219	1323	1423	1522	1625	1728	1825	1923	...	2132		0546	...	0627	0718
Grantham d.		▬	0631	0723	0816	...	0932	|	1127	1225	1327	1427	1526	1629	1732	1829	1926	...	2138		...	...	0631	0724
Sleaford d.		Ⓐ	0657	0751	0845	...	1003	1044	1153	1250	1355	1452	1552	1655	1801	1855	1955	2120	2203		...	...	0657	0751
Boston d.		0625	0725	0818	0912	...	1026	1111	1219	1315	1421	1517	1620	1721	1826	1921	2019	2153	2229		...	0625	0725	0818
Wainfleet d.		0649	0751	0843	0936	...	1050	1135	1244	1340	1447	1542	1645	1748	1851	1946	2044	...	...		...	0649	0751	0843
Skegness a.		0703	0805	0856	0949	...	1100	1150	1258	1354	1500	1556	1659	1800	1905	1959	2057	...	...		...	0703	0805	0856

	⑥	⑥	⑥	⑥	⑥	⑥	⑥	⑥	⑥	⑥	⑥	⑥	⑥ A	⑥	⑦	⑦	⑦	⑦	⑦	⑦	⑦	⑦	⑦	⑦
Nottingham 206 d.	0731	0840	0955	1045	1145	1245	1345	1445	1545	1645	1744	1845	...	2051		0815	0915	1000	1157	*1240*	1456	1623	1831	2045
Grantham 206 a.	0809	0923	|	1123	1219	1325	1423	1522	1625	1728	1825	1923	...	2131		0849	0950	1035	1229	*1313*	1531	1703	1908	2118
Grantham d.	0817	0930	|	1127	1225	1329	1427	1526	1629	1732	1829	1926	...	2136		...	...	...	1233	1350	1536	1707	1913	...
Sleaford d.	0846	0956	1044	1153	1250	1355	1452	1552	1655	1801	1855	1955	2121	2201		...	...	...	1259	1416	1602	1736	1941	...
Boston d.	0912	1022	1111	1219	1315	1421	1517	1620	1721	1826	1921	2019	2153	2229		...	...	...	1324	1445	1629	1802	2010	...
Wainfleet d.	0936	1047	1135	1244	1340	1446	1542	1645	1748	1851	1946	2043	...	...		...	...	...	1349	1509	1653	1827	...	...
Skegness a.	0948	1100	1150	1258	1354	1500	1556	1659	1800	1905	1959	2057	...	...		...	...	...	1400	1524	1708	1838	...	...

A – From Lincoln (Table **185**).

TL — LONDON - KINGS LYNN — 196

km		⚒	Ⓐ	⑥	Ⓐ	⚒	Ⓐ	⑥	Ⓐ	Ⓐ	⚒	Ⓐ	⚒	⚒	⚒	⚒	⚒	⚒	⚒	⚒	⚒	⑥	Ⓐ	⚒	⑥	Ⓐ
0	**London** Kings Cross **197** d.		...	...	0542	0644	0714	0744	0744	0814	0844	0914	0944	1014	1044	1114	1144	1214	1244	1314	1344	1414	1414	1444	1514	1514
93	Cambridge .... **197** d.		0615	0635	0652	0733	0806	0835	0838	0909	0935	1015	1035	1104	1135	1204	1235	1304	1335	1404	1435	1504	1507	1535	1604	1606
117	Ely .... d.		0633	0651	0708	0751	0822	0851	0854	0928	0951	1037	1051	1121	1151	1222	1251	1321	1351	1421	1451	1521	1524	1551	1621	1623
142	Downham Market .... d.		0653	0707	0725	0807	0838	0907	0910	...	1007	...	1107	...	1207	...	1307	...	1407	...	1507	...	...	1607	...	...
160	**Kings Lynn** .... a.		0707	0721	0740	0821	0852	0921	0925	...	1021	...	1121	...	1221	...	1321	...	1421	...	1521	...	...	1621	...	...

	⑥	Ⓐ	Ⓐ	⚒	⑥	Ⓐ	Ⓐ	⚒	⑥		Ⓐ	⑥	Ⓐ	Ⓐ	⑥	Ⓐ	Ⓐ	⑥	Ⓐ	⑥	Ⓐ	⑥	Ⓐ	Ⓐ	Ⓐ	⑥
London Kings Cross **197** d.	1544	1544	1558r	1614	1644	1644	1707r	1714	1744	...	1744	1814	1814	1807r	1844	1844	1907r	1914	1914	1944	1944	2014	2014	2004	2044	2044
Cambridge .... **197** d.	1635	1635	1721	1704	1735	1740	1817	1805	1835	...	1839	1905	1909	1919	1935	1939	2014	2007	2008	2035	2040	2107	2110	2128	2140	2140
Ely .... d.	1651	1652	1742	1723	1751	1757	1833	1823	1851	...	1856	1919	1924	1935	1951	1956	2030	2023	2025	2051	2056	2123	2126	2146	2156	2159
Downham Market .... d.	1707	1710	...	...	1807	1813	1850	...	1907	...	1912	1935	1939	1952	2007	2012	2047	2039	...	2108	2112	2139	2142	...	2212	...
Kings Lynn .... a.	1721	1724	...	...	1821	1827	1908	...	1921	...	1927	1951	1954	2010	2021	2026	2105	2053	...	2121	2126	2153	2156	...	2226	...

	⑥	Ⓐ	⑥	Ⓐ	⚒	Ⓐ	⚒	⑦	⑦	⑦	⑦	⑦	⑦	⑦	⑦	⑦	⑦	⑦	⑦	⑦	⑦	⑦	⑦b	⑦h	⑦b	⑦h
London Kings Cross **197** d.	2114	2114	2144	2144	2214	2244	2314		0752a	0915f	1015f	1115f	1215f	1315f	1415f	1515f	1615f	1715f	1815f	1915f	2015f	2115f	2215	2215	2315	2315
Cambridge .... **197** d.	2207	2210	2237	2240	2310	2340	0010		0906	1006	1106	1206	1306	1406	1506	1606	1706	1806	1906	2006	2106	2206	2306	2317	0007	0028
Ely .... d.	2223	2228	2254	2300	2328	2359	0026		0922	1022	1122	1222	1322	1422	1522	1622	1722	1822	1922	2022	2122	2222	2322	2333	0023	0044
Downham Market .... d.	2239	2244	...	...	2344	...	0042		0938	1038	1138	1238	1338	1438	1538	1638	1738	1838	1938	2038	2138	2238	2338	2349	0039	0100
Kings Lynn .... a.	2253	2258	...	...	2358	...	0058		0953	1053	1153	1253	1353	1453	1553	1653	1753	1853	1953	2052	2153	2253	2353	0004	0054	0114

	⚒	Ⓐ	⑥	Ⓐ	Ⓐ	⑥	Ⓐ	Ⓐ	Ⓐ	⑥	Ⓐ	Ⓐ	Ⓐ	Ⓐ	⑥	Ⓐ	Ⓐ	⑥	⑥	Ⓐ	Ⓐ	⑥	Ⓐ	⚒	Ⓐ	⑥
Kings Lynn .... d.		0454	...	0517	0551	0554	0610	0617	0651	0654	...	0714	0725	...	0754	0754	0827	...	0854	0857	...	0925	0930	0954	...	1026
Downham Market .... d.		0508	...	0531	0605	0608	0622	0631	0705	0708	...	0728	0737	...	0808	0808	0841	...	0908	0911	...	0937	0949	1008	...	1038
Ely .... d.		0525	0526	0550	0622	0625	0647t	0650	0722	0726	0730	0748	0756	0800	0825	0826	0858	0859	0925	0928	0949	0956	1007	1025	1058	1058
Cambridge .... **197** a.		0544	0545	0610	0639	0644	0704	0710	0739	0742	0747	0804	0810	0820	0841	0843	0915	0915	0941	0945	1006	1013	1023	1041	1115	1115
London Kings Cross **197** a.		0636	0639	0725r	0737	0734	0806	0825r	0838	0836	0920r	0909	0909	0950r	0935	0945	1015	1007	1036	1043	1110	1105	1132	1135	1205	1209

	⚒	⚒	⚒	⚒	⚒	⚒	⚒	⚒	⚒	Ⓐ	⑥	Ⓐ	⚒	⚒	Ⓐ	⑥	Ⓐ	⚒	Ⓐ	⑥	Ⓐ	⑥	⚒	Ⓐ	⑥	Ⓐ
Kings Lynn .... d.	1054	...	1154	...	1254	...	1354	...	1454	...	...	...	1554	...	1636	1654	...	...	1736	1754	...	...	1835	...	1935	1937
Downham Market .... d.	1108	...	1208	...	1308	...	1408	...	1508	...	...	...	1608	...	1651	1708	1710	...	1750	1808	...	...	1849	...	1949	1953
Ely .... d.	1125	1158	1225	1258	1325	1358	1425	1458	1525	1532	1558	1605	1625	1658	1709	1725	1726	1754	1808	1825	1858	1859	1906	1959	2006	2010
Cambridge .... **197** a.	1141	1215	1241	1315	1342	1416	1441	1515	1541	1553	1615	1623	1642	1715	1725	1741	1743	1812	1824	1841	1915	1916	1924	2016	2023	2026
London Kings Cross **197** a.	1238	1308	1335	1406	1435	1510d	1535	1608	1636	1719	1707	1735	1738	1823p	1833	1836	1839	1908	1937	1938	2005	2006	2036d	2107	2132	2133

	Ⓐ	⚒	Ⓐ	Ⓐ	⑥	Ⓐ	⑥	Ⓐ	⑥	⑦	⑦	⑦	⑦	⑦	⑦	⑦	⑦	⑦	⑦	⑦	⑦	⑦	⑦	⑦	⑦	⑦
Kings Lynn .... d.	...	2035	...	...	2135	2136	2226	2231	2310		0827	0927	1027	1127	1227	1327	1427	1527	1627	1727	1757	1827	1927	2027	2127	2227
Downham Market .... d.	...	2049	...	...	2149	2151	2240	2245	2324		0841	0941	1041	1141	1241	1341	1441	1541	1641	1741	1809	1841	1941	2041	2141	2241
Ely .... d.	2059	2106	2126	2157	2206	2209	2257	2302	2343		0858	0958	1058	1158	1258	1358	1458	1558	1658	1758	1826	1858	1958	2058	2158	2258
Cambridge .... **197** a.	2116	2124	2143	2214	2223	2225	2313	2321	0001		0915	1015	1115	1215	1315	1415	1515	1615	1715	1815	1840	1915	2015	2115	2215	2314
London Kings Cross **197** a.	2205	2232	2238	2305	2332	2336	0042	0051	...		1009g	1108g	1208g	1308c	1408c	1508c	1609c	1709c	1808g	1909c	1936b	2009g	2109c	2210g	2311c	0042

a – Departs 0805 Feb. 18 - Mar. 25.
b – Until Feb. 11 and from April 1.
c – Arrives 6–8 minutes later Feb. 18 - Mar. 25.
d – Arrives 3–4 minutes earlier on ⑥.
f – Departs 10 minutes earlier Feb. 18 - Mar. 25.
g – Arrives 9–12 minutes later Feb. 18 - Mar. 25.
h – Feb. 18 - Mar. 25.
p – Arrives 1807 on ⑥.
r – London **Liverpool Street**.
s – Stops to set down only.
t – Arrives 5 minutes earlier.

TL — LONDON KINGS CROSS - CAMBRIDGE — 197

km		Ⓐ	Ⓐ	Ⓐ	Ⓐ	Ⓐ	Ⓐ	Ⓐ	Ⓐ	Ⓐ	Ⓐ	Ⓐ	Ⓐ		Ⓐ	Ⓐ	Ⓐ	Ⓐ	Ⓐ	Ⓐ	Ⓐ	Ⓐ	Ⓐ	Ⓐ	Ⓐ	Ⓐ
0	**London** Kings X d.		0004	0542	0608	0644	0714	0744	0814	0844	0914	0944	1014	and at the same minutes past each	1514	1544	1552	1614	1644	1714	1744	1814	1823	1844	1914	1944
93	**Cambridge** ....a.		0129b	0650	0703	0731	0804	0833	0904	0930	1009	1030	1102	hour until	1602	1630	1655	1703	1735	1804	1834	1908	1928	1934	2005	2035

	Ⓐ	Ⓐ	Ⓐ	Ⓐ	Ⓐ	Ⓐ	Ⓐ	Ⓐ	⑥	⑥	⑥	⑥		⑥	⑥	⑥	⑥		⑥	⑥	⑥	⑥	⑥	⑥	⑥	⑥
London Kings X d.	2014	2044	2114	2144	2214	2244	2314	2344		0004	0031	0544	...	0644	0716	0744	0814	and at the same minutes past each	1944	2014	2044	2052	2114	2144	2152	2214
Cambridge........ a.	2105	2135	2205	2235	2305	2335	0005	0040		0124	0129	0655	...	0730	0810	0830	0903	hour until	2030	2101	2135	2155	2202	2235	2255	2305

	⑥	⑥	⑦	⑦	⑦c	⑦d	⑦d	⑦c	⑦d	⑦d	⑦c	⑦d	⑦c		⑦d	⑦c	⑦d	⑦c	⑦d	⑦c	⑦c	⑦d		⑦c	⑦c	⑦d
London Kings X d.	2244	2314		0014	0635	0638	0738	0752	0805	0838	0852	0905	0915	and at the same minutes past each	2038	2052	2105	2115	2138	2152	2215	2215	...	2252	2315	2315
Cambridge........ a.	2337	0005		0122	0745	0751	0849	0855	0901	0949	0955	1001	1001	hour until	2153	2155	2201	2201	2249	2255	2301	2312	...	2355	0006	0023

	Ⓐ	Ⓐ	Ⓐ	Ⓐ	Ⓐ	Ⓐ	Ⓐ	Ⓐ	Ⓐ	Ⓐ	Ⓐ	Ⓐ	Ⓐ	Ⓐ	Ⓐ	Ⓐ		Ⓐ	Ⓐ	Ⓐ	Ⓐ	Ⓐ	Ⓐ	Ⓐ	Ⓐ	Ⓐ
Cambridge........ d.		0514	0545	0614	0645	0715	0745	0815	0851	0920	0927	0950	1017	1047	1117	1147	and at the same minutes past each	1647	1717	1749	1815	1845	1916	1945	2017	2047
London Kings X a.		0610	0636	0716	0737	0806	0838	0909	0945	1015	1033	1043	1110	1135	1205	1238	hour until ☆	1738	1823	1839	1908	1939	2005	2039	2107	2135

	Ⓐ	Ⓐ	Ⓐ	Ⓐ	⑤	Ⓐ	⑥	⑥	⑥	⑥	⑥	⑥		⑥	⑥	⑥	⑥	⑥	⑦	⑦	⑦	⑦	⑦c	⑦d	⑦	⑦c
Cambridge........ d.	2117	2145	2217	2231	2256	2322		0546	0615	0646	0717	0748	and at the same minutes past each	2117	2147	2217	2229	2315		0628	0728	0828	0920	0920	0928	1020
London Kings X a.	2205	2238	2305	2336	0007	0051		0639	0704	0734	0805	0836	hour until ☆	2205	2235	2304	2332	0043		0740	0836	0937	1009	1018	1030f	1108

	⑦d	⑦	⑦c	⑦d	⑦	⑦		⑦	⑦	⑦	⑦	⑦c	⑦c	⑦d	⑦c	⑦d	⑦		⑦	⑦c	⑦d	⑦	⑦c	⑦d	⑦	⑦
Cambridge........ d.	1020	1028	1120	1120	1128	1220	and at the same minutes past each	1720	1728	1820	1828	1845	1920	1920	1928	1928	2020	...	2028	2120	2120	2128	2220	2220	2228	2316
London Kings X a.	1120	1130f	1208	1220	1230f	1308f	hour until ☆	1808e	1832g	1909f	1930f	1936	2009	2018	2030	2040	2109f	...	2130f	2210	2222	2230f	2311	2316	2330f	0042

a – Until Oct. 22.
b – Arrives 0124 ②–⑤.
c – Until Feb. 11 and from April 1.
d – Feb. 18 - Mar. 25.
e – Arrives 1819 Feb. 18 - Mar. 25.
f – Arrives 6–8 minutes later Feb. 18 - Mar. 25.
g – Arrives 1836 Feb.18 - Mar. 25.
☆ – Timings may vary by up to 3 minutes.

CC, LE — LONDON - SOUTHEND and CAMBRIDGE — 199

Typical off-peak journey time in hours and minutes
READ DOWN ↓ READ UP ↑

Journey times may be extended during peak hours on Ⓐ (0600 - 0900 and 1600 - 1900) and also at weekends.
The longest journey time by any train is noted in the table heading.

LONDON FENCHURCH STREET - SOUTHEND CENTRAL — Longest journey: 1 hour 08 minutes — CC

km	A				A
0	0h00	↓	d.**London** F Street ....a.	↑	1h04
8	0h09		d.West Ham..............d.		0h56
12	0h14	↓	d.Barking ....d.	↑	0h50
39	0h34		d.Basildon.................d.		0h29
56	0h53	↓	a.**Southend** Central..d.	↑	0h10
63	1h03		a.Shoeburyness........d.		0h00

From London Fenchurch Street: 0500⚒/0634⑦ and at least every 30 minutes (every 10 - 20 minutes 0840Ⓐ - 2010Ⓐ) until 2341.
From Southend Central*: 0424⚒/0549⑦ and at least every 30 minutes (every 15 minutes 0424Ⓐ - 2020Ⓐ) until 2249⑦, 2335⚒.
A – During peak hours on Ⓐ (0600 - 0900 and 1600 - 1900) trains may not make all stops.
* – Trains depart Shoeburyness 10 minutes before Southend Central.
☛ On ⑦ passengers for Basildon and Shoeburyness should change at Barking.

LONDON LIVERPOOL STREET - SOUTHEND VICTORIA — Longest journey: 1 hour 14 minutes — LE

km					
0	0h00	↓	d.**London** L Street....a.	↑	0h58
6	0h07		d.Stratford.................d.		0h49
32	0h25	↓	d.Shenfield ....d.	↑	0h35
53	0h43		d.Rayleigh ....d.		0h16
64	0h54	↓	a.**Southend** Airport...d.	↑	0h05
66	1h01		a.**Southend** Victoria .d.		0h00

From London Liverpool Street: 0535⚒/0714⑦ and at least every 30 minutes (every 20 minutes 0635⚒ - 2213⚒) until 2344.
From Southend Victoria: 0400⚒/0615⑦ and at least every 30 minutes (every 20 minutes 0626⚒ - 2130⚒) until 2249⑦/2300⚒.

LONDON LIVERPOOL STREET - CAMBRIDGE — Longest journey: 1 hour 39 minutes — LE

km					
0	0h00	↓	d.**London** L Street....a.	↑	1h23
10	0h12		d.Tottenham Hale .....d.		0h57
36	0h29	↓	d.Harlow Town..........d.	↑	0h38
48	0h42		d.Bishops Stortford ...d.		0h28
67	0h54	↓	d.Audley End ....d.	↑	0h15
89	1h23		a.**Cambridge**............d.		0h00

From London Liverpool Street: on Ⓐ at 0528, 0558 and every 30 minutes until 1528, 1558, 1628, 1643, 1707, 1713, 1737, 1743, 1807, 1813, 1837, 1843, 1907, 1911, 1928, 1958, 2028 and every 30 minutes until 2258, 2328, 2358⑤; on ⑥ at 0520, 0558, 0628, 0658 and every 30 minutes until 2328, 2358; on ⑦ at 0742, 0828, 0857 and at the same minutes past each hour until 2228, 2257.
From Cambridge: on Ⓐ at 0448, 0520, 0548, 0551, 0618, 0621, 0647, 0651, 0717, 0721, 0747, 0751, 0818, 0821, 0848, 0918, 1004, 1021 and at the same minutes past each hour until 1521, 1551 and every 30 minutes until 1921, 2004, 2021, 2102, 2121, 2204, 2221, 2251; on ⑥ at 0438, 0521, 0604, 0621 and at the same minutes past each hour until 2221, 2251; on ⑦ at 0732, 0751 and at the same minutes past each hour until 2132, 2232.

200 LONDON - HARWICH, IPSWICH and NORWICH

Most Norwich trains convey 🍷 LE

For Rail - Sea - Rail services London - Amsterdam and v.v. via Harwich and Hoek van Holland see Table **15a**.

km			Ⓐ P	Ⓐ	Ⓐ	Ⓐ	Ⓐ	Ⓐ	Ⓐ C	Ⓐ	Ⓐ	Ⓐ	Ⓐ	Ⓐ	Ⓐ	Ⓐ		Ⓐ	Ⓐ	Ⓐ	Ⓐ	Ⓐ	Ⓐ	Ⓐ	Ⓐ	Ⓐ	Ⓐ	Ⓐ	Ⓐ
0	**London** L St ‡ .. d.	Ⓐ	...	...	...	0600	...	0625	...	0638	0700	0730	0755	...	0830	0900	and	1530	1600	...	*1602*	1630	1644	1700	1702	1730	...	1750	...
48	Chelmsford .... d.		...	...	...	0630	...	0658	...	0710	|	0803	|	...	0903	|	at	1600	|	...	*1635*	|	1715	|	1736	|	...	|	...
84	Colchester .... d.		0540	0610	...	0650	...	0723	...	0743	0751	0823	0847	...	0923	0947	the	1621	1647	...	*1705*	1717	1748t	|	1801	|	...	1843	...
97	Manningtree .... d.		0549	0618	...	0658	0724	0731	...	0751	0759	0831	0855	0900	0931	0955	same	1629	1655	1700	1724	|	1757	|	1809	1827	1835	1852	1902
112	**Harwich** Int'l .. d.		|	0636	...	|	0741	|	0750	0810	|	|	|	0917	|	|	minutes	|	|	1717	1741	|	1815	|	|	|	1852	|	1919
115	**Harwich** Town a.		|	0641	...	|	0746	|	|	0815	|	|	|	0922	|	|	past	|	|	1722	1746	|	1822	|	|	|	1857	|	1924
111	**Ipswich** .... **205** d.		0600	...	0639	0712	...	0744	0820	...	0812	0844	0908	...	0944	1008	each	1641	1708	...	...	1736	...	1800	1825	1839	...	1904	...
130	Stowmarket .. **205** d.		0611	...	0651	0723	...	0755	0834	...	0823	0855	|	...	0955	|	hour	1652	1719	...	...	1747	...	|	1836	1850	...	1916	...
153	Diss .... d.		...	...	0704	0735	...	0808	...	...	0836	0908	0929	...	1008	1029	until	1705	1732	...	...	1800	...	1821	1848	1904	...	1929	...
185	**Norwich** .... a.		...	...	0724	0755	...	0827	...	...	0855	0927	0948	...	1027	1050		1724	1753	...	...	1822	...	1842	1909	1925	...	1950	...

	Ⓐ	Ⓐ	Ⓐ	Ⓐ	Ⓐ	Ⓐ	Ⓐ	Ⓐ	Ⓐ	Ⓐ	Ⓐ	Ⓐ	Ⓐ L	Ⓐ	Ⓐ	Ⓐ	Ⓐ	Ⓐ	Ⓐ	Ⓐ	Ⓐ	Ⓐ		⑥ P	⑥	⑥	⑥	⑥	⑥ C	⑥
London L St ‡ ... d.	1810	1830	...	1820	1900	...	1930	1932	...	2000	...	2030	...	2100	...	2102	2130	2200	...	2230	...	2330	⑥	...	...	0534	...	0630	...	0638
Chelmsford .... d.	|	|	...	1857	|	...	|	2002	...	|	...	2103	...	|	...	2134	2203	2228	...	2303	...	0003		...	...	0610	...	0703	...	0712
Colchester .... d.	1902	1923	...	1930	1947	...	2020	2025	...	2047	...	2123	...	2147	...	2204	2223	2247	...	2323	...	0023		0540	0553	0640	...	0723	...	0740
Manningtree .... d.	1911	1932	1938	1940	1955	2000	2028	2034	2038	2055	2100	2132	...	2156	2200	2212	2232	2255	2300	2332	2336	0032		0549	0601	0648	0700	0731	...	0748
Harwich Int'l .. d.	|	|	1955	2002	|	2017	|	2054	2055	|	2117	|	2138	|	2217	2228	|	|	2317	|	2353	|		|	0618	|	0717	|	0750	0809
Harwich Town a.	|	|	2000	...	|	2022	|	...	2100	|	2122	|	|	|	2222	...	|	|	2322	|	2358	|		|	0623	|	0722	|	|	...
Ipswich ...... **205** d.	1923	1944	...	...	2008	...	2041	...	...	2108	...	2145	2204	2209	...	...	2245	2308	...	2345	...	0045		0600	...	0700	...	0744	0820	...
Stowmarket. **205** d.	1934	1955	...	...	2019	...	2052	...	...	2119	...	2156	...	2220	...	...	2257	...	...	2357	...	0057		0611	...	*0721*	...	0755	0834	...
Diss .... d.	1947	2008	...	...	2032	...	2105	...	...	2132	...	2209	...	2233	...	...	2311	...	...	0011	...	0111		...	...	*0734*	...	0808	...	...
Norwich .... a.	2009	2030	...	...	2051	...	2124	...	...	2151	...	2229	...	2253	...	...	2330	...	...	0030	...	0136		...	...	*0753*	...	0827	...	...

	⑥	⑥	⑥	⑥	⑥		⑥	⑥	⑥	⑥	⑥	⑥	⑥	⑥ L	⑥	⑥	⑥	⑥	⑥	⑥	⑥	⑥	⑥		⑦ C	⑦	⑦	⑦	⑦
London L St ‡ ... d.	0700	...	0730	0800	...	and	1900	...	1930	1932	2000	...	2030	...	2100	...	2102	2130	2200	...	2230	...	2330	⑦	...	...	0755	0802	0830
Chelmsford .... d.	|	...	0803	|	...	at	|	...	2003	2007	|	...	2103	...	|	...	2134	2203	2228	...	2303	...	|		...	...	0836	0843	|
Colchester .... d.	0747	...	0823	0847	...	the	1947	...	2023	2032	2047	...	2123	...	2147	..	2204	2223	2248	...	2323	...	0026		...	0818	0859	0913	0925
Manningtree .... d.	0755	0800	0831	0855	0900	same	1955	2000	2031	2040	2055	2100	2132	...	2155	2200	2212	2232	2256	2300	2332	2336	0036		...	0826	0907	0921	0933
Harwich Int'l .. d.	|	0817	|	|	0917	minutes	|	2017	|	2056	|	2117	|	2138	|	2217	2228	|	|	2317	|	2353	|		0830	0843	0925	|	|
Harwich Town a.	|	0822	|	|	0922	past	|	2022	|	...	|	2122	|	|	|	2222	...	|	|	2322	|	2358	|		|	0848	*0948*	|	|
Ipswich ...... **205** d.	0808	...	0844	0908	...	each	2008	...	2044	...	2108	...	2145	2203	2208	...	...	2245	2308	...	2345	...	0049		0902	...	...	0935	0946
Stowmarket. **205** d.	|	...	0855	|	...	hour	|	...	2055	...	|	...	2156	...	...	...	...	2257	...	...	2357	...	0101		0917	...	...	...	0957
Diss .... d.	0829	...	0908	0929	...	until	2029	...	2108	...	2129	...	2209	...	...	...	...	2311	...	...	0011	...	0114		...	...	...	...	1010
Norwich .... a.	0850	...	0927	0950	...		2050	...	2127	...	2150	...	2229	...	...	...	...	2330	...	...	0036	...	0140		...	...	...	...	1031

	⑦ P	⑦	⑦	⑦		⑦	⑦	⑦		⑦	⑦	⑦	⑦	⑦	⑦	⑦	⑦	⑦	⑦	⑦	⑦	⑦	⑦	⑦	⑦	⑦	⑦	⑦	⑦
London L St ‡ ... d.	...	0902	...	0930	and	1702	...	1730	...	1802	...	1830	1900	1902	...	1930	*1932*	2002	...	...	2030	2102	...	2130	2202	2230	2302	2330	2332
Chelmsford .... d.	...	0943	...	|	at	1743	...	|	...	1843	...	|	|	1943	...	|	*2011*	2043	...	...	|	2143	...	|	2243	|	2343	|	0011
Colchester .... d.	0932	1013	...	1025	the	1813	...	1825	...	1913	...	1925	1955	2013	...	2025	2046	2113	...	...	2125	2213	...	2225	2313	2325	0013	0025	0043
Manningtree .... d.	0940	1021	1026	1033	same	1821	1826	1833	...	1921	1926	1933	2003	2021	2026	2033	2055	2121	...	2126	2134	2221	2226	2234	2321	2334	0021	0034	...
Harwich Int'l .. d.	|	|	1043	|	minutes	|	1843	|	...	|	1943	|	|	|	2043	|	2114	|	2110	2143	|	|	2243	|	|	|	|	|	...
Harwich Town a.	|	|	1048	|	past	|	1848	|	...	|	1948	|	|	|	2048	|	...	|	|	2148	|	|	2248	|	|	|	|	|	...
Ipswich ...... **205** d.	0955	1033	...	1046	each	1833	...	1846	...	1933	...	1946	2016	2033	...	2046	...	2133	2137	...	2147	2233	...	2247	2333	2347	0039	0047	...
Stowmarket. **205** d.	1006	...	...	1057	hour	...	...	1857	...	...	...	1957	2027	...	...	2057	...	...	...	...	2158	...	...	2259	...	2359	...	0059	...
Diss .... d.	...	...	...	1110	until	...	...	1910	...	...	...	2010	2040	...	...	2110	...	...	...	...	2211	...	...	2313	...	0013	...	0113	...
Norwich .... a.	...	...	...	1131		...	...	1931	...	...	...	2031	2101	...	...	2131	...	...	...	...	2231	...	...	2332	...	0032	...	0137	...

		Ⓐ	Ⓐ		Ⓐ		Ⓐ	Ⓐ		Ⓐ	Ⓐ	Ⓐ L	Ⓐ	Ⓐ	Ⓐ	Ⓐ	Ⓐ	Ⓐ	Ⓐ	Ⓐ	Ⓐ	Ⓐ	Ⓐ	Ⓐ	Ⓐ		Ⓐ	Ⓐ	Ⓐ
Norwich .... d.	Ⓐ	...	...	...	0500	...	0530	...	...	0600	...	...	0624	0648	...	...	0705	0740	...	...	...	0800	0830	...	0900	and	1530	...	1600
Diss .... d.		...	...	...	0518	...	0548	...	...	0618	...	...	0642	0706	...	...	0723	0758	...	...	...	0817	0847	...	0917	at	1547	...	1617
Stowmarket. **205** d.		...	...	...	0530	...	0600	...	...	0630	...	...	0654	0718	...	...	0735	|	...	0810	...	0829	|	...	0929	the	|	...	1629
Ipswich ...... **205** d.		0512	...	...	0544	...	0614	...	...	0644	...	0659	0708	0732	...	...	0749	0820	...	0826	...	0843	0909	...	0943	same	1609	...	1643
Harwich Town d.		|	0524	...	|	...	|	0624	...	|	0652	|	|	|	...	0716	|	|	0758	|	0828	|	|	0928	|	minutes	|	1628	|
Harwich Int'l .. d.		|	0529	...	|	...	|	0629	...	|	0657	0727	|	|	0715	0721	|	|	0803	|	0833	|	|	0933	|	past	|	1633	|
Manningtree .... d.		0524	0546	...	0554	...	0624	0646	...	0654	0714	...	0718	0743	0731	0738	0759	|	0820	0836	0850	0853	0919	0950	0953	each	1619	1650	1653
Colchester .... d.		0534	...	...	0605	...	0635	...	...	0705	...	...	0730	|	0742	0754t	0810	|	0837t	0845	...	0903	0930	...	1003	hour	1630	...	1703
Chelmsford .... d.		0558	...	...	|	...	|	...	...	|	...	...	|	|	0814	0819	|	|	0859	0904	...	0921	|	...	1021	until	|	...	1721
London L St ‡ ... a.		0634	...	...	0654	...	0727	...	...	0758	...	...	0824	0842	0854	0858	0904	0924	0936	0939	...	0958	1019	...	1055		1719	...	1758

	Ⓐ	Ⓐ	Ⓐ	Ⓐ	Ⓐ	Ⓐ	Ⓐ	Ⓐ	Ⓐ	Ⓐ	Ⓐ	Ⓐ	Ⓐ	Ⓐ	Ⓐ	Ⓐ	Ⓐ	Ⓐ C	Ⓐ	Ⓐ P	Ⓐ	Ⓐ	Ⓐ	Ⓐ	Ⓐ P	Ⓐ	Ⓐ		⑥	⑥
Norwich .... d.	...	1630	...	1700	1730	...	...	1800	1830	...	...	1900	1930	...	...	2000	...	...	2030	...	...	2100	...	2200	...	...	2305	⑥	0500	0530
Diss .... d.	...	1647	...	1717	1747	...	...	1817	1847	...	...	1917	1947	...	...	2017	...	...	2047	...	...	2117	...	2217	...	...	2323		0517	0547
Stowmarket. **205** d.	...	|	...	1729	1759	...	...	1829	|	...	...	1929	|	...	...	2029	...	2045	|	2114	...	2129	...	2229	2308	...	2336		0529	|
Ipswich ...... **205** d.	...	1709	...	1743	1813	...	...	1843	1909	...	...	1943	2010	...	...	2043	...	2101	2109	2128	...	2143	...	2243	2322	...	2349		0543	0609
Harwich Town d.	1653	|	1728	|	|	1800	1826	|	|	1905	1928	|	|	2005	2028	|	...	|	|	|	2128	|	2228	|	|	2328	...		|	|
Harwich Int'l .. d.	1658	|	1733	|	|	1805	1831	|	|	1910	1933	|	|	2010	2033	|	2045	2129	|	|	2133	|	2233	|	|	2333	...		|	|
Manningtree .... d.	1715	1719	1750	1753	|	1822	1848	1853	1919	1927	1950	1953	2020	2027	2050	2053	2058	...	2119	2138	2150	2153	2250	2253	2332	2350	...		0553	0619
Colchester .... d.	...	1730	...	1803	1830	*1843*	...	1903	1930	*1946*	...	2003	2030	*2045*	...	2103	2112f	...	2130	2151	...	2203	...	2303	2343	2359	...		0603	0630
Chelmsford .... d.	...	|	...	1821	|	*1909*	...	1921	|	...	...	2021	|	...	...	2121	2140	...	|	...	...	2221	...	2325	...	...	...		0621	|
London L St ‡ ... a.	...	1819	...	1855	1917	*1945*	...	1955	2020	...	...	2055	2119	...	...	2155	2214	...	2219	...	...	2255	...	0003	...	...	...		0655	0719

	⑥	⑥	⑥	⑥	⑥	⑥	⑥	⑥	B	⑥	⑥	⑥	⑥	⑥	⑥	⑥	⑥	⑥	⑥	⑥ C	⑥	⑥ P	⑥	⑥	⑥	⑥	⑥	⑥ P	⑥
Norwich .... d.	...	0600	...	0630	...	...	0700	0730	and	1730	...	1800	1830	...	1900	...	...	2000	...	...	...	...	...	2100	...	...	2200	...	...
Diss .... d.	...	0617	...	0647	...	...	0717	0747	at	1747	...	1817	1847	...	1917	...	...	2017	...	...	...	...	...	2117	...	...	2217	...	...
Stowmarket. **205** d.	...	0629	...	|	...	...	0729	|	the	1759	...	1829	|	...	1929	...	...	2029	...	2045	...	2114	...	2129	...	...	2229	2308	...
Ipswich ...... **205** d.	...	0643	0659	0709	...	...	0743	0809	same	1813	...	1843	1909	...	1943	2009	...	2043	...	2101	2109	2128	...	2143	2223	...	2243	2322	...
Harwich Town d.	0628	|	|	|	...	0728	|	|	minutes	|	1828	|	|	1928	|	|	2028	|	...	|	|	|	2128	|	|	2228	|	|	2328
Harwich Int'l .. d.	0633	|	0727	|	0720	0733	|	|	past	|	1833	|	|	1933	|	|	2033	|	2045	2129	|	|	2133	|	|	2233	|	|	2333
Manningtree .... d.	0650	0653	...	0719	0733	0750	0753	0819	each	|	1850	1853	1919	1950	1953	2019	2050	2053	2058	...	2119	2138	2150	2153	2233	2250	2253	2332	2350
Colchester .... d.	...	0703	...	0730	0743	...	0803	0830	hour	1830	...	1903	1930	...	2003	2030	...	2103	2112f	...	2130	2149	...	2203	2243	...	2303	2343	2359
Chelmsford .... d.	...	0721	...	|	0809	...	0821	|	until	|	...	1921	|	...	2021	|	...	2121	2140	...	|	...	...	2221	2309	...	2325	...	...
London L St ‡ ... a.	...	0755	...	0819	0846	...	0855	0919		1919	...	1955	2019	...	2055	2117	...	2155	2214	...	2217	...	...	2255	2351	...	0010	...	...

	⑥		⑦	⑦	⑦	⑦	⑦	⑦	⑦	⑦	⑦	⑦	A	⑦ P	⑦	⑦	⑦	⑦	⑦ C	⑦	⑦	⑦	⑦ P	⑦	⑦	⑦	⑦	⑦	⑦
Norwich .... d.	2305	⑦	...	0700	...	...	0800	...	...	0900	...	...	and	...	1900	...	...	...	...	2000	...	...	...	2100	...	...	2200	...	2305
Diss .... d.	2322		...	0717	...	...	0817	...	...	0917	...	...	at	...	1917	...	...	...	...	2017	...	...	...	2117	...	...	2217	...	2323
Stowmarket. **205** d.	2336		...	0729	...	...	0829	...	...	0929	...	...	the	1911	1929	...	...	...	2018	2029	...	...	2111	2129	...	...	2229	...	2336
Ipswich ...... **205** d.	2349		...	0743	0751	0809	0843	...	0909	0943	...	1009	same	1925	1943	...	2009	...	2036	2043	...	2109	2125	2143	...	2209	2243	...	2351
Harwich Town d.	...		...	|	|	|	|	0853	|	|	0953	|	minutes	|	1953	1953	|	...	|	|	2053	|	|	|	2153	|	|	2253	...
Harwich Int'l .. d.	...		0720	|	0816	|	|	0858	|	|	0958	|	past	|	|	1958	|	2035	2105	|	2058	|	|	|	2158	|	|	2258	...
Manningtree .... d.	...		0734	0753	...	0819	0853	0915	0919	0953	1015	1019	each	1935	|	2015	2019	2048	...	2053	2115	2119	2135	2153	2215	2219	2253	2315	...
Colchester .... d.	...		0748r	0803	...	0830	0903	...	0930	1003	...	1030	hour	1946	2003	...	2030	2057	...	2103	...	2130	2146	2203	...	2230	2303	2324	...
Chelmsford .... d.	...		0810	|	...	0858	|	...	0958	|	...	1058	until	...	|	...	2058	2115	...	|	...	2158	...	|	...	2258	2325	...	...
London L St ‡ ... a.	...		0859	0904	...	0944	1003	...	1044	1103	...	1144		...	2103	...	2144	2202	...	2204	...	2240	...	2303	...	2340	0007	...	...

A – Additional Norwich - London departure at 1620, calling at Diss 1638, Stowmarket 1650, Ipswich 1705, Colchester 1723 and London Liverpool Street 1831.

B – The 0800, 0900 and 1000 departures from Norwich do not call at Colchester or Chelsmsford and arrive London Liverpool Street 3 minutes earlier.

C – To / from Cambridge (Table **205**).

P – To / from Peterborough (Table **205**).

L – To / from Lowestoft (Table **201**).

f – Arrives 2107.

r – Arrives 0743.

t – Arrives 7 – 8 minutes earlier.

‡ – **London** Liverpool Street.

LE — IPSWICH - LOWESTOFT — 201

km		⚒ Ⓐ 2	Ⓐ 2	⑥ 2	Ⓐ 2	⑥ 2	⚒ 2		⚒ 2	Ⓐ 2	⑥ 2	⚒ 2	Ⓐ 2	⑥ 2	⚒ 2	⚒ 2	⚒ 2	⚒ H	⑦		⑦ 2	⑦ 2	⑦ 2	⑦
0	**Ipswich** d.	0620	...	0717	0735	0817	0917	and at	1517	1554	1617	1717	1813	1817	1917	2017	2117	2217	1002	and every	1802	1907	2002	2202
17	Woodbridge d.	0637	...	0732	0753	0832	0932	the same	1532	1618	1632	1732	1830	1832	1932	2032	2132	2232	1019	**two** hours	1819	1924	2019	2219
36	Saxmundham d.	0658	0744	0754	0815	0854	0954	minutes	1554	1640	1654	1754	1851	1854	1954	2054	2154	2254	1040	until	1840	1945	2040	2240
65	Beccles d.	...	0816	0825	0846	0925	1025	past each	1625	1719	1725	1825	1925	1925	2025	2125	2225	2325	1112	☆	1912	2021	2112	2312
79	**Lowestoft** a.	...	0833	0843	0906	0943	1043	hour until ☆	1643	1736	1751	1843	1943	1943	2043	2143	2243	2343	1130		1930	2039	2130	2330

	⚒ Ⓐ H	⑥	Ⓐ	Ⓐ 2	⑥	Ⓐ 2	⑥ 2	⚒		⚒	⑥ 2	Ⓐ 2	Ⓐ	⑥	⚒ 2	⚒ 2	⚒ 2	⚒ 2	⑦		⑦ 2	⑦ 2	⑦ 2	⑦
Lowestoft d.	0525	0607	0614	0641	0707	0727	0807	0907	and at	1507	1607	1607	1702	1707	1807	1907	2007	2107	0805	and every	1605	1705	1805	2005
Beccles d.	0541	0625	0630	0657	0725	0743	0825	0925	the same	1525	1625	1625	1725	1725	1825	1925	2025	2125	0821	**two** hours	1621	1721	1821	2021
Saxmundham d.	0613	0657	0703	0729	0757	0817	0857	0957	minutes	1557	1657	1707**t**	1757	1757	1857	1957	2057	2157	0853	until	1653	1753	1853	2053
Woodbridge d.	0635	0718	0725	0751	0818	0839	0918	1018	past each	1618	1718	1728	1818	1818	1918	2018	2118	2218	0914	☆	1714	1814	1914	2114
Ipswich a.	0653	0736	0744	0809	0836	0857	0936	1036	hour until ☆	1636	1736	1746	1836	1836	1936	2037	2136	2236	0932		1732	1832	1932	2132

H – To/from Harwich International (Table **200**).

t – Arrives 6 minutes earlier.

☆ – All trains are 2nd class only except the following which also convey 1st class: From Ipswich at 0917⑥, 1002⑦, 1117Ⓐ, 1317⑥, 1517Ⓐ, 1602⑦, 1717⑥, 1917Ⓐ, 2117⑥, 2202⑦, 2217⚒. From Lowestoft at 0525Ⓐ, 0607⑥, 0614Ⓐ, 0707⑥, 0805⑦, 0907Ⓐ, 1107⑥, 1307Ⓐ, 1405⑦, 1507⑥, 1702Ⓐ, 1907⑥, 2005⑦.

LE 2nd class — NORWICH and IPSWICH local services — 203

NORWICH - GREAT YARMOUTH

Journey time ± 32 minutes *30 km (33 km via Reedham)*

From Norwich: Trains noted '**r**' call at **Reedham** 18–21 minutes later.

Ⓐ: 0506, 0611, 0652, 0736**r**, 0809, 0836, 0936, 1036, 1136**r**, 1236, 1336, 1440, 1536, 1638, 1706, 1736, 1804, 1840, 1933, 2038, 2140, 2300.

⑥: 0530**r**, 0636, 0706, 0736**r**, 0809, 0836, 0936, 1036, 1136**r**, 1236, 1336, 1436, 1536, 1640, 1706, 1736, 1806, 1840, 1933, 2040, 2140, 2300.

⑦: 0736**r**, 0845, 0936**r**, 1045, 1136**r**, 1245, 1336**r**, 1445, 1536**r**, 1645, 1736**r**, 1845, 1936**r**, 2045, 2136**r**, 2236.

From Great Yarmouth: Trains noted '**r**' call at **Reedham** 12–14 minutes later.

Ⓐ: 0543, 0624, 0658, 0730, 0817, 0846, 0917, 1017, 1117, 1217, 1317, 1417, 1517**r**, 1617, 1717, 1747**r**, 1817, 1847**r**, 1917, 2017, 2117, 2217, 2334**r**.

⑥: 0615, 0717, 0745, 0817, 0847, 0917, 1017, 1117, 1217, 1317, 1417, 1512**r**, 1617, 1717, 1747**r**, 1817, 1847**r**, 1917, 2017, 2117, 2217, 2334**r**.

⑦: 0817**r**, 0922, 1017**r**, 1122, 1217**r**, 1322, 1417**r**, 1522, 1617**r**, 1722, 1817**r**, 1922, 2017**r**, 2122, 2217**r**, 2317**r**.

NORWICH - LOWESTOFT

Journey time ± 43 minutes *38 km*

From Norwich: Trains noted '**r**' call at **Reedham** 18–21 minutes later.

Ⓐ: 0536**r**, 0627**r**, 0645**r**, 0755**r**, 0855, 1005**r**, 1058, 1205**r**, 1258, 1405**r**, 1455**r**, 1550**r**, 1658**r**, 1750**r**, 1902**r**, 2005**r**, 2105**r**, 2205**r**, 2240**r**.

⑥: 0540**r**, 0650**r**, 0750**r**, 0855, 1005**r**, 1058, 1205**r**, 1258, 1405**r**, 1458**r**, 1550**r**, 1658**r**, 1750**r**, 1905**r**, 2005**r**, 2105**r**, 2205**r**, 2240**r**.

⑦: 0725, 0858**r**, 1058**r**, 1258**r**, 1458**r**, 1658**r**, 1858**r**, 2058**r**.

From Lowestoft: Trains noted '**r**' call at **Reedham** 20–23 minutes later.

Ⓐ: 0542**r**, 0635**r**, 0735**r**, 0747**r**, 0850**r**, 0948**r**, 1057, 1148**r**, 1257, 1348**r**, 1457, 1548**r**, 1648**r**, 1748**r**, 1848**r**, 1955**r**, 2057, 2148**r**, 2248**r**, 2330**r**.

⑥: 0638**r**, 0740**r**, 0848**r**, 0948**r**, 1057, 1148**r**, 1257, 1348**r**, 1457, 1548**r**, 1648**r**, 1748**r**, 1848**r**, 1955**r**, 2057, 2148**r**, 2248**r**, 2330**r**.

⑦: 0946**r**, 1146**r**, 1346**r**, 1546**r**, 1746**r**, 1946**r**, 2146**r**, 2335**r**.

NORWICH - SHERINGHAM (🚂)

Journey time ± 57 minutes *49 km*

From Norwich:
Trains call at **Hoveton and Wroxham** 🚂 ± 15 minutes, and **Cromer** ± 45 minutes later.

⚒: 0510Ⓐ, 0520⑥, 0540Ⓐ, 0545⑥, 0715, 0821, 0945, 1045, 1145, 1245, 1345, 1445, 1545, 1645, 1745, 1855, 1955, 2115, 2245①–④, 2305⑤⑥.

⑦: 0836, 0945, 1036, 1145, 1236, 1345, 1436, 1545, 1636, 1745, 1836, 1945, 2036.

From Sheringham:
Trains call at **Cromer** ± 11 minutes, and **Hoveton and Wroxham** 🚂 ± 39 minutes later.

⚒: 0007⑥, 0621⑥, 0631Ⓐ, 0716, 0822, 0944, 1047, 1144, 1247, 1344, 1447, 1546, 1649, 1749, 1852, 1956, 2110, 2217, 2347①–④ (also 0553Ⓐ from Cromer).

⑦: 0007, 0942, 1041, 1142, 1241, 1342, 1441, 1542, 1641, 1742, 1841, 1942, 2041, 2142.

IPSWICH - FELIXSTOWE

Journey time ± 25 minutes *25 km*

From Ipswich:

Ⓐ: 0504, 0604, 0714, 0825, 0857, 0958 and hourly until 2058, 2228.

⑥: 0558, 0658, 0758 and hourly until 2058, 2228.

⑦: 1055 and hourly until 1955.

From Felixstowe:

Ⓐ: 0534, 0636, 0747, 0854, 0928 and hourly until 2128, 2301.

⑥: 0628, 0728, 0828 and hourly until 2128, 2258.

⑦: 1125 and hourly until 2025.

r – Via Reedham.

🚂 – Heritage and Tourist railways:
NORTH NORFOLK RAILWAY: Sheringham - Holt and v.v. *8 km*. ✆ 01263 820800. www.nnrailway.co.uk
BURE VALLEY STEAM RAILWAY: Wroxham - Aylsham and v.v. ✆ 01253 833858. www.bvrw.co.uk

LE — IPSWICH - CAMBRIDGE and PETERBOROUGH — 205

km		⚒ 2	⚒ C	⚒	Ⓐ	⑥	⑥	Ⓐ	⚒ H	⚒	⑥	Ⓐ	⚒	⚒	⚒	⚒	⚒	⚒	⚒	⚒	⚒	⚒	⚒
0	**Ipswich** 200 d.	0510	0600	0616	0654	0720	0800	0803	0820	0920	0958	1000	1020	1120	1158	1220	1320	1358	1420	1520	1558	1620	1720
19	Stowmarket 200 d.	0526	0612	0631	0709	0735	0812	0816	0835	0935	1011	1012	1035	1135	1211	1235	1335	1411	1435	1535	1611	1635	1735
42	Bury St Edmunds d.	0549	0629	0654	0733	0757	0829	0832	0857	0957	1029	1029	1057	1157	1229	1257	1357	1429	1457	1557	1629	1657	1757
65	Newmarket d.	0609	|	0714	0752	0817	|	|	0916	1017	|	|	1116	1217	|	1316	1417	|	1516	1617	|	1717	1817
88	**Cambridge** 208 a.	0633	|	0739	0819	0839	|	|	0939	1039	|	|	1139	1239	|	1339	1439	|	1539	1639	|	1739	1839
82	Ely 208 d.	...	0656	...	...	...	0858	0858	...	...	1058	1058	...	...	1258	...	...	1458	...	...	1658	...	...
108	March 208 d.	...	0714	...	...	...	0916	0916	...	...	1116	1116	...	...	1316	...	...	1516	...	...	1716	...	...
132	**Peterborough** 208 a.	...	0737	...	...	...	0939	0939	...	...	1139	1139	...	...	1339	...	...	1539	...	...	1739	...	...

	Ⓐ	⑥	Ⓐ	⑥	Ⓐ	⑥	⚒	⚒	⚒ 2	⚒ 2	⑦ 2	⑦ H	⑦ C	⑦	⑦	⑦	⑦	⑦	⑦	⑦	⑦	⑦	⑦ 2
Ipswich 200 d.	1749	1758	1817	1820	1913	1920	1958	2018	2117	2219	0732	0902	0955	1102	1155	1302	1355	1502	1555	1702	1755	1902	2102
Stowmarket 200 d.	1804	1811	1832	1835	1928	1935	2011	2035	2133	2235	0748	0918	1007	1118	1207	1318	1407	1518	1607	1718	1807	1918	2118
Bury St Edmunds d.	1830**b**	1829	1857**b**	1857	1957**c**	1957	2029	2057	2156	2257	0811	0941	1024	1141	1224	1341	1424	1541	1624	1741	1824	1941	2141
Newmarket d.	|	|	1916	1916	2017	2017	|	2116	2217	...	0831	1001	|	1201	|	1401	|	1601	|	1801	|	2001	2201
Cambridge 208 a.	|	|	1939	1939	2039	2039	|	2140	2240	...	0857	1025	|	1225	|	1425	|	1625	|	1825	|	2024	2224
Ely 208 d.	1858	1858	...	...	...	...	2059	...	...	...	...	...	1052	...	1252	...	1452	...	1652	...	1852	...	...
March 208 d.	1916	1916	...	...	...	...	2116	...	...	...	...	...	1108	...	1308	...	1508	...	1708	...	1908	...	...
Peterborough 208 a.	1939	1939	...	...	...	...	2139	...	...	...	...	...	1131	...	1331	...	1531	...	1731	...	1931	...	...

	⚒ Ⓐ	Ⓐ 2	⑥ 2	⚒ 2	⚒	⚒		⚒	⚒	⚒	⚒	⚒		⚒	⚒	⚒	⚒		⚒	⚒	⚒	⚒	⚒
Peterborough 208 d.	...	...	...	...	...	0750	...	...	...	0950	...	...	...	1150	...	...	1350	...	...	...	1550	...	...
March 208 d.	...	...	...	...	...	0809	...	...	...	1009	...	...	...	1209	...	...	1409	...	...	...	1609	...	...
Ely 208 d.	...	...	...	...	...	0832	...	...	...	1032	...	...	...	1232	...	...	1432	...	...	...	1632	...	...
Cambridge 208 d.	...	...	...	0642	0744	|	...	0844	0944	|	1044	1144	...	|	1244	1344	|	...	1444	1544	|	1644	1744
Newmarket d.	...	...	...	0702	0805	|	...	0904	1005	|	1104	1205	...	|	1304	1405	|	...	1504	1605	|	1705	1805
Bury St Edmunds d.	0531	0621	0623	0723	0824	0858	...	0924	1024	1058	1124	1224	...	1258	1324	1424	1458	...	1524	1624	1658	1725	1825
Stowmarket 200 d.	0552	0642	0644	0745	0845	0914	...	0945	1045	1114	1145	1245	...	1314	1345	1445	1514	...	1545	1645	1714	1745	1845
Ipswich 200 a.	0607	0700	0702	0802	0902	0928	...	1002	1102	1128	1202	1302	...	1328	1402	1502	1528	...	1602	1702	1728	1804	1902

	⚒	⚒	⚒ H	⚒ C	⚒	⚒	⚒ C	⚒ 2		⑦ 2		⑦	⑦	⑦	⑦	⑦	⑦	⑦	⑦ C	⑦ H	⑦ C	⑦	⑦ 2
Peterborough 208 d.	1750	...	...	1950	...	...	2145	...	...	...	...	...	1150	...	1350	...	1547	...	1745	...	1947	...	...
March 208 d.	1809	...	...	2009	...	...	2204	...	...	...	...	...	1209	...	1409	...	1606	...	1804	...	2006	...	...
Ely 208 d.	1832	...	...	2032	...	...	2226	...	...	...	...	...	1232	...	1432	...	1629**b**	...	1829**b**	...	2029**b**	...	...
Cambridge 208 d.	|	1844	1944	|	2044	2144	|	2244	...	0912	...	1112	|	1312	|	1512	|	1712	|	1912	|	2112	2250
Newmarket d.	|	1904	2005	|	2104	2205	|	2306	...	0934	...	1134	|	1334	|	1534	|	1734	|	1934	|	2134	2312
Bury St Edmunds d.	1858	1924	2024	2058	2124	2224	2252	2327	...	0955	...	1155	1258	1355	1458	1555	1655	1755	1855	1955	2055	2155	2333
Stowmarket 200 d.	1914	1945	2045	2114	2145	2245	2308	2348	...	1018	...	1218	1314	1418	1514	1618	1711	1818	1911	2018	2111	2218	2355
Ipswich 200 a.	1928	2004	2100	2128	2202	2302	2322	0005	...	1036	...	1236	1328	1436	1528	1636	1725	1836	1925	2036	2125	2236	0011

C – To/from Colchester (Table **200**).

H – To/from Harwich International (Table **200**).

b – Arrives 4–6 minutes earlier.

c – Arrives 1948.

206 NORWICH - NOTTINGHAM - SHEFFIELD - MANCHESTER - LIVERPOOL

2nd class EM

km	Station	Ⓐ	Ⓐ	Ⓐ	Ⓐ	Ⓐ	Ⓐ	Ⓐ	Ⓐ	Ⓐ	Ⓐ	Ⓐ	Ⓐ	Ⓐ	Ⓐ	Ⓐ	Ⓐ	Ⓐ	Ⓐ AD	⑥	⑥	⑥	⑥	⑥
0	**Norwich** 207 d.	...	...	...	0550	0651	0757	0857	0957	1057	1157	1257	1357	1457	1548	1657	1754	1857	...	...	...	...	0550	0653
49	Thetford 207 d.	...	...	...	0624	0719	0824	0924	1024	1124	1224	1324	1424	1524	1623	1727	1827	1924	...	...	...	...	0623	0722
86	Ely 205 207 208 d.	...	...	...	0651	0744	0848	0946	1053	1148	1248	1348	1448	1547	1647	1752	1852	1952	...	...	...	...	0648	0748
111	March 205 208 d.	...	...	...	0707	0800	0907	|	|	1208	|	|	|	|	|	|	1908	|	...	...	...	...	0707	0804
135	**Peterborough** 180 205 208 d.	...	...	...	0727	0824	0927	1028	1128	1226	1326	1426	1528	1627	1724	1828	1926	2027	2131	...	...	...	0727	0829
181	Grantham 180 194 d.	...	...	...	0758	0855	0958	1100	1200	1259	1358	1458	1601	1658	1757	1858	1959	2059	|	...	...	...	0758	0859
218	**Nottingham** 194 a.	...	...	...	0840	0926	1035	1134	1235	1336	1435	1534	1635	1735	1835	1935	2031	2133	2254	...	...	...	0839	0935
218	**Nottingham** 171 d.	0521	0639	0746	0847	0947	1047	1147	1247	1347	1447	1547	1647	1747	1847	1941	*2047*	*2146*	...	0520	0640	0746	0847	0947
247	Alfreton 171 d.	|	0659	0810	0908	1008	1108	1208	1310	1408	1508	1610	1708	1810	1908	2002	|	*2211*	...	|	0700	0809	0908	1008
264	Chesterfield 171 d.	0549	0710	0820	0920	1020	1120	1220	1320	1420	1520	1620	1720	1820	1920	2012	*2131*	*2222*	...	0549	0711	0819	0920	1020
283	**Sheffield** 171 193 d.	0618	0732**a**	0840	0940	1040	1140	1240	1340	1440	1540	1640	1740	1840	1940	2031	*2158*	*2236*	...	0620**a**	0732	0840	0940	1040
343	Stockport 193 a.	0722	0824	0924	1025	1125	1224	1325	1425	1525	1625	1725	1825	1924	2025	2124	...	...	...	0722	0824	0925	1025	1125
352	**Manchester** Piccadilly 193 a.	0734	0836	0937	1036	1136	1236	1336	1436	1536	1636	1736	1836	1936	2036	2133	...	...	...	0734	0836	0936	1036	1136
378	Warrington Central 188 a.	0753	0857	0957	1057	1157	1257	1357	1457	1557	1657	1802	1857	1957	2057	...	...	...	...	0753	0857	0957	1057	1157
399	**Liverpool** SP ▷ 188 a.	0818	0915	1015	1115	1215	1315	1415	1515	1615	1715	1821	1918	2018	2118	...	...	...	...	0818	0915	1015	1115	1215
408	**Liverpool** Lime Street 188 a.	0832	0932	1026	1131	1231	1331	1426	1529	1631	1731	1832	1934	2035	2136	...	...	...	...	0831	0931	1026	1131	1231

Station	⑥	⑥	⑥		⑥	⑥	⑥	⑥	⑥	⑥ D	⑦	⑦	⑦	⑦	⑦	⑦	⑦	⑦	⑦	⑦	⑦	⑦	⑦	⑦
Norwich 207 d.	0757	0857	0957	B	1457	1552	1654	1750	1857	...	...	...	...	...	1047	...	...	1347	1453	1554	1654	1754	1856	2052
Thetford 207 d.	0824	0924	1024		1524	1623	1724	1823	1924	...	...	...	...	...	1114	...	...	1414	1520	1621	1721	1821	1923	2119
Ely 205 207 208 d.	0848	0946	1048	and	1547	1647	1747	1848	1948	...	...	...	...	...	1139	...	...	1440	1546	|	1748	1848	1948	2144
March 205 208 d.	0905	|	|	at	|	|	|	1905	|	...	...	...	...	...	|	...	...	|	1603	|	|	|	|	|
Peterborough 180 205 208 d.	0925	1022	1123	the	1627	1725	1826	1930**a**	2026	2127	...	...	...	...	1216**a**	...	1431	1523**b**	1624	1723**c**	1826**a**	1926	2030**a**	2223**d**
Grantham 180 194 d.	0953	1055	1156	same	1658	1759	1858	2003**a**	2058	2202	...	...	...	...	1252**a**	...	1509	1555	1656	1755	1858	1957	2102	2255
Nottingham 194 a.	1035	1136	1235	minutes	1735	1834	1933	2036	2132	2232	...	...	...	...	1330	...	1539	1624	1731	1827	1933	2031	2134	2328
Nottingham 171 d.	1047	1147	1247	past	1744	1847	1939	*2117*	...	...	0947	1048	1144	1240	1342	1447	1547	1642	1739	1840	1943	*2133*	...	...
Alfreton 171 d.	1108	1208	1310	each	1808	1908	2000	*2144*	...	...	1004	1108	1207	1304	1405	1510	1607	1711	1804	1903	2003	*2205*	...	...
Chesterfield 171 d.	1120	1220	1320	hour	1818	1920	2010	*2155*	...	...	1018	1119	1218	1317	1416	1521	1618	1721	1815	1914	2013	*2216*	...	...
Sheffield 171 193 d.	1140	1240	1340	until	1837	1940	2032	*2214*	...	...	1041**a**	1139**a**	1239**a**	1338**a**	1437	1543**a**	1639**a**	1744**a**	1837**a**	1935**a**	2035**a**	*2236*	...	...
Stockport 193 a.	1224	1325	1425	♤	1924	2025	2117	...	...	...	1126	1225	1325	1425	1525	1625	1728	1825	1926	2025	2124	...	...	...
Manchester Piccadilly 193 a.	1236	1336	1436		1935	2036	2127	...	...	...	1137	1237	1337	1437	1537	1637	1738	1837	1939	2038	2137	...	...	...
Warrington Central 188 a.	1257	1357	1457		1957	2057	...	...	...	...	1158	1258	1358	1458	1558	1658	1758	1858	1959	...	...	...	...	...
Liverpool SP ▷ 188 a.	1315	1415	1515		2015	2120	...	...	...	...	1216	1316	1416	1516	1616	1716	1816	1916	2017	...	...	...	...	...
Liverpool Lime Street 188 a.	1331	1431	1531		2031	2133	...	...	...	...	1230	1330	1432	1530	1630	1730	1830	1930	2032	...	...	...	...	...

Station	Ⓐ A	Ⓐ D	Ⓐ A	Ⓐ	Ⓐ	Ⓐ	Ⓐ	Ⓐ		Ⓐ	Ⓐ	Ⓐ	Ⓐ	Ⓐ	Ⓐ	Ⓐ	Ⓐ	⑥ A	⑥ D	⑥ A	⑥	⑥	⑥
Liverpool Lime Street 187 d.	...	...	...	...	...	0647	0742	0852		1352	1452	1552	1652	1752	1852	1952	2137	...	...	...	...	...	0649
Liverpool SP ▷ 188 d.	...	...	...	...	...	0657	0753	0903		1403	1503	1603	1703	1803	1903	2003	2147	...	...	...	...	...	0659
Warrington Central 188 d.	...	...	...	...	...	0715	0813	0919	and	1419	1519	1619	1719	1819	1919	2019	2203	...	...	...	...	...	0715
Manchester Piccadilly 193 d.	...	...	...	...	...	0742	0843	0943	at	1443	1543	1643	1743	1843	1943	2043	2228	...	...	...	...	...	0742
Stockport 193 d.	...	...	...	...	...	0754	0854	0954	the	1454	1554	1655	1754	1854	1954	2054	2238	...	...	...	...	...	0754
Sheffield 171 193 d.	...	...	...	*0603*	*0724*	0837	0937	1037	same	1537	1637**a**	1745**a**	1852**a**	1937	2041**a**	2137	2337	...	...	...	*0554*	*0737*	0837
Chesterfield 171 d.	...	...	...	*0619*	*0737*	0852	0952	1052	minutes	1553	1653	1801	1907	1952	2056	2155	0002	...	...	...	*0619*	*0750*	0852
Alfreton 171 d.	...	...	...	*0630*	*0748*	0903	1002	1103	past	1603	1704	1811	1918	2003	2108	2205	|	...	...	...	*0629*	*0801*	0903
Nottingham 171 a.	...	...	...	*0701*	*0823*	0927	1027	1126	each	1627	1727	1831	1941	2027	2133	2231	0040	...	...	...	*0702*	*0825*	0927
Nottingham 194 d.	0456	0507	0610	0752	0835	0934	1034	1134	hour	1635	1734	1837	...	2034	...	...	...	0505	0507	0610	0745	0834	0934
Grantham 180 194 d.	|	0551**a**	|	0828**a**	0912**a**	1011**a**	1110	1211**a**	until	1713**a**	1811	1909	...	2110	...	...	...	|	0551**a**	|	0820**a**	0910	1007
Peterborough 180 205 208 d.	0627**a**	0623	0736	0859	0940	1045**a**	1141	1242	♤	1744	1845**a**	1942	...	2139	...	...	...	0627	0625	0735	0858	0943	1040
March 205 208 a.	0642	...	0752	|	|	|	|	|		|	1859	|	...	|	...	...	...	0642	...	0750	|	|	|
Ely 205 207 208 a.	0701	...	0811	0942	1013	1118	1213	1314		1817	1919	2015	...	2213	...	...	...	0701	...	0811	0931	1016	1113
Thetford 207 a.	0728	...	0836	1006	1037	1143	1238	1339		1841	1950	2038	...	2237	...	...	...	0730	...	0836	1006	1043	1137
Norwich 207 a.	0813	...	0913	1044	1112	1215	1313	1413		1910	2022	2113	...	2318	...	...	...	0813	...	0915	1043	1115	1213

Station	⑥	⑥		⑥	⑥	⑥	⑥	⑥	⑥	⑥	⑥	⑥	⑦	⑦	⑦	⑦	⑦	⑦	⑦	⑦	⑦	⑦	⑦	⑦
Liverpool Lime Street 187 d.	0742	0852		1352	1452	1552	1652	1752	1852	1952	2052	2137	...	...	...	1252	1352	1452	1552	1654	1752	1852	1952	2121
Liverpool SP ▷ 188 d.	0752	0903		1403	1503	1603	1703	1803	1903	2003	2103	2147	...	...	...	1303	1403	1503	1603	1705	1803	1903	2003	2131
Warrington Central 188 d.	0813	0919	and	1419	1519	1619	1719	1819	1919	2019	2119	2203	...	...	...	1319	1419	1519	1619	1721	1819	1919	2019	2147
Manchester Piccadilly 193 d.	0843	0944	at	1443	1543	1643	1743	1843	1943	2043	2143	2228	...	...	1243	1344	1444	1544	1644	1746	1844	1944	2044	2211
Stockport 193 d.	0854	0954	the	1454	1554	1654	1754	1854	1954	2054	2152	2238	...	...	1255	1354	1454	1553	1654	1755	1854	1954	2054	2228
Sheffield 171 193 d.	0937	1037	same	1537	1637	1741**a**	1840	1937	2039**a**	2138	2242**f**	2338	*1103*	1243	1348**b**	1441**a**	1539**a**	1643**a**	1740**a**	1839	1940**a**	2040**a**	2140**a**	2330**a**
Chesterfield 171 d.	0952	1052	minutes	1552	1653	1757	1857	1952	2054	2154	2256	2353	*1120*	1257	1402	1455	1553	1657	1754	1854	1954	2054	2156	2344
Alfreton 171 d.	1003	1103	past	1603	1704	1808	1908	2003	2105	2205	2307	|	*1130*	1308	1412	1508	1603	1707	1805	1905	2005	2105	2206	2355
Nottingham 171 a.	1027	1127	each	1627	1727	1829	1930	2027	2133	2234	2328	0030	*1158*	1334	1435	1532	1628	1730	1834	1933	2030	2133	2236	0023
Nottingham 194 d.	1034	1134	hour	1634	1734	1837	...	2034	...	...	...	...	1240	1347	1445	1550	1645	1736	1846	...	2045	...	...	...
Grantham 180 194 d.	1106	1209**a**	until	1706	1814**a**	1909	...	2107	...	...	...	...	1315	1422	1520**a**	1622	1721**a**	1817	1925	...	2120	...	...	...
Peterborough 180 205 208 d.	1141**a**	1240	♤	1740**a**	1844	1941	...	2140	...	...	...	...	1343	1458**a**	1558**a**	1659**a**	1757**a**	1849	1959	...	2154	...	...	...
March 205 208 a.	|	|		|	1900	|	...	|	...	...	...	...	|	|	|	|	1812	|	|	...	|	...	...	...
Ely 205 207 208 a.	1213	1313		1813	1919	2014	...	2213	...	...	...	...	1416	1531	1631	1732	1832	1922	2032	...	2227	...	...	...
Thetford 207 a.	1238	1337		1837	1943	2038	...	2237	...	...	...	...	1443	1555	1655	1756	1856	1949	2056	...	2251	...	...	...
Norwich 207 a.	1313	1413		1908	2016	2113	...	2319	...	...	...	...	1524	1635	1726	1830	1929	2026	2137	...	2325	...	...	...

A – Via Melton Mowbray (Table **208**).
B – The 1057 from Norwich also calls at March (d.1205).
D – From / to Spalding (Table **185**).

a – Arrives 4 – 6 minutes earlier.
b – Arrives 10 minutes earlier.
c – Arrives 1712.
d – Arrives 2216.

f – Arrives 2231.

♤ – Timings may vary by up to 5 minutes.
▷ – **Liverpool** South Parkway.

207 CAMBRIDGE - NORWICH

LE

km	Station	Ⓐ	⑥	⑥	Ⓐ	⚒	Ⓐ	⑥	⚒		⚒	⚒	⑥	Ⓐ	⑥	Ⓐ	⑥	Ⓐ	⚒2	⚒		⑦	⑦	⑦
0	**Cambridge** d.	0602	0605	0700	0700	0810	0906	0910	1010	and at	1710	1810	1910	1922	2010	2019	2110	2115	*2140*	2255	...	0850	1050	1150
24	Cambridge North d.	0606	0609	|	0704	0814	0911	0914	1014	the same	1714	1814	1914	1926	2014	2023	2114	2120	*2144*f	2259	...	0854	1054	1154
63	Ely 206 d.	0619	0622	0716	0719	0828	0926	0928	1028	minutes	1728	1828	1928	1940	2028	2037	2128	2133	2216	2312	...	0907	1107	1207
84	Thetford 206 d.	0644	0647	0743	0747	0853	0951	0953	1053	past each	1753	1853	1953	2004	2053	2101	2153	2157	2237	2337	...	0934	1134	1232
94	Attleborough d.	0703	0706	0803	0806	0908	1006	1008	1108	hour until	1808	1908	2008	2019	2108	2116	2208	2212	2251	2352	...	0949	1149	1247
110	Wymondham d.	0711	0714	0813	0816	0915	1015	1015	1115	△	1815	1915	2015	2027	2115	2124	2215	2220	2258	2359	...	0957	1157	1254
	Norwich 206 a.	0727	0728	0830	0830	0930	1030	1030	1130		1830	1930	2030	2041	2130	2138	2232	2235	2319	0013	...	1013	1213	1312

Station	⑦	⑦	⑦	⑦	⑦	⑦	⑦	⑦	⑦2	⑦	⑦2
Cambridge d.	1250	1350	1450	1550	1650	1750	1850	1950	*2006*	2150	*2206*
Cambridge North d.	1254	1354	1454	1554	1654	1754	1854	1954	|	2154	|
Ely 206 d.	1307	1407	1507	1607	1707	1807	1907	2007	2036	2207	2230
Thetford 206 d.	1334	1432	1532	1634	1732	1832	1932	2032	2057	2232	2251
Attleborough d.	1349	1447	1547	1649	1747	1847	1947	2047	2111	2247	2305
Wymondham d.	1357	1454	1554	1657	1754	1854	1954	2054	2118	2254	2312
Norwich 206 a.	1413	1513	1613	1713	1813	1910	2013	2110	2137	2313	2325

Station	Ⓐ	⑥	Ⓐ	⑥	Ⓐ	⑥	⚒		⚒
Norwich 206 d.	0533	0537	0633	0640	0737	0740	0840	and at the	1440
Wymondham d.	0545	0549	0645	0652	0749	0752	0852	same	1452
Attleborough d.	0552	0556	0652	0659	0756	0759	0859	minutes	1459
Thetford 206 d.	0606	0610	0706	0713	0810	0813	0913	past each	1513
Ely 206 d.	0631	0635	0733	0738	0838	0838	0938	hour until	1538
Cambridge North d.	0644	0648	0746	0751	0851	0851	0951	△	1551
Cambridge a.	0652	0656	0753	0759	0859	0859	0959		1559

Station	⑥	Ⓐ	⚒	⚒	⑥	Ⓐ	Ⓐ	⑥	⑥	Ⓐ	⚒		⑦	⑦	⑦	⑦	⑦	⑦	⑦	⑦	⑦	⑦	⑦2	⑦	⑦2	⑦
Norwich 206 d.	1535	1540	1638	1735	1838	1840	1937	1940	2110	2115	2240	...	0903	1003	1103	1203	1303	1403	1503	1603	1703	1803	1856	2003	2052	2203
Wymondham d.	1547	1552	1650	1747	1850	1852	1950	1952	2122	2127	2252	...	0915	1015	1115	1215	1315	1415	1515	1615	1715	1815	|	2015	|	2215
Attleborough d.	1554	1559	1659	1754	1857	1859	1957	1959	2129	2134	2259	...	0922	1022	1122	1222	1322	1422	1522	1622	1722	1822	|	2022	|	2222
Thetford 206 d.	1613	1613	1713	1813	1911	1913	2012	2013	2143	2148	2313	...	0936	1036	1136	1236	1336	1436	1536	1636	1736	1836	1923	2036	2119	2236
Ely 206 a.	1638	1638	1738	1838	1938	1938	2039	2038	2210	2216	2338	...	1003	1103	1203	1303	1403	1503	1603	1703	1803	1903	1944	2103	2140	2303
Cambridge North d.	1651	1651	1751	1851	1951	1951	2052	2051	2223	2229	2351	...	1016	1116	1216	1316	1416	1516	1616	1716	1816	1916	|	2116	|	2316
Cambridge a.	1659	1659	1759	1901	1959	1959	2058	2059	2231	2235	2359	...	1022	1122	1222	1322	1422	1522	1622	1722	1822	1922	*2007*	2122	*2207*	2322

f – ⑥ only.

△ – Timings may vary by up to 2 minutes.

XC STANSTED AIRPORT - CAMBRIDGE - PETERBOROUGH - LEICESTER - BIRMINGHAM 208

km		⚒	⑥	Ⓐ	Ⓐ	⑥	⚒	⚒	⚒	⚒🍷	⚒🍷	⚒🍷	⚒🍷	⚒🍷	⑥🍷	Ⓐ🍷	⚒🍷	⚒🍷	⚒	⚒	ⒶB	Ⓐ	⑦	⑦
0	**Stansted Airport** ... ▽ d.	...	0525	0516	0612	0627	0721a	0821a	0921a	1027	1127	1227	1327	1427	1527	1527	1627	1727	1821a	1921a	...	2021	1025	1125
40	**Cambridge** .... ▽ d.	0515	0555	0555	0656	0657	0758	0901	1001	1101	1201	1301	1401	1501	1601	1601	1701	1801	1901	2001	...	2101	1100	1200
64	Ely .... **205** d.	0530	0610	0610	0712	0712	0815	0915	1015	1115	1215	1315	1415	1515	1615	1615	1715	1815	1915	2015	...	2115	1115	1215
89	March .... **205** d.	0546	0628	0628	0729	0728	0832	0932	1032	1132	1232	1332	1432	1532	1632	1632	1732	1834	1932	2032	...	2132	1132	1232
113	**Peterborough** .... **205** d.	0610	0652	0652	0752	0752	0852	0952	1052	1152	1252	1352	1452	1552	1652	1652	1752	1852	1952	2052	2131	2159	1153	1253
131	Stamford .... d.	0623	0705	0705	0805	0805	0905	1005	1105	1205	1305	1405	1505	1605	1705	1705	1805	1905	2005	2105	2145	2212	1206	1306
154	Oakham .... d.	0635	0719	0719	0819	0819	0919	1019	1119	1219	1319	1419	1519	1619	1719	1719	1819	1919	2019	2119	2201	2226	1220	1320
174	Melton Mowbray .... d.	0646	0730	0730	0830	0830	0930	1030	1130	1230	1330	1430	1530	1630	1730	1730	1830	1930	2030	2130	2214	2237	1231	1331
197	**Leicester** .... d.	0710	0748	0751c	0848	0848	0948	1048	1148	1248	1348	1448	1548	1648	1748	1748	1848	1948	2048	2148	...	2255	1250	1350
227	Nuneaton .... d.	0729	0810	0817	0910	0910	1010	1110	1210	1310	1410	1510	1610	1710	1810	1815	1910	2010	2110	2210	...	2314	1310	1409
244	Coleshill Parkway .... d.	0745	0825	0832	0925	0925	1025	1125	1225	1325	1425	1525	1625	1725	1825	1830	1925	2025	2125	2225	...	2329	1325	1425
259	**Birmingham** New St.. a.	0803	0838	0845	0938	0938	1038	1138	1238	1338	1438	1538	1638	1738	1838	1844	1938	2038	2138	2238	...	2342	1338	1438

	⑦	⑦	⑦	⑦🍷		⑦🍷	⑦🍷	⑦	⑦
Stansted Airport ... ▽ d.	1225	1325	1425	1525	...	1625	1725	1825	1925
Cambridge .... ▽ d.	1300	1400	1500	1600	...	1700	1800	1900	2000
Ely .... **205** d.	1315	1415	1515	1615	...	1715	1815	1915	2015
March .... **205** d.	1332	1432	1532	1632	...	1732	1832	1932	2032
Peterborough ..... **205** d.	1353	1453	1553	1653	...	1753	1853	1953	2053
Stamford .... d.	1406	1506	1606	1706	...	1806	1906	2006	2106
Oakham .... d.	1420	1520	1620	1720	...	1820	1920	2020	2120
Melton Mowbray .... d.	1431	1531	1631	1731	...	1831	1931	2031	2131
Leicester .... d.	1450	1550	1650	1750	...	1850	1950	2050	2150
Nuneaton .... d.	1509	1609	1709	1809	...	1909	2010	2110	2210
Coleshill Parkway .... d.	1525	1625	1725	1825	...	1925	2025	2125	2225
Birmingham New St . a.	1538	1638	1738	1838	...	1938	2038	2138	2238

	ⒶA	⑥A	Ⓐ	⑥	⚒A	⚒🍷	⚒🍷	⚒C	⚒🍷	⚒🍷	⚒🍷
Birmingham New St .... d.	...	...	0519	0522	...	0622	0722	0822	0922	1022	1122
Coleshill Parkway .... △ d.	...	...	0534	0536	...	0636	0735	0836	0936	1036	1136
Nuneaton .... d.	...	...	0549	0552	...	0652	0751	0852	0952	1052	1152
Leicester .... d.	...	...	0615	0615	...	0718c	0818	0918c	1018	1118c	1218c
Melton Mowbray .... d.	0536	0540	0632	0632	0653	0735	0835	0935	1035	1135	1235
Oakham .... d.	0549	0552	0643	0643	0705	0746	0846	0946	1046	1146	1246
Stamford .... d.	0605	0608	0657	0657	0719	0800	0900	1000	1100	1200	1300
Peterborough .... **205** d.	0627c	0627	0712	0712	0736	0818	0918	1018	1118c	1218c	1318c
March .... **205** d.	0643	0643	0731	0731	0751	0834	0934	1034	1134	1234	1334
Ely .... **205** d.	0701	0701	0752	0752	0811	0852	0952	1052	1152	1252	1352
Cambridge .... ▽ d.	...	...	0810	0810	...	0910	1010	1110	1210	1310	1410
Stansted Airport .... ▽ a.	...	...	0839	0839	...	0940	1040	1140	1240	1340	1440

	⚒🍷	⚒🍷	⚒🍷	⚒	⚒	Ⓐ	⑥	⚒	⚒	⚒	⑥	Ⓐ	⚒	⑦🍷	⑦🍷	⑦🍷	⑦	⑦	⑦	⑦	⑦	⑦	⑦	⑦	⑦D
Birmingham New St . d.	1222	1322	1422	1522	1622	1652	1652	1722	1822	1922	2022	2025	2222	1122	1222	1322	1422	1522	1622	1722	1822	1922	2022	2052	2152
Coleshill Parkway ... △ d.	1236	1336	1436	1536	1636	1706	1707	1736	1836	1936	2036	2038	2235	1136	1236	1336	1436	1536	1636	1736	1836	1936	2036	2105	2205
Nuneaton .... d.	1252	1352	1452	1552	1652	1722	1723	1752	1852	1952	2052	2054	2252	1152	1252	1352	1452	1552	1652	1752	1852	1952	2052	2129	2222
Leicester .... d.	1318c	1418c	1518c	1618c	1718c	1755b	1750	1818	1918c	2018c	2118c	2118c	2320	1219c	1319c	1419c	1519c	1619c	1716	1819c	1919c	2019c	2116	2148	2248
Melton Mowbray .... d.	1335	1435	1535	1635	1735	1813	...	1835	1935	2035	2135	2135	...	1236	1336	1436	1536	1636	1736	1836	1936	2036	2136	...	...
Oakham .... d.	1346	1446	1546	1646	1746	1825	...	1846	1946	2046	2146	2146	...	1247	1347	1447	1547	1647	1748	1848	1948	2048	2147	...	...
Stamford .... d.	1400	1500	1600	1700	1800	1840	...	1900	2000	2100	2200	2200	...	1301	1401	1501	1601	1701	1801	1902	2001	2101	2201	...	...
Peterborough ..... **205** d.	1418c	1518c	1618c	1718c	1818c	1859	...	1918	2018c	2118c	2214	2218c	...	1318	1418	1518	1618	1718	1818	1918	2018	2118	2216	...	...
March .... **205** d.	1434	1534	1634	1737	1834	1915	...	1934	2034	2134	2229	2236	...	1334	1434	1534	1634	1734	1834	1934	2034	2134	2232	...	...
Ely .... **205** d.	1452	1552	1652	1800	1852	1934	...	1952	2052	2152	2248	2254	...	1352	1452	1552	1652	1752	1852	1952	2052	2152	2251	...	...
Cambridge .... ▽ d.	1510	1610	1710	1817	1910	1952	...	2010	2110	2210	2303	2310	...	1410	1510	1610	1710	1810	1910	2010	2110	2210	2306	...	...
Stansted Airport ... ▽ a.	1540	1640	1740	1853	1940	...	...	2040	2140	2252	...	...	...	1445	1545	1645	1745	1845	1945	2045	2145	2245	...	...	...

A – [2] Nottingham - Norwich (Table **206**).
B – [2] Spalding - Nottingham (Tables **185** and **206**).
C – [12] 🍷 Gloucester - Stansted Airport (Table **121**); 🍷 Birmingham - Peterborough.
D – [12] Cardiff Central - Leicester (Table **121**).

a – Departs 6 minutes later on ⑥.
b – Arrives 9 minutes earlier.
c – Arrives 4–6 minutes earlier.

△ – 🚌 connections available to the National Exhibition Centre (NEC) and Birmingham International Airport.

☛ **Full service Leicester - Birmingham New Street and v.v.**

From Leicester: On ⚒ at 0549⑥, 0617Ⓐ, 0643Ⓐ, 0649⑥, 0710, 0722Ⓐ, 0748⑥, 0751Ⓐ, 0816, 0848, 0918, 0948 and every 30 minutes until 2018, 2048, 2116, 2148, 2216⑥, 2227Ⓐ, 2255Ⓐ.

On ⑦ at 1022, 1119, 1219, 1250 and then at 19 and 50 minutes past each hour until 2019, 2050, 2150, 2219.

From Birmingham New Street: On ⚒ at 0519Ⓐ, 0522⑥, 0550Ⓐ, 0552⑥, 0622, 0652, 0722, 0752, 0822, 0852 and every 30 minutes until 1522, 1552, 1609Ⓐ, 1622, 1652, 1709Ⓐ, 1722, 1752, 1822, 1852, 1922, 1952, 2022⑥, 2025Ⓐ, 2052, 2222.

On ⑦ at 0952, 1052, 1122, 1152 and every 30 minutes until 2022, 2052, 2152.

▽ – **Full service Cambridge - Stansted Airport and v.v.**

From Cambridge:

On ⚒ at 0444Ⓐ, 0456⑥, 0517Ⓐ, 0542⑥, 0610⑥, 0632Ⓐ, 0640⑥, 0710⑥, 0740, 0810, 0826⑥, 0910, 0926⑥, 0931Ⓐ, 1010, 1026, 1110, 1126, 1210, 1226, 1310, 1326, 1410, 1426, 1510, 1526, 1610, 1626⑥, 1710, 1726⑥, 1817⑥, 1818Ⓐ, 1826⑥, 1910, 1926⑥, 2010, 2026⑥, 2110, 2126, 2210.

On ⑦ at 0739, 0824, 0915, 0924, 1015, 1024, 1115, 1124, 1215, 1224, 1315, 1324, 1410, 1424, 1510, 1524, 1610, 1624, 1710, 1724, 1810, 1824, 1910, 1924, 2010, 2024, 2110, 2124, 2210.

From Stansted Airport:

On ⚒ at 0516Ⓐ, 0525⑥, 0612Ⓐ, 0627⑥, 0648⑥, 0721Ⓐ, 0727⑥, 0748⑥, 0821Ⓐ, 0827⑥, 0905⑥, 0921Ⓐ, 0927⑥, 1005, 1027, 1105, 1127, 1205, 1227, 1305, 1327, 1405, 1427, 1505, 1527, 1605, 1627, 1705⑥, 1727, 1805⑥, 1821Ⓐ, 1827⑥, 1905⑥, 1921Ⓐ, 1927⑥, 2005⑥, 2021Ⓐ, 2027⑥, 2105⑥, 2127, 2205, 2227, 2257Ⓐ, 2327⑥.

On ⑦ at 0840, 0909, 1009, 1025, 1109, 1125, 1209, 1225, 1309, 1325, 1409, 1425, 1509, 1525, 1609, 1625, 1709, 1725, 1809, 1825, 1909, 1925, 2009, 2025, 2104, 2118, 2209, 2225, 2304.

NT 2nd class MIDDLESBROUGH - NEWCASTLE 210

km		ⒶA	⚒	⚒	⚒	⚒	and at	⚒	⚒	⚒	⚒	⑥Y	Ⓐ	⑦	⑦	⑦	⑦	and at	⑦	⑦Y	⑦	⑦	⑦	⑦
0	**Middlesbrough** . d.	...	...	0655	0732	0832	the same	1632	1743	1832	1942	2047	2110	0833	0934	1033	1131	the same	1634	1732	1831	1933	2032	2114
9	Stockton .... d.	...	...	0706	0743	0843	minutes	1643	1754	1843	1954	2058	2121	0844	0945	1044	1142	minutes	1646	1743	1842	1944	2043	2125
28	Hartlepool ... **183** d.	...	0703	0725	0802	0902	past each	1702	1813	1902	2013	2117	2140	0904	1005	1104	1202	past each	1706	1802	1901	2003	2102	2145
57	Sunderland . **183** d.	0540	0730	0755	0830	0930	hour until	1729	1843	1929	2039	2142	2211a	0930	1030	1130	1227	hour until	1731	1828	1928	2028	2128	2211
77	**Newcastle** .... a.	0556	0751	0816	0853	0953	✣	1753	1907	1955b	2104	2204	2232	0950	1050	1150	1247	✣d	1750	1848	1953	2048	2148	2233

	Ⓐ	⑥	⑥	Ⓐ	⚒	and at	⚒	Ⓐ	⑥	Ⓐ	⑥	ⒶA	⑦	⑦Y	⑦	⑦	⑦Y	⑦	and at	⑦	⑦	⑦	⑦	⑦
Newcastle .... d.	0600	0600	0700	0700	0730	the same	1930	2030	2033	2118	2130	2300	0830	0932	1030	1130	1230	1330	the same	1727	1830	1930	2030	2130
Sunderland **183** d.	0620	0628a	0721	0720	0750	minutes	1951	2051	2055	2138	2151	2320	0850	0952	1050	1150	1251	1351	minutes	1750	1850	1951	2051	2150
Hartlepool .. **183** d.	0646	0653	0745	0749	0815	past each	2017	2115	2122	2203	2215	...	0913	1015	1113	1213	1314	1414	past each	1814	1913	2014	2114	2213
Stockton .... d.	...	...	0804	0808	0833	hour until	2036	2133	2140	2221	2234	...	0932	1034	1132	1232	1333	1433	hour until	1832	1932	2033	2133	2232
Middlesbrough a.	...	...	0825	0825	0848	✣e	2049	2148	2155	2236	2248	...	0943	1045	1143	1243	1344	1444	✣c	1844	1943	2044	2144	2243

A – To / from London Kings Cross (Table **180**).
Y – From Whitby (Table **211**).

a – Arrives 6–8 minutes earlier.
b – Arrives 1951 on Ⓐ.

c – The 1530 departure from Newcastle calls at Sunderland 1553, Hartlepool 1619, Stockton 1638 and Middlesbrough 1649 and continues to Whitby (Table **211**).
d – The 1431 departure starts from Whitby (Table **211**).

e – Additonal Newcastle - Middlesbrough departure at 1653, calling at Sunderland 1751, Hartlepool 1739, Stockton 1758 and Middlesbrough 1815.
✣ – Timings may vary by ± 3 minutes.

NT 2nd class MIDDLESBROUGH and PICKERING - WHITBY 211

km		⚒	⑦D	⚒	⑦B	⑦B	⚒	⑦B	⚒	
0	**Middlesbrough** .... d.	0704	0842	1028	1050	1346	1403	1651	1740	...
18	Battersby .... d.	0734	0910	1058	1129	1419	1435	1725	1810	...
41	Glaisdale .... d.	0808	0944	1131	1203	1453	1509	1758	1843	...
46	Grosmont .... d.	0817	0952	1139	1211	1501	1517	1806	1851	...
56	**Whitby** .... a.	0837	1011	1159	1230	1519	1536	1825	1911	...

	⚒	⑦D	⚒	⑦B	⑦B	⚒	⑦	Ⓐ	⑥B
Whitby .... d.	0845	1022	1215	1247	1546	1559	1831	1918	1918
Grosmont .... d.	0902	1039	1232	1304	1603	1617	1848	1935	1935
Glaisdale .... d.	0913	1050	1243	1315	1614	1627	1859	1946	1946
Battersby .... d.	0947	1124	1318	1349	1655	1702	1933	2020	2020
Middlesbrough .... a.	1015	1151	1345	1416	1724	1729	2002	2047	2047

km		🚂	🚂		🚂	🚂	🚂		🚂	🚂
0	**Pickering** .... d.	...	0925	...	1100	1200	1300	...	1500	1610
29	Grosmont .... a.	...	1025	...	1205	1305	1405	...	1615	1710
29	Grosmont .... d.	0915	1040	...	...	1315	1430	...	...	1715
39	**Whitby** .... a.	0945	1110	...	...	1345	1500	...	...	1745

	🚂	🚂		🚂	🚂	🚂	🚂	🚂	
Whitby .... d.	1000	...	...	1245	1400	...	1640	1800	...
Grosmont .... a.	1025	...	...	1315	1425	...	1705	1825	...
Grosmont .... d.	1030	1130	...	1330	1430	1540	1715	...	...
Pickering .... a.	1140	1240	...	1440	1540	1650	1820	...	...

B – To / from Newcastle (Table **210**).
D – To / from Darlington (Table **212**).

🚂 – Easter - October 2018. Service to be announced. National rail tickets **not** valid. An amended service operates on most ⑦ and on certain other dates - please confirm with operator. The North Yorkshire Moors Railway (✆ 01751 472508. www.nymr.co.uk).

212 BISHOP AUCKLAND - DARLINGTON - MIDDLESBROUGH - SALTBURN

2nd class NT

km		⚒	⚒	Ⓐ	⑥	⚒		⚒	Ⓐ	⑥	⚒	Ⓐ	⑥	⚒	⑦A	⑦	⑦	⑦	⑦	⑦	⑦	⑦	⑦
0	**Bishop Auckland** d.	0717	0821	0926	0925	1023		1623	1725	1726	1805	1900	1920	2110	...	0810	1006	1206	1506	1706	1806	1906	...
4	Shildon d.	0722	0826	0931	0930	1028	and at	1628	1730	1731	1810	1905	1925	2115	...	0815	1011	1211	1511	1711	1811	1911	...
8	Newton Aycliffe d.	0727	0831	0936	0935	1033	the same	1633	1735	1736	1815	1910	1930	2120	...	0820	1016	1216	1516	1716	1816	1916	...
19	**Darlington** a.	0743	0847	0953	0952	1050	minutes	1650	1750	1753	1831	1926	1947	2136	...	0837	1033	1233	1533	1733	1833	1934	...
19	**Darlington** ▶ d.	0744	0900	0955	0955	1051	past each	1653	1752	1754	1833	1928	1955	2138	0813	0839	1035	1235	1535	1735	1835	1935	2252
43	**Middlesbrough** ▶ d.	0811	0927	1022	1024	1121	hour until	1720	1822	1825	1900	1958	2023	2206	0840	0906	1103	1303	1603	1803	1903	2003	2320
55	Redcar Central ▶ d.	*0907*	0938	1034	1036	1133	✣	1732	1834	1837	1910	2010	*2110*	2218	...	0918	1115	1315	1615	1815	1915	2015	...
63	**Saltburn** ▶ a.	*0926*	0955	1051	1053	1150		1750	1850	1854	1926	2026	*2126*	2235	...	0933	1130	1331	1630	1831	1931	2031	...

	⚒	⚒	⑥	Ⓐ	⚒	⚒	⚒	⚒	⚒	⚒		⚒	⚒	⚒	⚒	⑦	⑦	⑦	⑦A	⑦	⑦	⑦	⑦
Saltburn ▷ d.	...	...	0621	0624	...	0754	0830	0958	1057	1157		1555	1630	1730	1930	...	...	1037	...	1336	1536	1636	1736
Redcar Central ▷ d.	...	...	0634	0637	...	0807	0843	1011	1110	1210	and at	1608	1643	1743	1943	...	...	1050	...	1349	1549	1649	1749
Middlesbrough ▷ d.	0544	...	0647	0650	...	0820	0908f	1023	1121	1221	the same	1619	1657	1755	1955	...	0850	1102	1149	1402	1602	1705	1802
Darlington ▷ a.	0614	...	0719	0720	...	0851	0938	1053	1150	1252	minutes	1649	1727	1825	2026	...	0919	1129	1216	1429	1629	1734	1829
Darlington d.	...	0647	...	...	0749	0851	0953	1054	1152	1254	past each	1651	1728	1832	2032	0741	0929	1131	...	1431	1631	1735	1834
Newton Aycliffe d.	...	0701	...	...	0804	0906	1007	1108	1206	1308	hour until	1705	1742	1846	2046	0755	0943	1145	...	1445	1645	1750	1848
Shildon d.	...	0706	...	...	0808	0910	1012	1113	1211	1313	✣	1710	1747	1851	2051	0800	0948	1150	...	1450	1650	1754	1853
Bishop Auckland a.	...	0715	...	...	0816	0918	1019	1120	1219	1320		1717	1755	1858	2058	0806	0955	1158	...	1457	1658	1802	1901

A – To/from Whitby (Table **211**).

f – Arrives 0855.

✣ – Timings may vary by ± 4 minutes.

▶ – All trains Darlington - Middlesbrough - Redcar - Saltburn:
⚒: 0629, 0658, 0725Ⓐ, 0730⑥, 0823⑥, 0831Ⓐ, 0900, 0931, 0955, 1032, 1051, 1131, 1153, 1232, 1252, 1332, 1353, 1432, 1451, 1531, 1553, 1631, 1653, 1730, 1752Ⓐ, 1754⑥, 1833, 1928Ⓐ, 1930⑥, 2030, 2138.
⑦: 0839, 0933, 1035, 1135, 1235, 1333, 1434, 1535, 1635, 1735, 1835, 1935, 2035, 2157.

▷ – All trains Saltburn - Redcar - Middlesbrough - Darlington:
⚒: 0621⑥, 0624Ⓐ, 0710, 0725Ⓐ, 0728⑥, 0754, 0830, 0930, 0958, 1030, 1057, 1130, 1157, 1230, 1257, 1330, 1357, 1430, 1457, 1530, 1555, 1630, 1655, 1730, 1757, 1829, 1857, 1930, 2030Ⓐ, 2034⑥, 2130, 2239.
⑦: 0937, 1037, 1136, 1236, 1336, 1436, 1536, 1636, 1736, 1836, 1940, 2040, 2153, 2256.

213 NEWCASTLE - CARLISLE

2nd class NT

km		⑥	Ⓐ	⚒	⚒	⚒	⚒	⚒	⚒	⚒	⚒	⚒W	⚒	⚒	⚒	⚒	⚒	⚒	Ⓐ	⑦	⑦	⑦	⑦
0	**Newcastle** ▶ d.	0630	0646	0824	0924	1022	1122	1222	1323	1424	1524	1622	1716	1754	1824	1925	2016	2118	2235	0845	0935	1035	1135
6	MetroCentre ▶ d.	0638	0654	0832	0932	1033	1132	1232	1333	1432	1532	1630	1724	1802	1833	1934	2024	2126	2243	0853	0943	1043	1143
19	Prudhoe ▶ d.	0650	0704	0844	0942	1043	1142	1242	1344	1442	1542	1642	1737	1814	1848	1947	2039	2138	2258	0907	0957	1055	1157
36	Hexham ▶ d.	0709	0717	0858	0955	1055	1155	1255	1357	1455	1556	1701	1750	1833	1906	2005	2100	2157	2318	0926	1016	1116	1216
62	Haltwhistle d.	0732	0740	0921	1014	1118	1214	1318	1416	1518	1616	1724	1813	1855	1925	2028	...	2220	...	0948	1038	1138	1234
99	**Carlisle** a.	0807	0815	0957f	1046	1157f	1247	1356	1451	1557f	1651	1800	1852	1932	1959	2103	...	2256	...	1022	1112	1209	1308
	Glasgow Central 214 a.	1037	1037	...	...	...	...	...	1737	...	...	...	2140	...	...	...	...	...	...	...	...	...	...

	⑦	⑦	⑦	⑦	⑦	⑦	⑦	⑦	⑦
Newcastle ▶ d.	1235	1335	1435	1535	1632	1735	1835	1935	2034
MetroCentre ▶ d.	1243	1343	1443	1543	1640	1743	1843	1943	2042
Prudhoe ▶ d.	1255	1357	1455	1557	1652	1757	1855	1957	2057
Hexham ▶ d.	1314	1416	1514	1616	1711	1816	1914	2016	2116
Haltwhistle d.	1336	1434	1536	1634	1733	1834	1936	2038	2138
Carlisle a.	1407	1508	1607	1708	1804	1908	2007	2112	2212
Glasgow Central 214 a.	...	...	...	...	...	...	...	...	...

	⚒	⑥	Ⓐ	⚒D	⚒E	⚒	Ⓐ	⑥	⚒	⚒
Glasgow Central 214 d.	...	...	...	...	...	0707	...	...	...	...
Carlisle d.	...	0625	0628	0718	0828	0943	1025	1030	1135	1228
Haltwhistle d.	...	0657	0700	0750	0900	1011	1058	1100	1203	1300
Hexham ▷ d.	0612	0719	0722	0812	0922	1029	1120	1122	1222	1322
Prudhoe ▷ d.	0630	0737	0740	0829	0934	1041	1132	1134	1234	1334
MetroCentre ▷ d.	0645	0750	0753	0846	0946	1053	1144	1146	1246	1346
Newcastle ▷ a.	0655	0807	0807	0901r	0959	1106	1157	1159	1259	1400

	⚒	⚒	⚒	⚒	⚒	Ⓐ	⑥	⚒	⚒	⚒	Ⓐ	⑦	⑦	⑦	⑦	⑦	⑦	⑦	⑦	⑦	⑦	⑦	⑦	⑦
Glasgow Central 214 d.	...	1213	...	...	...	1613	1613	...	...	...	...	...	...	...	...	...	...	...	...	...	...	...	...	...
Carlisle d.	1332	1436	1528	1628	1728	1838	1841	1941	...	2128	...	0834	0939	1038	1139	1238	1338	1438	1539	1633	1742	1837	1934	2038
Haltwhistle d.	1404	1505	1556t	1700	1800	1910	1913	2010	...	2200	...	0906	1007	1110	1207	1310	1407	1510	1607	1710	1810	1909	2006	2110
Hexham ▷ d.	1426	1523	1615	1722	1822	1932	1935	2028	2112	2222	2322	0928	1029	1128	1229	1328	1429	1528	1629	1727	1832	1927	2028	2128
Prudhoe ▷ d.	1438	1535	1626	1734	1840	1949	1952	2045	2130	2240	2340	0945	1047	1145	1247	1345	1447	1545	1647	1745	1845	1944	2045	2145
MetroCentre ▷ d.	1450	1547	1638	1746	1853	2003	2006	2059	2145	2253	2353	1000	1100	1200	1300	1400	1500	1600	1700	1800	1903	1959	2100	2200
Newcastle ▷ a.	1503	1558	1650	1759	1907	2017	2017	2113	2156	2306	0004	1010	1110	1210	1310	1410	1510	1610	1710	1810	1914	2009	2110	2211

D – From Dumfries (Table **214**).
E – On Ⓐ from Dumfries (Table **214**).
W – To Whitehaven (Table **159**).

f – On ⑥ arrives 4–5 minutes earlier.
r – On Ⓐ arrives 0857.
t – Ⓐ only.

▶ – Additional Trains Newcastle - Hexham. Journey time 43–45 minutes:
0625Ⓐ, 0753⚒, 0854⚒ and houly until 1454⚒, 1554⚒, 1654Ⓐ, 1656⑥ 1724⚒.

▷ – Additional Trains Hexham - Newcastle. Journey time 42–47 minutes:
0742⚒, 0845⚒, 0943⚒, 1045⚒, 1143⚒, 1245⚒, 1342⚒, 1445⚒, 1543⚒, 1645⚒, 1743⚒, 1843⚒.

214 CARLISLE - DUMFRIES - GLASGOW

2nd class SR

km		⚒	⚒	⑥	Ⓐ	⚒	⑥	Ⓐ	⚒	⚒	⚒	⚒	⑦	⑥	Ⓐ	⚒	⑦	⚒	⑦	⑥	Ⓐ	⚒	⑦	⚒	Ⓐ	⑥	⚒	⑦	⚒
	Newcastle 213 d.	...	...	...	...	...	0630	0646	...	...	...	...	...	...	...	1323	...	...	...	...	...	...	...	1716	...	...	...	...	...
0	**Carlisle** 154 d.	...	...	0525	0531	0608	0815	0815	0955	1115	1220	1312	1313	1422	1430	1512	1515	1617	1712	1716	1727	1757	1912	1917	2017	2022	2112	2126	2310
16	Gretna Green d.	...	...	0536	0542	0619	0826	0826	1006	1126	1232	1323	1324	1433	1441	1523	1526	1628	1723	1727	1739	1808	1923	1928	2028	2033	2123	2137	2321
28	Annan d.	...	...	0545	0553	0627	0834	0834	1014	1134	1240	1331	1332	1441	1449	1531	1534	1636	1731	1735	1749	1817	1931	1937	2036	2041	2131	2145	2329
53	**Dumfries** d.	0513	0545	0602	0610	0646	0853	0853	1035	1153	1258	1350	1351	1459	1507	1550	1552	1654	1749	1753	1806	1835	1950	1955	2054	2059	2150	2203	2347
124	Auchinleck d.	0601	0634	...	...	0734	0941	0941	...	1241	...	1438	1439	...	...	1638	...	...	...	...	...	1924	2038	2044	...	...	2238	...	...
146	**Kilmarnock** ▽ d.	0620	0652	...	...	0755	0959	0959	...	1259	...	1458	1457	...	...	1656	...	...	...	...	...	1957a	2057	2101	...	...	2257	...	...
185	**Glasgow** Cent 154 ▽ a.	0711f	0732	...	...	0838f	1037	1037	...	1336	...	1538	1542	...	...	1737	...	...	...	...	...	2037	2135	2140	...	...	2336	...	...

	⚒	⚒	Ⓐ	⚒	⚒	⚒	⚒	⚒	⑦	Ⓐ	⑥	⚒	⚒	⑦	⚒	⑦	⚒	⚒	⚒	⑦	⚒	⚒	⑥	⑥	Ⓐ	Ⓐ	⑦	⑥	Ⓐ
Glasgow Cent 154 ▽ d.	...	...	...	...	0707	0837	...	1013	...	...	...	1213	1313	...	...	1503	...	1613	...	...	1742	1913	2013	...	2013	2113	2212	2213	2313
Kilmarnock ▽ d.	...	...	...	...	0754	0918	...	1051	...	...	...	1250	1350	...	...	1551	...	1652	...	...	1825	1952	2058	...	2058	2153	2249	2253	0002
Auchinleck d.	...	...	...	...	0811	0935	...	1108	...	...	...	1307	1407	...	...	1608	...	1709	...	...	1842	2009	2114	...	2125	2210	2306	2309	0020
Dumfries d.	0458	0618	0713	0743	0901	1025	1102	1158	1300	1304	1314	1357	1457	1501	1602	1700	1707	1759	1841	1901	1933	2100	2218	2220	2222	2300	2356	2359	0115
Annan d.	0513	0633	0728	0758	0916	1040	1117	1213	1315	1319	1329	1413	1512	1516	1617	1715	1722	1814	1856	1916	1948	2115	...	2235	...	2315	0011	0014	...
Gretna Green d.	0522	0642	0737	0807	0925	1049	1126	1222	1324	1328	1338	1421	1521	1525	1626	1724	1731	1823	1905	1925	1957	2124	...	2244	...	2324	0020	0023	...
Carlisle 154 a.	0535	0655	0753	0820	0941	1104	1139	1235	1337	1341	1354	1435	1534	1538	1639	1737	1744	1836	1918	1938	2011	2143	...	2257	...	2337	0033	0036	...
Newcastle 213 a.	...	0901r	...	0959t	1106	...	...	...	...	...	...	1558	...	...	...	...	...	2017	...	...	...	...	...	...	...	...	...	...	...

a – Arrive 1941. f – On ⑥ arrives 4 minutes earlier. r – On Ⓐ arrives 0857. t – Ⓐ only. ▽ – Frequent additional services are available (half-hourly on ⚒, hourly on ⑦).

215 GLASGOW and KILMARNOCK - STRANRAER

2nd class SR

For ⛴ Cairnryan - Belfast and v.v. see Table 2002.

km		⚒	⚒	⚒	⚒	⚒	⚒	⑦	⚒	⚒	⑦	⚒	⚒	⑦	⚒	⚒	⚒	⑦	⚒	⚒	⑦	⚒	⚒	⚒	Ⓐ	⑥
0	**Glasgow** Central 216 d.	...	...	...	...	0807	...	...	...	...	...	...	...	...	1413	...	...	...	1713	1813	...	...	...	...	2213	...
39	**Kilmarnock 214** a.	...	...	...	...	0849	...	...	...	...	...	...	...	...	1450	...	...	...	1752	1852	...	...	...	...	2252	...
39	**Kilmarnock** d.	...	...	...	0801	0900	...	...	1104	...	...	1303	...	...	1458	...	1700	...	1804	1904	...	...	2104	...	2305	2305
56	Troon 216 d.	...	...	...	0814	0912	...	...	1116	...	...	1315	...	...	1510	...	1712	...	1818	1916	...	...	2116	...	2317	2317
64	**Ayr** 🚌 216 a.	...	...	...	0827	0923	...	...	1129	...	...	1328	...	...	1524	...	1723	...	1828	1927	...	...	2127	...	2330	2330
64	**Ayr** d.	0525	0621	0716	0828	0923	1026	1106	1131	1226	1227	1329	1424	1505	1525	1625	1723	1805	1829	1927	1927	2032	2128	2230	2331	2331
97	Girvan d.	0552	0648	0756	0855	0954f	1055	1136f	1201f	1253	1253	1359f	1453	1535f	1555f	1652	1754f	1835f	1856	1958f	1953	2059	2153	2257	0001f	0001f
121	Barrhill d.	...	...	0816	...	1013	...	1155	1220	...	1318f	1418	...	1554	1614	...	1813	1854	...	2017	2017f	...	...	...	0020	0020
162	**Stranraer** a.	...	...	0852	...	1049	...	1231	1256	...	1354	1454	...	1630	1650	...	1849	1930	...	2053	2053	...	...	...	0056	0056

	⚒	⚒	⚒	⚒	⚒	⚒	⚒	⑦	⚒	⑦	⚒		⚒	⑦	⚒	⚒	⚒	⑦	⚒	⚒	⚒	⑦	⑥	Ⓐ	⚒	⚒
Stranraer d.	...	...	0702	...	0858	...	1106	1041	...	1241	1304	...	...	1440	1500	...	1659	1740	...	1903	...	1940	2103	2103	...	...
Barrhill d.	...	...	0736	...	0932	...	1140	1116	...	1316	1338	...	...	1514	1534	...	1733	1814	...	1937	...	2015	2137	2137	...	...
Girvan d.	0557	0653	0754	0900	0952	1100	1159	1134	1300	1334	1357	...	1500	1533	1553	1659	1751	1833	1901	1956	2104	2033	2157	2157	2230	2302
Ayr a.	0627	0721	0823	0928	1020	1128	1229	1202	1328	1402	1429	...	1528	1601	1626	1728	1820	1901	1929	2026	2132	2101	2225	2225	2309	2330
Ayr 🚌 216 d.	...	0722	0824	...	1021	...	1229	...	...	...	1430	...	...	...	1627	1728	1821	...	...	2027	...	...	2226	2226	...	...
Troon 216 d.	...	0733	0836	...	1029	...	1238	...	...	...	1441	...	...	...	1638	1739	1829	...	...	2038	...	...	2239	2239	...	...
Kilmarnock a.	...	0749	0852	...	1044	...	1254	...	...	...	1456	...	...	...	1653	1756	1844	...	...	2055	...	...	2256	2303	...	...
Kilmarnock 214 d.	...	...	0857	...	...	...	...	...	...	...	...	...	...	...	...	...	1857	...	...	...	...	...	...	...	...	...
Glasgow Central 216 a.	...	...	0937	...	...	...	...	...	...	...	...	...	...	...	...	...	1937	...	...	...	...	...	...	...	...	...

f – Arrives 5 minutes earlier.

☛ 🚌 connections to/from Cairnryan are available from Ayr for pre-booked Rail & Sail ticket holders - www.stenaline.co.uk/rail

Typical off-peak journey time in hours and minutes
READ DOWN ↓ READ UP ↑

Journey times may be extended during peak hours on Ⓐ (0600 - 0900 and 1600 - 1900) and also at weekends.
The longest journey time by any train is noted in the table heading.

GLASGOW CENTRAL - AYR

Longest journey: 1 hour 04 minutes SR

km	△				△
0	0h00	↓	**Glasgow** Central ......d.		0h49
43	0h25		Kilwinning ....d.	↑	0h22
48	0h29	↓	Irvine ....d.		0h18
56	0h37		Troon........................d.	↑	0h11
61	0h41	↓	Prestwick Airport ✈ ..d.		0h07
67	0h52		**Ayr**..........................a.	↑	0h00

From Glasgow Central: On ⚒ at 0015②–⑥, 0600, 0630, 0700, 0730, 0746, 0800, 0830, 0838, 0900, 0930, 1000, 1030 and every 30 minutes until 1500, 1530, 1600, 1628, 1640, 1701, 1716Ⓐ, 1728Ⓐ, 1730⑥, 1747Ⓐ, 1800 and every 30 minutes until 2330.
On ⑦ at 0900 and every 30 minutes until 1900, 2000, 2100, 2200, 2300.

From Ayr: On ⚒ at 0513, 0540, 0602, 0620Ⓐ, 0633, 0650, 0705, 0717, 0734Ⓐ, 0740, 0805, 0829, 0851, 0924, 0950, 1025, 1050, 1124, 1152, 1223, 1250, 1325, 1350, 1426, 1450, 1525, 1548, 1623, 1654, 1706, 1724, 1753, 1805, 1825, 1850, 1915 and every 30 minutes until 2215, 2300.
On ⑦ at 0845 and every 30 minutes until 1945, 2045, 2145, 2300.

△ – Trains at 0015⚒ - 0838⚒ and 1900⚒ - 2330⚒ and all day on ⑦ call additionally at Paisley Gilmour Street.

GLASGOW CENTRAL - ARDROSSAN - LARGS

Longest journey: 1 hour 10 minutes SR

km					
0	0h00	↓	**Glasgow** Central ......d.	↑	0h59
12	0h10		Paisley Gilmour St ....d.		0h46
43	0h29	↓	Kilwinning ....d.	↑	0h25
50	0h38		**Ardrossan** Sth Beach ..d.		0h17
64	0h49	↓	Fairlie ....d.	↑	0h05
69	0h56		**Largs** ....a.		0h00

From Glasgow Central:
On ⚒ at 0615, 0715, 0848 and hourly until 1448, 1548, 1631, 1714⑥, 1723Ⓐ, 1749, 1850, 1945, 2045, 2145, 2245, 2315①–⑤, 2345⑤.
On ⑦ at 0940 and hourly until 2140, 2242.

From Largs:
On ⚒ at 0642, 0722Ⓐ, 0742, 0833Ⓐ, 0853⑥, 0953 and hourly until 1553, 1648, 1733, 1852, 1952, 2052, 2152, 2252.
On ⑦ at 0854 and hourly until 2154, 2300.

SR 2nd class GLASGOW - OBAN, FORT WILLIAM and MALLAIG 218

km		⚒	⚒	⚒ A	Ⓐ Ba	⚒ 🍷	⚒ 🍷	⑦ d		⑦ 🍷	⚒ 🍷	Ⓐ Bb	⑦ 🍷	⑦ 🍷 d	⚒ 🍷	⚒ 🍷		Ⓐ	⚒	⑦ 🍷	⑦ 🍷	⚒ 🍷	①–④ 🍷	⑤ 🍷	⑥ 🍷
	Edinburgh **220**..........d.	...	...	0450	...	*0715*	*0715*	...	...	*0830*	*0930*	...	*1100*	*1100*	*1115*	*1115*	...	...	*1530*	*1700*	*1700*	*1715*	*1715*	*1715*	*1715*
0	**Glasgow** Queen St .....d.	...	0520	0548‡	...	0821	0821	...	...	0956	1037	...	1220	1220	1221	1221	...	...	1637	1821	1821	1821	1821	1821	1821
16	Dalmuir........................d.	...	0539	0604	...	0842	0842	...	...	1016	1057	...	1234	1234	1242	1242	...	...	1657	1836	1836	1841	1841	1841	1841
26	Dumbarton Central.......d.	...	0548	0615	...	0852	0852	...	...	1026	1106	...	1247	1247	1251	1251	...	...	1706	1847	1847	1850	1850	1850	1850
40	Helensburgh Upper .....d.	...	0603	0632	...	0907	0907	...	...	1041	1127	...	1306f	1306f	1306	1306	...	...	1722	1905f	1905f	1906	1906	1904	1906
51	Garelochhead ....d.	...	0614	0645	...	0918	0918	...	...	1052	1140	...	1318	1318	1318	1318	...	...	1733	1916	1916	1917	1917	1917	1917
68	Arrochar & Tarbet........d.	...	0634	0709	...	0938	0938	...	...	1112	1200	...	1338	1338	1338	1338	...	...	1757f	1936	1936	1937	1937	1937	1937
81	Ardlui..........................d.	...	0652f	0724x	...	0951	0951	...	...	1128	1214	...	1356f	1356f	1356f	1356f	...	...	1810	1951	1951	1951	1951	1951	1951
95	**Crianlarich**..................a.	...	0708	0745	...	1007	1007	...	...	1145	1230	...	1412	1412	1412	1412	...	...	1826	2007	2007	2007	2007	2007	2007
95	**Crianlarich**..................d.	...	0718	0747	...	1015	1021	...	...	1147	1233	...	1418	1424	1418	1424	...	...	1829	2014	2020	2014	2020	2020	2020
	Dalmally ....d.	...	0751f	|	...	1042	|	...	...	1215	1259	...	1444	|	1444	|	...	1705	1855	2040	|	2040	|	|	|
	Taynuilt ....d.	...	0811	|	...	1103	|	...	...	1240f	1320	...	1504	|	1505	|	...	1724	1920	2100	|	2100	|	|	|
162	**Oban** ....a.	...	0835	|	...	1127	|	...	...	1304	1343	...	1527	|	1528	|	...	1747	1943	2124	|	2124	|	|	|
115	Bridge of Orchy ....d.	...	...	0818	...	...	1048	...	...	...	...	...	...	1449	...	1449	...	...	...	...	2045	...	2045	2045	2045
140	Rannoch......................d.	...	...	0846	...	...	1109	...	...	...	...	...	...	1512	...	1512	...	...	...	...	2108	...	2108	2108	2108
177	Roy Bridge ....d.	...	...	0931x	...	...	1148	...	...	...	...	...	...	1550	...	1550	...	...	...	...	2146	...	2146	2146	2146
183	Spean Bridge...............d.	...	...	0939	...	...	1155	...	...	...	...	...	...	1556	...	1556	...	...	...	...	2153	...	2153	2156	2153
197	**Fort William**...............a.	...	...	0955	...	...	1208	...	...	...	...	...	...	1609	...	1609	...	...	...	...	2206	...	2206	2209	2206
197	**Fort William**...............d.	0830	...	...	1015	...	1212	1212	...	...	...	1430	...	1619	...	1619	...	...	...	...	2214	...	2214	2217	2214
223	Glenfinnan ....d.	0905	...	...	1122	...	1246	1246	...	...	...	1545	...	1655	...	1655	...	...	...	...	2247	...	2247	2250	2247
251	Arisaig ....d.	0938	...	...	|	...	1319	1319	...	...	...	|	...	1727	...	1727	...	...	...	...	2320	...	2320	2323	2320
259	Morar...........................d.	0946	...	...	|	...	1327	1327	...	...	...	|	...	1736	...	1736	...	...	...	...	2328	...	2328	2331	2328
264	**Mallaig**.......................a.	0953	...	...	1225	...	1334	1334	...	...	...	1629	...	1743	...	1743	...	...	...	...	2335	...	2335	2338	2335

	⚒	⚒ 🍷	⚒ 🍷	⚒ 🍷	⚒ 🍷	⑦ 🍷	⑦ d	Ⓐ 🍷	Ⓐ Ba	⑦ 🍷	⑥ 🍷		Ⓐ		⚒ 🍷	⚒ 🍷	⑦ 🍷	⑦ 🍷	⑦ A	⑦ d	⚒ 🍷	⚒	Ⓐ A	Ⓐ Bb
Mallaig................................d.	...	0603	...	...	1010	...	1010	...	1410	...	...	...	...	...	1605	...	1605	...	...	1815	1815	...	...	1838
Morar.....................................d.	...	0609	...	...	1017	...	1017	...	|	...	...	...	...	...	1612	...	1612	...	...	1822	1822	...	...	|
Arisaig ....d.	...	0619	...	...	1027	...	1026	...	|	...	...	...	...	...	1621	...	1621	...	...	1831	1831	...	...	|
Glenfinnan ....d.	...	0651	...	...	1059	...	1059	...	1518	...	...	...	...	...	1654	...	1654	...	...	1904	1904	...	...	1947
Fort William..........................a.	...	0725	...	...	1132	...	1132	...	1600	...	...	...	...	...	1728	...	1728	...	...	1937	1937	...	...	2031
Fort William..........................d.	...	0744	...	...	1140	...	1140	...	...	...	...	...	...	...	1737	...	1737	...	1900	...	...	...	1950	...
Spean Bridge..........................d.	...	0757	...	...	1156	...	1156	...	...	...	...	...	...	...	1751	...	1751	...	1917	...	...	...	2008	...
Roy Bridge ....d.	...	0804	...	...	1202	...	1202	...	...	...	...	...	...	...	1757	...	1757	...	1923x	...	...	...	2014x	...
Rannoch..................................d.	...	0847f	...	...	1242	...	1242	...	...	...	...	...	...	...	1838	...	1838	...	2012	...	...	...	2107	...
Bridge of Orchy ....d.	...	0907	...	...	1303	...	1303	...	...	...	...	...	...	...	1858	...	1858	...	2046	...	...	...	2133	...
Oban ....d.	0521	|	0857	1211	|	1211	|	1441	...	1611	1611	...	1611	...	|	1811	|	1811	|	...	...	2036	|	...
Taynuilt ....d.	0544	|	0920	1235	|	1238	|	1506	...	1638	1634	...	1634	...	|	1833	|	1833	|	...	...	2101	|	...
Dalmally ....d.	0603	|	0940	1300f	|	1259	|	1526	...	1658	1654	...	1654	...	|	1856	|	1856	|	...	...	2120	|	...
Crianlarich............................a.	0631	0931	1008	1332	1327	1326	1332	1554	...	1726	1722	...	...	...	1922	1927	1922	1927	2114	...	...	2147	2202	...
Crianlarich............................d.	0633	0933	1014	1337	1337	1337	1337	1556	...	1727	1724	...	...	...	1932	1932	1932	1932	2116	...	...	2148	2206	...
Ardlui.....................................d.	0651	0952	1029	1355	1355	1355	1355	1611	...	1743	1742	...	...	...	1952	1952	1952	1952	2133x	...	...	2204	2224x	...
Arrochar & Tarbet.................d.	0710f	1006	1043	1409	1409	1409	1409	1627	...	1757	1756	...	...	...	2006	2006	2006	2006	2151	...	...	2218	2242	...
Garelochhead ....d.	0730	1032f	1104	1431	1431	1429	1429	1649	...	1819	1819	...	...	...	2026	2026	2026	2026	2218	...	...	2238	2306	...
Helensburgh Upper...............d.	0742	1044	1116	1443	1443	1440	1440	1700	...	1831	1831	...	...	...	2037	2037	2040	2040	2232	...	...	2249	2320	...
Dumbarton Central................a.	0756	1059	1129	1501f	1501f	1453	1453	1713	...	1847	1844	...	...	...	2051	2051	2053	2053	2247	...	...	2302	2334	...
Dalmuir...................................a.	|	1112	1138	1513	1513	1505	1505	1723	...	1858	1854	...	...	...	2103	2103	2104	2104	2302	...	...	2311	2347	...
Glasgow Queen St................a.	0837	1130	1156	1530	1530	1526	1526	1747	...	1918	1920	...	...	...	2121	2121	2119	2119	2326¶	...	...	2333	0012¶	...
Edinburgh **220**....................a.	*0953*	*1237*	*1307*	*1638*	*1638*	*1650*	*1650*	*1853*	...	*2025*	*2026*	...	...	...	*2250*	*2250*	*2223*	*2223*	0030	...	...	...	0111	...

A – 🅁. 🛏12 (limited accommodation), 🛏 1, 2 cl. and ✕ London Euston - Fort William and v.v. (Table **161**).
B – THE JACOBITE – 🚂. 🅁. National Rail tickets **not** valid. To book ✆ 0844 850 4685 or visit www.westcoastrailways.co.uk.

a – Dec. 11–22, 27–29, Mar. 30 - Oct. 26 (also ⑥⑦ Mar. 31, April 1, June 2 - Sept. 30).
b – May 14 - Sept. 14 (also ⑥⑦ June 16 - Sept. 2).
d – From Mar. 25.
f – Arrives 5–7 minutes earlier.
s – Calls to set down only.

u – Calls to pick up only.
x – Calls on request.
‡ – Low-level platforms. Calls to pick up only.
¶ – Low-level platforms. Calls to set down only.

SCOTTISH ISLAND FERRIES 219

Caledonian MacBrayne Ltd operates numerous ferry services linking the Western Isles of Scotland to the mainland and to each other. Principal routes – some of which are seasonal – are listed below (see also the map on page **90**). Service frequencies, sailing-times and reservations: ✆ +44 (0)800 066 5000; fax +44 (0)1475 635 235; www.calmac.co.uk

Ardrossan – Brodick (Arran)
Ardrossan – Campbeltown (Kintyre)
Barra – Eriskay
Claonaig – Lochranza (Arran)
Colintraive – Rhubodach (Bute)
Fionnphort – Iona (Iona)
Kennacraig – Port Askaig (Islay)
Kennacraig – Port Ellen (Islay)
Kilchoan – Tobermory (Mull)
Largs – Cumbrae (Cumbrae)
Leverburgh (Harris) – Berneray (North Uist)
Lochaline – Fishnish (Mull)
Mallaig – Armadale (Skye)
Mallaig – Eigg, Muck, Rum and Canna
Mallaig – Lochboisdale (South Uist)
Oban – Castlebay (Barra)
Oban – Coll and Tiree
Oban – Colonsay, Port Askaig (Islay) and Kennacraig
Oban – Craignure (Mull)
Oban – Lismore
Portavadie (Cowal & Kintyre) – Tarbert (Loch Fyne)
Sconser (Skye) – Raasay
Tayinloan – Gigha
Tobermory (Mull) – Kilchoan
Uig (Skye) – Lochmaddy (North Uist)
Uig (Skye) – Tarbert (Harris)
Ullapool – Stornoway (Lewis)
Wemyss Bay – Rothesay (Bute)

① – Mondays ② – Tuesdays ③ – Wednesdays ④ – Thursdays ⑤ – Fridays ⑥ – Saturdays ⑦ – Sundays Ⓐ – Not Saturdays 79

220 EDINBURGH - GLASGOW

GR, SR, XC

EDINBURGH - FALKIRK - GLASGOW QUEEN STREET

km			⚒	⚒	Ⓐ	⑥	Ⓐ	⚒	⚒	⚒	⚒	⚒	⚒	⚒	⚒		⚒	⚒	⚒	⚒	Ⓐ	⑥	⚒	⚒
0	**Edinburgh** Waverley .... d.	⚒	0555	0630	0645	0700	0700	0715	0730	0745	0800	0815	0830	0845	0900	and at	1800	1815	1830	1845	1900	1900	1915	1930
2	Haymarket .... d.		0600	0635	0650	0704	0705	0720	0734	0749	0805	0819	0835	0851	0905	the same	1806	1821	1835	1849	1905	1905	1920	1934
28	Linlithgow .... d.		0615	0650	0706	|	|	0735	0749	0805	|	0834	|	0906	|	minutes	|	1836	|	1905	|	|	1935	1952
41	Falkirk High .... d.		0626	0701	0714	0724	0728	0744	0801	0814	0828	0846	0856	0918	0924	past each	1825	1847	1856	1916	1924	1926	1946	2000
76	**Glasgow** Queen Street. a.		0649	0725	0738	0744	0752	0808	0825	0840	0855	0906	0920	0938	0948	hour until ☆	1850f	1909	1923	1937	1944	1949	2008	2024

	Ⓐ	⑥	⚒	⚒	⚒	Ⓐ	⑥	⚒	⚒	⚒		⑦	⑦	⑦	⑦	⑦	⑦	⑦		⑦	⑦	⑦	⑦	⑦
Edinburgh Waverley .... d.	2000	2000	2030	2100	2130	2200	2200	2230	2300	2330	⑦	0800	0830	0900	0930	1000	1030	1100	and at	2130	2200	2230	2300	2330
Haymarket .... d.	2004	2006	2035	2105	2134	2204	2205	2235	2305	2334		0804	0834	0904	0934	1004	1034	1104	the same	2136	2204	2234	2304	2334
Linlithgow .... d.	2017	2021	2052	2120	2149	2217	2218	2250	2320	2350		0825	0855	0925	0954	1024	1049	1119	minutes	2151	2219	2249	2319	2349
Falkirk High .... d.	2027	2032	2100	2131	2158	2226	2228	2258	2331	0003		0836	0904	0936	1003	1035	1058	1130	past each	2200	2230	2258	2330	0002
Glasgow Queen Street. a.	2049	2052	2125	2152	2221	2244	2248	2322	2359	0027		0900	0928	0957	1026	1055	1122	1151	hour until ⊡	2224	2251	2322	2354	0026

		⚒	Ⓐ	⑥	Ⓐ	⚒	⚒	⚒	⚒	⚒	⚒	⚒	⚒	⚒	⚒	⚒	⚒		⚒	⚒	⚒	⚒	Ⓐ	⑥
Glasgow Queen Street d.	⚒	0600	0630	0630	0645	0700	0715	0730	0745	0800	0815	0830	0845	0900	0915	0930	0945	and at	1800	1815	1830	1845	1900	1900
Falkirk High .... d.		0619	0651	0654	0707	0721	0734	0753	0804	0822	0835	0853	0904	0923	0935	0952	1005	the same	1824	1834	1852	1904	1920	1922
Linlithgow .... d.		0630	0703	0705	0715	0733	0745	0801	0816	|	0845	|	0916	|	0946	|	1016	minutes	|	1846	|	1915	|	|
Haymarket .... ▽ a.		0646	0718	0720	0731	0750	0801	0819	0833	0847	0903	0917f	0934	0948	1001	1017	1032	past each	1848	1901	1913	1934	1942	1946
Edinburgh Waverley ... a.		0651	0723	0725	0736	0755	0806	0824	0838	0852	0908	0922f	0939	0953	1007	1023	1037	hour until ☆a	1854	1907	1918	1940	1947	1951

	⚒	⚒	⚒	⚒	⚒	⚒		⚒	⚒	⚒	⚒		⑦	⑦	⑦	⑦	⑦	⑦	⑦		⑦	⑦	⑦	⑦
Glasgow Queen Street. d.	1915	1930	2000	2030	2100	2130	...	2200	2230	2300	2330	⑦	0750	0830	0900	0930	1000	1030	1100	and at	2200	2230	2300	2330
Falkirk High .... d.	1934	1950	2022	2050	2121	2150	...	2222	2249	2323	2353		0812	0848	0922	0949	1022	1050	1122	the same	2222	2249	2322	2352
Linlithgow .... d.	1945	2001	2030	2101	2128	2201	...	2230	2300	2334	0004		0823	0859	0930	1000	1030	1101	1130	minutes	2230	2300	2330	0003
Haymarket .... ▽ a.	2005f	2021	2047	2117	2143	2218	...	2245	2316	2350	0021		0849	0920	0949	1020	1046	1117	1148	past each	2245	2315	2345	0018
Edinburgh Waverley .... a.	2010	2028	2052	2123	2148	2225	...	2250	2322	2356	0026		0854	0925	0954	1025	1051	1122	1153	hour until ☆	2250	2321	2352	0023

EDINBURGH - MOTHERWELL - GLASGOW CENTRAL

km			⚒	⚒	Ⓐ2	⑥2	⑥A	ⒶA	⚒2	⚒A	⚒2	⚒A	⚒2	⚒A	Ⓐ2	⑥2	⚒A	⚒2	⚒2	⚒A	ⒶB	⑥A	ⒶA	⚒2
0	**Edinburgh** Waverley .... d.	⚒	0624	0727	0740	0754	0914	0918	1019	1111	1153	1312	1352	1512	1549	1548	1712	1740	1826	1911	2017	2113	2114	2313
2	Haymarket .... d.		|	0731	0746	0758	0920	0924	1024	1116	1158	1316	1357	1516	1554	1553	1717	1746	1831	1916	2022	2118	2119	2317
71	Motherwell .... a.		0704	0812	0833	0900	0954	1002	1133	1152	1309	1353	1504	1552	1635	1704	1752	1834	1933	1953	2103	2159	2207	0021
92	**Glasgow** Central .... a.		0721	0829	0855	0923	1015	1025	1154	1212	1325	1412	1525	1612	1657	1723	1811	1856	1954	2015	2125	2220	2224	...

		⑦	⑦A	⑦A	⑦A	⑦A	⑦A	⑦A	⑦B
Edinburgh Waverley .... d.	⑦	1023	1217	1313	1510	1711	1918	2112	2122
Haymarket .... d.		|	1221	1318	1514	1715	1923	2117	2126
Motherwell .... a.		1103	1258	1353	1554	1755	1959	2156	2203
Glasgow Central .... a.		1128	1318	1412	1611	1812	2019	2213	2224

		⚒A	⚒B	⑥2	Ⓐ2	⚒A	⚒A	Ⓐ2	⑥2
Glasgow Central .... d.	⚒	0601	0650	0703	0705	0750	0900	0933	0948
Motherwell .... d.		0616	0706	0721	0721	0805	0915	1000	1004
Haymarket .... d.		0657	0748	0822	0829	0851	0957	1050	1113
Edinburgh Waverley .... a.		0701	0752	0829	0834	0857	1002	1054	1121

	⚒A	⚒2	⚒A	⚒2	⚒A	⚒2	⚒A	⚒A	Ⓐ2	⑥2	⑥	Ⓐ			⑦A	⑦A	⑦A	⑦A		⑦A	⑦A	⑦	
Glasgow Central .... d.	1100	1146	1300	1405	1500	1546	1700	1900	1947	1948	2105	2105	...	⑦	1055	1200	1348	1455	...	1655	1900	2058	...
Motherwell .... d.	1116	1202	1316	1427	1516	1602	1716	1916	2006	2006	|	2122	...		1113	1217	1404	1512	...	1712	1915	2118	...
Haymarket .... d.	1154	1249	1354	1519	1556	1705	1754	1954	2054	2053	2154	|	...		1151	1256	1442	1552	...	1751	1959	2204	...
Edinburgh Waverley .... a.	1159	1256	1359	1524	1600	1711	1800	1958	2100	2058	2200	2221	...		1156	1300	1447	1556	...	1755	2005	2208	...

OTHER SERVICES EDINBURGH - GLASGOW

EDINBURGH WAVERLEY – SHOTTS – GLASGOW CENTRAL

76 km Journey time: ±75 minutes (trains marked * ±90 minutes)

From Edinburgh Waverley:

⚒ : 0552*, 0636 Ⓐ, 0642 ⑥, 0655*, 0757, 0826*, 0857, 0925*, 0956 and at the same minutes past each hour (⊡) until 1555, 1626*, 1656, 1723*, 1749, 1758*, 1856, 1926*, 2125* ⑤⑥ and 2256* ⑤⑥.

All trains call at **Haymarket** 4 minutes later and **Shotts** 38 minutes later (trains marked * 53 minutes later).

⑦: Service by 🚌 at 0839, 1049, 1249, 1449, 1649, 1849 and 2049.

Journey time to **Haymarket** 9 mins; **Shotts** 105 mins; **Glasgow** 186 mins.

From Glasgow Central:

⚒ : 0005* ⑥, 0616*, 0700, 0713*, 0803, 0817*, 0903, 0917*, 1003, 1016*, 1103, 1116* and at the same minutes past each hour until 1616*, 1702, 1718*, 1803, 1816*, 1903 Ⓐ, 1907 ⑥, 1916*, 2116 ⑤⑥* and 2303 ⑤⑥*

Trains call at **Shotts** 27 minutes later (trains marked * 36 minutes later) and **Haymarket** 59 minutes later (trains marked * 83 minutes later).

⑦ : Service by 🚌 at 0816, 1016, 1216, 1416, 1616, 1816 and 2016.

Journey time to **Shotts** 85 mins; **Haymarket** 168 mins and **Edinburgh** 189 mins.

EDINBURGH WAVERLEY – AIRDRIE – GLASGOW QUEEN STREET LOW LEVEL

71 km Journey time: ±74 minutes.

From Edinburgh Waverley:

⚒: 0608, 0620, 0639, 0651, 0707, 0721, 0737, 0749 ⑥, 0752Ⓐ, 0807, 0821, 0839, 0849Ⓐ, 0852⑥, 0911⑥, 0913Ⓐ, 0921, 0938, 0951, 1007, 1023, 1038, 1048, 1107, 1122, 1137, 1150, 1208, 1221, 1237, 1253, 1308, 1319Ⓐ, 1322⑥, 1338, 1349, 1407Ⓐ, 1411⑥, 1421, 1438, 1449, 1508, 1520, 1541, 1552, 1608, 1621⑥, 1623Ⓐ, 1640Ⓐ, 1642⑥, 1648, 1708, 1719, 1737, 1753, 1806, 1823, 1838Ⓐ, 1840⑥, 1848, 1919⑥, 1922Ⓐ, 1949⑥, 1951Ⓐ, 2022⑥, 2024Ⓐ, 2054, 2121, 2150, 2222, 2251 and 2309**c**.

⑦: 0838, 0906, 0938, 1006, 1040, 1110, 1140, 1210, 1240, 1309 and every 30 minutes until 1809, 1840, 1940, 2040, 2140 and 2240.

All trains call at **Haymarket** 4 minutes later, **Bathgate** 25 minutes later and **Airdrie** 44–49 minutes later.

From Glasgow Queen Street Low Level:

⚒: 0545, 0601, 0616, 0638, 0647, 0707, 0717, 0738, 0747, 0808, 0818, 0838, 0848, 0909, 0917, 0938, 0947, 1007, 1016, 1038, 1047, 1108, 1117, 1138, 1147, 1208, 1217, 1238, 1247 and at the same minutes past each hour until 1808, 1817, 1838, 1847, 1908, 1938, 2023, 2053, 2123, 2153, 2224, 2253**b**, 2323**b**, and 2353**b**.

⑦: 0811, 0845, 0915, 0945, 1015, 1045 and every 30 minutes until 1815, 1845, 1945, 2045, 2145 and 2245**b**.

All trains call at **Airdrie** 23 minutes later, **Bathgate** 40–45 minutes later and **Haymarket** 63–67 minutes later.

A – To/from destinations on Tables **120** and **124**.
B – To/from London Kings Cross (Table **180**).

a – The 1730 from Glasgow also calls at Linlithgow (d. 1803).
b – Terminates at Bathgate.
c – Terminates at Airdrie.
f – Arrives 4 minutes earlier on ⑥.

☆ – Timings may vary by ± 5 minutes.
▽ – Trains call to set down only.
⊡ – Timings may vary by ± 2 minutes.

221 EDINBURGH - TWEEDBANK

2nd class SR

km			Ⓐ	⑥	⚒	⚒	Ⓐ	⑥	Ⓐ	⑥	⚒	⚒	⚒		⚒	⚒	⚒	Ⓐ	⑥	⚒	⚒	Ⓐ	⑥	⚒	Ⓐ	⑥
0	**Edinburgh** Waverley. d.	⚒	0544	0555	0620	0650	0723	0723	0753	0756	0824	0852	0923	and at	1524	1552	1624	1653	1654	1722	1754	1823	1826	1854	1924	1925
13	Eskbank .... d.		0608	0614	0641	0711	0742	0745	0812	0815	0843	0913	0942	the same	1543	1613	1643	1713	1715	1743	1814	1842	1845	1914	1943	1945
15	Newtongrange .... d.		0612	0617	0644	0714	0745	0748	0815	0818	0846	0916	0945	minutes	1546	1616	1646	1716	1718	1746	1817	1845	1848	1917	1946	1948
43	Stow .... d.		|	|	0706	0736	0807	0811	0837	0840	0908	|	1008	past each	1608	|	1708	1738	1741	1808	1839	1907	1910	1939a	2008	2010
53	Galashiels .... d.		0644	0646	0715	0745	0816	0819	0846	0849	0917	0945	1017	hour until	1617	1646	1717	1747	1749	1817	1848	1916	1919	1948	2017	2019
57	**Tweedbank** .... a.		0648	0650	0719	0750	0820	0824	0850	0853	0922	0950	1021	♡	1623	1650	1722	1751	1754	1821	1853	1921	1923	1952	2021	2024

	⚒	⚒	Ⓐ	⑥	⚒	⚒		⑦	⑦		⑦	⑦
Edinburgh Waverley .. d.	1954	2053	2153	2156	2254	2354	⑦	0911	1011	and at	2212	2311
Eskbank .... d.	2014	2115	2212	2215	2315	0013		0930	1030	the same	2232	2330
Newtongrange .... d.	2017	2118	2215	2218	2318	0016		0933	1033	minutes	2235	2333
Stow .... d.	2039	2140	2237	2240	2339	0038		0955	1055	past each	2257	2355
Galashiels .... d.	2048	2149	2246	2248	2348	0047		1004	1104	hour until	2306	0004
Tweedbank .... a.	2053	2153	2250	2253	2355	0053		1008	1108	♡	2310	0009

		Ⓐ	⑥	⚒	⚒	Ⓐ	⑥	Ⓐ	⑥	⚒
Tweedbank .... d.	⚒	0520	0528	0558	0628	0658	0659	0726	0729	0757
Galashiels .... d.		0524	0532	0602	0632	0702	0703	0730	0733	0801
Stow .... d.		0533	0541	0611	0641	0711	0712	0739	0742	0810a
Newtongrange .... d.		0553	0601	0631	0701	0731	0732	0800	0802	0830
Eskbank .... d.		0556	0604	0634	0704	0734	0735	0803	0805	0833
Edinburgh Waverley . a.		0615	0623	0656	0729	0759	0755	0821	0824	0854

	Ⓐ	⑥	⚒	⚒	⚒	⚒		⚒	⚒	Ⓐ	⑥	Ⓐ	⑥	⚒	Ⓐ	⑥	⚒	⚒	⚒d		⑦	⑦		⑦	⑦
Tweedbank .... d.	0828	0832	0859	0930	0959	1029	and at	1730	1759	1830	1832	1859	1903	1931	2029	2032	2129	2229	2328	⑦	0845	0945	and at	2145	2246
Galashiels .... d.	0832	0836	0903	0934	1003	1033	the same	1734	1803	1834	1836	1903	1907	1935	2033	2036	2133	2233	2332		0849	0949	the same	2149	2250
Stow .... d.	0841	0845	|	0943	|	1042	minutes	1743	|	1843	1845	|	|	1944	2042	2045	2142	2242	2341		0858	0958	minutes	2158	2259
Newtongrange .... d.	0901	0905	0931	1003	1031	1102	past each	1803	1831	1903	1905	1931	1935	2004	2102	2105	2202	2302	0001		0918	1018	past each	2218	2319
Eskbank .... d.	0904	0908	0934	1006	1034	1105	hour until	1806	1834	1906	1908	1934	1938	2007	2105	2108	2205	2305	0004		0921	1021	hour until	2221	2322
Edinburgh Waverley .. a.	0923	0929	0954	1028	1056b	1129b	♤c	1829	1853	1925	1931	1955	1957	2026	2124	2127	2227	2326	0023		0940	1041		2241	2341

a – Not ⑥.
b – Arrives 3–4 minutes earlier on Ⓐ.

c – The 1557 and 1658 departures also call at Stow on Ⓐ.
d – On ⑥ runs 3 minutes later.

♤ – Timings may vary by ± 4 minutes.
♡ – Timings may vary by ± 2 minutes.

km		⚒	⚒	⚒	⚒	⚒	⚒	⚒	⚒	⚒	⚒	⚒	⑥	Ⓐ	⑦	⚒	⚒	⑥	Ⓐ	⚒	⑦	Ⓐ	⑥	⑦	⑥	Ⓐ	⑦
		G	**A**	**H**			**K**	2	2	**H**		2	2	2		**H**		**E**	**E**	2							
0	**Edinburgh** Waverley d.	...	...	...	...	0530	...	0630	0700	0730	...	0734	0800	0801	0804	0828**h**	...	0831	0834	0900	0910	0930	0930	0915	...	...	...
2	Haymarket d.	...	...	...	...	0534	...	0634	0704	0734	...	0739	0804	0807	0808	0833	...	0836	0839	0904	0915	0934	0934	0921	...	...	...
42	Kirkcaldy d.	...	0520	...	...	0603	...	0706	0736	0802	...	0812	0836	0839	0840	|	...	0907	0910	0936	0950	|	|	1007	...	...	...
54	Markinch d.	...	|	...	...	0612	...	0715	0745	|	...	0822	0845	0848	|	|	...	0916	0919	0945	|	|	|	1016	...	...	...
82	Leuchars △ d.	...	0548	...	...	0633	...	|	0806	0825	...	|	0909	0911	0906	0925	...	|	|	1005	1014	|	1023	1037	...	...	...
	Glasgow Queen Str d.	...	|	...	...	|	0556	|	|	|	0742	|	|	|	|	|	0841	|	|	|	|	|	|	|	0941	0941	0937
	Stirling d.	...	|	...	...	|	0625	|	|	|	0809**u**	|	|	|	|	|	0908	|	|	|	|	|	|	|	1008	1008	1010
	Perth d.	...	|	0600	...	|	0700	0746	|	|	0842	0857	|	|	|	|	0942	0946	0949	|	|	|	|	|	1040	1040	1047
95	**Dundee** d.	0539**a**	0608	0625	0642	0652**f**	0723	0812	0822	0843	0904	...	0925	0927	0920	0940	1005	...	...	1022	1029	1034	1037	1052	1102	1102	1111
112	Carnoustie d.	0559**a**	0622	0640	|	0704	0735	...	...	|	0916	...	...	...	|	|	|	...	...	...	|	|	|	|	1117	1117	1126
123	Arbroath d.	0606**a**	0631	0648	0701	0712	0742	...	...	0859	0923	...	...	...	0936	0959	1021	...	...	...	1046	1051	1054	1109	1124	1124	1132
145	Montrose d.	0626	0647	0704	0716	0726	0757	...	...	0914	0938	...	...	...	0950	|	1041	...	...	...	1102	1105	1108	1124	1138	1144**f**	1148
184	Stonehaven d.	0651	0712	0726	0737	0751	0821	...	...	0935	|	...	...	...	1010	1036	1102	...	...	...	1125	1126	1129	1146	1203	1212	1213
210	**Aberdeen** a.	0714	0735	0749	0758	0813	0847	...	...	0955	1017	...	...	...	1029	1055	1125	...	...	...	1145	1146	1149	1210	1223	1235	1237

	⑦	Ⓐ	⑥	⚒	⚒	⚒	⚒	⑦	⑦	⚒	⑥	Ⓐ	⑦	⚒	⑥	Ⓐ	⑦	⑥	Ⓐ	⚒	⚒	⚒	⑦	⑦	⚒	⚒	⑦
	E	2	2	2	**C**		2**E**			2			2		2	2		2	2	**H**		2			2	**J**	2
Edinburgh Waverley d.	0933	0936	0936	1000	1028	...	1036	...	1050	1100	1130	1131	1132	...	1135	1139	...	1200	1203	1230	...	1235	1241	...	1300	1330	1334
Haymarket d.	0937	0940	0943	1004	1033	...	1041**u**	...	1054	1104	1134	1135	1136	...	1141	1143	...	1204	1207	1234	...	1241	1245	...	1304	1334	1338
Kirkcaldy d.	1012	1012	1015	1036	1105	...	1113**u**	...	1123	1136	|	|	1208	...	1213	1215	...	1236	1239	|	...	1313	1314	...	1336	|	1410
Markinch d.	1022	1022	1024	1045	|	...	1122	...	|	1145	|	|	1217	...	1222	1225	...	1245	1248	|	...	1322	|	...	1345	|	1419
Leuchars △ d.	|	|	|	1105	1130	...	|	...	1147	1205	1223	1224	1239	...	|	|	...	1305	1308	1323	...	|	1338	...	1405	1423	1441
Glasgow Queen Str. d.	|	|	|	|	|	1041	|	1045	|	|	|	|	|	1141	|	|	1145	|	|	|	1241	|	|	1245	|	|	|
Stirling d.	|	|	|	|	|	1109	|	1111	|	|	|	|	|	1207	|	|	1211	|	|	|	1307	|	|	1311	|	|	|
Perth d.	1054	1054	1056	|	|	1139	1154	1142	|	|	|	|	|	1237	1254	1257	1246	|	|	|	1339	1355	|	1342	|	|	|
Dundee d.	...	...	...	1122	1144	1202	...	1210**f**	1210**g**	1221	1240	1238	1255	1300	...	...	1310	1321	1324	1339	1402	...	1352	1407	1421	1437	1457
Carnoustie d.	...	...	...	...	|	|	...	|	|	...	|	|	...	1312	...	...	|	...	...	|	|	...	|	|	...	|	...
Arbroath d.	...	...	...	...	1202	1218	...	1227	1227	...	1256	1255	...	1319	...	...	1326	...	...	1355	1418	...	1408	1423	...	1454	...
Montrose d.	...	...	...	...	1218	1233	...	1241	1241	...	|	|	...	1333	...	...	1341	...	...	1410	1433	...	1422	1439	...	|	...
Stonehaven d.	...	...	...	...	1241	|	...	1303	1303	...	1330	1328	...	|	...	...	1402	...	...	1431	1454	...	1446	1500	...	1527	...
Aberdeen a.	...	...	...	...	1301	1313	...	1323	1323	...	1350	1351	...	1415	...	...	1422	...	...	1450	1514	...	1506	1520	...	1549	...

	⚒	⑦	⚒	⑦	⚒	⚒	⑦	⚒	⑦	⑥	Ⓐ	⚒	⚒	⑦	⚒	⑦	⚒	⑦	⚒	⑦	⚒	⚒	⚒	⑦	⑦	⚒	⚒
			E	**E**	2	**C**	**C**	**F**		2	2	2	**H**	2			2	**E**	2		**H**	2			**CE**	2	**CE**
Edinburgh Waverley d.	...	...	1336	1356	1400	1428	1433	...	...	1434	1437	1500	1530	1534	...	...	1535	1550	1600	1605	1630	...	...	...	1632	1634	1634
Haymarket d.	...	...	1340**u**	1400	1404	1433	1439	...	...	1438	1441	1504	1534	1538	...	...	1539	1554	1604	1609	1634**u**	...	...	...	1637	1639	1639
Kirkcaldy d.	...	...	1411**u**	1432	1436	1506	1511	...	...	1514	1513	1536	|	1610	...	...	1613	1626	1636	1640	|	...	...	...	|	1713	|
Markinch d.	...	...	1420	|	1445	|	|	...	...	1523	1523	1545	|	1621	...	...	1623	1635	1645	1649	|	...	...	...	|	1722	|
Leuchars △ d.	...	...	|	|	1505	1531	1536	...	...	|	|	1605	1624	1642	...	...	|	|	1705	1709	1726	...	...	...	|	|	|
Glasgow Queen Str. d.	1341	1345	|	|	|	|	|	1441	1449	|	|	|	|	|	1541	1545	|	|	|	|	|	1611	1641	1645	|	|	|
Stirling d.	1408	1413	|	|	|	|	|	1507	1518	|	|	|	|	|	|	1612	|	|	|	|	|	1639	1713**e**	1711	1722	|	1723
Perth d.	1438	1450	1450	1509	|	|	|	1540	1552	1555	1555	|	|	|	1636	1647	1655	1707	|	|	|	1719	1741	1740	1756	1754	1758
Dundee d.	1502	1513	...	...	1521	1548	1552	1602	1615	...	...	1622	1639	1658	1658	1710	...	..	1722	1723	1740	1746	1804	1802	...	...	...
Carnoustie d.	1517	1525	...	...	...	|	|	1614	|	...	...	...	|	...	1710	|	...	....	...	1738	|	1803	1817	|	...	...	...
Arbroath d.	1524	1532	...	...	...	1605	1610	1621	1631	...	...	...	1655	...	1717	1726	...	...	...	1744	1756	1813	1824	1819	...	...	...
Montrose d.	1541	1548	...	...	...	1621	1626	1636	1645	...	...	...	1709	...	1732	1741	...	...	...	1800	1812	...	|	1837	...	...	...
Stonehaven d.	|	1610	...	...	...	1644	1649	|	1707	...	...	...	1733	...	1753	1805	...	...	...	1822	1837	...	1858	1858	...	...	...
Aberdeen a.	1626	1633	...	...	...	1704	1706	1715	1726	...	...	...	1753	...	1813	1825	...	...	...	1842	1901	...	1919	1918	...	...	...

	⚒	⑦	⑦	⚒	⚒	⚒	⑦	⚒	⑦	Ⓐ	⑦	⑥	Ⓐ	⑦	⚒	⑦	⚒	⚒	⑦	⚒	⚒	⑦	Ⓐ	⚒	⚒	⑦	⑥
	2		2		2			**E**		2	2	**D**	**D**	**D**	**C**	**C**		2	2	2	2	2	**C**	**B**			**E**
Edinburgh Waverley d.	1700	1705	1734	1736	...	...	...	1741	1750	1800	1806	1811	1810	1813	1833	1836	...	1837**d**	1855	1900	...	1915	1925	1929	...	...	1941
Haymarket d.	1705	1709	1738	1741	...	...	...	1746**u**	1754	1805	1811	1815	1815	1816	1838	1841	...	1841**d**	1859	1904	...	1919	1932	1933	...	...	1945
Kirkcaldy d.	1737	1739	1810	|	...	...	...	1817	1826	1842	|	1844	1847	1845	1913	1913	...	1919	|	1936	...	2002	|	|	...	...	2017
Markinch d.	1746	|	1819	|	...	...	...	1827	1836	1851	|	1853	1857	1854	|	|	...	1929	2003	1945	...	2011	|	|	...	...	2026
Leuchars △ d.	1809	1804	1841	1834	...	...	...	|	|	1911	|	1914	1923	1915	1940	1937	...	|	|	2006	...	2032	|	2029	...	...	|
Glasgow Queen Str. d.	|	|	|	|	1704**b**	1740	1745	|	|	|	|	|	|	|	|	|	1841	|	|	|	1909	|	|	|	1941	1945	|
Stirling d.	|	|	|	|	1746	1816	1813	|	|	|	1900	|	|	|	|	|	1907	|	|	|	1937	|	2015	|	2008	2012	|
Perth d.	|	|	|	|	1825	1855	1845	1858	1906	|	1936	|	|	|	|	|	1943	2001	2035	|	2012	|	...	|	2038	2047	2058
Dundee d.	1827	1818	1857	1848	1855	1918	1909	...	...	1927	...	1930	1936	1931	1955	1952	2005	...	...	2023	2038	2048	...	2043	2100	2110	...
Carnoustie d.	...	|	...	|	1918	1930	1921	...	...	...	...	|	|	|	|	|	2019	...	...	...	...	...	...	|	|	|	...
Arbroath d.	...	1835	...	1905	...	1937	1928	...	...	...	...	1949	1952	1947	2012	2009	2026	...	...	...	...	...	...	2059	2117	2126	...
Montrose d.	...	1850	...	1922	...	1951	1944	...	...	...	...	2003	2006	2001	2028	2025	2041	...	...	...	...	...	...	2114	2131	2141	...
Stonehaven d.	...	1912	...	1944	...	2015	2009	...	...	...	...	2024	2027	2023	2051	2048	|	...	...	...	...	...	...	2135	2155	2205	...
Aberdeen a.	...	1935	...	2007	...	2035	2029	...	...	...	...	2042	2048	2042	2111	2108	2122	...	...	...	...	...	...	2156	2215	2225	...

	Ⓐ	⚒	Ⓐ	⑥	Ⓐ	⚒	⑥	Ⓐ	⑦	⚒	⚒	①–④	⑤	⑦	⚒	⑥	Ⓐ	⚒	⑦	⑦	⚒	⑦	Ⓐ	⑥	⑤⑥	⚒	⚒
	E	2	**D**	**D**	**C**		2	2		2		2			2			2	2	2	2	🚌	2	2	2	2	2
Edinburgh Waverley d.	1942	2000	2014	2014	2032	...	2037	2040	2100	2105	2143	...	...	...	2134	2150	2153	2210	2226	2236	2237	...	...	...	...	2309	2319
Haymarket d.	1946	2004	2017	2018	2037	...	2041	2044	2105	2109	2147	...	...	...	2139	2155	2157	2214	2230	2241	2241	...	...	...	...	2313	2323
Kirkcaldy d.	2019	2047	|	2052	2111	...	2115	2116	2135	2151	2215	...	...	...	|	|	|	2257	2313	|	2324	...	...	...	...	2356	|
Markinch d.	2028	2056	2102	2102	|	...	2124	2126	2144	2200	|	...	...	...	|	2258	2258	2306	2322	|	2333	...	...	...	...	0005	0024
Leuchars △ d.	|	2116	2127	2128	2139	...	|	|	2205	2222	2239	...	...	...	|	|	|	2328	2343	|	|	...	...	...	...	0025	|
Glasgow Queen Str. d.	|	|	|	|	|	2041	|	|	|	|	|	2105*	2142	2045*	|	|	|	|	|	|	|	2145	2248**r**	2252	2337	|	|
Stirling d.	|	|	|	|	|	2108	|	|	|	|	|	2208	2208	2136*	2225	|	|	|	|	2328	|	2235**s**	2333	2333	0005	|	|
Perth d.	2100	|	|	|	|	2143	2156	2158	|	|	|	2241	2241	2248	2304	2333	2333	|	|	0008	0005	2338**s**	0013	0009	0044	|	0056
Dundee d.	...	2132	2142	2143	2153	2209	...	...	2221	2238	2253	2303	2303	2310	...	...	...	2344	2359	...	...	0009**s**	0036	...	...	0041	...
Carnoustie d.	...	...	...	...	|	2220	...	...	|	...	|	2320	2320	2322	...	...	...	...	...	...	...	0035**s**	...	...	...	...	...
Arbroath d.	...	...	...	...	2211	2227	...	...	2240	...	2309	2327	2327	2329	...	...	...	...	...	...	...	0051**s**	...	...	...	...	...
Montrose d.	...	...	...	...	2227	2241	...	...	2255	...	2324	2341	2341	2344	...	...	...	...	...	...	...	0111**s**	...	...	...	...	...
Stonehaven d.	...	...	...	...	2250	2302	...	...	2316	...	2345	0005	0005	0005	...	...	...	...	...	...	...	0147**s**	...	...	...	...	...
Aberdeen a.	...	...	...	...	2310	2322	...	...	2339	...	0008	0025	0025	0025	...	...	...	...	...	...	...	0213	...	...	...	...	...

A – [R]. 🛏 1, 2 class and 💺 London Euston - Aberdeen. Departs London previous day. Train stops to set down only. See Table **161**.
B – To Inverness (Table **225**).
C – From destinations on Table **180**.
D – From destinations on Table **124**.
E – To Inverness (Table **223**).
F – On Ⓐ to Inverness (Table **225**).
G – To Inverness (Table **225**); conveys 💺 only on ⑥.
H – To Inverurie (Table **225**).
J – On ⑥ to Inverurie (Table **225**).
K – To Dyce (Table **225**).

a – Ⓐ only.
b – Departs 1711 on Ⓐ.
d – Departs 4 minutes later on Ⓐ.
e – ⑥ only.
f – Arrives 5 – 6 minutes earlier.
g – Arrives 1200.
h – Departs 0831 on Ⓐ.
r – ⑤ only.
s – Stops to set down only.
u – Stops to pick up only.

△ – Frequent 🚌 connections available to / from **St Andrews**. Journey 10 minutes. Operator: Stagecoach (routes 94, 96, 99).
* – Connection by 🚌.

222 ABERDEEN - DUNDEE - EDINBURGH and GLASGOW

🍷 on most trains — GR, SR, XC

km		Ⓐ	Ⓐ	⚒	⑥	Ⓐ	⚒	⚒	⑥	Ⓐ	⚒	⑥	Ⓐ	⚒	⚒	⚒	⚒	⑦	⚒	⚒	⚒	⚒	⚒	⑦	⚒	⑦	⑦
		C	2	2	2	2	2	2	D	D	2	2	2			2	2	2	2F			G	2	2	F	2	
0	**Aberdeen** d.	...	...	...	...	...	...	...	...	...	...	...	...	0526	0546	...	...	...	...	0634	...	0703	...	...	...	...	...
26	Stonehaven d.	...	...	...	...	...	...	...	...	...	...	...	...	0546	0603	...	...	...	...	0653	...	0720	...	...	...	...	...
65	Montrose d.	...	...	...	...	...	...	...	...	...	...	...	...	0611	0624	...	...	...	...	0715	...	0744	...	...	...	...	...
87	Arbroath d.	...	...	...	...	...	...	...	...	...	...	...	...	0626	0638	...	...	...	...	0728	...	0758	...	...	...	...	...
97	Carnoustie d.	...	...	...	...	...	...	...	0603	0603	...	...	...	│	0645	...	...	...	...	0735	...	0805	...	...	...	...	...
115	**Dundee** d.	...	...	...	...	...	0553	0605	0632	0632	...	...	...	0650h	0658	0709	0738	0724	...	0753	0817	0820	0828	...	...	...	0845
149	**Perth** d.	...	0513	0518	0535	0614	0619	│	│	│	0639	0656	0656	0715	│	│	│	│	0801	0814	0841	│	│	...	0850	0850	0906
202	Stirling d.	0526	│	0554	│	│	0655	│	│	│	0717	│	│	0753	│	│	│	│	│	0845	0915	│	│	0905	│	│	0939
249	**Glasgow** Queen Str. a.	│	│	0635	│	│	0734	│	│	│	│	│	│	0834	│	│	│	│	│	0915	0945	│	│	│	│	│	1014
	Leuchars △ d.	│	│	...	│	│	...	0618	0646	0646	│	│	│	...	0711	0723	0751	0737	│	...	...	│	0841	│	│	│	...
	Markinch a.	│	0545	...	0604	0646	...	0640	0710	0708	│	0737	0737	...	│	0747	0811	0759	0830	...	...	│	0904	│	│	0919	...
	Kirkcaldy a.	│	0555	...	0614	│	...	0649	0720	0717	│	0746	0746	...	0739	0756	0821	0808	0839	...	...	│	0913	│	0925	0928	...
	Haymarket a.	0611	0642	...	0701	0753	...	0734	0755	0758	0812	0821	0825	...	0818	0839	0857	0858	0919	...	...	0925	0954	0959	1003	1018	...
	Edinburgh Waverley a.	0617	0647	...	0706	0800	...	0739	0801	0804	0817	0826	0830	...	0823	0845	0903	0903	0924	...	...	0930	0959	1004	1011	1023	...

	⚒	⑦	⚒	⚒	⑦	Ⓐ	⑥	⑦	⚒	⚒	⚒	⚒	⑦	Ⓐ	⑥	⚒	⑦	⚒	⑦	⚒	⑦	⚒	⑦	⚒	⑦	⚒	⚒
	J	2	C	D	2	2	2	2	CF	2			2	2	2	2		H	C	C	2		CF	F			
Aberdeen d.	0739	...	0752	0820	...	...	...	...	...	...	0842	0907	...	...	...	...	0924	0935	0947	0952	...	...	...	...	1030	1038	...
Stonehaven d.	0756	...	0810	0838	...	...	...	...	...	...	│	│	...	...	...	...	0941	0954	1005	1010	...	...	...	...	1047	│	...
Montrose d.	0817	...	0833	0859	...	...	...	...	...	...	0918	0946	...	...	...	...	1006	1016	1028	1033	...	...	...	...	1108	1114	...
Arbroath d.	0831	...	0849	0915	...	...	...	...	...	...	0932	1000	...	...	...	...	1020	1030	1044	1049	...	...	...	...	1123	1128	...
Carnoustie d.	0838	...	│	│	...	...	...	...	...	...	0939	│	...	...	...	...	1027	1036	│	│	...	...	...	...	│	1135	...
Dundee d.	0854	...	0907	0933	0924	0944	0943	...	...	...	0954	1017	...	1030	1034	...	1046	1054	1103	1107	1120	1128	...	...	1144	1150	1213
Perth d.	0915	0916	│	│	│	│	│	0936	0957	1003	1016	│	1010	│	│	1102	1108	1116	│	│	│	│	1159	1202	1209h	1212	1238
Stirling d.	0943	0951	│	│	│	│	│	│	1032	│	1043	│	1046	│	│	│	1143	1144	│	│	│	│	1235	│	1243	1243	1313
Glasgow Queen Str. a.	1017	│	│	│	│	│	│	│	│	│	1116	│	│	│	│	│	1214	1216	│	│	│	│	│	│	1314	1316	1347
Leuchars △ d.	...	│	0921	0946	0937	0957	0956	│	│	│	...	1030	│	1043	1047	│	...	...	1117	1123	1133	1141	│	│	...	...	...
Markinch a.	...	│	│	1008	0959	1020	1018	1005	│	1032	...	│	│	1104	1108	1131	...	...	│	│	1155	1203	│	1231	...	...	...
Kirkcaldy a.	...	│	0943	1016	1008	1029	1027	│	│	1041	...	│	│	1113	1117	1141	...	...	1139	1145	1204	1212	│	1240	...	...	...
Haymarket a.	...	1040	1019	1049	1055	1107	1108	1111	1111	1123	...	1130f	1135	1149	1158	1217	...	...	1216	1220	1240	1248	1315	1319	...	...	...
Edinburgh Waverley a.	...	1046	1025	1055	1101	1113	1115	1116	1117	1129	...	1135f	1141	1154	1203	1223	...	...	1222	1226	1245	1253	1321	1324	...	...	...

	⚒	⑦	⑥	Ⓐ	⑦	⚒	⑦	⚒	⑦	⑥	Ⓐ	⑦	⚒	⚒	⑦	⚒	⑦	⚒	⚒	⚒	⑦	⚒	⑦	⚒	⚒	⑦	⑦
	J	D	2	2	F	F	J		C	J	J	2	2	2					2	F			C	2		2	F
Aberdeen d.	1103	1110	...	...	...	...	1129	1142	1147	1205	1205	...	...	...	1229	1240	1245	1308	...	...	1331	1337	1347	...	1404	...	...
Stonehaven d.	1120	1127	...	...	...	...	1145	│	1205	1224	1224	...	...	...	1246	1256	1305	1325	...	...	1348	1356	1405	...	1421	...	...
Montrose d.	1144	1148	...	...	...	...	1208	1218	1228	│	│	...	...	...	1307	1320	1330	1346	...	...	1409	1418	1428	...	│	...	...
Arbroath d.	1158	1204	...	...	...	...	1222	1232	1244	1258	1258	...	...	...	1322	1334	1344	1400	...	...	1424	1432	1444	...	1458	...	...
Carnoustie d.	│	│	...	...	...	...	│	1239	│	│	│	...	...	...	│	│	1351	│	...	...	│	1439	│	...	│	...	...
Dundee d.	1217	1224	1233	1236	...	...	1243	1254	1302	1317	1320r	1320	1333	...	1343	1354	1407	1417	1434	...	1445	1454	1502	1513	1517	1515	...
Perth d.	│	│	│	│	1255	1302	1305	1316	│	│	│	│	│	1402	1406	1415	│	│	│	1504	1508	1516	│	1537	│	│	1532
Stirling d.	│	│	│	│	│	│	1338	1344	│	│	│	│	│	│	1438	1444	│	│	│	│	1542	1544	│	1614	│	│	│
Glasgow Queen Str. a.	│	│	│	│	│	│	1409	1416	│	│	│	│	│	│	1509	1518	│	│	│	│	1617	1617	│	1652t	│	│	│
Leuchars △ d.	1230	1237	1246	1249	│	│	...	...	1317	1330	1333	1333	1346	│	...	...	1420	1430	1447	│	...	...	1516	...	1530	1528	│
Markinch a.	│	1257	1307	1310	1322	1330	...	...	│	│	│	1355	1408	1431	...	...	│	│	1508	1531	...	...	│	...	│	1550	1600
Kirkcaldy a.	│	1306	1316	1319	1332	1340	...	...	1339	│	│	1404	1417	1440	...	...	1445	│	1517	1540	...	...	1538	...	│	1559	1609
Haymarket a.	1323	1337	1352	1357	1407	1419	...	...	1420	1423	1426	1440	1453	1518	...	...	1518	1525	1553	1618	...	...	1618	...	1623	1635	1645
Edinburgh Waverley a.	1328	1343	1357	1404	1412	1425	...	...	1426	1428	1433	1445	1458	1524	...	...	1523	1530	1558	1623	...	...	1625	...	1628	1640	1650

	⚒	⚒	⑦	⚒	⚒	⑦	⑦	⚒	⑥	Ⓐ	⚒	⚒	⑦	⑦	⚒	⑦	⚒	Ⓐ	⑥	⚒	⑦	Ⓐ	⑥	⚒	⚒	⑦	⑥
	2	2			C				2	2	2	J	F	2	2		F			K		2	2	2		G	
Aberdeen d.	...	...	1431	1439	1452	1509	1528	1533	...	...	...	1602	...	...	...	1628	...	1627	1636	1709	1709	...	...	...	1736	1747	1818
Stonehaven d.	...	...	1448	│	1510	1529	1544	1549	...	...	...	1619	...	...	...	1645	...	1645u	1655	│	1726	...	...	...	1753	1804	1836
Montrose d.	...	...	1509	1515	1533	1550	1609	1610	...	...	...	│	...	...	...	1706	...	1710	1717	1751	1747	...	...	...	1817	1828	1859
Arbroath d.	...	...	1524	1529	1549	1604	1623	1624	...	...	...	1655	...	...	...	1721	...	1726	1731	1805	1801	1820	1822	...	1832	1843	1915
Carnoustie d.	...	...	│	1536	│	1610	│	│	...	...	...	1702	...	...	...	│	...	│	│	│	│	1827	1828	...	1839	│	│
Dundee d.	1533	...	1545	1551	1607	1624	1643	1646	1650	1651	...	1717	...	1721	1734	1742	...	1748	1750	1822	1818	1844	1846	...	1854	1903	1932
Perth d.	│	1600	1608	1613	│	│	1705	1712	│	│	1703	│	1722	│	│	1805	1806	1814	1814	│	│	│	│	1910	1916	1926	│
Stirling d.	│	│	1640	1641s	│	│	1738	1744	│	│	│	│	│	│	│	1837	│	1844	1844	│	│	│	│	│	1945	1958	│
Glasgow Queen Str. a.	│	│	1713	1717	│	│	1813	1817	│	│	│	│	│	│	│	1908	│	1917	1917	│	│	│	│	│	2015	2029	│
Leuchars △ d.	1547	│	...	...	1622	1637	...	...	1703	1704	│	1731	│	1734	1747	...	│	...	...	1835	1831	1857	1859	│	...	...	1946
Markinch a.	1608	1629	...	...	│	│	...	...	1725	1726	1732	│	1750	1756	1810	...	1835	...	...	│	│	1919	1920	1940	...	...	│
Kirkcaldy a.	1617	1638	...	...	1644	1702	...	...	1734	1735	1741	│	1759	1805	1820	...	1844	...	...	│	1856	1928	1929	1949	...	...	2011
Haymarket a.	1653	1714	...	...	1720	1734	...	...	1820	1821	1826	1829	1835	1841	1855	...	1920	...	...	1929	1928	2003	2005	2028	...	...	2043
Edinburgh Waverley a.	1700	1722	...	...	1726	1740	...	...	1825	1828	1831	1834	1842	1846	1903	...	1927	...	...	1936	1933	2009	2011	2033	...	...	2048

	Ⓐ	⑦	⚒	⚒	⚒	⑦	⚒	⑥	Ⓑ	⑦	⑤⑥	①–④	⑦	⚒	⑤⑥	①–④	⚒	⑤⑥	①–④	⑦	⚒	⚒	Ⓑ	⑦	①–④	⑥	⑤
	C	2	2		J		2	F	F					J				F	F			2	B				
Aberdeen d.	1818	...	...	1828	1911	1907	...	...	...	1936	1946	1946	2006	2009	2042	2042	2104	...	...	2129	2131	...	2143	2226	2226	2226	2323
Stonehaven d.	1836	...	...	1849	1928	1924	...	...	...	1952	2005	2005	2026	2025	2059	2059	2121	...	...	2146	2149	...	2201u	2246	2246	2246	2343
Montrose d.	1859	...	...	1912	1952	1946	...	...	...	2014	2027	2027	2050	2046	2120	2120	2145	...	...	2207	2210	...	2226u	2310	2310	2310	0007
Arbroath d.	1915	...	...	1926	2006	2000	...	...	...	2028	2041	2041	2104	2100	2134	2134	2159	...	...	2223	2226	...	2244u	2324	2324	2324	0021
Carnoustie d.	│	...	...	1933	│	2007	...	...	...	│	│	│	│	2107	│	│	│	...	...	│	│	...	2253u	2331	2331	2331	0028
Dundee d.	1933	1916	...	1949	2023	2022	2042	...	...	2050	2101	2101	2122	2119	2156	2156	2216	...	...	2241	2245	...	2307u	2349	2349	2348	0046
Perth d.	│	│	2002	2011	│	│	│	2106	2106	2110	2122	2122	│	│	2217	2217	│	2238	2238	│	│	2243	│	0013	0012	...	0110
Stirling d.	│	│	│	2042	│	│	│	│	│	2229*	2150	2150	│	│	2248	2248	│	2310	2310	│	│	│	│	...	...	...	...
Glasgow Queen Str. a.	│	│	│	2115	│	│	│	│	│	2338*	2226	2250*	│	│	2318	2350*	│	2343	0010*	│	│	│	│	...	...	...	...
Leuchars △ d.	1947	1929	│	...	2036	2035	2055	│	│	...	...	...	2135	2132	...	...	2229	...	...	2254	2258	│	2326u	...	...	...	...
Markinch a.	│	1951	2031	...	│	│	2117	2133	2133	...	...	...	2157	2154	...	...	2251	...	...	2315	2318	2312	│	...	...	...	...
Kirkcaldy a.	2009	2000	2041	...	│	2101	2126	2142	2142	...	...	...	2206	2203	...	...	2300	...	...	2323	2327	│	2355u	...	...	...	...
Haymarket a.	2044	2047	2117	...	2130	2133	2212	2216	2220	...	...	...	2239	2249	...	...	2346	...	...	2357	2358	0018	...	...	...	...	...
Edinburgh Waverley a.	2050	2052	2122	...	2137	2138	2217	2222	2225	...	...	...	2244	2254	...	...	2352	...	...	0002	0007	0023	...	...	...	...	...

OTHER SERVICES EDINBURGH and GLASGOW - STIRLING

From Edinburgh Waverley to Stirling: *75 km* Journey time: 54 minutes

⚒: 0518, 0633 and every 30 minutes (⊡) until 1705, 1733, 1803, 1835, 1904, 1933⑥ 1943Ⓐ, 2033⑥, 2034⑤, 2134⑥, 2135⑤, 2233⑤⑥, 2303⑥, 2304⑤, 2333⑤⑥.

⑦: 0934, 1035 and hourly until 1935 (also 1106 and hourly until 1806).

All trains call at **Haymarket** 4 minutes later, **Linlithgow** 22 minutes later and **Falkirk Grahamston** 35 minutes later.

From Stirling to Edinburgh Waverley:

⚒: 0530, 0637, 0717, 0749Ⓐ, 0805 and every 30 minutes (⊡) until 1837, 1907, 1937, 2007, 2037, 2107⑤⑥, 2207⑤⑥, 2317⑤⑥.

⑦: 0905, 0951, 1046, 1110 and hourly until 1810, 1919, 2010 (also 1146 and hourly until 1646).

Trains call at **Falkirk Grahamston** 17 minutes later, **Linlithgow** 30 minutes later and **Haymarket** 50 minutes later.

From Glasgow Queen Street to Stirling: *47 km* Journey time: 45 minutes

⚒: 0556, 0614, 0650, 0718, 0749, 0818, 0849 and every 30 minutes (⊡) until 1918, 1948, 2018, 2048**a**, 2118**a**, 2148**a**, 2218**a**, 2248⑤, 2252⑥, 2319**a**, 2348**a**.

⑦: 0937, 1015 and hourly until 2015.

From Stirling to Glasgow Queen Street:

⚒: 0554, 0623, 0655, 0723, 0739, 0753, 0811, 0823 and every 30 minutes until 1723, 1751, 1819, 1853, 1923, 1953, 2021, 2053**a**, 2123**a**, 2153**a**, 2223**a**, 2253**a**.

⑦: 0926, 1026, 1125 and hourly until 2025.

B – Ⓡ. 🛏 1, 2 class and (2) Aberdeen - London Euston. Train stops to pick up only. See Table **161**.
C – To destinations on Table **180**.
D – To destinations on Table **124**.
F – From Inverness (Table **223**).
G – From Inverness (Table **225**).
H – From Dyce (Table **225**).
J – From Inverurie (Table **225**).
K – From Dyce on Ⓐ; from Inverurie on ⑥.
a – ⑤⑥ only.
f – Arrives 6 minutes earlier on ⑥.
h – Arrives 4 minutes earlier.
r – Arrives 1314.
s – Stops to set down only.
t – Arrives 1648 on ⑥.
u – Stops to pick up only.
⊡ – Timings may vary by up to ± 5 minutes.
△ – Frequent 🚌 connections available to / from **St Andrews**. Journey 10 minutes. Operator: Stagecoach (routes 94, 96, 99).
* – Connection by 🚌.

Most Inverness trains convey 🍴.

Table 223 (first section)

km	Station	Times
0	Edinburgh Waverley d.	0630 … 0831 0834 … 0933 0936 0936 … 1036 1035 … 1135 1139 … 1336 … 1356 … 1434 … 1550
2	Haymarket d.	0634 … 0836 0839 … 0937 0940 0943 … 1041u 1039 … 1141 1143 … 1340u 1400 … 1438 … 1554
42	Kirkcaldy d.	0706 … 0907 0910 … 1012 1012 1015 … 1113u … 1213 1215 … 1411u 1432 … 1513 … 1626
54	Markinch d.	0715 … 0916 0919 … 1022 1022 1024 … 1122 … 1222 1225 … 1420 … 1523 … 1635
	Glasgow Queen St d.	0710 0841 … 0937 … 1011 1041 … 1111 … 1209 1341 … 1345 … 1438 … 1509 1545
	Stirling d.	0453 … 0736 0908 … 1010 … 1037 1039 … 1126 1141 … 1237 1408 … 1413 … 1507 1537 1612
91	Perth d.	0508 0538 0745 0810 0941 0950 0950 1046 1055 1054 1056 1116 1138 1155 … 1217 1254 1257 1313 1437 1451 1449 1514c 1546 1555 1616 1646 1708
116	Dunkeld & Birnam d.	0525 0600 0830 … 1111 … 1137 … 1235 … 1330 1508 … 1531 … 1633 … 1725
137	Pitlochry d.	0538 0615 0843 … 1022 1022 … 1124 … 1150 … 1224 1248 … 1343 1521 … 1544 1613 … 1646 … 1738
148	Blair Atholl d.	0547 0628 0852 … 1031 1031 … 1134 … 1233 … 1352 1530 … 1553 … 1655
186	Dalwhinnie d.	0613 0659 0917 … 1056 1056 … 1158 … 1259 … 1555 1622c
202	Newtonmore d.	0710 0927 … 1208 … 1309 … 1632 … 1728
207	Kingussie d.	0643f 0719 0936 … 1109 1109 … 1213 … 1235 1315 1336 … 1428 … 1608 1637 1657 … 1733 … 1822
226	Aviemore d.	0704r 0742 0950 … 1123 1123 … 1225 … 1247 1333 1348 … 1440 1619 … 1649 1710 1744 … 1833
237	Carrbridge d.	0719c 0755 0959 … 1233 … 1342 1401c … 1658 … 1752
282	Inverness a.	0749 0839 1028 … 1158 1158 … 1302 … 1329 1415 1429 … 1523 1654 … 1727 1745 1821 … 1908

Table 223 (second section)

Edinburgh W'ley d.	1633 … 1632 … 1741 1750 … … 1941 1942
Haymarket d.	1638 … 1637 … 1745u 1754 … … 1945 1946
Kirkcaldy d.	… 1817 1826 … 2017 2019
Markinch d.	… 1827 1836 … 2026 2028
Glasgow Q St. d.	1641 … 1645 … 1740 … 1811 1811 1941
Stirling d.	1713a 1723 1711 1722 1816 … 1841 1842 2008
Perth d.	1742 1802 1738 1801c 1852 1900 1906 1917 1923 2037 2101 2101
Dunkeld & Birnam d.	… 1920 … 1933 1940 … 2118 2118
Pitlochry d.	1831 … 1832 … 1933 … 1946 1953 … 2133 2135c
Blair Atholl d.	… 1956 2002 … 2142 2144
Dalwhinnie d.	… 2020 2026 … 2207 2213c
Newtonmore d.	… 2031 2036 … 2217 2223
Kingussie d.	1916 … 1917 … 2016 … 2036 2041 … 2222 2228
Aviemore d.	1929 … 1931 … 2027 … 2047 2053 … 2234 2239
Carrbridge d.	… 2056 … 2243 2248
Inverness a.	2004 … 2006 … 2102 … 2125 2127 … 2311 2316

Table 223 (Inverness → Edinburgh/Glasgow, upper right)

Inverness d.	0536 … 0650 … 0755 … 0845 … … 0940 … 0941
Carrbridge d.	… 0916 … 1011
Aviemore d.	0612 … 0725 … 0830 … 0924 … 1019 … 1027
Kingussie d.	0627 … 0737 … 0843 … 0936 … 1032 … 1039
Newtonmore d.	… 0940 … 1037
Dalwhinnie d.	0640 … … 1053
Blair Atholl d.	0712r … … 1109 … 1115
Pitlochry d.	0726 … 0818 … 0925 … 1022 … 1123 … 1125
Dunkeld & Birnam d.	0739 … 0830 … 1033 … 1137 … 1137
Perth d.	0801 0814 0850 0915 0957 1016 1056 1102 … 1159 1249 1202c 1212
Stirling d.	0845 … 0943 1032 1044 1129 … 1235 1243 … 1243
Glasgow Q St. a.	0915 … 1017 … 1116 1213 … … 1314 … 1316
Markinch a.	0830 … … 1131 … … 1231
Kirkcaldy a.	0839 … 0925 … … 1141 … … 1240
Haymarket a.	0919 … 1003 … 1111 … 1217 … 1315 … 1319
Edinburgh W a.	0924 … 1011 … 1117 … 1223 … 1321 … 1324

Table 223 (lower section, Inverness → Edinburgh)

Station	Times
Inverness d.	1045 … 1050 … 1244 1253 … 1330 … 1447 … 1522 … 1551 … 1623 … 1730 … 1845 … 1850 … 2015 2015 … 2026 2045
Carrbridge d.	… 1317 1325 … 1627 … 1658 … 1807 … 1916 … 1923 … 2100 2100
Aviemore d.	1123 … 1125 … 1325 1333 … 1407 … 1523 … 1557 … 1635 … 1710 … 1814 … 1928 … 1931 … 2108 2108 … 2116 2134
Kingussie d.	1136 … 1137 … 1337 1345 … 1419 … 1535 … 1609 … 1647 … 1722 … 1826 … 1940 … 1943 … 2120 2120 … 2130 2151
Newtonmore d.	… 1341 1349 … 1651 … 1945 … 1947 … 2124 2124 … 2136 2157
Dalwhinnie d.	1151 … … 1548 … 1957 … 1959 … 2136 2136 … 2151 2211
Blair Atholl d.	… 1413 1421 … 1723 … 1755 … 2019 … 2021 … 2157 2157 … 2216 2239
Pitlochry d.	1224t … 1220 … 1423 1432 … 1500 … 1618 … 1650 … 1733 … 1805 … 1907 … 2029 … 2031 … 2207 2207 … 2230 2250
Dunkeld & Birnam d.	1237 … 1235 … 1434 1444 … 1633 … 1702 … 1745 … 1818 … 1920 … 2042 … 2042 … 2219 2219 … 2244 2304
Perth d.	1302c 1316 1255 1305 1454 1504 1516 1532 1608 1654 1703 1702 1805 1806 1814 1839 … 1942 2002 2106c 2122 2122 2106c 2120 2238 2238 2243 2307 2330
Stirling d.	1344 … 1338 1524 … 1544 … 1640 1729 … 1837 … 1844 1909 1919 2016 … 2150 2150 … 2229 2310 2310
Glasgow Q St. a.	1416 … 1409 1558 … 1617 … 1713 1810 … 1908 … 1917 1941 … 2046 … 2226 2250* … 2338 2343 0010*
Markinch a.	1330 1322 … 1531 … 1600 … 1732 1750 … 1835 … … 2031 2133 … 2133 … 2312
Kirkcaldy a.	1340 1332 … 1540 … 1609 … 1741 1759 … 1844 … … 2041 2142 … 2142
Haymarket a.	1419 1407 … 1618 … 1645 … 1826 1835 … 1920 … 2008 2117 2218 … 2220 … 0018
Edinburgh W'ley a.	1425 1412 … 1623 … 1650 … 1831 1842 … 1926 … 2013 2122 2223 … 2225 … 0023

A – ℝ. 🛏 1, 2 class and 🍴 London Euston - Inverness.
  Departs London previous day. Train stops to set down only. See Table **161**.
B – ℝ. 🛏 1, 2 class and 🍴 Inverness - London Euston.
  Train stops to pick up only. See Table **161**.
K – From London (Table **180**). Via Falkirk Grahamston (d. 1705).
L – To London (Table **180**). Via Falkirk Grahamston (d. 1046☓/1249⑦).
P – To Elgin (Table **225**).

a – ⑥ only.
c – Arrives 5–7 minutes earlier.
f – Arrives 0625.
r – Arrives 10 minutes earlier.
t – Arrives 1216.
u – Calls to pick up only.

* – Connection by 🚌.

Table 225 (Inverness → Aberdeen)

km	Station	Times
0	Inverness d.	0453 0554 … … 0709 0900 … 1057 1246 1427 … … 1529 1711 1813 2004 2133 … 0959 1233 1529 1713 1800 2103 2142
24	Nairn d.	0508 0609 … 0725 0916 … 1114 1301 1442 … 1546 1730 1828 2020 2148 … 1014 1248 1544 1729 1815 2118 2157
40	Forres d.	0519 0620 … 0737 0927 … 1125 1312 1453 … 1557 1741 1839 2031 2158 … 1025 1259 1555 1740 1826 2129 2208
59	Elgin d.	0533 0634 … 0752 0952r … 1141 1330 1509 … 1611 1759r 1857 2047 2213 … 1039 1313 1609 1754 1841 2143 2223
89	Keith d.	0554 0655 … 0813 1011 … 1202 1349 1530 … 1635 1820 1919 … 2234 … 1100 1334 1631 1815 … 2205 …
109	Huntly d.	0609 0711 0746 … 0839 1026 … 1216 1403 1545 … 1650 1847 1942 … 2251 … 1120 1352 1646 1830 … 2221 …
130	Insch d.	0624 0729 0802 … 0857 1048r … 1235 1419 1603 … 1706 1902 1958 … 2306 … 1136 1408 1702 1846 … 2237 …
147	Inverurie d.	0637 0743 0816 … 0909 1100 1134 1247 1431 1616 … 1719 1915 2010 … 2319 … 1148 1420 1714 1858 … 2249 …
164	Dyce + d.	0651 0759 0830 0907 0921 1113 1146 1302 1443 1630 1639 1705 1735 1929 2024 … 2332 … 1201 1435 1728 1912 … 2301 …
174	Aberdeen a.	0702 0811 0841 0917 0933 1125 1156 1313 1455 1641 1650 1717 1746 1940 2035 … 2343 … 1212 1446 1739 1923 … 2313 …

Table 225 (Aberdeen → Inverness)

Station	Times
Aberdeen d.	… 0614 0715 0819 0849 1013 1200 1338 1527 1619 1644 1722 1726 1822 2014 2057 2156 2201 2250 … 1000 1300 1522 1801 2127
Dyce + d.	… 0623 0727 0830 0857 1022 1209 1347 1537 1629 1652 1732 1735 1833 2024 2106 2205 2210 2259 … 1009 1309 1531 1810 2136
Inverurie d.	… 0639 0743 0843 … 1034 1221 1359 1549 … 1750r 1751 1844 2037 2119 2217 2222 2312 … 1021 1321 1543 1822 2148
Insch d.	… 0651 0755 0858 … 1047 1234 1412 1602 … 1803 1803 1857 2049 … 2229 2234 … 1034 1334 1556 1835 2201
Huntly d.	… 0713r 0812 0914 … 1103 1250 1428 1618 … 1820 1820 1913 2107 … 2250 2255 … 1050 1351 1612 1858 2222
Keith d.	… 0727 0826 0928 … 1118 1305 1443 1640 … 1834 1834 1928 2121 … 2304 2309 … 1108 1406 1635 1913 2236
Elgin d.	0658 0723 0753 0847 0950 … 1140 1329 1508 1702 … 1857 1857 1950 2142 … 2325 2330 … 1129 1427 1656 1935 2258
Forres d.	0711 0743 0806 0902 1004 … 1153 1342 1522 1716 … 1913 1911 2003 2205 … 2339 2344 … 1142 1440 1710 1949 2311
Nairn d.	0727r 0754 0817 0918r 1015 … 1204 1353 1545t 1731r … 1924 1922 2021r 2216 … 2350 2355 … 1153 1451 1730j 2000 2322
Inverness a.	0745 0812 0835 0936 1033 … 1211 1411 1603 1749 … 1942 1940 2039 2234 … 0008 0013 … 1211 1509 1749 2018 2340

Other trains **Inverurie - Dyce - Aberdeen**: On ☓ at 0713**C**, 0817⑥, 0846Ⓐ, 1038**A**, 1333, 1524**A**, 1638⑥**A**, 1647Ⓐ, 1750Ⓐ, 1752⑥, 1845**A**, 1946**A**, 2124;
On ⑦ at 1102**C**, 1255, 1458, 1620, 1730, 2122.

Other trains **Aberdeen - Dyce - Inverurie**: On ☓ at 0750**E**, 0958**A**, 1103**A**, 1250, 1457**A**, 1552**F**, 1622Ⓐ, 1755**A**, 1918**A**;
On ⑦ at 1035, 1225, 1426, 1550, 1648, 2035.

A – To / from Edinburgh (Table **222**).
B – From Glasgow (Table **223**).
C – To / from Glasgow (Table **222**).
D – From Dundee on Ⓐ; Montrose on ⑥ (Table **222**).
E – From Perth (Table **222**).
F – From Edinburgh on ⑥ (Table **222**).
G – Conveys 🍴 on ⑥; 🛏 only on ⑥.
H – Conveys 🍴 on ⑥; 🛏 only on Ⓐ.
J – 🛏 only on Ⓐ.
K – From Kyle of Lochalsh (Table **226**).

f – Arrives 2226.
j – Arrives 1722.
r – Arrives 5 – 7 minutes earlier.
t – Arrives 1532.

226 INVERNESS - THURSO, WICK and KYLE OF LOCHALSH

2nd class SR

km		⚒ 🍸	⚒ a	⚒ 🍸	⚒ a	⚒		⚒	⚒ 🍸	⚒	⚒		⚒	⚒ 🍸	⚒	⑤⑥	⑦	⑦	⑦	⑦	⑦ 🍸		⑦
0	**Inverness** d.	0700	0855	1041	1056	1142	...	1335	1400	1450	1712	...	1754	1830	2107	2333	0940	1059	1253	1533	1754	...	2108
16	Beauly d.	0715	0910	|	1113	1157	...	1350	1415	1505	1727	...	1809	1845	2122	2348	0955	1115	1308	1548	1809	...	2123
21	Muir of Ord d.	0723	0916	1101	1119	1207	...	1356	1423	1511	1733	...	1815	1851	2128	2354	1001	1121	1314	1556	1815	...	2129
30	Dingwall d.	0739	0929	1112	1132	1219	...	1411	1437	1524	1747	...	1829	1906	2141	0007	1014	1134	1327	1609	1831	...	2142
49	Garve d.	|	0952	|	1155	...	...	1433	|	|	|	...	1853	|	|	|	|	1158	|	|	|	...	|
75	Achnasheen d.	|	1018	|	1221	...	...	1500	|	|	|	...	1920	|	|	|	|	1225	|	|	|	...	|
104	Strathcarron d.	|	1048	|	1253	...	...	1530	|	|	|	...	1949	|	|	|	|	1255	|	|	|	...	|
116	Stromeferry d.	|	1105	|	1310	...	...	1547	|	|	|	...	2006	|	|	|	|	1312	|	|	|	...	|
124	Plockton d.	|	1117	|	1322	...	...	1559	|	|	|	...	2018	|	|	|	|	1324	|	|	|	...	|
133	**Kyle of Lochalsh** a.	|	1130	|	1335	...	...	1612	|	|	|	...	2031	|	|	|	|	1337	|	|	|	...	|
51	Invergordon d.	0758	...	1130	...	...	...	...	1454	1541	1804	...	...	1926	2158	0024	1032	...	1345	1626	1848	...	2200
71	Tain d.	0817	...	1149	...	...	...	...	1513	...	1824	...	...	1945	2217	0043	1050	...	1403	...	1901	...	2218
93	Ardgay d.	0833	...	1205	...	...	...	...	1529	...	1839	...	...	2001	...	...	...	...	...	...	1923	...	...
108	Lairg d.	0853	...	1221	...	...	...	...	1545	...	...	...	...	2017	...	...	...	...	...	...	1942	...	...
136	Golspie d.	0918	...	1246	...	...	...	...	1610	...	...	...	...	2042	...	...	...	...	...	...	2007	...	...
146	Brora d.	0929	...	1257	...	...	...	...	1621	...	...	...	...	2052	...	...	...	...	...	...	2018	...	...
163	Helmsdale d.	0947	...	1312	...	...	...	...	1636	...	...	...	...	2108	...	...	...	...	...	...	2033	...	...
201	Forsinard d.	1021	...	1346	...	...	...	...	1712	...	...	...	...	2142	...	...	...	...	...	...	2107	...	...
237	Georgemas Jcn a.	1045	...	1410	...	...	...	...	1736	...	...	...	...	2206	...	...	...	...	...	...	2131	...	...
248	**Thurso** a.	1059	...	1424	...	...	...	...	1750	...	...	...	...	2220	...	...	...	...	...	...	2145	...	...
248	**Thurso** d.	1102	...	1427	...	...	...	...	1753	...	...	...	...	2223	...	...	...	...	...	...	2148	...	...
237	Georgemas Jcn d.	1114	...	1439	...	...	...	...	1805	...	...	...	...	2235	...	...	...	...	...	...	2200	...	...
260	**Wick** a.	1131	...	1456	...	...	...	...	1822	...	...	...	...	2252	...	...	...	...	...	...	2217	...	...

	⑥	⚒	⚒	⚒ a	⚒ 🍸	⚒ 🍸	⚒	⚒ a		⚒	⚒	⚒ 🍸	⚒ E	⚒ 🍸	⚒	⚒	⑦	⑦	⑦	⑦ 🍸	⑦	⑦	⑦
Wick d.	...	...	...	...	0618	0802	...	...	...	...	...	1234	...	1600	...	...	...	...	...	1158	...	...	...
Georgemas Jcn. d.	...	...	...	...	0636	0820	...	...	...	...	...	1252	...	1618	...	...	...	...	...	1216	...	...	...
Thurso a.	...	...	...	...	0646	0830	...	...	...	...	...	1302	...	1628	...	...	...	...	...	1226	...	...	...
Thurso d.	...	...	...	...	0650	0834	...	...	...	...	...	1306	...	1632	...	...	...	...	...	1230	...	...	...
Georgemas Jcn. d.	...	...	...	...	0703	0847	...	...	...	...	...	1319	...	1645	...	...	...	...	...	1243	...	...	...
Forsinard d.	...	...	...	...	0727	0913	...	...	...	...	...	1347	...	1711	...	...	...	...	...	1309	...	...	...
Helmsdale d.	...	...	...	...	0800	0946	...	...	...	...	...	1421	...	1744	...	...	...	...	...	1342	...	...	...
Brora d.	...	...	...	...	0816	1002	...	...	...	...	...	1436	...	1800	...	...	...	...	...	1358	...	...	...
Golspie d.	...	...	...	...	0825	1012	...	...	...	...	...	1447	...	1810	...	...	...	...	...	1408	...	...	...
Lairg d.	...	...	0626	...	0852	1038	...	...	...	...	...	1512	...	1836	...	...	...	...	...	1433	...	...	...
Ardgay d.	...	0614	0643	...	0907	1054	...	...	...	...	...	1530	...	1852	1928	...	...	...	...	1449	...	...	...
Tain d.	0048	0630	0659	...	0923	1110	...	...	...	...	...	1546	...	1908	1946	2221	0048	1055	1408	1505	...	...	2223
Invergorgon d.	0105	0649	0719	...	0942	1131	...	...	...	...	1551	1606	...	1925	2005	2240	0105	1114	1427	1524	1631	...	2242
Kyle of Lochalsh d.	|	|	|	0611	|	|	...	1208	...	1346	|	|	1713	|	|	|	|	|	|	|	|	1512	|
Plockton d.	|	|	|	0627	|	|	...	1221	...	1359	|	|	1726	|	|	|	|	|	|	|	|	1525	|
Stromferry d.	|	|	|	0639	|	|	...	1233	...	1411	|	|	1738	|	|	|	|	|	|	|	|	1537	|
Strathcarron d.	|	|	|	0658	|	|	...	1252	...	1430	|	|	1757	|	|	|	|	|	|	|	|	1556	|
Achnasheen d.	|	|	|	0726	|	|	...	1320	...	1501	|	|	1825	|	|	|	|	|	|	|	|	1624	|
Garve d.	|	|	|	0753	|	|	...	1347	...	1527	|	|	1852	|	|	|	|	|	|	|	|	1651	|
Dingwall d.	0121	0708	0738	0816	1001	1153	1245	1410	...	1550	1611	1626	1919	1941	2024	2258	0121	1135	1445	1543	1649	1714	2300
Muir of Ord d.	0131	0722	0751	0830	1014	1206	1258	1422	...	1603	1624	1639	1931	1952	2037	2311	0131	1148	1457	1555	1702	1726	2313
Beauly d.	...	0728	0757	0835	1020	1211	1304	1427	...	1609	1629	1645	1936	|	2042	2316	...	1153	1502	1601	1707	1732	2318
Inverness a.	...	0743	0812	0850	1035	1226	1319	1442	...	1626	1646	1702	2000	2010	2057	2331	...	1208	1517	1616	1722	1747	2333

E – To Elgin (Table **225**).

a – Conveys 🍸 on ①–⑤.

227 🚌 INVERNESS - ULLAPOOL - STORNOWAY

Valid until March 29, 2018

	①–⑥ 🚌	①–⑥ ⛴		①–⑤ 🚌	①–⑤ ⛴		⑦ 🚌	⑦ ⛴		⑥ 🚌	⑥ ⛴
Inverness d.	0810	...	...	1500	...	...	1540	...	...	1640	...
Garve d.	0844	...	...	1534	...	...	1614	...	...	1714	...
Ullapool a.	0930	...	...	1620	...	...	1700	...	...	1800	...
Ullapool d.	...	1030	...	...	1730	...	...	1830	...	...	1900
Stornoway a.	...	1300	...	...	2000	...	...	2100	...	...	2130

	①–⑥ ⛴	①–⑥ 🚌		①–⑤ ⛴	①–⑤ 🚌		⑦ ⛴	⑦ 🚌		⑥ ⛴	⑥ 🚌	
Stornoway d.	0700	...	...	1400	...	...	1430	...	...	1530	...	...
Ullapool a.	0930	...	...	1630	...	...	1700	...	...	1800	...	...
Ullapool d.	...	0950	...	...	1650	...	...	1720	...	...	1820	...
Garve d.	...	1032	...	...	1732	...	...	1802	...	...	1902	...
Inverness a.	...	1110	...	...	1810	...	...	1840	...	...	1940	...

☛ Latest passenger check-in for ⛴ is 30 minutes before departure.

Operators: 🚌 Scottish Citylink (service **961**). www.citylink.co.uk. ✆ (0) 871 266 3333.
⛴ Caledonian MacBrayne. www.calmac.co.uk. ✆ (0)800 066 5000.

228 🚌 INVERNESS - FORT WILLIAM - OBAN

Valid until May 20, 2018

Service number	915	919	919	19	919	916	919	919	919	19
		①–⑥	①–⑥	①–⑥			①–⑥	①–⑥	⑦	①–⑤
Inverness bus station d.	...	0905	1105	1300	1405	...	1735	1905	1915	2015
Fort Augustus bus stance d.	...	1008	1208	1403	1508	...	1838	2008	2018	2122
Invergarry Jct. bus bay A82 d.	0948j	1023	1223	1423	1523	1738j	1853	2023	2033	2128
Fort William bus station a.	1030	1105	1305	1500	1605	1820	1935	2105	2115	2205
Service number		918			918					
		①–⑥			①–⑥					
Fort William bus station d.	...	1115	...	...	1710	...	...	...	...	...
Ballachulish Tourist Office d.	...	1142	...	...	1737	...	...	...	...	...
Oban Station Road a.	...	1242	...	...	1837	...	...	...	...	...

Service number	919	19	919	916	918	915	919	19	918	919	917
	①–⑥	①–⑥	①–⑥		①–⑥		①–⑥	①–⑤	①–⑥	⑦	
Oban Station Road d.	...	...	...	...	0930	...	...	...	1500	...	...
Ballachulish Tourist Office d.	...	...	...	...	1029	...	...	...	1559	...	...
Fort William bus station a.	...	...	...	...	1058	...	...	...	1628	...	...
Service number					919				919		
					①–⑦				①–⑥		
Fort William bus station d.	0625	0730	0855	1015	1115	1400	1415	1530	1645	1700	1840
Invergarry Jct. bus bay A82 d.	0707	0807	0937	1054j	1157	1439j	1457	1625	1727	1742	1919j
Fort Augustus d.	0722	0819	0952	...	1212	...	1512	1640	1742	1757	...
Inverness bus station a.	0825	0920	1055	...	1315	...	1615	1741	1845	1900	...

j – On A87 at Invergarry Hotel.

Operator: Scottish Citylink. www.citylink.co.uk. ✆ (0) 871 266 3333.

229 ISLE OF MAN RAILWAYS

2017 service ✆ +44 (0)1624 662525

Service shown is for 2017. The 2018 service was not available when we went to press. For more details please call ✆ +44 (0)1624 662525.

km	*Manx Electric Railway*	A	A	A	A	A	A	A		
0	**Douglas** Derby Castle ‡ d.	0940	1040	1140	1240	1410	1510	1610	...	...
4	Groudle d.	0952	1052	1152	1252	1422	1522	1622	...	...
11	Laxey d.	1010	1110	1210	1310	1440	1540	1640	...	...
29	**Ramsey** a.	1055	1155	1255	1355	1525	1625	...	...	...

	A	A	A	A	A	A	A		
Ramsey d.	...	1110	1210	1340	1440	1540	1640	...	...
Laxey d.	1055	1155	1255	1425	1525	1625	1725	...	...
Groudle d.	1113	1213	1313	1443	1543	1643	1743	...	...
Douglas Derby Castle ‡ a.	1125	1225	1325	1455	1555	1655	1755	...	...

km	*Snaefell Mountain Railway*	B	B	B	B	B	B	B		
0	**Laxey** d.	1015	1115	1215	1315	1400	1455	1545	...	...
8	**Summit** a.	1045	1145	1245	1345	1430	1525	1615	...	...

	B	B	B	B	B	B	B		
Summit d.	1110	1215	1315	1415	1500	1555	1645	...	...
Laxey a.	1140	1245	1345	1445	1530	1625	1715	...	...

km	*Isle of Man Steam Railway*	C	C	C	C			D 🍴		
0	**Douglas** Railway Station ‡ d.	0950	1150	1350	1550	...	...	1900	...	...
9	Santon d.	1011x	1211x	1411x	1611x	...	...	|	...	...
13	Ballasalla d.	1120	1220	1420	1620	...	...	1940	...	...
16	Castletown d.	1027	1227	1427	1627	...	...	1947	...	...
25	**Port Erin** a.	1050	1250	1450	1650	...	...	2015	...	...

	C	C	C	C		D 🍴			
Port Erin d.	1000	1200	1400	1600	...	2115	...	...	...
Castletown d.	1027	1227	1427	1627	...	2142	...	...	...
Ballasalla d.	1035	1235	1435	1635	...	2149	...	...	...
Santon d.	1047x	1247x	1447x	1647x	...	|	...	...	...
Douglas Railway Station ‡ a.	1105	1305	1505	1705	...	2230	...	...	...

A – Mar. 9 - Oct. 1 (not Mar. 13, 17, 20, 24, 27, 31, Apr. 3) (also ⑥⑦ in Oct.). Minimum service shown. Additional services operate on most dates. A reduced service operates on ②③④ Oct. 10 - Nov. 2; also ⑥⑦ Oct. 28 - Nov. 5.

B – Apr. 7 - Nov. 5 (not Oct. 2, 6, 9, 13, 16, 20, 23, 27, 30, Nov. 3). Minimum service shown. Additional services operate on most dates June - September.

C – Mar. 18 - Nov. 5. **Does not run every day**. Enhanced services with different timetables operate on most ④⑥⑦ in July and ④⑤⑥⑦ in August and on certain other dates.

D – ④ June 15 - Nov. 2. Reservation essential.

x – Calls on request.

‡ – 🚌 services **1**, **1H**, **2A**, **12**, **12A**, connect Derby Castle and Lord Street Bus Station which is near the Steam Railway Station.

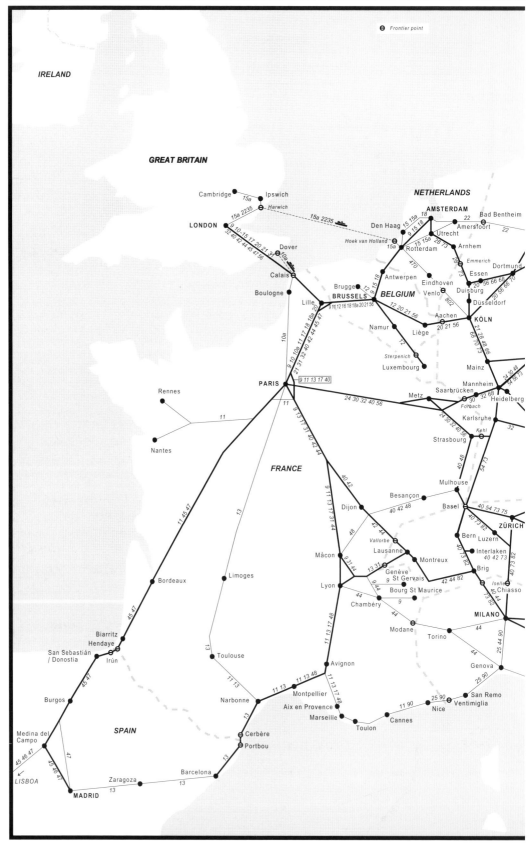

⊖ Frontier point

IRELAND

GREAT BRITAIN

NETHERLANDS

Cambridge · 15a Ipswich
15a 2235 Harwich
LONDON · 15a 2235
9 10 -15 17 20 21 32
32 40 41 42 44 45 47 56
Dover
10a
Calais ⊖
Boulogne ·
Brugge · 12 9 15 18
BRUSSELS
BELGIUM
Lille 9 11 12 16 18 18a 20 21 56
Namur
Sterpenich
Luxembourg

AMSTERDAM 18 22 Bad Bentheim
Den Haag 15 15a
9 15 18 Amersfoort 22
Utrecht
Hoek van Holland 15a Rotterdam Arnhem
470 Emmerich Dortmund
28 73
Antwerpen Essen 20 56 66 68
Eindhoven 20 66 66 70
Venlo Duisburg
802 Düsseldorf
Aachen KÖLN
Liège 20 21 56
12 24 28 48 66
68 70 73

Rennes
11
Nantes

PARIS 9 11 13 17 40
11
24 30 32 40 56 Metz
Saarbrücken
Mannheim
Mainz
30 Heidelberg
Forbach
24 30 32 40 56 Karlsruhe
Kehl 32
Strasbourg

FRANCE

11 45 47
13
40 42
Dijon 9 11 13 17 31 44
48
42 44
Vallorbe
Mâcon Lausanne
13 31 Genève g
Lyon 9 St Gervais
9 44 Bourg St Maurice
44 9
Chambéry
Modane
Torino
44

Mulhouse
Besançon
40 42 48 Basel 40 54 73 75
40 73 82
ZÜRICH
Bern Luzern
Interlaken
Montreux 40 42 73
Brig
42 44 82
Iselle
73 82 Chiasso
73 82 40 44
MILANO
25 44 90

Bordeaux
Limoges
13
45 47
Biarritz
Hendaye ⊖
San Sebastián / Donostia Irún ⊖
Toulouse
11 13
13
Burgos
Narbonne
11 13 11 13 48
Montpellier
Aix en Provence
Marseille
Toulon
Cannes
11 90 Nice
25 90 Ventimiglia
San Remo
25 90
Genova
44
25 90

SPAIN
Medina del Campo
45 46 47
45 46 47
47
LISBOA
45 46 47
Zaragoza 13
Barcelona
13
MADRID 13
Cerbère
Portbou
13

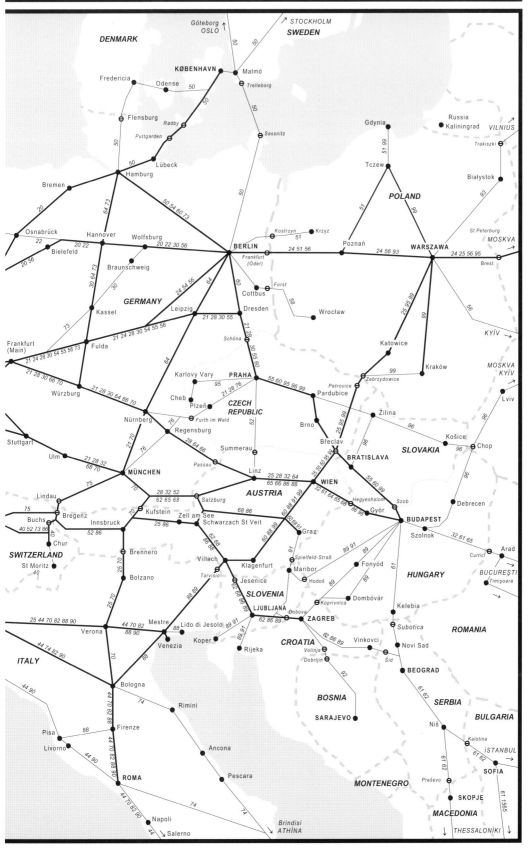

MP Middleton Press

EVOLVING THE ULTIMATE RAIL ENCYCLOPEDIA

Easebourne Midhurst GU29 9AZ. Tel:01730 813169

www.middletonpress.co.uk email:info@middletonpress.co.uk

A-978 0 906520 B- 978 1 873793 C- 978 1 901706 D-978 1 904474
E - 978 1 906008 F - 978 1 908174 G - 978 1 910356

All titles listed below were in print at time of publication - please check current availability by looking at our website - www.middletonpress.co.uk or by requesting a Brochure which includes our *LATEST RAILWAY TITLES* also our TRAMWAY, TROLLEYBUS, MILITARY and COASTAL series